The
Heritage
of
Missouri

Third Edition

The Heritage of Missouri

Duane G. Meyer

Emden Press
Springfield, Missouri

First Printing January 1982
Second Printing August 1983
Third Printing August 1986
Fourth Printing August 1988
Fifth Printing August 1990
Sixth Printing August 1992
Seventh Printing November 1993
Eighth Printing August 1998

Published by Emden Press

Printed in the United States of America

Library of Congress Catalog Number: 81-51710

Cover Designed by Jerry Moore and Janet Moody

To
Andrea
James
Mark
and
Paul

PREFACE

Twenty-five years ago, as a Colonial American historian newly-graduated from the University of Iowa, I was assigned to teach a class of college-age Missourians the history of their state. During the hours of reading and research required for preparation, I became intrigued by the fascinating saga of this, my adopted state. In 1963 this interest resulted in the publication of the first edition of *The Heritage of Missouri*. The intervening years have shed new light on the prehistory of the state and have brought changes in the social, political and economic story of Missouri. This new material and my continued interest in the "Mother of the West" has led to this third edition.

For their assistance in preparing this new edition, two scholars deserve special appreciation. Dr. James E. Price, archaeologist, member of the staff of Southwest Missouri State University, and manager of the Field Station at Naylor, has graciously reviewed Chapter One and revised it to reflect the latest research findings. Dr. Price has adjusted the dates of the cultural periods and has added a new period—the Middle Archaic Period, 5000 B.C. to 3000 B.C. The projectile points from this period were drawn by Dr. Price, and the changes made in all the archaeological illustrations were in response to his suggestions. Dr. Art Mattingly of the department of history, Southeast Missouri State University, has made numerous helpful suggestions for the revision of the book.

Gratitude is also due Erby Young of River City Publishers for his assistance in the technical aspects of the production of the book.

My wife, Marilyn Hansen Meyer, has once again been my chief associate in preparing this revised edition. She edited and typed the text, drew revised and new archaeological illustrations, read the galleys, and placed new photographs in the last three chapters. All original artwork and maps, except where noted, were drawn by her. Her concern for accuracy and her critical questions regarding content have been of great help to me.

There are others, of course, who helped in the preparation of the original edition and their contribution should be remembered: Dr. Robert F. Karsch and Dr. Carl Chapman, who were then at the University of Missouri-Columbia; Dr. David Adams and Dr. B. B. Lightfoot of Southwest Missouri State University; and James E. Moss, formerly of the State Historical Society of Missouri. Edward Pierce served as my research assistant, constructed the chronology, drew the statistical maps and graphs, and compiled the index.

Students, teachers, and other interested readers should be aware of the rich opportunities for research in Missouri history. Throughout the state, museums, libraries, and historical and archaeological societies have made literature and research material available to scholars and interested citizens. The two leading storehouses of documents and artifacts are the State Historical Society of Missouri at Columbia and the Missouri Historical Society of St. Louis. A bargain in historical information is the *Missouri Historical Review* which is published by the State Historical Society and is available to any person, school, or organization for the annual membership fee of only $5.00. Another highly usable source of information is the book entitled *Missouri: A Guide to the "Show Me" State*, New York: Hastings House, Revised Edition, 1954. The book summarizes the historical developments in the state related to many economic, social, and political topics and then sketches the major events associated with each community.

I am impressed with the growing number of fine scholars writing about Missouri history. Eight histories which have appeared since 1963 are particularly recommended as reference sources. They are arranged in order of their year of publication:

David D. March, *The History of Missouri*, 4 volumes, Lewis Publishing Co., 1967.

William E. Foley, *A History of Missouri: Volume I, 1673 to 1820*, (William E. Parrish, editor), University of Missouri Press, 1971.

Perry McCandless, *A History of Missouri: Volume II, 1820 to 1860*. (William E. Parrish, editor), University of Missouri Press, 1972.

William E. Parrish, *A History of Missouri: Volume III, 1860 to 1875*, University of Missouri Press, 1973.

Russel L. Gerlach, *Immigrants in the Ozarks*, University of Missouri Press, 1976.

Paul C. Nagel, *Missouri, A Bicentennial History*. Norton, 1977.

Lorenzo J. Greene, Gary R. Kremer, and Anthony F. Holland, *Missouri's Black Heritage*, Forum Press, 1980.

William E. Parrish, Charles T. Jones, Jr., and Lawrence O. Christensen, *Missouri: The Heart of the Nation*, Forum Press, 1980.

Duane Meyer
Southwest Missouri State University
Springfield, Missouri

CONTENTS

CHAPTER I

Early Man in Missouri

As o'er the verdant waste I guide my steed,
Among the high rank grass that sweeps his sides . . .
I think of those upon whose rest he tramples:
Are they here, the dead of other days? . . .
Let the mighty mounds that overlook the rivers,
Or that rise in the dim forest . . . answer.
A race that long has passed away built them;
A disciplined and populous race heaped,
With long toil, the earth, while yet the Greek
Was . . . rearing on its rock
The glittering Parthenon.
—from William Cullen Bryant, "The Prairies"

The first Europeans to reach Missouri—the members of the Marquette-Joliet expedition—were quietly skimming the Mississippi River in 1673 when they suddenly beheld two green, red, and black "monsters" peering at them. "They have horns on their heads like those of deer, a horrible look, red eyes, a beard like a tiger's, a face somewhat like a man's, a body covered with scales . . ." The creatures were horned and bearded "thunderbirds" painted on a large rock on the Illinois side of the river near what is now the city of Alton. Father Marquette admits in his journal that the beasts "at first made us afraid." After their initial fear had passed, the party continued the voyage downstream. As they paddled they discussed the unusual art work they had seen. Marquette refused to believe that Indians were responsible for the two figures since they were "so well painted." Most Americans today, like Father Marquette in the seventeenth century, tend to underrate the Indian cultures which preceded ours. Sometimes in our histories we completely ignore them. But, in spite of such slights, the Indians remain as an indelible page of Missouri history.

People of our culture have inhabited the Mississippi Valley for only 300 years. Indians in various stages of development lived here for over 10,000 years before the European explorers arrived. However, the barns and billboards of Western Civilization have so changed the face of the countryside that unless we are alert, we may fail to see the remaining traces of these first Missourians. Before we learn more about these prehistoric people, let us examine the land that was their home.

The Geographic Setting

The basins of three great rivers, the Ohio, the Missouri, and the Mississippi, form the heartland of the North American continent. The midlands of the other continents are either too hot or too cold, too drenched or too dry to encourage development, but the heartland of North America is ideally suited for settlement and agriculture. The rolling prairies of deep black soil are remarkably fertile. The climate is agreeable to people and plants, with adequate rainfall and a sufficiently long growing season for important crops such as wheat and corn. Little wonder then that land-hungry Europeans scrambled over the Appalachian Mountains or paddled up the St. Lawrence River or poled up the Mississippi to reach this thousand-mile-wide land of promise.

Missouri is located at the confluence of mid-America's three main streams, with the Mississippi River forming the entire eastern boundary of the state. Starting as a clear, icy trickle in the mountains of western Montana, the Missouri River meanders across the Great Plains gathering silt and then bisects the state of Missouri before its muddy flow, "too thick to drink but too thin to plow," joins the Mississippi. At the southeast corner of the state the Ohio River empties into the mighty Father-of-Waters after draining the plains region as far east as Pittsburgh. All of these streams are navigable. In those early periods of North American history when the rivers provided the roadways for exploration, settlement, and commerce, Missouri occupied the choice corner lots at the crossroads of the Midwest.

Missouri offers a greater variety of scenery than her plains-state neighbors to the west, north, and east. Like them, she has great areas of plains, but Missouri also possesses sizeable stretches of bottomland and an extensive region of forested high-lands. Let us take an imaginary tour of the state to become ac-

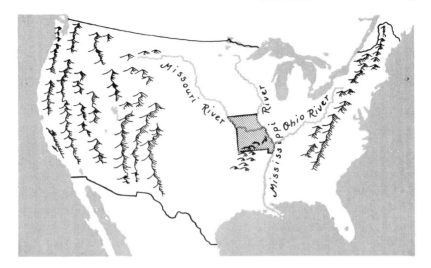

quainted with these various sections. There are four main regions: the Glacial Plains, the Old Plains, the River Lowlands, and the Ozark Highlands.

The Glacial Plains

The area north of the Missouri River is the Glacial Plains. During the Ice Age great glaciers grated over the surface of this region leaving behind varying depths of the deposits of crushed rock that geologists call drift. Following the glaciers, the rock layers were blanketed with wind-carried soil, or loess (LO ehs). The heaviest concentration of loess is found near the Missouri River. For uncounted centuries this surface soil was further enriched by a luxuriant growth of prairie grasses. Valuable coal and fire clay deposits are located in several parts of northern Missouri, particularly in the central section near the towns of Moberly and Mexico. This region of the Glacial Plains is well drained by a network of rivers flowing into the Missouri and the Mississippi.

The Old Plains

Next we come to the Old Plains region which can best be described as a wedge-shaped area stretching southward from the Missouri River along the Kansas border. The dark brown or gray soils are mostly a sandy clay derived from shale (rock made of pressed clay, mud, or silt) and sandstone. Crops such as corn, wheat, and soybeans are grown in this productive section. Drainage is provided by the twisting Osage River which crosses the Old Plains and reaches far into Kansas. Part of the Old Plains north of the Osage River is called the Osage Plains after the tribe that had its main settlements there. Since coal deposits are so near the surface of the Old Plains, open "strip mining" is possible in many places.

The Ozark Highlands

The lovely Ozark Highlands comprise about two-fifths of the land area of Missouri and form the third distinctive geographic region. They stretch diagonally across the state from St. Louis in a southwestward direction and continue into northern Arkansas and eastern Oklahoma. Centuries of erosion have eaten away the mountain peaks and have left the region a rugged tableland. The slopes and ridges of the hilliest parts are clothed with oak, pine, walnut, hickory, gum, redbud, and dogwood. These hillsides provide a canvas for the artistry of the changing seasons as the trees exhibit the colors of blossoms or turning leaves. The roughest terrain in the Ozarks is found where the rivers cut through the highlands, and at the outside edges of the plateau as the surface descends to the level of the surrounding plains.

Located at the eastern end of the Ozark Highlands are the so-called St. Francois Mountains. But Taum Sauk, the highest peak, reaches only 1772 feet above sea level. This cluster of hills and knobs in Iron, Reynolds, Madison, St. Francois, and Washington counties is formed of a hard rock with visible crystals called granite, and other igneous (formed by the melting action of heat within the earth) rocks which have been better able to resist erosion than the sedimentary (formed by material that has settled in water) rocks which covered them. The area is of special importance in Missouri history since the French made their earliest settlements near here in order to exploit the rich mineral deposits.

The soil in the Ozarks is a rocky limestone (sedimentary rock consisting of remains of marine animals, chiefly shells) clay, usually gray or light brown. However, along the outsides of the Ozark plateau the gash of the plow in the rocky surface is often brick red. Of great importance to the development of the state are the valuable mineral and rock deposits in the Ozarks—lead, zinc, iron ore, barite, granite, and cement mate-

A Regional Map
of Missouri

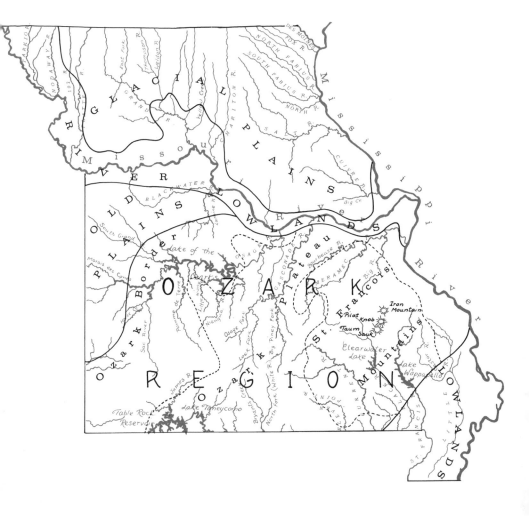

rials. Many caves and springs add to the charm of this section. The Missouri Ozarks have more than 10,000 springs, ninety-eight of which have a daily flow of over a million gallons each. The Ozark Highlands, with their caves, springs, lakes, and tree-clad slopes contribute much to the beauty and variety of Missouri and attract millions of tourists yearly.

The River Lowlands

The fourth and last region of the state is called the River Lowlands. This area, estimated to be one-fifth the land surface of the state, is composed of the floodplains of the Missouri and Mississippi rivers and their major tributaries. Asia has its fertile crescent and Missouri has its somewhat distorted fertile T. When Kentucky and Tennessee immigrants poured into Missouri after the Louisiana Purchase, they quickly recognized the value of this rich valley land. By 1830 the major settlements in the state formed a T with most people living along the Missouri and Mississippi rivers. The bottomland varies from one to ten miles wide except in the southeast corner—the bootheel—where the floodplains reach a width of sixty miles. In the river-

The rugged and beautiful Ozark Highlands have great mineral, timber, and water resources.
(Courtesy State Historical Society)

The fertility of the flat River Lowlands is evident in this Boone County farm scene.

bottom regions the water-deposited soils are deep alluvial deposits of sandy loam and clay loam, or "gumbo." The bottoms are highly productive when properly drained. Before the bootheel was ditched at the beginning of this century, it was a swampy, snake-infested wasteland overgrown with cypress, magnolia, and gum trees. After 1500 miles of drainage canals were dug, it was transformed into a booming cotton plantation area typical of states farther to the south.

Recognizing these four geographic regions in the state should help us to understand the later development of certain economic and social distinctions in each section. Furthermore, a consideration of the location and resources of the state explains why Europeans flocked to Missouri. If the European was attracted by geographic factors, so was prehistoric man.

The First Missourians

The first people to inhabit North America entered the continent across a land bridge that connected Asia with North America where the Bering Strait exists today. All Indians both in the prehistoric and historic past descended from this common Mongoloid stock. Man entered the region presently within the bounds of Missouri at least 12,000 years ago, but written records exist for only the past four centuries—a mere three percent of that great time span. It is not the historian, but the archaeologist or prehistorian, with his systematic techniques of excavating, sifting, mapping, and comparing, who has the task of illuminating this long night. Archaeological research points to considerable variety in the type of prehistoric settlements in the state and the lifestyles in those settlements. Missouri was the focal point of several different cultures throughout the prehistoric past, probably because of its central location, diverse topography, and river connections with other regions. Certainly the state is a fruitful area for archaeological research.

The nature of prehistoric man's settlement and subsistence strategies in what is now Missouri has received more detailed research in the past decade. Due to federal legislation mandating cultural resource management studies during the planning and execution of federally funded or federally licensed undertakings that modify the landscape, the study of prehistoric man has greatly accelerated. Currently over forty archaeologists are actively involved in archaeological research in Missouri and data are being compiled at a rapid rate in areas of the state where research had not previously been conducted.

The archaeologist has several methods for determining the age and sequence of prehistoric cultures. Particularly popular in the southwestern part of the United States is the system of counting and comparing the annual growth rings of wood. This technique, called dendrochronology, makes possible the dating of wooden objects, thus sites or strata within sites where wood is discovered can be dated. Another more common archaeological technique is to carefully excavate and analyze surviving artifacts such as stone implements, pottery fragments called sherds, and bone tools according to such attributes as design, size, texture, and skill of workmanship relative to their stratigraphic location in archaeological sites. This is based on the fact that as archaeological materials accumulate on sites over thousands of years the first or oldest specimens are on the bottom with progressively more recent specimens in layers above these. This produces a relative chronology or sequence of human occupations on sites. A more precise technique which is probably the most dramatic and widely-known system for determinining the age of organic materials is the carbon-14 method. All living things contain the same proportions of carbon-14. Since carbon-14 disappears at a known rate after the death of an organism, the time which has lapsed since its death can be determined by measuring the amount of carbon-14 remaining in a specimen of faunal or floral material. Other dating techniques employed by archaeologists are archaeomagnetic and thermoluminescence methods. Like carbon-14 dating these methods are highly complex and require specialists in the physical sciences.

Using the various methods of their discipline, Missouri archaeologists have divided the prehistoric era into several cultural periods. These were first adapted for use in the state by Dr. Carl Chapman of the University of Missouri and have been further refined by research over five decades. These periods are:

Paleo-Indian Period	12,000 B.C. − 8,000 B.C.
Early Archaic Period	8,000 B.C. − 5,000 B.C.
Middle Archaic Period	5,000 B.C. − 3,000 B.C.
Late Archaic Period	3,000 B.C. − 1,000 B.C.
Early Woodland Period	1,000 B.C. − 500 B.C.
Middle Woodland Period	500 B.C. − A.D. 400
Late Woodland Period	A.D. 400 − A.D. 900
Early Mississippi Period	A.D. 900 − A.D. 1350
Late Mississippi Period	A.D. 1350 − A.D. 1700

We will describe each of these archaeological periods in chronological order. The illustrations are an artist's conceptions of some aspects of life in each period. Selected sites from each period which have been explored by archaeologists are indicated on the maps.

The Paleo-Indian Period

We do not know precisely when man first entered Missouri but there is evidence that during the Ice Age or Pleistocene, man coexisted with the mastodon—a tusked mammal similar in size and shape to the present-day elephants in India. Archaeologists have carbon-14 proof that these great beasts still roamed America as late as 8000 years ago. In 1838 a German fossil trader named Albert C. Koch unearthed the charred skeleton of a mastodon while digging in Gasconade County along the Bourbeuse River. Two years after his original find, Dr. Koch discovered a more complete mastodon skeleton near the Pomme de Terre River in Benton County. In both cases Koch found adjacent stone projectile points which may have been used by the early Missourians to kill or weaken the huge animals helplessly mired in the mud. Although Koch found mastodon bones at what is now Mastodon State Park near Kimmswick in Jefferson County he did not find specimens of human manufacture associated with them. One hundred forty years later, while excavating at the same site, the Illinois State Museum funded by a grant from the Missouri Department of Natural Resources recovered fluted Clovis projectile points in direct association with mastodon bones.

Evidence of Paleo-Indians has been found throughout the state but such finds are sporadic. Few large habitation sites yielding multiple specimens of Paleo-Indian artifacts have been discovered. Although Paleo-Indians hunted large Ice Age mammals such as the mastodon it is highly likely that they depended mostly on hunting of small mammals and the gathering of wild floral resources for their subsistence. At best the remains of this important occupation in Missouri are scanty and to date we cannot produce a detailed picture of the life of these ancient peoples.

Typical projectile points of this period are fluted (longitudinally grooved) of exquisite workmanship.

The meticulous work of the archaeologist can be seen in this excavation at Hidden Valley Shelter II in Jefferson County. The area is carefully plotted so that each item found can be located in relation to other objects.

(Courtesy State Historical Society)

THE PALEO-INDIAN PERIOD
12000 B. C. - 8000 B. C.

★ Sites of Koch's discoveries

▲ Distribution of Clovis-type points

Koch's find

Clovis-type points

A bog-mired mastodon was fair game for Early Missouri hunters.

The Early Archaic Period

The Early Archaic Period follows the disappearance of such animals as the mastodon, mammoth, and prehistoric bison and is best known by the presence of the Dalton Culture whose remains occur throughout most areas of the state. These peoples manufactured basally thinned, serrated projectile points differing little in appearance from those of the previous Paleo-Indians. Other artifacts in the Dalton tool kit are chipped stone adzes, steeply flaked endscrapers, and small flaked gravers and burins. Dalton people lived approximately seven to nine thousand years ago and were the first people to leave substantial evidence of their habitation loci. Often their artifacts are made of exotic lithic resources evidencing trade over great distances.

Although the people were still dependent on hunting and gathering for their food, they appear to have moved somewhat less than the Paleo-Indians and to have lived in larger groups. Although they had no agriculture it is likely that resources were abundant and easily extractable in a natural environment that had witnessed little exploitation by man. For shelter from wind, rain and snow they probably constructed skin or grass frame huts called wickiups or made use of natural shelters inside caves or under rock ledges. It is in such places of natural protection that archaeologists have discovered abundant evidence of this period. Late in this period grinding stones for foodstuffs were made. There is no evidence that these people made or used pottery.

The Middle Archaic Period

The middle Archaic Period witnessed the development of regionally diverse cultures utilizing various projectile point shapes usually with stems, side-notches, concave bases and serration. Apparently these people formed different adaptations to the environments of the Ozark Highlands, the Plains, and the Southeast Lowlands in what is now Missouri. Regional settlement patterns and subsistence strategies developed which are recognizable one from another. The full-grooved pecked and ground stone ax was introduced during this period as were stone gorgets, and atlatl weights.

The Late Archaic Period

The period witnessed rather large populations throughout most areas of the state with a wide subsistence base involving

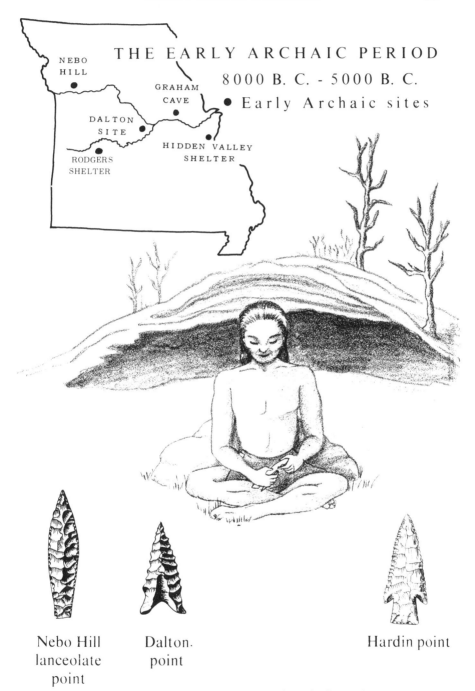

THE EARLY ARCHAIC PERIOD
8000 B. C. - 5000 B. C.
● Early Archaic sites

NEBO
HILL

GRAHAM
CAVE

DALTON
SITE

HIDDEN VALLEY
SHELTER

RODGERS
SHELTER

Nebo Hill
lanceolate
point

Dalton.
point

Hardin point

Shaping stone projectile points was a precise and tedious task.

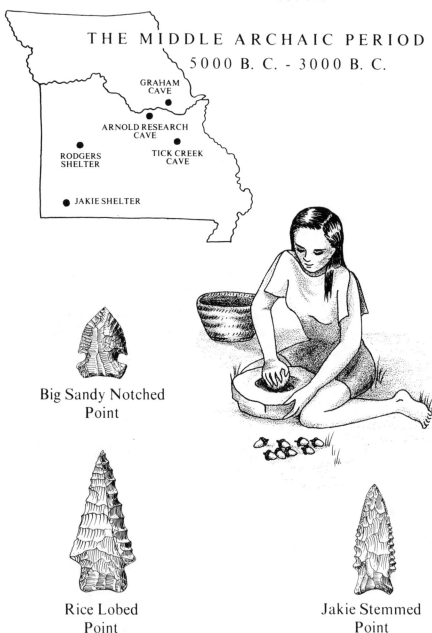

THE MIDDLE ARCHAIC PERIOD
5000 B. C. - 3000 B. C.

GRAHAM CAVE

ARNOLD RESEARCH CAVE

RODGERS SHELTER

TICK CREEK CAVE

JAKIE SHELTER

Big Sandy Notched Point

Rice Lobed Point

Jakie Stemmed Point

Acorns were ground in stone mortars to make flour.

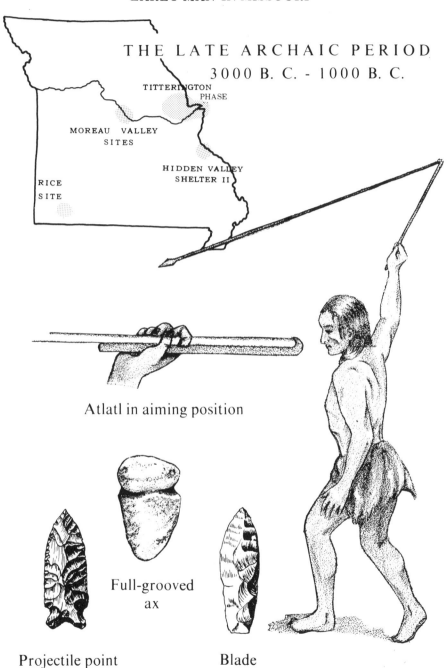

THE LATE ARCHAIC PERIOD
3000 B. C. - 1000 B. C.

TITTERINGTON PHASE

MOREAU VALLEY SITES

HIDDEN VALLEY SHELTER II

RICE SITE

Atlatl in aiming position

Full-grooved ax

Projectile point

Blade

The atlatl made it possible for the Indian to throw his spear faster and farther.

exploitation of a great variety of faunal and floral resources. Recent evidence from the Truman Reservoir area of southwestern Missouri indicates that limited horticulture was introduced during this period. At a site called Phillips Spring evidence of squash in the form of charred seeds and rind were discovered in a Late Archaic context.

Stylistic differences in artifact assemblages varied greatly among the people living in the major river drainages. The Late Archaic people were riverine adapted and the terraces and natural levees of most Missouri streams are dotted with habitation sites formed through repeated use of the same loci over great lengths of time. In fact large accumulations of fire-cracked rock, animal bone, and mussel shells often collected on these sites creating middens, rather deep mounds of heavy organic soils and cultural debris. Projectile points used by these peoples were often quite large, stemmed and cornernotched specimens. Other artifacts, stone beads, fullgrooved axes, atlatl weights, plumments, and gorgets, associated with Late Archaic sites demonstrate an exquisite lapidary industry. The Indians of this period made not only stone tools such as mortars, pestles, axes, digging tools, scrapers, drills, and adzes, but they also used bone and shell for tools of various kinds. Bone needles and shell beads appear in sites of this period. In this pre-pottery era the bow and arrow was not used widely, if at all. Instead, the Indian depended upon his spear which he threw with the help of an atlatl. In effect this wooden throwing stick lengthened the arm of the hunter and made it possible for him to hurl his spear a greater distance at a higher velocity.

The Early Woodland Period

The Early Woodland Period witnessed the first use of ceramics in Missouri and a greater dependence on horticulture. Although much of the Late Archaic lifestyle continued into Woodland times, certain changes took place in settlement and subsistence strategies reflected in the distribution of their sites or habitation loci. Not only are these sites located in major stream valleys but also extend up small tributaries and into environmental zones not extensively occupied previously. Early Woodland peoples made contracting stemmed and cornernotched projectile points and their ceramic vessels often had conical bottoms. The importance of the invention of pottery should not be underemphasized. Early man needed water-tight storage vessels to retain liquids and waterproof containers to protect objects from rain. Gourds were not per-

THE EARLY WOODLAND PERIOD
1000 B. C. - 500 B. C.

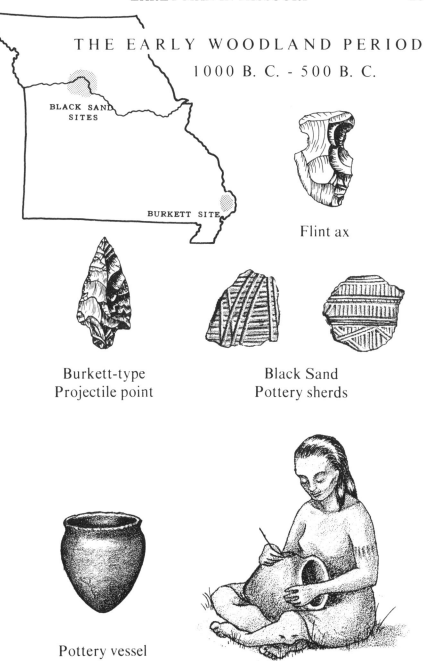

BLACK SAND
SITES

BURKETT SITE

Flint ax

Burkett-type
Projectile point

Black Sand
Pottery sherds

Pottery vessel

The invention of pottery was an important cultural advance in prehistoric Missouri.

manent and decomposed in water. Wooden vessels were difficult
to shape with stone tools. Thus, the crude pottery of the Early
Woodland Period solved some of the problems of transportation,
storage, and food preparation. Surfaces of pottery vessels were
often plain or cordmarked, that is, impressed with a cordwrapped
paddle while the clay was still plastic. Sometimes the surface was
decorated with incised lines, fabric impressions, pinching, punc-
tutations, and bosses. The tempering agent used in the ceramic
past was most often burned and ground limestone or sand.

We know the Missourians of this period had established trade
networks with Indians on the Gulf of Mexico. They used Gulf
seashells for beads and other ornaments.

The Middle Woodland Period

Middle Woodland occupation of Missouri witnessed a rise in
the importance of horticulture. At this time certain parts of the
state received cultural influence and perhaps even migrations of
people from the Ohio and Illinois area in the form of the Hopewell tradition. The major Hopewell development in Missouri
took place along the Missouri River from the Big Bend area in
Saline County to the present site of Kansas City. The Hopewell
people are known from the conical burial mounds they constructed on eminences overlooking major stream valleys. The
Hopewell tradition had little influence in most parts of the
state where many of the same preceding lifeways continued
essentially unmodified. Mound building became an established
practice, however; and these were both of earthen construction
or made of rocks piled to form a mound. The latter are called
cairns.

Middle Woodland projectile points are generally large cornernotched specimens. Other artifacts diagnostic of Middle Woodland
are platform stone pipes and three-quarter grooved axes. Some
Middle Woodland ceramics are elaborately decorated with incised
motifs in the form of stylized raptorial birds.

One characteristic of the Hopewell culture is their more highly
developed agriculture. Corn and beans were their chief crops. Perhaps this easier method of food procurement with a resultant increase of leisure time explains the development of another characteristic—new artifacts and skills. However, they still hunted. Their
favorite prey were deer, bison, and wapiti.

The Hopewell people were widely scattered east of the Rocky
Mountains, and they carried on commerce between the different

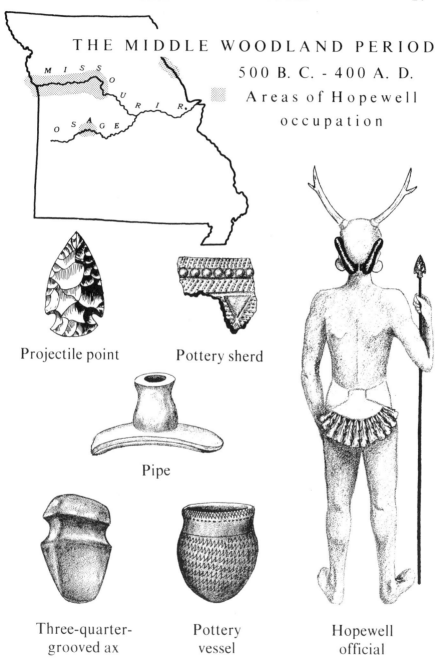

THE MIDDLE WOODLAND PERIOD
500 B. C. - 400 A. D.
Areas of Hopewell
occupation

Projectile point

Pottery sherd

Pipe

Three-quarter-
grooved ax

Pottery
vessel

Hopewell
official

A turkey-feather bustle and an antler headdress adorn this Hopewell official.

major settlements. They distributed copper from the Great Lakes area, quartz, and mica from the Appalachian Mountains, obsidian from the Rocky Mountains, and sea shells from the Gulf Coast.

In excavating Hopewell burial mounds archaeologists have found copper ear plugs which were inserted in the lobe of the ear to stretch it, sea shell beads, freshwater pearls, and shark tooth necklaces, all brought from afar.

Not only was life different for the Hopewell people, but death practices were too. The dead were often placed in mounds enclosed by ceremonial earthworks in geometric forms such as circles, squares, and crescents.

The Late Woodland Period

This period witnessed the decline of the elaborate Hopewell tradition. Subsistence patterns did not change drastically from earlier Woodland Periods. They practiced horticulture and grew corn, pumpkins, sunflowers and beans in small plots. They were primarily a hunting and gathering people who left only moderate evidence of other subsistence activities.

Of paramount importance during this period was the introduction of the bow and arrow. Arrow points are much smaller than those hurled by an atlatl and were probably quite effective in hunting because of their ability to penetrate game when launched by a powerful bow.

The Early Mississippi Period

Approximately A.D. 900 great changes began to take place in the sociopolitical organization and technology of aboriginal groups in the alluvial valley of the Mississippi and in the eastern Ozarks. Rich alluvial soils of the major stream valleys became much sought after for agricultural purposes. As the Mississippian lifeway evolved there was greater dependence on agriculture and large populations began to cluster into villages and towns. Major technological innovations took place in ceramic manufacture and there was a shift to the use of burned and pulverized river mussel shells as a tempering agent in pottery vessels. There was a greater variety of vessel shapes produced including bottles, bowls, and jars. Many of their pottery vessels were modeled into likenesses of animals or human beings. They also produced ceramic ear plugs, ladles, beads, trowels, and marbles.

The more sophisticated technology and agricultural efficiency freed segments of society for public works such as the building of

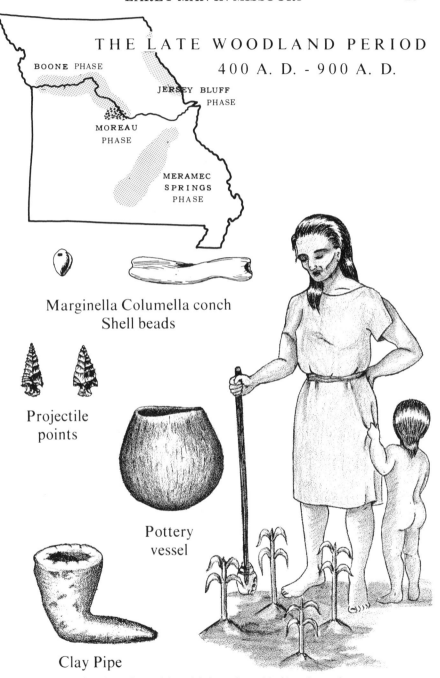

THE LATE WOODLAND PERIOD
400 A. D. - 900 A. D.

BOONE PHASE

JERSEY BLUFF PHASE

MOREAU PHASE

MERAMEC SPRINGS PHASE

Marginella Columella conch Shell beads

Projectile points

Pottery vessel

Clay Pipe

Early Missourians cultivated their gardens with chipped-stone hoes.

large platform mounds and artistic works in sheet copper and ground stone. An elite ruling class arose that formed the paramount authority in the socio-political system. Enormous human labor was expended in the construction of elaborate moats and palisades around towns that sometimes exceeded forty acres in size. They constructed the large mounds by transporting soil in baskets and heaping it up. Such mounds served as bases for large public structures of religious significance.

Trade in many commodities flourished. Among these was chert from southern Illinois widely employed in the manufacture of hoes and large digging implements. Another stone raw material traded from southern Illinois was fashioned into woodworking adzes and gouges. The Mississippian lifeway was shared throughout most of southeastern North America and generated the highest aboriginal population densities in Pre-Columbian times.

The best documented Mississippian manifestation in Missouri is the Powers Phase, a large fortified mound center, subsidiary villages, hamlets, and farmsteads located near the Ozark Border in the Western Lowland of southeast Missouri. Extensive excavations on a series of these sites by a cooperative research effort by the University of Michigan and the University of Missouri indicated that all had been burned and abandoned ca. A.D. 1350. Excavations of whole villages indicated that they were highly planned and structured with walled segments, each with its own courtyard, isolating social groups from each other. Remains of dwellings, specialized public structures, and maize storage structures were discovered in the form of charred building timbers. Fire is generally thought of as a destructive force but to the archaeologist it is often a boon because it sometimes preserves perishable materials such as wood, grass, and food remains by reducing them to charcoal which does not decay. Such was the case in the Powers Phase villages. Architectural elements were abundant enabling archaeologists to accurately reconstruct the kinds of structures employed by these Mississippian peoples.

The Late Mississippi or Protohistoric Period

Shortly before the arrival of European explorers the Mississippian culture began to decline much as the decline following classic Hopewell. Disruption brought about by European diseases and encroachment brought further decline to aboriginal populations. In protohistoric times many areas of the state were devoid of human occupation except for hunting forays by the Osage and

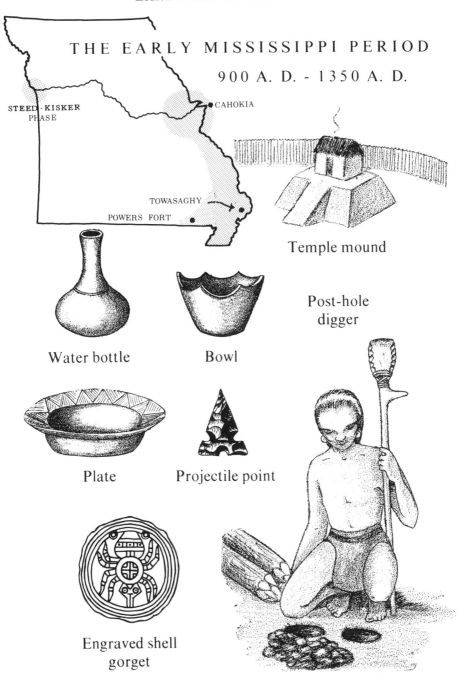

THE EARLY MISSISSIPPI PERIOD
900 A. D. - 1350 A. D.

STEED-KISKER PHASE

CAHOKIA

TOWASAGHY

POWERS FORT

Temple mound

Water bottle

Bowl

Post-hole digger

Plate

Projectile point

Engraved shell gorget

Early Mississippians dug post holes to erect a stockade fence around the village.

Missouri (Oneota) Indians who lived in southwest and northwest Missouri respectively. Most areas of the Ozarks and Bootheel of southeast Missouri were abandoned except for a series of villages on Pemiscot Bayou in the extreme southeastern tip of southeast Missouri occupied by peoples carrying on the Mississippian lifeway. These villages were abandoned in the seventeeth century and the region remained essentially vacant until the arrival of Euro-American trappers, traders, and settlers in the eighteenth century.

Both the Osage and Missouri Indians continued to occupy the prairie regions of the western part of the state until the eighteenth century. According to Osage tradition their tribe originally came from the Ohio Valley. The legends of the Missouri tribe stated that their group moved down the Grand River from the region to the north.

Both tribes combined hunting, gathering, and agriculture to sustain themselves. The Missouri also fished for food. The two tribes carried on the usual occupations of making pottery, stone weapons, bows and arrows, and clothing from animal skins. They also knew how to weave cloth. Pipe smoking and painting the skin with red iron ore called hematite were important parts of their tribal ceremonies. They lived in large—sometimes 100 feet long—frame lodges covered with skins or mats. These houses sheltered extended families and were located around an open area which was used for meetings and dances.

About the year 1719 these Indians began regular trade with the Euro-Americans. As the Indians turned more and more to the business of preparing skins for sale to these traders they gave up most of their old arts and adopted European-type weapons, tools and clothing. In a later chapter more will be said about these Indians during the historic periods of the state.

That Missouri was an important region during several parts of the prehistoric past is evidenced by the complex of mounds that once stood in the St. Louis area and the few that remain across the Mississippi River near Cahokia, Illinois. Much research has been done, but much remains to be done. Even with the present incomplete evidence we can sketch the slow development of man in Missouri as we observe the gradual improvement in weapons, tools, pottery, agriculture, and home constuction. We can even chart an evolution in religious ceremonies, commerce, and social practices. A new civilization was slowly, painfully emerging in North America. This process of social evolution was halted by the waves of Euro-American settlers that surged over the continent pushing

THE LATE MISSISSIPPI PERIOD
1350 A. D. - 1700 A. D.

House

Bevelled
knife

Bison-
scapula hoe

Projectile
point

Pipe

Pottery vessel

Disk-bowl pipe

A framework of saplings was the foundation for Late Mississippi lodges.

aside the Indian and bringing in European customs, languages, and beliefs.

Missouri is now clearly part of Western Civilization, but this has been so for only a minute segment of her history. No doubt future archaeological finds will help us know better the people who struggled here so long before the white man arrived.

Although archaeologists are extremely active in the discovery and assessment of archaeological sites in Missouri they cannot begin to keep pace with the rapid destruction of our prehistoric cultural resources. St. Louis was once known as "Mound City" for the numerous Indian embankments in the area. The early residents of St. Louis even made use of some mounds. The first city water works was constructed on top of a mound at the corner of Dickson and Collins Streets. The elevation increased the water pressure. In 1819, after some had already been destroyed, there were still twenty-seven mounds left in the north end of the city. Only one of those mounds remains in St. Louis today. Cultural resources are nonrenewable and finite in number. They contain all the data that archaeologists can ever anticipate generating from research. Urban expansion, agricultural landleveling, and forest clearing are taking a heavy toll in destruction of these resources. Fortunately, as Americans become more concerned with environmental consider- ations so has concern risen for our cultural heritage. Numerous federal mandates and directives have generated programs for cultural resources management. During the planning of federally licensed or federally funded projects, archaeologists now play an active role in the discovery and assessment of archaeological properties in direct impact zones. Adverse impacts are mitigated through avoiding or systematically studying significant sites so that important information on the first Missourians is not irre- trievably lost.

BIBLIOGRAPHY

GEOGRAPHY

Branson, Edwin B. *The Geology of Missouri.* The University of Missouri Studies, Vol. XIX, No. 3 (Columbia: The University of Missouri, 1944).

Collier, James E. *Agricultural Atlas of Missouri.* University of Missouri College of Agriculture Bulletin, No. 645 (February, 1955).

Collier, James E. "Geographic Regions of Missouri," *Annals of the Association of American Geographers*, Vol. XLV, No. 4 (December, 1955), pp. 369-392.

Collier, James E. *The Geography of the Northern Ozark Region in Missouri.* The University of Missouri Studies, Vol. XXVI, No. 1 (Columbia: The University of Missouri, 1953).

Garland, John H., ed. *The North American Midwest: A Regional Geography.* New York: John Wiley & Sons, Inc., 1955.

Gist, Noel P., et al., eds. *Missouri: Its Resources, People and Institutions.* Columbia: The Curators of the University of Missouri, 1950.

Rutledge, Wiley B. "Missouri, Crossroads of the Nation," *Missouri Historical Review*, Vol. XXXVIII (October, 1943), pp. 1-11.

PREHISTORY

Chapman, Carl H. *The Archaeology of Missouri.* Vols. I-II. Columbia: University of Missouri Press, 1975 and 1980.

Chapman, Carl H. and Eleanor F. Chapman. *Indians and Archaeology of Missouri.* Missouri Handbook No. 5, Fourth Printing.Columbia: University of Missouri Press, 1978.

Cottier, Randy, Susan B. Traub and Don C. Traub. *A Selected Bibliography of Missouri Archaeology.* Columbia: Missouri Archaeological Society Research Series No. 10, 1973.

Early Man. Quarterly magazine published by Northwestern Archeology, a program jointly sponsored by Northwestern University and the Foundation for Illinois Archaeology.

Hester, Thomas R., Robert F. Heizer, and John A. Graham. *Field Methods in Archaeology.* Palo Alto: Mayfield Publishing Company, 1975.

Jennings, Jesse D. and Edward Norbeck, eds. *Prehistoric Man in the New World.* Chicago: The University of Chicago Press, 1964.

Price, James E., and James B. Griffin. *The Snodgrass Site of the Powers Phase of Southeast Missouri.* Ann Arbor: University of Michigan Museum of Anthropology, Anthropological Papers No. 66, 1979.

The Missouri Archaeologist. 41 vols. Columbia: The Missouri Archaeological Society, 1935-1981.

Willey, Gordon R. *Introduction to American Archaeology.* Vol. I, North and Middle America. Englewood Cliffs: Prentice-Hall, 1966.

CHAPTER II

The European Arrives

The Missionaries and others, who have had the most
perfect Knowledge of Louisiana, give us so great an Idea
of its uncommon Beauties and Productions, that one would
take it for the French-Men's Paradise.
—anonymous eighteenth-century observer

Today the United States is in a race with other nations of
the world to explore and exploit outer space. There was a similar race in the sixteenth, seventeenth, and eighteenth centuries
to claim and conquer North America. Although Spain, England,
France, and Holland all took part in this competition, Spain and
France were the first to be active in the Missouri region.

De Soto's Expedition

Sixteenth-century Spain had a surplus of courageous, reckless young men thirsting for adventure. These conquistadors
found what they were looking for in the huge uncharted wilderness that was America. Encouraged by the Spanish monarchs
with their desire for empire and by the Church with its missionary motives, these young men dreamed of discovering such
fabulous places as the Seven Lost Cities. Spanish mythology
assured them these cities were constructed of gold and the
streets inlaid with precious jewels. The fact that several conquistadors did discover high Indian civilizations with much gold
and silver in Mexico and Peru only whetted their appetite for
more such treasure.

Hernando De Soto, a dashing, handsome, headstrong, young
swashbuckler, was a member of Pizarro's small expedition into
Peru. He shared in the $15,000,000 loot of that amazingly suc-
cessful and frequently brutal conquest. Returning to Spain to
be knighted, he organized an expedition of his own to probe the

"DeSoto Discovering the Mississippi" is a painting by Oscar E. Berninghaus who was born in St. Louis in 1874. Berninghaus has painted many colorful scenes of early Missouri history, some of which are in the state capitol in Jefferson City.

interior of North America. Landing his 720 men on the west coast of Florida in 1539, he immediately moved inland in search of rich cities, precious metals, and jewels. Pushing aside or cutting down Indians in his path, the ruthless explorer followed the mirage of "riches just ahead" through the present-day states of Florida, Georgia, South Carolina, North Carolina, Tennessee, Alabama, and Mississippi. Those Indians who were not cowed by the size of his army were often terrified by the sight of his horses, his huge wolfhounds, and his eighteen primitive guns which gave off a cloud of smoke when fired.

After two years of futile wandering, De Soto's weary, ragged, and rusty-armor-clad expedition reached the Mississippi River. This gave Spain claim to ownership of the great Mississippi Valley. He crossed the river in 1541 and spent ten months exploring the Ozarks of Arkansas. Although he was close to Missouri, he did not enter the state. Just before he died De Soto ordered the slaughter of an entire nearby Indian settlement as an object lesson to natives in the area to encourage obedience to his commands. As in some of the other Indian massacres, men, women, and children all were butchered. Thus did Western Civilization come to the Mississippi Valley. When De Soto died in Arkansas in 1542 his companions knew that his grave would certainly be molested by vengeful Indians. To prevent this, his weighted body was submerged secretly in the Mississippi. The survivors fled south to the Gulf of Mexico.

De Soto sought treasure in mid-America. He did not find it. Although the Spanish failed to appreciate the fact, he did discover a great fertile region far more valuable than golden trinkets. The Spanish did not follow this exploration with settlement. The Mississippi Valley remained undisturbed by Europeans for another century.

The French Period (1673-1770)

French Beginnings

Because of numerous problems at home, England and France were unable to begin the colonization of North America until about 1600. The English settled in the area that is today the eastern United States. Hedged in by the Appalachian Mountains, the English were slow to move westward into the middle of the continent. The earliest French settlements, however, were made farther north along the St. Lawrence River. This waterway immediately lured the inquisitive Frenchmen inland. Quebec was founded in 1608. By 1615 the French had reached Lake Huron; by 1634, Green Bay, Wisconsin; by 1673, Missouri. In contrast, it was 1671 before the first English colonist ventured so far west as to cross the Appalachians.

There are several reasons why the French were so active in exploring the interior of the continent. First, it was part of French national policy to develop a great empire. This was particularly true under Louis XIV whose expansionist policies provoked war after war. The French crown hoped that by seizing the interior of North America, particularly the Ohio Valley, they would contain the British to the area east of the Appalachians. Second, the French as well as other Europeans were looking for a Northwest Passage to the Pacific. Rich rewards were sure for those who could control the passageway for the trade of the Orient. Third, the Catholic secular orders of France, especially the Jesuits, were imbued with a strong missionary zeal. Fourth, the French wanted to enlarge their lucrative fur trade. Fifth, the Frenchmen were curious about all aspects of the New World including rumors of wealth and high civilization.

In contrast to the Spanish, the French usually went west

in small groups that were at the mercy of the Indians. These men lived with the Indians, traded with them, and sometimes took Indian wives. French-Canadians who went out as traders and trappers were known as *coureurs de bois* (koo ruhr duh BWAH). The boatmen who transported goods and people far into the heart of the continent were called *voyageurs* (vwah yah ZHUR). These French-Canadians were fearless people, particularly suited to the conquest of a great continent. Crude, superstitious, volatile, often illiterate, they would work under the most primitive conditions for scant wages and little food. Scorning blizzards, mosquitoes, bears, plagues, Indian attacks, and starvation, they seemed addicted to suffering.

These were men who would paddle and portage 2000 miles in a summer. Marquette and Joliet traveled over 2500 miles in their frail birch-bark canoes. Not even Indian tortures could scare them into leaving the West. The accounts of the slow horrible executions of Jesuit priests by the Indians only encouraged more Jesuits to set up new missions. Such French persistence was personified by Pierre Radisson. As a boy of fifteen the plucky Frenchman was captured by Indians who tied him to a rack, pulled out four of his fingernails, and scorched his feet and legs. A small Indian boy spent part of a day attempting to chew off one of Radisson's fingers. The young Frenchman was lucky enough to be set free and went on to a long and fruitful career as an explorer in North America.

"Marquette Descending the Mississippi, 1673" by Oscar E. Berninghaus

(Courtesy August A. Busch, Jr.)

It took more than occasional Indian violence to discourage the French.

French Explorers

Who were the first Frenchmen in Missouri? Some authors give this honor to Radisson and Groseilliers (groh zay YAY) since their records show that sometime in the 1650's they discovered a stream "wch we believe runns toward Mexico." However, there is no clear evidence that they followed this stream to Missouri. Probably Marquette and Joliet during their expedition of 1673 were the first Europeans to reach Missouri. Louis Joliet was the experienced Canadian-born *voyageur* in charge of the expedition. Jacques Marquette was a dedicated Jesuit missionary noted for his ability to speak six Indian dialects. Taking along only five *voyageurs* in two canoes, they left Lake Michigan at Green Bay, traveled down the Fox River, portaged two miles to the Wisconsin River and descended the Wisconsin until it emptied into the Mississippi.

As the party floated downstream on the Father-of-Waters they marveled at the huge catfish, the curious-appearing spadefish, the great buffalo, the friendly Illinois Indians, and the rock paintings mentioned earlier. But the greatest discovery of the voyage came when they arrived at the junction of the

In 1715 Antoine de la Motte Cadillac, the Governor of Louisiana, crossed the Mississippi from Kaskaskia looking for silver deposits which had been reported in Missouri. Cadillac's party discovered a rich vein of lead ore in what is today northern Madison County. Although Cadillac remained only a brief time, the site became known as Mine La Motte in his honor. About a decade later Philippe Renault came to work the lead mines of the region.

(Cadillac etching by Charles A. Barker. Courtesy Burton Historical Collection, Detroit Public Library)

Missouri and the Mississippi rivers. These are the words Marquette used to describe the event.

> . . . sailing quietly in clear and calm water, we heard the noise of a rapid, into which we were about to run. I have seen nothing more dreadful. An accumulation of large and entire trees, branches, and floating islands, were issuing from the mouth of the river *Pekitanoui,* with such impetuosity that we could not without great danger risk passing through it. So great was the agitation that the water was very muddy, and could not become clear.

On the map made by Marquette he called this new muddy stream the *Pekitanoui.* Near the river he located an Indian village called *Ou-Missouri.* Later French explorers assigned the name Missouri to the river for which the state is named.

From the flow of the river which they had discovered, the French reasoned that this new stream must be lengthy. Since it appeared to be coming from the northwest, they considered the possibility that it might be a passage to the Pacific. Marquette immediately began planning another voyage up the new river. "I hope by its means to discover the Vermillion or California Sea" he wrote in his journal. Not only did he wish to explore and claim new regions, but he desired to "preach the Gospel to all the peoples of this new world who have so long grovelled in the darkness of infidelity." Marquette was unable to complete his plan. After traveling down the Mississippi as far as the mouth of the Arkansas River, the party returned to Lake Michigan. Two years later on the shore of this lake the dedicated Jesuit, weakened by long illness, died. The Marquette-Joliet expedition is significant because it demonstrated that the Mississippi did not flow into the Pacific. It opened a new possibility that the Missouri River might be a channel to Asia.

The French were not slow to follow up their first exploration of the Mississippi. In 1682 a Frenchman named La Salle canoed down the Mississippi with his one-armed friend Tonty and fifty-two French and Indian comrades. As they descended the great river, La Salle envisaged a new French empire in America stretching from the St. Lawrence in Canada, along the Great Lakes and Mississippi, south to the Gulf of Mexico. He planned a great chain of French settlements along the waterways to control the Indian trade and exploit the land and mines.

Arriving at the mouth of the Mississippi, the French erected a column with the royal coat of arms, planted a cross next to it, and buried an inscribed lead plate. Then La Salle with great pomp proclaimed to his little assemblage:

> In the name of the most high mighty, invincible and victorious Prince, Louis the Great . . . I . . . do now take, in the name of his Majesty and of his successors to the crown, possession of this country of Louisiana. . . .

Thus, the new French empire on the Mississippi came to be named after Louis XIV. La Salle, the architect of a greatly enlarged New France, was murdered several years later, but his far-sighted blueprints inspired French policy in America for the next eighty years.

After La Salle, French explorers appeared in Missouri with increasing frequency. Some came to save souls, others to find furs, tin, salt, and lead or an easy route to the Pacific or the silver mines of New Mexico. To many the unknown stretches of land on the Missouri River were an irresistible temptation. Joutel appeared in 1687; Derbanne in 1706; Darac in 1710; and Du Tisne in 1719. Their reports of the area speak of "great quantities of buffalo, bear, deer," "the most beautiful prairies and woods," "a very, very rich lead mine," and "so great a quantity of wild pigeons, that the air was darkened and quite covered by them."

While these Frenchmen were alternately amazed and delighted at the resources of the region, they were sometimes puzzled by the superstitions of the natives. Henri Joutel and his expedition navigating up the Mississippi in 1687 came upon the Indian thunderbird painting Marquette had seen earlier. Joutel reported that when their party came upon the scene:

> Our *Indians* paid Homage by offering Sacrifice to that Stone; tho' we endeavor'd to give them to understand, that the said Rock had no Manner of Virtue, and that we worship'd something above it, pointing up to Heaven; but it was to no *Purpose*, and they made Signs to us, that they should die if they did not perform that Duty.

First French Settlements

Today's territorial distinctions between Illinois and Missouri did not exist during the period of French control of Louisiana. The area on both sides of the Mississippi River in mid-America was called Illinois. Following the earliest explorers came a stream of Canadians into Illinois to establish missions, trading posts, and mining operations. The missionary sometimes objected to traders who set up their posts near missions and gave the Indians brandy. Because the Indians were not used to strong drink their use of it frequently led to debauchery and violence in Indian villages and undid much of the work of the missionaries. However, since the missionaries themselves depended upon the traders for supplies it was difficult and perhaps unwise to attempt to drive the traders away.

The first two settlements in the area were on the east side of the Mississippi at Cahokia (1699) and Kaskaskia (1700). The first French settlement west of the Mississippi occurred about the year 1700. The scanty information available indicates that a group of Frenchmen lived at an Indian encampment on the River Des Peres where they built cabins, a chapel, and fortifications. Father Pinet, a Jesuit, was a priest in the settlement. The location is part of St. Louis today. The site was abandoned about the year 1703 when the settlers moved to Kaskaskia.

It sometimes happens that an isolated event can make an unknown part of the world famous. This happened to the Mississippi Valley in the years 1717-1720. John Law, a Scottish financier, headed the so-called Mississippi Company, which had been granted a monopoly of the trade in the Mississippi Valley. Law, like La Salle, had grand plans for the Mississippi Valley and he soon persuaded thousands of Frenchmen to invest in his company. As reports of his plans spread, a mania developed in France. People bid higher and higher for stock in his Mississippi venture. But in 1720 when public confidence in Law suddenly ended, the great Mississippi Bubble burst. The value of the stock fell to almost nothing and the company was forced into bankruptcy. Law did not establish any settlements in Missouri, but he did focus the attention of France on the Mississippi Valley for a time.

In the 1720's and the 1730's a new wave of French people moved into Illinois. East of the Mississippi, Fort Chartres was established in 1720, St. Philippe in 1723, and Prairie du Rocher in 1733. West of the Mississippi, Philippe Renault, an ambitious mining promoter, set up the first extensive lead mines in 1720 with 200 workers, mining tools from France, and black slaves, from the West Indies. His main mining operations were on the Meramec River and in the area around Mine La Motte. He continued this operation for about twenty years.

Etienne de Bourgmond (sometimes spelled Bourgmont) was another man who played an important role in the early years of French occupation. Before he came to Missouri he was noted both for his bravery in an Indian battle at Fort Detroit and for having deserted his military post. While at Fort Detroit in Michigan he fell in love with an Indian maiden whom he followed to her home in Missouri. During his stay in Missouri from 1712-1718, he made an exploration up the Missouri River at least as far as the mouth of the Platte River and perhaps farther. After returning to France in 1719 with his half-breed son, he found French officials worried about reports of a Spanish expedition from Santa Fe in the area of the Missouri River. Wishing to protect the Missouri Valley from Spanish encroachment, the Company of the Indies, which was then in charge of Louisiana, sent Bourgmond back to America in 1722 with the title of "Commandant of the Missouri." He and his son returned to their Indian village on the Missouri River late in 1724. He built, as ordered, a fortification named Fort Orleans on the north bank of the river in what is today Carroll County. Although it was a simple structure it included living quarters, a chapel, a storage area and a stockade. The next year, under orders from Paris, he made a journey into Kansas to conclude a peace treaty between the fierce Comanches and the Missouri tribes. He was not able to go on to Santa Fe as he had hoped. In 1725 he returned to France, having established friendly relations with the Indians of the Missouri area and some of the tribes between Santa Fe and Missouri. He felt sure that French traders would soon be able to carry their goods to Santa Fe to exchange for Spanish silver dollars. His assurance was justified in 1739 when the Mallet brothers did reach Santa Fe.

When Bourgmond returned to Paris in 1725 he took along a delegation of Indians from the Missouri area including a princess of the Missouri tribe. These first Americans delighted the Parisians, King Louis XV, and the entire royal court with their unusual appearance and curious customs. They demonstrated a stag hunt for the court to show their prowess as hunters. They performed their Indian dances at the opera and presented gifts to the King. The Indian princess was baptized at the Cathedral

(Courtesy Massie-Missouri Commerce)

Ernest L. Blumenschein's painting in the Missouri capitol portrays the return of the French soldier and his Indian bride to Fort Orleans in the late 1720's.

Notre Dame de Paris and later was married to one of Bourgmond's soldiers, a Sergeant Dubois.

The French were fascinated by the Indians. The Indians, who returned to America in rich and beautiful French costumes, were mutually impressed. The old Indian chief, Chicagou, for the rest of his long life carefully kept in his possession a snuffbox that had been given to him by the Duchess of Orleans. The Indian princess returned to Missouri with "a beautiful repeating watch, adorned with diamonds, which the savages called a spirit, because of its movement, which seemed to them supernatural." Even thirty years after the Paris visit one Indian recalled his impression of the perfumed women of France who, as he described them, "smelled like alligators."

Ste. Genevieve—First Permanent Missouri Settlement

Missouri's first two settlements—at River Des Peres and Fort Orleans—were both temporary. Fort Orleans was abandoned after only six years of occupation and the River Des Peres site after an even briefer period. The first permanent French settlement in Missouri was made at Ste. Genevieve sometime during the second quarter of the eighteenth century. Tradition assigns the date 1735 to the founding. Unfortunately, we know little about the character of this early settlement. Two factors —salt springs and lead mines in the area—probably were responsible for the location of the town. The town itself was in a low region about three miles below the site of Ste. Genevieve today. Probably there was a scattered group of homes situated on a narrow road. We know that the houses were constructed in the typical French fashion with the hewn logs arranged vertically instead of horizontally as in the usual American log cabin.

The census of 1752 reveals that the settlement had only twenty whites and three blacks. There were eight registered owners of land but only six were in residence in 1752. By 1769 one official estimated a population of 600 people in the settlement. Ste. Genevieve had a nickname. It was called "Misere" (mee ZAHR) which means wretchedness or in want. Perhaps this is descriptive of the character of that early settlement. Ste. Genevieve played a significant role in the early lead trade. It was the point from which lead from the mines at Mine La Motte, Fourche a Renault, and Mine a Breton was shipped down the river. The miners shaped the lead into horse collars, put them over horses' heads and led the animals to Ste. Genevieve. Because of frequent floods the town of Ste. Genevieve was moved in the last quarter of the eighteenth century to its present location.

The Founding of St. Louis

Auguste Chouteau, who was only thirteen, hardly seemed old enough for the job, but in August, 1763, he was in charge of a heavily-loaded boat moving up the Mississippi River. He shouted as his crew of solemn *voyageurs* alternately paddled, cordelled, or poled the pirogue (canoe-like boat) upstream. His craft was only one of a flotilla carrying supplies from New Orleans to the Illinois Country for Maxent-Laclede and Company. Since the company had an exclusive franchise for eight years to trade with the Indians on the Missouri River, their cargo was mainly merchandise which the Indians sought such as cloth, shirts, guns, powder, flints, knives, blankets, kettles, hatchets, and hooks.

In the first boat leading the flotilla was Auguste's stepfather, Pierre Laclede Liguest, who has come to be known in Missouri history simply as Laclede. He and a man named Antoine Maxent of New Orleans were partners in this business

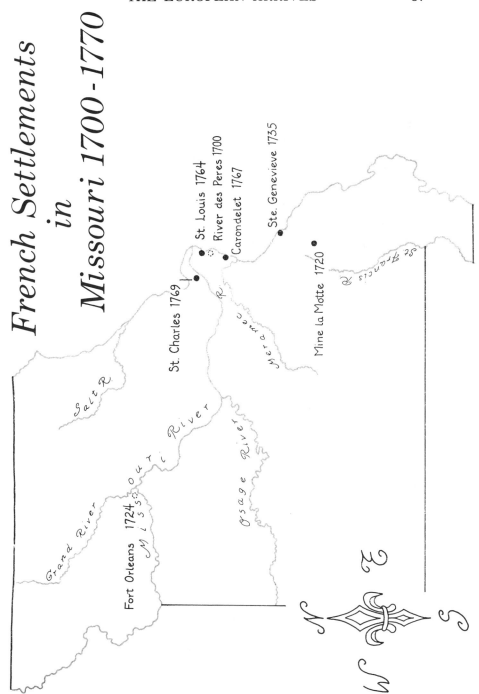

French Settlements in Missouri 1700-1770

St. Louis 1764
River des Peres 1700
Carondelet 1767
Ste. Genevieve 1735
St. Charles 1769
Mine la Motte 1720
Fort Orleans 1724
St. Francis R.
Meramec R.
Salt R.
Grand River
Missouri River
Osage River

Pierre Laclede Liguest, a fur merchant who had been trained in civil engineering in France, selected the site and directed the establishment of St. Louis.
(*Courtesy Missouri Historical Society, St. Louis*)

venture. Maxent remained in New Orleans, but the dark-eyed, olive-skinned Laclede was to direct their activities on the Missouri River. Laclede, who was a graduate of the University of Toulouse in France and a civil engineer, had previously been a planter in southern Louisiana and a soldier. Now he was a merchant who hoped to tap the great reservoir of fur in the Missouri region.

After a three-month struggle against the river the weary Frenchmen finally came to the little village of Ste. Genevieve. To their great disappointment the group found that in Ste. Genevieve there were not enough available buildings for holding even one-fourth of their merchandise. Laclede then accepted the kind offer of shelter from the commandant at Fort Chartres.

In December, 1763, Laclede and Chouteau crossed to the west side of the Mississippi in order to find a place for the establishment of a trading post. Looking for a site on the Mississippi where boats could easily unload their cargo and a place which would not flood during the high water period in the spring, he picked an elevated area on the west bank of the Mississippi about twelve miles below the mouth of the Missouri. There Laclede marked several trees. He told young Chouteau that it would be his responsibility to return in the early spring and begin the construction work. When the two returned to Fort Chartres, Laclede informed his associates that he believed the new settlement "might become, hereafter, one of the finest cities of America." He was right.

By the early part of February enough of the ice on the Mississippi had cleared so that the river could be crossed with boats. Although it may seem strange to us today, in Chouteau's time boys who early displayed intelligence and responsibility were given positions of command. Auguste Chouteau was barely fourteen years old, but Laclede placed him in command of the crew of thirty construction workers sent to begin the building of a town. He was ordered to clear the land, build a warehouse for the company merchandise, and construct cabins for the workers. Chouteau completed the task assigned him, then Laclede himself crossed the river in April to direct the main construction. Shortly after his arrival, Laclede named the city St. Louis in honor of the kind, just French King Louis IX.

As soon as the Indians in the area heard of the new settlement, a group of 150 warriors together with their women and children encamped immediately next to Laclede's site. The curious aborigines not only hampered construction but they were soon "appropriating everything they could lay their hands on." Hoping that the prospect of hard labor would drive them away, Laclede ordered the Indians to begin digging a cellar for a house

"LaClede Landing at the Present Site of St. Louis" by Oscar E. Berninghaus.

(Courtesy of August A. Busch, Jr.)

he planned to construct. The tribal leaders were not so easily outwitted. The braves ordered their women to do the work while the men continued their loitering and pilfering. Finally, Laclede threatened to call in troops from Fort Chartres and the tribe reluctantly left. But though the French disliked the immediate presence of the Indians in St. Louis, the city clearly was built upon the trade with them. Only five years after the city was established, in 1769, the traders exported between 1200 and 1500 packs of furs which they had procured from their Indian neighbors. Obviously the natives whom Laclede considered a nuisance were necessary to the success of the French in St. Louis.

The French settlers had a tradition of assigning nicknames to their villages. These names often are humorous to us now, but they were probably descriptive of the conditions of life in the villages. St. Louis was called "Pain Court" which means "short of bread." Only five miles south of St. Louis was the little village of Carondelet which was settled in about the year 1767. It was called "Vide Poche" or "empty pocket." One historian suggests that Carondelet was given this nickname because of the gambling in that area.

St. Charles

St. Charles was established in 1769 on the north bank of the Missouri River about twenty-one miles from the point where the Mississippi and Missouri unite. A hunter named Louis Blanchette started the village as a trading post. He located the buildings just far enough north of the river to escape the periodic flood waters. As in the other French settlements, the inhabitants planted crops and grazed their animals in the large common fields surrounding the town. However, most settlers also engaged in hunting and the Indian trade. Blanchette, who married a Pawnee woman named Angelique, exemplified the close association with the Indians that was typical of the people at St. Charles. Because of this, the inhabitants of St. Louis were sometimes contemptuous of their St. Charles neighbors. It is not unusual in the history of frontier America for the inhabitants of the older settlements to consider the people of the new frontier towns as being inferior in culture. Lieutenant-Governor Zenon Trudeau wrote of St. Charles in 1795, "the customs are so depraved there due to its being in a most out of the way location and its residence of the savages, mongrels and the worst scoundrels in Illinois." Trudeau asked the Governor-General in New Orleans to send a priest to St. Charles in order to "restrain them in their vices." St. Charles was not a large settlement. At no time before the United States took possession of Louisiana in 1804 did more than 100 families reside in St. Charles.

The Spanish Period (1770-1804)

The Transfer of Louisiana

The eighteenth century, like the century in which we live, was a time of many world wars. These wars usually started in Europe and then spread to the colonies ruled by the warring powers. France and England were enemies in each of these conflicts.

For the French empire in North America, the crucial contest of the century was the French and Indian War (1754-1763). The conflict began when English colonists attempted to claim and settle the Ohio Valley. In 1754 a twenty-two year old Virginia surveyor named George Washington led a small English military unit across the Appalachian Mountains to attack the French forces in the Ohio Valley. The war which followed this skirmish was disastrous for French interests in America. One by one the French forts and principal settlements were captured—Fort Duquesne on the Ohio River, Quebec and Montreal on the St. Lawrence, and many lesser forts. It was clear by 1762 that France must give up her valuable St. Lawrence settlements and probably much of North America, since she had been defeated at sea, in Canada, in the Ohio Valley, and in the West Indies.

Spain was drawn into the war early in 1762 on the side of almost-defeated France. The French and Spanish monarchs were closely allied since both were members of the House of Bourbon—a noble French family from which were descended several European kings. But the Spanish had no more success than the French in the war against England. Late in 1762 both France and Spain were ready to make peace.

The negotiations to conclude the French and Indian War began in Paris in the fall of 1762. Since the English had won the war, they made extensive territorial demands on France and

Spain. The English wanted Canada and all French territory in North America as far west as the Mississippi River. If the French were to lose their valuable settlements on the St. Lawrence and the Great Lakes, it seemed futile to try to retain the area west of the Mississippi. Louisiana had been a financial drain on France for many years. The slight revenues from the region did not provide enough money for the governmental expenses. Thus, Louis XV of France made a secret treaty with Charles III of Spain which transferred to Spain "the country known by the name of Louisiana, as well as New Orleans and the island in which the city is situated." By this secret deal known as the Treaty of Fontainebleau of 1762, the area that is now Missouri became Spanish property. Three months later the Treaty of Paris of 1763 stripped the French of Canada and all the area east of the Mississippi. The great French empire in North America vanished. La Salle's grandiose plan was shattered.

The Spanish were no more anxious than the French to bear the heavy expense of administering Louisiana, but there were several compelling reasons why Spain accepted the gift. There was always the chance that the region might become more valuable later if it were heavily settled or if precious metals were discovered. The defense of Mexico and New Mexico was an even more important consideration. The Spanish thought of Louisiana as a buffer zone to protect their silver-producing regions from British traders or settlers. When Louisiana was transferred from Bourbon France to Bourbon Spain, it meant the territory was being kept in the family and out of the hands of their common enemy.

The Migration

The French and the English were traditional enemies in the eighteenth century, having fought three wars by mid-century. In addition to this war hatred there was a religious conflict between the two countries. France was a Catholic nation; England was Protestant. One can understand the distress of many French colonists living east of the Mississippi when they discovered in 1763 that they were living in English territory. As an example of the attitude of the French residing on the Illinois side of the Mississippi River, every family in the village of St. Philippe left, except one. The family that remained owned

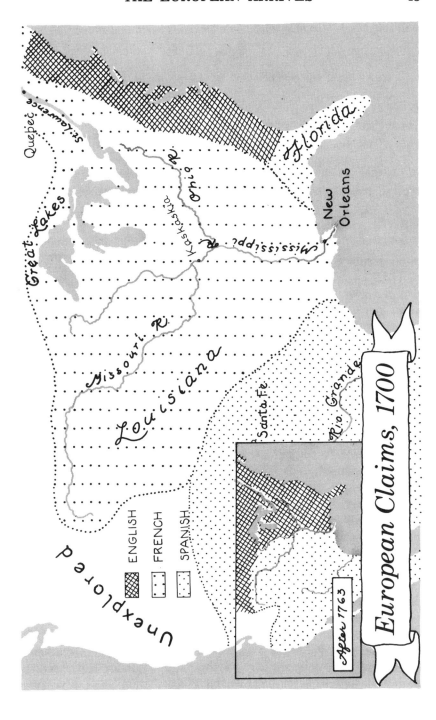

European Claims, 1700

ENGLISH
FRENCH
SPANISH

After 1763

a mill for which they could not find a buyer. Some of the refugees went to lower Louisiana or France, others crossed the Mississippi and settled in Missouri.

When Laclede established St. Louis early in 1764, he knew about the dissatisfaction of the French settlers with the transfer of Illinois to Britain. His plan to attract many of these unhappy people to his own settlement was successful. As soon 'as Fort Chartres was formally transferred to the English, the French commander, St. Ange, moved his garrison of troops to St. Louis. Thus the city was founded at just the right time to receive many new inhabitants. It was a happy combination of geography and history which aided Laclede and the city he founded.

Spanish Political Control

Although the treaty for transfer of Louisiana was signed in 1762, the Spanish government did not officially assume control of the Missouri region until May, 1770. This occurred when quiet, sensitive Pedro Piernas appeared in St. Louis to replace St. Ange, the acting French governor of Upper Louisiana.

The administrative structure of the Spanish empire in America was clear-cut and simple. Louisiana was divided into Upper and Lower Louisiana and Missouri was part of the former. Upper Louisiana was governed by a lieutenant-governor residing in St. Louis. This lieutenant-governor was subordinate to a governor-general in New Orleans, and a captain-general in Havana, Cuba. The lieutenant-governor could be, and sometimes was, overruled by his superiors. Below the lieutenant-governors were commandants who had military, political, and judicial responsibility in a given area. In isolated, small settlements, syndics were named to do the work of the commandant.

Spanish government in Missouri certainly was not democracy as we know it today. Of the major nations of Europe in the eighteenth century only England had a government which allowed popular participation. Both France and Spain had monarchs who ruled without interference from a parliament. The English colonists who came to America at once demanded assemblies and a part in government. This was part of their political tradition. French and Spanish colonists made no such demands. They were not used to participation in government. Therefore, self-government did not exist during the Spanish period of control in Missouri from 1770 to 1804.

We can catch a glimpse of the political life of Missouri during this time if we trace the duties of the Spanish officials from the humblest to the most exalted. The syndic was the subordinate of the commandant. Syndics were unsalaried officials who had jurisdiction over only minor cases and were similar to our present-day justice of the peace. Legal training was not considered necessary for the office.

The commandant was a busy, important official. He was a judge in civil cases and also presided in criminal cases when the lieutenant-governor was unable to attend court. Of course, his decision could be appealed to the lieutenant-governor. The commandant was the official who gave permission to settle in the area. Furthermore, if anyone wished to travel over twenty miles, it was necessary to secure a pass from the commandant. It was the commandant who took the census, kept the official records, commanded the local militia unit, witnessed wills, presided over the settling of estates, and directed forced sales for the payment of debts. Although they often had little education, the commandants were usually respected men who acted in a fatherly way to direct the community. Only three of the commandants—those at Ste. Genevieve, New Bourbon, and Cape Girardeau—received pay for their services. Francois Dunegant, the honest, dedicated commandant in Florissant, lived in poverty. A Spanish official who visited Florissant found Dunegant

Carlos Dehault De Lassus, the last Spanish lieutenant-governor in Upper Louisiana (1799-1804), arranged the details of the transfer to American control.
(Courtesy of Missouri Historical Society, St. Louis)

embarrassed that he could "neither read nor write." No doubt
Dunegant had to rely upon some educated person for the maintenance of his records.

The lieutenant-governors who were sent to St. Louis (the
Spanish called it San Luis) were the chief administrators in
Upper Louisiana. They were usually men of ability and good
will. It is noteworthy, considering the isolated character of the
area and the distance from their New Orleans superiors, that
the governmental officers were so upright. The lieutenant-
governor had control of the militia units in the area and the
regular Spanish garrison. He could make decrees and demand
obedience to them. The lieutenant-governor was the chief justice
for the area. He could also issue grants of land to settlers. The
lieutenant-governor controlled the Indian trade which was of
primary importance to the life of the settlement. He was also
in charge of all Indian affairs. Observance of activities across
the Mississippi was another responsibility of the lieutenant-
governor. This reconnaissance was carried on by sending intelligence agents across the river and by entertaining guests from
that area. The lieutenant-governor's position was obviously an
important one.

The lieutenant-governors did not serve for a set term of
years. They remained at their post until relieved. The following is a list of lieutenant-governors and the year of their appointment:

> 1770   Pedro Piernas
> 1775   Don Francisco Cruzat
> 1778   Fernando De Leyba
> 1780   Don Francisco Cruzat
> 1787   Don Manuel Perez
> 1792   Zenon Trudeau
> 1799   Carlos Dehault De Lassus

Although the government of Upper Louisiana was theoretically Spanish, the people were French. Even the lieutenant-
governors Spain sent to Upper Louisiana are illustrative of this
fact. Both Piernas and Trudeau married French women. Trudeau was born of French stock. De Lassus was born in France.
It would appear that the Spanish government was attempting to
select officials who would be accepted by the French inhabitants
of the Missouri area.

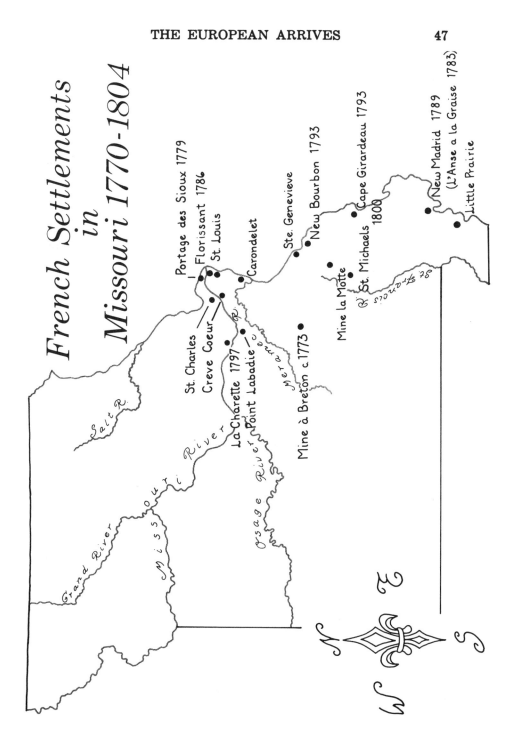

French Settlements in Missouri 1770-1804

Portage des Sioux 1779
Florissant 1786
St. Louis
Carondelet
Ste. Genevieve
New Bourbon 1793
Cape Girardeau 1793
St. Michaels 1800
New Madrid 1789 (L'Anse a la Graise 1783)
Little Prairie

St. Charles
Creve Coeur
La Charette 1797
Point Labadie
Mine à Breton c.1773
Mine la Motte

Salt R.
Grand River
Missouri River
Osage River
Meramec R.
St. Francois R.

New Settlements

The construction of new villages continued during the Spanish period. These new settlements were largely French—as their names testify.

For administrative purposes Spain divided Upper Louisiana into districts. In the St. Charles District there were several early settlements. Portage des Sioux was established in 1779 and La Charette in 1797. Spanish officials promoted the building of Portage des Sioux as a defensive measure. It was to be a fortification to discourage any invasion of Spanish territory or unauthorized use of the Missouri River. La Charette was located about forty miles up the river from St. Charles. Both were weak and sparsely populated outposts. Cote Sans Dessein was founded in 1808 on the north bank of the Missouri River just opposite the mouth of the Osage River. For administrative reasons, the area north of the Missouri River was called the St. Charles District. Since there were so few Europeans there, the district was a huge one, extending all the way up the Mississippi River to Dubuque, Iowa.

The St. Louis District was the region between the Meramec and the Missouri rivers. Besides St. Louis, the district included two other notable centers of population—Carondelet, which we have already mentioned, and Florissant. The latter town was located over ten miles north of St. Louis about midway from the city and the Missouri River. Florissant was founded in 1786 or 1787 and, like all the villages named so far, was peopled by French-Canadians. There were still many Indians in the area. Three residents of the town were massacred by an Indian band in 1793. In 1799, there were only 300 residents. Other, even smaller, settlements in the St. Louis District were Creve Coeur and Point Labadie.

The Ste. Genevieve District included several smaller towns. Mine a Breton was founded by Francois Azor, who was known as "Breton." He is noted for having lived 111 years. The town developed around the lead mine "Breton" discovered in 1773. Another settlement in the district was New Bourbon, which was founded in 1793 several miles south of the old location of Ste. Genevieve. Although it was originally planned as a residence for a group of dissatisfied Frenchmen living in Ohio, few of these Ohio people agreed to move to New Bourbon. It became a typical small hunting and trading settlement. Among the other small villages in this area was St. Michaels, which is known today as Fredericktown.

The Cape Girardeau District is the next area south of Ste. Genevieve. Cape Girardeau was established in 1793 by a Montreal-born Frenchman named Louis Lorimier. Typical of the Canadians of his time, he went out as a trader into the Ohio Valley. After the American Revolution, he moved west to avoid living under the American government. Lorimier, whose first wife was half Shawnee, was noted as a friend of the Indians. The Spanish government believed Lorimier was a valuable ally because of his control of many Indians. They assured themselves of his service by granting him the exclusive trading rights with the Shawnee and Delaware tribes residing between the Mississippi and the Arkansas rivers. To carry on the trade, he set up a post at Cape Girardeau in 1793, although he did not secure title to the land until 1795. During the Spanish period, the settlement was always a tiny, struggling one, but its location on a high point overlooking the Mississippi River made it a strategic military site.

The New Madrid District had a high percent of English-speaking colonists in the Spanish Period. New Madrid was established on a bend of the Mississippi which originally was referred to as L'Anse a la Graise—the cove of grease or fat. It has been suggested that the name was given to the spot because fatty bear meat was stored here. Although there were French settlers at L'Anse a la Graise by 1783, the major influx of settlers came in 1789 when Colonel George Morgan and a large group of Americans moved in and changed the name of the town to New Madrid. Morgan was a man of education and refinement, a promoter of several colonization schemes, and a tireless adventurer. After having gone bankrupt in one land specula-tion venture, he secured the approval of the Spanish minister to the United States, Don Diego de Gardoqui, for the establishment of a large new settlement in Spanish Missouri. Morgan, who had traveled up and down the Mississippi before, proposed to establish a colony on the west bank of the Mississippi River where the Ohio flows into the Mississippi. He made elaborate plans in surveying the site of the city and in laying out the neighboring farms. But, although the settlement was started with the blessing of Gardoqui and the help of Lieutenant-Governor Perez in St. Louis, Governor-General Miro in New Orleans opposed the

George Morgan was a disgruntled, bankrupt promoter who received a preliminary land grant of over twelve million acres from the Spanish ambassador to the United States. Arriving in Missouri on February 14, 1789, he established New Madrid. His elaborate plans for the city included many public parks and streets 100 feet wide. Governor Miro disapproved of his plans for the settlement, which included self-government and religious freedom. Miro refused to confirm the land grant, and Morgan returned to Pennsylvania.

(Courtesy Washington County Historical Society; Washington, Pennsylvania)

project. Miro refused to legalize the huge grant of land to Morgan or to grant self-government to the settlers of New Madrid as they requested. The dejected Morgan returned to the United States, but some of his colonists remained in New Madrid. The Spanish sent in a garrison of troops, and the government and economy of New Madrid functioned in much the same way as any other Missouri village. The only adjacent village in the New Madrid section was Little Prairie.

The Battle of St. Louis

Few people realize that one of the battles of the American Revolution was fought in Spanish Missouri. The American colonists officially declared their independence from Britain on July 4, 1776, initiating the American Revolution which continued for seven years. France entered the American Revolutionary War in 1778 on the side of the American rebels. Spain declared war on Britain in 1779. The Spanish did not take up arms to help the rebels; Spain was not anxious to encourage colonial rebellion because she had many colonies of her own in America. She did, however, share France's antipathy toward Britain who had taken Gibraltar, Spain's prized fortress, from her. This alliance was Spain's opportunity to regain the mammoth rock which controls the entrance to the Mediterranean.

The area across the Mississippi from Missouri was British territory at the beginning of the war, but a dauntless, red-

(Courtesy State Historical Society)

Route of the British and Indian attack force, May, 1780

headed Virginian named George Rogers Clark led a small but capable force of American frontiersmen out to Illinois. Clark and his moccasin-shod men moved so quietly that when they appeared at the British fort at Kaskaskia in 1778 the British were taken completely by surprise. The Americans walked into the British fort and took control. With subsequent victories at Cahokia— a few miles from Kaskaskia—and Vincennes, George Rogers Clark was in control of the major British forts along the Ohio and the Mississippi.

The French people of Missouri tended to be pro-American in this conflict. One reason for this was that France was officially the ally of the Americans. Another reason was the traditional rivalry between the French and the English. However, since Missouri was so far west and so far removed from British forts, there was no immediate concern over fighting in Missouri itself. But British officers in Canada were anxious to reoccupy their former forts in Illinois. In their desire for revenge, they

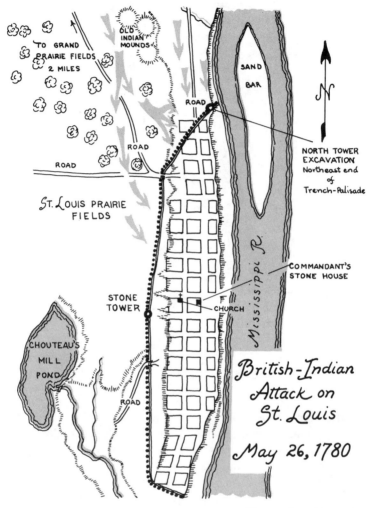

After map in "The British-Indian Attack on St. Louis, May 26, 1780," by Don Rickey, Jr. in Missouri Historical Review, October, 1960.

planned an expedition which would march down the Mississippi Valley to attack the Illinois forts held by George Rogers Clark, and the Spanish city of St. Louis. The British enlisted about 1000 Indians from the Great Lakes region to do the fighting.

Captain De Leyba was in charge of the Spanish militia and the small army garrison at St. Louis. De Leyba had slightly less than two months to prepare for the attack he feared would come. Near St. Louis was an ancient fort in bad repair. De Leyba removed the five cannons from the fort and stationed them at prominent points around the perimeter of the city. In addition he directed the digging of a trench around the city.

At 1:00 p.m. on May 26, 1780, the first shrieking waves of Indians began the attack. It is estimated that De Leyba had only 350 men against an Indian force of 650 warriors. However, the defenders of St. Louis were able to use their cannons to great effect. After two hours of attack the Indians withdrew to the east side of the Mississippi.

The failure of their attack so angered some of the braves that they committed atrocities on the field—mutilating, scalping, torturing, and dismembering those French settlers they had captured before the battle started. These vicious acts were carried out in full view of the men who defended the city. Little wonder that the participants could never escape the memory of that day. Official British reports of the Battle of St. Louis show that the Indians took thirty-three French scalps and twenty-four prisoners.

By defeating the English attack in 1780, the people of St.

Detail from the lunette "Indian Attack on the Village of Saint Louis, 1780" by Oscar E. Berninghaus in the capitol building in Jefferson City.
(Courtesy Massie-Missouri Commerce)

Louis gave valuable assistance to the American cause in the American Revolution. The English were unsuccessful in their attempts to seize a part of Missouri. Missouri remained Spanish until 1804 when Thomas Jefferson was so fortunate as to secure possession of the area as a part of one of the biggest bargains in history—the Louisiana Purchase.

BIBLIOGRAPHY

Costain, Thomas B. *The Mississippi Bubble*. New York: Random House, 1955.

De Voto, Bernard. *The Course of Empire*. Boston: Houghton Mifflin Co., 1952.

Emmons, Ben L. "The Founding of St. Charles and Blanchette, Its Founder," *Missouri Historical Review*, Vol. XVIII (July, 1924), pp. 507-520.

Folmer, Henri. "Etienne Veniard De Bourgmond in the Missouri Country," *Missouri Historical Review*, Vol. XXXVI (January, 1942), pp. 279-298.

Garraghan, Gilbert J. "Fort Orleans of the Missouri," *Missouri Historical Review*, Vol. XXXV (April, 1941), pp 373-384.

Glenn, Robert A. "The Osage War," *Missouri Historical Review*, Vol. XIV (January, 1920), pp. 201-210.

Gregg, Kate L., ed. "Explorers in the Valley," *Missouri Historical Review*, Vol. XXXIX (April and July, 1945), pp. 354-388, 505-540.

Gregg, Kate L. "The Building of the First American Fort West of the Mississippi," *Missouri Historical Review*, Vol. XXX (April, 1935), pp. 345-364.

Gregg, Kate L. "The History of Fort Osage," *Missouri Historical Review*, Vol. XXXIV (July, 1940), pp. 439-488.

Hodge, Frederick W., ed. "The Narrative of the Expedition of Hernando De Soto, By the Gentleman of Elvas," *Spanish Explorers in the Southern United States, 1528-1543* ("Original Narratives of Early American History," Vol. II). New York: Scribner's Sons, 1907.

Houck, Louis. *A History of Missouri*. Vol. I. Chicago: R. R. Donnelley & Sons Co., 1908.

Kellogg, Louise Phelps. "The Mississippi Voyage of Jolliet and Marquette, 1673," *Early Narratives of the Northwest, 1634-1699* ("Original Narratives of Early American History," Vol. XIII). New York: Charles Scribner's Sons, 1917.

McDermott, John Francis. "The Confines of A Wilderness," *Missouri Historical Review*, Vol. XXIX (October, 1934), pp. 3-12.

McDermott, John Francis. "The Exclusive Trade Privilege of Maxent, Laclede and Company," *Missouri Historical Review*, Vol. XXIX (January, 1935), pp. 272-278.

Nasatir, A. P. "Ducharme's Invasion of Missouri, An Incident in the Anglo-Spanish Rivalry for the Indian Trade of Upper Louisiana," *Missouri Historical Review*, Vol. XXIV (October, 1929; January and April, 1930), pp. 3-25, 238-260, 420-439.

Parkman, Francis. *The Discovery of the Great West: La Salle.* New York: Rinehart & Co., Inc., 1956.

Penn, Dorothy and Marie George Windell, eds. "The French in the Valley," *Missouri Historical Review,* Vol. XL (October, 1945; January, April, July, 1946), pp 90-122, 245-275, 407-430, 562-578; Vol. XLI (October, 1946; January, April, July, 1947), pp. 77-106, 192-216, 305-314, 391-399.

Peterson, Charles E. "Early Ste. Genevieve and Its Architecture," *Missouri Historical Review,* Vol. XXXV (January, 1941), pp. 207-232.

Rickey, Don, Jr. "The British-Indian Attack on St. Louis, May 26, 1780," *Missouri Historical Review,* Vol. LV, No. 1 (October, 1960), pp. 34-45.

Schaff, Ida M. "The Founding of Ste. Genevieve, Missouri," *Missouri Historical Review,* Vol. XXVII (January, 1933), pp. 145-150.

Sheldon, Addison E. "The Missouri River Region As Seen by the First White Explorers," *Missouri Historical Review,* Vol. XXII (January, 1928), pp. 176-186.

Shoemaker, Floyd C. "Cape Girardeau, Most American of Missouri's Original Five Counties," *Missouri Historical Review,* Vol. L (October, 1955), pp. 49-61.

Shoemaker, Floyd C. "Fort Orleans: The Heritage of Carroll County," *Missouri Historical Review,* Vol. LI (January, 1957), pp. 105-112.

Shoemaker, Floyd C. "New Madrid, Mother of Southeast Missouri," *Missouri Historical Review,* Vol. XLIX (July, 1955), pp. 317-327.

Shoemaker, Floyd C. "St. Charles, City of Paradoxes," *Missouri Historical Review,* Vol. XXXVI (April, 1942), pp. 184-189.

Stipes, M. F. "Fort Orleans, The First French Post on the Missouri," *Missouri Historical Review,* Vol. VIII (April, 1914), pp. 121-135.

Thwaites, Reuben Gold. *France in America, 1497-1763.* ("The American Nation Series"). New York: Harper & Brothers Publishers, 1905.

Violette, E. M. "Early Settlements in Missouri," *Missouri Historical Review,* Vol. I (October, 1906), pp. 38-52.
Vol. I (October, 1906), pp. 38-52.

Williams, Walter and Floyd Calvin Shoemaker. *Missouri, Mother of the West.* Vol. I. Chicago and New York: American Historical Society, Inc., 1930.

CHAPTER III

Problems of Settlement

From the wilds of the North comes the young voyageur,
With his buoyant canoes well laden with fur.
There's a song on the lips of the young voyageur,
And his voice, sounding far, sets the forest astir.
—from the folksong *The Young Voyageur*

The white men who came to Missouri to establish themselves in what was then a wild and remote part of the world were faced with a variety of tasks and problems. They had to build homes, churches, barns, and fences. Making use of the natural resources of the region, they had to create an economy to support the population. They had to learn to live with strange and frequently hostile tribes of Indians. They had to work out a system of transportation which would minimize their isolation. Each of these problems is an important part of the early history of Missouri.

The Establishment of Villages

We usually envision the first frontier families living in isolated wilderness homes far from other white men. This was a true picture of some English-speaking settlers, but the Frenchmen who first settled in Missouri built villages patterned after those they knew in France. They were a gregarious people who appreciated the advantages of group living. Devout Catholics, the French settlers felt the need of a parish church, and they enjoyed such community pleasures as billiards and dances. They preferred to plow their fields, to sow their crops, to gather their harvests, and to herd their cattle cooperatively. Communal living also offered greater protection from Indian attack—as illustrated by the Battle of St. Louis. And so, rather than build isolated homesteads as did their fellow pioneers to the east, the Frenchmen who settled Missouri established communities.

During the periods of French and Spanish control in Missouri, the settlers did not purchase land from the king for their

A typical French Missouri house by Charles E. Peterson.

homes and villages. Grants of land were made without charge, either to an individual, or to the residents of a village as a group holding. These grants were usually made by the highest official in the area—the lieutenant-governor, or the commandant acting for him. Occasionally, unauthorized persons made grants. Laclede parceled out many plots of land to the first settlers of St. Louis. Although he had no legal right to do this, the proper authorities later recognized his grants. To secure permanent title to the land, the settler was obliged to take an oath of loyalty to the king, to clear part of the land, and to construct a house on it within a year and a day. If he failed to meet these three requirements, the land was to be forfeited to the crown.

The first French settlements (such as Ste. Genevieve, St. Louis, or Carondelet) had three distinct areas: (1) a residential zone divided into blocks and lots where the settlers built their houses and other private buildings and planted orchards and gardens; (2) a wooded "common" where all of the cattle, horses, and pigs were herded and where firewood was secured; (3) a "common field" which was divided into strips that were assigned to each family as farm land.

In the residential zone the colonists usually fenced their lots. At the front of the lot, facing the narrow farm lane that served as a street, the settler built his quaint little house. Behind the house he constructed such outbuildings as a barn, corn crib, and, if he were a slave owner, a cabin for his slaves.

Since logs were the cheapest, most accessible, building material on the frontier, these French Missourians built log houses. These houses were unlike the typical log cabin of the American frontier in that the logs were set vertically in the manner of a stockade fence rather than horizontally. The logs were hewn flat on two or four sides and anchored several feet in the soil. The cracks between the logs were filled with a clay mortar and straw filler. The houses, usually single-storied, were covered with a high-pitched shingled roof. The many-paned windows had shutters that could be closed against the weather. There were several variations of this basic house. Those people who had sufficient money built a porch around the house. This gave protection from sun and rain and expanded the usable living area. As more and more of the colonists built porches about their houses, the porch became one of the chief distinguishing characteristics of French colonial architecture in the Mississippi Valley. Some colonists covered the exterior of their houses with a sandy mortar or with clapboards and coated the interior walls with a clay plaster. Others built their houses of stone.

Buildings constructed by driving wooden posts into the ground were not permanent. As soon as sufficient time and money were available, stone foundations were adopted. The Bishop of Louisiana was disturbed when he received a report in 1798 that the log church in St. Louis could not "be kept from falling into ruin." As Lieutenant-Governor Manuel Perez explained to the Bishop, "since it is built on posts in the earth . . . the timbers rot very readily." Perez reported that the people of St. Louis wanted to build a stone church which would not need the constant repairs that a log building required, but they did not have money enough to construct a church of stone.

The typical house was only about thirty feet wide by twenty feet deep and usually was divided into two rooms. A stone chimney in the middle of the house provided a smoke outlet for the two fireplaces. The more affluent settlers built larger, more elaborate houses. In 1765, Jean Marie Papin built a fine stone house on First Street in St. Louis. Papin's home was fifty-six feet wide by thirty-six feet deep and contained seven rooms. The original Chouteau house in St. Louis had two chimneys and four fireplaces.

There was room in most houses for little more than the necessary articles of furniture. In the simplest home one could find a bedstead, table, chairs, cupboard, trunk, and dresser. In the homes of the wealthier settlers were such articles as silverware, crystal glasses, books, and ornate four-poster beds. Remembering that such articles and furnishings usually had to be brought from Quebec or New Orleans by boat, we can imagine that these possessions were treasured by the fortunate Missourians who owned them.

Henry Brackenridge, who came to Missouri from Pennsylvania, lived in Ste. Genevieve during the 1790's and the early years of the next century. Here, in the words of this contemporary, we have a description of a typical house in colonial Missouri:

> The house of M. Beauvais was a long, low building, with a porch or shed in front and another in the rear; the chimney occupied the center, dividing the house into two parts, with each a fireplace. One of these served for diningroom, parlor, and principal bed-chamber; the other was the kitchen; and each had a small room taken off at the end for private chambers or cabinets. There was no loft or garret, a pair of stairs being a rare thing in the village. The furniture, excepting the beds and the looking-glass, was of the most common kind, consisting of an armoire [cupboard], a rough table or two, and some coarse chairs.

The basic house design of the time was adapted to a two-story structure for the residence of Maria Therese Chouteau in St. Louis.

(Courtesy Missouri Historical Society)

The houses may have been crude by our standards, but they fulfilled the basic need for shelter from the elements and from enemies. This need had to be met before other problems could be faced.

Indian Relations

Government Policies

The establishment of a friendly relationship with their Indian neighbors was a task of high priority for the French settlers. The French and Spanish governments seem to have been eager to foster friendship and trust between the natives and the newcomers. At the time that Don Pedro Piernas took control of the Missouri settlements, he was given the following unusual command:

> Whenever any party of Indians brings any scalps, and makes a present of them to the commandant of the post, he shall receive them and ask what Indian tribe the above-mentioned scalps were taken from. By the reply, he will be able to tell whether they were the scalps of friendly tribes. If they are of a friendly tribe, he will restore them to those Indians.

The Spanish official in New Orleans who wrote this order knew the importance of Indian diplomacy. For one to retain a scalp that had been taken from a member of a certain tribe was to declare that tribe one's enemy. Most officials wished to protect the Indian from exploitation. Indian slavery was prohibited. Traders were forbidden to give guns or brandy to the Indians, and dishonest traders were barred from Indian areas.

In spite of the inevitable instances of conflict, exploitation, and irritation, it is probably true that Indian relations were better west than east of the Mississippi River. The Spanish and French authorities made efforts to treat the Indians fairly. On the other hand, cases of injustice and exploitation seem to have been more frequent among the English-speaking settlers and their Indian neighbors. In the Missouri area the tribes were remarkably law-abiding when one considers the circumstances. The white traders, often carrying large quantities of valuable highly-desired goods, moved freely about the area that was unpatrolled by Spanish officials. Indians must have been greatly tempted by the opportunity to overpower the trader and seize his goods. As the illustrations in this chapter indicate, an occasional Indian did yield to temptation, and the threat of more doing so was always present; but relatively few traders were molested. Appreciation of the fair treatment by Spanish officials may explain, at least in part, Indian obedience to Spanish law. The following instance testifies to Indian respect for Spanish justice.

In 1801 five Indians who were members of a tribe living in the New Madrid district murdered a certain David Trotter. The Indians were captured by a militia unit and brought to New Madrid for their trial which was held in the presence of the two principal chiefs of the tribe. One of the Indians, Tewanaye, was found guilty and sentenced to death by a firing squad. The tribal chieftains did not protest. The four other Indians captured were ordered released after they watched the execution of their companion. The reports indicate that there was no complaint from the members of their tribe and that the chiefs considered the sentence a just one.

Several policies were adopted by the colonial government in an attempt to control the Indians. The bribing of influential chiefs was one method used. As one Spanish official explained, "it is better to fatten one who rules as a despot over various tribes, than to feed many at less expense." Another technique employed was the halting of all trade with a tribe. Such an embargo had a pacifying effect upon the Osage. A third tactic was to flatter a chief by giving him an ornate medal. Like chil-

Bodmer's sketch of a Missouri, an Oto, and a Punca Indian chief shows the chieftain with his prized medal.

(Courtesy State Historical Society)

dren, the several tribal heads competed with one another for the largest, most colorful decorations. Victor Collet, who visited Missouri and other parts of the Mississippi Valley in the 1790's, spoke of the medals given to the chiefs as follows: "These medals serve as presents for the chiefs. It ought to be observed that they should have only one figure upon them; for when an Indian sees more, he will not accept the medal: *"I have but one heart,* he tells you, *I cannot love more than one person."* It was hoped that seeing their chief accept and wear medals bearing the likeness of the Spanish king would lead members of the tribe to feel a kinship for the monarch. A fourth and less commendable practice was the exploiting of intertribal rivalries. Colonial officials sometimes resorted to inciting warfare to punish troublesome tribes.

Despite policies to promote good relations and to prevent or punish misdeeds, many tribes went unpunished for crimes against the whites. In the 1740's the Missouri tribe killed a trader named La Grillade. Several months earlier the Osage killed a French trader and carried his head about to display it to neighboring tribes. A. P. Nasatir, an expert on the Osage Indians, says of that tribe, "When pinched and hurt, or in imminent danger of revenge, punishment, or starvation, they always cringed before the superior power and profusely shed crocodile tears until their immediate objective was attained." Perhaps such Indian histrionics were performed by the guilty ones in the two atrocities mentioned above, for in both instances the murderers escaped without punishment. Indian dramatics were not the only impediment to justice in colonial Missouri. The difficulty in administering the two major modes of punishment —war or embargo—was another obstacle colonial officials encountered. War was expensive, bloody, and difficult to win since the mobility of the tribes made them elusive opponents. And because the French *coureurs de bois* were an independent group of men, a strict embargo was difficult to enforce.

In 1750, however, the Little Osage tribe displayed an amazing zeal to cooperate with French officials. A member of the tribe killed a French trader on the Des Moines River. When the French demanded that the murderer be punished, the Little Osage seized the man they believed to be guilty, executed him, and sent his scalp to the French commandant. Later the tribe discovered that they had mistakenly executed the guilty man's brother. At last they seized the real murderer who was delivered to the French for execution.

Mistakes were made, and there were instances of injustice attributed to the whites and to the Indians. Still, considering the weakness of French and Spanish law enforcement agencies and the multitude of opportunities for plunder, the overall pattern of respect between the Indians and the colonial government was remarkably good.

The Meeting of Cultures

Even though we live in a rapidly-changing society today, nothing in our experience is similar to the cultural revolution that occurred in Indian society when the white men appeared.

(from John Musick, Stories of Missouri, 1897)

The flintlock musket gave the Frenchman an advantage over his primitively-armed Indian adversary.

Suddenly, a late stone-age people learned about iron knives, hatchets, files, scissors, fishhooks, needles, and pots. They received woolen cloth, mirrors, burning glasses, and porcelain. Even more mysterious was the flintlock musket and that magical water called brandy. Once they were introduced to these European innovations, the Indians were eager to share them.

It seemed futile to spend a day chipping stones to produce crude and hard-to-use scrapers, blades, or projectile points when far superior tools and weapons were available. Clay pottery could not compare with iron pots which were almost unbreakable, did not leak, and could be hung over the fire. It seemed foolish to try to build a dugout canoe with stone tools when an iron axe or hatchet made the process so much 'easier. In a similar manner, the introduction of firearms and metal scalping knives made Indian hunting more productive and Indian warfare more terrible. To obtain the tools, weapons, and materials they coveted, the Indians spent more and more time seeking the furs the whites desired. Tribes modified their migrations so that their paths would cross those of the French traders. Indian artisans abandoned old skills when the final product failed to compete with trade goods. Having developed an insatiable thirst for products they could not produce themselves, the Indians of Missouri became, by 1800, almost totally dependent on the white man and his goods.

Although there was an almost immediate bond of economic interdependence between the whites and the Indians, there was not an immediate social unity. The cultural gap was too great for the rapid development of a mutual understanding between the two groups. The Frenchmen were horrified by the brutality of the Indians. The Europeans were shocked by such Indian customs as dipping newborn babies into a stream regardless of the weather. It also was difficult at times for the French to accept the Indian diet. One trader had this to say of his visit to the Miami Indians: "I ate there, for the first time in my life, dog's flesh, with which they always regale themselves on these occasions. Although this food was extremely disagreeable to me, I was obliged to commend and praise it."

The whites were, of course, influenced by this Indian environment. They adopted the Indian's moccasin and some of his foods such as corn and pumpkin. Some Frenchmen, especially those with extensive debts, joined tribes and became permanent residents of Indian villages. Many chose Indian wives.

Although the Europeans came to know the Indians well, several Indian habits were difficult to tolerate and proved resistant to change. The Indian enjoyed no solitude in his camp and was unable to understand the white man's concept of privacy. Indians—particularly those who had been successful in obtaining liquor—would race shrieking and screaming up and down the streets of St. Louis and would burst into whichever door took their notice. Many a Frenchwoman was startled by the sudden appearance of a savage in her kitchen. Zenon Trudeau at times despaired of changing the thieving habits of some Indians. In 1793 he cordially entertained six Indians in his home and gave them a gift when they departed. On the way out of St. Louis they stole three horses. Trudeau wrote, "This is the way these pests have always been and they will remain this way with no other remedy than a large population to punish these abuses from time to time."

The Europeans were not blameless reformers, however, for although some white men sought through example and missionary activity to civilize the Indian, others introduced more efficient means to promote Indian savagery. The gun contributed to greater loss of life in Indian warfare. Scalping knives, in which white traders were able to do a lucrative business, only facilitated a brutal and bloody practice. One chief named Big Rabbit was able to control tribal leaders who opposed him by seasoning their food with arsenic obtained from European friends.

In view of the great cultural differences, the many sources of misunderstanding and animosity, and the fact that the whites had few military units, it is remarkable that Indian-White relations were as peaceful as they appear to have been in colonial Missouri.

Developing An Economy

Farming

Although many French colonists engaged in mining and the fur trade, agriculture was the activity in which almost every colonist spent part of his time. The Europeans found that they could not depend upon the Indians for food. Indian agriculture was not so highly developed in North America as in Central America. Since the areas under cultivation were small and the yields sparse, the Indians did not have much extra food to trade. In those days of slow and expensive shipping, it was not feasible to transport most of the food from great distances. Therefore, the Europeans were forced to engage in farming to produce their own food.

The colonists practiced strip farming as they had done in France and along the St. Lawrence River. A large fertile region was set aside for cultivation and then divided into strips. At that time in history, fencing a field was an expensive and laborious activity. By centralizing their cultivated fields, much less fence was required—especially if one side of the field joined a river. These fields had to be large. For example, the St. Charles field was at least 10,000 acres. The strips were frequently long. At Carondelet the strips in the common field were at least a mile and a half long. The regulations of each settlement provided that each farmer was to be responsible for the fence adjoining his land. Of course, if only one farmer failed to keep up his fence, all the crops were in jeopardy. Even as late as the year 1826 Father Van Quickenborne of Florissant lamented that a break in the fence allowed the hogs to ruin half of the wheat crop. Thus, when St. Ange gave his farewell message in 1764 to the people of the Missouri area he stressed the fact that the settlers should "keep up their fences, it being to the public interest that the cattle should not pass from the commons to the grain fields."

To plant, cultivate, and harvest their usual crops of Indian corn, wheat, barley, oats, beans, pumpkins, flax, tobacco, and cotton, the settlers employed the simplest of tools—a hoe, scythe, spade, axe, rake, and pitchfork. The latter two items as well as their plows were usually made of wood. Oxen were employed to pull plows, harrows, and often farm carts. Instead of placing a yoke on the neck of the oxen, a beam was fastened to the horns of the beast and the vehicle or implement was then attached to the beam.

The French settlers discovered buffalo in eastern Missouri; but since the buffalo could not be domesticated for use as a beast of burden, it was necessary to bring in European cattle. We know there were such cattle on the Illinois side of the Mississippi by 1712. The other familiar farmyard animals appeared shortly afterward—pigs, horses, sheep, chickens, ducks, and geese. Most animals were herded by day and returned to the barnyard at night, but the cattle and hogs were often allowed to roam without any restraint on the meadows and in the forests, feeding on the prairie grasses, nuts, roots and berries. They could be coaxed home regularly when salt was put out for them. The hogs were marked with registered ear clips to prove ownership.

Fur Trade

The economic activity of second importance in colonial Missouri was the trade in furs. From the time of Laclede, the fur

PLAN OF FORT ORLEANS

Its location and that of the lands on the river of the Missouri
at XXXIX degrees XLV minutes of latitude.
Scale: one hundred and fifty feet.

Explanation of the alphabetical letters: A, Commandant's house. B, Officers' house. C, Chapel. D, Blacksmith's house. E, Forge. F, Chaplain's house. G, Storekeeper's house. H, Store. J, Guard-house. K, Drummer's house. L, Laundry. O, Barracks. P, Flag-staff. Q, Powder magazine. R, Embrasures for the cannon.

Explanation of the figures: 1, M. DeBourgmont's house. 2, His poultry-house. 3, His oven. 4, Ice-house. 5, Big garden. 6, His yard. 7, Little garden. 8, Store. 9, Field of tobacco. 10, Plot used as a kitchen-garden. 11, M. St. Ange's yard. 12, His house. 13, Storeroom. 14, House of M. St. Ange. *fils*, officer. 15, Storeroom. 16, His yard. 17, Little garden. 18, Soldiers' field. 19, Pond. 20, Island. 21, Prairie. 22, Big hills two leagues distant from the fort. 23, Road from the river to the fort. 24, Little embankment fifteen feet high.

(Courtesy Mid-America, July, 1930, p. 259)

trade was a major factor in the rapid development of St. Louis. Although some Frenchmen canoed or tramped through the great stretches of North America for missionary reasons or because of a love of adventure, most of the French were motivated by a desire for wealth. The fur trade was so easy a way to make money that it attracted many men. Furs were in great demand in Europe both for the robes of the nobility and for the manufacture of beaver skin hats. The Indians at first were so much interested in European trade goods that they gave away large numbers of skins for a few trinkets. Knowing this, the traders made great efforts to reach obscure, isolated tribes where they could secure great piles of furs for a rusty hatchet or knife.

In the French villages of Missouri it was usually true that the married men of the community cultivated the soil, mined the lead, or worked the salt springs. The single men, having fewer ties, were freer to make the long voyages to Montreal or New Orleans, or to move up the Missouri with boats of supplies to be traded for furs.

Although many of the early traders operated alone or in small groups, it was soon clear that a larger organization was necessary to finance, direct and carry on the trade along the Missouri River. The French and Spanish governments believed in the mercantile theory, as did most of the governments of Europe. Under this theory, trade was to be controlled by the mother country. One of the techniques employed was to grant certain individuals or companies a monopoly of the trade in a certain region. Throughout the colonial period the Missouri trade was alternately granted to large companies and then opened to many small traders. We have already referred to the contract given to Maxent and Laclede, but there were other earlier grants for the trade of the Missouri River region. The first such grant was made in 1745 to a Canadian named Deruisseau. He was given "the exclusive trade of the entire Missouri River and all of its tributary streams" for a five-year period. The lengthy contract mentions the fact that individual *voyageurs* from Canada had caused disorder and dissension among the Indians and had competed against each other in such a way that they had even given their trade goods away at low prices. The government felt that this competition might spoil the Indians and that such easy trading might discourage them from seeking the maximum number of furs. By granting Deruisseau a monopoly it was hoped that the traders could be controlled and that the Indians could be kept busy acquiring more furs.

We know that the fur trade was large even as early as the 1750's. One French official estimated an annual trade of eighty packs of deer and bear skins annually from the Osage and Missouri tribes. The Kansas Tribe produced a hundred packs of skins which were mostly beaver, deer, and bear. Eighty packs of skins were secured from the Otos and Iowas. According to Maxent, there was a great increase in the fur trade during the 1760's. In 1769 he estimated that his company was able to export 1200 to 1500 packs—about fifty-four to sixty-eight tons—of fur each year.

The French carried such fine furs as beaver, marten, mink, and otter to Canada where the cooler climate allowed less chance for the fur to spoil. Less delicate and less valuable pelts such as deerskins and buffalo skins were floated down to New Orleans.

The companies and the large, well-financed traders usually established trading outposts in Indian territory. Canoes were filled with trade goods and floated to the chosen site. There a fur trading fort was built to serve as a warehouse for the goods

Fur traders descending the Missouri with their valuable cargoes
(Courtesy State Historical Society)

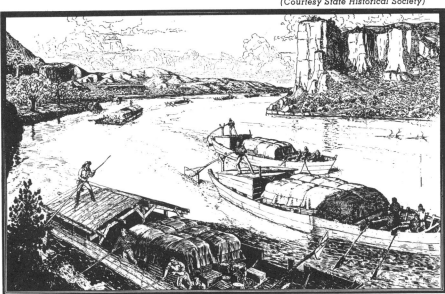

and as a center to which the Indians might bring their furs. The Indians, eager for trade goods, flocked to the fort with their hard-won furs. After elbowing their way into the crowded room, braves would stand silently eyeing the white man's wares as children today study the toy counters before Christmas. Kettles, guns, bullets, powder, wire, knives, hatchets, picks, awls, and hooks would so simplify the daily tasks of the red man. As all of us today seek the style that is new, the Indian sought the white man's gingham shirts, calico cloth, and woolen blankets. There is a certain wry humor in the fact that furs, since they were so plentiful, were not greatly coveted among the Indians before the white man came. But the white man wanted the red man's fur, and the red man wanted the white man's cotton and woolen goods.

The fur forts would set a certain price for each kind of fur and then hold that price constant through the year. A fluctuation of price or granting of more favorable terms to one person always led to unrest among the Indians.

Because of the expense of building a fort, securing trade goods, and making advance payments to tribal chieftains, it often took three years before a fur trading post made money for the owners. Thus, the holders of such fur monopoly charters complained when the crown declared the contract void and opened the area to other traders before the full contract had run out. If a monopoly lasted past the time required to recover the initial investment, the returns were most satisfying. Profits from one hundred to three hundred percent were considered normal for the traders who dealt with the Indians before 1793. The Chouteaus of St. Louis were able to secure a monopoly of the Osage trade, and much of the family wealth stemmed from that trade.

At various times during both the French and Spanish periods, the government allowed any colonist with a license to trade with the Indians. This encouraged many small traders to enter the business. Lacking the capital to establish trading posts, these small traders either invested their money in merchandise and then moved upstream to trade, or secured trade goods from a St. Louis merchant in return for a promise to bring their furs back to the same merchant.

Before the furs were moved downstream they were pressed into packs or bales weighing between eighty and one hundred pounds. When it was necessary to hide the skins for a time while the traders carried on other activities, the skins and extra supplies were put in a *cache*. A hole was dug in the cool clay of a river bank and then lined with branches and leaves. The furs were put into the hole, and then the entrance was closed and camouflaged.

(Courtesy Metropolitan Museum of Art)

George Caleb Bingham's "Fur Traders on the Missouri" shows a pirogue, or dugout canoe.

The policy of free trade open to a large number of licensed colonists led inevitably to sharp competition. The Indians then could force the traders to bid against each other. This economic rivalry also led to attempts by some traders or their Indian allies to capture or capsize their competitors' boats. There were grumbles of complaint when trade was restricted. There were protests from the privileged when such restrictions were revoked. Even as today, government officials could not escape criticism regardless of the policy they adopted.

In 1793 the Spanish governor-general in New Orleans gave permission for the merchants of St. Louis to form a single company in order to exploit the trade along the Missouri River. The company of merchants operated under the leadership of Jacques Clamorgan and was to have exclusive trading rights with the Indians of the Missouri River for ten years. In addition to its trading activities, the company was encouraged to explore the area to the west in order to find the passage to the Pacific. The discoverer was assured a reward of 200 pesos which was later raised to 3,000. This dual role in business and exploration explains why the company was called during part of its existence the "Company of Explorers of the Upper Missouri." It will be referred to here by its better-known name, the Spanish Missouri Company.

The company sent three major trading-exploring expeditions up the Missouri from St. Louis. The first, under the command of a teacher, Jean Baptiste Truteau (not to be confused with Zenon Trudeau, the lieutenant-governor), left in 1794 and, since the party was robbed of much of its trade goods by the Sioux, the trip was probably a financial failure. A second expedition in 1795 under different leadership was pillaged by the Ponca tribe. Then in 1796 the Spanish Missouri Company sent a naturalized Scotchman named James Mackay as the leader of an expedition. He was an intelligent, loyal, honest man who became Spanish by choice. All who met him attested to his great ability.

In spite of Mackay's efforts, the company was not a success. Poor leadership in St. Louis, Indian depredations, and British competition were too much. Several reorganizations failed to revive the company. The volume of business continued to diminish as British traders secured more and more of the available furs.

During his trip up the Missouri River, James Mackay sent his Welsh companion, John Evans, ahead of the party. We can catch a glimpse of the danger, suspense, and constant tension these traders endured in the following section of Evans' instructions from Mackay:

> You will take heed not to fall in with some parties of savages, where there are neither women nor children, as they are almost always on the warpath. It would not be prudent to appear at any nation if you can avoid it, unless it be their villages; and in spite of this be well on your guard. You will never fire any guns except in case of necessity; you will never cut wood except with a knife unless it should be strictly necessary; you will never build a fire without a true need, and you

will avoid having the smoke seen from afar, camping if it is possible in the valleys. You will not camp too early and you will always leave before daybreak; you will always be on guard against ambushes and will always have your arms in good condition, changing the tinder evening and morning, and you will never separate them from you or place them in the hands of the savages. When you will see some nations, raise your flag a long way off as a sign of peace, and never approach without speaking to them from a distance. When you will enter a village, stop and ground arms at a small distance until they come to receive and conduct you. Appear always on guard and never be fearful or timid, for the savages are not generally bold, but will act in a manner to make you afraid of them. If, however, they see that you are courageous and venturesome, they will soon yield to your wishes. You will recollect that the pipe is the symbol of peace and that when they have smoked with you there is no longer any danger; nevertheless you must beware of treason.

In the trade that followed this approach to an Indian village there were certain to be some attempts to defraud. The Indians were sometimes gullible because of the amazing qualities they had observed in the traders' goods. Thus, it was possible on one occasion for a trader to secure a fine pack of beaver skins in exchange for a small quantity of unusual gunpowder. The Indian was told that the powder could be planted and that it would then grow and produce great yields of gunpowder. Ignorant of the method by which gunpowder was produced, the Indian made the deal and no doubt waited in vain during the next summer to harvest his valuable crop. This type of trading was sure to lead to bitterness and encouraged the Indian to seek revenge.

Lead Mining

Lead mining ranks immediately after farming and fur trading in importance to the economy of colonial Missouri. The first explorers found lead deposits in many locations in the area now divided into Ste. Genevieve, Jefferson, Washington, and Madison counties. Both French and Spanish government officials were pleased to receive reports of lead ore (galena) in their domain. Lead was a particularly valuable metal in colonial days because it was used to make shot. It also was utilized in several other ways, such as in setting window panes, printing, and glazing pottery. In Mexico the Spanish had been delighted to find silver near the lead deposits. Colonial officials hoped that this pleasant discovery would be repeated in Missouri.

The lead mining process, as it was first practiced, was relatively simple. Using a pick and shovel, the miners would dig a hole in the rocky soil and remove the bluish-gray ore. They did not attempt to make tunnels or mine shafts under the earth; all mining was on the surface with holes that rarely exceeded six feet in depth. The ore was smelted in a crude way. After a quantity of ore had been placed in a pile on the ground, the miners would build a great bonfire atop the pile. The heat caused the metal to fuse and form puddles which, when cooled, solidified into chunks of lead. Using this crude system the miners recovered only about a thirty-three percent yield from the lead ore. Moses Austin, who came to Missouri from Virginia in 1797, was able to improve greatly the smelting process. He constructed a new stone furnace which increased the yield to sixty-five percent.

It has been noted earlier that lead mining was a factor in the establishment of the first permanent settlement in Missouri —Ste. Genevieve. Throughout the colonial period, Ste. Genevieve was the exporting settlement for lead. The trails from Mine a Breton and Mine La Motte to Ste. Genevieve soon were turned into roads as the valuable metal was regularly transported on horses or mules, or in crude two-wheeled carts. Most of the lead was mined in the fall of the year from August through November. Lighter rainfall during this season facilitated the working of the surface pits.

Associated with the lead mining industry were several names important in Missouri history. We have already discussed Renault who was the first miner to make a major effort to exploit the Missouri deposits. Renault worked the mines for about twenty years. His two main mining operations were at Old Mines and Mine La Motte. Other names associated with the lead industry were Francois Valle and his brother Jean Baptiste Valle of Ste. Genevieve, John Smith T., and Moses Austin.

The Valle brothers were the wealthy leading citizens of Ste. Genevieve. Both served terms as commandants in that settlement. Francois was buried beneath his church pew when he died in 1804. The Valle house still stands in Ste. Genevieve.

(Courtesy Massie-Missouri Commerce)

"Early Lead Mining in Washington County," a lunette by Berninghaus, in the state capitol in Jefferson City, shows the winch used by the miners to remove ore from the deeper holes.

The Valle brothers and several associates operated Mine La Motte. John Smith T. is best known for his curious name. Having been confused with several other men of the same name, he added a T—for his home state Tennessee—to distinguish himself. John Smith T. operated Mine Shibboleth—a highly productive mine at the turn of the century.

Moses Austin, originally from Connecticut, had spent time in Virginia before moving to Missouri in 1797. He was an alert, intelligent, vigorous man who knew the mining industry. He was able to secure a large Spanish grant in the lead district which included Mine a Breton. Changing the techniques of mining, he was able to improve and expand the industry. He built new furnaces, constructed a shot tower at Herculaneum, and was influential in establishing the town of Potosi.

Salt Making

Salt making was another activity of importance in colonial Missouri. Although there were salt springs at several points, those south of Ste. Genevieve and those along the banks of the Salt River were used most frequently. The usual technique was to construct furnaces using large kettles in which the water could be boiled away and the salt left as a deposit. After 1800, much Missouri salt was exported to settlers living along the Ohio River. One can picture the trials of the early salt maker from the following official testimony given in 1811:

> Albert Tison saith . . . that he saw the salt fur-
> naces in operation by Fremon Delauriere; that the
> family of the said Delauriere had been residing on
> the said saline since either 1801 or 1802, in fact, a
> long time before the land was surveyed, at least
> two years before; that they made a great quantity
> of salt at said works for the supply of inhabitants;
> that they sustained losses by boats upsetting in
> the Mississippi, and yet more in Salt river itself;
> that at the beginning of their undertaking there
> was a great danger on account of the Indians; that
> they were obliged to fortify themselves; had a
> piece of cannon, and were several times threatened
> of being attacked; that the place where they made
> salt was the extreme frontier of the settlements;
> that by this undertaking Fremon Delauriere was
> reduced to poverty.

Not all the salt manufacturers were so unfortunate as poor Delauriere. The extraction and sale of salt supported many families and provided a substance necessary for nutrition and food preservation in frontier society.

And so, by utilizing the resources that Missouri provided— arable land, pelts, and minerals—the French developed an economy which successfully supported the white population and which provided sufficient export products to pay for their foreign imports.

Transportation

Although it was possible to go overland for great distances by following Indian trails, the easiest and most popular routes of transportation for the explorers and early settlers were the waterways. Of course, there were problems with river transportation. Rivers could not be used during the winter when they were frozen. During the flood time of the spring the streams frequently overflowed, were turbulent, rapid, and difficult to navigate. During the normal periods of the year there were constant problems with partly or barely submerged trees, and impassable rafts of wood (called wooden islands) which covered the surface of the rivers. In this respect it should be noted that the *voyageurs* found the Missouri River more difficult to navigate than the Mississippi.

The French settlers had several types of vessels for the rivers. For rapid travel and ease of portage the first explorers from Canada used a birch bark canoe such as the Indians employed. But a more common craft on the Mississippi and Missouri was the *pirogue*. The pirogue was a dugout hollowed out of a tree trunk until it resembled a canoe in shape. Then the

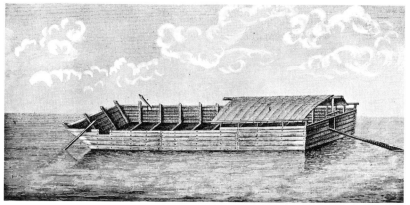

Courtesy State Historical Society

This sketch by Collet shows the type of flatboat used to transport goods downriver.

boat was split lengthwise into two sections and planking was inserted between the two sides, thus widening the vessel. The pirogues varied in length, but they frequently were about twenty feet long. Birch bark canoes were of about the same length, although there are reports of some birch bark canoes used in Canada which were forty feet long, six feet wide, and capable of carrying a load of four tons and a crew of fourteen.

Another kind of boat used was the flat bottomed *bateau*. The floor structure was really a raft, but a shelter which included both a roof and sides was built at the stern of the craft. The bateau was sometimes fifty feet long and was used to carry freight downstream propelled by the current and the activity of several oarsmen. The craft was crudely constructed and it was abandoned or sold for lumber at the end of a trip.

The Indians of the plains taught the white men to make a simple, temporary boat up to fourteen feet long. Called a *bull boat,* it was created by stretching buffalo skins over a willow frame. It could be used in an emergency, but the craft was not sufficiently sturdy to warrant regular use. The buffalo robes had to be greased regularly with hot tallow to avoid leaks.

The greatest transportation problem was the movement of quantities of heavy freight upstream great distances. To transport heavy cargoes the French designed what they called a *keel boat*. It was a shallow, covered boat up to seventy feet long with a keel. For power, the boat relied upon a crew of ten to thirty men who walked along the bank pulling a rope which was attached both to the mast and the bow of the boat. This procedure was called cordelling a boat. The keel boat also had a sail which could be raised when the wind was right. Long poles were sometimes used to push the boat along.

In 1780 a Creole named Jean Baptiste de Gamache established ferry service over the Meramec. Captain James S. Piggott secured permission to operate a ferry service between St. Louis and Cahokia in 1797. Thus, regular commercial transportation began in Missouri at the end of the eighteenth century.

Much of the early travel was dangerous. The birch bark canoe and the bull boat could be easily torn on a snag or rock in the water. This was a factor in the trip to and from Montreal, since the men usually tried to shoot the many rapids instead of portaging around them. With all vessels there was the danger of capsizing. When the men were ashore there was the peril of wild animals and of robbers, white or red, who preyed upon travelers. These bandits were more common on the Mississippi than on the smaller, less heavily traveled rivers.

The colonists and fur traders in the mid-continent needed trade goods from the East and were willing to pay for them. This meant there were profits to be made in transportation, and there were *voyageurs* who would take the necessary risks. English settlers were frequently impressed by the stamina of the *voyageurs*. Amos Stoddard wrote of the boatmen as follows:

> They are seldom known to be impatient of labor, or to be affected by the heat; and on these accounts they are to be preferred to others. They are also accustomed to live on what would starve an English American. A small amount of corn meal, and bear's grease, are all the articles of nourishment allowed them in Indian countries, except when they are so fortunate as to kill game. They are seldom furnished with salted meat, except when employed in the neighborhood of the whites, where it can be occasionally obtained.

(Courtesy State Historical Society)

Bodmer has sketched this view of Indians with their bull boats. The tail left on the buffalo skin in the front boat could serve as a handy tow rope.

Since space was so valuable in the canoe, a *voyageur* could take along only his blanket, his pipe and tobacco, and a small bundle of other articles. Despite the inconveniences, the French boatmen were willing to travel in all kinds of weather from early spring to early winter. It was a difficult way to earn a living.

On the trip between the Mississippi and Montreal there were approximately thirty-six portages, some up cliffs and others through bogs. The French tied their trade goods or furs into packages weighing about ninety pounds. The *voyageur* would trot with two such packages resting on his back and secured across his forehead by a cord. There were legends among the French of *voyageurs* who could carry eight packs at a time.

Even after the English received control of Canada at the end of the French and Indian War, the same system of transportation to the West was used. Zenon Trudeau estimated in 1792 that the English were able to send at least one hundred and fifty canoes of goods to the Mississippi each year.

Throughout the seventeenth and eighteenth centuries there was a great passion on the part of the French colonists of North America to find the water route to the Pacific. Such a route would be valuable as a channel for goods to and from the Orient. By the year 1763, Frenchmen had explored all of the Mississippi River and a great part of the Missouri River. They were somewhat retarded in their explorations of the Missouri River by the ferocity of the plains Indians.

It is only natural that certain myths should develop about the unknown areas to the West. Rumor populated the region with strange tribes of dwarf Indians, white Indians, and bearded Indians. There were reports of Indians whose eyes bulged out an inch farther than their noses. Strange to say, such legends were one of the factors promoting settlement. Stories of richly clad, bejeweled Oriental peoples in the West spurred interest in exploration, which in turn opened new lands for settlement.

One of the most incredible legends is associated with the brave, remarkable Welshman, John Evans. Evans came to America in search of a tribe of Welsh Indians who were believed to live somewhere up the Missouri River. Word of his project reached high places; even Thomas Jefferson expressed an interest in the search. Evans crossed the Atlantic in 1792 and had followed the clues to the whereabouts of his lost red kinsmen as far as Missouri by 1795. Recognizing his trustworthiness and his determination, the Spanish Missouri Company made use of the services of Evans in 1796 when they hired him to follow the Missouri River to its source across the continent. As he went, Evans was to carve the name of King Charles IV on rocks and trees giving proof of his discoveries. But Evans, like many other brave *voyageurs*, was unable to accomplish his task. The savage plains Indians, who either detained the travelers to keep trade goods from other tribes or who made war upon the pale interlopers, were the main obstacle to the fulfillment of his goal.

Whether the whites were seeking silver, rubies, the Pacific, long-lost tribes, or just adventure, they pushed their way westward and broadened the knowledge of Europeans. White persistence, ingenuity and gunpowder was sure to have its way. The first explorer was always followed by another. Though the blood of white men was to stain many bluffs along the Missouri, there were always new young men ready to risk their lives for the adventure of travel into the unknown. In this exciting and dangerous process of exploration, boats were the chief vehicles of travel.

The colonists, like the Indians, traveled by horseback within the French communities or to outlying areas away from the waterways. Horses were also used to pull buggies when roads were sufficiently developed to accommodate such vehicles. Christian Schultz, a German visitor to St. Louis in 1807, described the horse he rode as follows:

> I accordingly set out on a Spanish horse, at a round gallop of six miles to the hour. These are a kind of animal you have probably never seen. They are generally about thirteen hands high, hardy, and full of mettle, and may almost be said to live by hard riding, as they are frequently galloped fifty to sixty miles in a day, without even halting to feed.

When Schultz had ridden about twenty miles out of St. Louis, he lost his way. Schultz blamed himself for his "stupidity and ignorance in expecting to find anything like a road through this wilderness."

The first roads frequently were only Indian trails that had been widened by felling a few trees. The stumps usually remained in the right of way, and infrequent use allowed the weeds and brush to overgrow the road, camouflaging the impediments. The wagons and buggies that later traveled the road had great trouble with the stumps. Broken wagon or buggy wheels were a common occurrence. French vehicles were the

Cordelling a keel boat upstream required the services of a large crew of strong men. Sails and poles were employed wherever possible.

(*Courtesy Missouri Historical Society*)

most vulnerable, because the French did not usually apply an iron band to their wooden wheels.

As one might expect, the two oldest roads in Missouri were in the Ste. Genevieve area. The oldest was the Three Notch Road from Ste. Genevieve to Mine La Motte. It was so named because of the early habit of marking a road by notching trees along the way. This is why many early roads were called traces. The second earliest road was the King's Highway (*Rue Royale* or *El Camino Real*) which ran along the Mississippi north and south connecting St. Louis, Ste. Genevieve, Cape Girardeau, and New Madrid. Today Federal Highway 61 follows approximately the same path. Few colonists made the difficult and dangerous trip from St. Louis to Cape Girardeau overland. The Indian threat and the inconvenience of land transportation caused the French to use the water whenever possible.

Certainly there were many more problems in settlement than those of building homes and pirogues, establishing an economy, and maintaining friendly relations with the Indians. But these were the major tasks, and the colonists were forced to wrestle with each of them. This struggle of European man with his new environment is one of the most dramatic chapters of the history of Missouri.

BIBLIOGRAPHY

Broadhead, G. C. "Early Missouri Roads," *Missouri Historical Review*, Vol. VIII (January, 1914), pp. 90-92.

De Voto, Bernard. *The Course of Empire*. Boston: Houghton Mifflin Co., 1952.

Dolch, Isabel S. "Some Aspects of Early Indian Fur Trade," *Missouri Historical Review*, Vol. XXXVI (April, 1942), pp. 190-198.

Espinosa, J. Manuel. "Spanish Louisiana and the West: The Economic Significance of the Ste. Genevieve District," *Missouri Historical Review*, Vol. XXXII (April, 1938), pp. 287-297.

Gardner, James A. "Business Career of Moses Austin in Missouri," *Missouri Historical Review*, Vol. L (April, 1956), pp. 235-247.

Gentry, North Todd. "Plank Roads in Missouri," *Missouri Historical Review*, Vol. XXXI (April, 1937), pp. 272-287.

Gregg, Kate L., ed. "Indians in the Valley," *Missouri Historical Review*, Vol. XXXIX (October, 1944; January, 1945), pp. 75-97, 224-255.

Houck, Louis. *A History of Missouri*. Vols. I and II. Chicago: R. R. Donnelley & Sons Co., 1908.

Houck, Louis. *The Spanish Regime in Missouri*. Vols. I and II. Chicago: R. R. Donnelley & Sons Co., 1909.

Holmes, Jack D. L., ed. "A 1795 Inspection of Spanish Missouri," *Missouri Historical Review*, Vol. LV (October, 1960), pp. 5-17.

Klein, Ada Paris, ed. "Lead Mining in Pioneer Missouri," *Missouri Historical Review*, Vol. XLIII (April, 1949), pp. 251-270.

Klein, Ada Paris. "Ownership of Land Under France, Spain and United States," *Missouri Historical Review*, Vol. XLIV (April, 1950), pp. 274-294.

Klein, Ada Paris. "The Fur Trade," *Missouri Historical Review*, Vol. XLIII (July, 1949), pp. 360-380; Vol. XLIV (October, 1949; January, 1950), pp. 48-65, 168-178.

McDermott, John Francis. "The Confines of a Wilderness," *Missouri Historical Review*, Vol. XXIX (October, 1934), pp. 3-12.

McDermott, John Francis. "The Exclusive Trade Privilege of Maxent, Laclede and Company," *Missouri Historical Review*, Vol. XXIX (July, 1935), pp. 272-278.

Nasatir, A. P. "An Account of Spanish Louisiana, 1785," *Missouri Historical Review*, Vol. XXIV (July, 1930), pp. 521-536.

Nasatir, A. P. *Before Lewis and Clark: Documents Illustrating the History of the Missouri, 1785-1804*, Vols. I and II. St. Louis: St. Louis Historical Documents Foundation, 1952.

Nasatir, A. P. "Ducharme's Invasion of Missouri, An Incident in the Anglo-Spanish Rivalry for the Indian Trade of Upper Louisiana," *Missouri Historical Review*, Vol. XXIV (October, 1929; January and April, 1930), pp. 3-15, 238-260, 420-439.

Nasatir, A. P. "John Evans, Explorer and Surveyor," *Missouri Historical Review*, Vol. XXV (January, April, July, 1931), pp. 219-239, 432-460, 585-608.

Nasatir, A. P., "The Formation of the Missouri Company," *Missouri Historical Review*, Vol. XXV (October, 1930), pp. 10-22.

Penn, Dorothy and Marie George Windell, eds. "The French in the Valley," *Missouri Historical Review*, Vol. XL (October, 1945; January, April, July, 1946), pp. 90-122, 245-275, 407-430, 562-578; Vol. XLI (October, 1946; January, April, July, 1947), pp. 77-106 192-216 305-314, 391-399.

Peterson, Charles E. "Early Ste. Genevieve and Its Architecture," *Missouri Historical Review*, Vol. XXXV (January, 1941), pp. 207-232.

Schaaf, Ida M. "The First Roads West of the Mississippi," *Missouri Historical Review*, Vol. XXIX (January, 1935), pp. 92-97.

Swartzlow, Ruby Johnson. "The Early History of Lead Mining in Missouri," *Missouri Historical Review*, Vol. XXVIII (January, 1934), pp. 184-194; Vol. XXIX (October, 1934; January and April, 1935), pp. 27-34, 109-114, 195-205.

Williams, Walter and Floyd Calvin Shoemaker. *Missouri, Mother of the West*. Vol. I. Chicago and New York: American Historical Society, Inc., 1930.

Wood, Martha May. "Traces in Early Missouri," *Missouri Historical Review*, Vol. XXXVIII (October, 1943), pp. 12-24.

CHAPTER IV

French Society in Missouri

> In the old French portion of the town [St. Louis] the
> thoroughfares are narrow and crooked, and some of the
> houses are very quaint and picturesque. . . . Some of
> these ancient habitations . . . have a kind of French
> shrug about them; and being lop-sided with age, appear
> to hold their heads askew as if they were grimacing in
> astonishment at the American improvements.
>
> —a description of St. Louis in 1840
> by Charles Dickens, printed in his
> *American Notes*

The threads of many national groups are woven together
to form the fabric of America's culture. Each strand of custom
and tradition adds new color and texture to the whole. So it
was in Missouri when Frenchmen met Indians and when the
two groups were joined by Spanish officials, English-speaking
immigrants, and settlers of other European nationalities. As the
years passed, a silent compromise of living habits resulted in
the development of a new society not exclusively identified with
any one of the original groups, but a mixture of the social traditions of all.

The French who first settled Missouri formed a society that
was possibly the most colorful on the American frontier. Because of the importance of this picturesque society in colonial
Missouri, a look at French costume, custom, and cuisine has a
place in any history of the state.

Religion

In Europe the sixteenth, seventeenth, and eighteenth centuries were times of great religious turmoil born of the conflict
between Protestants and Roman Catholics. In general it can be
said that the Catholics emerged victorious in southern Europe
and the Protestants in northern Europe. In France, the result-

(*Walker—Missouri Commerce*)

This painting by Oscar E. Berninghaus in the Missouri capitol building gives the artist's view of the people, houses, and church of colonial Ste. Genevieve. Note the ox-drawn charette with its solid wooden wheels.

ant civil war was settled when the Catholic forces secured the upper hand. The French Protestants—called Huguenots—sought to migrate to the colonies, but permission to do so was denied them. French policy was designed to insure that their colonies would be Catholic. In contrast to the French, the English government encouraged religious dissenters and non-conformists to settle in their American colonies. Thus, while French America was uniformly Catholic, English America had a variety of churches.

Since the Catholic Church was the established church of France, it was supported with government funds. The government provided the land for a church, a rectory, and a cemetery. In addition, the crown made an annual grant of money for the church building and paid the priest's salary. Because of this official encouragement and because of the Catholic background of the colonists, it is little wonder that churches were constructed soon after settlement was begun.

There was little change in the relationship of church and state when Louisiana became Spanish territory. The Catholic Church was the established church in Spain, just as in France.

In fact, the Spanish king was addressed as His Catholic Majesty. Spanish monarchs were noted for their orthodoxy and for their devotion to the Catholic Church. The Spanish crown immediately assumed the responsibilities of the French government in support of the churches in Missouri.

In 1776, the church and parish residence were completed in St. Louis. A temporary log church had been used for several years before this sanctuary was constructed. The scene was drawn by C. Heberer under the direction of F. L. Billon.

The first churches were simple in structure and built in a manner similar to that used in the construction of houses. We have already noted the complaints of the people in St. Louis that their church built in 1776 was in danger of collapsing twenty years later because the beams making up the walls were rotting where they entered the ground. In 1792 Governor-General Carondelet ordered "all the inhabitants to contribute in proportion to their ability to the said work and that those who do not have money will employ themselves, personally making up the amount of money which they should contribute by a few days work" for the rebuilding of the church at St. Louis. The church at New Madrid was constructed later than the St. Louis church, but the following description of it, written in 1804, gives us a picture of the early churches:

That building is sixty feet long, twenty-eight wide,

and sixteen feet high between the ground and the ceiling. Its carpenter work is constructed of cypress timber doubled on the outside with planks of the same wood. It has . . . an altar with a tabernacle of cherry wood, and a picture of the most holy Virgin Mary, eight feet high by five and one-half feet wide, framed in wood, a railing in front where communion is taken, a pulpit of cherry wood, a belfry with a metal bell weighing fifty pounds.

A group of appraisers estimated the value of the church at 1200 pesos.

The cemetery was a consecrated place for the burial of the dead. Priests, however, and those who contributed 100 pesos to the upkeep of the church, could be interred within the church itself. Because the cemeteries were considered consecrated ground, only Catholics could be buried there. An unconsecrated cemetery was soon necessary in St. Louis for the burial of Protestants and Indians. It is believed to have been located in the area of the Old Courthouse at Market and Broadway. Pontiac, the Ottawa Indian chief who was murdered near St. Louis in 1769, was buried in this cemetery.

From Father Marquette's time on through the period of French control, the Jesuits were the main religious order in the Mississippi Valley. These fearless men with a passion for service acted as explorers, missionaries to the Indians, diplomats, and priests to the struggling new churches. But the very aggressiveness of the Jesuits created enemies for the group within the Catholic Church, and in 1767 the Jesuits were banned in Spain and in the Spanish empire. Six years later Pope Clement XIV officially outlawed the Jesuits. This act encouraged other religious orders to carry on the work. During the time of Spanish control in Missouri the Capuchins, with their brown robes and pointed hoods, were the leading order of monks although men from other orders also served from time to time.

There were never enough priests for the new communities developing in the Missouri region. This was true of both the Spanish and French periods. For devoted Catholics this was a serious matter, since only a priest could celebrate the Mass. In communities without a priest a devout layman was sometimes authorized to preside at prayer meetings, weddings, and funerals. At Florissant, Rene Kiercereaux, a layman, was the leading chanter of the church. Garbed in a long black cassock and white surplice, he also held weddings and funerals.

During the Spanish period there was an interesting attempt to solve the priest shortage by bringing in Irish priests. In fact, the Spanish government even agreed to pay Irish priests forty dollars per month, ten dollars more than Spanish or French priests received. What was the background of this development? In the late eighteenth and early nineteenth century the almost solidly Catholic Irish were still ruled by the English whom they considered exploiters and religious enemies. To secure a Catholic education many Irishmen went to Spain where many of them later entered the Spanish army or government service. In 1798 Lieutenant-Governor Zenon Trudeau approved plans to make use of priests "of the Irish nation" who were being trained at Irish College, Salamanca, Spain. He felt they would be acceptable to the French settlers and Spanish officials. In addition, he stated they would be effective in working with the English-speaking Americans moving into the area and with the Irish soldiers serving in the Spanish army. Thus, in the 1790's, Father James Flynn was sent to St. Louis and Father James Maxwell to Ste. Genevieve.

Although the priests were to supplement their government salaries by receiving offerings for performing marriages, baptisms, and low Masses, they were not to collect the tithe as was done in Europe. When Father Hilaire of Ste. Genevieve, a Capuchin, attempted to collect the tithe in 1774, his parishioners sent protests to Lieutenant-Governor Pedro Piernas in St. Louis. Piernas sent their remonstrance on to the Governor-General in New Orleans adding only that his own priest in St. Louis, Father Valentine, was not collecting the tithe. In their petition the people of Ste. Genevieve asserted that Father Hilaire had not earned the money since he had "given no instruction to the children or preached a sermon or given an exhortation to his parishioners." Even if their priest had earned such an increase in pay, the churchmen of Ste. Genevieve protested that because of adverse weather conditions and poor crops "there is nothing else left for us of it, than air, which, although it is good, is not sufficient for the support of our families. . . ." The priest was immediately ordered to halt the collections.

When a priest was available, the Mass was celebrated each Sunday morning. There were, of course, special services for funerals, weddings, church holidays, and particularly midnight Mass at Christmas. After church services on Sunday morning, town officials would make announcements and sometimes hold sales in front of the church. Sunday was a time of entertainment, too, with dances and billiard games the rest of the day.

The French colonists maintained a Catholic tradition now rarely seen in Missouri—religious processions on the city streets. They formed processions led by a priest and marched to the homes of the dying where the priest would perform the last rites of the Catholic Church. A German visitor has described a procession of the chanting faithful who marched down to the Mississippi River and prayed for the flooding to cease.

Both the French and Spanish governments had laws forbidding the entrance of Protestants into Missouri, but the laws were slightly revised in 1795. Protestants were then permitted to enter Missouri, but the "Privilege of enjoying the liberty of conscience is not extended beyond the first generation." Non-Catholic services were still prohibited by law. All marriages and baptisms were to be Catholic. Colonial officials anticipated that, through observing these restrictions, any Protestant population would be Catholic by the second generation.

It is difficult to determine the ethical impact of a religious movement. In colonial Missouri there is evidence both positive and negative. When Pedro Piernas came to Missouri in 1769, he wrote the following about Ste. Genevieve: "Religion is given but scant respect, or to speak more correctly, is totally neglected. . . ." He described St. Louis as a place of "Trade, looseness of conduct, the abandonment of life." It must be admitted that the records of the French fur traders who went West show that they often departed from Christian ethical standards when they lived with, and exploited, the Indians.

The criticism by Piernas, however, should not lead us to feel that the settlers of Missouri were, to a man, irreligious or unmoved by their faith. No doubt some today would describe our own society in words similar to those of Piernas. Probably the best tribute to the effectiveness of the Catholic faith comes from Henry Brackenridge, a Protestant, who described his childhood in Ste. Genevieve as follows:

> Madam Beauvais caused me every night to kneel
> by her side, to say my *pater noster* and *credo*, and
> then whispered those gentle admonitions which

seep deep into the heart. To the good seed thus
early sown I may ascribe any growth of virtue in
a soil that might otherwise have produced only
noxious weeds. . . .

Food

Although those who came to Missouri in the late fall and
winter may have experienced difficulties in procuring food,
usually the newcomer was surrounded by natural provisions.
Buffalo were still grazing along the Mississippi River when the
first colonist arrived. Elk, antelope, and black bear were common in the area. Deer, rabbit, raccoon, squirrel, opossum, quail,
pheasant, wild turkey, goose, and duck can be added to the list
of other animals hunted for food. The rivers provided catfish,
bass, crappie, sunfish, perch, and pike. Living in the midst of
a hunter's and angler's paradise, many of the early settlers
spent their lives in the forest or along the streams in a search
for food. Some Spanish government officials were highly critical of the French colonists for spending so much time hunting
and so little time farming. They complained that the French
settlements were not as highly developed as they might have
been because the Frenchmen were wasting time in hunting. The
officials warned the settlers that they would have nothing to
show for their efforts once all the game was shot.

Gathering and gardening provided fruits and vegetables for
the colonists' diet. Wild persimmons, pawpaws, cherries, plums,
gooseberries, strawberries, grapes, and mushrooms added variety to French-American menus. The settlers gathered wild
honey and produced sugar from the sap of the maple trees. In
addition, peas, cabbage, beets, carrots, potatoes, melons, and
cucumbers were grown in the garden found on every homestead.
Indian crops such as corn, beans, and pumpkins were immediately adopted by the settlers. In the common fields they produced Indian corn, wheat, rye, oats, buckwheat, and barley.
Each family also owned livestock to provide beef, pork, mutton,
chicken, eggs, milk, and butter for their table.

Prior to the building of gristmills in Missouri, the colonists
were forced to the tedious use of mortars or hand mills to grind
their corn into meal and their wheat into flour. In 1766 Joseph
Taillon constructed a horse or ox-powered gristmill in St. Louis
where the Cupples Station freight terminal stands today. A
year later he dammed the small stream that flowed through

what is now known as Mill Creek Valley to provide water power for the mill. This time-saving facility contributed to the self-sufficiency of the young town and freed many hours for more constructive labors.

It was necessary to preserve food for winter consumption by several processes. Fruit was dried or made into preserves. Meat was smoked or salted. Grains could be stored either in baskets or on the ear. Nuts were gathered in the fall and stored in a cool, dry place. Root vegetables were buried in sand. To give variety to winter meals, rabbit, squirrel, wild turkey, or pheasant were shot.

In early Missouri, as now, Frenchmen took pride in their cooking when they had a variety of provisions and the time to prepare their dishes. One early observer noted that even in the house of the poorest peasants "cookery is an art well understood." It is difficult to describe a typical meal. We know that

This photograph of a colonial goblet and silverware from the collections of the Missouri Historical Society of St. Louis originally appeared in St. Louis, A Fond Look Back.

the French seem to have preferred wheat bread to cornbread, and meat simmered in gravy—fricasseed—to that fried or roasted. The Creoles (as the American-born French and Spanish were called) also enjoyed tastily prepared vegetables and salads. They particularly delighted in gumbo soups, fricassees, or stews, well seasoned with garlic, onion, or pepper and containing a variety of vegetables. They used bear grease for salad oil and shortening, and maple sugar for sweetening. The favorite beverage was the wine—usually red—that was prepared from available fruits—gooseberries, currants, and especially grapes. Perhaps time-dimmed memory may account for the following description which is rather inconsistent with the usual reputation of French cuisine. Henry Brackenridge wrote that on a visit to New Madrid as a child "coarse, black bread, a kind of catfish soup, hot with pepper and seasoned with garlick, [sic] was about the only food they gave us." General David Forman was more pleasantly entertained when he visited the Spanish commandant in New Madrid in 1790 and reported, "He gave us a splendid dinner in the Spanish style, and plenty of good wines and coffee without cream." Inventories of estates show that some of the wealthier settlers were able to buy foods brought in from great distances—tea, coffee, chocolate, mustard, and olive oil. Although most were unable to afford such delicacies, the French colonists in America had an abundance of easily secured food which was, on the whole, superior to that consumed by their fellow countrymen in France.

Health

It was widely believed both in Europe and in America that colonists on the American frontier were usually weak, sickly people. The physical deterioration of the frontier settler was thought to result from the musty vapors produced by decaying vegetation. The colonist usually picked a wooded area for his home since the wood was so necessary for building materials, fuel, and fences; such wooded areas always had many layers of decaying leaves on the ground. There was also a belief that a colonist could expect to be sick the first summer in his new home. The months when sickness was most prevalent were August and September. Called "autumn fevers," the sickness probably was caused, not by vile vapors, but by the mosquitoes that swarmed about every man or animal on the frontier.

Although the white men had many health problems which required medical advice, the Indians were in a much more difficult position. Because they had no immunity to the white man's diseases, entire tribes were wiped out by maladies such as measles and smallpox.

Probably no aspect of culture has changed so much since the eighteenth century as the practice of medicine. Medicines and medical techniques have both been greatly altered by the scientific discoveries of the 19th and 20th centuries. Eighteenth-century concepts of health, sanitation, and medicine would be unacceptable today. Few people today who live along the Mississippi or Missouri rivers will drink the unpurified river water as did the first colonists.

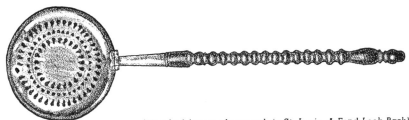

(Sketched from a photograph in St. Louis, A Fond Look Back)

French settlers used this copper bedwarmer on cold winter nights in Missouri. It is now in the collections of the Missouri Historical Society.

One of the primary medical treatments was the bleeding of a patient, thereby, it was believed, removing the bad blood which had caused the disease. In 1791 Lieutenant-Governor Zenon Trudeau lamented that the mortality rate in the colony was so high because no "blood letter" was available to cure the people. A strong laxative or purge was commonly prescribed for a variety of ailments. Some placed great faith in the drinking of mineral water or the use of Indian medicine such as powdered rattlesnake's rattle.

Though most of the medical practices of the period were founded on ignorance and superstition, some advances were made. In an attempt to avoid fevers, the people of Ste. Genevieve decided to drain a marshy area adjacent to the city in 1797. Since fever-carrying mosquitoes bred in these swamps, the strategy was a good one. A second advance in medicine occurred when vaccination against smallpox was begun. Finally,

Young Auguste Chouteau, one of the founders of St. Louis, was a wealthy merchant and community leader during the Spanish and American periods. This sketch was made from a portrait in the possession of the Missouri Historical Society of St. Louis.

we must not fail to mention that two physicians came to Missouri during the Spanish period. Dr. Andre Auguste Conde came to St. Louis in 1766 and Dr. Antoine Francois Saugrain in 1800. The latter was brought as part of a government campaign to improve health. Another feature of this campaign was the government's promise to build a hospital for the new physician. This promise was not fulfilled.

Clothing

The Frenchman in colonial Missouri found new foods unknown in Europe which he prepared in his own French way. Fricasseed buffalo tongue is thus a combination of the European and American. In the area of dress there was a similar merging of traditions; buckskin often replaced calico for aprons, and Indian moccasins were worn beneath layers of European petticoats. Colonists who lived with the Indian tribes as traders often adopted most of the Indian wearing apparel. Those, however, who lived in the villages did not make such radical changes in their garb.

The clothing of the colonist was usually sewn of a coarse cotton material or a mixture of cotton and wool. Each family produced enough cotton and wool so that they could spin and weave fabric for their own needs. Winter was an ideal time for such indoor work. Men who were traveling, hunting, or engaging in heavy work wore clothes of buckskin or other animal hides. For special occasions the Creoles donned expensive garments of satin, taffeta, silk, or velvet.

Both men and women often tied a blue handkerchief about their hair. For festive occasions the women placed colored ribbons on their blue head scarves. For at least half of the year the colonists required a coat or, as they called it, a *capote*. The *capote* was a loose fitting white coat with a hood that hung down the back when not in use. Women delighted in bright polka dot, checked, or striped calico blouses and skirts with several petticoats. The men wore coarse blue cotton trousers and shirts in summer. During the winter most of them donned buckskin garments. Both men and women were shod in moccasins during the winter, but during the summer often went barefoot.

For Mass on Sunday and for the ball which followed, the colonists appeared in more elegant attire. Women aped what they believed to be the Paris fashions and in garments of satin and lace, in silk stockings and morocco slippers, they displayed their dancing ability. They were all the more alluring for their chiffon scarves, combs of ivory, ornate fans, beads, and ear-

Madame Marie Therese Bourgeois Chouteau is sometimes known as "the Mother of St. Louis." Her home was the chief meeting place in the first years of the settlement. She is pictured in the typical French-Missouri headdress.
(Sketch from an old portrait in the collection of the Missouri Historical Society in St. Louis.)

rings. The men wore brightly colored coats with gold buttons and tied their powdered hair in cues with silk ribbons. Such an ensemble would be complete if the gentleman carried a sword, a lace handkerchief, and a silver snuff box.

(This sketch was made from a photograph in St. Louis, A Fond Look Back)

Auguste Chouteau and his bride wore these garments on their wedding day, September 26, 1786. Notice the embroidered vest, the elegant fleur-de-lis lace at the wrists of the handsome satin coat, and the yards of ruffled silk lace decorating Madame Chouteau's gown. These garments are now the property of the Missouri Historical Society of St. Louis.

Visitors to Missouri remarked at the ability of the humblest colonist to dress regally for special occasions. John Bradbury, who toured the American frontier in 1809-11, reported that the French colonists "retain as much fondness for showy dress as the most foppish of their ancestors." On a Saturday he visited the lead mines and watched a particular digger throw ore out of his trench. On Sunday morning, Bradbury reported, "I met him in the village, dressed in a white gown, with red slippers, and a blue silk waistcoat, embroidered with silver lace."

The washing of clothes was an important and, in the absence of modern laundry equipment, laborious chore for the women. Since a river bank was usually the gathering place for such an activity, the company of neighbors similarly engaged and the opportunity to visit with them must have lightened the task to a degree. In St. Louis the women carted their soiled clothing to the bank of Chouteau's Pond near Taillon's grist mill. There the laundry was boiled in great iron pots and then beaten with paddles. The women hung their clean wash to dry on hazel bushes, scrub oaks, persimmon, and grapevines which covered the nearby hill.

Entertainment

There were sure to be hardships and privations in any frontier area. But when the colonists lived in settlements where families were in close proximity to one another, they at least enjoyed the benefit of one another's company and avoided the terrible loneliness of those settlers who built isolated homesteads. The French in Missouri, like the Puritans of New England, lived in towns or settlements where they were able to organize community activities to entertain themselves. English-speaking frontiersmen who visited Missouri remarked at the

The coureur de bois wore both French and Indian clothing. The hooded capote often topped buckskin shirt and trousers.
(Sketch from painting in Laut's The Story of the Trapper)

importance the French assigned to such matters as holidays and social etiquette. Americans often looked down upon these French as a frivolous, lazy people, but one suspects that there was envy in the hearts of many of those Americans and that, perhaps, they coveted the fun of these gay French communities.

Catholic sections of Europe were noted for the many religious festivals they observed. The Creoles of Missouri maintained the same calendar of celebrations including such days as Christmas, New Years, Epiphany, Easter, Corpus Christi Sunday, Whitsunday, and Michaelmas. Each holiday could be the occasion for a family to gather for a banquet of fine foods and wines after the church service. Following, and sometimes preceding, their festive meals the celebrants engaged in card games—especially a game called loo—or they crowded into one of the several billiard halls. An indication of the popularity of billiards can be seen in the fact that when the lieutenant-governor wanted an announcement to be widely circulated he had notices posted in "all the billiard halls." The colonists enjoyed gambling and played both cards and billiards for money.

The Creoles also imported the French love of music and dancing. Not all children were taught to read, but all were taught to dance. After Mass each Sunday a ball was held somewhere in the town. These Sabbath dances were attended by all —rich and poor, young and old. Those too young or too old to dance watched the others. Cotillions, waltzes, reels, two-steps, and minuets were performed to the music of a fiddle with as much grace as might have been expected anywhere in Europe. There were several pianos in St. Louis in the 1790's and we can surmise that they were also put to use at the frequent balls.

In general, the French colonists were a fun-loving people who so arranged their lives that they were able to enjoy the same social activities that they had known in the Old Country. The accounts of their colorful folk celebrations form a large and fascinating segment in the social history of Missouri.

Education

It is fair to say that a formal education was not so highly prized among the Creoles of Upper Louisiana as it seems to have been in such English colonies as Massachusetts or Connecticut. It was, of course, desirable to be able to read and

(Howe, The Great West)

The younger people in the French communities danced from house to house on New Year's Day singing La Guignolee, a traditional French song.

write, and, in time, a few schools were organized to teach such rudimentary skills. But there was no popular demand for, or support of, an educational system which could serve a large part of the children in the colony. There are, no doubt, a number of reasons for this. In France itself, the common people did not expect to receive an education. Furthermore, an education did not appear to be of immediate value to most men who spent their days digging for lead, boiling for salt, or paddling a canoe as a *coureur de bois.* It is also well to remember that even if the colonists had demanded an education for all their children, frontier conditions made it difficult to secure teachers, books, and facilities necessary for the founding and operation of schools. The French colonists were not opposed to education, but they did not have sufficient zeal for it to overcome immediately the obstacles to the establishment of an inclusive school system.

The village priests are known to have given some training to the children of the parishes. However, this schooling seems to have been in religion or in social graces as much as in reading and writing. In 1792, the people of St. Louis petitioned the governor-general asking that a Benedictine monk, Friar Pierre Joseph Didier, be sent to them to educate their children. Two years later he was moved to St. Louis, after he became involved in a quarrel with the commandant in Florissant.

Aside from the priests, there were several lay people who acted as teachers for a small part of the population. The best known was Jean Baptiste Truteau who established his own school in a log cabin in St. Louis in 1774 and taught there for almost fifty years. Truteau was the author of a poem entitled "Ballad of the Year of the Surprise" which described the British attack on St. Louis in 1780. This was probably the first poem composed in Missouri. Truteau was an excellent teacher and he served well those families who could afford to pay the tuition charged. We know that a Madame Rigauche operated another school in St. Louis in the 1790's. At the same time a similar school was opened in Ste. Genevieve by a young man named Fremonde Lauriere.

The lack of education in the colony becomes apparent when we observe the number of people who were unable to sign their names on public documents. Only about one-third of the people could write. However, the signatures of those who could write display great care and concern over flourishes. Illustrations of such signatures clearly demonstrate that writing was a skill not to be considered lightly.

(Houck's History of Missouri, Vol. II)

The pride and great care with which lettered Creoles signed their names is illustrated by the signatures of Laclede, Pedro Piernas, Zenon Trudeau, and Thomas Portelle.

A survey of the libraries in St. Louis gives statistics as to the books available in the settlement and the type of literature which was read. Of the 659 whites in St. Louis in 1800, approximately 56 owned books. It is estimated that there were 2000 to 3000 volumes in the town. Laclede had in his library of 150 books the works of such important European scholars as Rousseau, Locke, and Descartes. He had treatises on such varied subjects as agriculture, law, and surgery. When Laclede died on a trip from New Orleans to St. Louis he was carrying with him a twelve volume history of the Roman emperors. Thus, amid the general indifference to literature and language there were those who were reading the best books Europe had to offer at the time.

When Perrin du Lac visited Ste. Genevieve in 1802, he found much to criticize. In particular he deplored the fact that the people were "without learning or the desire of learning." Instead of working or studying, the young people spent their time riding, hunting, and dancing. While his criticism of the people is probably extreme, du Lac was close to the truth in describing their educational lethargy.

American Immigrants

When Zenon Trudeau was appointed lieutenant-governor of Upper Louisiana in 1792, he received the following order:

> You will not give any passport or permit the English and Americans to cross the Mississippi River or introduce themselves into the Dominions of His Majesty situated to the west of that river.

It was traditional Spanish policy to exclude such Protestant people from their areas of control. The Protestant Reformation, which swept across Europe in the sixteenth century, had been stamped out in Spain by prompt and violent action. The Spanish did not want what they considered a heretical movement to get started in the colonies. Furthermore, one reason for Spanish acceptance of the territory of Louisiana from France in 1762 was Spain's desire to protect her valuable Mexico and New Mexico settlements from the westward-moving Americans. Louisiana was a buffer area. If the Americans were allowed to enter the Louisiana territory, what would keep them from New Mexico?

It is usually easier to hand down an edict than it is to enforce it. The Spanish authorities who were ordered to keep the Americans out had only a few troops garrisoned in the settlements. As one official explained the problem, "You can't lock up an open field." There was no effective patrolling of the Mississippi River to keep out the silent invaders who usually did not even need the cover of darkness to cross unnoticed into the forbidden territory.

The Americans pressed ever westward across the continent.

Fed by a growing stream of immigrants from Europe, these Americans sought the solitude and promise of the frontier. Often unmindful of property rights and government regulations, they moved West to seek a better situation whenever they felt cramped by neighbors. Acquainted with few luxuries, they could move their few possessions and animals easily. As one observer described it, "a carbine and a little cornmeal in a sack is sufficient for an American to range the forests for a month." It was impossible to defend such an unpatrolled boundary line against the invasion of these restless, resourceful people who became ever more numerous in the 1790's.

There was a sudden change in Spanish policy in 1795. Governor-General Carondelet informed Lieutenant-Governor Trudeau that Americans could be given a permit to enter and settle west of the Mississippi. How can this policy change be explained? One major factor behind this development was Spanish fear of British encroachment in Upper Louisiana. Traders from Canada were taking control of the Indian trade in that province. The Spanish feared that the British might try to seize the area by force. A larger population—even if most of the settlers were Americans—would make it easier to organize a defense force in the colony. The other factor was a change in attitude toward the Americans. Zenon Trudeau appears to have developed respect for some of the Americans whom he met when they visited St. Louis. He wrote of the Americans in 1795, "A certain number of these men, the good cultivators, can do nothing but great good for our inhabitants, who need an example to put aside their old methods of cultivation, and to substitute a better one." The summer of 1795 he gave "many honest families" permission to cross over into Missouri.

Since their old policy of exclusion had failed, the Spanish officials, who had not had the money necessary to support the policy, decided that by being hospitable and tolerant they might win the affection and loyalty of the Americans. Although the Spanish did not change their religious laws requiring that all inhabitants be Catholic, they did not enforce this requirement. Furthermore, the Spanish government offered each family approximately six hundred arpents (492 acres) of land with slight variations depending upon the size of the family. The only charge was a small fee for survey and registration. In addition, for a time, the Americans were given as gifts such tools as a hoe, scythe, axe, spade, and sickle plus a pig, three chickens, and a barrel of corn for each immigrant over twelve years of age, and a half-barrel for each child between the ages of twelve and six. The Americans responded to these generous terms. Trudeau reported in 1796, "American families are coming to us daily."

The change in Spanish policy not only allowed the officials to give land to these immigrants, but it led them to offer larger grants to important individuals. Thus, Daniel Boone, who was well known as a leader in the settlement of the West, in 1798 was offered one thousand arpents if he would settle in Missouri. Boone accepted the offer and moved across the Mississippi. He acted as syndic of the Femme Osage section of the St. Charles district from 1800 to 1804. By the time the Louisiana territory became a part of the United States in 1804, there were approximately ten thousand white men in the district of Upper Louisiana; approximately half of the whites were Americans. This illustrates the great influx of Americans during the years 1795-1804. There were, of course, some people in Louisiana who disliked the new policy. The Bishop of Louisiana was outspoken in his opposition, but his voice was lost in the clatter and clamor of Americans building new homes and a new life in the fertile river valleys of the Spanish colony.

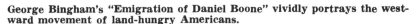

George Bingham's "Emigration of Daniel Boone" vividly portrays the westward movement of land-hungry Americans.

The contrast in the living habits of the Creoles and the Americans was immediately apparent. The latter were a pushing, building, improving, exploiting group who shunned the villages and settled in isolated sections. They erected their log cabins with horizontally placed logs and carved out farms in the wilderness. They produced more corn than their French neighbors and built mills to grind it. They were not so attracted as the French to the fur trade and they were unwilling to act as *voyageurs*.

In their more isolated existence, the Americans did not have so gay a social life as the Creole Missourians. Dancing was far less frequently indulged in and, therefore, much less graceful than that of the French settlers. While the French colonists, when occasion demanded, could bring out dress clothing of style and beauty, the Americans lived in brown, style-less, homespun woolen clothing and had less use for fancy dress.

The people, of course, differed in religion. While many of the earliest Americans who entered Missouri were not affiliated with a specific denomination, they were usually Protestant in

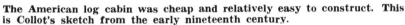

The American log cabin was cheap and relatively easy to construct. This is Collot's sketch from the early nineteenth century.

The unshorn American frontiersman was used to working and living in isolation.

tradition. It was illegal to hold non-Catholic worship services or for people either to be married or baptized by a Protestant clergyman. Some Missourians were forced to make a trip to the east side of the Mississippi in order to receive such church services from a Protestant minister. However, a Methodist minister named John Clark did secretly enter Missouri from Illinois each month in order to minister to the Protestant settlers. Lieutenant-Governor Trudeau was aware of this, but regularly gave Clark three day's notice to leave the colony. Thus, Clark had an opportunity to complete his pastoral duties while Trudeau had acted to uphold the law.

The unpampered palate of the American was accustomed to simpler fare than that which the Frenchman enjoyed. Variety in kinds of foods and methods of preparation were not expected by the hardy newcomers whose staple foods were salt pork, cornbread, and whiskey.

The Creoles in Missouri felt they were part of a French society—even though ruled by Spain. They maintained their French delight in style, in light-hearted amusements, in good eating, in their church. The Americans were immigrants from a new, fast-growing, energetic country. They were not by tradition concerned with form, etiquette, style, and graces. Their first task was to build homes and gain a livelihood; social graces and culture were secondary to roofs, beds, and rail fences. The two groups—so different—complemented each other. The Americans served as an example of industry and ambition for the

French, who in turn were a model of gentility and good taste for their rough-hewn neighbors.

BIBLIOGRAPHY

Clark, Thomas D. "Manners and Humors of the American Frontier," *Missouri Historical Review,* Vol. XXXV (October, 1940), pp. 3-24.

Goodwin, Cardinal L. "Early Exploration and Settlement of Missouri and Arkansas," *Missouri Historical Review,* Vol. XIV (April, 1920), pp. 385-425.

Houck, Louis. *A History of Missouri.* Vols. I and II. Chicago: R. R. Donnelley & Sons Co., 1908.

Houck, Louis. *The Spanish Regime in Missouri.* Vols. I and II. Chicago: R. R. Donnelley & Sons Co., 1909.

Kirkpatrick, R. L. "Professional, Religious and Social Aspects of St. Louis Life, 1804-1816," *Missouri Historical Review,* Vol. XLIV (July, 1950), pp. 373-386.

Lass, William E. "Tourist's Impression of St. Louis 1766-1859," *Missouri Historical Review,* Vol. LII (July, 1958), pp. 325-338.

Liljegren, Ernest R. "Frontier Education in Spanish Louisiana," *Missouri Historical Review,* Vol. XXXV (April, 1941), pp. 345-372.

McMillan, Margaret and Monia Cook Morris. "Educational Opportunities in Early Missouri," *Missouri Historical Review,* Vol. XXXIII (April and July, 1939), pp. 307-325, 477-498.

Nasatir, A. P. *Before Lewis and Clark: Documents Illustrating the History of the Missouri, 1785-1804.* Vols. I and II. St. Louis: St. Louis Historical Documents Foundation, 1952.

Penn, Dorothy and Marie George Windell, eds. "The French in the Valley." *Missouri Historical Review,* Vol. XL (October, 1945; January, April, July, 1946), pp. 90-122, 245-275, 407-430, 562-578; Vol. XLI (October, 1946; January, April, July, 1947), pp. 77-106, 192-216, 305-314, 391-399.

Robins, Ruby Matson, ed. "Americans in the Valley," *Missouri Historical Review,* Vol. XLV (October, 1950; January, April, July, 1951), pp. 1-15, 158-169, 275-293, 386-403.

Shoemaker, Floyd C. "Missouri's Tennessee Heritage," *Missouri Historical Review,* Vol. XLIX (January, 1955), pp. 127-142.

Shoemaker, Floyd C. "The Pioneer," *Missouri Historical Review,* Vol. XIX (January, 1925), pp. 241-255.

Squires, Monas N. "Merry-Making in Missouri in the Old Days," *Missouri Historical Review,* Vol. XXVIII (January, 1934), pp. 91-102.

Vestal, Stanley. *The Missouri.* New York: Farrar & Rinehart, Inc., 1945.

Viles, J. "Population and Extent of Settlement in Missouri Before 1804," *Missouri Historical Review,* Vol. V (July, 1911), pp. 189-207.

Whitaker, Arthur Preston. *The Mississippi Question, 1795-1803.* New York: D. Appleton-Century Co., Inc., 1934.

Williams, Walter and Floyd Calvin Shoemaker. *Missouri, Mother of the West.* Vol. I. Chicago and New York: American Historical Society, Inc., 1930.

CHAPTER V

Territorial Missouri

> Upper Louisiana, from its climate, population, soil, and productions, and from other natural advantages attached to it, will, in all human probability, soon become a star of no inconsiderable magnitude in the American constellation. —report by Captain Amos Stoddard

The French flirted with Missouri for a century before deserting her. The Spanish courted Missouri for about thirty years, but finally rejected her as a bride. She was just too expensive to maintain. The United States greeted Missouri with open arms in 1804, held her as a betrothed for a proper seventeen years, and finally led her to the altar of full statehood in 1821. In this chapter we shall examine the engagement time which is known as the territorial period.

The Louisiana Purchase

In 1800, St. Louis was still a French village of about 1,000 inhabitants and 180 houses. As the Creoles gathered before their fireplaces on the cold winter evenings or gossiped in groups around the dance floor, there was much to discuss. They could speak of the many new English-speaking settlers from east of the Mississippi, and lament that the French would soon be outnumbered in Upper Louisiana if the influx of Americans continued as it had the past five years.

Belatedly, the villagers received snatches of news from France which they eagerly told and retold. Of course they knew of the great revolution which had toppled the French king and had ushered in years of turmoil. No doubt they took pride in the brilliant military victories of France under their new military leader, Napoleon Bonaparte. But Europe was far away. At home in Missouri they could, if they were perceptive, observe the slow deterioration of Spanish power in the decaying ramparts and rusty cannon of the Spanish forts. Although there were hints of changes to come and possibly some speculation concerning the nature of these changes, the colonists could not have predicted the amazing transactions that took place in the next four years.

The revolutionaries in France had attacked the monarchy, the nobility, and the Catholic Church with great savagery. Although these revolutionary ideas had spread to other parts of Europe, they did not find popular response among the French of Missouri. The only instance of revolutionary activity in Missouri occurred in the year 1796 when General Ccllot, a French official of the revolutionary government, visited the area. He attempted to organize a revolutionary society and to introduce such innovations as the revolutionary calendar. The one major revolutionary act of the St. Louis society was to serenade the village priest on September 22—the first day of the revolutionary year—wishing him a "Happy New Year." This insolence, no doubt, irritated the priest and probably worried a few Spanish officials who feared that the Creoles in Upper Louisiana might attempt to overthrow Spanish control, but there was no real danger. The Creoles of Missouri were not flaming revolutionaries. They were quiet spectators of the great conflicts of Europe.

In their isolation, the French settlers in Missouri could not guess that they would be part of Napoleon's future plans. Napoleon, like Hitler in our century, had great plans for his country. Bonaparte envisioned an American empire which would enrich France and increase his prestige. Since sugar was a most important item in European commerce, Napoleon wanted to encourage sugar production in his West Indies islands. In order to free farm land for sugar cane, the islanders needed to import food. Napoleon decided that he could secure the wheat, corn, pork, and beef for his islanders from Louisiana which had been a French territory until 1762. All that was necessary was to persuade the Spanish to give Louisiana back to France.

This task was not so difficult as one might imagine. In 1800 the Spanish Secretary of State for Foreign Affairs had written, "Between ourselves, Louisiana costs us more than it is worth. . . ." The Spanish found that they could not balance their budget for Louisiana. In spite of keeping only skeleton forces in the forts—32 soldiers at New Madrid, 110 at St. Louis

—the financial deficit continued. Spanish military forces in Louisiana managed to maintain law and order in the colony, but they were far too weak to withstand a British or American attack.

When Napoleon came asking for Louisiana, Spain was ready to negotiate. The Spanish king, Charles IV, was seeking an area in Europe where his son-in-law might be given a throne. Since Napoleon's conquests had included such an area, a trade was proposed whereby the Spanish royal family was to receive a section of Italy called Tuscany in return for Louisiana. As originally negotiated, this Treaty of San Ildefonso of 1800 was considered a great victory by the Spanish. They were relieved of a financial drain, and in the process they were to acquire an Italian area with one million people in return for an American population of only fifty thousand. Both Napoleon and Charles IV were pleased with the arrangement.

The Americans were not so happy when the secret treaty was finally publicized. It was a shock for the citizens of the young country suddenly to discover that Napoleon, the greatest military leader in Europe, was standing at their back door, peering in. President Jefferson considered this new development a great crisis, for he knew of Bonaparte's dreams of world conquest. Jefferson immediately announced plans for a military

The signing of the Louisiana Purchase is commemorated in this bronze relief on the river front side of the Missouri capitol. It was originally created for the Louisiana Purchase Exposition in St. Louis in 1904. Monroe is standing at left, Livingston is seated, and Napoleon's treasurer Marbois is at right signing the document.
(Courtesy Massie-Missouri Commerce)

alliance with the British against the French, and he began to strengthen the American army.

The Ohio, Kentucky, and Tennessee frontiersmen were troubled by another problem at the same time. It is well known that there was a rush of American settlers into the trans-Appalachian area in the two decades after the Revolutionary War. By the year 1785 at least fifty thousand pioneers had crossed the mountains to claim land in Ohio, Kentucky, and Tennessee, along the Ohio River and its tributaries. The land in the area was highly productive, and the settlers had a major problem in marketing their surplus. It was most difficult to transport their corn, wheat, whiskey, tobacco, and pork to market on the Atlantic Coast. Roads to the east were primitive, bridges frequently non-existent, and wagons subject to hazards such as upsets or wheel breakage. Thus it was both expensive and dangerous to try to send produce overland to New York, Pennsylvania, Maryland, or Virginia. The easier method was to build a flatboat or barge and float down the Ohio and the Mississippi rivers to the Gulf of Mexico where sea-going sailing ships could carry the cargo to the Atlantic ports. In 1802, approximately 550 river craft carried goods from the American West down to New Orleans.

Unfortunately, there was one obstacle for the Americans who wished to use this all-water route to market. The Spanish who owned both Louisiana and West Florida controlled the land on both sides of the mouth of the Mississippi. From 1784 to 1788 the Spanish halted American use of the river. This tourniquet on the West's economic jugular vein brought cries of rage from the American farmers. In 1788 the Spanish relented partially, allowing trade to go through if the Americans paid duties. In Pinckney's Treaty of 1795 the Spanish were forced to grant more favorable terms, allowing Americans free navigation of the Mississippi River and the "right of deposit" at New Orleans. The right of deposit was the privilege of unloading the river barges and storing the cargo on shore, free of duty, until an American seagoing ship came to carry it away.

Pinckney's Treaty halted the grumbling of the American frontiersmen for seven years. But in 1802, shortly after it was announced that Napoleon had secured Louisiana by treaty, the Spanish officers who were still in charge suddenly withdrew the right of deposit at New Orleans. Both Jefferson and the frontiersmen now were worried. There was much talk of war in the West, and the Spanish ambassador in Washington sent hurried notes of concern to his government. The westerners were people accustomed to violence, and a violent reaction to the Spanish closure edict could be expected. The situation was further complicated by the uncertainty of how much the French government was responsible for the Spanish action in halting the right of deposit.

President Jefferson admired French culture, had an affection for the French people, and took a tolerant view of the French Revolution. But faced with this crisis, he developed a new stern policy toward France. Referring to New Orleans and the strangle hold on Mississippi commerce, he wrote, "There is on the globe one single spot the possessor of which is our natural and habitual enemy." Jefferson then set his strategy to secure that "single spot" which to him meant New Orleans and the rest of the east bank of the mouth of the Mississippi. If the United States could secure the east bank all the way to the Gulf, then the Spanish, who presently controlled the west bank, or the French, who would soon claim it, could not halt American use of the river. In order to abolish the constant threat to western commerce, Jefferson ordered the American Ambassador to France, Robert Livingston, and James Monroe, a special diplomat, to attempt to buy New Orleans and West Florida, for which they might pay up to ten million dollars.

Napoleon Bonaparte was a calculating man who usually knew when to change his tactics. In 1803 he found that Louisiana had ceased to be of value to him and was, in fact, a potential liability. After losing his brother-in-law and fifty thousand men in a futile campaign to put down a revolution in Haiti, Napoleon no longer needed Louisiana for a storehouse to supply his sugar islands. Furthermore, Louisiana would be easily lost in the war with Britain that he expected to erupt at any time. Finally, Napoleon was short of cash, and he thought that the Americans would be willing to pay well for the territory so important to their interests.

The American diplomats sent by Jefferson did not even propose the purchase of all of Louisiana. Imagine the surprise of Livingston, the deaf and aged ambassador, when Napoleon's finance minister suddenly offered to sell all of Louisiana. After eighteen days of haggling, on April 30, 1803, the elated Yankee diplomats agreed to purchase the huge area—some 828,000 square miles which now comprise six states and parts of seven others—for fifteen million dollars, or about three cents an acre. After signing the treaty Livingston declared, "We have lived long but this is the noblest work of our whole lives." And Napoleon rightly predicted, "This accession of territory . . . strengthens forever the power of the United States."

Curiously, the French sold Louisiana before their military or government officials ever came to America to claim it. In fact, the French sold Louisiana despite the promise Napoleon made the Spanish that he would never sell the territory, and despite his failure to deliver the Tuscany kingdom to the Spanish king. The Americans, however, were so happy with their acquisition that they refused to inquire into the legality of the prior transfers. The Spanish were too weak to stand up to the unscrupulous Frenchman and, as a result, Napoleon made a clear profit of fifteen million dollars for shuffling some papers.

The bewildered Spanish officials in Louisiana reluctantly carried out the details of the transfer. At New Orleans, the French occupation lasted only twenty days. On December 20, 1803, the Americans were declared rulers of the area. The transfer did not take place in Upper Louisiana until eighty days later.

Captain Amos Stoddard of the United States Army was appointed to receive "the quiet and peaceable possession of Upper Louisiana, together with the military posts at St. Louis and its dependencies," from the Spanish officials. He was to act for both the Republic of France and for the United States. Captain Meriwether Lewis of the Lewis and Clark expedition was in St. Louis at the time and assisted in the planning for the transfer. After making careful preparations by letter, Captain Stoddard and his men landed at St. Louis on March 9, 1804. The Americans marched to the Government House, at the southeast corner of Main and Walnut, where the formal but friendly ceremony of exchange took place. Both the soft-spoken Lieutenant-Governor De Lassus and the polite, correct Stoddard spoke to the people gathered to witness the ceremony. After the signing of an agreement there was the firing of cannon salutes and an exchange of flags, then banquets and balls in fine French style. Captain Stoddard wrote, "[I] took possession of Upper Louisiana in the name of the French Republic on the 9th day of

March; and on the next day, I assumed the Country and Government in the name of the United States."

No doubt the French settlers were both bewildered and troubled by these changes. One report declares that the "older inhabitants took it sadly to heart." Once again they had been traded away by their own countrymen. Stoddard described the reaction of the Creoles to the deal as follows, "they seemed to feel as if they had been sold in open market, and by this means degraded. . . ."

In fairness to Napoleon—usually considered as cold, hard-hearted, and oblivious to human suffering—it should be noted that he himself wrote Article 3 of the Louisiana Purchase Treaty which stipulated that the people of Louisiana should be admitted to the Union as soon as possible and that their rights, liberties, property, and religion be protected. Napoleon added with remarkable concern:

> Let the Louisianians know that we separate our-
> selves from them with regret; . . . and let them

On March 9, 1804, when the Stars and Stripes replaced the French Tricolor, Upper Louisiana became part of the United States. The painting is from the George Rogers Clark Memorial in Vincennes, Indiana.

(Courtesy Read Studio, Vincennes)

hereafter . . . recollect that they have been
Frenchmen, and that France, in ceding them, has
secured for them advantages which they could not
have obtained from a European power, however
paternal it might have been. Let them retain for
us sentiments of affection; and may their common
origin, descent, language and customs perpetuate
the friendship.

St. Louis and Exploration

President Jefferson and most other Americans had long
been curious about the West. They were intrigued with the
idea of a route to the Pacific. They were anxious for information about the people, the resources, and the animals of the
mysterious West. Even a decade before the Louisiana Purchase,
Jefferson had begun plans to explore the region. With the purchase of Louisiana there was all the more reason for exploring
the area.

St. Louis was the logical base for exploration in the West.
Most expeditions started their trips by water, and St. Louis was
ideally located on streams running either north or west. St.
Louis was large enough to have many merchants and sufficient
supplies to outfit an expedition. Finally, St. Louis was a place
where one could obtain information from the *coureurs de bois*
about their experiences in the West, and where *voyageurs* could
be hired to accompany the explorers.

In 1803, shortly before the completion of the Louisiana
Purchase, President Jefferson chose his private secretary, Meriwether Lewis, and William Clark, the red-haired younger brother of George Rogers Clark, to lead an expedition up the Missouri
to its source and from there to the Pacific. Although most of
the expedition members were Americans, Lewis and Clark did
hire two French settlers to accompany them. The Spanish officials still in command in St. Louis at first hesitated, then decided to cooperate with the project.

Lewis spent most of the winter of 1803-04 buying supplies
in St. Louis and conferring with fur traders. On March 9 and
10, 1804, he witnessed the signing of the Louisiana Purchase.
In the meantime, Clark remained at River Dubois (Wood River)
in Illinois across from the mouth of the Missouri River drilling
troops, collecting additional supplies, and preparing the three
boats.

The Americans bought a varied and complete collection of

supplies for the expedition. There was clothing to protect them from an uncertain climate; tools to build shelters and to repair equipment; weapons and ammunition to help procure food and to protect the explorers from unknown and possibly hostile tribes; drugs and medical instruments to alleviate the effects of illness and accident; and even scientific instruments—including a thermometer made by Dr. Saugrain, the St. Louis physician, with the mercury scraped from the back of his wife's mirror. Almost as important as the supplies were the bales of presents for the Indians they would encounter—richly laced coats, ornate medals, bright flags, knives, tomahawks, beads, mirrors, handkerchiefs, paints, and other items chosen to suit a red man's fancy.

The expedition set out from Wood River on May 14, 1804. Clark and his men met Lewis in St. Charles seven days later. The explorers then paddled up the Missouri not to return until September 23, 1806, after successfully travelling 7,689 miles across the continent and back. On their return they were warmly welcomed by the city and entertained by Pierre and Auguste Chouteau. This accomplishment, and the glowing descriptions of the West which the explorers brought back, were a great encouragement to the westward movement.

Jefferson, as curious about the North as he was the West, and intending to determine the boundary between Canada and

"The Lewis and Clark Expedition" by Dean Cornwell
(Commissioned by and used through the courtesy of the New York Life Insurance Company)

the United States, secured the services of Zebulon Pike to chart and scout the headwaters of the Mississippi River. This trip into the Minnesota region in 1805 was followed by a longer and more difficult trek the next year, when Pike was sent southwest to explore the Arkansas River. He followed the Arkansas to Colorado and explored the mountains there where he discovered the peak that bears his name. After great suffering in the cold winter of 1807, Pike pushed south into Spanish New Mexico. The Spanish officials did not approve of his invasion of their territory. His forces were imprisoned for a time before they were allowed to return to St. Louis in 1808.

The other American explorer to use St. Louis as his base of operations was Stephen H. Long, who was sent out to the Central Rocky Mountains in 1820. Major Long is best known for his inaccurate observations of the West. However, he may be remembered in Missouri history as the person who named the Ozark Mountains.

Each of these expeditions was organized at St. Louis and departed from the St. Louis area. Many of the men accompanying the explorers and most of the supplies they carried came from Missouri. Some of these venturesome Missourians profited from their experience when they returned to the West as traders and merchants.

Territorial Government

The United States had a well-developed governmental system for its territories by the time Louisiana was added in 1804. Under federal regulations, territorial governors were appointed

William Clark was called the "Red Head" by many of his Indian friends. After his well-publicized expedition he married, settled in St. Louis, and acted as territorial governor for a time and as superintendent of Indian affairs. Clark named his first son Meriwether Lewis Clark for his friend and fellow-explorer.

(Courtesy State Historical Society)

Meriwether Lewis had a short and brilliant career. As President Jefferson's secretary, he accepted the opportunity to lead an expedition overland to the Pacific. He returned to St. Louis as territorial governor. Sensitive, intelligent, and serious, he died under mysterious circumstances on a trip to Washington in 1809.
(Courtesy State Historical Society)

by the President. Citizens were gradually given greater legislative power and thus were educated politically as the territory advanced through several stages toward full statehood.

In 1804 the Louisiana Purchase was divided into two sections. The area south of the thirty-third parallel was called the Territory of Orleans. North of the thirty-third parallel the region was known as the District of Louisiana. The District of Louisiana was assigned as part of the Territory of Indiana, the capital of which was Vincennes. The inhabitants of the District of Louisiana disliked this arrangement and held a protest convention in St. Louis. The people complained that they had no voice in the government, the officials were too far away, and the institution of slavery—on which many Missourians depended for labor—was not fully protected by law.

Responding to these protests, the United States Congress in 1805 declared that the District of Louisiana should be renamed the Territory of Louisiana with the capital located at St. Louis. As residents of a first class territory, the inhabitants of Louisiana still had no voice in government, but the chief government officials (four appointive officers—the governor and three judges) were located more closely to the governed. When the governor and three judges sat as a single body they were the legislature for the territory. At this stage, the inhabitants of the territory had no more political rights than they had possessed under Spain.

Seven years later, in 1812, Congress raised Missouri to the rank of a second class territory. The people of a region of this rank could vote and take part in their own government.

For the first time, the citizens elected representatives—one for every 500 free white male inhabitants—for a two-year term to the lower house of the legislature, the territorial House of Representatives. They also chose a delegate without vote to the United States House of Representatives. The nine members of the upper house, the Legislative Council, were selected by the President from a list of eighteen nominees suggested by the lower house. The bicameral legislative process functioned just as our state government does today. It was at this time that the name Missouri was officially associated with the area for the first time. Because the District of Orleans had been admitted to the Union as the state of Louisiana, the name of the area formerly known as the Territory of Louisiana was changed to the Territory of Missouri.

The next change in territorial status occurred in 1816, when the Territory of Missouri was advanced in rank to a third class territory. The major difference was that at this rank both houses of the legislature were elected by the people. This system prevailed until Missouri was admitted to the Union as a state in 1821.

These territorial governments served several important functions: They provided the necessary government during the years when the area was filling with settlers. They instructed the Creoles in the American democratic process. They provided an orderly transition from Spanish to American laws and procedures.

Of the five well-known men who served Missouri as territorial governors, four were conscientious public servants who gave their best efforts to serve the people of the territory. One —James Wilkinson—was a traitor to his country.

Amos Stoddard temporarily acted as the Commandant of all of Upper Louisiana until provisions for government were made. Under orders from President Jefferson, he made few changes in government during his half-year tenure.

In 1805 President Jefferson appointed General James Wilkinson as the first resident governor of the newly-created Territory of Louisiana. General Wilkinson was, at the time, a brigadier general of the United States Army.

Wilkinson was a grafter, conniver and traitor. Because of his conduct, he twice was forced to resign his commission during the Revolutionary War. Thereafter he went west to live in

Kentucky, but he was unwilling to play the usual role of a frontier farmer. Wilkinson found much unrest among the settlers in Kentucky and Tennessee because Spanish control of the mouth of the Mississippi endangered American use of the all-water route to eastern markets. The Spanish plotted to use this unrest to instigate a revolution. Wilkinson offered to aid the Spanish in their scheme. In 1787 he went to New Orleans where, after taking an oath of loyalty to the Spanish king, he became Spain's Secret Agent 13 for a promised salary of $2,000 per year for twenty years. Amazingly, he then reentered the American army where, after 1796, he was the highest ranking officer. Brigadier General Wilkinson connived with the Spanish and with another American adventurer—Aaron Burr—to foment revolution in the West. Burr was Jefferson's Vice-President from 1801-1805 and may have secured Wilkinson's appointment as governor of the Louisiana Territory. We do know that Burr and Wilkinson held lengthy negotiations before Wilkinson came to St. Louis.

Although Governor Wilkinson was received with politeness and the citizens of St. Louis greatly enjoyed the celebration at the time of his inauguration, the people were not attracted to the new governor. He was too loud and too fond of liquor. The Creole fur merchants were annoyed by his attempts to elbow his way into their business. The English-speaking settlers were suspicious of his actions—and rightly so. Wilkinson had even sent a message to Spanish officials in Santa Fe suggesting that they arrest Lewis and Clark if the explorers could be discovered in the West.

The governor had a continuous correspondence with Burr, who spent two weeks visiting him in St. Louis in the fall of 1805. But the Burr-Wilkinson plans for a western revolution in the fall of 1806 had been shared with too many westerners. Burr talked too much. The story spread, and was soon reported in Washington. In a typical traitor's way, Wilkinson wrote a letter to President Jefferson in which he attempted to place all blame on Burr. There was sufficient evidence against Wilkinson, however, so that he was removed from the governorship in March, 1807. No doubt some of the residents of the Missouri region contrasted this corrupt American official with the capable and generally upright officials of the French and Spanish periods.

Subsequent American officials were great improvements over their predecessor. When the Lewis and Clark "Corps of Discovery" returned to St. Louis in September, 1806, the members of the party were treated as heroes by the inhabitants. Poems and songs were written in their honor and recited at banquets and balls. Thus, Jefferson's choice was a popular one when in 1807, he appointed Meriwether Lewis the next governor.

Lewis was governor of the Territory of Louisiana for two and a half years. His partner, William Clark, was made a brigadier general and given an appointment in St. Louis, too, as Superintendent of Indian Affairs. Clark married before returning to St. Louis and asked the unwed Lewis to make his home with him and his bride, but Lewis chose to reside with Auguste Chouteau. Lewis carried on his duties satisfactorily, but he was not happy either in his new popularity or in his position. Lewis had always been moody; now he began to drink heavily. In 1809 on a trip back to Washington he died under suspicious circumstances which seem to indicate that he took his own life.

The third governor appointed was Benjamin Howard, a Kentucky Congressman and soldier, who served from 1810-1813. It will be noted later that he served effectively during the War of 1812. He resigned the governor's post when he was promoted to the rank of brigadier general in 1813.

William Clark, the quiet, likeable explorer, was made governor of the Territory of Missouri in 1813. The last territorial

Benjamin Howard, who served as territorial governor of the Territory of Louisiana from 1810 to 1813, supervised the organization of the Rangers during the War of 1812.
(Courtesy State Historical Society)

governor, Clark served with distinction until Missouri secured statehood in 1821. His integrity and pleasant disposition together with his firmness made him a close friend of many Indians and a leader respected by the settlers.

The New Madrid Earthquake

During the term of Governor Benjamin Howard, a catastrophe struck the territory. The residents of what is now southeast Missouri went to bed on the night of December 15, 1811 to be abruptly awakened at 2 a.m. by the creaking of house timbers and the crash of falling chimneys. An earthquake, stronger than the one at San Francisco a century later, gave the earth a great shaking. The quake which extended deep into South America originated and was most severe in the New Madrid area.

People were terrified. "The earth was in continual agitation, visibly waving as a gentle sea." One observer reported twenty-seven shocks before daylight and several the next day. Great crevices opened in the earth. Trees toppled or split. The banks of the Mississippi crumbled into the stream in some places and great waves of water rushed over the surface of the land as the earth changed its conformations. Momentarily, the Mississippi River ran backward. The Culbertson family on the Pemiscot River had a smokehouse and well between their home and the river. During the night the earthquake caused a huge fissure between the home and the outbuildings. The river rushed into the great crevasse. When morning came, the Culbertsons found their well and smokehouse on the opposite bank of the river.

Incredibly, only a few persons were killed—one in a collapsed house and several who were on the river when the disaster struck. The loss of life probably would have been much greater had the settlers lived in two-story homes.

The tremors, which continued for another year, were again violent in February, 1812. Colonel John Shaw has given us the following description of the events on February 7:

> I was in New Madrid, when nearly two thousand people, of all ages, fled in terror from their falling dwellings, in that place and the surrounding country, and directed their course north about thirty miles to Tywappety Hill, on the western bank of the Mississippi, and about seven miles back from the river. This was the first high ground above

New Madrid, and here the fugitives formed an encampment. It was proposed that all should kneel, and engage in supplicating God's mercy, and all simultaneously, Catholics and Protestants, knelt and offered solemn prayer to their Creator.

Because of these developments, the bootheel area of the state lost many settlers. They left either from fear of further quakes or because the change in the course of the Mississippi had turned their farms into swamps. The present-day counties of Pemiscot and New Madrid were most affected.

The residents of the area requested Congress to provide relief for them in their distress. Tardily, Congress passed an act in 1815 permitting the settlers to transfer their former lands back to the government. In return, the settlers were issued New Madrid certificates which could be used to purchase any government land that was for sale. But almost four years had passed since the first quake. Many settlers had sold their land for a few dollars and moved on. Speculators took advantage of the situation to buy cheap farms—$40 to $60 for up to 640 acres—in the area in order to turn the land in for certificates to obtain other, valuable, acreage. The New Madrid certificates were sometimes issued without any statement as to the acreage returned to the government. Thus, there was much fraud in the wake of the disaster. Then, as always, there were those anxious to exploit the misfortune of others for their own personal gain.

Indians of Missouri

The American flag, then spangled with seventeen stars, was first flown above St. Louis on March 10, 1804. That day retiring Lieutenant-Governor De Lassus addressed a gathering of Delaware, Shawnee, and Sac Indians:

Your old fathers, the Spaniards and the Frenchmen, who grasp by the hand your new father, the Chief of the United States, by an act of their Good Will, and in virtue of their last treaty, have delivered up all of these lands. The new father will keep and defend the land and protect all of the white and redskins who live thereon. You will live as happily as if the Spaniard was still here.

These words may have comforted the Indians at the time of the land transfer, but they were not accurate. The French settlers were not the threat to the Indians that the English-

The great New Madrid Earthquake of December 16, 1811 was followed by occasional tremors through 1812.
(From Howe, The Great West, 1851)

speaking immigrants were. The French took little Indian land, lived mostly in villages along the major rivers, and sought Indian trade items. The English-speaking farmers, on the other hand, came in such great numbers that they carved up large parts of the state. It is not difficult to understand why Indian leaders often hated the white men who seized their tribal homes.

In describing the history of America we often discuss the way in which the Indian was forced to move because of the encroachment of white settlers. However, it should also be made clear that the Indians were a mobile society long before the first explorers arrived. Defeat in intertribal warfare or the decimation of game in one area often forced tribes to move to other camping and hunting grounds. The influx of white settlers did not initiate tribal migrations, but provided another—certainly a most powerful—incentive for such wanderings.

During the early years of the nineteenth century there was a steady procession of tribes who, pushed from their lands east of the Mississippi, moved through Missouri. Their entrance into the area disturbed the Indians who had settled there earlier and led to new intertribal friction.

The main tribes in Missouri during this period were the Osage, the Little Osage, the Missouri, the Sac (sometimes spelled Sauk) and Fox, and the Delaware and Shawnee. The exact limits of the Indian habitations cannot be known because the Indians, who roamed the land in search of game, were not so precise as we in locating land plots. However, we can indicate the general limits of their wanderings.

The Osage Indians of southwest Missouri, northern Arkansas, and northeast Oklahoma were a respected and feared tribe. A member of the Sioux family of tribes, they could be in turn hospitable and generous or sullen and brutal. The tribe included many men who were at least six feet tall. J. J. Audubon described them as "well formed, athletic and robust men of noble aspect." The Osage were usually friendly to the whites —especially after the Chouteaus were given a monopoly of their trade—but they could not be taken for granted. Quick to be offended, they made reprisal raids on both whites and other Indians. The Osage had a chief as did the other tribes, but major decisions were reached at pow wows by a vote of all the warriors. The federal government built a trading post and military position called Fort Osage in 1808. Located near Sibley in Jackson County, the fort was part of an attempt to control the Osage.

The Little Osage had their headquarters in the area between the Osage River and the Missouri River in what today is Saline County. The Little Osage, for reasons not now known, united with another Sioux tribe, the Missouri Indians, for whom our state is named. The Missouri Indians were a small tribe. Their numbers were reduced by an epidemic of smallpox and the persistent raids of the Sac and Fox. The Missouri finally fled westward to the protection of their Indian relatives the Oto Indians in 1798. The Missouri tribe is now extinct.

The Sac and Fox Indians had great land claims in the Midwest in the present-day states of Wisconsin, Illinois, Iowa, and Missouri. They claimed ownership of all the area north of the Missouri River and east of the Grand River. The two tribes united, and lived and fought as one group. They were good farmers and produced much corn in their fields along the Mississippi River. As members of the Algonquin family, they were related to the Illinois Indians. The tribe disliked the Missouri and Little Osage. This enmity led to much bloodshed. Although they were finally crushed by the American army, the Sac and Fox put up great battles during the War of 1812 and in the Black Hawk War two decades later.

Two Algonquin tribes, the Shawnee and Delaware, entered Missouri during the Spanish period upon invitation of the Spanish authorities in the 1790's. The two tribes maintained their own tribal organizations, but they acted together on major matters. Louis Lorimier, a French adventurer, had great influence over the tribes. At the request of Spanish officials, Lorimier accompanied the tribes across the Mississippi and helped them to settle the region around what is now Cape Girardeau. The Spanish hoped the Delaware and Shawnee would protect the whites against the Osage, whom they did not trust. The two tribes generally proved loyal to the Spanish and American authorities in Missouri.

The largest Shawnee settlement was probably at Old Appleton, twenty miles north of Cape Girardeau, with scattered groups at Bloomfield and Kennett and on the Meramec and Current rivers. As more of these tribes entered the Missouri region and as the pressure of whites increased, the Shawnee and Delaware moved westward to settlements in Taney County near Forsyth, in Christian County at James Fork, and in Greene County on Wilson's Creek. The Shawnee and Delaware were considered more advanced than the majority of tribes. They built log homes and carried on a highly productive agriculture. They even operated a ferry across the Mississippi. As one white observer described them:

> We were surprised at the neatness of their houses, and their fine gardens and fields, in which they equal if they do not excel us. They appear to be honest, industrious, and generally virtuous.

Not all observers would agree with this estimate of their virtue, but it is clear that the Shawnee and Delaware were successful in adopting the white man's agricultural tools and techniques.

Artist George F. Green's painting shows Fort Osage in Jackson County with Indian huts and canoes in the foreground and two keel boats arriving with supplies from St. Louis.

(Courtesy State Historical Society)

FT. OSAGE.
1808-1825

A group of Miami Indians migrated into Missouri at the turn of the century and settled in Saline County. They later played a minor role in the War of 1812. The Kickapoo Indians had two villages in Missouri in the early years of the nineteenth century. One was near St. Louis; the other was either in Webster or Greene County. The Peoria were originally driven from northwest Missouri by the Sac and Fox. They settled later on the outskirts of St. Louis and Ste. Genevieve and in Taney County. The Iowa tribe was one which was forced to move frequently. They resided along the northern border of the state on the Des Moines River, then on the headwaters of the Chariton and Grand rivers, and finally along the western border in Platte County. Other small Indian groups were the Potawatomies in Platte County and the Piankeshaw Indians in Taney County. The Oto tribe at one time lived on the Des Moines River, but later they moved west to occupy the area where the Platte drains into the Missouri River.

From the above listing of tribes, it may seem that Missouri had a large Indian population. This was not the case, since the tribes were generally small. For example, Lewis and Clark estimated that there were eight hundred Iowa Indians, five hundred Osage warriors (this number did not include women and children), and about half as many members of the Little Osage tribe in Missouri in 1804. Had all the Indians engaged in intensive agriculture, the area could have supported a much higher Indian population. But a sparse population was ideal for people who depended primarily on hunting for their food.

Much has been written of the way in which the white man debauched and debased the red man. We must not, however, think that European contact had nothing but a corrupting influence on the Indian, or that all Indians became debased as a result of this contact. Many Indians used European innovations to improve their living standards while proudly retaining their Indian heritage. A writer in frontier Missouri wrote of the Indians he observed:

> Indians of various tribes—the Potawatomi, the Foxes (Musquakee), Kickapoo, Iowa, and Oto— one sees constantly in this town [St. Louis], particularly at the landing where they take the ferryboat to cross the river. They conduct themselves in a very dignified manner. Now and then, to be sure, when one of them has drunk too much of the

An Osage mother and child
(From a portrait in the collection of the State Historical Society)

forbidden whiskey, he is somewhat quarrelsome, but no more so than an intoxicated white man; nor is an Indian under those conditions any more dangerous than a drunken American.

In the tribal system of government which prevailed, the chief ruled with the advice of his Council; but there was always a number of young Indians who were resentful of authority. Kioway, a Fox chief, told an American Indian agent, "Your work is hard and my work is hard. Among all nations the young men are foolish and will not be governed by their chiefs." This was one of the reasons for Indian massacres during the War of 1812. The young warriors did not follow tribal policies established by the ruling elders. The Osage appear to have had greater participation in important tribal decisions, since all the warriors assembled to express their will. In all the tribes the men were responsible for war and hunting. The women, old men, and children did the menial work of cleaning game, cooking food, building shelters, dressing skins, planting and harvesting the crops, and making moccasins and clothing.

Although many of the externals of Indian life differed from those of the white man, the Indian himself was very much like his pale brother. The visitors to Indian camps speak of the gay laughter of the people and their appreciation of the humor of children. The red man mourned the loss of loved ones just as his white neighbors, although because of Indian funeral customs his wails of grief may have been louder and his sorrow more physically evident. Washington Irving tells of his visit to the Osage shortly after the death of the beautiful little daughter of an important warrior. The grieving father slew his child's favorite pony and buried the pet with her that she might ride to the spirit world.

Although the women did the menial work in Indian camps and were obviously under the control of the male leaders of the tribe, still the squaws were not entirely submissive. Observers noted that Indian women were constantly tongue-lashing their husbands, who appear to have paid little heed to the scolding. History and everyday experience show that these sharp-tongued women and conveniently-deaf men have their counterpart in any race and in any century.

While there were bloodshed and brutality in Indian territory before the European arrived, and while many Indians escaped the corrupting influence of the evils in European society, the white man—particularly the American—must bear the guilt for the anguish suffered by thousands of his red brothers in the last days of Indian freedom. The final major Indian episode in Missouri was associated with the Cherokee. A large group of Georgia and Tennessee Cherokees was forced to flee to the West in 1838. Driven brutally by an army detachment, about one-fourth of the 16,000 Indian men, women, and children died on the trek west. The Indians crossed the Mississippi at Cape Girardeau and travelled across the state to Springfield where they paused before continuing toward their destination in Oklahoma. Because of the suffering caused by this forced migration, the journey has been called "The Trail of Tears."

This Indian movement is symbolic of the indifference of most of the Americans to the plight of the Indian. The French settler wanted to trade with the Indian. The American settler wanted to drive him out and seize his land. The Indian probably would have resisted, except that the chances of his winning against the military might of the United States were slight. The Indian was a realist. When the American government put a bayonet to his back, he moved westward.

The War of 1812

President Madison had sincerely tried to avert war with Britain, but popular pressure was so great that he was forced to agree to a declaration of war in 1812. There were several reasons for war. The British had seized American sailors and ships, and they had frequently violated American rights on the high seas. Secondly, the United States government knew the British were supplying many Indian tribes with guns and ammunition and this caused trouble on the American frontier. Thirdly, some Americans looked covetously at Canada believing that we could seize it easily during a war.

Those Americans who lived along the Atlantic coast lived in fear of the British fleet or an invading British Army. The Americans who lived far inland feared Indian attacks. Tecumseh, a canny Shawnee chief, was responsible for much of the fear on the frontier. He had carefully examined the history of Indian-white relations, and had accurately diagnosed the two primary Indian weaknesses. First, Tecumseh called on the tribes to unite in an Indian Confederation to oppose the westward movement of the whites. In the past, the whites had always been able to secure the services of one Indian group to fight another one. Tecumseh preached political and military union. Secondly, Tecumseh knew that the Indians who drank the white man's liquor often gave away Indian lands. He called on the red man to take a pledge of total abstinence.

In 1811, General William Henry Harrison, Governor of Indiana decided that he would attack Tecumseh's forces before they became more numerous. The battle which ensued was the Battle of Tippecanoe. After this initial inconclusive struggle, Indian warfare began throughout the trans-Appalachian West with ambushes, massacres, and skirmishes. The British government provided guns and other weapons for the red warriors.

Missourians, surrounded by Indian groups, were in a precarious situation. The Indians were restless. Watching the constant encroachment of white men on their lands they were fearful of the future. Of immediate concern was the disappearance of game so necessary to sustain the tribes. With British agents agitating the tribes to action and offering military assistance, it is no wonder that violence resulted.

Fortunately, the American officials had made a treaty with the Osage in 1808. Before the treaty was negotiated, Osage bands had been raiding isolated American settlements. Under the treaty, the Osage nation assigned to the United States government ownership of land between the Missouri River and the Arkansas River east of a line running due south from Fort

Osage in Jackson County. In return the Osage were to be given an annual grant of $1,000. The Little Osage were to receive half that sum. The government was to provide a mill, a blacksmith shop and smith, a government trading house, plows, tools, and a house for the two main chiefs. This treaty had a pacifying effect on the Osage. They were promised the right to continue hunting on the land ceded. The government was to use its military power to keep the Sac and Fox out of the area. The Osage felt their hunting territory was thus protected from their traditional enemies.

That same year, 1808, Fort Osage was established on the bank of the Missouri River in what is today Jackson County. George C. Sibley was the factor in charge of the fort. The Indians were invited to move close to the fort to facilitate trading and to give Sibley an opportunity to watch them for any change in their attitude or policies.

When war did develop in 1812, all the tribes were suspected of being sympathetic to the British. East of the Mississippi most tribes did take up the tomahawk and scalping knife, but not so west of the river. In spite of the fear and suspicion in the minds of the white Missourians, few of the tribes in Missouri joined the British-inspired offensive.

In Missouri the main Indian troublemakers were the Sac

Fort Osage, near Sibley in Jackson County, has been effectively restored. The factor's house, where George Sibley maintained his bachelor's quarters is pictured below.

(Courtesy State Historical Society)

During the War of 1812 many settlers lived in fear of attack by the Sac and Fox tribes. "War Dance of the Sauks and Foxes" is from an early nineteenth century engraving by Peter Rindisbacher.

(Courtesy State Historical Society)

and Fox—although not all the Sac and Fox took the war trail. Smaller tribes such as the Miami and the Potawatomi also joined in the uprising. Missourians suffered greatly from raiding parties of Sac and Fox who came down from northern Illinois and southern Wisconsin. Washington Irving, who visited a camp of the Sac and Fox at about this time, has given us the following description of the Sac and Fox warriors:

> They were all armed with spears, clubs, guns, and knives. Many of the warriors had a long tuft of red horsehair tied to their elbows, and bore a necklace of grizzly bear's claws. Their headdress consisted of red dyed horsehair, tied in such a manner to the scalp lock to present the shape of the decoration of a Roman helmet. The rest of the head was completely shaved and painted. . . . They beat drums. They uttered yells at definite points. . . . They looked the very spirit of defiance. Their leader stood as a prince, majestic and frowning. The wild native pride of man, in the savage state, flushed by success in war, and confident in the strength of his arm, was never so fully depicted to my eyes.

This was the white man's adversary.

There were no major or lengthy battles in Missouri during the War of 1812. The British did not have an army available to send into the upper Mississippi Valley. Instead, the war took the character of a series of Indian raids, skirmishes, and atrocities. In small bands the savages would sweep down on a frontier settlement, attack those people who could be found in the fields, steal the livestock, and burn the undefended cabins and outbuildings. The Indian customs of scalping or beheading their victims made the conflict all the more horrible.

These attacks were almost all north of the Missouri River either in the Boon's Lick region in the central part of the state, or in the scattered settlements along the Mississippi and Missouri rivers. In particular, the Indians struck at Femme Osage, Cap au Gris, Portage des Sioux, Wood's Fort, Charette, St. Charles, Cote sans Dessein, and Loutre Island.

The whites, anticipating a major British offensive down the Mississippi River coupled with Indian attacks from all sides, made anxious preparations for war. The *Missouri Gazette* for February 20, 1813, carried the following editorial:

> Let those who live in frontier positions build or repair their forts, have a good supply of ammunition and their arms in good order, let the planting be conducted by numbers in each field, with centinels [sic]; let the village inhabitants build in each a stockade for the women and children, and above all divide the men into companies or squads for frequent drilling and examination into the state of their arms and ammunition. . . .

Advice of this sort was heeded immediately. There were approximately 250 American soldiers west of the Mississippi in 1812. The American government did not have enough soldiers in the West to defend their own federal forts; they certainly could not protect the population. There were two federal forts located in what is presently Missouri—Fort Bellefontaine in St. Louis County, and Fort Osage in Jackson County. Because Fort Osage was in the more exposed position, the troops and traders abandoned it in 1813 for the duration of the war.

To protect themselves, the colonists built sturdy log forts with projecting second stories. Since these forts really constituted only one large house, they were not sufficient for populous settlements. In such situations, the settlers built a stockade fence which would enclose several cabins and an open area.

Wood's Fort in 1812, now Troy in Lincoln County, protected the settlers from the Indians. This painting by William Knox is in the state capitol.

These forts or stockades were constructed at strategic points which could be more easily defended. Usually the Indians did not attack such a fortification. In 1815 the Indians did attack Fort Roy at Cote sans Desseins. They succeeded in setting the stockade afire, and they danced about the flaming fortification in preparation for the anticipated massacre of the frightened settlers huddled within the enclosure. The besieged colonists were spared this horror, for their attackers had set fire to the powder magazine. In the ensuing explosion twenty Indians were killed. The stockade wall was a shambles, but the surviving Indians fled in fear.

In the struggle with the Indians the Missourians were fortunate to have an ample supply of shot. In 1809, John Nicholas Maclot, a political refugee from France, set up a system at Herculaneum for the manufacture of lead shot. Maclot built a shot tower on a bluff above the Mississippi River about thirty-two miles south of St. Louis. Molten lead was poured through sieves into tubs of water below. The drops of liquid lead solidified into pellets upon contact with the cold water. The Missouri bullets made at Herculaneum were used in many parts of the West; Andy Jackson used Missouri shot at the Battle of New Orleans.

Captain Nathan Boone's Rangers patrolled the banks of the Missouri River during the War of 1812.
(Courtesy Missouri Historical Society)

The citizens of St. Charles and St. Louis protested the inadequate defenses for the area and called on Washington to send more troops. Their complaints were not adequately answered, and the settlers were forced to improvise their own defense forces. The territorial officials organized companies of rangers who were sometimes dubbed "the Minute Men of the Frontier." Each ranger was expected to provide his own horse, rifle, and provisions. In all kinds of weather these men patrolled the settlements from Salt River on the Mississippi to Loutre Island in the Missouri. Daniel Boone's son Nathan was the first leader of the rangers.

To this point we have spoken only of defensive policies. The Missourians did send out several offensive expeditions. In 1813 General Benjamin Howard led 1400 Missouri militiamen in a raid on the Sac and Fox settlements in northern Illinois. The tribe avoided a battle with Howard, so he could only destroy their crops and villages. Another expedition of Missourians, this time under the leadership of General William Clark, went up the Mississippi to Prairie du Chien in 1814 and built a fort at the mouth of the Wisconsin River. The fort was later taken by the Indians.

A dramatic event of the war occurred when General Henry Dodge led 350 rangers and about 50 Shawnee and Delaware braves out to the Boon's Lick area to relieve the settlers under siege by the Miami Indians. Dodge finally surrounded the tribe in Saline County. The Miami agreed to surrender if General Dodge would promise to spare their lives. A crisis developed when Captain Cooper of Boon's Lick found a certain rifle in the possession of the Indians. The gun had been the property of Cooper's friend who had been murdered. Captain Cooper threatened to kill all the Indians if they did not produce the murderer. General Dodge, who had pledged the safety of the surrendered Miamis, refused to cooperate with Cooper. Cooper's men prepared to carry out their leader's threat, but General Dodge drew his sword and held it to Captain Cooper's breast. At this tense moment Captain Nathan Boone arrived and he—although a resident of the area—upheld General Dodge. Cooper and his men finally withdrew, and the crisis passed. One hundred and fifty-three Miami Indians owed their lives to the integrity and bravery of General Dodge.

The peace treaty ending the war was signed in December, 1814, but it was not made official in Missouri until the summer of 1815. There were two peace conferences. In July, 1815, nineteen tribes came to Portage des Sioux to make treaties with William Clark, Auguste Chouteau, and Ninian Edwards, the American representatives. The following summer ten more tribes came to St. Louis to formalize the end of the war.

The War of 1812 was a serious threat to the settlements along the Mississippi and Missouri rivers. Fortunately for the settlers, however, the English lacked the power to prosecute

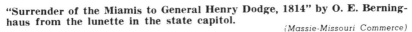

"Surrender of the Miamis to General Henry Dodge, 1814" by O. E. Berninghaus from the lunette in the state capitol.

(*Massie-Missouri Commerce*)

the war vigorously in the American Midwest. The Indians, by themselves, were not strong enough to seize the American settlements. 1816 marked the end of the Indian threat to the whites of Missouri.

Territorial Developments

A glance at the population statistics of the territorial period makes it clear that, in spite of earthquakes and Indian attacks, Missouri was a rapidly developing area. The following rounded figures speak for themselves: 1800—7,000 population; 1804—10,000 population; 1810—20,000 population; 1820—67,000 population. The population doubled during the first six years of American control; it tripled in the next decade.

The people who came were English-speaking frontiersmen, usually from Kentucky, Tennessee, Virginia, and North Carolina. Under the provisions of the Northwest Ordinance, it was illegal to hold slaves north of the Ohio River. Thus, southerners with slaves could not immigrate into Illinois, Indiana, and Ohio. For these southerners Missouri was the logical western destination. The territory had good timber, excellent soil, fine rivers for transportation, and an abundance of other natural resources. These southerners sought rich land, and they found it in central Missouri in the area bordering on the Missouri River.

The region first had been settled by Daniel Boone's sons in 1807 when they began to make salt from a saline spring in present-day Howard County. Thus the region became known as Boon's Lick. The next year Benjamin Cooper and his family also entered the area—although he was temporarily forced to withdraw by the Indians. Despite Indian opposition, Americans forced their way into the region. The town of Franklin was established in 1817. By 1820 it had grown to a population of 1,000. Chariton was settled in 1818 and Boonville in 1819. To illustrate the growth of the period, Howard and Cooper counties developed so rapidly that they had over 20,000 residents in 1820 or about one-third the population of the whole Territory of Missouri.

Of course, some settlers secured land in the western sections of the original counties along the Mississippi. There was activity particularly in the region joining the Salt River.

The population influx forced the territorial government to adjust the county boundaries frequently. In 1804 there were

Victor Higgins has painted this scene in the state capitol building showing Daniel Boone's sons making salt in Saline County. The iron pot used by the Boones is on display in the capitol in Jefferson City.

only five counties. By 1821 the territory had twenty-five counties.

Missouri was a bustling, booming carnival of activity as the immigrants pushed their way in like anxious hordes of circus-goers trying to find seats in the arena. In October, 1819, 400 to 500 people daily were crossing the Mississippi to St. Louis. The *Missouri Gazette* in 1819 gave the following description of the immigrants who,

> . . . flowing through St. Charles with men servants and maid servants, their flocks and their herds, remind the citizens of the patriarchal ages. . . . Some turn to Boon's Lick, some to Salt River —lands of promise. The tinkling bells, the cloud of dust, the throng of hogs and cattle, the white headed children, the curly headed Africans, smiling infancy, blooming virgins, athletic manhood, and decrepit age, altogether form groups too interesting to be painted by the pencil of Teniers.

This population expansion made it necessary to work out some arrangement with the Indians. Fortunately, the territorial governor at this time was William Clark, who had years of valuable experience as an Indian agent. The Indians liked and trusted Clark. He knew their ways. Clark once described the requisites for making an Indian treaty as "a lot of time and a lot of smoking." During his years as governor he smoked

many peace pipes as one tribe after the other was forced to
move west into present-day Kansas or south into the Indian
Territory that is now the state of Oklahoma. In 1819 the Sac,
the Fox, and the Iowa relinquished control of the lands north
of the Missouri River. The Osage and the Little Osage gave
up claim to Missouri in 1825. The Shawnee in 1825 and the
Delaware in 1829 sold their property rights. Finally, in 1832,
the remaining tribes—the Kickapoo, Peoria, and Piankeshaw—
agreed to move out. The last Indian claim to land in Missouri
was thus extinguished.

In 1828 a group of Peoria Indians visited St. Louis to complain wistfully of their treatment:

> You have become the possessor of the country
> where the bones of our forefathers are scattered.
> You have built large houses with our stones and
> the clay that covered the bones of our ancestors,
> and your Friend and children the Peoria, are poor
> and helpless.

It was during the territorial period that Missouri became
American in culture. In 1804 the population was about equally
divided between French and Americans. By 1821 Creoles constituted less than ten percent of the population. The American
majority now controlled Missouri and its society.

Some observers believed that the Americans with their
gambling, drunkenness, duels, and frontier gang fights had
lowered the level of civilization in Missouri. There were, of
course, some uncouth and depraved Americans in the hordes
who crossed the Mississippi; and one could hardly expect that
life on the frontier in Kentucky and Tennessee would encourage
the social graces. However, all was not bad that was American.
One of the most significant cultural advances during the territorial period was the establishment of schools throughout
the area.

By 1821 there were schools at St. Louis, St. Charles, Ste.
Genevieve, Florissant, Cape Girardeau, Franklin, Potosi, Jackson, and Herculaneum. There were schools even in the west, in
Cooper and Howard County, and an Indian school in what is
today Bates County. Many of the Protestant missionaries, who
could enter Missouri legally after 1804, taught school in addition to proclaiming their faith; but most schools were taught
by individuals as a livelihood and were not church or mission
projects.

There was greater emphasis on education for boys than for girls. The schools for boys stressed language training, mathematics, drawing, and moral instruction. Christoph Friederick Schewe established a boys' school in St. Louis in 1809, where he taught English, French, German, arithmetic, geography, geometry, "as well as any other branch of mathematics," and drawing. In case anyone doubted his ability to teach so wide a range of courses, Schewe offered to "bear an examination by competent persons in order to avoid suspicion of a want of talents." Schewe was a teacher of undisputed excellence, but the wide range of subjects often taught by one person and the frequency with which these pedagogues were required to defend their competence leads one to suspect that many teachers who depended on students for income exaggerated their own academic abilities. Some parents were disillusioned by the quality of education their children received.

There were eleven schools for girls which operated in the period from 1797 to 1821. The school for girls at Franklin, a typical "female seminary," was started in 1820 and offered three basic courses: "Reading, Writing and Plain Work." The curriculum also included such electives as needlework, embroidery, filigree, and piano.

"Harmony Mission for the Osage Indians in Bates County in 1821," a lunette in the state capitol painted by William Knox
(Photograph by Hammond and Irwin, Jefferson City, Missouri)

Training in one particular skill was also available for boys and girls alike. Dancing teachers were common. One of them advertised instruction in "all the new European dances (particularly the waltz) in the handsomest style." Another teacher taught boys fencing as a sideline—perhaps to teach his clumsier pupils to defend themselves in altercations arising on the dance floor. There were music teachers who taught the piano, flute, clarinet, and organ, and teachers of penmanship who promised students that the result of their training would be "elegant handwriting."

During the territorial period several changes in education took place. The first schools of Missouri were available only to those who were able to pay tuition. A move toward free schools, however, was beginning. In 1818 Bishop Du Bourg, the leader of the Catholic Church in Missouri brought in five French nuns of the Society of the Sacred Heart to establish a convent school for girls. The school, first located at St. Charles but later moved to Florissant, was under the leadership of Mother Philippine Duchesne whose beatification was proclaimed by Pope Pius XII in 1940. As in the other schools of the day, the scholars were required to pay for their education. However, the school of Mother Duschesne was different in that the poor children of the parish could attend without charge. About this same time, the Protestant churches established Sunday schools which met to teach reading and writing. These Sabbath schools were free to all who attended.

Another change in education—the trend toward coeducational schools—began late in the territorial period. The early schools were founded mainly in the large settlements and specialized in the education of either boys or girls. Coeducation first occurred in the rural areas where limited resources made the establishment of separate schools impractical. The coeducational system spread to the settlements, and schools for both boys and girls were functioning in Potosi, Jackson, and Franklin in 1821.

Another educational development occurred toward the end of Missouri's years as a territory. This development was the appearance of "community academies." These schools, unlike those founded by an individual or sponsored by a church, were established by committees of the leading citizens of a community. These academies had a guarantee of steady financial

Mother Philippine Duchesne
(Courtesy State Historical Society)

support which gave them a stability often lacking in the other schools. While fees were charged, such community-sponsored academies were a first feeble step in the direction of public education. Academies of this type were established in Ste. Genevieve, Franklin, Jackson, and St. Charles, and were chartered by the territorial legislature.

Religiously, there were important developments during the territorial period. The Catholic Church had been supported by tax money during the time of French and Spanish rule. When Missouri became American, this favored position ceased. Other religious groups could enter the area freely. Prior to the Louisiana Purchase the Creoles had not paid the priests' salaries directly. The three priests serving St. Louis, St. Charles, and Ste. Genevieve each received 370 dollars annually from the king. With such financial and legal support gone, many priests left Missouri after the transfer in 1804. Amos Stoddard lamented the departure of these men whom he described as "learned and liberal in their principles." Although Bishop Flaget of Kentucky traveled occasionally to Missouri to minister to the Catholic people in the territory, the Catholics of Missouri were virtually leaderless from 1804 to 1818.

However, in 1818, Bishop William Du Bourg arrived in St. Louis to lead the reconstruction of the Catholic Church. The bishop was a man of vigor and foresight. Two months after his arrival, he broke ground for the construction of the St. Louis Cathedral.

During the fourteen years when the Catholics of Missouri were without leadership, there was a new wave of vigorous, dedicated Protestant ministers who entered the territory to work among the English-speaking settlers. Traveling light with a few clothes, an axe, a rifle, a hymn book, and a Bible, the missionaries—usually Baptist, Methodist or Presbyterian— went from cabin to cabin into the most isolated areas to share their gospel. Living among the settlers, they came to know the people and problems of the frontier. These missionaries found a response in the rural areas. In the winter, neighbors would gather in a cabin for a worship service. During pleasant weather, meetings were held out-of-doors. Before long, the missionaries began to organize individual congregations. Then circuits or associations were established to allow ministers to serve several congregations in an area. The rural character of these Protestant churches can be seen in the following list of congregations which were the first for each denomination:

> Baptists—Tywappity Bottom near Cape Girardeau in 1805 and Bethel Church near Jackson in 1806; Methodists—McKendree Church near Jackson in 1806; Presbyterians—ten miles south of Potosi in 1816; Christian Church—Salt Creek Church in Howard County in 1817.

The one early congregation that did not share the rural nature of the first Protestant churches of Missouri was Prot-

Frontier rivers failed to stop the Methodist circuit rider from making his rounds.
(*Harpers*, October 12, 1867)

Bethel B a p t i s t
Church, the first
Protestant church
building west of
the Mississippi was
constructed n e a r
Jackson, Missouri,
in 1806.
(Courtesy State Historical Society)

estant Episcopal Christ's Church which was organized in St. Louis in 1819.

Not all the missionaries were men of great ability, but there were some excellent leaders among the early Protestant clergymen. Such men as Baptist John Mason Peck and Presbytrian Salmon Giddings and Timothy Flint, were intelligent and sensitive to the needs of the people. They provided a counterbalance to the emotional excesses of some open-air camp meetings.

The work of the Protestant groups was hampered greatly by divisions and denominational bickerings; but in spite of their shortcomings, these churches made several important contributions to frontier life. First, the Protestant clergy were insistent that their parishioners read the Bible, and this insistence resulted in more widespread reading ability.

Secondly, the missionaries were a prod to the conscience of the frontiersman. The use of profanity, drunkenness, gambling, and Sabbath-breaking were condemned. A church member found guilty in a church trial of any of the above practices was in danger of excommunication. The clergy not only condemned what they considered corrupt practices, but they also preached concern for one's fellowmen. Such concern did develop and was evidenced by such institutions as Harmony Mission, in present-day Bates County, which was established by the United Foreign Missionary Society to convert and educate the Osage. Even the Baptist settlers of Howard County, who themselves were considered residents of a mission area by the eastern churches, had their "Mite Society" for the support of other, probably more isolated, missions. This religious influence had a steadying and somewhat softening effect on the rough-hewn frontiersman so accustomed to the self-centered, toughening struggle for existence.

Thirdly, the church was a social institution in a time and place of few diversions. Church services and social activities gave the often lonely settlers a chance to escape the isolation of their farms.

Growth and change marked the territorial period in Missouri. And both the growth and the change were distinguished by the speed with which they occurred. Once-Creole Missouri grew and changed so rapidly during her seventeen years as a territory that by 1821 the population and culture were distinctly American—with only a slight French accent.

BIBLIOGRAPHY

Anderson, Hattie M. "The Evolution of Frontier Society in Missouri, 1815-1828," *Missouri Historical Review,* Vol. XXXII (April and July, 1938), pp. 298-326, 458-483; Vol. XXXIII (October, 1938), pp. 23-44.

Anderson, Hattie M. "Frontier Economic Problems in Missouri, 1815-1828," *Missouri Historical Review,* Vol. XXXIV (October, 1939; January, 1940), pp. 38-70, 182-203.

Anderson, Hattie M. "Missouri 1804-1828: Peopling a Frontier State," *Missouri Historical Review,* Vol. XXXI (January, 1937), pp. 150-180.

Cable, John Ray. "Some Early Missouri Bankers," *Missouri Historical Review,* Vol. XXVI (January, 1932), pp. 117-125.

Covington, James W. "A Peoria Indian States His Case," *Missouri Historical Review,* Vol. LI (July, 1957), pp. 382-385.

Dorsey, Dorothy B. "The Panic of 1819 in Missouri," *Missouri Historical Review,* Vol. XXIX (January, 1935), pp. 79-91.

Eaton, David W. "Echoes of Indian Emigration," *Missouri Historical Review,* Vol. VIII (January, April and July, 1914), pp. 93-99, 142-153, 198-205.

Ferril, W. C. "Missouri Military in the War of 1812," *Missouri Historical Review,* Vol. IV (October, 1909), pp. 38-41.

Finley, Helen Deveneau, and Ada Paris Klein, (ed.). "The Lewis and Clark Expedition," *Missouri Historical Review,* Vol. XLII (April and July, 1948), pp. 249-270, 343-366; Vol. XLII (October, 1948; January, 1949), pp. 48-70, 145-159.

Fisher, Robert L. "The Western Prologue to the War of 1812," *Missouri Historical Review,* Vol. XXX (April, 1936), pp. 267-281.

Fuller, Myron L. *The New Madrid Earthquake.* Cape Girardeau, Missouri: Ramfre Press, 1958.

Goodwin, Cardinal L. "Early Explorations and Settlements of Missouri and Arkansas 1803-1822," *Missouri Historical Review,* Vol. XIV (April-July, 1920), pp. 385-424.

Gregg, Kate L. "Building the First American Fort West of the Mississippi," *Missouri Historical Review*, Vol. XXX (July, 1935), pp. 345-364.

Gregg, Kate L. "The War of 1812 on the Missouri Frontier," *Missouri Historical Review*, Vol. XXXIII (October, 1938; January and April, 1939), pp. 3-22, 184-202, 326-348.

Hagan, William T. *The Sac and Fox Indians.* Norman, Oklahoma: University of Oklahoma Press, 1958.

Hagan, William T. "The Sauk and Fox Treaty of 1804," *Missouri Historical Review*, Vol. LI (October, 1956), pp. 1-7.

Hammond, Bray. *Banks and Politics in America from the Revolution to the Civil War.* Princeton: Princeton University Press, 1957.

"Indians in the Valley," *Missouri Historical Review*, Vol. XXXIX (October, 1944; January, 1945), pp. 75-97, 224-258.

King, Roy T. "Portraits of Daniel Boone," *Missouri Historical Review*, Vol. XXXIII (January, 1939), pp. 171-183.

La Force, Alice F., (ed). "The Missouri Reader: The Louisiana Purchase," *Missouri Historical Review*, Vol. XLII (October, 1947; January, 1948), pp. 50-71, 153-172.

Lightfoot, B. B. "The Cherokee Emigrants in Missouri, 1837-1839," *Missouri Historical Review*, Vol. LVI (January, 1962), pp. 156-167.

Nutter, Charles. "Robert R. Livingston, the Forgotten Architect of the Louisiana Purchase," *Missouri Historical Review*, Vol. XLVIII (January, 1954), pp. 117-133.

Pratt, Julius W. "Western Aims in the War of 1812," *Mississippi Valley Historical Review*, Vol. XII (June, 1925), pp. 36-50.

Sampson, Francis A. "The New Madrid and Other Earthquakes of Missouri," *Missouri Historical Review*, Vol. VII (July, 1913), pp. 179-199.

Shaw, John. "The New Madrid Earthquake," *Missouri Historical Review*, Vol. VI (January, 1912), pp. 91-92.

Shoemaker, Floyd C. "Louisiana Purchase, 1803, and the Transfer of Upper Louisiana to the United States, 1804," *Missouri Historical Review*, Vol. XLVIII (October, 1953), pp. 1-22.

Shoemaker, Floyd C. *Missouri and Missourians.* Vol. I. Chicago: The Lewis Publishing Company, 1943.

Shoemaker, Floyd C. *Missouri's Struggle for Statehood 1804-1821.* Jefferson City: The Hugh Stephens Printing Company, 1916.

Shoemaker, Floyd C. "A Sketch of Missouri Constitutional History During the Territorial Period," *Missouri Historical Review*, Vol. IX (October, 1914), pp. 272-277.

Still, Bayrd. "An Interpretation of the Statehood Process, 1800-1850," *Mississippi Valley Historical Review*, Vol. XXIII (September, 1936), pp. 189-204.

Viles, Jonas. "Missouri in 1820," *Missouri Historical Review*, Vol. XV (October, 1920), pp. 36-52.

Windell, Marie G., (ed). "The Road West in 1818; Diary of Henry Vest Bingham," *Missouri Historical Review*, Vol. XL (October, 1945; January, 1946), pp. 21-54, 174-204.

CHAPTER VI

The New State

Missouri is born into the Union, . . . a manchild; his birth
no secret in the family, but a proud and glorious event,
proclaimed to the nation with the firing of cannon, the
ringing of bells and illumination of towns and cities.
—St. Louis *Enquirer*
March 29, 1820

The preceding statement—though written prematurely—
describes accurately the fanfare and hullabaloo with which Missouri entered the Union. Before this finally occurred, however,
the entire nation became involved in the struggle over Missouri
statehood. Missouri, after all, was a frontier area and displayed
characteristics typical of frontier people—individualism, impa-
tience, intemperance, and brashness. These qualities often led to
political and personal conflicts. They also gave color to the era.
This chapter is devoted to the brawling and bawling infant state
born of the union of the Territory of Missouri and the United
States of America.

Demands for Statehood

Although statehood was frequently a topic of discussion
during the territorial period, it was not until the year 1817 that
a petition requesting statehood was circulated in Missouri. Such
a petition was normally the first step in a long and complicated
procedure whereby a territory was transformed into a state.
Under this procedure the statehood petition would be submitted
to Congress, and Congress would—if it were so inclined—pass an
enabling act. Such an act authorized or enabled the territory to
prepare a state constitution. Delegates were then elected to a
state constitutional convention at which the document was written. After its completion, the constitution was sent to Washington for an examination by Congress. When the state constitution
was accepted by Congress, the territory would be granted statehood.

Potosi or Mine a Burton (Breton) from H. R. Schoolcraft, A View of the Lead Mines of Missouri, 1819

There were many reasons why Missourians took the first step toward statehood in 1817 and 1818. One important reason was the feeling among the people of Missouri that the United States Government had not kept its promise—clearly stipulated in the Louisiana Purchase Treaty of 1803—that the area of Louisiana would be divided into states and admitted to the Union "as soon as possible." This promise to the Creoles of Louisiana had been added to the treaty by Napoleon himself. However, fifteen years had gone by, and the people of Missouri still did not live as citizens of a state. There were many who argued that the United States Government was morally bound to admit Missouri to full statehood immediately because of the promises in the treaty signed in 1803.

A second factor hastening the demand for statehood was the Spanish land grant conflict. Carlos De Lassus, the last Spanish governor of the Missouri area, often ignored Spanish law in his issuance of land grants. He made a large number of grants during the last years of Spanish control when he knew the area was to be transferred to France or the United States. The United States Congress believed that many of these land grants were fraudulent and, therefore, refused to recognize Spanish land grants made after the transfer of Louisiana from Spain to France in 1800. As a consequence, those colonists—Creoles and Americans alike—who received land grants during the period 1800 to 1804 found their land titles questioned. In particular, American officials questioned the legality of the many large grants made by De Lassus to his family and friends, since Spanish instructions forbade grants of over 640 acres. The legal conflict over land titles was further complicated by the failure of many settlers to register and "perfect" their titles. The perfecting of a title required the signatures of Spanish officials at New Orleans. Obtaining such signatures was a complex and cumbersome procedure, and only about one-twentieth of all titles were perfected. Land titles which had not been perfected were called into question by American authorities.

A special federal commission investigated titles to some 5000 holdings and found approximately half of the titles illegal. During the territorial period this dispute over land titles was the main conflict between the United States Government and the territorial authorities. There were those Missourians who believed that if the territory were made a state, Missourians would be in a better position to secure liberal title treatment. Thus, they petitioned for statehood. Gradually, Congress did pass laws confirming the Spanish grants, but the last of these congressional acts was not passed until the year 1836.

The establishment of newspapers in Missouri during the territorial period was a third factor stimulating the settlers to request full membership in the Union. In the year 1808 an Irish refugee named Joseph Charless established the first newspaper in Missouri. Known as the *Missouri Gazette,* it was published in St. Louis. The paper was small in size—only eight inches by twelve inches—but it was printed with both English and French sections. Subscription prices were $3 a year in cash or $4 a year if payment were made in "country produce." In the early papers of Missouri the editor was the frequent target of complaints and often found himself waging a campaign against another editor or against a faction in the community. This personal journalism usually influenced public opinion as the citizens took sides on the issues discussed in the papers. Such journalism also stimulated the development of political factions.

In St. Louis several papers appeared in opposition to Joseph Charless and his *Gazette.* The first opposition papers—the *Western Journal* and the *Western Immigrant*—were unable to support themselves financially. The first financially successful opposition newspaper was the St. Louis *Enquirer,* established in the fall of 1818. This paper was edited for two years by Thomas Hart Benton, who was later to gain political fame at the national level. Benton and Charless carried on a continuous literary debate. In 1819 they were joined by Benjamin Holliday when he began publishing the *Missouri Intelligencer and Boon's Lick Advertiser.* These three publications did much to stimulate political interest in a region of earlier political lethargy.

A fourth factor influencing the Missourians to petition for statehood was the desire for political equality. As citizens of a territory, Missourians had no vote in national or international issues. They did, however, have strong convictions concerning political issues. The newspapers of the time clearly show that the settlers were vitally interested in such problems as tariff laws, the national bank, and development of the West. They wanted a voice and vote in Washington.

A fifth factor inciting a demand for statehood was the influx of settlers who had been politically active in other states. When the first Americans crossed the Appalachians and spread out to settle in the fertile river valleys, they brought with them a desire for self-rule and a knowledge of the workings of government. It was not long before such western districts as Kentucky, Tennessee, and Ohio sought, and at length received, admission to the Union as states on an equal footing with the original thirteen. Many of these same frontiersmen, and people with similar political experience, came to Missouri. Having tasted political power, they were not satisfied with so unpalatable a substitute as territorial government.

The Missouri petition which had begun to be circulated in the year 1817 was presented to the House of Representatives in 1818. The petition emphasized the loyal and responsible role Missourians had played in the War of 1812. To reinforce the petition request, the Missouri territorial legislature adopted a resolution in 1818 declaring that Missouri was ready to take her

Joseph Charless, publisher of the first English language newspaper west of the Mississippi, printed the first copies of the Missouri Gazette in St. Louis in July, 1808.
(Courtesy State Historical Society)

place in the Union. As a result of the petition and the resolution, a bill was introduced in Washington in December, 1818, which was designed to be an enabling act authorizing the citizens of the Missouri area to call a constitutional convention as a step toward statehood.

At this point, the slavery issue suddenly appeared. Slaves had been used in the American South all through the colonial period. Although at that time there was little criticism of slavery on moral grounds, late in the eighteenth century some of the leaders of the South felt that the institution of slavery was actually a detriment to the southerners. George Washington and Thomas Jefferson were two of these slave owners who disliked the system. While there were critics of slavery, there was no concerted effort to halt the practice in the South. An attempt was made, however, to halt the expansion of the institution to the territories. In the year 1787 the Articles of Confederation Congress passed the Northwest Ordinance, which provided that slavery would not be permitted in the area north of the Ohio River. As a consequence of this, slave-holding farmers from Virginia and North Carolina who moved west in order to acquire cheap land could not take their slaves into the area presently comprising the states of Michigan, Illinois, Indiana, and Ohio. Therefore, those southerners who wished to retain their slaves moved across the Mississippi into Missouri. People who were critical of slavery—they tended to be individuals from the North where slavery was not practiced—opposed the spread of the institution into the Missouri area. The opposition of these northerners to the extension of slavery led to the Missouri statehood conflict.

In 1819 Missouri had approximately 10,000 blacks in her population of 66,000, and more southerners were arriving daily with their slaves. Taking note of this development, Representative James Tallmadge of New York in 1819 submitted an amendment to the Missouri Enabling Act. The amendment provided that Missouri would be allowed to frame a constitution only if that constitution (1) prohibited the introduction of slaves into Missouri, and (2) stipulated that all slave children born in the state of Missouri would become free at the age of 25. This was a highly controversial proposal which immediately precipitated national debate. Up to this point in American history there had been a balance between slave and free states. By advocating the

The approximate boundaries of the first five counties of Missouri as described in 1812 and of Howard County as described in 1816
(Courtesy State Historical Society)

prohibition of slavery in Missouri, Representative Tallmadge
tipped the balance in favor of the free states and greatly angered
the South. Since the House of Representatives was chosen on the
basis of population, and since there was a greater population in
the northern states, the Tallmadge Amendment passed the
House. In the Senate, where representation of North and South
was equal, the Tallmadge Amendment caused the defeat of the
Missouri Enabling Act. Missouri's petition for statehood was
rejected because of the slavery issue.

Missourians were outraged at this treatment. Throughout
the territory there was a flurry of political activity with conferences, caucuses, public meetings, and banquets to protest the
matter. The public statements which were adopted at the time
would indicate that white Missourians were strongly resentful of
any attempt by the Federal Government to dictate state policies
with regard to slavery. Grand juries in seven counties adopted
resolutions deploring the Tallmadge Amendment. The St. Louis

grand jury referred to the amendment as an "unwarrantable usurpation of power over our unalienable rights and privileges as a free people." The Jefferson County grand jury expressed both "surprise and regret" at the Tallmadge proposal. The jurymen went on to add the following statement: "That slavery is an evil we do not pretend to deny, but, on the contrary, would most cheerfully join in any measure to abolish it, provided those means were not likely to produce greater evils to the people than the one complained of. . . ." The Montgomery County grand jury declared the amendment "unlawful, unconstitutional, and oppressive." In this crisis they called upon "the genius of '76, and the interposition of Divine Providence" to protect them. Even the Mount Pleasant Baptist Association issued a lengthy statement criticizing the Tallmadge proposal.

In the early nineteenth century it was popular for political leaders to hold banquets at which many toasts were given. These toasts were frequently highly polished and violently received with shouts of favor or disfavor. At the Fourth of July celebration at St. Louis in 1819 a toast was made to Representative Tallmadge and his associate, Representative Taylor, as follows: "Messrs. Tallmadge and Taylor—politically insane—May the next Congress appoint them a dark room, a straight waistcoat [straight jacket] and a thin water gruel diet." Following that toast the crowd gave nineteen cheers and the band played "Yankee Doodle." At a banquet in Franklin, Duff Green, the political leader who later became an adviser to Andrew Jackson, gave the following toast: "The Union—It is dear to us, but liberty is dearer."

The conflict was also discussed in the papers of the day. The *Gazette* editor, Joseph Charless, who disliked slavery, declared that he "never hesitated to state his opposition to the interference of Congress, but still felt desirous that some limitation be put by the people to the importation of slaves." Thomas Hart Benton and the *Enquirer* took a clear anti-restriction stand. Benton both spoke and wrote on the subject. He declared that the issue was not "slavery or anti-slavery." Instead, he suggested that it was a matter of freedom versus coercion. The *Enquirer* was convinced that Congress was stepping outside the bounds of its authority. In the fall of 1819 the paper noted the many new immigrants streaming in from Kentucky and Tennessee. "They bring great numbers of slaves, knowing that Congress has no power to impose the agitated restriction, and that the people of Missouri will never adopt it."

There were some in Missouri who even considered the possibility of rebellion and the establishment of an independent government separate from the United States if Missouri were denied admission to the Union. Such seditious thoughts were not uncommon on the American frontier; westerners had frequently considered rebellion during the 1790's and the early years of the nineteenth century. The aging Thomas Jefferson, retired from active political life but still profoundly interested in his young country, was much troubled over the Missouri crisis. He wrote to former President John Adams, "The Missouri question is a breaker on which we lose the Missouri country by revolt and what more God only knows."

Simply stated, the Missourians who looked forward to statehood as something they deserved, felt that they were not being treated justly. They believed that Congress had no right to make the decision to halt or to continue slavery in their territory. Missouri slave owners were threatened with the loss of their property. Land speculators and merchants feared that a ban on the introduction of slaves would halt both the stream of southerners into Missouri and the profits these immigrants would bring to the territory. Thus, there were both economic and political reasons for the defiant attitude Missourians took when, in 1819, Congress refused their first appeal for admission to the Union.

New Madrid in 1848 from Das Illustrirte Mississippithal by Henry Lewis

(Courtesy State Historical Society)

The Missouri Compromise

It soon became clear to the nation at large that the people of Missouri were incensed by congressional attempts to restrict their constitution. The slavery question, however, was not an isolated problem of an individual state. Once the question of slavery had been raised with regard to westward expansion, the issue was sure to arise each time a territory applied for admission to the Union. Congressmen from both North and South sought a formula which would allow them to defend their own positions regarding slavery while providing a basis for the settlement of similar conflicts in the future. From this search for a solution among both pro- and anti-slavery congressmen, a compromise developed. In fact, two compromises were negotiated before Missouri became a state.

The first compromise was suggested in 1820 when the Territory of Maine requested admission to the Union. Henry Clay, skilled statesman from Kentucky, was speaker of the House of Representatives in 1820. During the troubled years from 1820 to 1850 Clay, more than anyone else, acted as the mediator in the growing conflicts between North and South. Congressional leaders saw in Maine's request for statehood an opportunity for "horse trading." Maine, a northern state without slaves, could be allowed to enter the Union as a free state. Missouri would then be accepted as a slave state. However, the antislavery forces were still unhappy over the prospect of the spread of the despised institution. Their opposition finally led Senator Jesse B. Thomas of Illinois to propose an amendment. The Thomas Amendment, which had speaker Clay's support, provided that, although Missouri could enter the Union as a slave state, the remaining portion of the Louisiana Purchase north of the line 36° 30′ was to be forever free of slavery. This compromise solution was finally passed and became law. Thus on March 6, 1820, Congress authorized the people of Missouri to write a state constitution and establish a state government. The hated Tallmadge Amendment was not part of this enabling act. The only restrictions on the people of Missouri were that the government should be republican in form and that the state constitution should not conflict with the federal constitution.

The news of this first Missouri compromise reached the state on March 21, when a man from Cincinnati brought the news to Jackson, Missouri. Such important information spread rapidly through the territory, and it was known at Franklin, Missouri, by April 1. There were immediate plans throughout the territory to celebrate the congressional decision. The St. Louis *Enquirer,* in its issue of March 25, carried the headline, "GRATIFYING NEWS FROM WASHINGTON." The paper went on to describe the reception of the news by announcing that the paper was being published "amidst the ringing of the bells, the firing of cannons, and the joyful congratulations of the citizens." Both St. Louis papers carried the following announcement:

Upon the request of many citizens of the town of St. Louis, it is resolved by the board of trustees that an illumination of the town be recommended to the citizens on Thursday night, 30th inst. to commence precisely at 8 o'clock p.m. in consequence of the admission of Missouri into the Union upon an equal footing with the original states.

A national salute under the direction of the trustees will be fired precisely at 8 o'clock.

Pierre Chouteau.
Chairman.

It was reported later that all but four or five of the houses in St. Louis were illuminated by candles flickering in the windows. Many of the candles glowed behind designs painted on transparent paper. Dr. Heely displayed a transparency showing "a beautiful representation of the American Eagle, from the beak [of which floated] the words, 'Missouri and no restrictions!'" Another citizen displayed a transparency which showed a black dancing joyously because "Congress had voted to permit the slaves to come and live in such a fine country as Missouri."

The next step for the citizens of Missouri was the election of delegates to a constitutional convention. Forty-one delegates were chosen and were ready to begin the writing of the constitution when the convention opened on June 12, 1820. The meeting was held in St. Louis in the commodious, three-story Mansion House Hotel located at the present corner of Third and E Streets. Only thirty-two days after the convention convened, the delegates adopted and published the first Missouri constitution. As everyone anticipated, this Constitution of 1820 legally protected the practice of slavery.

A little over a month after the constitution was proclaimed, in keeping with the instructions of Congress, the first state election was held on August 28, 1820. On this occasion a governor, a congressman, and members of the two houses of the legislature were chosen. Shortly thereafter the legislature met to select the two United States senators. When these organizational proceedings were complete in September, 1820, the Missourians believed they had met the conditions of the enabling act. They now considered themselves members of the Union.

The ensuing celebrations were premature, however, for one section of the constitution became a new focal point for conflict. Section 26 of Article 3 of the Missouri constitution assigned to the state legislators the following power: "It shall be their duty as soon as may be, to pass such laws as may be necessary, to prevent free Negroes and mulattoes from coming to, and settling in this state, under any pretext whatsoever." This portion of the constitution was intended to protect slavery by excluding free blacks. No doubt the framers of the constitution felt that the presence of free blacks in the state might make the slaves restless. However, since blacks were citizens in many northern states, the Missouri proviso seemed to be contrary to the provision in the United States Constitution which states that "citizens of each state shall be entitled to all privileges and immunities of citizens in the several states." The discrepancy between these constitutional provisions created a new volcano of political oratory and threatened to halt once more Missouri's plans for statehood.

When Missouri's congressmen arrived in Washington they were not immediately admitted to seats in Congress. The antislavery forces declared that the Missouri constitution with its provision for the exclusion of free blacks and mulattoes was unacceptable and that Missouri could not be admitted to the Union unless her constitution were changed. During the year of debate before the dispute was settled, Missouri's congressmen drew salaries, but they were not seated as voting members of Congress.

In 1820 a presidential election was held. The Missourians had rushed the organization of their government in order to have a part in the choosing of the new president. However, there was a question as to the validity of the Missouri votes since Congress had not yet approved the controversial Missouri constitution. While some congressmen—northern and southern alike—protested, the majority in Congress allowed the following procedure in canvassing the presidential ballots:

> The votes of Missouri were read, and the results of
> all the votes having been read—The president of

the Senate announced that the total number of
votes for James Monroe, as President of the United
States, was 231, and, if the votes of Missouri were
not counted, was 228; that in either event James
Monroe had a majority of the whole number of
votes given.

This procedure satisfied Missouri's desire to be heard in the
presidential election, but it did not solve the dispute over acceptance of her constitution. At this point, Henry Clay assumed
once more the role of mediator and secured congressional approval of the second Missouri Compromise. Missouri was required to pass a "solemn act" promising that the offending
Section 26 would never be construed as restricting the rights
guaranteed by the federal constitution of any citizen of any
other state. Such a promise from the Missouri legislature would
then be accepted as proof that the legislators did not intend to
carry out the intent of the disputed section. Missouri political
leaders knew—as did thinking politicians in Washington—that
such a "solemn act" was, in fact, meaningless. Missouri's constitution still would be the supreme law of the state. The Missouri
legislature, quite willing to adopt such a statement if it would
satisfy the objections of the northern politicians, passed the act
in June, 1821. Finally, on August 10, 1821, four years after the
beginning of the petition movement, President Monroe issued the
following statement: "The admission of the said State of Missouri into this Union is declared to be complete."

The Constitution of 1820

The people of Missouri elected capable delegates to the constitutional convention in 1820. The speed with which they completed their labors and the general effectiveness of the constitution speak well of their abilities. The Missouri founding fathers

**Lawyer David Barton, one of Missouri's
first two senators, served as the president of the first constitutional convention of Missouri and was influential in
the framing of the Constitution of 1820.**
(Shoemaker, Missouri's Struggle for Statehood,
Courtesy State Historical Society)

were prominent lawyers, land owners, or merchants of the state, most of whom had previous political experience either in Missouri or in such states as Virginia, Kentucky, and Tennessee. Only two of the forty-one delegates were born in Upper Louisiana. The other thirty-nine were immigrants. The prosperity of the region can be seen in the fact that all but four delegates were men of means. Some of the most influential participants were John Rice Jones, Duff Green, Edward Bates, John Cook, Jonathan Findlay, John Scott, Alexander McNair, and Henry Dodge. David Barton was chosen chairman of the convention.

Thomas Hart Benton, the editor of the St. Louis *Enquirer*, was not among the convention delegates, although he had expected to be chosen. A caucus of St. Louis politicians had decided upon a slate of delegates which did not include his name. Benton later received a petition bearing 138 signatures requesting him to run as a delegate. However, he declined to oppose the members of his own political faction. This political loyalty was later rewarded. At the time, however, the opposition editor, Joseph Charless, had great fun chiding Benton over this slight. Angered by these *Gazette* jeers, Benton's partner, Isaac N. Henry, accosted Charless on the street and struck him "several blows with a heavy cudgel." The next day Charless described the attack in his paper and stated that he returned the blows "with a stick disproportionately small." At the time of the street assault, Mr. Charless was accompanied by the Reverend Joseph Piggot. Charless reported that the peace-loving clergyman attempted to part the two combatants, but one of Henry's friends drew "a pistol from his bosom," and told the minister "he would blow him through if he interfered." The minister finally went for help, and the fight ended. Such conduct by some of the leading citizens of St. Louis demonstrates the passion and violence of politics at the time of the constitutional convention.

In an orderly and efficient manner, the delegates to the convention divided into committees and proceeded immediately to prepare the charter. After approximately five weeks, the work was completed. A comparison of the Missouri constitution with other constitutions of the time shows that the delegates liberally selected portions of other constitutions to include in the Missouri document. In particular, the delegates adopted the language and procedures of the constitutions of Kentucky, Alabama, Illinois, and Maine.

"Stump Speaking" by George Caleb Bingham. An earnest candidate addresses a gathering of Missourians while his opponent, seated behind him, studiously takes notes.

It is usual for states to point to the unique provisions of their own constitutions. In truth, however, the most startling characteristic of American state constitutions is their similarity. Congress did not set requirements for the state constitutions other than the qualification that the governments should be republican in form. But in state after state the governments are remarkably alike. The founding fathers of Missouri wrote a constitution which was consistent with their English political heritage, and parallel to the other state governments of the time. The Missouri bill of rights is a repetition of similar bills in the federal constitution and those of her sister states. The government itself was made up of the familiar three departments—executive, legislative, and judicial.

At the executive level, the governor was the chief state administrator, and it was his responsibility to maintain a government which would enforce the law. As head of the militia of the state, he was responsible for preserving peace and order. He had legislative power since he could call the legislature into session, and could veto laws. Finally, he had judicial responsibilities because he could extend clemency. The governor enjoyed a powerful position, but he could not succeed himself after his four-year term. The lieutenant-governor's primary duty during his four-year term was to preside over the Senate. The governor, the lieutenant-governor, the state legislators, and the United

States congressman were elected by popular vote. All other officials of the state government and the two United States senators were appointed by the two houses of the legislature. The auditor, attorney-general, and secretary of state were nominated by the governor and approved by the Senate.

Just as the federal legislature had two houses, so the Missouri General Assembly was made up of a House of Representatives and a Senate. House members served for two years and senators for four. Each county was to have at least one member in the House of Representatives, but the maximum number of delegates was set at 100. The Senate was to be a smaller body of 14 to 33 members, depending upon the number of senatorial districts established. In procedure, a bill had to pass both houses in identical form before it became law. This gave each house a veto in the legislative process.

The judicial branch of the government was established in a supreme court, the court of chancellery (abolished in 1822), and the circuit courts. The judges were appointed by the governor and the Senate and served "during good behavior."

This general structure of government was typical throughout the United States. However, the Missouri constitution differed from those of other states in several respects. First, the constitution did provide laws for the humane treatment of slaves. It is evident that a great majority of the citizens of the state wished to maintain the institution of slavery. In the constitutional elections in the spring of 1820, antislavery candidates stood for election in one-third of the counties. Not one of these candidates was elected as a delegate to the constitutional convention. Although the delegates were in favor of slavery, they wrote a constitution which outlawed brutal treatment of slaves. Any owner who attempted to kill or maim his slave would be liable to the same punishment as though his victim were white. Another constitutional provision provided that owners could free their blacks, but the freed slaves could not become public charges; the owner was forced to insure that the slave could maintain himself after manumission. This law was designed to protect aged blacks. Without this provision, an unscrupulous slave owner might seek to free his aged, unproductive slaves in order to escape his responsibility for their support. The Missouri constitution further provided that slavery could not be abolished in the state by action of the state government unless each owner was compensated for the full value of his slaves. This provision was to cause difficulty at the time of the Civil War.

A second distinguishing feature of the Constitution of 1820 was the concern given to the separation of church and state. From the colonial period on, the American frontiersman disliked established churches—that is, churches recognized as the official religious body and supported financially by taxes. Established churches forced all citizens to pay for religious programs which were not acceptable to all. In New England, the Congregational Church had been established. In the southern colonies, the Anglican (Episcopal) Church was supported by tax money. In colonial Missouri, the Catholic Church was tax supported. In each case, religious minorities felt imposed upon when they were forced to contribute their tax dollars for the support of a church which was not their own. Furthermore, many unchurched frontiersmen wanted "freedom from religion" not "freedom of religion". The framers of the Constitution of 1820, therefore, made a special effort to separate church and state. The constitution clearly provided that priests or clergymen or officials of a particular religious group were ineligible for the legislature. The only public office to which a clergyman might aspire was that of justice of the peace.

There are several ways in which the Constitution of 1820 was in line with the future. It provided for biennial legislative sessions which later became popular throughout the Union. It provided for long terms of office for state officials. Only members of the House of Representatives served for two years. Judges served during "good behavior"—which in most cases meant life —and all other state officials for four years. The constitution also was forward-looking when it allowed any free, white man, 21 or over, the right to vote. There were no property qualifications for the franchise.

After the delegates had complied, corrected, and polished their constitution, the document was issued without ratification by the people. Although this procedure would not be tolerated today, it was not so unusual in the early nineteenth century. The convention was anxious to create a government so that Missouri might speedily become part of the Union. Among other incentives for the rapid establishment of government was the Missourians' wish to have a part in the presidential election of 1820. The constitution appears to have been generally popular in Mis-

Missouri's first governor, Alexander McNair, served from 1820 to 1824. In the new state's first gubernatorial race, Alexander McNair campaigned against the proposed $2000 annual governor's salary, which he considered excessive.

(Courtesy State Historical Society)

souri, and it probably represented the wishes of the majority. At noon on July 9, 1820, the delegates to the convention signed the constitution "amidst a great concourse of citizens, [who seem always to have been eager to celebrate!] and under a national salute of twenty-four guns, fired by the St. Louis Guards." Only one delegate, Joseph McFerron, of Cape Girardeau County, refused to sign, because he objected to a provision referring to the election of the governor.

The constitution was well received in Missouri, and Alexander McNair properly evaluated the document for the people of that time as follows: "We have found for ourselves a constitution which, though perhaps not free from imperfections incident to all human institutions, does honor to the character and intelligence of our infant state, and gives us every reason to expect that we shall, without further difficulty, be admitted into the federal union."

The constitutional convention also approved a five-point agreement which the Federal Government submitted for their consideration. The state of Missouri agreed to exempt all publicly-owned land from state, county, or township taxes for five years, and to exempt from taxation those pieces of property granted to veterans of the War of 1812. In return the Federal Government made five promises. (1) One section of land in each township was to be used to facilitate the establishment of public schools. (2) The state was granted ownership of twelve salt springs, to prevent anyone from securing a salt monopoly. Few of us realize today how important salt was to the frontier people and how they often struggled to secure an adequate supply. (3) Five per cent of the sale price of public lands was to be set aside for the financing of internal improvements—roads and canals. (4) Four sections of land were granted to the state to aid in the construction of a new state capitol building. (5) The state government was given thirty-six sections of land to finance a state university. Thus, the Federal Government was using its main resource—land—to assist the new state in establishing conditions which would benefit her future citizens. Public education in Missouri was greatly stimulated by this agreement.

The delegates to the constitutional convention were also instrumental in locating a capital for the new state. Article 11 of the constitution provided for the creation of a commission to pick the exact location "on the bank of the Missouri river, and within forty miles of the mouth of the river Osage." The delegates also discussed a name for the seat of government, and "Missouriopolis" was one frequently mentioned. When the first General Assembly met in 1821, a commission was selected to examine the general area in order to suggest the specific site. In December, 1821, the present location was accepted by the legislature, and

"The Assembling of the First Legislature, St. Charles, Missouri, 1821" by Richard E. Miller from the lunette in the state capitol
(Courtesy Walker-Commerce)

the name "City of Jefferson" was adopted. This name, though officially correct, is rarely used today. Although the site was agreed upon in 1821, several years were required to build a suitable structure. The governor and legislature met in St. Louis during 1821. From 1821 to 1826 St. Charles was the temporary seat of government. Finally, in the fall of 1826 the government records and officials were moved to the present promontory in Jefferson City overlooking the Missouri River.

The Rise of Thomas Hart Benton

The first half of the nineteenth century was a time of political giants in the United States. Henry Clay of Kentucky, John C. Calhoun of South Carolina, Andrew Jackson of Tennessee, Martin Van Buren of New York, and Daniel Webster of Massachusetts, all were powerful protagonists in the halls of Congress. From the frontier state of Missouri came another giant who feared not to debate with the greatest. Thomas Hart Benton, one of Missouri's first two senators, represented the state in the United States Senate and in the highest councils of government for thirty years. Although he was one of the most influential leaders of the Democratic Party, he took independent positions when his convictions demanded it. No other political personality in the history of the state was the center of controversy for so long a period as was Benton.

Benton was born in 1782 and spent his childhood in the Piedmont region of North Carolina. Because of the early death of his father, Thomas was reared under the supervision of his mother. She carefully directed his reading in English literature, history, and law to prepare him to become a lawyer as his father had been. At the age of sixteen he entered the University of North Carolina at Chapel Hill. His experience at Chapel Hill was not a pleasant one. Several months after his arrival he was charged with thievery when his roommates discovered money missing from their pocketbooks. Benton was trapped into an admission of guilt and was dismissed from the University in 1799. He returned to his home in humiliation. This bitter experience prodded Thomas into a great drive to demonstrate his honor and abilities to the world.

Several years later the Bentons joined the many other families from Virginia and North Carolina who moved westward into the Cumberland Valley of Tennessee. They claimed a 2,560-acre homestead bordering the Natchez Trace twenty-five miles south of Nashville. The farm was in a dangerous location, for it lay immediately beside the Indian hunting grounds of the southern tribes. Young Thomas was a restless, intelligent boy who was not satisfied with the routine duties of the farm. He soon re-entered the academic life to teach school and to study law. Thomas was twenty-four years old when he was admitted to the bar in 1806. He immediately began his practice, which at that time meant following the judges about on the circuits in Tennessee, seeking clients and representing them before the bar of justice.

One of the judges in Tennessee was Andrew Jackson. Jackson was impressed with the abilities of the young lawyer and frequently had Benton in his home. Like Jackson, Benton soon entered politics. He ran for the state senate in 1809 and was elected. He immediately led a reform movement to increase the number of courts in Tennessee, and he and his supporters were successful in thus speeding justice for those accused of crimes. His friendship with Jackson also helped secure a commission when the War of 1812 began. He was granted a captaincy in a company of infantry volunteers. Benton longed for active service and military glory, but in spite of his frequent letters to army officials begging for battle duty, he had to be satisfied with routine army life and a period as a recruiter.

"Colonel Thomas Hart Benton as a Young Man," an oil portrait by Matthew Harris Jouett (1787-1827)
(Courtesy The Clevelend Museum of Art, Gift of Mrs. Otto Miller)

(Courtesy State Historical Society)

Thomas Hart Benton's home in Tennessee

Among the proud, vain men of the frontier, it was common-place for one who had suffered some insult to challenge his de-tractor to a duel. This senseless activity led to the death of many people—particularly those of the upper class who were most sensitive of their prestige and reputation. In 1813, while Thomas Hart Benton was on a trip to Washington, D. C., his younger brother, Jesse, became involved in a quarrel with Major William Carroll, a friend of Andrew Jackson. Although Carroll was anxious to avoid the duel if he could do so with honor, the hot-blooded Jesse insisted on a showdown battle. In the duel that followed, Jesse fired first and missed. Thus, Carroll had ample time to aim carefully at his opponent. In this moment of crisis Jesse Benton turned about and was wounded in the back. The ridiculousness of this duel made young Benton the laughingstock of Nashville, and when Tom Benton returned home, he felt a re-sponsibility to defend his brother's honor. Benton was infuriated to discover that while he had been in Washington acting as a spokesman for Andrew Jackson, Jackson had served as Carroll's second against Jesse Benton. When Tom Benton publicly assailed Jackson's action as treachery, a conflict with his former friend was imminent.

On September 4, 1813, Andrew Jackson and several friends went to Nashville to precipitate a showdown. The inevitable battle occurred when Jackson and his associates arrived at Clayton Talbot's Tavern where the Bentons had a room. Jackson and his friends produced guns; the Bentons followed suit. In the melee which followed, Jesse seems to have fired first, but Andy and Tom also exchanged shots. After the first exchange of gunfire, General Jackson fell to the floor, blood spurting from his left arm. The battle at this point turned into a free-for-all as Jackson's friends attempted to dispatch the Bentons with drawn daggers. In the midst of this struggle, the overweight Tom Benton fell down the flight of stairs at the rear of the hotel, and others who were nearby halted the fight. For ten years from that night, Jackson and Benton were bitter enemies.

The next year General Andrew Jackson won the famous Battle of New Orleans, and he became the great hero of the West. The popularity of Jackson in Tennesssee meant that Benton had to leave the state if he wished to rise in politics. Thus, in the fall of 1815, when he was thirty-three years old, Thomas Hart Benton moved to St. Louis, Missouri. He arrived with only $400, but he had much experience as a lawyer, and his time in the legislature had given him a taste for politics. He was to follow both inclinations in Missouri.

When Benton arrived in St. Louis he was fortunate to meet Charles Gratiot, who invited him into his home. Gratiot was a wealthy merchant and the husband of Victoria Chouteau. This meeting was an opportune one, for it gave Benton access to the highest levels of society in the city, and he was soon acquainted with the community leaders. During his early years in St. Louis, the young lawyer followed the judges of the circuit courts, handling routine cases of the time. In particular, he became involved in the many suits associated with the recognition of Spanish land grants. Benton, who had had difficulty in Tennessee over land titles, believed the United States Government should act in a sympathetic manner in recognizing the land grants made by the Spanish.

In time he met Judge John B. C. Lucas, who acted as U. S. Land Commissioner to investigate the authenticity of land titles. Lucas was a French immigrant (his real name was Jean Baptiste Charles) who had risen rapidly to prominence in Missouri. As a judge, he strictly enforced the federal regulations concerning land titles, and his commission rejected as invalid about half of the Spanish grants examined. Judge Lucas had a favorite son named Charles, who was also a lawyer. In a court case in 1816, the two young men, Lucas and Benton, carried on a violent exchange in the courtroom. In the ensuing months their hatred for each other grew. When Benton approached the election judges in August, 1817, Charles Lucas challenged his right to vote, declaring that Thomas had failed to pay his taxes. Benton then said to the election judges, "Gentlemen, if you have any questions to ask, I am prepared to answer, but I do not propose to answer charges made by any puppy who may happen to run across my path!" This word "puppy" rankled Lucas, and he sent Benton a letter demanding "that satisfaction which is due from one gentleman to another for such an indignity." Benton accepted the challenge, and a duel followed on Bloody Island in the Mississippi. The two men chose pistols which were not to exceed eleven inches in length, and they took position thirty feet apart. Simultaneously they answered the command, "Fire!" Benton's bullet entered Lucas' neck and the duel was over. Benton received only a slight wound on the leg.

Sometimes duels would result in the healing of a breach, but the Benton-Lucas meeting did not end the participants' antagonism. After their encounter, both men declared themselves unsatisfied. Gossip and rumors in St. Louis kept both men aroused and led eventually to another duel. After rowing out to Bloody Island on September 27, 1817, the two men met once more. On this occasion they aimed at a distance of only 10 feet. Benton again proved to be the better shot. This time the ball from his gun entered Lucas' heart, and as Benton watched, the young man died. For the rest of his life Thomas Hart Benton was haunted by memories of the scene.

In 1818 Benton became the editor of the newly-organized St. Louis *Enquirer*. Now his opinions were more widely publicized. He was a strong advocate of the westward movement and was much disturbed when the United States gave up her claim to Texas during the Monroe administration. Another issue that interested him was the distribution of federal land. As a typical westerner, he called for rapid distribution at low prices. Because of his speaking ability and his position as an editor, as well as his general competence, Benton was soon deeply immersed in Missouri politics. In 1819 he was part of a group called the "little junto" by Editor Charless. This group included the largest landowners and merchants, and it represented those people who anxiously sought vindication of their Spanish land grants. Among the leaders of the "little junto" were Auguste Chouteau, Charles

Gratiot, Bernard Pratte, Territorial Governor William Clark, lawyer Edward Hempstead, and John Scott of Ste. Genevieve, who was the territorial delegate to Congress. Opposing Benton and his friends was the "anti-junto" group including Judge Lucas, Joseph Charless, David Barton, William Russell, and Rufus Eaton. These men were land speculators who came to the region after the transfer to America. Thus, they did not stand to profit from the vindication of Spanish land grants.

The election in 1820 of John Scott of Ste. Genevieve as Missouri's congressman pleased Benton and his friends. However, William Clark, the territorial governor, was unsuccessful in his attempt to win the governorship. Instead, Alexander McNair was chosen. Under the provisions of the federal constitution, Missouri's two United States senators were to be chosen by the General Assembly. Throughout 1820, Benton carefully planned his strategy to secure his election to the Senate. It was soon clear that David Barton was the most popular candidate for this office. Barton's popularity was pleasing to Benton, who had come to like the intelligent man during the preceding year, despite his periods of drunkenness which Benton referred to as "frolics."

Shortly before the General Assembly was to make the choice of senators, Benton's supporters discovered they lacked one vote to assure his election. John Scott and Auguste Chouteau, who were in charge of his strategy, together with Chouteau's brother Pierre, and other wealthy Creoles Jean P. Cabanne and Sylvestre Labadie, gave their assistance to secure the vote of Representative Marie Philippe Leduc. Leduc, who disliked Benton, intended to vote for Judge Lucas. However, his friends warned Leduc, who

Daniel Ralls, for whom Ralls County was named, was carried in his sickbed to vote for his friend Thomas Hart Benton.
(From John R. Musick, Stories of Missouri, 1897)

had several large Spanish land grants, that Lucas was not sympathetic to his best interests. They pictured Benton as one who would secure land titles. Finally, after nearly a night of argument, the old man relented and agreed to vote for Benton.

Another dramatic episode in the selection of the senators in 1820 is associated with the name of Representative Daniel Ralls of Pike County. Representative Ralls, a staunch supporter of Benton, was near the point of death, but while the Assembly was in session he was carried into the meeting on his bed by four blacks. Too faint to lift his head, Ralls could only cry out the names, "Barton and Benton," when it was time for him to vote. When Representative Ralls died soon after this incident, the St. Louis *Enquirer* honored him with this poem comparing him with the great English statesman, Chatham, who died under similar circumstances:

> When rack'd by disease in his litter he lay,
> He was borne in that litter the tribute to pay
> To his friend, his loved Country, while Senate beheld
> The last moments of Chatham by Ralls paralled'd.

When the roll call was completed, David Barton had received a clear majority, and by a margin of only one vote Thomas Hart Benton was elected to a term as the other of Missouri's first two United States senators. Such was the troubled beginning of his tumultuous career in the U. S. Senate.

Political Alignments

When Missouri entered the Union in 1820 the United States did not have a two-party system. The old Federalist Party had died at the time of the War of 1812. The remaining political party was made up of the followers of Thomas Jefferson who called themselves the Democratic-Republicans. This time of one-party government in America is sometimes called the Era of Good Feeling, because of the reduction in political conflict.

Whenever the two-party system disappears and one party is in control of the government—as is frequently true in our southern states today—rivalries develop within the ruling party. So it was when Missouri became a state. All the political leaders were Democratic-Republicans, but there were contending factions within the party. Governments are frequently operated through coalitions of certain politically powerful individuals, and this, too, was true of Missouri during the early years of statehood.

"County Election" by George Caleb Bingham from an engraving by John Sartain. The voter at the top of the county courthouse steps is swearing that he has not voted at another precinct. The ambitious politician doffing his silk hat is working hard at winning friends and influencing voters.

Looking at the political history of Missouri from 1820 to 1840 one cannot help being amazed at the frequency with which political leaders changed their alliances. This was possible because the political leaders were dedicated not so much to ideals as to friendship with certain individuals. Subsequent personal differences would then result in the formation of a new political alliance or coalition.

The politicians of the time engaged in vigorous personal battles. This can be seen on the pages of the St. Louis *Enquirer* and the *Gazette*. For example, the *Enquirer* charged the *Gazette* with fabricating up to 100 lies concerning John Scott. Editor Charless immediately demanded that Benton prove his statements. Benton thereupon published a "List of One Hundred Lies fabricated by the old communications maker." This kind of journalism delighted and stimulated the politicians of Missouri.

Before beginning a chronological description of Missouri politics from 1820 to 1840, several characteristics of the period should be stressed. First, except for Governor McNair, all the men who served in the United States House of Representatives and Senate, or as governor, were from southern slave-holding states. In a time when sectionalism was a major factor in politics, Missouri leaders were westerners, but they also had ties of interest and sympathy with the South. Second, Thomas Hart Benton was such a strong personality and was involved in so many issues that politics tended more and more to orbit about him during the period. Third, in this era of a rapidly expanding economy and a boom-and-bust cycle, problems associated with

Missouri's second governor,
Frederick Bates, served only
one year before dying of
pleurisy at the age of forty-
eight.   Bates   County   was
named in his honor.
(Courtesy State Historical Society)

money and banking came to be the chief political issues. Fourth,
Missouri gradually developed a two-party system. The parties
were organized around national issues. The followers of Jackson
and Benton came to be known as Democrats. Those who opposed
the two and advocated a national bank or greater federal expenditure for the construction of roads and canals to the West
were known as National-Republicans. In 1834 the National-
Republicans became known as the Whig Party.

The election of 1820 marks the beginning of an independent
state government in Missouri. Alexander McNair, a Pennsyl-
vania-born official who directed the United States Land Office
in St. Louis, won an easy election victory over Territorial Governor William Clark. Clark was with his sick wife in Virginia and
did not campaign. McNair received seventy-two per cent of the
votes. His administration as governor was relatively quiet and
uneventful. The site of the new capital was chosen. The state
adopted a seal. When a depression struck the state, he secured
the passage of emergency loan legislation to aid those in danger
of foreclosure. McNair was a diplomatic man with many friends
and few, if any, enemies.

In the election of 1824 Frederick Bates of St. Louis was
chosen governor. Bates had much previous experience in govern-

ment. Although he was born in Virginia, he had moved to the Michigan Territory where he had taken part in the organization of the territorial government of Michigan. He was chosen secretary of the Louisiana Territory in 1807, and he had been an interim governor of Missouri on several occasions. Bates may be remembered not only for his political activities, but for the fact that he compiled the first book to be printed in Missouri, *The Laws of the Territory of Louisiana,* published in 1808.

Unfortunately, Governor Bates died the year after his election, and this created a complicated political crisis. The lieutenant-governor had already resigned. Under the constitution the president *pro tempore* of the Senate, Abraham J. Williams of Boone County, became the interim governor until a special election could be called. Williams served for five and a half months until December, 1825, when the people elected John Miller of Cooper County the chief executive of the state.

Miller, like Bates, had been born in Virginia. He was so popular that he was re-elected in 1828, when he ran without opposition. During Miller's term, the Assembly passed a law to attempt to halt the practice of dueling. Under this law any person convicted of dueling was to be publicly flogged. Although Governor Miller opposed duels, he was unwilling to take this strong action, and he vetoed the law. Under Miller's administration the state debt was reduced to $37,000 by 1833.

John Miller, governor of Missouri from 1826 to 1832, held office longer than any other governor except Phil M. Donnelly who served two four-year terms.
(Strauss portrait, Courtesy State Historical Society)

At the national level, there was no change in the Missouri delegation to Congress until the year 1826. John Scott was re-elected in 1822 and 1824. David Barton was re-elected in 1824.

Although Senator Barton was more popular than Benton in 1820, Senator Benton soon proved to be a much more colorful and successful politician. Benton utilized his newspaper experience in writing speeches which he printed and distributed in great numbers to his constituents. In his first years of service in the Senate, Benton supported several policies intended to help those who had aided in his election. For example, he secured the passage of bills which made it possible for most of the holders of Spanish land grants to secure American titles to their property. He also arranged congressional action to halt the old government "factory" system for the Indian trade. Under this system, government agents called factors acted as traders offering the Indians goods at cost. This discouraged exploitation and provided for uniform treatment of the Indians. However, the individual Missouri merchants and fur companies were unhappy with what they considered unfair competition, and Benton's action forced the closing of these government trading posts.

Having paid some of his political debts, Senator Benton turned to legislative plans of broader appeal. He became known in particular for two propositions, neither of which was ever adopted. (1) He called for the establishment of a graduation-donation system for the sale of government land. He disliked the old system under which the land was auctioned at a minimum price of $1.25 per acre. Under Benton's plan the Federal Government would lower the price of land regularly in order to encourage settlers to purchase it. In the event that no one wished to purchase the land, it could then be donated to those who wished to live upon it. As one could imagine, this plan was most popular in the West. (2) He also proposed that a new system be adopted for the election of the president and vice-president. He wished to destroy the electoral college and use a direct vote of the people instead. Again, this proposal was popular with the many frontier people who believe in the importance of the ballot for common people. These two proposals made Benton the advocate for the small farmer and artisan.

The election of 1824 produced a new crisis. Henry Clay, a candidate for president that year, married Lucretia Hart, a cousin of Benton. Clay campaigned in 1824 on a platform calling for federal money for internal improvements (the construction of roads and canals), a high protective tariff, and a national bank. Clay believed this program would establish a sound, balanced, prosperous economy. Benton was impressed with Clay's arguments, and returned to Missouri where he traveled some 800 miles about the state campaigning for his relative-by-marriage. Benton's arguments were accepted by the citizens of Missouri, and Clay received 2,042 votes to 1,166 for Andrew Jackson and 218 for John Quincy Adams.

Under the provisions of the federal constitution, when a candidate for the presidency fails to secure a majority of the electoral votes the selection is made by the House of Representatives. In 1824 the electoral college failed to give any one candidate a majority. As a consequence, the House was asked to choose between Andrew Jackson, John Q. Adams, and William Crawford, the three candidates who received the most electoral votes. Clay was no longer eligible. In the House of Representatives, John Scott was to cast Missouri's lone vote. After careful consideration, Scott decided that he would cast Missouri's vote for Adams. He did this in spite of the fact that few Missourians had shown

Lithograph of "The Verdict of the People" by George Caleb Bingham. An election judge announces the results of the balloting.

(Courtesy State Historical Society)

a preference for Adams. Scott made the decision primarily because he admired Adams, and Clay had thrown his support to Adams. Missouri's other senator, David Barton, also supported Adams. It was at this moment that Thomas Hart Benton made one of the greatest decisions in his life.

Andrew Jackson had come from Tennessee to the United States Senate in 1823. In fact, he had been assigned to the same committee as Benton—the Committee on Military Affairs. One might have anticipated an explosion of hatred at the meeting of these two enemies. However, both men acted in a civil manner, and as time went on a new friendship developed. In 1824, before the House of Representatives voted for the president, Benton suddenly made an announcement. He declared his support for Andrew Jackson since Clay was no longer a candidate. Furthermore, Benton stated that the people of the state of Missouri had voted their feeling of greater confidence in Jackson than in Adams. In spite of bitter denunciations from Senator Benton, Congressman Scott cast his vote for John Quincy Adams, and Adams was the victor. In doing this, Scott cut his political ties with Benton. When Scott ran for re-election in 1826, he was defeated by Edward Bates.

Senator Benton was creating a new political party in Missouri, the foundations of which were evident in 1824. Clearly, he was tying himself to the large body of tillers of the soil who made up the common people. William Nisbet Chambers, who wrote the biography, *Old Bullion Benton,* says of the senator, "He was now fighting, all-out, for a political economy of popular, majority-rule democracy, based on a population of small farmers, small producers, and small traders." Benton saw that the future was with this group. At the same time, he was cutting his ties with the merchants and large landowners who had supported him originally.

In the election of 1828 Benton displayed his political power by securing the election of his hand-picked candidate for Congress, Spencer Pettis. Benton thus defeated Bates who, like his predecessor Scott, turned out to be an Adams man. In addition to Pettis, John Miller, another Benton candidate, was elected governor without opposition. That same year, in the Missouri vote for president, Andrew Jackson received 8,372 votes, but John Quincy Adams polled only 3,407. No doubt Benton's campaign was an influential factor in Jackson's victory. There were many who believed that Benton's proposals for lowering the price of land were a major factor in Jackson's success in Missouri and in the nation at large.

In the year 1830 David Barton—now Benton's enemy, although originally Barton had aided Benton in securing a Senate post—was defeated in his attempt to be renamed as the United States senator. The legislature chose Alexander Buckner instead. Buckner was not in sympathy with either Benton's or Jackson's proposals. Thus, he was only a little more acceptable than Barton had been.

At this time, a new issue appeared on the political horizon in 1831. The Bank of the United States—frequently referred to at that time as the B. U. S.—was under sharp criticism by Benton, since he considered it a privileged corporation with too much power. Benton gave sympathy and advice to Andrew Jackson in the latter's war upon the B. U. S. Benton was also concerned about another economic development—the increasing issuance of paper money by banks. It was a common practice for banks to issue more paper than they could redeem. This inflated or worthless money circulated freely on the frontier, and was often called "shin plasters" or "wild cat currency." Benton, believing that the poorer people were frequently defrauded by this practice, proposed that it be made illegal to print paper money for bills below $20. Instead, he suggested the use of gold or silver coins. Be-

Innkeeper Daniel Dunklin of Potosi served as governor of Missouri from 1832 to 1836. One of Governor Dunklin's special interests was the establishment of a public school system in Missouri.
(Strauss portrait, Courtesy State Historical Society)

cause he long advocated this policy, the Senator became known as Old Bullion Benton.

In the election of 1832, Benton found a new coalition of political opponents in Missouri. This coalition included some people who previously had supported Jackson, but were now outraged over Jackson's attempts to weaken or destroy the B. U. S. Party names appeared in this election. Those who were opposed to Benton, the National-Republicans, tended to be the large merchants, those engaged in the mining industry, and the people who operated plantations along the Mississippi and Missouri rivers. Benton's supporters, the Democrats, were the small farmers of the outlying counties beyond the two major rivers, and the growing number of working-class town and city dwellers. In this election of 1832 Daniel Dunklin—originally the operator of a tavern in Potosi—was chosen governor. Dunklin, like his predecessor Miller, was a Benton-Jackson man. During his term of office he is noted particularly for his encouragement of public education and his plans for the establishment of a state bank. In the same election Benton was re-elected for a third term in the United States Senate.

By this time, Thomas Hart Benton was known as Andrew Jackson's leading spokesman in the Senate. This new friendship is remarkable in view of their earlier difficulties. During 1833 it is reported that Jackson finally had the bullet removed which had lodged in his arm during the earlier encounter with Benton at Nashville. According to the story, after the bullet was removed one of Jackson's associates offered to return it to Senator Benton. Benton declined the souvenir, declaring that "twenty years peaceful possession" gave Jackson full ownership of the metal.

In 1833 a cholera epidemic struck Missouri. Among those who died was Senator Buckner of Cape Girardeau. Under the terms of the state constitution, the governor could name the succeeding senator. Governor Dunklin selected Lewis Linn of Ste. Genevieve. Linn, like Benton and Dunklin, was a Jackson supporter. Now, for the first time, Benton had a Missouri associate in the Senate with whom he agreed politically.

Benton's next major show of strength occurred in the year 1836. At this time Andrew Jackson was retiring, and his hand-picked successor was Martin Van Buren of New York. Benton, now one of the strong men of the Democratic Party, campaigned for Van Buren and those who supported the Benton-Jackson program. The success of this campaign can be seen in the complete sweep made by the Benton ticket. Lilburn W. Boggs, of Jackson County, was chosen governor, Albert Harrison and John Miller were sent to Congress, and Lewis Linn was named senator for another term by the Assembly.

The Boggs administration was one of the most eventful in the early history of the state. Boggs was governor at the time the new capitol building was being erected in Jefferson City. Although the structure was planned to cost only $75,000, the governor spent over $200,000. An investigation absolved Boggs of any irregularities—he had simply wished to build a fine capitol. Another event was the Mormon crisis, which ultimately resulted in the expulsion of that religious group from the state. The Bank of the State of Missouri was also chartered during the Boggs administration, giving a new financial structure to the state. Other matters of importance were the establishment of the first state university west of the Mississippi and the passage of Missouri's first public school law.

Shortly after President Van Buren took office in 1837 a great depression struck the nation. That depression was felt in Missouri, but not so severely as in other parts of the country. Benton's popularity with the common people of the state was sufficiently strong to counteract the adverse effect of the depression

Jefferson City in 1850 from Dana, The United States Illustrated
(Courtesy State Historical Society)

on his constituents' confidence. Harrison and Miller, both Benton men, were both re-elected to Congress.

By the 1830's Missouri was a two-party state. The Democrats were stronger in the inland counties. The Whigs—as the National-Republicans came to be called—had great strength in the commercial areas and the river counties. There was a growth in the number of Whig votes in the elections from 1828 to 1840; but, although the Whigs were always a threat to the Democrats and occasionally defeated them, the period up to 1840 was a time of great popularity and political power for Thomas Hart Benton and the Democratic Party.

The Platte Purchase

In the year 1820 Congress established a policy of moving Indian tribes west of the Mississippi River. At that time there were only two states west of the Mississippi—Louisiana and Missouri. The Congressional Act of 1820 authorized President Jackson to give the Indians assurance that the new lands they would receive in the West could be held in perpetuity. Immediately, the Federal Government began the plan of moving the eastern Indians across the Mississippi. At the Treaty of Prairie du Chien in 1830 the so-called Platte region was set aside as a permanent Indian zone.

The Platte region was a wedge-shaped district presently occupied by six northwest Missouri counties—Platte, Buchanan, Andrew, Holt, Nodaway, and Atchison. It was hemmed in between the Missouri River and the original western boundary of the state of Missouri. The Missouri Enabling Act of 1820 had drawn the western boundary of Missouri as a straight line passing north and south through the point where the Kansas River empties into the Missouri River. The Platte area was highly attractive because of the rich bottoms lying along the Nodaway and Platte rivers and because of its close proximity to the Missouri River. This latter factor would greatly facilitate transportation and communication for any who settled the area. The Indians recognized the desirability of the fertile area, and in their legends they referred to the region as the "beginning of the road to Paradise."

In the 1820's and 1830's a growing number of settlers moved into the northwestern parts of Missouri. They were aware of the boundaries but did not always respect them. The residents of the

The Platte Purchase as pictured in the mural by George Gray in the Robidoux Hotel, St. Joseph. Notice the inset map.

border counties of Clinton, DeKalb, and Gentry found it easier to transport their goods to market by way of the Missouri River, crossing Indian territory to get there, than to make the long overland trip south to Clay County. There were also some settlers who quietly moved into the Indian region and occupied the fertile lowlands, clearly in violation of Indian rights.

Obviously, the settlers of northwest Missouri felt it was wrong to waste such fine land on the redskins, and exerted great pressure on both the state and federal governments to have the region annexed to Missouri and opened to settlers. These pioneers did not feel personally responsible for solemn government promises made to the Indians.

As early as the year 1831 the Missouri legislature began to petition Congress for the annexation of the Platte region. In 1834 the Missouri constitution was amended to allow for the extension of the state boundaries. It was clear that the leaders of the state were looking at the Platte region with covetous eyes. Finally, in June, 1836, after much work by Senators Benton and Linn, Congress repudiated its earlier promises and agreed that the Platte region would be added to the State of Missouri as soon as the Indian titles to the section could be extinguished.

Immediately, government Indian agents began working with

the various tribes, cajoling or threatening in order to secure their withdrawal. William Clark and Henry Dodge were leaders in the government campaign to secure the Indian land titles. A Sioux group gave up their title in 1836 in exchange for $400 in presents. The Iowa and the Sac and Fox relinquished their claims for the sum of $7,500 and the promise of new homes west of the Missouri River. That same fall a group of other tribes— the Missouri, the Omaha, the Oto, the Yankton, and the Santee, accepted the inevitable and sold their claims for $4,520 in merchandise. When several other tribes, including the Medawah-Kanton, the Sissitong, and the Wahapakoota, finally capitulated in November of 1836, all Indian claims to the region were extinguished.

On March 28, 1837, the Platte area was officially declared to be part of Missouri by the new president, Martin Van Buren. In great haste white settlers rushed in to seize the best areas. The highly productive soil proved to be such an attraction that settlers soon were to be found throughout the entire two-million acre area.

The Honey War

One of the most ludicrous episodes in Missouri history occurred in 1839. In that year the governor of Missouri and the governor of the Territory of Iowa entered into a ridiculous dispute which, for a time, threatened to result in warfare. The disagreement concerned the exact location of the Iowa boundary line. The act of Congress which authorized Missouri to organize as a state decreed that the northern boundary was "the parallel of latitude which passes through the rapids of the river Des Moines, making the said line to correspond with the Indian boundary line."

The northeast corner of the state had few settlers until the 1830's. When people began to move into this area, the legislature passed a law in 1836 authorizing Governor Lilburn W. Boggs to have the northern boundary surveyed. The Missouri surveyors went to work and, although they had difficulty identifying "the rapids of the river Des Moines," they did establish a boundary line which was officially approved by the state legislature in February, 1839.

The region to the north of Missouri was part of the Territory of Michigan from 1834 to 1836, and in the latter year was declared part of the Territory of Wisconsin. In 1838 the Territory of Iowa was formed. Congress, wishing to delineate clearly this new territory from the state of Missouri, insisted upon a federal survey and appointed Major Albert Miller Lea to survey the area. Major Lea laid out four lines, any one of which, he said, could be considered the boundary. The discrepancy in the survey lines led the state and local officials of both Iowa and Missouri to contest the boundary.

The area in dispute was approximately nine miles wide at the Des Moines River and eleven miles wide in the western part of the state. There were few settlers in the region and only one town, Farmington, presently in Van Buren County, Iowa.

Trouble occurred in late summer of 1839 when Governor Robert Lucas of Iowa and Governor Boggs of Missouri each issued proclamations warning the officers of the other's government not to extend their jurisdiction over the area claimed by both. Sheriff Uriah Gregory of Clark County, Missouri, however, felt an obligation to collect taxes in the zone considered part of Missouri by Governor Boggs. Sheriff Gregory attempted to make his collections in the region near Farmington, but his requests made to a group of settlers at a house-raising earned him a hostile reception in August, 1839. He decided to retreat. Three months later he returned to Farmington, and was immediately arrested by the sheriff of Van Buren County, Iowa. He was charged with usurpation of authority and jailed for a short time at Muscatine. This act alerted both governments. Governor Boggs called up part of the Missouri militia in order to protect the territorial integrity of the state. Governor Lucas requested that Congress be authorized to draw a line, but this conciliatory gesture was turned down by the adamant Boggs. Lucas then mobilized his own militia. War seemed imminent.

Some 2200 Missouri militiamen were called to arms; but, when the units from Lewis, Clark, and Knox counties assembled in Clark County, there were only 600 to 800 men. There was much grumbling among the Missouri troops, for whom the state had provided no supplies. In desperation, the militia from Lewis County broke into a store at La Grange to get food, blankets, and other provisions. The outraged merchant was later partially reimbursed. Governor Lucas of Iowa immediately called up 1200 men to face the Missourians. At the time when battle seemed inevitable, cooler heads on both sides saw the folly of fighting

Governor Lilburn W. Boggs, a native of Lexington, Kentucky, was a storekeeper and an Indian trader at Fort Osage and Harmony Mission before entering politics.
(Courtesy State Historical Society)

over the issue. Committees from both militia units negotiated a truce. Before the two armies parted for home, however, they adopted a novel means of displaying their contempt for the two governors who had interrupted their pursuits and nearly engaged them in war. A slab of venison was cut in two and suspended in a tree. The label "Governor Lucas of Iowa" was placed under one slab of meat, and the label "Governor Boggs of Missouri" was placed under the other. After duly executing the two effigies, the soldiers solemnly took them down and buried them with great funeral solemnity and all the honors of war.

The conflict cost the state of Missouri $20,000—the price of alerting the militia. The boundary line was ultimately decided by a court case which reached the United States Supreme Court in 1849. The decision resulted in an almost equal division of the disputed region. In order to avoid future conflict, the court ordered the line to be marked carefully. Twenty-two cast iron pillars were ordered to be set on the boundary at about ten-mile intervals. To insure against misunderstanding, the pillars had the word "Missouri" inscribed on the south side and "Iowa" on the north side. Even after the court decision, the line was not officially surveyed and set until 1850. At last, almost thirty years after her acceptance as a state, Missouri had an officially recognized northern boundary.

The Honey War was so named because of an episode that occurred early in the conflict. A Missourian who cut down several bee trees in the disputed area was sued in an Iowa court, found guilty, and assessed $1.50 in costs and damages. The court decision inspired John I. Campbell to write a poem which was published December 26, 1839, in the Palmyra *Missouri Whig and General Advertiser*. Sung to the tune of "Yankee Doodle," it was a favorite in Missouri during the 1840's.

"The Honey War"

Ye freemen of the happy land,
Which flows with milk and honey,
Arise! To Arms! Your ponies mount,
Regard not blood or money.
Old Governor Lucas, tiger-like
Is prowling round our borders,
But Governor Boggs is wide awake,
Just listen to his orders:
Why shed our brothers' blood in haste,
Because big men require it;
Be not in haste our blood to waste,
No prudent men desire it.
Now if the Governors want to fight,
Just let them meet in person,
And when noble Boggs old Lucas flogs,
'Twill teach the scamp a lesson.
Then let the victor cut the trees,
And have three bits in money,
And wear a crown from town to town,
Anointed with pure honey.
And then no widows will be made,
No orphans unprotected;
Old Lucas will be nicely flogged,
And from our line ejected
Our honey trade will then be laid
Upon a solid basis;
And Governor Boggs,
Where'er he jogs,
Will meet with smiling faces.

BIBLIOGRAPHY

Anderson, Hattie M. "The Jackson Men in Missouri in 1828," *Missouri Historical Review*, Vol. XXXIV (April, 1940), pp. 301-334.

Boggs, William M. "Sketch of Governor Lilburn W. Boggs," *Missouri Historical Review*, Vol. IV (January, 1910), pp. 106-110.

Broadhead, G. C. "The Location of the Capital of Missouri," *Missouri Historical Review*, Vol. II (January, 1908), pp. 158-163.

Chambers, William Nisbet. *Old Bullion Benton*. Boston and Toronto: Little, Brown, and Company, 1956.

Chambers, William Nisbet. "Thomas H. Benton: Editor," *Missouri Historical Review*, Vol. XLVI (July, 1952), pp. 335-345.

Fagg, Thomas J. C. "Thomas Hart Benton," *Missouri Historical Review*, Vol. I (October, 1906), pp. 22-37.

Gordon, Joseph F. "Political Career of Lilburn W. Boggs," *Missouri Historical Review*, Vol. LII (January, 1958), pp. 111-122.

Hodder, Frank H. "Side Lights on the Missouri Compromise," *Missouri Historical Review*, Vol. V (April, 1911), pp 138-149.

King, Roy T. "Robert William Wells, Jurist, Public Servant, and Designer of the Missouri State Seal," *Missouri Historical Review*, Vol. XXX (January, 1936), pp. 107-131.

Lehmann, F. W. "The Constitution of 1820," *Missouri Historical Review*, Vol. XVI (January, 1922), pp. 239-246.

Loeb, Isidor. "Constitutions and Constitutional Conventions in Missouri," *Missouri Historical Review*, Vol. XVI (January, 1922), pp. 189-238.

Loeb, Isidor. "The Development of Missouri's State Administrative Organization," *Missouri Historical Review*, Vol. XXIII (October, 1928), pp. 49-60.

McCandless, Perry. "Political Philosophy and Political Personality of Thomas Hart Benton," *Missouri Historical Review*, Vol. L (January, 1956), pp. 145-158.

McCandless, Perry. "Rise of Thomas Hart Benton in Missouri Politics," *Missouri Historical Review*, Vol. L (October, 1955), pp. 16-29.

McClure, C. H. "Early Opposition to Thomas Hart Benton," *Missouri Historical Review*, Vol. X (April, 1916), pp. 151-196.

McKee, Howard I. "The Platte Purchase," *Missouri Historical Review*, Vol. XXXII (October, 1937), pp. 129-147.

McMurtrie, Douglas C. "The Early Career of Joseph Charless, the First Printer in Missouri," *Missouri Historical Review*, Vol. XXVI (July, 1932), pp. 342-353.

Magers, Roy V. "An Early Missouri Political Feud," *Missouri Historical Review*, Vol. XXIII (January, 1929), pp. 261-269.

Meigs, William M. *The Life of Thomas Hart Benton*. Philadelphia and London: J. B. Lippincott Company, 1904.

Newhard, Leota. "Beginning of the Whig Party in Missouri, 1824-1840," *Missouri Historical Review*, Vol. XXV (January, 1931), pp. 254-280.

Rader, Perry S. "The Location of a Permanent Seat of Government," *Missouri Historical Review*, Vol. XXI (October, 1926), pp. 9-18.

Rader, Perry S. "The Great Seal of the State of Missouri," *Missouri Historical Review*, Vol. XXIII (January, April, 1929), pp. 270-297, 447-462.

Ravanel, Samuel W. "Honorable David Barton," *Missouri Historical Review,* Vol. VIII (July, 1914), pp. 216-219.

Roach, Cornelius. "Missouri's Eleven State Capitols," *Missouri Historical Review,* Vol. VII (July, 1913), pp. 224-231.

Roosevelt, Theodore. *Thomas Hart Benton.* Boston and New York: Houghton, Mifflin and Company, 1886.

Sharp, James Roger. "Gov. Daniel Dunklin's Jacksonian Democracy in Missouri, 1832-1836," *Missouri Historical Review,* Vol. LVI (April, 1962), pp. 217-229.

Shoemaker, Floyd C. "A City That Is Set on a Hill Cannot Be Hid," *Missouri Historical Review,* Vol. XXXVII (January, 1943), pp. 123-133.

Shoemaker, Floyd C. "Fathers of the State," *Missouri Historical Review,* Vol. X (October, 1915), pp. 1-32.

Shoemaker, Floyd C. "First Constitution of Missouri," *Missouri Historical Review,* Vol. VI (January, 1912), pp. 51-63.

Shoemaker, Floyd C. *Missouri and Missourians.* Vol. I. Chicago: The Lewis Publishing Company, 1943.

Shoemaker, Floyd C. *Missouri's Struggle for Statehood, 1804-1821.* Jefferson City: The Hugh Stephens Printing Company, 1916.

Shoemaker, Floyd C. "Traditions Concerning the Missouri Question," *Missouri Historical Review,* Vol. XVI (January, 1922), pp. 253-262.

Squires, Monas N. "A New View of the Election of Barton and Benton to the United States Senate," *Missouri Historical Review,* Vol. XXVII (October, 1932), pp. 28-45.

Stevens, Walter B. "Alexander McNair," *Missouri Historical Review,* Vol. XVII (October, 1922), pp. 3-21.

Stevens, Walter B. "The Travail of Missouri for Statehood," *Missouri Historical Review,* Vol. XV (October, 1920), pp. 3-35.

Thomas, John L. "Some Historic Lines in Missouri," *Missouri Historical Review,* Vol. III (October, 1908; January, July, 1909), pp. 5-53, 210-233, 251-274.

Viles, Jonas. "Missouri in 1820," *Missouri Historical Review,* Vol. XV (October, 1920), pp. 36-52.

Viles, Jonas. "Missouri Capitals and Capitols," *Missouri Historical Review,* Vol. XIII (January, April, 1919), pp. 135-156, 232-250.

CHAPTER VII

Missouri and the West

Oh, don't you remember sweet Betsey from Pike
Who crossed the big mountains with her brother Ike,
With two yoke of cattle, a large yellow dog,
A tall Shanghai rooster and one spotted hog?
—American folksong

For the first half of the nineteenth century Missouri served as a great funnel to channel the stream of traders and settlers going west. Missouri was the entrance to the West both because of her central location and her waterways. Since Missouri was situated in the middle of the Mississippi Valley, some westbound travelers found easy access to her supply centers and river highways from the Gulf of Mexico. Others who journeyed westward learned that they could travel the Ohio River to reach Missouri. Once in the state, migrants going west soon discovered that the broad and navigable Missouri River would provide almost three hundred miles of water transportation before it was necessary to take up the more difficult overland trek.

The waves of migrants carried an enthusiasm that infected the settlers through whose land they flowed. Many Missourians —like Sweet Betsey and Ike from Pike County—were swept into the stream of pioneers and carried across the Rockies.

The Fur Trade

During the seventeenth and eighteenth centuries, long before the tide of western migrants flowed through Missouri, French *coureurs de bois* roamed the wilderness in a quest for furs rather than farms. Indeed, the elegant pelts from the American wilds were the resource most sought after—gold and silver excepted. The *voyageurs* who provided the power for the transportation of goods into the interior were primarily active in providing transportation for the French fur interests. Later, during the first century of the history of St. Louis, fur trading constituted the major economic activity of the city. The very founding of St.

Raccoon skin cap and buckskin
pants and moccasins are worn
by this well-armed trapper. Notice his flintlock rifle and the
pack of furs slung over his back.
*(Courtesy Remington Art Memorial,
Ogdenburg, N. Y.)*

Louis is associated with the attempts of Laclede and Chouteau
to establish a post for the trading of furs. From the earliest days
of Missouri, fur trading made two important contributions to the
area. It provided an economic activity for the employment of
many colonists, and it furnished an incentive for exploration.

The fur trade attracted many bold men. Any age and any
culture will produce daring young men eager to be part of a
dangerous adventure. The fur traders answered the call of adventure by setting off into barely known—or unexplored—regions in whose unknown depths death might wait in the form of
a savage, or a wild beast, or a sudden terrible storm. There was
also the lure of travel. North America, with its remarkable contrasts of pine-clad mountains and grass-clothed plains, of roaring
silver rivers and quiet sapphire lakes, was an intriguing opportunity for travel. Furthermore, there was always the possibility
that some obscure, isolated Indian tribe might be willing to part
with its furs for a few trade items. Stories were well known of
fortunate traders who craftily secured great piles of valuable

furs for a few trinkets. Thus, despite its promise of hazard and hardship, the fur trade was a popular occupation for men with spirit and energy.

During the French and Spanish periods of occupation the fur trade was carried on both by individual traders and by large companies. At times traders were given a monopoly of trading rights with specific tribes. More frequently, the government granted licenses to any reputable person, and the trader sought out the Indians with whom he wished to trade. We already have noted that Maxent, Laclede, and Company held a monopoly on the Missouri trade for the first years after the establishment of St. Louis. Auguste Chouteau in 1794 was given a monopoly over the Osage trade in return for his construction of Carondelet. In 1802 the Osage monopoly was granted to Manuel Lisa, but it was returned to Chouteau in 1804.

The fur trade did not flourish during the Spanish period. The British traders moved in from Canada and with their superior trade goods secured the good will of the Indians. The St. Louis traders had difficulty meeting British competition in the valuable trading territory north of the Des Moines River and in the upper reaches of the Missouri River. The Spanish Government, because of grave financial difficulties, was unwilling to support adequately explorations of the West and the establishment of forts to subdue the tribes west and north of the settled areas of Missouri. As a result, the Spanish traders found such harassment from the Indians of the Upper Missouri and Upper Mississippi and such competition from the British that they were unsuccessful in developing a lucrative trade. This failure was unfortunate, since St. Louis was the natural drainage point for the products of the Missouri Valley.

Beginning in 1804 with the American control of the Louisiana Territory, there was a new growth of the fur industry. We can point to five new aspects of the fur trade during this period. First, there was a great enlargement of the area exploited by most traders and trappers. With the increased protection afforded by occasional American military units in the West and the greater frequency of parties of white explorers and pioneers in the Northwest, it soon became relatively common for Missourians to roam the Upper Missouri Valley and the Rocky Mountains. Second, during the American period, the fur companies made greater use of white trappers, whom they found to be a much more reliable source of furs than the unpredictable Indians. Third, as the fur traders and trappers moved farther into the West greater capitalization and organization were necessary to develop the industry. Thus, larger and larger companies were organized, until the fur industry became a monopoly in the 1830's. Fourth, the American fur companies added certain innovations such as pack trains and the rendezvous system to drain the furs from the more isolated areas. Fifth, the demand for beaver skins for the hats worn by gentlemen of station and style led the fur traders to place greater emphasis on the acquisition of that valuable pelt.

In following a typical fur expedition to the upper reaches of the Missouri River—where Lewis and Clark reported mountain valleys teeming with beaver—we can see the problems and the organizational techniques of the industry. During the Spanish period, the St. Louis traders had great difficulty attempting to reach the Upper Missouri because tribes along the way wished to obtain the white man's trade supplies for their own use or for sale to other tribes. In order to get by nations such as the Arikara and the Sioux, the traders organized large flotillas with mounted guns. Such large groups were able to transport additional supplies to trade for larger numbers of beaver skins from the Upper Missouri region, but the payroll for the necessary boatmen, the traders, and trappers was a major expense. For this reason, large amounts of capital were required for trading on the Upper Missouri. Frequently, the major stockholders accompanied the expedition in order to give immediate leadership and to protect their own investments.

The keelboats, loaded with trade goods, moved up the river with difficulty. Although sails were attached, the main power of locomotion came from poling, paddling, or pulling (cordelling) the craft. When a broad, dry, treeless shore was available, it was simple for the crews of twenty to forty men to pull the keelboats, often loaded with as much as twenty tons of freight. However, when sharp bluffs, swamps, or trees lined the shore, cordelling was more difficult. Often the *voyageurs* stumbled, strained, and crawled along the slimy banks both in and out of the water as they haltingly inched their craft upstream. They wryly described themselves as "half horse and half alligator." The task was made all the more difficult by the rafts or islands of timber floating on the river and such other impediments as sandbars, hidden snags, and rock-strewn rapids. Moving at a pace of ten to fifteen miles a day, ever alert for a possible Indian ambush, the members of the trading parties must have found their voyage of 1,500 to 2,000 miles long and exhausting.

Fur Traders on the Missouri Attacked by Indians by W. M. Cary from Harpers Weekly, May 23, 1868

Arriving at their destination, the men would build a typical frontier log fort to protect their goods and to provide a safe place of residence during the trading season to come. The traders and trappers did not place all their furs in forts for safekeeping. Many employed the cache system described in Chapter III. In addition to their regular fur trade activities, the men of the forts planted gardens, bought food and buckskin garments from the Indians, and carried on the usual chores of living. Cats were highly prized animals by the men of the fur trade. Many traders brought tabbies from St. Louis to protect their possessions and furs from the multitude of mice in the West.

The fur companies, depending on their plan of organization, usually employed boatmen and traders. Later companies also hired white trappers and skinners. All the men worked under hazards. There were dangers of ambush or a hostile reception for those white traders who visited Indian villages to purchase pelts. The white trappers who attempted to snare the beaver needed both diplomacy and daring, since they were considered interlopers by the Indians who claimed the area.

The furs most frequently secured were beaver, mink, otter, civet, raccoon, fox, and badger. Since beaver skins were in great demand for coats and hats, the price was high. Indians did not like beaver-trapping since it involved working in the icy, fast-moving mountain streams. Snaring beaver ashore was usually unsuccessful, for a trapped beaver would not hesitate to gnaw off his leg to achieve his freedom. The white men adopted a technique of trapping the beaver under the water where he would drown before freeing himself. The white trappers spent the trapping season, from September 1 to December 1 and from late March to June 1, in the streams setting and resetting their traps. Because of the strong, rapid current of the snow-chilled streams it was dangerous, cold work. After a beaver was caught, the animal was skinned and the pelt was scraped, cured, and pressed into bundles of eighty skins. The bundles were then transported down-river to the fur warehouses of St. Louis.

The fur industry was a "feast or famine" endeavor. When a company was successful in transporting its take to St. Louis, the investors were assured of great profits. The mansions of St. Louis testify that some of the fur merchants were remarkably successful. People such as the Chouteaus, Bernard Pratte, William Sublette, Robert Campbell, and William Ashley were richly rewarded for their original investments in the fur trade. For those less favored by Lady Luck, the story had another ending. Indian attacks, boatwrecks, and highjacking by rival companies resulted in many bankruptcies.

Although hundreds of Missourians gave their lives to the fur trade, three men should be remembered for their special contributions of leadership—Manuel Lisa of the Missouri Fur Company, General William Ashley of the Rocky Mountain Fur Company, and John Jacob Astor of the American Fur Company.

Manuel Lisa, a Creole of Spanish descent who was born in New Orleans, made his way to St. Louis in the 1790's. After a decade of trading in St. Louis and with the Osage Indians, he became interested in the possibilities of the Upper Missouri region. In 1807 he conducted his first expedition to that region with a party of forty-two men. Impressed by the enthusiastic reports of William Clark, he determined to tap the great reservoir of furs in the Northwest. After a difficult voyage, he built a two-room fort at the point where the Big Horn River empties into the Yellowstone. Lisa returned to St. Louis with only twenty packs of the 300 he originally gathered, but with the assurance that a successful trade could be established in the North.

Upon Lisa's return to St. Louis, a number of prominent citizens, including Auguste and Pierre Chouteau, Andrew Henry, and William Clark invested money to form the Missouri Fur Company in 1808. The company sent a larger expedition of 350 men up the Missouri in 1809 in nine carefully-packed keelboats. Lisa was an excellent organizer and a dauntless leader. With seemingly endless energy he directed the building of forts along the river to protect his supply line and to carry on the trade. Lisa was usually successful in negotiating with the Indians. H. M. Chittenden, historian of the fur trade, describes him as a man of courage, diplomacy, and superior intelligence. Lisa, himself, described his treatment of the Indians as follows:

> I appear as the benefactor, and not as the pillager of the Indians. . . . I lend them traps, only demanding a preference in their trade. My establishments are the refuge of the weak, and of the old men no longer able to follow their lodges; and by these means I have acquired the confidence and friendship of these nations and the consequent choice of their trade.

Lisa, however, probably overestimated his own diplomatic abilities. His attempts to trade with the hated and feared Blackfoot Tribe—who were still angry over the killing of several of their warriors by the Lewis and Clark group—only provoked an attack upon him and his forts. Due to the hostility of this tribe, the Missouri Fur Company was unsuccessful in the Upper Missouri region, but the company did continue to trade on the Middle Missouri for many years. The United States Government displayed its confidence in Lisa by requesting him to secure treaties of peace and alliance from the western tribes during the War of 1812, whereupon Lisa brought forty-three "chiefs and headmen" to St. Louis for the negotiation of treaties of alliance.

The Missouri Fur Company was reorganized several times. Lisa continued as the leader of the company until his death in 1820. The company was unable to survive the growing competition in the fur industry, and the organization disappeared in the early 1830's.

William Henry Ashley, a native of Virginia who came to

Manuel Lisa (c. 1776-1820) one of the founders of the Missouri Fur Company is said to have traveled more than 26,000 miles in three years of trading expeditions on the Missouri River.
(Courtesy State Historical Society)

Ste. Genevieve about the year 1803, was another leader of the fur trade industry. During his early years in Missouri, Ashley mined saltpeter and lead, manufactured gunpowder, and acted as surveyor. He was a friend of Andrew Henry, from whom he learned much about the fur trade. In the first state election in Missouri in 1820 Ashley was chosen lieutenant-governor. During his term of office, Ashley, with Andrew Henry, organized expeditions to the Upper Missouri in 1822 and 1823. The partnership thus initiated became known in time as the Rocky Mountain Fur Company.

Ashley and Henry placed the following notice in the *Missouri Republican*, February 13, 1822:

> To enterprising young men. The subscriber wishes to engage one hundred young men to ascend the Missouri River to its source, there to be employed for one, two or three years. For particulars enquire of Major Andrew Henry near the lead mines in the County of Washington, who will ascend with, and command, the party; or of the subscriber near St. Louis.
>
> (Signed) William H. Ashley

Ashley and Henry intended to use as trappers free white men who would work under contract to them. The company did not wish to depend upon Indians as the source of supply for their furs.

The Indians—particularly the Arikaras, who were disgruntled over their treatment by the Missouri Fur Company—caused so much trouble in his first two attempts to establish a trade on the Upper Missouri that Ashley developed a new system for trapping and collecting the furs of the Northwest. Since the tribes along the Missouri River were hostile, Ashley determined to bypass these Indians by crossing the Great Plains to the Rocky Mountains region with pack trains of mules. Another innovation by Ashley was the rendezvous system. The fur forts were a source of Indian-white friction because the Indians grew to be suspicious of forts built on the territory they claimed. Ashley decided to eliminate fur forts. His new plan involved the sending of large numbers of trappers called "Mountain Men" into the West to trap beaver along the Big Horn, Platte, Wind, Sweetwater, and Green rivers. Each year a rendezvous would be held when representatives of the fur company would meet the trappers at a prearranged site. The trappers would then sell their furs to the company, and the company would distribute the necessary supplies. In defense of his system of operation, Ashley wrote in December, 1825, "Nor have we in the whole four years lost a single man by death except those who came to their end prematurely by being either shot or drowned."

Ashley was remarkably successful in finding a large number of resourceful, capable men who agreed to work in his employ. William and Milton Sublette, Jedediah Smith, David Jackson, Hugh Glass, Robert Campbell, Thomas (Broken Hand) Fitzpatrick, Jim Bridger, Joe Meek, and Christopher (Kit) Carson are men, now famous in the history of the West, who were at one time employees of the Rocky Mountain Fur Company. Ashley's company proved to be a highly successful enterprise, and by 1826 he had made a fortune. In that year the company was sold to William Sublette, Jedediah Smith, and David Jackson. These men continued the fur trading procedures established by Ashley.

Under changing management, the company continued as a profitable venture until the 1830's. In 1824 a group of employees of the company, under the direction of Thomas Fitzpatrick, were the first to discover South Pass—the important route through the Rocky Mountains. Ashley should be remembered also for his role as an explorer; he was the first white man to explore the Green River and almost paid with his life for this distinction. After retiring from the fur trade, he re-entered the field of politics and served as a National-Republican congressman from Missouri during the years 1831-1837.

(Courtesy Denver Public Library Western Collection)

"The Trappers' Summer Rendezvous" from Frances Fuller Victor, The River of the West, Hartford, 1870

German immigrant John Jacob Astor arrived in America in 1783. During a shipboard conversation, he learned of the opportunities for gain in the fur trade. When he arrived in New York he sold the flutes he had brought to America and used the money to enter the fur business. Astor had visions of a great fur trade network spanning the continent. Methodically, he established control over the fur trade of the Great Lakes region and the Mississippi Valley. Then he attempted to cross the continent by establishing a line of forts stretching all the way to the mouth of the Columbia River. He hoped to defeat the two British companies—the Hudson Bay Company and the Northwest Fur Company—by his large-scale operations. Since furs were greatly desired in Asia, he planned to transport the furs from the Columbia River to the Far East for sale. His scheme was a brilliant one, but, unfortunately for Astor, the War of 1812 erupted shortly after he established the Columbia River post named Astoria. Because of the threat of seizure by the British-directed land and sea forces, the Astorians under duress were forced to sell their post to their British rivals.

Astor was not easily defeated. In 1822 he opened a branch of his American Fur Company in St. Louis. He was ruthless in his tactics. After combining with several of the smaller firms, he proceeded to crush all competitors, using price cutting, liquor, and Indian ambush to secure his ends. With these techniques, the American Fur Company did achieve a near monopoly of the fur trade by 1834. Astor and his men were much hated by the trappers and small traders of the West. One of the major reasons for his success was his great financial resources. He could take great losses, and he could sacrifice profits for a time, knowing that eventually the financial rewards would be great.

Keelboat transportation up the Missouri River was so laborious and so treacherous that the company decided to experiment with another technique. In 1831 the American Fur Company sent its first steamboat up the Missouri River. The boat, named the *Yellowstone,* went as far as the mouth of the Teton River in present-day South Dakota. The *Yellowstone* returned to St. Louis with great quantities of furs and buffalo skins, together with 10,000 pounds of buffalo tongues—a great delicacy on the frontier. With this new mode of transportation, the later trappers and traders found it much easier to ascend the Missouri. Astor later sold out his fur interests to Pratte, Chouteau, and Company. He left Missouri for New York where he devoted his talents and attention to real estate speculation and continued to develop the great fortune associated with his name.

Of all those people involved in the fur trade, the Mountain Men led the most colorful lives. They lived in isolation in a region of breathtaking splendor—and hair-raising peril. Never completely sure of the friendship of the Indians about them, they were constantly forced to court the Indians for their own protection. The predators of the area—wolves, mountain lions, and bears—were another hazard. On one occasion a mother bear grabbed Hugh Glass and tore out a chunk of his flesh which she tossed to her cub. Fortunately for Glass, he was rescued by a friend before the baby bear was served another course. The weather was another problem for these hardbitten men of the mountains. Winter brought the twin threats of starvation and freezing; spring, the hazards of lightning-sparked forest fires, thaw-swollen floods, and landslides.

Historians have estimated that the mortality rate among the Mountain Men was very high, running perhaps to seventy-five per cent during the time they were in the mountains. Even those who were spared the agony of death from the fangs of a rabid wolf, or a rattlesnake, and from famine, freezing, fire, or flood, were troubled by the scourge of rheumatism. Working all day in the cold mountain streams, without a change of clothing, chilled bone, nerve, and muscle until limbs ached. Observers have remarked that the buckskin clothing of the Mountain Men often became vermin-infested. When the irritation became too great to bear, they would remove their clothing and place it on an ant heap for the ants to clean. For these men, the annual rendezvous was an eagerly anticipated carnival, market, and celebration. In the midst of gambling, drinking, and trading, the trappers prepared for the year to come, purchasing the necessary supplies and tools and sometimes gambling away the few dollars remaining.

The importance of the fur industry in Missouri waned with the advent of the silk hat and the virtual disappearance of fur-bearing animals in some regions. However, the fur trade constituted a most important episode in the history of Missouri and the mountain territory of the West. The traders established posts about which towns and cities later developed. They discovered the passes through the mountains, and they marked the trails which later became roads to cross the Great Plains and the Rocky Mountains. They brought guns and knives to the Indians of the West, making them a more formidable enemy of the western migrants. They brought also whiskey and disease to the western tribes, thus beginning the slow process of defeating that enemy. In the fur trade of the early nineteenth century, most of these traders, trappers, and boatmen came from Missouri, and Missouri prospered for a time because of the packs of skins her sons transported back to St. Louis.

The steamboat Yellowstone on the upper Missouri from a painting by Charles Bodmer

(Courtesy State Historical Society)

The Mormons

Joseph Smith was a young man of 18 when, according to his own statement, he had a vision of an angel. This revelation occurred in the year 1823 in upstate New York. The angel directed him to a set of golden plates buried near Manchester, New York. The plates were inscribed with a strange script which Smith could not read, but with the help of a magic shield, sword, and a pair of spectacles provided by the angel, the young man was able to decipher the strange writing. Aided by a friend, Smith translated and copied all of the text, which subsequently was published as the Book of Mormon. This book, accepted as scripture by Joseph Smith's followers, is particularly interesting in that it declares the American Indians to be descendants of the Lost Tribes of Israel.

Although many of Joseph Smith's neighbors and friends were contemptuous of his theological concepts, Smith organized a new religious group known as the Mormons, or more formally, the Church of Jesus Christ of Latter Day Saints. Because of the hostility of the people in his New York community, Smith with his few disciples moved to Kirtland, Ohio, where he established a growing church and became involved in a number of business enterprises, including a bank.

The Mormons had a special message for the American Indians, and in the winter of 1830-31, the church sent missionaries to Missouri to make preparations for work among the Kansas Indians immediately to the West. While several of the missionaries went on to labor in Kansas, the remaining Mormons worked in Independence, Missouri, to support their associates. One of the group returned to Kirtland to relate to Smith his impressions of the West. In response to favorable reports of western Missouri as a land "flowing with milk and honey," Joseph Smith and a group of his associates hiked across Missouri from St. Louis and arrived in Independence in 1831.

Joseph Smith was delighted with the city of Independence, and announced that by special revelation he had been told that Independence was "the land of promise and the place for the city of Zion." He called upon his Saints to buy land in this place appointed for the gathering of the faithful. A lot in Independence was consecrated as the future site of the temple in a special ceremony in August, 1831. Smith then returned to Ohio, but other Mormons began to arrive in numbers. One estimate places the

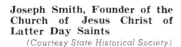

Joseph Smith, Founder of the
Church of Jesus Christ of
Latter Day Saints
(Courtesy State Historical Society)

number of Mormons in Jackson County in 1833 as 1,200, or approximately one-third of the population. While Smith was pleased with the natural endowments of Missouri, he was not favorably impressed by the people of the state. He described the inhabitants of western Missouri as people who "roamed about without the benefit of civilization, refinement, or religion." He considered them "nearly a century behind the time."

At first the people of the Independence area were merely curious about Joseph Smith's disciples. Within two years their interest turned to suspicion, fear, and hostility. The records of the time show several reasons for the development of this attitude. First, the Mormons were frank to speak of their intention to dominate the community, where they planned to build the New Jerusalem. They began purchasing large areas of land. The non-Mormons were apprehensive about their own future in the event that the Mormons' scheme to dominate Independence was realized. Second, the Mormons lived as a closely-knit community. Outsiders, ignorant of Mormon social and religious concepts, distrusted them for their clannishness. Third, the Mormons were outspoken abolitionists. Many of the settlers along the Missouri River were originally from the South and held slaves. The slaveholders accused the Saints of attempting to corrupt their slaves or incite them to rebellion. Fourth, there were many petty charges, including attempts to brand the Mormons as thieves and counterfeiters. Fifth, their unorthodox religious teachings were considered sacrilege by leaders of the other churches.

In July, 1833, a mass meeting was held in the Independence courthouse to enforce a list of grievances against the Mormons. This statement provided:

> That no Mormon shall in future move or settle in this county. That those now here who shall give a definite pledge of their intention within a reasonable time to remove out of the county shall be allowed to remain unmolested until they have sufficient time to sell their property and close their business without any material sacrifice.

In a sarcastic manner the Jackson County declaration ended with the taunting statement that Mormons who failed to comply with the request should speak to "their brethren who have the power of divination or of unknown tongues to inform them of the lot that awaits them." The proclamation was signed by approximately 500 citizens and presented to the leaders of the Mormon church.

When the Saints did not immediately agree to this ultimatum, mobs proceeded to destroy the Mormon newspaper, *The Evening and Morning Star;* and two Mormon leaders, Bishop Partridge and Charles Allen, were tarred and feathered. Intimidated by this violence, the Mormons agreed to leave the county. One-half of the Saints were to depart by January 1, 1834; the remainder were to leave by April 1, 1834. The Mormon leaders at Independence requested guidance from headquarters in Kirtland. The church officials in Ohio appealed to Governor Dunklin of Missouri, who promised protection for the Mormons and declared that he would use the powers of the state to prevent the Jackson County mobs from carrying out their threats. Thus reassured, the Mormons brought in more settlers and publicly announced, in October, 1833, their intention to remain.

Angered by this reversal, the anti-Mormon forces of Jackson County organized again in late October and early November, 1833. Mobs stormed Mormon homes, stores, and churches. All attempts on the part of the Mormons to secure protection from the violence were futile. Courts, peace officers, and militia all acted against them, refusing both protection and redress of their grievances. In the early winter of 1833, the Mormons were forced to flee Jackson County under most difficult circumstances and with considerable loss of money.

For almost three years the Mormons lived in the Clay County region with their headquarters at Liberty. At first the hospitality of the Clay County people was in marked contrast to the treatment received in Jackson County. However, in 1836, the ever-recurring request to leave was delivered to the Saints, it being suggested that they move on to some unorganized territory.

Due in part to the lobbying of the Mormons' capable lawyer, Alexander Doniphan of Liberty, the state legislature authorized the formation of Caldwell County as a new settlement site for the beleaguered Mormons. In the summer and fall of 1836 the unhappy, unwanted Saints directed their wagons north to their new home. The Mormons established Far West as the chief town of their new county. Far West, located eight miles west of the present town of Kingston, no longer exists.

A depression swept over the United States in 1837 bringing economic ruin to many. The banks west of the Appalachians were particularly hard hit since some had issued great quantities of paper money which they could not redeem. When Joseph Smith's bank failed in Kirtland, Ohio, in 1837, many people lost their deposits. Charged with failing to obey Ohio banking laws, Smith and his chief associate, Sidney Rigdon, fled to Far West in 1838.

The city of Far West experienced a rapid growth. By 1838 there was such an influx of Mormons that the population swelled to approximately 3,000 people. At this point in their history, the Mormons adopted a new policy of belligerence. In the past, they had moved when disgruntled neighbors demanded their departure. Thus, they had fled New York, Ohio, and Jackson and Clay counties in Missouri. Failing to defend themselves, they had been abused again and again. Rigdon, an apostle of the church, delivered the dedicatory message at the time of the consecration of the new temple at Far West. Basing the message upon the scripture, "If the salt hath lost its savor, wherewith shall it be salted?", Rigdon called for a new attitude toward those who would persecute the Saints. He declared that the faithful should forcefully resist any future infringement of their rights.

Because of the influx of Saints from the East, Caldwell County soon was a solidly Mormon county. The area around Far West filled with Mormon farmers. Other Saints moved into nearby Daviess and Carroll counties. A Mormon settlement in Daviess County on the Grand River was called Adam-ondi-Ahman. Joseph Smith assigned the name to the settlement because, in his own words, "It is the place where Adam shall come to visit his people, or the Ancient of Days shall sit, as spoken of by David the Prophet."

In August, 1838, the state elections were held in Missouri. Both the Whig and the Democratic parties courted the Saints for their votes. Since most of the Mormons voted for the Democratic Party in 1838, Caldwell County was Democratic; but Daviess County was about evenly divided. The Whigs in Daviess County attempted to prevent the Mormons from casting their ballots, and several clashes occurred at Gallatin, the county seat. One eyewitness described the scene of the voting at Gallatin:

> There was a big pile of house logs piled up in front of the little cabin where they were voting. My father and I climbed to the very top of that pile of logs and witnessed the whole battle. I had witnessed many knock downs in my time, but none on so grand a scale. Pistols were not used. Rocks and clubs were in demand, and an occasional butcher knife slipped in. Men dropped on all sides.

Hearing of the battle, Joseph Smith mobilized Mormon forces at Far West and rode to Daviess County to force the officials to accept Mormon votes. One threat of force led to another and soon both Mormons and non-Mormons were arming and roaming about in force. These mob maneuvers led to raids on isolated farmsteads, the destruction and theft of property, and even murders. The most tragic episode was the raid on Jacob Haun's mill—about eight miles south of the present town of Breckenridge—when a party of non-Mormons attacked the Mormon families who had assembled there. Although these Mormons had not engaged in any previous battles, the non-Mormons swept down upon them and shot or hacked to death with corn knives seventeen Saints. Even little children were among the victims.

Governor Lilburn Boggs reacted immediately to the reports of bloodshed in the Mormon area by raising a militia unit of 400 men to be sent to the area of conflict. In his order to the militia, Governor Boggs stated, "The Mormons must be treated as enemies and must be exterminated or driven from the state if necessary for public peace."

The Mormons realized that they could not withstand an attack from state forces, and the Mormon military leader surrendered. Joseph Smith and other leading officials of the group were imprisoned. Far West was raided and looted. Immediately a court-martial was held for Smith and his four chief associates.

(From Mormonism Unveiled, Courtesy State Historical Society)
The fight at Gallatin, Missouri, between Mormons and "Gentiles"

They were sentenced to be shot in the public square at Far West. Alexander Doniphan, a brigadier general in the Missouri militia and a former lawyer for the Mormons, was ordered to carry out the execution. Doniphan refused the order with the following note: "It is cold-blooded murder, I will not obey your order." General Lucas then moved the prisoners to the jail at Independence. Trials were held at Richmond, Independence, and Gallatin. Some were found not guilty and released; others, like Smith, escaped from the authorities. All the surviving Saints eventually made their way to Illinois where they attempted a new settlement.

The suffering of the Mormon people who were harried out of the state during the winter of 1838-39 is vividly pictured in the records of Mrs. Amanda Smith:

> I started the 1st of February, very cold weather, for Illinois, with five small children and no money. It was mob all the way. I drove the team, and we slept out of doors. We suffered greatly from hunger, cold, and fatigue; and for what? For our religion. In this boasted land of liberty. Deny your faith or die was the cry.

In retrospect, it appears the Mormons were likely to arouse hatred in any region because of their concepts of special revelation and preferred position in the eyes of God. Still, the treatment the Mormons received in Missouri is one of the sorriest episodes in the history of the state. It reveals frontier bigotry and intolerance at its worst. It also proves that during this period neither local nor state officials were willing to uphold the

rights of a persecuted minority. A later Mormon poet could
write with truth:

> The people of Missouri,
> Like a whirlwind in its fury,
> And without a judge or jury,
> Drove the Saints and spilled their blood.

**An engraving from an old book The Mormons or the Latter Day Saints
showing an encampment of Mormons on the Missouri River**

The Saints' attempt to establish the New Jerusalem at Nauvoo in Illinois ended soon after the brutal murder of Joseph
Smith. Brigham Young, a leader of outstanding ability, assumed
the presidency of the church. He directed the exodus of the
faithful across the wilderness, blazing a new trail to the West
just north of the Platte River in order, as he expressed it, to
avoid the "rowdy Missourians" who traversed the Oregon Trail.
The Saints established a thriving community in the basin of the
Great Salt Lake in Utah. In the years to follow, Brigham Young
and his Saints were instrumental in the development of one of
the great states of the West—Utah.

The Santa Fe Trail

Santa Fe, one of the oldest cities in America, was established
only a few years after Jamestown, Virginia, in the early seven-

teenth century. It was the northernmost fortress of the Spanish in New Mexico, and by the early nineteenth century it had a population of about 3,000 people. In addition to Santa Fe, there were a number of smaller villages nearby stretching along the banks of the Rio Grande River and its tributaries. It was difficult for the Spanish to provide trade goods for the people of this region. The Spanish unloaded their ships at Vera Cruz and transported the goods overland for approximately 2,000 miles through mountainous terrain to Santa Fe. The people of New Mexico were greatly in need of iron products, cutlery, tools, and particularly textiles. They had a surplus of mules, horses, and silver. Many Missouri merchants were aware of the rich trading possibilities at Santa Fe, but the Spanish officials were under strict instructions to arrest and jail any American traders entering Spanish territory. Many such traders, including Auguste Pierre Chouteau, had been captured and their goods confiscated.

In 1821 the Mexican people were successful in their revolution against Spain, and as a result Santa Fe became Mexican territory. Immediately a number of western traders saw an opportunity to profit from the change of government. William Becknell and Colonel Benjamin Cooper set out from Franklin, Missouri, early in 1821 with pack trains of goods bound for Santa Fe. Cooper was waylaid by Indians and forced to return home, but Becknell completed the expedition, though with considerable difficulty. He found a ready market for his goods and, after only five months, returned to Franklin with an account of the profits to be made in the Santa Fe trade. Although he cautioned Missouri merchants that the particular buyers of Santa Fe wanted only "goods of excellent quality and unfaded colors," he reported that goods purchased in St. Louis could be sold in Santa Fe for five times the purchase price. The percentage of profit encouraged others to join William Becknell on the Santa Fe Trail.

On Becknell's second trip, in 1822, he took twenty-one men and three wagons of much-wanted goods to Santa Fe. This trip was even more financially successful than his first venture. Returning by a new route, he cut the travel time between Franklin and Santa Fe to forty-five days. More and more traders wished to take part in the lucrative enterprise, and by 1824 trading parties on the Trail numbered twenty-five wagons, eighty men, and one hundred and fifty horses. Those who made the trip in

1824, among whom was M. M. Marmaduke, later governor of the state, carried $30,000 worth of goods. They returned with merchandise valued at $190,000.

Franklin, across the Missouri River from Boonville, was the point of organization for early caravans. Merchants in the area either sold goods to the traders or sent wagons of their own goods along. The train crossed the Missouri by way of the ferry at Arrow Rock, then moved on to Fort Osage and out into the Kansas Indian Territory.

Because of the Indian threat and the difficulties of following the trail, Missouri settlers soon demanded that the Federal Government set up a system of military protection for the merchants, send men to mark the trail, and sign treaties with the Indians to insure the safety of the traders. Many Missourians died on the trail, including Jedediah Smith who was set upon by Indians as he looked for water in the dry bed of the Cimarron River. For the trip of 1829, the secretary of war ordered a military unit from Jefferson Barracks to escort the traders to Spanish territory. In 1832 Congress authorized regular mounted military forces to protect the traders. But small groups without escorts continued as targets of sporadic attacks. In 1825-26 the trail was officially marked by United States surveyors.

After the town of Franklin was washed away by the change in the channel of the Missouri River in 1827, Independence became the starting point for the trading expeditions. Independence was a flurry of excitement during the spring as traders purchased their wagons and supplies; arranged their oxen, mules, and horses; haggled with other merchants over the purchase price of trade goods; and made plans for the long trip. The prairie schooners, originally manufactured in Pittsburgh but later produced in Independence, were packed carefully for the difficult trip to insure transportation without damage. Drivers, nicknamed bull whackers or mule skinners, used six yoke of oxen or three to five teams of mules to pull each wagon.

For protection, the traders traveled to Santa Fe in one large group. The most common perils and problems of the trip were Indian attacks, runaways, breakdowns, water shortage, and injuries to the oxen's tender feet. To secure protection against the Indians, the caravan was organized under a captain whose orders each mule skinner and bull whacker was obliged to follow. It was the captain who determined the manner in which the train moved, the number of miles—about fifteen—traveled daily, and the choice of campsites. It was also the captain's responsibility to direct the train to the all-important water holes along the way.

Of course there were many technical problems associated with the 900-mile journey. Wagons and harness had to be repaired along the way. Sometimes the tender feet of the oxen were shod in buffaloskin boots to protect them. It was usually difficult to ford streams, and the traders were sometimes forced to leave wagons hopelessly mired in mud holes. In spite of all these difficulties, the traders pushed ahead and finally, after about six weeks, they reached the adobe houses of old Santa Fe. An observer has given us the following description of the reaction of the people of Santa Fe to the arrival of the Missouri traders:

> I doubt, in short, whether the first sight of the walls of Jerusalem were beheld by the crusaders with much more tumultuous and soul enrapturing joy. The arrival produced a great deal of bustle and excitement among the natives. "Los Americanos!"—"Los Carros"—"La Entrada de la Caravana!" were to be heard in every direction; and crowds of women and boys flocked around to see the newcomers; while crowds of leperos hung about as usual to see what they could pilfer.

After paying a duty which varied year to year from $10 per wagon to $750, depending upon the greed of the governor, the traders were free to sell their goods. Those who were anxious to return to Missouri might sell their entire stock to Santa Fe merchants. Those who were willing to spend more time haggling in the Mexican fashion could usually secure higher prices. In return

"Wagon Train" by Oscar E. Berninghaus
(Courtesy August A. Busch, Jr.)

for their frying pans, hammers, mirrors, cotton goods, handkerchiefs, silk shawls, crepes, and gay calico, the Americans purchased mules, jacks, jennets, furs, and Mexican silver and dollars. The Americans were amazed by the sights of Santa Fe. In particular they noted the contrast between their own somber brown or gray clothing and the many-colored, silver-spangled, silk-embroidered riding costumes of the Spanish men. They observed with astonishment the *senoritas* who smoked *cigarritos* even while they danced, and remarked at the great number of beggars lining the streets.

The Santa Fe trade did not involve a large number of people. It is estimated that only ninety merchants engaged in this trade at its height. However, it did provide for the introduction of considerable sums of silver money much needed in Missouri. Josiah Gregg states that the trade resulted in a total profit of approximately $3,000,000 between the years 1822 and 1843. We should also note that the introduction of the Santa Fe jackass was the basis for the development of a mule industry in Missouri.

In addition to the money and materials brought to Missouri, the trade also gave many Missourians experience in crossing the Great Plains. They were to use this experience later, at the time of the Mexican War and during the westward movement, to direct groups of colonists to the West. Christopher Carson was apprenticed to a harness maker in Franklin, Missouri, at the age of sixteen. Dissatisfied with the tedium of a craftsman's life, he decided to run away from home and his apprenticeship, and seek a life of adventure. In 1826 he joined the caravan to Santa Fe. During the rest of his life—renowned as Kit Carson—he acted as frontier scout and trail blazer.

The Oregon Trail

The great Northwest of green mountain slopes, primeval forests, and verdant valleys, including both the snow-capped mountain peaks of the Cascade range and the shores of the Pacific, was an intriguing and inviting area to many Americans in the first half of the nineteenth century. At that time the whole region from the present-day northern boundary of California to the southern boundary of Alaska was called the Oregon country. In 1792 a Boston ship captain named Robert Gray discovered the mouth of the Columbia River. In 1804 Lewis and Clark made their epochal journey to the Pacific coast into the

(Courtesy State Historical Society)

The courthouse at Independence in 1849. Notice the Conestoga-type wagon in the left foreground and the lighter, canvas-covered farm wagons often used on the Oregon trail at the left near the fence.

Oregon region. Their trip was duplicated by the employees of John Jacob Astor in 1811 when an expedition under the leadership of Wilson Price Hunt pushed up the Missouri River and trekked across the Rocky Mountains to Oregon. The United States, because of these early exploratory activities, claimed the Oregon territory as her own.

Other nations were also interested in Oregon. Spain, Russia, and Great Britain all declared ownership of the region. But the claims of Spain and Russia were theoretical and tenuous. Spain soon relinquished any property rights north of the 42nd parallel. Russia in turn dropped her claims south of the 54° 40′ line. Only the United States and Great Britain remained to contend for the Oregon Territory.

Neither nation was willing to fight over the area in dispute. The scattered settlers in the sparsely-populated region were in no position to carry on a conflict. From the beginning, the United States had been willing to divide the area along the 49th parallel, but the English hoped to secure the land as far south as the Columbia River. Unable to make an immediate decision, the two nations made an agreement in 1818 to occupy the region jointly for ten years. Thus, the citizens of both nations had access to the hunting, trapping, and farming areas. Although this treaty was to last for only ten years, in 1827 the privileges of

Astoria

Whitman Mission

Fort Walla Walla

Portland

Columbia

Lee Mission

Yellowstone

Lisa's

Snake R.

Fort Boise

Snake River

Wind R.

Big Horn R.

Fort Hall

Sweetwater

South Pass

Rende

Fort Bridger

Salt Lake City

Green R.

Rende

Sutter's Fort

Pony Express

San Francisco

Colorado River

Pike

Los Angeles

Rio Grande River

Sa

Fort Yuma

El

Missouri and the West

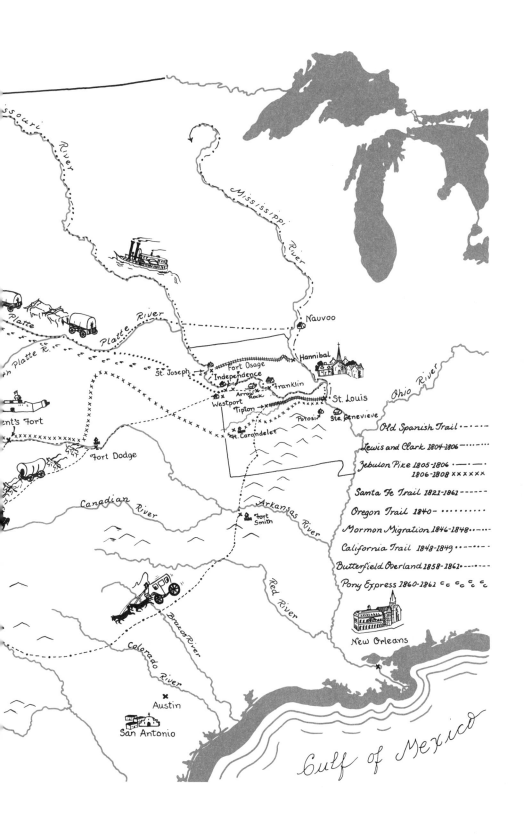

Missouri River

Mississippi River

Platte River

North Platte R.

North Platte R.

Ohio River

Nauvoo

Hannibal

St. Joseph

Fort Osage

Independence

Franklin

Arrow Rock

Westport

Tipton

Potosi

St. Genevieve

St. Louis

Bent's Fort

St. Carondelet

Fort Dodge

Canadian River

Arkansas River

Fort Smith

Red River

Brazos River

Colorado River

Austin

San Antonio

New Orleans

Gulf of Mexico

Old Spanish Trail ⋅ ⋅ ⋅ ⋅ ⋅

Lewis and Clark 1804-1806 ⋅—⋅—⋅—

Zebulon Pike 1805-1806 —⋅—⋅—⋅
1806-1808 ×××××

Santa Fe Trail 1821-1861 - - - - -

Oregon Trail 1840- ⋅⋅⋅⋅⋅⋅⋅⋅

Mormon Migration 1846-1848 ⋅⋅—⋅⋅—

California Trail 1848-1849 ⋅—⋅—⋅—

Butterfield Overland 1858-1861⋅- ⋅- ⋅-

Pony Express 1860-1861 ᴄ ᴄ ᴄ ᴄ ᴄ

joint occupation were extended indefinitely, the only stipulation being that if either nation wished to terminate the arrangement, one year's notice should be given to the other.

Although there were national leaders who spoke of the importance of settling and controlling Oregon during the 1820's, only a few wandering trappers and traders made their way to that far region. An event in 1832 brought the area to national attention and, in particular, stirred the churches to action. In the fall of 1831, four Indians from Oregon arrived in St. Louis with a group of fur traders. The Indians were taken to see General William Clark, who was at that time the superintendent of Indian affairs. Clark invited a literate Christian Indian named William Walker to meet his visitors from Oregon. Walker then learned the following story from them:

> It appeared that some white man had penetrated into their country, and happened to be a spectator at one of their religious ceremonies, which they scrupulously perform at stated periods. He informed them that their mode of worshipping the Supreme Being was radically wrong, and instead of being acceptable and pleasing, it was displeasing to him; he also informed them that the white people away toward the rising of the sun had been put in possession of the true mode of worshipping the great Spirit. . . . They accordingly deputed four of the chiefs to proceed to St. Louis to see their father, General Clark, to inquire of him, having no doubt but he would tell them the whole truth about it.

Two of the Indians died in St. Louis, and Walker feared that the other two might never reach their home since the change of environment had had an evil effect upon their health. But Walker added, "If they died on their way home, peace be to their names! They died inquirers after the truth."

As a result of Walker's description, the Methodist Church became much interested in missions in Oregon. Describing Clark's four visitors as "The Wise Men from the West," the Methodist *Christian Advocate* demanded missionary action. The story of these Indians was accompanied by an account of the manner by which the Flathead Indians of Oregon deformed their papooses' heads. The combination of this Macedonian call and the account of infant mutilation was so compelling that many Methodists immediately sent money to finance a mission enterprise. In 1834 the first Methodist missionary team, headed by Jason Lee, left Missouri to establish a mission station in Oregon.

Soon after the Methodists had arrived the Presbyterian Church became interested in the region. Dr. Marcus Whitman of New York came to Missouri in 1835 preparing to go to Oregon as a medical missionary. He and his associates joined a pack train of the American Fur Company and traveled to the Green River rendezvous with the group. On the way, Dr. Whitman treated Jim Bridger at Fort Bridger, removing an iron arrow which had been shot into the shoulder of the mountain man three years earlier. Both Jason Lee and Marcus Whitman returned to the East in the late 1830's to speak of the need for missions among the Indians of Oregon. Whitman's ill-fated return to the Northwest will be mentioned later.

In most regions, the missionaries followed the settlers. Oregon is unusual in that American missionaries led the way for American migrants. The missionaries played an important role not only in attracting settlers by publicizing the region, but also in helping the migrants to their destination by developing and marking the Oregon Trail.

During the late 1830's Lewis F. Linn, senator from Missouri, became the leading advocate of American occupation of Oregon. In 1838 he introduced a bill calling for the Federal Government to encourage the movement of people into Oregon with the con-

Lewis Fields Linn, frontier physician, statesman, and promoter of Missouri industries, is known as the state's "model senator." His bill to promote the settlement of the Oregon territory won for him the title "Father of Oregon." *(Courtesy State Historical Society)*

struction of forts, the marking of the trail, and other incentives. Year after year Linn worked for the passage of his Oregon bill. In 1843 it passed the Senate, but was defeated in the House of Representatives. Linn died in the fall of 1843 without having secured the desired legislation. However, he had focused American attention upon the Oregon region, and it is fitting that he is now known as the "Father of Oregon."

Only a few fur traders, missionaries, and government officials had made the long trip to Oregon before 1841. In that year, an emigrant group gathered at Sapling Grove, Missouri, to prepare for a journey to the West. Some members of the party wished to go to California, others to Oregon. The sixty-nine colonists were fortunate to have as their guide Thomas Fitzpatrick, who had traveled into the West many times for the Rocky Mountain Fur Company. Father Pierre Jean De Smet, the remarkably successful Catholic missionary, joined them for his first of many trips west. The accomplishments of this devoted priest will be discussed later. After the group arrived in Oregon, they sent back reports so full of enthusiasm for the region that a new wave of immigrants appeared. The population of the Mississippi Valley had grown so rapidly in the early nineteenth century that there was now a body of pioneers ready for a new frontier. Oregon was a logical destination.

The Oregon Trail originally began at Independence, Missouri. However, the washing away of the loading docks along the Missouri River encouraged the development of another town in the immediate vicinity of Independence. In 1833 Westport was founded and later grew to be the great metropolitan center now known as Kansas City. A few of the Oregon-bound settlers began their journey from northern points such as St. Joseph or Council Bluffs, but the large majority started at Independence or Westport. The Oregon Trail and the Santa Fe Trail were the same for the first forty miles beyond Independence. Then the trail branched, the Oregon fork following the Platte River to Fort Laramie, thence north to Independence Rock and southwest to Fort Bridger. From Fort Bridger the trail ran into southeast Idaho to the point known as Fort Hall, from which it followed the Snake River much of the way to its confluence with the Columbia River.

The trail was approximately 2,000 miles long over plains, across rivers, through mountainous areas. Most of the trail was

Fort Bridger in Utah Territory served as a way station for travelers on the Oregon Trail. Notice the typical farm wagon fitted with a frame for a canvas cover.

unmarked, but, as the years went by, the growing number of wagons left their imprint. Along the way there were the same difficulties and dangers encountered on the Santa Fe Trail, but since the Oregon Trail was twice as long, the hazards were doubled. In addition, the problems of mountain travel were added on the Oregon trip. Rugged, rocky mountain paths took their toll in broken wagons; swift, frigid mountain streams placed additional obstacles in the path of the Oregon-bound pioneers.

In 1843 a great body of people—estimated at approximately 1,000 men, women, and children—converged on Independence in preparation for the journey across the continent. The leader of this immigration party was Peter H. Burnett of Platte County, who, in lectures throughout Missouri, painted with fervent phrases the unlimited opportunities for settlement in Oregon. In May, 1843, Burnett's party together with some 5,000 cattle began the trip to the Northwest. This trip has been described in the writings of Jesse Applegate, and as a result we know all the intimate details of the troubles of transportation to the West.

Although later artists have frequently pictured the Oregon immigrants as traveling in Conestoga wagons, these heavy, cumbersome vehicles were not used on the Oregon Trail. Some were employed in the Santa Fe trade, but that journey was much shorter and less difficult than the Oregon trip. Those going to the Northwest adopted a typical farm wagon of the day with a canvas or water-proofed material as a cover. Either oxen or mules were employed to pull them. There were many arguments at the time among the settlers as to the relative merits of each beast. Mules were easy to feed, but ineffective in mud and more likely to be stolen by Indians. Oxen, on the other hand, more frequently developed sore feet. The most common breakdowns on the trail resulted from wagon tongues or axles which would snap under great pressure. The immigrants, crowded for space, did not carry spare parts. They would find the nearest tree and carve out the needed part. It was fortunate that the metal wheels were much stronger than tongues or axles, for the immigrants could not make a new wheel on the trail. The jolting, slow-moving wagons were not equipped with springs or brakes; the only maintenance they required, aside from necessary repairs, was an occasional lubrication of the wheels with the tar and animal fat carried for the purpose. The pioneer's wagon was his home and fortress. In the evening, the wagons were arranged in a circle to provide a protective fort. The Indians rarely attacked such a night encampment; their chances of success were better if the attack were made by day when the wagons were strung out along the trail.

After the year 1843 a growing torrent of settlers followed the Oregon Trail to the Northwest. How can one explain why so many frontiersmen risked their lives and the lives of their children to make the long, exhausting, agonizing trip? They endured enervating heat, choking dust, and maddening swarms of mosquitoes. They lost their own lives or those of their loved ones in epidemics of cholera and typhoid, and in Indian attacks. Even the normal activities of everyday life were carried out under the most difficult circumstances. They were men and women of courage, with a vision for the future, with a great curiosity about the regions beyond their own view, and, no doubt, with a desire for better land and a higher standard of living. Whatever their motives, they settled the West. Missouri both aided their migration and contributed many of her own people.

The editor of the *Independence Expositor* looked out the window of his shop and wrote:

> Even while we write, we see a long train of wagons coming through our busy streets; they are hailed with shouts of welcome by their fellow voyagers, and, to judged [sic] from the pleased expression on every face, it "all goes merry as a marriage bell." . . . But they are past, and now comes team after team, each drawn by six or eight stout oxen, and such drivers! positively sons of Anak! not one of

them less than six feet two in his stockings. Whoo ha! Go it boys! We're in a perfect *Oregon fever.*

It may seem strange that the settlers from Missouri and Iowa would travel 2,000 miles to establish themselves as farmers when there was a great abundance of land immediately to the west in the present-day states of Nebraska and Kansas. There are several reasons why the pioneers ignored the plains region. First, this area had been assigned to the Indians, and government opposition to plans for settlement could be expected. Second, the area was largely treeless, and most settlers did not know how to establish a homestead without the help of trees. In the past, the farmer had chosen a forest area as an indication of soil fertility. He used the wood to build his home, outbuildings, fences, furniture, and to provide fuel for his fireplace. Third, the inaccurate report of Zebulon Pike, who had described the Great Plains as a desert, led to a belief that rainfall would be inadequate for agriculture. Fourth, much exaggerated publicity had circulated during the 30's and 40's concerning the resources and desirability of Oregon and California. Settlers who saw the treeless monotony of the Great Plains were easily attracted to the forested utopia of the Pacific slopes.

Although British claims to the region south of the 49th parallel were not removed until 1846, the continually expanding American population strengthened the American hand in Oregon. Before his death in 1843 Senator Linn had offered "to take 10,000 Missourians and settle the trouble with Great Britain in sixty days." When President Polk threatened Britain with war over Oregon in 1845, the British decided that the 49th parallel would be an acceptable division point. And so it was that Oregon south of the 49th parallel became American. Missouri, by affording a starting point and by providing both supplies and pioneers, played a major role in the exploration and settlement of the territory.

The Settlement of Texas

Most Missourians were themselves immigrants, and they looked with the eye of a prospector at any description of available lands in new areas of settlement. One new possibility for occupation was Texas. As a northern province of Spanish Mexico, Texas largely had been ignored by the officials in Spain. Settlement in the region was sparse for at least two reasons. First, the fierce Indians of the southern plains discouraged coloniza-

Stephen Fuller Austin, elder son of Moses Austin of Potosi, has been called the "Father of Texas" for his part in the settlement of the territory and her struggle for independence.

(From the collection of the Ellison Photo Company, Austin, Texas)

tion. Only those settlements carefully organized with military power adequate to repel the plains tribes were successful. Second, the arid region between Mexico and Texas discouraged the movement of Mexicans to the northeast.

Though the Mexicans were not much attracted to the region, the Americans were. The soil in eastern Texas was known to be excellent. The better-drained areas were ideal for the expansion of a cotton-producing southern-type economy. By 1820, the western states of Louisiana and Missouri had scores of restless frontiersmen beginning to feel crowded and anxious to move on. To many men on the frontier, utopia always seemed just beyond the next boundary. Such settlers would give serious consideration to promoters eager to fill the open spaces of Texas.

When Spain owned the Louisiana Territory, she had helplessly observed the onrush of American frontiersmen and had been unable to halt them at the Mississippi River. That same westward movement had reached the borders of Texas by 1820, and the Spanish Government was forced to make another decision: Should Spain allow American colonists to enter Texas? A well-known Missouri leader helped Spain decide.

Moses Austin was an enterprising son of Connecticut who had acted as a merchant in New Haven, in Philadelphia, and in Richmond, Virginia. A man of great ability and daring, he was willing to attempt the most difficult tasks. In 1797 he moved to Missouri and secured a huge grant in the lead mine area near Ste. Genevieve. Due to his adoption of improved mining and smelting techniques, he became a leader in the lead industry. It was Austin who produced the first sheet lead and cannon balls around the year 1800. Financial success permitted him to build a large, comfortable home at Potosi, known as Durham Hall. The second decade of the century brought financial reverses. Profits from the lead mines declined. The Bank of St. Louis, which he helped establish in 1816, failed three years later. Financially ruined, he was imprisoned for a short time for the nonpayment of debts.

At the time of this financial difficulty, Austin conceived of a plan to establish a new colony in Texas. During the summer of 1820, he set out on horseback for Texas, followed by his mule-mounted slave. The two travelers made their way to Louisiana, where they secured a Spanish passport.

At San Antonio Austin sought Spanish approval of his plan to bring 300 families into Texas. He made the proposal more palatable by informing the officials that he was himself a Catholic, that the new settlers would be Catholics, and that many of the settlers had formerly been Spanish subjects during the time Louisiana was the property of His Catholic Majesty. This proposal finally secured the approval of the government at San Antonio—in January, 1821, he received permission to begin the project. The return trip to Missouri was difficult, and the hardships and exposures of the journey led to a fatal illness—probably pneumonia. Moses Austin died in Ste. Genevieve County in June, 1821, and was buried in Potosi.

The resourceful, intelligent Austin was the father of an equally well-endowed son, Stephen. This young man had been educated at Transylvania University, had worked with his father in the mining business, and had inherited his father's ability to plan and execute difficult assignments. At the age of twenty he was elected to the Missouri territorial legislature where he gained excellent experience as a delegate from 1814 to 1820. Stephen, only 27 years old at his father's death, immediately accepted the responsibility of fulfilling the settlement project. He set out at once for Texas to inspect the area and to make the necessary arrangements.

There were large numbers of settlers in Missouri, Kentucky, and Tennessee who were anxious for the opportunity to move into the new region. When Austin's plan was made public, the response was immediate and favorable. Stephen's mother reported that she expected a third of the people of Missouri to migrate to Texas, since such a move was the only topic of conversation. Austin wrote Governor Martinez of Texas, "I am convinced that I could take on fifteen hundred families as easily as three hundred if permitted to do so."

Stephen Austin brought his first groups to Texas in December of 1821. Shortly after the settlers arrived, the Mexican Revolution made Mexico independent of Spain. Due to this change of government, Austin was forced to make a trip to Mexico City in order to re-establish his rights to settle the area. The Mexican government confirmed his request in 1823, stipulating once more that the immigrants be Roman Catholic and promising farms of 177 acres for each of 300 families brought to the region. Those settlers who were to engage in stockfarming were to receive 4,428 acres. The leader of the immigration, or *impresario,* as he was called, was to receive a grant of 26,000 acres for himself for every 100 families brought into Texas.

Austin returned to Texas and continued to act as the leading American official of the growing settlement. Other *impresarios* soon arrived with emigrants—both respectable and disreputable —from the American frontier, but it was Austin who gave the necessary direction and leadership which the colony required. In all, Austin brought some 1200 families to Texas. It is understandable that the colonists named him commander-in-chief of the Texas army at the time of the Revolution of 1835, and that today this Missourian is given the title "Father of Texas."

Statue of Moses Austin in San Antonio, Texas
(Photograph by Smith's Studio, San Antonio, Texas; Courtesy State Historical Society)

The Mexican War

The American settlers in Texas, so many of whom had come from Missouri, secured their independence from Mexico in 1836. Although these Texans wished to become part of the United States, the Republic of Texas was not admitted to the union immediately. Texas stood, sombrero in hand, at the back door of America seeking admission for nine years. Those who lived in such border states as Missouri and Louisiana were anxious to open the door to their relatives, but the issue of slavery kept the states of the Northeast from encouraging this admission. Texas was settled by southerners, many of whom surreptitiously brought slaves to their new homes, in defiance of the Mexican constitution. To accept Texas as a state would add two more proslavery votes in the Senate. The issue was so explosive politically that Andrew Jackson, an ardent expansionist, refused to admit Texas, and nothing was done about Texas statehood until 1845.

James K. Polk of Tennessee, the Democratic candidate for president in 1844, campaigned on a platform calling for the annexation of Oregon and Texas. His subsequent election, therefore, seemed to place the citizens' stamp of approval upon expansion. Immediately after the election results were known, Congress acted to admit Texas to the Union. The Mexican government had long feared that the United States would take this move. The Mexicans warned the Yankees to the north that American acceptance of Texas might well mean war. President Polk, a son of the West, where challenges were answered on the field of honor, met the Mexican threat by sending an American army into the disputed southern boundary region claimed by both Texas and Mexico. The inevitable conflict occurred, and the United States declared war in April of 1846.

There were reasons why Missourians would be especially interested in the war. The movement to settle Texas had been directed by a Missourian. The original group Austin took with him to Texas, sometimes known as "The Old Three Hundred," included more Missourians than people from any other state. Most Missouri families had at least one relative who had forsaken Missouri to settle in Texas. Another factor should not be forgotten. The legend of Cortez lived on in the Mississippi and Missouri valleys. The accounts of huge stores of gold and silver in the country to the south was a great lure to many young Missourians. They dreamed of a glorious and lucrative invasion of Mexico. Finally, Missourians, and most other westerners, believed in the doctrine of "Manifest Destiny"—that the United States was destined eventually to control most, if not all, of North America.

In spite of Missouri interests in Texas and Mexico and the resultant sentiment in favor of war, Thomas Hart Benton declared his opposition to the "immediate annexation," which he believed would provoke an armed conflict with Mexico. He called Mexico a "peaceable neighbor," and he deplored the possibility of transforming her into an armed foe. The retired president, Andy Jackson, at the Hermitage in Tennessee, was saddened by Benton's stand. Jackson wrote to a friend that he felt the senator's new statement would enable his enemies "to put Col. Benton politically down in Missouri." Benton's stand is all the more interesting since at the time of Missouri's demands for statehood he had actively supported the admission of a slave state into the Union. But in 1844 he declared, "I will not engage in schemes for extension [of slavery] into regions where [legally] it was never known." After twenty-five years in the Senate, Benton had changed his ideas.

Despite his opposition to the immediate annexation of Texas and his attempts to secure the passage of a moderate bill for negotiating the differences between Texas and Mexico, Thomas Hart Benton cooperated with President Polk and Congress after war finally was declared in 1846. He did, however, continually seek ways to bring about a swift end to the hostilities. Benton suggested that the simplest way to bring the war to a close would be to land an army at Vera Cruz and march them inland to Mexico City. He also suggested a plan for the appointment of a civilian lieutenant-general to direct the army and to seek peace with the Mexican people. The proposal was sent to Congress and Polk, who supported the plan, probably intended to name Benton himself as the civilian officer in charge of the army. The Senate refused the plan, but the army did make a Vera Cruz landing in 1847.

At the beginning of the Mexican War the officer in charge at New Orleans, General E. P. Gaines, became alarmed at the prospect of an invasion by Mexico and asked the western states to send troops immediately to protect New Orleans. Some 650 Missouri volunteers sailed down the Mississippi River and pre-

A Mexican War volunteer from J. T. Hughes, Doniphan's Expedition, U. P. James Publishers, Cincinnati, 1847
(Courtesy State Historical Society)

sented themselves to General Gaines. Their courage was for nought. Since Gaines had not been authorized to raise the forces, the troops were disbanded and sent home.

In the middle of May, 1846, Governor John C. Edwards of Missouri called for volunteers to join the United States forces training to seize Santa Fe. There was an immediate response to this request: 856 men volunteered to serve in the cavalry, 250 men in light artillery, and 145 men in the infantry. All told, the commanding officer, General Stephen W. Kearny, organized a force of 1,658 men. About 400 of these were Missourians.

The period of basic training was short. After only twenty days of drilling at Fort Leavenworth, the training site for the Army of the West, Kearny's army was ready to depart for Santa Fe. The eight companies of Missouri troops were organized into the First Regiment of Missouri Volunteers. The men elected Colonel Alexander Doniphan of Liberty as their leader in the event that General Kearny could not direct the army. Doniphan —wise, dependable, and courageous—proved worthy of their confidence.

Since many Missourians had made the trip to Santa Fe, the army followed the already-established trail. Kearny sent a supply train of 100 wagons and 800 cattle ahead of the army. On the trail Colonel Doniphan received an intelligence report that the Mexican government, determined to defend the city, had 7,000 soldiers in Santa Fe.

The major military obstacle between the American army and

Santa Fe was Galisteo Pass. The Mexicans, who could have defended this position with ease and effectiveness, had not completed their preparations when the Army of the West arrived. One explanation is that an argument between two rival Mexican generals had prevented the completion of the arming of the pass. Kearny's army, having traveled 900 miles in 50 days, marched into Santa Fe without firing a shot. General Kearny seized the governor's mansion and raised the Stars and Stripes. The American forces were in control.

(Copyright Princeton University Press; used by permission)

A sketch of a camp washing day during Doniphan's march to Santa Fe from Jacob S. Robinson, A Journal of the Santa Fe Expedition under Colonel Doniphan.

General Kearny left Colonel Doniphan in charge of Santa Fe and proceeded west to California with 300 men. When Kearny's force was only 150 miles out of Santa Fe they came upon a group of Indians and a white man—Kit Carson. Although Carson had orders to take secret messages to Washington, D. C., he entrusted the messages to his friend, Broken Hand Fitzpatrick, and turned about to direct Kearny's force on their 1,090-mile march to California. When Kearny's troops arrived in California, he engaged in skirmishes with Mexican forces, and soon defeated them.

Colonel Doniphan, who had been left in charge of the American forces in Santa Fe, waited for reinforcements from Missouri before beginning his expedition against other Mexican armies to the south. Colonel Sterling Price arrived on September 28, 1846, with 1,200 Missouri men. Bolstered by these reinforcements, Doniphan's men carried out an expedition against the Navajo Indians who had been causing great difficulties by their raids. The extreme cold and heavy snows were a major handicap, but Doniphan finally was able to subjugate the Indians and to arrange a peace.

Colonel Sterling Price, who remained in charge of the military forces in Santa Fe, did not have an easy time in his assignment. Missourian Charles Bent was murdered soon after his appointment as governor of Santa Fe, and the Mexican citizens of the area attempted a rebellion. Because of the troubles in and around Santa Fe, it was necessary to send Missouri reinforcements to Colonel Price.

Meanwhile Doniphan, having pacified the Indians of New Mexico, moved south to invade the province of Chihuahua. At the Brazito River on Christmas Day, 1846, his forces of about 500 men defeated a Mexican army of 1,200. The city of El Paso was taken without opposition. When his artillery finally arrived from Santa Fe, Doniphan began the march from El Paso to Chihuahua. Much of the journey was over desert land and sun-baked prairies. Men and beasts suffered greatly from thirst, from blowing sand, and from the heat and smoke of a prairie fire. Fifteen miles from Chihuahua the Mexican army of about 4,000 attempted to halt the Americans at Sacramento Pass. But Doniphan and his 900 remarkable men pushed the Mexican troops aside to win the day and seize Chihuahua. The Missouri forces lost only one man in this battle, while the Mexican dead numbered 304. After these two epic victories the army marched to Saltillo and then to Matamoras, where they embarked by ship for New Orleans and home.

General Alexander Doniphan, lawyer, military hero and statesman won lasting fame for his leadership during the Mexican War.
(Courtesy State Historical Society)

Doniphan's army had marched 2,200 miles into enemy territory over difficult terrain. Although often greatly outnumbered,
they were victorious in every encounter. Fewer than fifty men
were lost in the entire campaign. The arrival of Doniphan and
his ragged troops in St. Louis in 1847 signaled the beginning of
a great celebration to honor the heroes. Thomas Hart Benton
gave a speech of praise and welcome, and great throngs lined the
streets to greet the triumphant sons of Missouri.

Benton, who reluctantly voted for war in 1846, had great
sympathy for the Mexicans. Many thoughtful Americans recognized the Mexican War as an act of aggression against a weak
neighbor. Most Missourians, however, were more concerned
about expansion than about the morals of power politics. The
energy, enthusiasm, and willingness of the Missouri men to volunteer for duty indicates that the people of Missouri favored the
conflict, and history shows that they played a major part in
American victories in north Mexico and California.

The Forty-niners

The Treaty of Guadalupe Hidalgo of 1848 ended the Mexican
War. Under the terms of the treaty, Texas as far south as the
Rio Grande River, New Mexico, and California, were now American territory. The virtues of California had been sung for many
years by those Mountain Men and occasional traders who had
made the difficult journey to and from that Pacific region. No
doubt, a stream of settlers would have pushed westward to California in the late 1840's and 1850's regardless of conditions.
However, a dramatic event which occurred in January of 1848
intensified, almost to the point of hysteria, interest in California.
While building a water mill on the American River, workmen
discovered gold. The news spread rapidly to Utah and then on
east to Missouri and other settlements. Gold was a magic word
in the early nineteenth century, as throughout history, and there
was an immediate rush of people from all walks of life to frontier
California.

It was possible to reach California by several routes. Some
traveled by ship around the Horn; others sailed as far as Panama
and then, after crossing the Isthmus on foot or on mule, completed the trip by Pacific ship; still others chose the less costly
but more difficult cross-country trek. Missouri was the popular
jumping-off spot for those who wanted a share of the nuggets

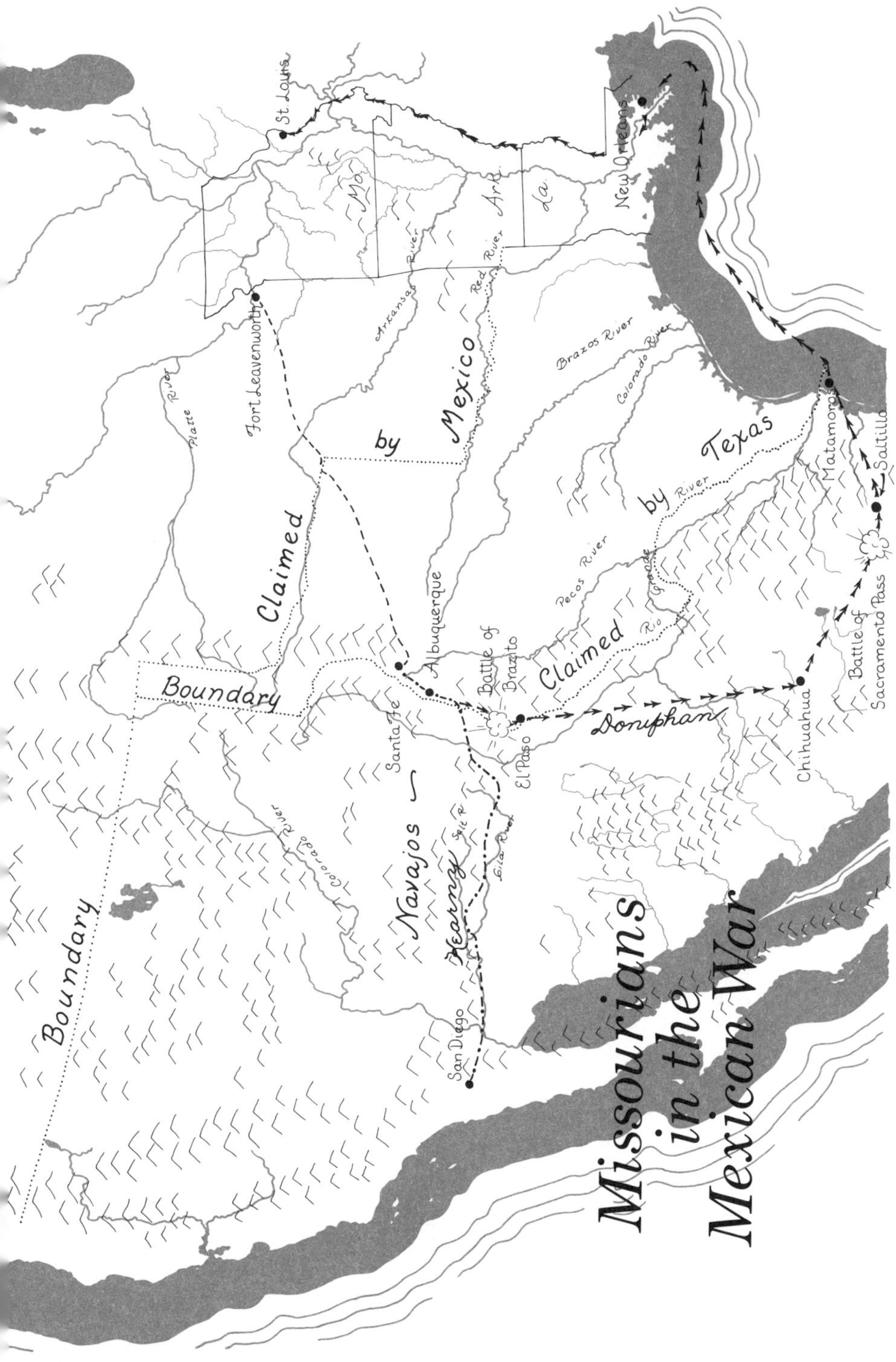

St. Louis

Mo.

Ark.

La.

New Orleans

Platte River

Fort Leavenworth

Arkansas River

Red River

Brazos River

Colorado River

Claimed

by

Mexico

by

Texas

Pecos River

Rio Grande

Matamoros

Saltillo

Battle of
Sacramento Pass

Boundary

Albuquerque

Battle of
Brazito

Claimed

Doniphan

Chihuahua

Santa Fe

Navajos

Kearny

El Paso

Gila R.

Colorado River

San Diego

Boundary

Missourians
in the
Mexican War

Colonel Christopher "Kit" Carson, trapper, Indian agent, and soldier, served as a guide on John C. Fremont's first three expeditions.
(Courtesy State Historical Society)

of the West. The great army of people bound for California left from Independence, Westport, or St. Joseph. Those who made the journey could follow the well-established Oregon Trail with its branch leading to northern California, or the Santa Fe Trail with its extension to southern California. Missouri merchants, outfitters, and artisans made money from these westward-moving gold seekers, just as Missourians earlier had profited from the Oregon-bound pioneers.

Captain J. A. Pritchard and thousands of others rushed to western Missouri in the spring of 1849. Pritchard described the scene:

> By noone to-day we came to where the St. Joseph road and Independence road come togeather —It was allarming to see the long strings of wagons that were on the road—I counted just passing before us as we came into the St. Jo road 90 Ox teams in one string—And as far as the Eye could reach forward and back the road was just lined with them—It would appear from the sight befor us—that the nation was disgorgeing its self and sending off its whole inhabitance—

By mid-May 5,000 wagons had left Missouri for California. By the first of June one observer estimated 12,000 wagons on the way. Not even a cholera epidemic in St. Louis in the spring of 1849 slowed the flow of 1,000 immigrants a week into the city. Small wonder that an estimated 5,000 people died of cholera on the trails that summer.

Many Missourians joined the throng to the West. Two of

the familiar songs of the forty-niners which have been passed down in several versions through the years refer to the people from Pike County, Missouri. Sweet Betsey from Pike was introduced earlier. Her fellow-Missourian immortalized in song is Joe Bowers.

> My name it is Joe Bowers
> And I've got a brother Ike;
> I came from old Missouri,
> And all the way from Pike.

Because of these songs and the multitude of Missourians who joined the wagon trains, "Pike" came to be known in the West as a term referring to the "poor white" settlers from the Mississippi Valley.

Just as Missouri was closely involved in the California gold rush of 1849, Missourians also were active in the later gold rushes of the West, particularly the gold rush of 1859. It is estimated that 100,000 Americans made the trip to Colorado in that year. Most of these passed through Missouri. As in the California gold rush and that of Nevada and other states of the West, few who went to Colorado discovered wealth. At least half of those who made the trip were forced to return home, empty-handed, the same year. One of these disillusioned prospectors was probably the first to sing this old Missouri ballad:

> Come join in the chorus and sing its fame,
> You poor lonely settler that's stuck on a claim.
> 'Farewell to this country; Farewell to the West.
> I'll travel back east to the girl I love best.
> I'll stop in Missouri and get me a wife,
> And live on corn dodger the rest of my life.'

"The Pathfinder" by Oscar E. Berninghaus.
Thomas Hart Benton's son-in-law John C. Fremont gained fame as the "Pathfinder" for his explorations in the West.

(Courtesy August A. Busch, Jr.)

The history of Missouri is an important part of the history of every western state. The explorers, the traders, the trappers, the missionaries, and the soldiers of Missouri played a major role in creating the new western commonwealths. Jedediah Smith, Jim Coulter, Jim Bridger, Kit Carson, and Father De Smet cannot be confined to Missouri history. The biography of each of them will testify to their courage and accomplishments. We know much of the contribution of the Austins to Texas, of the Chouteaus to the Indian territories later to become Oklahoma, and of the Bents to the development of Colorado and New Mexico. We cannot list here the many Missourians who settled throughout the West and who were instrumental in organizing the governments in their new homes. It is appropriate that the first elected governor of California should be Peter H. Burnett, a Missourian who took part in the settlement of both Oregon and California. The first elected governor of Oregon was a Missourian named John L. Whitaker. The state of Oregon has counties named Linn and Benton. Missourians made their mark on the West.

Some gained not only their destination, but fame as well. Others fell by the way, the vanquished in a mortal struggle with the wilderness. Most of them left no vestige on the Great Plains. Occasionally, an isolated tombstone such as the one that bears the following epitaph is found in barren sections of the West, bearing silent witness to the closing scene in the life of some pioneer.

Samuel McFarlin, of Wright Co Mo. died
27th Sep. 1849, of fever, Aged, 44 years
*May he rest peaceably in this
savage unknown country.*

BIBLIOGRAPHY

Atherton, Lewis E. "Business Techniques in the Santa Fe Trade," *Missouri Historical Review,* Vol. XXXIV (April, 1940), pp. 335-341.

Bailey, Thomas A. *A Diplomatic History of the American People.* New York: Appleton-Century, Inc., 1958.

Becknell, William. "Journal from Boone's Lick to Santa Fe and from Santa Cruz to Green River," *Missouri Historical Review,* Vol. IV (January, 1910), pp. 65-84.

Bek, William G., translated by. "From Bethel, Missouri to Aurora, Oregon: Letters of William Keil 1855-1870," *Missouri Historical Review,* Vol. XLVIII (October, 1953; January, 1954), pp. 23-41, 141-153.

Bieber, Ralph P. "Diary of a Journey from Missouri to California in 1849," *Missouri Historical Review,* Vol. XXIII (October, 1928), pp. 3-43.

Bieber, Ralph P. "Some Aspects of the Santa Fe Trail, 1848-1880," *Missouri Historical Review,* Vol. XVIII (January, 1924), pp. 158-166.

Bott, Emily Ann O'Neil. "Joseph Murphy's Contribution to the Development of the West," *Missouri Historical Review,* Vol. XLVII (October, 1952), pp. 18-28.

Britton, Rollin J. "Early Days on Grand River and the Mormon War," *Missouri Historical Review,* Vol. XIII (January, April, July, 1919), pp. 112-134, 287-310, 388-398; Vol. XIV (October, 1919; January, April-July, 1920), pp. 89-110, 233-245, 459-473.

Chittenden, Hiram Martin. *A History of the American Fur Trade of the Far West.* 2 Vols. Stanford, California: Academic Reprints, 1954.

Clark, Thomas D. *Frontier America.* New York: Charles Scribner's Sons, 1959.

Cox, Isaac Joslin. "Opening the Santa Fe Trail," *Missouri Historical Review,* Vol. XXV (October, 1930), pp. 30-66.

Culmer, Frederic A. "California Letter of John Wilson, 1850," *Missouri Historical Review,* Vol. XXIV (January, 1930), pp. 200-213.

Culmer, Frederic A. "Emigrant Missourians in Mexico and Oregon," *Missouri Historical Review,* Vol. XXV (January, 1931), pp. 281-288.

De Voto, Bernard. *Across the Wide Missouri.* Boston: Houghton, Mifflin and Company, 1947.

Dolch, Isabel S. "Some Aspects of Early Indian Fur Trade," *Missouri Historical Review,* Vol. XXXVI (April, 1942) pp. 190-198.

Duffus, Robert Luther. *The Santa Fe Trail.* London, New York: Longmans, Green, and Company, 1930.

Gardner, James A. "Business Career of Moses Austin in Missouri," *Missouri Historical Review,* Vol. L (April, 1956), pp. 235-247.

Gregg, Josiah. *Commerce of the Prairies* (edited by Max L. Moorhead). Norman: University of Oklahoma Press, 1954.

Gregg, Kate L. "Boonslickers in the Gold Rush," *Missouri Historical Review,* Vol. XLI (July, 1947), pp. 345-360.

Gregg, Kate L. "Missourians in the Gold Rush," *Missouri Historical Review,* Vol. XXXIX (January, 1945), pp. 137-154.

Klein, Ada Paris, ed. "The Fur Trade," *Missouri Historical Review,* Vol. XLIII (July, 1949), pp. 360-380; Vol. XLIV (October, 1949; January, 1950), pp. 48-65, 168-178.

Larkin, Lew. *Vanguard of Empire: Missouri's Century of Expansion.* St. Louis: State Publishing Company, 1961.

McDermott, John Francis. "The Exclusive Trade Privilege of Maxent, Laclede and Company," *Missouri Historical Review,* Vol. XXIX (July, 1935), pp. 272-278.

McGroarty, William B. "Letters from Alexander Doniphan," *Missouri Historical Review,* Vol. XXIV (October, 1929), pp. 26-39.

McGroarty, William B. "William H. Richardson's Journal of Doniphan's Expedition," *Missouri Historical Review,* Vol. XXII (January, April, July, 1928), pp. 193-236, 331-360, 511-542.

McLarty, Vivian K., ed. "Letters of William H. H. Gist: a Volunteer from Weston, Missouri in the War with Mexico," *Missouri Historical Review,* Vol. XLVIII (April, 1954), pp. 237-248.

Nasatir, A. P. "The Formation of the Missouri Company," *Missouri Historical Review,* Vol. XXV (October, 1930), pp. 10-22.

Page, Elizabeth. *Wagons West, a Story of the Oregon Trail.* New York: Farrar and Rinehart, Inc., 1930.

Parkman, Francis. *The Oregon Trail: Sketches of Prairie and Rocky-Mountain Life.* Boston: Little, Brown, and Company, 1909.

Phillips, Paul C. *The Fur Trade.* Norman: University of Oklahoma Press, 1961.

Pritchard, J. A. "The Diary of a Journey from Kentucky to California, 1849," *Missouri Historical Review,* Vol. XVIII (July, 1924), pp. 535-545.

Read, Georgia Willis. "Diseases, Drugs and Doctors on the Oregon-California Trail in the Gold Rush Years," *Missouri Historical Review,* Vol. XXXVIII (April, 1944), pp. 260-276.

Read, Georgia Willis. "Women and Children on the Oregon-California Trail in the Gold Rush Years," *Missouri Historical Review,* Vol. XXXIX (October, 1944), pp. 1-23.

Sampson, F. A. "M. M. Marmaduke Journal, Santa Fe Trail," *Missouri Historical Review,* Vol. VI (October, 1911), pp. 1-10.

Shoemaker, Floyd Calvin. *Missouri and Missourians.* Vol. I. Chicago: The Lewis Publishing Company, 1943.

Smith, Herman C. "Mormon Troubles in Missouri," *Missouri Historical Review,* Vol. IV (July, 1910), pp. 238-251.

Stephens, F. F. "Missouri and the Santa Fe Trade," *Missouri Historical Review,* Vol. X (July, 1916), pp. 233-262; Vol. XI (April-July, 1917), pp. 289-312.

Stephens, F. F. "Wetmore's Diary of a Journey to Santa Fe," *Missouri Historical Review,* Vol. VIII (July, 1914), pp. 177-197.

Stewart, George R. "The Prairie Schooner Got Them There," *American Heritage,* Vol. XIII (February, 1962), pp. 4-17.

Sunder, John E. *Bill Sublette: Mountain Man.* Norman: University of Oklahoma Press, 1959.

Trexler, H. A. "Missouri-Montana Highways," *Missouri Historical Review,* Vol. XII (January, April, 1918), pp. 67-80, 145-162.

Webb, James J. *Adventures in the Santa Fe Trade 1844-1847* (edited by Ralph P. Bieber). Glendale, California: The Arthur H. Clark Company, 1931.

West, Ray Benedict. *Kingdom of the Saints: The Story of Brigham Young and the Mormons.* New York: Viking Press, 1957.

Whiteman, Susan H. "Mormon Troubles in Carroll County," *Missouri Historical Review,* Vol. VIII (July, 1914), pp. 220-222.

Winters, Ethel Massie. "Experiences of Lewis Bissell Dougherty on the Oregon Trail," *Missouri Historical Review,* Vol. XXIV (April, July, 1930), pp. 359-378, 550-567; Vol. XXV (October, 1930; January, April, 1931), pp. 102-115, 306-321, 474-489.

Young, Otis E. "Military Protection of the Santa Fe Trail and Trade," *Missouri Historical Review,* Vol. XLIX (October, 1954), pp. 19-32.

CHAPTER VIII

Economic Growth, 1820-1860

> Its rich and beautiful prairies are rapidly taking on the aspects of cultivated fields; farms are opening, houses are being built; towns and villages are springing up in all directions. Its rivers are enlivened with commerce, with emigrants, and with troops moving to the frontiers. . . . Gold and silver is more abundant than in any other part of the Union; the demand for money less pressing; and the whole community animated with the consciousness, that all the comforts of life lay within the reach of every industrious man.
>
> —St. Louis *Enquirer*
> June 25, 1819

Thomas Jefferson frequently expressed his hope that frontier America would develop into a haven of happiness where settlers could live in peace with their neighbors, secure from the wars and troubles of the rest of the world and happy in the enjoyment of the bounty made available by the Creator in the rich river valleys of the West. It would be wrong for us to think of pre-Civil War Missouri as an idyllic abode or a cove of contentment. It was, however, a place of new hope and economic blessings for those who made the difficult trip to the West.

Settlement and Industry

The remarkable population growth in America during the nineteenth century resulted primarily from a combination of two factors—a high birth rate and a great influx of immigrants. During this period, hoards of Europeans struggling to escape Europe with its rigid class system, its scarcity of land, and its frequent bloody wars moved to America. The stream of immigrants came from all parts of northern Europe, particularly England, Ireland, and Germany. They moved westward with America—like the older settlers from Kentucky and Tennessee, they elbowed their way into the frontier states.

The census figures for the years 1820 to 1860 clearly illustrate the phenomenal population growth in Missouri:

1820	66,586
1830	140,455
1840	383,702
1850	682,044
1860	1,182,012

From 1820 to 1840 the population more than doubled each decade. Such a population growth produced great problems of settlement and of government.

Missourians were delighted to be part of such a rapidly growing state, for the population increase tended to boost land prices—which pleased all land owners—and it provided customers for the merchants and craftsmen. During its 1824-1825 session the General Assembly of Missouri issued the following statement which seemed to be an invitation to the unfortunate:

> Our country is peculiarly the asylum of the oppressed and emphatically the poor man's home, every law then which opens before the poor man a way to independence, which lifts him above the grade of tenant, which gives to him and his children a permanent resting and abiding place on the soil, not only subserves the cause of humanity but advances and maintains the fundamental principles of our government.

In 1820 Missouri was twenty-third in population rank among the states of the Union. Such great numbers swarmed into the state in the next forty years that Missouri had climbed to eighth place by 1860.

Contemporary sources from St. Louis and St. Charles speak of the constant flow of people crossing the Mississippi River. Driven by hopes for a brighter future, these people were often impoverished, with only a few crude articles of clothing or tools to call their own. Sometimes all of the family's possessions could be tied on the back of a horse. Some more fortunate families owned a wagon and a cow. Others—particularly artisans or craftsmen who did not intend to farm—placed all their goods in a cart or wheelbarrow and pushed it before them to their new home. It was not an easy way to travel. William Cobbett, an English traveler, spoke of "The rugged roads, the dirty hovels, the fire in the woods to sleep by, the pathless ways through the wilderness, the dangerous crossings of the rivers." As early as 1818 the concerned citizens of St. Louis began to establish immigrant aid societies to help unfortunates arriving in the city. The first such society, established in 1818 to help Irish and German settlers, was intended "to prevent them from falling into penury and vice." For most settlers, neither St. Louis nor St. Charles was their destination. They pushed beyond to find the cheap but fertile land they sought.

In the first half of the eighteenth century the following song—here shortened—was sung in England. It was intended as a form of advertising to attract settlers to Missouri. The refrain ran:

> To the West, to the West,
> To the land of the free,
> Where the mighty Missouri
> Rolls down to the sea.
> Where a man is a man
> So long as he'd toil.
> Where the humblest may gather
> The fruits of the soil.

Thomas Hart Benton believed that the United States Government should adopt new, more lenient policies in the distribution of its western land so that "the great number of persons now idle" might be transformed into "the respectable class of farmers and freeholders." Although Benton's plan for lowering the price of less desirable land was not adopted as government policy until 1854, the penniless settlers themselves developed a technique to acquire a farm. Those without money to buy land would "squat" upon a likely plot and improve it as their own. Under the prevailing attitudes of the frontier, the squatters' right was usually unchallenged; and later, when he had acquired sufficient money, he could purchase the acreage. In this extralegal way even the humblest could "gather the fruits of the soil" in Missouri.

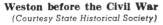
Weston before the Civil War
(Courtesy State Historical Society)

Until 1830 the areas of settlement usually followed the path of least resistance along the rivers. The wooded areas bordering the streams were known to be fertile and provided a supply of timber for building material and fuel. Prairie land inland from the streams was much more difficult to plow, and it had to lie fallow a year after plowing so that the grass roots would die. However, in the 1830's the settlers began to claim and till the Glacial Plains and Old Plains sections and to settle the Ozarks Highlands. For example, in 1820 the settled regions of the state were along such rivers as the Mississippi, Missouri, Gasconade, Osage, White, Current, Chariton, Grand, and Salt. By 1860 settlers had moved to all sections of the state. The last county to be admitted (except for St. Louis City, which was divided from St. Louis County in 1876) was Worth County, established in 1861. There were farms and villages in all four regions of the state by the outbreak of the Civil War. Of course the Ozarks area, with its less productive land, was much more sparsely populated than were either plains of the north or river lowlands.

The locations of the federal land offices in Missouri and the dates when they began making sales indicate the process of settlement in the state. Offices were located at St. Louis in 1816, Franklin in 1818, Jackson in 1818, Lexington in 1823, Palmyra in 1824, Fayette in 1832, Springfield in 1834, Plattsburg in 1842, Clinton in 1843, Milan in 1849, Warsaw in 1855, Boonville in 1858, Ironton in 1861, and Calhoun in 1863.

The new settler in Missouri had several alternatives in securing land. First, he might choose a likely plot of unsold government land and squat upon it in the expectation of later purchase. As an alternative he could claim the land and purchase it at auction for a minimum sum of $1.25 per acre. The sale price was frequently twice the minimum. Eighty acres was the smallest acreage sold under this arrangement. A third way to secure land was through the acquisition of New Madrid certificates issued by the Federal Government after the earthquake of 1811. These certificates were intended to help those whose land had been ruined in that cataclysm. As noted earlier, there was much fraud in the issuance of these certificates, and frequently the new settler in Missouri could secure some New Madrid certificates to present in payment for other land. In time the federal land offices honored five times as many New Mad d claims as there were heads of families in the earthquake region. A fourth way to secure land was to purchase plots that had already been claimed and improved. Land prices varied from time to time and place to place, but there were instances of improved farms, well located, which were sold by speculators to new immigrants for $8 to $20 per acre.

The usual frontiersman did not live in a community, but instead established a farm of his own in an isolated place. Those who chose wooded areas employed a technique which has been used all the way from North Carolina to California. The settler, after selecting his place of settlement, promptly killed the trees on approximately five-acre plots by "girdling," or removing a ring of bark. Since the dead trees dropped their foliage, the sun could reach the earth and such a field could produce crops the first year. The farmer did not have to wait until the underbrush had been removed, the trees cut, and the stumps rooted out. The fields thus planted with corn, wheat, and vegetables were dangerous places during windstorms, for great limbs and whole trees frequently crashed down into the planted area.

If there were no other settlers in the area, the frontier farmer built his typical log home without assistance. Where neighbors were present a community "raising" was held and everyone took part, perhaps singing as they built:

> Our cabins are made of logs of wood,
> The floors are made of puncheon,
> The roof is held by weighted poles
> And then we 'hang off' for luncheon.

House raisings were community projects. A group of neighbors could build a log house in a day.
(Harper's Weekly, January 24, 1874)

Usually the settler attempted to locate his house near a spring, which would provide him with a source of unpolluted water and a cool storage place for milk, butter, and meat. During the period before the Civil War those settlers who could afford to would construct a more permanent home once they were established, although the original log cabin often was kept for storage or other purposes. The second homes had rock foundations and were either of frame or rock construction with wooden shingles and a large fireplace. The German settlers in Cape Girardeau County were noted particularly for their fine stone homes.

The farmers, aiming at self-sufficiency, planted a variety of crops and raised several types of livestock. Corn grew well—the first crop grew stalks fifteen to twenty feet high—and was the most popular crop. It could be ground into cornmeal to provide a staple item for the diet of most early farmers. Corn could be fed to stock, sold, or turned into whiskey by the use of a still. The corn shucks were a useful material for chair bottoms, horse collars, mats, brooms, or mattress stuffing. The cobs could be burned for fuel, or used to make corn cob pipes, or dolls for the little girls in the family. Wheat was the second crop, although it was not grown in such quantities as corn. Garden crops, consisting of the vegetables most popular today except tomatoes, were of utmost importance. Cotton and flax were raised for the home production of cloth.

A crop especially popular in mid-Missouri was hemp. Before the age of wire cables, hemp ropes were much in demand. The crop had been raised in the South, and southerners brought it with them to Missouri where rope made from the fiber became an important product at such places as Lexington, Rocheport, Glasgow, Liberty, and Miami. Tobacco was another major crop along the Missouri River. Grape culture was introduced by German settlers in the Washington-Hermann area.

Horses, mules, cattle, hogs, sheep, and chickens were the common livestock found on Missouri farms of this period. The first farmers fenced in their fields of crops and allowed the stock to roam the woods. The wandering cattle and hogs were identified by ear marks. Because of the predators on the frontier, sheep had to be kept enclosed. By the 1840's many purebred cattle, especially Shorthorns, were being brought into the state. Berkshire hogs and purebred Shanghai chickens—kin to Pike County Betsey's traveling companion—were popular breeds in pre-Civil War Missouri.

(Courtesy State Historical Society)

Farmers brought their finest livestock to the first state agricultural fair in 1853.

Missouri also became noted in the first half of the nineteenth century for the production of mules. Because of the Santa Fe trade, many jacks had been brought back to Missouri to sire the first Missouri mules. The mule had many advantages over the horse. He had better resistance to disease. He did not need to be shod so frequently. He was able to work harder for longer periods, and he would not overeat. By 1835 Missourians were exporting mules to other parts of the country.

By the time of the Civil War there had been major improvements in several agricultural implements. Excellent iron plows of several designs were available. Reapers could be purchased to ease the back-breaking task of cutting grain. A crude threshing machine was introduced in Missouri shortly before the war started. In spite of these improvements, most Missouri farmers or their slaves spent a good part of their lives wielding a hoe or a scythe, or walking behind a mule-drawn plow.

Although most of the new settlers sought opportunities on the farm, a large number of new towns and cities developed in Missouri during the first four decades of statehood. The farmers required settlements where they might purchase necessary supplies and sell their produce. Many land speculators purchased a likely location with the intent of platting a region, building sev-

A reaper and mower in use during the 1860's

eral homes and stores, and selling lots at high prices. It is during this time that the inland cities developed.

The 1860 list of the ten most populous cities in Missouri shows the chief centers of population as follows:

St. Louis	160,773
St. Joseph	8,932
Hannibal	6,505
Kansas City	4,418
Lexington	4,122
Carondelet	3,993
St. Charles	3,239
Independence	3,164
Jefferson City	3,082
Cape Girardeau	2,663

Each of the these ten cities is located either on or near the Mississippi or Missouri rivers. To illustrate the relative size of St. Louis, it should be noted that the combined population of the next nine cities equaled approximately one-fourth the population of St. Louis.

The smaller cities served primarily as service centers for the rural population with the usual saw and grist mills, tanyards, merchants, smiths, harness makers, wagon makers, jewelers, and printers. Some settlements were also important for their manufacturing or mining activities. Iron smelters operated in Franklin County, Crawford County, Washington County, Iron County, and Phelps County. Probably the best known iron works was the "Maramec" Iron Works, later known as the James Iron Works, at St. James. Lead mining continued to be of importance in the Washington County area. The exploitation of lead mines also prompted the development of such isolated settlements in southwest Missouri as Neosho, Leadville, and Grandby. Many small communities profited from an export item related to the particular resources or skills of the area. Grapes from the vineyards surrounding Hermann yielded 10,000 gallons of wine in 1848. In the next eight years wine production was increased to 100,000 gallons. In 1845 Dr. William Keil, with a group of 500 followers of his religious and social theories, established a German community in Bethel, Missouri, in which all property was held in common. The settlement, under the efficient dictatorship of Dr. Kiel, was supported in part by a tailor shop, glove and shoe factories, and a tannery. Buckskin gloves from Bethel took first prize in the New York World's Fair of 1858.

St. Louis was the manufacturing and merchandising giant of the state. The city not only played a major role in supplying the westward movement and in serving as a shipping point on the Mississippi, but St. Louis also developed many new manufacturing industries, particularly in the years immediately preceding the Civil War. Industrial statistics show that the value of manufactured goods doubled between 1850 and 1860. St. Louis had many entrepreneurs with imagination and courage to establish new plants, and an abundance of laborers to man the enterprises. Workmen toiled from sunup to sundown before the year 1840, when the ten-hour day was adopted by many of the St. Louis industries.

Many of the major manufacturing concerns of St. Louis were active in the production of iron products. Plows, stoves, tools, furnaces, pipe, were all products of the fast-growing Mississippi metropolis. In addition St. Louis companies provided the guns, saddles, and wagons so necessary to the westward movement. They produced furniture, clothing, barrels, and steamboats. The German citizens brought with them Old World brewing techniques, and by the year 1860 some forty breweries were in operation in St. Louis. It is estimated that during this period the city produced approximately sixty per cent of the manufactured goods of Missouri. By the end of the period, Kansas City and St. Joseph began to emerge as factory centers.

Transportation and Communication

During the first forty years of statehood, when settlers pushed their way into the farthest corners of the state and farms and villages sprouted in all sections, it early became necessary to develop systems of transportation for the movement of goods and people from one area to another. Travelers and shippers had two choices of transport—land and water. The only exception was the balloon voyage of John Wise who ascended at St. Louis July 1, 1859, and landed nineteen hours later in New York State. The letters in a mail bag Wise was forced to discard during a storm were later found and delivered. Balloonist Wise is therefore credited by some as being the first man to transport air mail. His historic flight is, of course, atypical. Everyone else went by land or by water.

Near the end of Missouri's territorial period, the first steamboat arrived in St. Louis. The *Zebulon M. Pike* made the trip from Louisville, Kentucky, to St. Louis in 1817 moving upstream at the impressive pace of three miles per hour. The ship carried poles for the crew to supply extra power when necessary. Although the Indians at the wharf in St. Louis fled in terror at the sight of the hissing monster, other Missourians recognized the steam engine as a new, more rapid, and more convenient method of transportation. The *Pike* carried on regular four-week trips between Louisville and St. Louis with stops at Herculaneum, Ste. Genevieve, and Cape Girardeau. The first steamboat to make its way up the Missouri was the *Independence.* Choking and sputtering, the steam vessel, which had been constructed in Pittsburgh especially for use on the shallow Missouri, reached Franklin thirteen days after departing from St. Louis. She was greeted with great elation by those who witnessed her arrival. Amid congratulations, dinners, and thirty-one eloquent toasts, the people of Franklin declared their assurance of the "abundant development of our fertile and extensive region through contact with the Atlantic, West Indies, and European markets."

Another early steamboat designed for a particular purpose was the *Western Engineer.* Major Stephen H. Long, who was planning a voyage to the Upper Missouri River, had the boat constructed not only to transport his party, but also to terrify the Indians. As it was designed, the smoke from the engines was channeled out the serpent's head which formed the bow. The St. Louis *Enquirer* described the ship as follows:

> From under the boat, at its stern, issues a stream of foaming water, dashing violently along. All the machinery is hid. Three small brass field pieces, mounted on field carriages, stand on the deck. The boat is ascending the rapid stream at the rate of three miles an hour. Neither wind or human hands are seen to help her; and to the eye of ignorance, the illusion is complete, that a monster of the deep carries her on his back, smoking with fatigue, and lashing the waves with violent exertion.

In time, the white men learned that the Indian's initial fear of the steamboat was not unfounded. The steam that provided

(Courtesy State Historical Society)

Lunette by Victor Higgins in the Missouri capitol

(*Courtesy Missouri Historical Society*)

The Ornate Interior of the Grand Republic

the power to turn the great paddlewheels was generated in boilers which could—and did—explode in flaming disaster when fired beyond their endurance. This catastrophe was sometimes the result of races between rival steamers whose sweating boiler crews would cram wood—or, after 1840, coal—into the maw of the furnace until the overtaxed boiler burst, propelling the ship to glory—but not as victor in the race! The demand of the *Saluda's* captain for "More steam!" cost the lives of 100 Utah-bound Mormons near Lexington, Missouri, in 1852. The steamboats were imperiled, too, by the usual obstacles in the channel such as fallen trees, sandbars, and debris. The great boats were manuevered around such hazards with much more difficulty than lighter, smaller craft, and the toll of the river was such that, before 1850, the average life of a steamboat was five years.

In spite of the danger of explosion and navigation problems, the steamboat was a great improvement upon the earlier methods of upstream pulling, paddling, or poling. Steamboats were faster. They were larger and could carry greater loads. They could also provide passengers with room, board, and even entertainment.

There was a rapid growth of steamboat activity in Missouri during the early years of statehood. The steamboats not only served the usual ports of call such as New Madrid, Cape Girardeau, Ste. Genevieve, St. Louis, and St. Charles, but they also gave increasing service to Hermann, Jefferson City, Glasgow, Brunswick, Lexington, Independence, and St. Joseph. The steamboats were used on rivers such as the Grand, the Gasconade, and the Osage, which was navigated for 200 miles. Ships carried goods all the way to Warsaw and Osceola on the Osage, and in 1844 one boat ascended the river as far as Harmony Mission in Bates County. There is a report that a steamboat went as far north as Chillicothe in 1865. In southwest Missouri the White River provided a highway for steamboats all the way to the town of Forsyth.

The steamboat replaced the keelboat for moving the produce of the West. The lower decks of the boats supplied storage space for the freight, household goods, animals, and anything else that needed transportation. The tonnage figures for river shipping at St. Louis give a picture of the great growth of trade during the rise of the steamboats:

1824	90,000 tons
1834	174,000 tons
1844	716,000 tons
1854	1,370,000 tons

The steamboats provided comfortable passenger transport for part of the long journey west for immigrants and furnished a floating playground for those able to afford the luxury. The various steamboat companies spent great sums of money to fill their river-borne palaces with expensive and exotic appoint-

The Grand Republic
(Courtesy Missouri Historical Society)

ments. Crystal chandeliers, thick oriental rugs, plush-covered furniture, ornate bars, splendid dancing chambers, all were available to affluent Missourians. Some steamboats not only carried a string orchestra, but a brass band as well.

The splendid steamboats of the two decades before the Civil War are not in keeping with the usual drabness of life to be found in most of the West. They carried the glamour and sophistication of eastern cities to the frontier. The *Western Monthly Review,* a newspaper of the day, commented on the impact of the steamboat in 1827:

> An Atlantic [citizen] who talks to us under the name of backwoodsmen, would not believe that such fairy structures of oriental gorgeousness . . . had ever existed in the imaginative brain of a romancer, much less, that they were actually in existence, rushing down the Mississippi . . . bearing speculators, merchants, dandies, fine ladies . . . with pianos, and stocks of novels, and cards, and dice, and flirting, . . . and champagne, and on the deck, perhaps, three hundred fellows, who have seen alligators, and neither fear whiskey, nor gunpowder. A steamboat, coming from New Orleans, brings to the remotest villages of our streams, and the very doors of the cabins, a little Paris, a section of Broadway, or a slice of Philadelphia, to ferment in the minds of our young people, the innate propensity for fashions and finery.

The rapid development of the steamboat as a means of transportation and communication brought with it a new vocabulary and a new field of employment. Ship's officers, pilots, engineers, deckhands, stewards, clerks, and even barbers were among the large crews that managed the boat and tended to the passengers' needs. The captain of the ship had great responsibility and was paid accordingly. Even more important than the captain was the pilot who had to memorize every reef, sandbar, snag, and sunken wreck in the river to preserve the many lives in his hand. Pilots were probably the highest paid people in Missouri during this period. On the Mississippi they received $150 to $250 a month; on the more difficultly navigated Missouri River they frequently were paid $1,000 to $1,800 a month—a fabulous sum in that day. Samuel Clemens of Hannibal—alias Mark Twain—portrays in his *Life on the Mississippi* the colorful personalities of steamboat personnel, the puckish humor of their practical jokes, the breathless suspense of their hairbreadth escapes, and the horror and pathos of fiery wrecks.

The steamboat contributed much to Missouri. The transportation it furnished for goods and people facilitated communications, provided increased trade and employment, and lent a colorful backdrop for the life and literature of mid-nineteenth-century Missouri.

(Courtesy State Historical Society)

The painting of Missouri River snags by Bodmer shows why piloting on the Missouri required great skill.

Another important form of water transportation was the ferry established by an enterprising individual at a point where crossings were in frequent demand. Such great numbers of people were gathering in the American Bottom—the fertile section of southwest Illinois across the Mississippi from St. Louis—that a ferry boat was greatly needed. In 1797 Captain James Piggott received permission of Illinois officials and Spanish officials in St. Louis to operate a ferry across the Mississippi. An inventive gentleman named Samuel Wiggins acquired the St. Louis ferry in 1819 and experimented with new forms of propulsion. The earlier ferries had been paddled or poled across. Wiggins constructed horse-tread ferries which he named the *Sea Serpent,* the *Rhinoceros,* and the *Antelope.* Horse-tread ferries were also used in other parts of the state. In the year 1828 Wiggins began using steam power to ferry passengers and freight across the

Mississippi. Ferrying was an important occupation for many river people living at strategic points. The state granted permission for individuals to operate ferries, but they were required to purchase a license; and the fares, subject to regulation by the state courts, had to be posted.

There were also remarkable advances in transportation by land during the same period. Since the fertile lands bordering the rivers were the first to be occupied, later settlers were forced to choose homesteads more distant from the navigable streams. These farmers required roads for transportation and communication. During the territorial period the state legislature began the enactment of laws to encourage the improvement of such primitive roads as then existed. The first enactment came in 1808, and was supplemented by the road law of 1822. Under this legislation roads were to be cleared no wider than fifty feet nor less than twenty feet. The original law instructed officials to clear trees and brush from the road, and to leave no stump higher than ten inches in the roadway. State law required all male citizens to work on the roads for specified periods each year. These first roads were unsurfaced, and were virtually impassable during wet weather—and perhaps the rest of the time as well, to judge from a contemporary comment:

> . . .if the mud does not get quite over your boot tops
> when you sit in the saddle, they call it a middling-
> good road.

The stumps, even though restricted in size, provided a major hazard for wagons and buggies. Under the provision of the federal agreement with Missouri in 1820, three per cent of the money derived from the sale of federal land in Missouri was to be given to the state to assist in the construction of roads and bridges. This three per cent did not constitute a major source of funds. The small sums accumulated in this manner were used either for the construction of bridges or to assist counties in their road-building programs.

The most unusual innovation in road building was the plank road which became popular in the 1840's. Road planners, observing that timber was inexpensive and plentiful, devised a plan to construct a wooden road eight to twelve feet wide. Three oak sills were laid lengthwise with the road and then covered by planks placed across them. Some fifty companies secured state charters for the building of plank roads, but only seventeen such

Midnight Race on the Mississippi

thoroughfares were completed. Since tolls were usually collected on the plank roads, the cost of their construction was borne by those who traveled them. The longest plank road, used to transport ore from Iron Mountain to Ste. Genevieve, extended forty-two miles. The University of Missouri obviously considered accessibility to a plank road an important item of publicity. The following appeared in its catalogue for 1856:

> The University is easily accessible by river during the greater part of the year. At the landing in Providence, carriages will always be in readiness to convey passengers to Columbia. To this point a plank road is completed.

Since the wood soon warped and decayed, the plank roads were not practical. Road builders then adopted another form of surfacing—gravel.

It would be impossible here to list the new roads which appeared in Missouri during the pre-Civil War time. Those most frequently used were Three Notch Road from Ste. Genevieve to Mine La Motte, Boon's Lick Trail from St. Charles to Franklin, the Manchester Road from St. Louis to Manchester, and the Springfield Road from St. Louis to Neosho.

During this time, many bridges were constructed over smaller streams. To encourage this, the legislature frequently gave individuals permission to build toll bridges. Such bridges

(Courtesy State Historical Society)

A coach travels the plank road west of Hannibal in 1854

were usually built with walls and a roof to protect the wooden floor and supports from the elements. They were not built by professional engineers, but by capable, careful frontiersmen using the timbers available at the time.

In addition to the improved modes of water transportation and the new roads and bridges facilitating land travel, the overland mail and passenger services offered by private companies contributed to the development of transportation and communications. When Missouri became American territory in 1804, the nearest stage coach line was 1,000 miles away in western Pennsylvania. Couriers on horseback carried the mail to and from Pennsylvania about once a week. As the settlement of Missouri continued, post offices were erected in the major towns, and post riders were employed to distribute the mail within the state. With the introduction of stage coach lines in Missouri the post riders were no longer needed, as the coaches carried both passengers and mail.

The citizens of the new state of California were dissatisfied with the mail service furnished by steamers from Panama. They called for a faster, more efficient postal system. In 1857 Congress authorized the postmaster-general to subsidize a company which would establish an overland mail service from St. Louis to

San Francisco. The Butterfield Overland Mail Company secured this franchise and received a subsidy of $600,000 to help finance the project. The company prepared for the enterprise by purchasing 100 Concord coaches, 1,000 horses, and 500 mules. Seven hundred and fifty men worked for the company, either operating the way stations located every ten miles or driving the gaudy red and green coaches. In October, 1858, mail and passengers from St. Louis were transported by the Pacific Railroad to Tipton, where they boarded a Concord stage for the twenty-five-day trip. From Tipton the coach followed a route through Warsaw, Wheatland, Elkton, Bolivar, Brighton, Springfield, Clever, Cassville, and out into the Southwest.

Letters marked "By the Overland Mail" were transported for only three cents. Passengers were required to pay $200 for passage to San Francisco, but only $100 for the return trip. Patrons of the Butterfield Overland Line were at times delighted with the service, and at other times appalled at the food placed before them at the way stations. One traveler said of the accommodations at an Oklahoma station, "Our table and food were black with clustered flies which crowded even into our tea, and had to be shoveled out by wholesale." Another complaint frequently heard concerned the difficulty of traveling around the clock, attempting to sleep while sitting up in a crowded, jolting, lurching coach over bumpy dirt roads. The uncomfortable trip

Covered Bridge, Livingston County
(Courtesy State Highway Commission)

was made less attractive by the possibility of Indian ambush. Mark Twain tells of a driver for Overland who finally quit his job because "he came as near as anything to starving to death in the midst of abundance, because they kept him so leaky with bullet holes that he couldn't hold his vittles." Twain may have exaggerated a bit, but the trip was both difficult and dangerous for drivers and passengers alike.

Russell, Majors, and Waddell, a company with headquarters in Lexington, Missouri, became the most important freighters to the West during the 1850's. The company had between 3,500 and 4,000 ox-drawn wagons carrying freight to the scattered settlements of the West during the year 1858. The 4,000 to 5,000 employees of the company were called "The Mariners of the Plains," as they drove their 40,000 oxen and 10,000 mules back and forth across the Great Plains with goods—chiefly government freight for army posts—being delivered to the West. The company was financially successful in its transportation of freight, but unsuccessful in its attempts to enter the stage coach business and to operate the Pony Express. William H. Russell was more daring than his two partners and involved them in expensive operations. He initiated a daily stage coach service between Leavenworth and Denver, but the project lost money and was ultimately sold to another Missourian, Ben Holliday, from Weston.

The enterprise which brought great fame to Russell, Majors, and Waddell was the Pony Express. At the outset of the Civil War federal officials were concerned over the maintenance of communications with California, since the regularly used routes to the West—including the Butterfield Overland Route—tra-

"Stagecoach Being Attacked by Indians" by Oscar E. Berninghaus
(Courtesy August A. Busch, Jr.)

Interior View of an Overland Stage.
(Courtesy State Historical Society)

versed southern territory. William Russell offered to establish an express to carry messages from Missouri to California by couriers on fast horses. Although Majors and Waddell did not favor the project, they felt committed to carry it out because of promises Russell had made in Washington, D. C. Thus, in 1860, the company prepared to establish a more rapid communication system with the Pacific Coast by purchasing 500 swift horses, building 190 stations, and hiring 200 station attendants and eighty riders weighing 125 pounds or less. The following ad helped recruit daring young men for the Pony Express:

> WANTED: Young, skinny, wiry fellows, not over 18. Must be expert riders willing to risk death daily. Orphans preferred. Wages: $25 per week.

Letters delivered to St. Joseph by the Hannibal and St. Joseph Railway were immediately placed in especially-designed pouches. After securing the mailbags, the rider galloped off across the plains toward his destination 1,982 miles away. Usually a rider would travel seventy-five miles a day, although one famous rider, Buffalo Bill Cody, once rode 300 miles without rest. The fifteen pounds of mail was usually delivered in Sacramento ten days after leaving St. Joseph.

The Pony Express was a dramatic episode in Western history, and Americans all over the nation delighted to read of the brave young men who sped across the West through all extremes of weather and despite Indian perils to deliver the United States Mail. Although several riders died in carrying out their duties, it is to the credit of the company and their men that not one mail bag was lost during eighteen months of operation. The Pony Express was not a financial success, however, and when telegraph lines were completed in 1861, the service was discontinued.

It was not until 1847 that Missouri was connected with the East through a telegraph system. President Polk received the first telegram from St. Louis in December of that year. Originally, the telegraph lines extended to the Illinois side of the Mississippi River, and the messages were ferried across the river to be delivered. The telegraph company made several attempts to string the wires across the Mississippi using great masts planted on each shore and one in the middle of the river, on Bloody Island. However, passing boats and roosting birds disrupted service so frequently that a system was devised for laying the telegraph cable on the bed of the Mississippi. After reaching St. Louis by this means in 1850, the telegraph lines were then strung on trees across the state south to Cape Girardeau the same year, west to Weston in 1851, and farther west to St. Joseph in 1853.

In Missouri there was much interest in railroads long before the roads themselves were built. A state convention in St. Louis in 1836 recommended the immediate construction of two lines across the state. Although the legislature incorporated eighteen companies which intended to build railroads, the depression of 1837 halted all such plans. In 1849 a national railroad convention was held in St. Louis. Almost 1,000 delegates crowded into the city to consider the best means for encouraging the construction of railroads. Thomas Hart Benton spoke to the convention and, as a faithful Missourian and son of the West, recommended the creation of a road stretching from St. Louis to San Francisco. Although the convention strongly supported the immediate creation of a rail line to the West, the feat was not accomplished until the time of the Civil War.

In 1849 railroads had already been in operation successfully in the East for twenty years. Missourians could not wait for the completion of a western line, and enterprising promoters began the construction of railroads within the state. The Hannibal and St. Joseph Railroad received its charter in 1847 to construct a line across the northern part of the state between those terminal points. The Pacific Railroad was incorporated in 1849. Both companies were slow to begin construction because of money problems. Although railroads were recognized as being most important to the economic development of the state, it was difficult for promoters to secure the great sums necessary to construct the roads. Governor Austin A. King in 1850 suggested that the state use its credit to supplement private capital. The legislature agreed and issued a total of $24,950,000 in bonds to be loaned to the companies. According to the governor's plans, the railroads would repay the state government out of their profits.

The first two roads to begin building, the Hannibal and St. Joseph (now Burlington) and the Pacific (Missouri Pacific), received state grants in 1851. Later, state funds were also granted to the Southwest Branch of the Pacific (Frisco), the North Missouri (Wabash), the St. Louis and Iron Mountain (Missouri Pacific), the Platte County (Burlington), and the Cairo and Fulton (Missouri Pacific). In addition to further state loans in 1852, 1855, and 1857, the companies received land grants from the Federal Government to assist construction.

By 1855 the Pacific line reached from St. Louis to Jefferson City. Ten years later it extended to Kansas City. The St. Louis and Iron Mountain had laid its tracks from St. Louis to Pilot Knob by 1858. By 1859 the Hannibal and St. Joseph was complete. In fact, this railroad brought to St. Joseph the letters which were carried to California by the Pony Express. By 1860 Missouri had 817 miles of railroad.

However, all of the companies except the Hannibal and St. Joseph found themselves in financial trouble in the 1860's, and the state finally had to foreclose on them. Although the state resold the railroads, state officials were able to recover only about six million dollars. In effect the construction of these early railroads was heavily subsidized by the taxpapers. For many years charges and complaints could be heard in Missouri of alleged corruption in the handling of the railroad loans, the foreclosures, and the resale transactions.

Banks and Currency

There were three financial panics or depressions during the period 1820-1860. The first, although known as the depression of 1819, did not strike Missouri until 1821. The second was known nationally as the depression of 1837, and again Missouri's isolation postponed the evil effects until 1841. The third

"The Coming and Going of the Pony Express" by Frederic Remington

economic panic occurred in 1857. In each of these financial crises the banks of the state were severely tested. Today residents are spared the worry the early settlers endured concerning the safety of their bank deposits. The instability of the banks of Missouri in the last years of the Territorial Period and the first twenty years of statehood gave early Missouri depositors good cause for concern.

The first banks in Missouri, when making a loan, did not transfer specie (gold or silver coin) to the individuals seeking money. Instead they issued bank notes of various denominations. In most cases, the notes indicated that the bank would redeem the note in specie on presentation of the paper money. Thus, the bank note passed as currency because of the promise of redemption in coin. Overextension of credit, and the printing of excessive amounts of paper currency beyond the bank's capacity to redeem, were the two major causes of bank failures during this period. Four banks were chartered between 1813 and 1837. The first three closed within four years of their establishment.

The Bank of St. Louis was chartered in 1813 and opened in 1816 by a group of the leading citizens who believed that the growth of trade in Missouri necessitated the founding of a financial clearing house. Auguste Chouteau was the leader in the establishment of the bank; Moses Austin was a stockholder. In 1818 the stockholders were split over bank policies. Excessive loans had been granted to land speculators, and some of the stockholders wished the bank to adopt more conservative policies. Other proprietors favored liberal extension of loans. In 1819 the bank closed after several months of legal haggling between the two factions.

The Bank of Missouri, chartered in 1817, was the second to be established in the territory. This bank, like its competitors, was tempted to make extravagant loans. During the 1818-19 period, with the great influx of settlers, speculators were making large sums of money by purchasing land and reselling it, at a profit, to the immigrants. These speculators required cash to acquire land, and the bank provided it. However, the depression of 1819 struck the eastern states first, and in a year it curtailed the immigration of people into Missouri. This placed the speculators in a precarious situation since many had borrowed heavily for their land acquisitions. Because of the sharp decrease in the number of immigrants into the territory, both the speculators and merchants suffered. The banks, therefore, were unable to regain the money they had loaned. As a result, the Bank of Missouri was forced to suspend specie payments in August of 1821. In effect, the bank no longer had hard money with which to redeem the bank notes it had issued in denominations of $1, $3, $5, and $20. After examination of the assets and liabilities, the bank was liquidated and the stockholders were held partially liable for the losses sustained by the depositors. These two early bank failures taught many settlers of the dangers inherent in the excessive issuance of bank notes. Thomas Hart Benton had been involved as a stockholder in both banks, and his later stand for hard money in denominations under $20 probably resulted from these early experiences.

In the year 1829 the Bank of the United States, headed nationally by Nicholas Biddle of Philadelphia, established a branch in St. Louis. Biddle sent his brother Thomas to St. Louis to manage the Missouri branch of the B.U.S. The branch operated profitably in St. Louis until President Andrew Jackson began his attack upon it. Benton worked closely with Jackson to prevent the rechartering of the bank, and the senator approved the president's policy of removing federal deposits from the B.U.S. Thus, the Democratic party and political leaders of Missouri declared war on the bank in St. Louis. In 1831 Democrat Spencer Pettis, during his campaign for a seat in Congress, spoke critically of the B.U.S. and sharply criticized Thomas Biddle. As so frequently happened at that time, political controversy provoked physical violence. Biddle attacked the sleeping Pettis in his St. Louis hotel. Pettis was restrained from issuing an immediate demand for a duel until the election was called. Then, on August 26, 1831, Biddle immediately accepted Pettis' challenge to an encounter on Bloody Island. Because Biddle was nearsighted, the two stood only five feet apart. After an exchange of shots, both men fell wounded and died shortly thereafter.

Thus, the Missouri branch of the B.U.S. was closely tied to Missouri politics. The National Republicans (Whigs) supported Biddle and the Bank of the United States. Most of the mercantile interests in the state favored the continuation of the B.U.S. However, the bank was severely crippled when Jackson withdrew federal funds. The St. Louis branch was closed in 1833. John O'Fallon was in the charge of the Missouri branch of the B.U.S. at the time of its liquidation. When President Jackson withdrew the federal funds from the bank, it was forced to recall many of its loans. O'Fallon, however, was such a capable banker that he was able to close the St. Louis branch in 1833 with a loss of only $125.

During Jackson's second administration, 1832-36, a booming prosperity struck the West. This prosperity was built both on the growing productivity and trade of the country, and reckless money printing and lending by banks—particulary in the West. Jackson had encouraged this boom by depositing federal money in the state banks. Near the end of his administration, Jackson was alerted by Thomas Hart Benton and others to the dangers of the situation. Shortly before leaving the White House, the president issued his Specie Circular which prohibited further purchase of government land with paper money. Immediately, the people became suspicious of the abundant "shin plasters" or "wildcat currency" and the bank notes began to lose value in exchange. Since it was very difficult for the residents of Missouri to travel to the issuing bank in order to redeem bank notes from Ohio, Kentucky, or Tennessee, they would agree to accept less than face value for the paper they held. This practice contributed to the decrease in the value of paper money that began in 1837. Merchants or citizens who held paper found they could not easily pass it in trade.

The depression of 1837, however, was slow to reach Missouri. In part this can be explained by the fact that the Santa Fe trade

A view of Hermann in 1859 drawn on stone by E. Robyn. Notice the vineyards that cover the slope in the foreground.

brought coin and bullion into the state—approximately $100,000
annually during the period 1832-35. This source of specie continued during the depression of 1837. Another stabilizing factor
for the Missouri economy was the presence in St. Louis of large
government deposits to be used by six military forts and Indian
agencies, as well as federal funds received from the sale of land
This money was deposited in the St. Louis branch of the Cincinnati Commercial Agency until 1837. Still another reason for the
delayed arrival of the depression in Missouri was the establishment in 1837 of the new Bank of the State of Missouri. Federal
deposits were placed in this bank in 1837 when the branch of the
Cincinnati Commercial Agency withdrew.

The Bank of the State of Missouri was established to answer
a great need for sound banks which could provide credit, an
agency of exchange, and a safe place of deposit. In establishing
the Bank of the State of Missouri, the legislature was careful to
declare that the bank could not issue notes with a face value
of less than $10. Eventually branches of this bank were
established in Palmyra, Jackson, Fayette, Springfield, Cape
Girardeau, and Lexington. The bank was soon faced with a
crisis when St. Louis firms, such as the St. Louis Gaslight Company, attempted to deposit paper money issued by certain Illinois
banks which denied redemption of their bank notes in specie. The
Bank of the State of Missouri refused to accept notes from such
banks. Senator Benton and the rural inland population backed
the position of the bank, while the merchants sought a modifica-
tion of the decision, hoping thereby to be able to pass the paper
currency they received in trade. From this difference of opinion,

two groups developed in Missouri. The "Hards" insisted on the use of gold and silver coins for denominations under $20 and opposed the depositing of questionable paper money in the bank. The "Softs" favored the bank's acceptance of paper currency. The two factions engaged in political conflict in the state for almost a decade. The "Softs" were able, in 1841, to secure legislation forcing the Bank of the State of Missouri to accept paper money. Benton and his supporters, however, would not give up their constant demands for a sound, conservative banking system and for the use of hard money in place of paper currency of dubious value. Although the bank started in the midst of a national depression, it was successful because the directors, despite legislative intervention, operated on sound financial principles. The Bank of the State of Missouri continued as a strong financial

The currency pictured below is "scrip" issued by the Maramec Iron Works in 1869. On the face of the right side (above) is written "I will pay the bearer ONE DOLLAR in merchandise in presentation of this note at my store. Wm. James."

(Courtesy State Historical Society)

institution until finally sold to a private corporation after the Civil War.

Because the depression of 1837 was not felt in the state until 1841, Missouri did not have the great financial hardships of many other states in the West. Those neighboring states which had huge debts from vast internal improvement projects begun before the depression frequently were unable to pay their bonds. Having defaulted on earlier obligations, those states had difficulty securing new loans. Missouri, on the other hand, because of conservative banking, the influx of gold and silver from Santa Fe, and her moderate debt, did not suffer so greatly from the depression when it did come.

While Old Bullion Benton advocated hard money, a group of Missourians located near Hahatonka, in what is now Camden County, devised another solution for their money problems. These amateur economists set up printing presses in the caves of that lovely region and began to manufacture their own bank notes. The counterfeiters, who were christened the "Bank of Niangua" by Missouri wags, flooded the country with their notes. In time a group of vigilantes, who called themselves the "Slickers," publicized their determination to halt the illegal activity of the "Bankers." After the counterfeiters murdered a young man in retaliation, immediate popular pressure forced their capture in 1841. The activities of these outlaws, however, were of a longer duration than those of most of their legal counterparts, for they were able to operate some nine years before their "bank" failed.

The operation of banks and the type of money available became the most important political issue of the 30's and 40's. On the one hand Benton, acting as the leader of the Democratic Party, attacked the Bank of the United States as a monopoly and condemned it for its misuse of power. He also criticized state banks which printed bank notes recklessly and reaffirmed his belief that the common people of the country would be better protected if they were furnished gold coins, which were known as "yellow jackets." On the other hand, the Whigs were the advocates of the Bank of the United States. They believed that the B.U.S., properly run, would provide economic strength, uniformity, and great flexibility in the country's financial structure. Many of the political campaigns centered on this conflict of ideas. The following lyric entitled "To Promise, Yet Not Pay" was a Democratic song sung to the tune "To Sigh, Yet Feel No Pain":

> To promise, yet not pay
>   To cheat, to rob and lie;
> To trifle with the people's change,
>   To pass them proudly by,
> To pour at Biddle's shrine,
>   The offering of their cash,
> To waft it o'er the ocean brine,
>   And give us paper trash.
>
> This is Whiggery—Whiggery rank,
> This is Whiggery—Whiggery rank,
> Such as pleases Whig and Bank.
>
> Your cash, yourselves to save,
>   Unwon by paper charm;
> And "yellow jackets" plenty have,
>   In age to keep you warm.
> To feel that you endure
>   No fears that Bank men do,
> And tho' the Banks should break, you're sure
>   They cannot injure you.
>
> This is Jackson's—Benton's plan
> This is Jackson's—Benton's plan
> Such as charms the honest man.

*   *   *

In summary, the period from 1820 to 1860 was a time of great economic growth in Missouri. Large numbers of citizens were added to the state, the areas inland from the rivers were settled, and a multitude of towns and cities were established to serve the needs of the rural population. While Missouri was primarily an agricultural state, a growing industry developed to provide goods for her citizens and for the entire West as well.

This pre-Civil War period was the era when steamboats were the major carriers of freight and passengers. It was a time of slow development of roads and a valiant attempt to provide adequate transportation to, and communication with, the West. At the end of the period two important innovations, the telegraph and the railroad, made their appearance in Missouri. They were soon to push aside the other more cumbersome, less efficient systems of communications and transportation.

The last half of the period was a time of struggle to insure the stability of the emerging banking system and to promote responsibility in the issuance of paper currency. The combination of agriculture, merchandising, and manufacturing served by a developing transportation-communication network and a sound banking system was vital to the economic health of the state. It helped cushion the blows of intermittent depressions, and it contributed to the over-all prosperity of Missouri during the period 1820 to 1860.

BIBLIOGRAPHY

Anderson, Hattie M. "Frontier Economic Problems in Missouri, 1815-1828," *Missouri Historical Review,* Vol. XXXIV (October, 1939; January, 1940), pp. 38-70, 182-203.

Atherton, Lewis E. "James and Robert Aull—a Frontier Missouri Mercantile Firm," *Missouri Historical Review,* Vol. XXX (October, 1935), pp. 3-27.

Beebe, Lucius Morris. *Hear the Train Blow.* New York: Dutton, 1952.

Bloss, Roy S. *Pony Express, the Great Gamble.* Berkeley, California: Howell-North, 1959.

Broadhead, G. C. "Early Missouri Roads," *Missouri Historical Review,* Vol. VIII (January, 1914), pp. 90-92.

Broadhead, G. C. "Early Railroads in Missouri," *Missouri Historical Review,* Vol. VII (April, 1912), pp. 149-150.

Cable, J. Ray. "Some Early Missouri Bankers," *Missouri Historical Review,* Vol. XXVI (January, 1932), pp. 117-125.

Carpenter, Clifford D. "The Early Cattle Industry in Missouri," *Missouri Historical Review,* Vol. XLVII (April, 1953), pp. 201-215.

Clevenger, Homer. "The Building of the Hannibal and St. Joseph Railroad," *Missouri Historical Review,* Vol. XXXVI (October, 1941), pp. 32-47.

Cotterill, R. S. "National Railroad Convention in St. Louis, 1849," *Missouri Historical Review,* Vol. XII (July, 1918), pp. 203-215.

Culmer, Frederic A. "Selling Missouri Mules Down South in 1835," *Missouri Historical Review,* Vol. XXIV (July, 1930), pp. 537-549.

Dorsey, Dorothy B. "The Panic of 1819 in Missouri," *Missouri Historical Review,* Vol. XXIX (October, 1934), pp. 79-91.

Dorsey, Dorothy B. "The Panic and Depression of 1837-1843 in Missouri," *Missouri Historical Review,* Vol. XXX (January, 1936), pp. 132-161.

Eaton, Miles W. "Development and Later Decline of the Hemp Industry in Missouri," *Missouri Historical Review,* Vol. XLIII (July, 1949), pp. 344-359.

Gates, Paul W. "Railroads of Missouri, 1850-1870," *Missouri Historical Review,* Vol. XXVI (January, 1932), pp. 126-141.

Gentry, North Todd. "Plank Roads in Missouri," *Missouri Historical Review,* Vol. XXXI (April, 1937), pp. 272-287.

Gentry, North Todd. "Proposed Railroads in Northeast Missouri," *Missouri Historical Review,* Vol. XXVI (July, 1932), pp. 368-373.

Good-Knight, Asbury. "Wheat Raising in Pioneer Missouri," *Missouri Historical Review,* Vol. XVI (July, 1922), pp. 502-505.

Gregg, Kate L. "The Booneslick Road in St. Charles County," *Missouri Historical Review,* Vol. XXVII (July, 1933), pp. 307-314; Vol. XXVIII (October, 1933), pp 9-16.

Hagen, Olaf T. "The Pony Express Starts from St. Joseph," *Missouri Historical Review,* Vol. XLIII (October, 1948), pp. 1-17.

Harvey, Charles M. "Missouri from 1849 to 1861," *Missouri Historical Review,* Vol. II (October, 1907), pp. 23-40

Holt, Edgar A. "Missouri River Transportation in the Expansion of the West," *Missouri Historical Review,* Vol. XX (April, 1926), pp. 361-381.

Hunter, Louis C. *Steamboats on the Western Rivers.* Cambridge: Harvard University Press, 1949.

Korn, Anna Brosius. "Major Benjamin Holliday," *Missouri Historical Review,* Vol. XIV (October, 1919), pp. 16-28.

Lemmer, George F. "Early Leaders in Livestock Improvement in Missouri," *Missouri Historical Review,* Vol. XXXVII (October, 1942), pp. 29-39.

Lemmer, George F. "Farm Machinery in Ante-Bellum Missouri," *Missouri Historical Review,* Vol. XL (July, 1946), pp. 467-480.

Little, B. M. "The National Old Trails Road at Lexington," *Missouri Historical Review,* Vol. XXIII (January, 1929), pp. 207-213.

McLarty, Vivian K., ed. "The First Steamboats on the Missouri: Reminiscences of Captain W. D. Hubbell," *Missouri Historical Review,* Vol. LI (July, 1957), pp. 373-381.

May, David W. "Dan Carpenter, Pioneer Merchant and Horticulturist," *Missouri Historical Review,* Vol. XXII (April, 1928), pp. 285-295.

Meriwether, Lee. "Labor and Industry in Missouri During the Last Century," *Missouri Historical Review,* Vol. XV (October, 1920), pp. 163-175.

Moody, Ralph. *Riders of the Pony Express.* Boston, New York: Houghton, Mifflin, and Company, 1958.

Mumford, F. B. "A Century of Missouri Agriculture," *Missouri Historical Review,* Vol. XV (January, 1921), pp. 277-297.

Nettles, Curtis. "The Overland Mail Issue During the Fifties," *Missouri Historical Review,* Vol. XVIII (July, 1924), pp. 521-534.

Oliver, R. B. "Missouri's First Railroad," *Missouri Historical Review,* Vol. XXVI (October, 1931), pp. 12-18.

Rebbing, Virginia L. "Some Aspects of the Southern Overland Mail, 1857-1861," *Missouri Historical Review,* Vol. XL (July, 1946), pp.481-502.

Schaaf, Ida M. "The First Roads West of the Mississippi," *Missouri Historical Review,* Vol. XXIX (January, 1935), pp. 92-99.

Schultz, Gerald. "Steamboat Navigation on the Osage River Before the Civil War," *Missouri Historical Review,* Vol. XXIX (April, 1935), pp. 175-185.

Shoemaker, Floyd C. *Missouri and Missourians.* Vols. I and II. Chicago: The Lewis Publishing Company, 1943.

Shoemaker, Floyd C. "The Pony Express—Commemoration Stables and Museum," *Missouri Historical Review,* Vol. XLIV (July, 1950), pp. 343-363.

Squires, Monas N. "The Butterfield Overland Mail in Missouri," *Missouri Historical Review,* Vol. XXVI (July, 1932), pp. 331-341.

Sunder, John E. "St. Louis and the Early Telegraph," *Missouri Historical Review,* Vol. L (April, 1956), pp. 248-258.

Sunder, John E. "The Early Telegraph in Rural Missouri," *Missouri Historical Review,* Vol. LI (October, 1956), pp. 42-53.

Twain, Mark (Samuel L. Clemens). *Life on the Mississippi.* New York: Harper, 1950.

Vincent, J. W. "The 'Slicker War' and Its Consequences," *Missouri Historical Review,* Vol. VII (April, 1913), pp. 138-145.

Violette, Eugene Morrow. *A History of Missouri.* Cape Girardeau, Missouri: Ramfre Press, 1951.

Wallace, Agnes. "The Wiggins Ferry Monopoly," *Missouri Historical Review,* Vol. XLII (October, 1947), pp. 1-19.

Welsh, Donald H. "Butterfield Overland Mail, 1858-1861, and Its Centennial Observance in Missouri," *Missouri Historical Review,* Vol. LII (April, 1958), pp. 218-234.

White, Edward J. "A Century of Transportation in Missouri," *Missouri Historical Review,* Vol. XV (October, 1920), pp. 126-163.

Withers, Robert S. "The Pioneer's First Corn Crop," *Missouri Historical Review* Vol., XLVI (October, 1951), pp. 38-45.

CHAPTER IX

Social Development, 1820-1860

It is the fashion here for the females . . . to receive company, and the males to spend the day in making . . . calls . . . to exchange congratulations and mutual compliments. . . . Refreshments are set out in every house, in many places in great variety and costly profusion.
—description of New Year's Day
in St. Louis, in Edward Bates'
diary, January 1, 1848.

The American settlers in Missouri soon developed custom, protocol, and fashion. Although not all Missourians could offer guests refreshments in "costly profusion," the bounty of the land provided sustenance for all, with time and energy to spare for fun and cultural pursuits. The social whirl developed early. So did the desire for an educational system for Missouri's children. An increasingly literate population with leisure hours to spend provided subscribers for newspapers and magazines. The frontier supplied personalities and plots for a new body of literature to fill the columns of those publications. A new, progressive society was developing in pre-Civil War Missouri. Educational, scientific, and cultural advances were the by-products of that development.

Literature

There was a dramatic growth of publication in Missouri between 1820 and 1860, indicated by the number of newspapers published at the beginning of each of the following decades:

1820	5 papers
1840	35 papers
1850	54 papers
1860	148 papers

The newspapers, as we would expect, reflect the attitudes of the period, the habits, the political interests, and the dreams

The first page of the first issue of the Missouri Intelligencer and Boon's Lick Advertiser, Franklin, April 23, 1819.

(Courtesy State Historical Society)

of the settlers. In general, the newspapers seem different from those of today in several respects. The front page, unlike twentieth century dailies, was replete with advertisements. Poetry—both good and bad—was a popular form; many poems were printed to commemorate notable events, to comment on politics or practices, and to express the poet's sentiments and convictions.

Due to the lack of rapid communications—wire services were not yet available—the news, by the time it was published in Missouri, was very stale. The editorial feuding and personal political debate characteristic of newspapers of the period would be a rarity today. Before 1825 papers claimed to be independent. For years after that date they usually were openly pro- or anti-Jackson. Although the early newspapers of the period included some vague accounts of local happenings, they carried more national and international news. Often an editor would clip columns from other papers and print them in his newssheet. As the period neared its end, there was greater interest in narratives, serials, essays, and anecdotes. The papers of the later years, with their greater emphasis on American and local happenings rather than on European affairs, are of greater interest to us for they more clearly reveal local thinking and writing.

Since there was a continual population increase during the period, there was also a constant increase in circulation.

No doubt each paper was important in its own community and to those who shared the political view of the editor, but some papers had a greater impact upon the state than others. The *Missouri Statesman* was edited in Columbia by William F. Switzler, a partisan for the Whig Party. Switzler was noted for his attention to detail and his remarkable political power in the midsection of the state. He has properly been called the "Dean of Missouri Journalists." Another paper which had important influence on the state was the *Missouri Democrat* published in St. Louis. The *Democrat* departed from its original party alignment to support the new rising Republican Party in the 1850's. The two papers which gave Thomas Hart Benton his greatest support late in his career were the St. Louis *Union* and the *Enquirer* from Jefferson City. From the northeast section of the state we should note the appearance of the *Journal* published at Hannibal by two brothers, Orion and Samuel Clemens. The younger brother, Samuel, later to make a noted contribution to American literature as Mark Twain, amused the people of Hannibal with his anecdotes and witty comments.

Another important publication of the time was the St. Louis *Observer* published by a Presbyterian clergyman, the Reverend Elijah P. Lovejoy. Lovejoy, an outspoken foe of the institution of slavery, expressed his opinions in the *Observer*. He was warned persistently by irate citizens of St. Louis that his unpopular position might lead to violence. In 1836 a mob overturned his presses, scattered part of his printing equipment in the streets, and threw the remainder into the Mississippi River. Lovejoy, still persuaded of the righteousness of his stand, moved across the Mississippi to Alton, Illinois, a free state, where he resumed the publication of his convictions. It was in Alton that he met his death at the hands of a mob in 1837. We have already mentioned the Mormon publication, *The Evening and Morning Star,* which was printed at Independence beginning in the year 1832. The Independence mob threw the presses into the Missouri River the next year. Joseph Smith indicated the importance he assigned to the influence of the newspaper when he wrote this critical notice to the editor:

> We wish you to render the *Star* as interesting as possible, by setting forth the rise, program and the faith of the church, as well as the doctrine; for if

you do not render it more interesting than at present, it will fail, and the church will suffer a great loss thereby.

A few of the other newspapers of the time were the Palmyra *Spectator,* the Kansas City *Enterprise,* the *Ozark Standard* of Springfield, the St. Joseph *Gazette,* and the *Upper Missouri Enquirer* of Liberty.

The stretching of telegraph lines into Missouri in 1847 was of great importance to the newspapers. Before the telegraph, newspapers often depended for their appeal on slashing journalism or long didactic lectures to the citizenry. The telegraph line brought the news to the West shortly after its occurrence. Thus, the papers could promise their subscribers a description of the latest happenings throughout the nation.

Even with their weaknesses, the newspapers probably give us the best picture of Missouri as a frontier state. The life of the day can be seen in the legal notices, the foreclosures, the lotteries to produce money for road-building or schools, the notices about runaway slaves, or the steamboat schedules. The sarcasm of a frustrated saddler can be read in this ad in the *Missouri Intelligencer* printed in Fayette October 12, 1826:

> Notice is hereby given to all persons,
> THAT CHRISTOPHER CARSON, a boy about 16 years old, small of his age, but thick set; light hair, ran away from the subscriber, living in Franklin, Howard County, Missouri, to whom he had been bound to learn the saddler's trade, on or about the first of September last. . . . One cent reward will be given to any person who will bring back the said boy.
>
> DAVID WORKMAN

A mid-nineteenth century newspaper press from **E d w a r d** and Hopewell, Edward's Great West, 1860

Although the early editor had a busy life, it was often un-rewarding financially. The newspapers changed hands frequent-ly. Competition, or insufficient demand for advertising, or pub-lic disagreement with an editor's policy could and did lead to bankruptcy. Then there was always the possibility of mob vio-lence, or the danger that an irate reader might challenge the editor to a duel, with a result more disastrous than bankruptcy! The thought of this hazard may have prompted the editor of the Pike County paper to call his publication the *Olive Branch.*

Although most Missourians spoke English, there were those from Germany and France who desired to read the news in their native language. The Hermann *Volksblatt* began publication in 1854 for the German settlers in and near Hermann. In 1835 a pro-Benton German paper was started in St. Louis, the *Anzeiger des Westens,* but it was not so influential as the *Westliche Post* which began publication in 1857. The famous statesman and writer, Carl Schurz, acted as the publisher of this latter news-paper for a short time during the 1860's. A French paper, *La Revue de l'Ouest,* edited by Louis Richard Cortambert, son-in-law of Auguste Pierre Chouteau, appeared in St. Louis in 1854.

The authors of early Missouri depended very little on the literature of the past for either style or subject matter. Non-fiction of the day, aside from news reports and editorials, was chiefly in the form of biography or travel accounts. Thomas Hart Benton's biography entitled *Thirty Years' View, or a His-tory of the Working of the American Government for Thirty Years from 1820 to 1850* was widely read. Father De Smet and Henry Brackenridge were two of the travelers who wrote ac-counts of their journeys for publication in the newspapers.

The novel was a less important literary form in Missouri of the mid-nineteenth century, but despite criticism on religious or moral grounds, a few were published and were reviewed and quoted in the newspapers. Henry Boernstein's *The Mysteries of St. Louis* and the anonymous *Western Border Life; or What Fanny Hunter Saw and Heard in Kansas and Missouri* were products of Missouri authors.

Poetry, usually humorous comments on events or elements of frontier life or ornate treatments of unfamiliar subjects, was written by local poets and distributed via the newspaper columns.

The most characteristic literature of the time are the short stories and tall tales most frequently published in such papers as the *Reveille* or the *Peoples' Organ*. This literature was the actual by-product of a community whose members were often regaled with the thrilling tales of the returning hunter, trapper, and boatman. The Indian tales and stories of frontier and cabin life by Alphonso Wetmore in the *Gazetteer of the State of Missouri* appeared before 1840 and were typical examples of short stories in the young state. The tall tales were woven from the crude humor, the exaggerations, and the amorous exploits frequently assigned to certain frontier heroes. Missouri did not have a Davy Crockett or a Paul Bunyan, but for Missourians, Mike Fink, the legendary boatman, was a satisfactory substitute. This is Mike Fink as T. B. Thorpe described him in 1855:

> I'm from the Lightning Forks of Roaring River. I'm *all* man, save what is wild cat and extra lightning. I'm as hard to run against as a cypress snag —I never back water. I did hold down a buffalo bull, and tar off his scalp with my teeth. . . . I'm the man that, single-handed, towed the broadhorn over a sandbar—the identical infant who girdled a hickory by smiling at the bark, and if anyone denies it, let him make his will and pay the expenses of a funeral. I'm the genuine article, tough as bull's hide, keen as a rifle. I can out-swim, out-swar, out-jump, out-drink, and keep soberer than any man at Catfish Bend. I'm painfully ferocious. . . .

Fabulous riverboatman Mike Fink is shown displaying his shooting prowess. According to the story, the stunt ended in disaster when Mike's aim proved less than perfect. Mike was then dispatched by an onlooker.

(*Courtesy Missouri Historical Society*)

The *Reveille,* published by Joseph Field in St. Louis from 1844 to 1850, printed some of the best stories of early Missouri. Field himself contributed sketches flavored with legends, but employing less exaggeration. Theatre manager Sol (Solomon Franklin) Smith specialized in the anecdote often ending with a surprise for the reader. John S. Robb was a master of the tall tale. The following example from Robb's "Courting in French Hollow" illustrates the frontier sense of humor:

> One mornin', I was a leetle mite late to meetin', and when I got thar, the furst thing I seed war Jake Simins, sittin' close bang up agin Sofy, in the same pew with her daddy. I biled a spell with wrath, and then turned sour; I could taste myself. . . . I war so *enormous* mad that the new silk handkerchief round my neck lost its color!

The newspapers and books of this period reveal Missourians as they were—fun-loving, but concerned over serious issues; bigoted, yet anxious to debate all aspects of political issues; crude and clumsy, yet creative. From the frontier, the early Missourians derived not only their homes and their livelihood, but a new and typical literature.

Churches

The Anglo-American frontiersmen were, as a group, proudly independent and therefore suspicious of organized religion which might curtail their prized independence. Some were overtly hostile to religion; contemporary accounts describe such evidences of this animosity as Bible burnings, and drinking orgies parodying the Lord's Supper. Freethinking among the educated and wealthy, both French and American, was prevalent in Missouri for many years. In St. Louis of 1834 the *Western Examiner* began its "investigation of the credibility and general tendencies of the Christian Religion" and predicted that "perhaps, ere another century, the . . . prevailing . . . religion will be numbered among the exploded superstitions of past ages."

Despite such opposition, dedicated missionaries in Missouri, Catholic and Protestant alike, saw their labors rewarded. Congregations were established and churches, schools, and charitable institutions were built. The four decades from 1820 to 1860 were years of religious growth and activity in the young state.

Catholic influence in the Louisiana Territory was impaired by the exile of most of the clergy when the territory became

American in March of 1804. The Church suffered also from a tradition of liberalism among some of the wealthier class. The libraries of many well-to-do French families included volumes by Paine, Jefferson, Rousseau, Locke, Voltaire, Bacon, and other liberal writers, many of whom were included in a list of books condemned by the hierarchy. The feeling among some upper-class Creoles and French immigrants seemed to be that religion was for the ignorant and superstitious, philosophy was for gentlemen. The scarcity of clergy and the lack of leadership from the educated class left the Catholics of Missouri with little spiritual guidance from 1804 to 1818.

(Courtesy State Historical Society)

The Old Cathedral of St. Louis, built in 1831, was flanked on the right by the bishop's home and on the left by an orphan asylum.

Trappist Monks from a monastery established at Florissant in 1809 served the parishes north of Ste. Genevieve for about a decade. Then in 1818 a Catholic revival began with the arrival of the Right Reverend Louis William Valentine Du Bourg, Bishop of Louisiana and the Floridas, who chose St. Louis as his episcopal residence for several years. During Bishop Du Bourg's time in Missouri, he had an important part in the establishment in the territory of the religious orders of the Sisters of the

Sacred Heart, the Vincentians, and the Society of Jesus (Jesuits). He was also instrumental in the founding of the Indian schools, a seminary, and several churches. His successor, named in 1826, was Bishop Joseph Rosati, who had been a founder, professor and director of the first seminary west of the Mississippi, St. Mary's Seminary at the Barrens near Perryville, Missouri. Bishop Rosati's reign was one of activity and accomplishment. In 1828 the Sisters of Charity, with the financial support of John Mullanphy, Missouri's first millionaire, opened the first hospital west of the Mississippi. In 1829 St. Louis College was established by the Jesuits. The Sisters of St. Joseph founded the first asylum for the deaf and dumb at Carondelet in 1838.

Between the years 1830-1870 an influx of pious families from Ireland and South Germany strengthened the Catholic revival. Many Germans settled in central Missouri around the Boon's Lick Trail and built churches and schools to serve the growing communities. In the 1830's Father Verhaegen worked among the German settlers in Osage, Gasconade, Maries, and Cole counties. By 1833 there were twenty-nine congregations in the diocese of St. Louis, nineteen of which had built churches.

Many other priests labored among the scattered Indians and settlers in western Missouri, establishing churches throughout the state. By 1837 Kansas City had its first Catholic church. Ten years later the diocese of St. Louis was elevated to an archdiocese and Bishop Peter Richard Kenrick, Bishop Rosati's successor, was named the first archbishop of St. Louis. Archbishop Kenrick was a scholar, patriot and efficient administrator. He guided his people with patience and wisdom through years of turmoil when thousands of European immigrants flocked to Missouri, and through years of tension created by intolerance and the Civil War. Archbishop Kenrick was the first member of the American hierarchy to celebrate his golden jubilee when in 1891 he marked the fiftieth anniversary of his consecration as bishop.

Despite the pompous prediction that "God would never cross the Mississippi," by the year 1820 not only was the Catholic church revitalized, but the Baptists, Methodists, Presbyterians, Episcopalians, and Disciples of Christ were firmly established in Missouri. The Baptist and Methodist missionaries were the earliest protestants to appear on the frontier and were the most successful. The democratic church government of the Baptists and the "free grace, free will, and individual responsibility" taught by

The circuit rider braved the most inclement weather to carry his gospel to frontier areas.
(Harper's Weekly, October 12, 1876)

the Methodists appealed to the independent, individualistic frontiersman.

The settlers of the frontier were not used to contributing financially to the support of social institutions. It was difficult to persuade them to provide for ministers. Many of the early Baptist leaders were laymen—usually farmers—who preached to neighborhood groups. The early expansion of the Methodist church is also in part the responsibility of lay preachers. Since the circuit riders could be present only occasionally, these laymen met with weekly discussion groups for prayers, hymn singing, and scripture reading. The ministers who preached without pay were sometimes critical of the more highly-educated, salaried clergy, who often failed to understand the frontiersman. Those who received compensation were not overpaid, however. Salaries of $64 to $100 a year are recorded for early Methodist ministers.

These clergymen were allowed to supplement their incomes by peddling approved books of history, biography, travel, and philosophy. In this way, they contributed to the dissemination of information and culture on the frontier. Non-denominational Bible societies also provided reading material by distributing Bibles to the frontiersmen beginning in the 1820's.

John Mason Peck and James E. Welch were the first Baptist ministers sent to Missouri by the Baptist Board of Foreign Missions for the United States. These missionaries were the most influential clergymen of their denomination in the early years of Missouri. They established the first Sabbath school in St. Louis and founded the first Sunday school for blacks in 1818.

The latter school began with fourteen students and grew rapidly to provide a nucleus of membership for the first black Baptist church in St. Louis, organized about 1827.

By 1834 there were 150 Baptist churches in Missouri. In the next quarter of a century this growth continued, and Baptist churches numbered 750 in 1860.

The first Methodist church in Missouri was built near Jackson in 1819. The church was named McKendree Chapel for Elder William McKendree, the first presiding elder in Missouri. McKendree Chapel is the oldest Protestant church building still standing in the state. In the same year McKendree Chapel was built, the first session of the Missouri Conference was held there, and Elder McKendree and Jesse Walker directed the first camp meeting in Missouri on the "Old Camp-ground" at the chapel.

The camp meeting was a phenomenon of the frontier, a shadow of which may be seen even today in some of the brush arbor "protracted meetings" held in some parts of Missouri. In the early days of the state these meetings offered an occasion for religious instruction, for emotional outlet, and for visiting with friends, relatives, and neighbors. The dramatic scene of one camp meeting is described as follows by one who attended:

> The glare of the blazing camp fires falling on a
> dense assemblage . . . and reflected back from long

A camp meeting in early Missouri

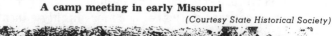

(Courtesy State Historical Society)

ranges of tents upon every side; hundreds of candles and lamps suspended among the trees, together with numerous torches flashing to and fro, throwing an uncertain light upon the tremulous foliage, and giving an appearance of dim and indefinite extent to the depths of the forest; the solemn chanting of hymns swelling and falling on the night wind; the impassioned exhortations, the earnest prayers; the sobs, shrieks, or shouts, bursting from persons under intense agitation of mind; the sudden spasms which seize upon scores, and unexpectedly dashed them to the ground; all conspired to invest the scene with terrific interest, and to work up the feelings to the highest pitch of excitement.

The educated clergymen of the towns often were critical of the emotional excesses of the camp meeting and frontier preaching. They called instead for the profession and practice of Christian principles in the lives of their parishioners.

The Presbyterian church did not grow so rapidly as the Baptist and Methodist denominations in early Missouri, but the Presbyterians made noteworthy contributions to the educational and cultural life of the frontier. Salmon Giddings, who has been called the "founder and father of Presbyterianism" in Missouri and Illinois, established twelve churches, including the first Protestant church in St. Louis, and a school for girls.

In 1821, in answer to the plea of seven Osage chiefs who had traveled to Washington to ask for missionaries, the Presbyterian, Dutch Reformed, and Associate Reformed churches, through the United Foreign Missionary Society, established Harmony Mission. The Mission, which provided for the secular and religious education of Osage children, was the first American settlement in Bates County. It also brought the Presbyterian church to the western part of the state.

The Congregationalists and the Presbyterians worked cooperatively under a "Plan of Union" until 1852. In this year, the Reverend T. M. Post was called by a formerly Presbyterian congregation to establish the first Congregational church in St. Louis.

Shortly before Missouri became a state, the first Protestant Episcopal church was founded in Missouri. In December, 1819, the sum of $1,714 was raised to build Christ Church in St. Louis. The Reverend John Ward served as rector for eighteen months. Then the congregation struggled without a rector until 1825, when the Reverend Thomas Horrel assumed the leadership of the church. A brick sanctuary was completed in 1830. From 1835 to 1844 the Right Reverend Jackson Kemper, the first missionary bishop of the Protestant Episcopal Church in America, served as rector of the St. Louis church, in addition to working to expand the church in Missouri, Iowa, Wisconsin, Minnesota, Nebraska, Kansas, and Indiana.

In 1844 Missouri became a separate diocese from Indiana and the Right Reverend Cicero Stephen Hawks was consecrated as the first bishop of Missouri and the rector of Christ Church. During Bishop Hawks' twenty-three years in Missouri he was faced with many difficulties—missionary problems, church debts, and the troubles arising from the Civil War. It was in 1859, during Bishop Hawks' tenure, that the Episcopal cathedral was built. In the mid-1800's, English clergyman-novelist Charles Kingsley described the cathedral as the "most churchly church" in the United States.

Among the German immigrants of the 1830's were three major religious groups: the Catholics mentioned earlier, members of the Reformed Evangelical Church of Germany, and the Saxon Lutherans. The second named group, the Reformed Evangelicals, were in fact liberal Lutherans. They established a German Evangelical Church Association of the West in 1840 to organize the few scattered congregations. To assure a supply of liberal pastors, the Association opened Eden Seminary in 1849 in Warren County. The seminary is now located in Webster Groves.

In 1839 a group of 600 Lutherans from the German province of Saxony came to Missouri under the leadership of Martin Stephan. Although some remained in St. Louis where they accepted the gracious invitation to use Christ Church as their first temporary church, most settled to the south in Perry County where they established Altenburg and Wittenburg. After charges were made against him, Martin Stephan was exiled to Illinois, and the Reverend Carl Walther of St. Louis emerged as the strong leader of the German Evangelical Lutheran Synod of Missouri. In 1839 the settlers at Altenburg built a one-room log cabin for the training of their ministers. This was the simple beginning of Concordia Theological Seminary which was moved to St. Louis in 1849.

The first congregations of the Disciples of Christ, also known as the Christian Church, were organized in central Mis-

(Courtesy State Historical Society)

Altenburg, the first Lutheran seminary in Missouri, built in 1853 in Perry County from a photograph taken in 1913

souri near Franklin in Howard County. The first Christian Church building was erected at Salt Creek four and one-half miles northeast of Franklin in 1817. The first Christian preacher was Elder Thomas McBride, who served the denomination for twenty years before moving to Oregon. The Disciples' freedom from ecclesiastical organization was well received by Missourians, and the group grew rapidly.

The brief residence of the Mormons in Missouri and their tragic exile from the state have already been discussed.

During the French and Spanish regimes, Jews could not legally enter Louisiana. After the Louisiana Purchase, Jewish families began to move into St. Louis. For over thirty years there were no synagogues for the Jewish immigrants. In 1836 the first regular Jewish service was held in rooms above a grocery store at Second and Spruce Streets. In 1839 the first group of worshipers, now joined by more recent immigrants, organized the first Jewish congregation in St. Louis, *Acduth Israel,* the United Hebrew Congregation. Under the leadership of Abraham Weigel as president, a place of worship was maintained at Sixth and St. Charles streets, a Jewish relief agency was established, and land was purchased for a Jewish cemetery.

In the late 1840's a new congregation was organized by a

The First Jewish Synagogue in St. Louis, 1857
(From Ballou's Pictorial, March 14, 1857)

group of the more liberal members of the United Hebrew Congregation. The majority of the founders of this congregation, called *Emanu-El,* were recently-arrived German immigrants. At about the same time, *B'nai B'rith,* the Sons of the Covenant, was organized by a Bohemian group.

William Greenleaf Eliot came to St. Louis shortly after his graduation from Harvard divinity school in 1834, and organized the first Unitarian congregation in November of that same year. Eliot was a distinguished public servant, especially in the field of public education, and was the founder of Eliot Seminary, the forerunner of Washington University. The Unitarians dedicated their first Missouri church in 1837 in St. Louis. The small group in St. Louis carried on humanitarian projects which included relief for the poor, a sewing school for needy girls, a day school for indigent children, and a school for black children. There were only two Unitarian congregations in Missouri before the Civil War.

During the first forty years of Missouri statehood there was a missionary zeal among most religious groups. Appeals for missionaries from Indians of the West inspired much of this enthusiasm for carrying the gospel beyond Missouri's boundaries. As in the case of explorers earlier, St. Louis served as the gateway to the West for many missionaries. The most noted Protestant missionaries of this period were the Presbyterian-Congregationalist-sponsored Dr. Marcus Whitman and his lovely wife, Narcissa. This dedicated couple departed from Missouri and struggled across the continent to Oregon to minister to the Cayuses of that region. American expansion into Indian territory and resultant Indian distrust of the white man defeated the

Whitmans. They and fourteen members of their medical mission were massacred in November, 1847.

Father Pierre Jean De Smet was sent out from St. Louis by Bishop Rosati about 1838. Father De Smet was a gifted linguist who mastered many Indian tongues and probably understood the Indians better than any other man of his day. He served as mediator at many historical conferences in the day of growing Indian-white tension. His journeys, during which he is estimated to have traveled over 180,000 miles, are recorded in his journals. These documents, now in the library of St. Louis University, are among the most valuable primary sources for students of western expansion.

Despite early opposition, religious institutions and ideals had taken root and grown strong in Missouri by 1830. As one might expect among independent and opinionated frontiersmen, there was not only inter-denominational competition but also disagreement within the individual churches concerning a wide variety of issues. Political and economic problems, both national and local, were debated along with doctrinal disputes. It is not surprising to see growing dissension within many of the churches when slavery became an increasingly provocative issue in 1830's and 1840's. Proslavery members of the Presbyterian, Methodist, and Baptist churches separated themselves from the national

Father Pierre-Jean DeSmet, missionary, author, and explorer shown wearing a medal bestowed by his native Belgium
(Courtesy State Historical Society)

organizations of their denominations in the 1840's. The Baptists of the Southern Convention, the Presbyterian Church in the Confederate States, and the Southern Methodists were organized by these factions. This dissension and the ensuing Civil War impaired the work of the churches for a time, but growth resumed soon after the end of the war.

Until 1804 Missouri was Catholic. During the Territorial Period, Protestant missionaries effectively moved into the region. From 1804-1818 the Catholic Church lost ground in Missouri. From 1818 to 1860 there was a revivification and constant growth of the Catholic Church, primarily because of the new German and Irish immigrants. Most of the newcomers to Missouri, however, were either unchurched or were Protestant in tradition. Thus, the Protestant groups constantly expanded during pre-Civil War years to blanket the state. By 1860 there was at least one church, Catholic or Protestant, in each county. In 1860 there were large Roman Catholic churches in French centers such as Ste. Genevieve, St. Louis, and St. Charles, as well as smaller parishes along the two major rivers. The Protestant churches had pushed to all areas. Although the following figures may be deceiving since they do not indicate the number of members in each church, the list does indicate the individual churches of each denomination:

Methodist	526	Roman Catholic	88
Baptist	457	Episcopalian	18
Christian	150	Lutheran	55
Presbyterian	127	Union	54
Cumberland		Jewish	2
Presbyterian	98	Unitarian	2

Schools and Colleges

In the years from 1820 to 1860 the population of Missouri increased eighteen times over. This enormous rate of population growth resulted in a rapidly expanding economy with great increase in wealth, and a new emphasis on education at its various levels. Many of today's respected educational institutions had their beginnings during this period.

Although there were great strides forward in the field of education, we must recognize that educational standards in the mid-nineteenth century were not uniformly high. Certainly, the schools and colleges of that period would suffer in comparison to our contemporary educational institutions. It was difficult to

(From a painting by L. D. Pomarede in Day, Pictorial St. Louis, 1876)

A view of St. Louis in 1832. The St. Clair, the first steam ferry in Missouri, was put into operation in 1828 by the Wiggins Ferry Company.

finance education, and the financial uncertainties led to instability in the schools. There were no recognized standards for the licensing of teachers, and accordingly teachers were not usually well-trained. Although Professor Everett Dick may be guilty of a slight exaggeration, he gives us an account of the candidate for a teaching position in Missouri who was being examined by the board of trustees of the school. They inquired of the young man whether he taught that the world is flat or round. The would-be teacher answered that he had never considered the matter, but that he would be willing to teach it either way. The board, pleased with this open-minded approach, hired the candidate and instructed him, after consultation, to teach his pupils that the world is flat.

The length of terms depended upon the financial condition of the school, the need for the children to work in the fields, and the availability of the teacher. Sometimes a school year would consist of only two to four months of study. Classes were held in any building available, and the textbooks and furniture were often scanty. In view of these handicaps, it is remarkable that the educational standards were not even lower.

There were a number of developments in Missouri education during the pre-Civil War period. The state government had recognized its responsibility to encourage education, but it was slow to provide financial assistance. By the Civil War, however, the state government was apportioning one-fourth of its revenues for the support of education. Second, the churches of Missouri played a leading role in the establishment of schools, academies

(Courtesy Missouri Historical Society)

Interior of Oakfield Academy showing the old blackboard

and colleges. A complete history of this period would list a multitude of such church-related institutions located in all parts of the state. Third, attempts were made, particularly by the churches, to educate the underprivileged. Fourth, the public slowly lost its disdain for free education. In 1820 and for many years thereafter, free education was considered a form of charity, and only paupers or those considered devoid of pride would attend free schools. With such a stigma attached to the free public school it is little wonder that many Missourians, unable to afford tuition but too proud to accept free education, kept their children at home. Lastly, the public high school appeared at the end of this period as a substitute for the private academy.

As we have noted, during the territorial period the schools were sometimes operated only for the profit of the teacher. In other cases, churches or groups of interested citizens or parents would sponsor schools, some of which were chartered by the state government. These teacher, church, or community-spon- sored schools were still in existence during the 1820-1860 period In these schools the student usually paid tuition for his educa tion. The *Boon's Lick Times,* dated October 26, 1844, carried the following advertisement:

NEW SCHOOL

The subscriber will commence a Male School, in Howard College in this place, on Monday, the 28th inst.

Instruction will be given in all the branches usually taught in High Schools and Academies. The terms for a session of 21 weeks will be as follows:

For the Primary Studies (Spelling, Reading,
Writing, Arithmetic, and Geography) ......$ 6.00
For Arithmetic, Grammar, and
Geography ....$ 8.00
For the Higher English Branches $10.00
For Latin and Greek $12.00

Satisfactory testimonials and qualifications can be given if required.

William T. Lucky

N.B. Students from a distance can procure good boarding in private families at from $1.50 to $2.00 per week.

The Constitution of 1820 declared that it was a responsibility of government to encourage education, and promised, "the children of the poor shall be taught free." However, it was thirty-

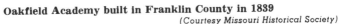

Oakfield Academy built in Franklin County in 1839
(Courtesy Missouri Historical Society)

three years before the state took effective action to aid education. In 1833 Governor Dunklin established a commission headed by Joseph Hertich to formulate plans for the establishment of a public school system in Missouri. Then in 1839 the General Assembly passed the Geyer Act which: (1) established, with money received from the sale of federal lands, a permanent fund to be invested to provide income for the financing of the schools; (2) established the office of state superintendent of schools, giving that officer responsibility to direct and encourage the Missouri school system; (3) named the township council as the local authority to encourage public education and to organize public schools. Henry S. Geyer, the author of this lengthy act—thirty-six pages—patterned the plan after the Virginia educational system with elementary schools, secondary schools, colleges, and a state university. Geyer has been called the "father of Missouri's public school system." Actually, the Geyer Act was not effective in encouraging public education, for it was difficult to interpret and provided only small sums of money.

Finally in 1853, a third of a century after the writing of the Constitution of 1820, the legislature passed a new education act which did provide the necessary state finances and supervision to be effective. It provided also for the establishment of county commissions to examine teachers as to their qualifications to teach. At that same time state officials suggested courses and textbooks. There was an immediate strengthening of the state school system as a result of this legislation. In 1858 the state provided $309,000 for aid to the schools, and in the ensuing years the figure continued to grow. The foundations for Missouri's vast public education system were laid before the Civil War. Most of the structure, however, was to be built after that war.

The churches of Missouri had been among the first to encourage education in the state, and during this time many new church schools appeared. In 1821 Harmony Mission was established in Bates County by the United Foreign Missionary Society to educate Osage children. In 1824, under the leadership of Bishop Rosati, two Catholic schools were organized at Florissant to teach Indian children—the Jesuits opened St. Regis School for Indian boys, and the Sisters of the Sacred Heart, under Mother Duchesne, founded a school for Indian girls. A Catholic school for deaf and dumb children was established at Carondelet in 1828 by the Sisters of St. Joseph. The state school for deaf children

On the second floor of Schoolhouse No. 3—Benton School—in St. Louis the first public high school west of the Mississippi opened in February, 1853. The high school was later moved to this $50,000 building dedicated on March 25, 1856.
(Courtesy State Historical Society)

at Fulton was not organized until 1851. Although a few black children were probably educated in several schools, the Unitarian Church in St. Louis demonstrated its concern for these young people by opening a school for them in 1841.

Howard High School at Fayette was founded in the year 1844 with a student enrollment of six boys. Although the school became inactive for several years, it was later reorganized and became Central College.

The first public school in St. Louis, which opened on April 2, 1838, was housed in a $3,170 two-story brick building on a small corner lot at Fourth and Spruce streets. "No. 1 School," as it was named, had an initial enrollment of 175 pupils. The first public high school in Missouri was opened in St. Louis in 1853. It was later housed in a new $50,000 building considered the model structure for schools of the time. Within a year, enrollment reached 115 students. It appears that standards in the school were high. The following courses were offered: "trigonometry, surveying, civil engineering, Latin history, mental philosophy, logic, political economy, German, French, penmanship, music, declamation, chemistry, geology, and astronomy." Most of these courses are considered part of a college curriculum today.

Missouri's first colleges and universities were established during the period 1820-1860. Saint Louis University, the first university west of the Mississippi, was chartered in 1832 and developed out of an earlier school known as Saint Louis College which had been established by the Jesuits in 1829. In 1834 a department was added to teach theology. Medical training began in 1842. Courses in law were first offered in 1843. Among the early teachers in Saint Louis University was Father De Smet, who acted as an instructor of English. The University of Mis-

James S. Rollins, Father of
the University of Missouri,
from an oil painting by
George Caleb Bingham
(Courtesy State Historical Society)

souri, founded by law in 1839 and opened officially in 1841, has
the distinction of being the first state university west of the
Mississippi. The University was located in Columbia on decision
of the state legislature after the inhabitants of Boone County
provided $117,000 to help establish the institution. The state
appropriated no money for the college until the year 1867. Captain J. A. Pritchard, stopping at Columbia on his way west to
California in 1849, reported:

> Six miles from Grant's we reached Columbia—one
> of the neatest and handsomest little Towns that I
> have seen in my life—In this place there is a fine
> College or institution of learning—

There were many other colleges established in Missouri before the Civil War, although most of the schools then founded
no longer exist. Among those which have survived is Linden-
wood of St. Charles, organized for young women in 1827 by
George C. and Mary Easton Sibley (George Sibley had earlier
served at Fort Osage). William Jewell College, established in
Liberty in 1849, was named after Dr. William Jewell of Columbia
who donated $10,000 to encourage the building of a Baptist col-
lege in Missouri. Westminster College grew out of the earlier
school known as Fulton College which opened in 1851. Christian
College, for women, supported by the Disciples of Christ, was
founded in Columbia the same year. Culver-Stockton College—
also associated with the Disciples of Christ—was founded in

1853. Washington University, established in St. Louis in 1853, is one of the few early colleges which was non-sectarian at its origin. Central College of Fayette began in 1855; it is now Central Methodist College. Stephens College—originally known as the Columbia Baptist Female College—was incorporated in 1857.

There were several institutions for specialized training in Missouri before the Civil War. St. Mary's Seminary at Perryville, a divinity school for Roman Catholic priests, was established in 1818. Concordia Seminary of Altenburg was founded in 1838 to train Missouri Synod Lutheran clergymen. Eden Theological Seminary was started in 1849 as Marthasville Seminary and was associated with the German Evangelical Church. Kemper College of St. Louis was founded in 1840 to train physicians.

In 1834 the report of the Hertich Committee announced to the state the need for the establishment of teacher training schools. Twenty-three years later, in 1857, St. Louis established a free normal school to train teachers for the city school system. This normal school later (1910) became Harris Teachers College. In 1856 the State Teachers Association was organized in Missouri. Horace Mann, the distinguished American educator, came to address the association at its organizational meeting.

There was much educational experimentation during the period, and many schools were short-lived. One such school was Marion College near Palmyra, which was established to train ministers, teachers, and professional people. The curriculum was classical and many students came from the East to attend. A novel feature of the college was the requirement that each stu-

The University of Missouri from an illustration in the 1859 catalog. The columns of the middle building, which stand today in the center of the University campus, have become a famous landmark. They were all that remained intact after a fire destroyed the main building. To the left is the president's house; to the right, the observatory.

(Courtesy State Historical Society)

William Greenleaf Eliot, clergyman, civic leader, founder of Washington University, and grandfather of celebrated poet T. S. Eliot

(Courtesy State Historical Society)

dent must work on the college farm as part of his training. David Nelson, the first president, was an outspoken abolitionist. His statements so angered proslavery Missourians that he left the college in 1835. The college closed soon after his departure.

Although many institutions of learning became defunct during the period, we can point statistically to a measure of success of the newly developing educational system. In 1840 fifteen per cent of the population of Missouri was illiterate. By 1850 the percentage had dropped to 13.5. In 1860 illiteracy was 12.5 per cent. It is estimated that in the year 1860, 200,000 white children and 155 free black children were attending schools. These last figures indicate that approximately one of every five Missourians was a student in 1860. Undoubtedly, free schools were losing their stigma, and the desire to educate children was growing stronger among Missourians.

Medicine

Although the physicians of the period were often poorly educated and labored in ignorance against the maladies afflicting Missourians, many advances were made in the field of medicine during the first half of the nineteenth century. The most common complaints were fevers, ague (malarial fever), cholera, scarlet fever, measles, mumps, smallpox, whooping cough, and diphtheria. The following poem printed in the *Missouri Intelligencer,* October 1, 1822, describes "The Ague," a complaint so common in the state that it was also called the "Missouri chills:"

> A painful yawn his muscles draw,
> Projecting out his under jaw,
> While chills run up and down his spine,
> To indicate that bark and wine
> Must swell the list of human ills,
> And follow up cathartic pills.
> Proboscis next, the cold assails
> And blue are thumb and fingernails;
> He shakes and runs, and runs and shakes . . .
> For thirteen years his autumn shakes
> Unstrung his nerves, like earth born quakes;
> His swelling ills, and bloated feet,
> His nose and chin that friend-like meet,
> No longer cold, but fever heat
> Now burns, and both his temples beat;

The last verses suggest the common belief that fevers were caused by forest air.

> I wish, instead of hunting bees,
> You'd clear away these cotton trees,
> And let the air and sun assail
> The damp recesses of this vale,
> Then garden vegetables would grow,
> And better soups we'd make, you know,
> That work on invalids such cures;
> 'Twould redden too, that face of yours.

In an age of limited medical knowledge, it was natural for people to use home remedies such as bear grease and sassafras. Some Missourians took small balls of spider web in liquor or tea as a remedy for fever. Hydrophobia, a dread and not uncommon disease on the frontier, was often treated by the application of a "mad stone" obtained from the stomach of a deer. An array of panaceas and patent medicines to cure all manner of ills were advertised in the newspapers. Calomel was a popular medicine of the period. Dr. Daniel Johnson wrote sarcastically in the Palmyra *Missouri Whig and General Advertiser* for February 29, 1840:

> I own that Calomel practice is both cheap and easy to the physician, for the whole extent of both theory and practice is, give Calomel, if that will not help, double and treble the dose of Calomel. If the patient recovers, Calomel cured him; if he dies, nothing in the world would have saved him.

**Dr. John Sappington by
George Caleb Bingham**
*(Courtesy State Historical
Society)*

Physicians still employed the ancient technique of bloodletting to treat many diseases. Purgatives and emetics were the physician's chief assistant. Opium offered welcome relief from painful disorders. One doctor described opium as "the monarch of medical powers, the soothing angel of moral and physical pain."

Dr. John Sappington of Arrow Rock, who carried on a medical practice along the Missouri River from Jefferson City to Lexington, deserves an important place in the history of medicine in Missouri. Dr. Sappington, highly critical of such ancient practices as bloodletting, attempted to improve the standards of medical treatment. Malaria was a real curse to the people of the frontier. Often an entire community would be ill with fever during the months of July, August, and September. Although quinine had been known as a drug for many years, it was Dr. Sappington who used it widely and informed other physicians of its effectiveness against fever. In 1832 he began the manufacturing of "Dr. John Sappington's Anti-Fever Pills," which he sold throughout the Mississippi Valley. His slaves were kept busy compounding the medicine which was composed of one grain quinine, $\frac{3}{4}$ grain licorice, $\frac{1}{4}$ grain myrrh, and oil of sassafras. Patients were instructed to take the medicine every two hours until the symptoms disappeared. The medicine became well known in mid-America. The following verse of the time, which sounds like a modern singing commercial, describes the popular demand for the drug:

> Quinine, Quinine
> Is our cry,
> Give us Quinine,
> Or we die.

Dr. Sappington also published a book in 1844 to popularize his methods of treating fever.

The training of physicians varied. Before 1840 an apprenticeship system was the usual method of training a doctor. A young man would act as an apprentice for three years and then receive a certificate of proficiency. As we have noted, in 1840 Kemper College in St. Louis began to teach medicine, and two years later, in 1842, Saint Louis University opened its medical department. The first doctors received education in anatomy, physiology, chemistry, and the accepted treatments of the day. In the early years of these schools, the great majority of students left school to begin practicing instead of completing their education. The physician often performed surgery in the patient's home, without the benefit of modern anesthetics. Ether was not used in Missouri until the late 1840's. Although schools, instru-

"Prairie Park" three miles southwest of Arrow Rock in Saline County was the handsome country home of Dr. John Sappington. Notice the two-story entrance porch typical of ante-bellum houses and the slave cabins to the rear of the house.

(Courtesy State Historical Society)

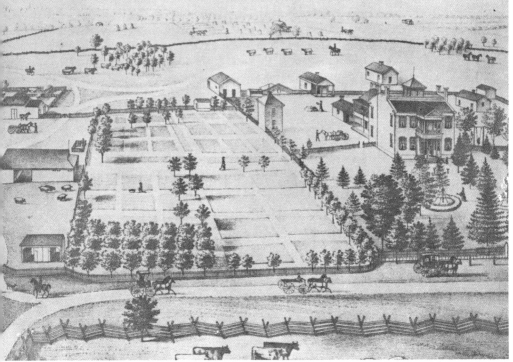

ments, and drugs were improving during the period, one candid physician, Dr. Daniel Johnson of Palmyra, declared that the physcans carried on their practice by guessing, and the best doctor was the luckiest.

St. Louis early became a medical center and was blessed with many distinguished physicians. Dr. William Carr Lane, who was elected the first mayor of St. Louis in 1823, established a public health system for the city during the first of his nine terms. Dr. Lane and Dr. Bernard Farrar, the first surgeon to locate permanently in St. Louis, were among the physicians who gave their lives during the terrible cholera epidemic of 1849. Dr. William Beaumont of St. Louis owes his fame to a wound that would not heal properly. During a tour of duty as an army doctor near the Canadian border he treated a patient, Alexis St. Martin, for a stubborn bullet wound in the stomach. With the cooperation of the remarkably obliging St. Martin, Beaumont was able to study for several years the workings of the digestive system through a "window" in his patient's stomach. Dr. Beaumont was later a professor of surgery in, and one of the founders of, the medical department of Saint Louis University.

The first modern hospital in St. Louis was established by Mother Seton's Sisters of Charity in 1828. Dr. F. Gratz Moses founded a free clinic in 1841 which was later taken over by the city. The first city hospital in St. Louis was opened in the year 1846. In 1847 the first state hospital was established by law, and nearly five years later, in December of 1851, it opened at Fulton under the direction of Dr. Turner R. Smith of Columbia. This was the first hospital for the mentally ill west of the Mississippi River.

Although ignorance and superstition still passed for medicine—especially in rural Missouri—between 1820 and 1840 the work of dedicated, intelligent physicians, the training provided by the new medical schools, and the establishment of modern hospitals laid the foundation for the excellent medical care available in the twentieth century.

Crime and Punishment

Much of the crime committed during the early years of statehood is similar in character to the crime reported in our own papers today—murder, theft, assault, jailbreaking. In addition, the papers reported the action taken against runaway indentured servants, the attempts to find and punish runaway slaves, the

Dr. William Beaumont
by Chester Harding
(Courtesy Beaumont Exhibit,
Washington University Med-
ical School)

imprisonment of those who failed to pay debts, and the evil consequences of duels.

Violence was more common in pre-Civil War Missouri than it is now. Since many people carried either a dirk or a gun, they could more easily commit violence when aroused. Whiskey, almost as popular a beverage as water, was quaffed not only in the tavern, but at all sorts of community gatherings from husking bee to camp meeting. The omnipresence of whiskey contributed to the irrational, passionate, and brutal character of frontier life.

The Missouri Intelligencer was particularly critical of horse-racing, and in 1834 the paper called such races "the perfect school of vice, immorality and drunkenness, where the rising generation becomes initiated in all manner of depravity." Then too, the intense pride of name or the personal sensitivity of the time led many to believe personal honor could be defended only on the dueling field. Cowardice was the unforgivable sin in ante-bellum Missouri society. In 1810 two men in St. Louis clashed over a card game. A challenge to meet at Bloody Island was made and accepted. One disputant asked his brother-in-law, Dr. Bernard G. Farrar, the first American surgeon in St. Louis, to second him. Farrar agreed reluctantly, for the doctor was a good friend of the opponent, James A. Graham. When the appointed time arrived, Farrar's brother-in-law failed to appear. The doctor, despite his friendship with Graham, was obligated as a second under the dueling code to carry out the contest. In the exchange of shots, both men were wounded. Immediately, Dr.

Farrar treated his friend whom he had shot, but the young lawyer died several days later. After several similarly sensational duels in 1823 and 1824, public pressure was so great that the practice was much curtailed. Although duels continued into the 1830's, there were many critics of the practice; ultimately it was outlawed by legislation.

The punishments meted out to convicted criminals were frequently severe. Courts often sentenced men to stripes or the pillory. For stealing a horse, the convicted man could be assigned 200 lashes, a fine of $500, the payment of double damages, and, in addition, he might be deprived of the right to give evidence in court, vote in elections, or seek public office. The court records of the time show that disobedient children could be placed in the county jail "until such time as they shall humble themselves."

In the early years of the state, the county governments used military prisons available at nearby posts when no community jails were available. In 1836 the state of Missouri built a penitentiary at Jefferson City at a cost of $25,000. The penitentiary consisted of several small buildings with accommodations for forty prisoners located on four acres of land and enclosed by a wooden stockade. The local jails were often weak structures which could not hold a strong or ingenious prisoner. Apparently even the state penitentiary had some difficulty in keeping its convicts. The *Boston Bee* declared "In Missouri if they wish to get rid of a man they put him in the state penitentiary. He is sure to get out and run away."

Violence—facilitated by the weapon-toting of private citizens and encouraged by whiskey, pride, and short tempers—was rife in the young state of Missouri. Punishment was correspondingly severe.

Recreation

The practical pioneer farmers of Missouri combined business with pleasure. Was there a house or barn or church to be built? A fence to lay? A crop of corn to shuck? "You help me, and I'll help you" was the byword of the frontier. The arrival of wagonloads of gay neighbors signaled a day of work sugarcoated with jokes and flirting, washed down with liquid lightning, and often followed by a dance to the tunes of the local fiddler. Were ever young men too weary to perform a jig for, or dance a three or four-handed reel with, bright-eyed maidens in calico?

Since corn was a crop raised on virtually every farm, the

(Scribner's Monthly, 1874, Courtesy State Historical Society)
At husking bees the lucky man who found a red ear was entitled to a kiss from the lady of his choice.

husking bee was a popular excuse for a party. The lucky man who found a red ear was, according to husking rules, entitled to kiss the girl of his choice. Corn husking was, therefore, an exciting as well as a useful activity which, according to Professor Walter Williams, ended in "much fuss and scuffle."

The rural folk also met socially for church functions and the summer camp meetings. The young men of the community would gather frequently for horse racing or games of skill such as running or shooting contests. Contemporaries speak of the "rough and tumble fight" which occurred when tempers were roiled. Without rules or refinements the men kicked, scratched, clawed, bit, and eye-gouged their opponents. Many a frontiersman went through life with a useless eye or missing a portion of his nose or ear as a consequence of this crude combat. For special celebrations such as the Fourth of July, community gatherings might include goose pulling (attempting to wring the neck of a goose suspended by its feet), greased-pig catching, and dog or cock fighting, in addition to the inevitable Independence Day orations.

The ministers of Missouri frequently attacked both public fighting and Sunday entertainments. In the towns of ante-bellum Missouri, Sunday was a time of trade, not rest, and irreligious activity abounded.

Tongues raced needles at quilting bees in old Missouri
(Harper's Weekly, April 13, 1861)

For rural folk, a trip to town was an eagerly anticipated diversion. Farmers who came to town were usually looking for the services of a blacksmith, saddler, wheelwright, or wagonmaker. There they might also secure the assistance of a printer, a doctor, or a lawyer. Each trip to town provided another adventure—especially for the children—a visit to the emporium of the local merchant who sold all kinds of merchandise—pills, pickles, candy, Calomel, tools, traps, aprons, and anise seed. The farmer seeking another hand would make his way to the courthouse square to purchase a slave at auction time. He could find both bed and board in the local tavern during his visit. Guests in the taverns or inns of the smaller cities slept in one of the several large rooms on the second floor. A common complaint concerning the inns was the lack of cleanliness and the inconvenience of sleeping in the same bed with several, possibly vermin-infested, strangers. Among the best known of the old taverns in Missouri is the Arrow Rock Tavern in Saline County, now restored and operated as a museum. Some of the other notable inns of the time were the Green Tree Hotel of Jackson, Mann's Tavern at Bowling Green, and the Square and Compass in Franklin. The hotels of the larger towns were usually more private and comfortable. The Planters House in St. Louis was both elegant and expensive—$1.25 per day.

In the towns and cities of early Missouri, social activities were somewhat more refined than in the rural areas. The larger towns provided cultural organizations and institutions, as well as professional entertainment. By 1850 there were libraries available in the following counties: St. Louis, St. Charles, Pike, Marion, Lafayette, Cooper, Cole, Clay, Boone, and Cape Girardeau. Debate clubs were formed such as that at Hannibal known as the Down East Debating Society, whose members discussed such hot issues as "When a house is on fire, does it burn up or down?" Literary societies, singing societies, and bands were organized in Missouri during this time.

Touring entertainers who gave musical, dramatic, or athletic displays appeared in the state during this period. One popular novelty organization known as the Druid Horn Blowers was made up of musicians who dressed in Druid costumes and blew ox horns. Often small family theatrical groups would travel from town to town giving a series of plays. Magicians, spiritualists, ventriloquists, fortune tellers, all came to entertain the curious and the gullible. To the river towns, an elaborate showboat might bring minstrels or melodramas. One steamboat transported an entire circus. Landbound circuses also toured the state bringing exotic animals and splendid spectacles to awe the populace. A 518-pound fat lady and a woman with two heads were exhibited in Jefferson City.

In the year 1825, Lafayette toured the United States at the invitation of retiring President James Monroe. The great Revolutionary hero was escorted to St. Louis by a committee consisting of Governor William Clark, Governor Edward Coles of Illinois, and Senator Thomas Hart Benton, who boarded his steamship, the *Natchez*, a half day's journey below the city. At his arrival, he was welcomed by Mayor Lane, Bunker Hill hero

Frontier beaux and belles danced to the fiddler's tune at rustic balls.
(Harper's Weekly)

Thespian Hall, Boonville, Missouri, erected in 1857, is said to be the oldest surviving theater building west of the Alleghenies.

Stephen Hempstead, and Auguste Chouteau. Lafayette rode in an open carriage, through the streets lined with cheering crowds, to a splendid reception at the handsome residence of Pierre Chouteau. He later toured the estate of William Clark, inspected a museum of Indian relics and, upon visiting the Lodge, was made a member of the Freemasons of St. Louis. In the evening, a dazzling ball was held in his honor in the City Hotel.

Missouri was still a place of great social contrast. While one could find libraries, gilt and velvet theatres, and elegantly-clad citizens waltzing beneath crystal chandeliers, he might stroll down the streets of St. Louis in 1840 and see

> A red gentleman of the Sac nation, in a green blanket, with his face painted in yellow stripes, . . . moving with dignified strides through our streets on Monday last. This wild man was preceded by his two wives, both clad in scarlet blankets and leggins of the same bright color. These distinguished strangers produced no great sensation here where we are accustomed to see them often, but in the eastern cities they would command a princely reception. The name of this gentleman Indian is Red Death, his eldest wife is called, when her name is rendered into English, Saddle-My-Nag and the younger is Mrs. Roast-My-Venison.

Growth and development, color and contrast—this was mid-nineteenth century Missouri.

BIBLIOGRAPHY

Anderson, Hattie M. "Missouri 1804-1828: Peopling a Frontier State," *Missouri Historical Review*, Vol. XXXI (January, 1937), pp. 150-180.

Anderson, Hattie M. "The Evolution of a Frontier Society in Missouri, 1815-1828," *Missouri Historical Review*, Vol. XXXII (April, July, 1938), pp. 298-326, 458-483; Vol. XXXIII (October, 1938), pp. 23-44.

Atherton, Lewis E. "Life, Labor, and Society in Boone County, Missouri, 1834-1854, as Revealed in the Correspondence of an Immigrant Slave-owning Family from North Carolina," *Missouri Historical Review*, Vol. XXXVIII (April, July, 1944), pp. 277-304, 408-429.

Banks, Loy Otis. "The Evening and The Morning Star," *Missouri Historical Review*, Vol. XLIII (July, 1949), pp. 319-333.

Bek, William G. "A German Communistic Society in Missouri," *Missouri Historical Review*, Vol. III (October, 1908; January, 1909), pp. 52-74, 99-125.

Bek, William G., translated by. "Gottfried Duden's Report, 1824-1827," *Missouri Historical Review*, Vol. XII (October, 1917; January, April, July, 1918), pp. 1-21, 81-89, 163-179, 258-270; Vol. XIII (October, 1918; January, April, 1919), pp. 44-56, 157-181, 251-281.

Bek, William G., translated by. "Nicholas Hesse, German Visitor to America 1835-1837," *Missouri Historical Review*, Vol. XLI (October, 1946; January, April, July, 1947), pp. 19-44, 164-183, 285-304, 373-390; Vol. XLII (October, 1947; January, April, 1948), pp. 34-49 140-152, 241-248.

Blake, Nelson Manfred. *A Short History of American Life*. New York, London: McGraw-Hill Book Company, 1952.

Bowen, Elbert R. "Amusements and Entertainments in Early Missouri," *Missouri Historical Review*, Vol. XLVII (July, 1953), pp. 307-317.

Bowen, Elbert R. *Theatrical Entertainment in Rural Missouri Before the Civil War*. Columbia: University of Missouri Press, 1959.

Britton, Wiley. "Pioneer Life in Southwest Missouri," *Missouri Historical Review*, Vol. XVI (October, 1921; January, April, July, 1922), pp. 42-85, 263-288, 388-421, 555-579; Vol. XVII (October, 1922; January, April, 1923), pp. 62-76, 198-211, 358-375.

Byars, W. V. "A Century of Journalism in Missouri," *Missouri Historical Review*, Vol. XV (October, 1920), pp. 53-73.

Chambers, William N. "Thomas H. Benton: Editor," *Missouri Historical Review*, Vol. XLVI (July, 1952), pp. 335-345.

Clark, Thomas D. "Manners and Humors of the American Frontier," *Missouri Historical Review*, Vol. XXXV (October, 1940), pp. 3-24.

Culmer, Frederic A. "Leonard-Berry Duel of 1824," *Missouri Historical Review*, Vol. XLIX (July, 1955), pp. 357-359.

Dearmont, W. S. "Building of the University of Missouri, an Epoch Making Step," *Missouri Historical Review*, Vol. XXV (January, 1931), pp. 240-244.

DeMenil, Alexander Nicholas. "A Century of Missouri Literature," *Missouri Historical Review*, Vol. XV (October, 1920), pp. 74-125.

Dillon, Merton L. *Elijah P. Lovejoy, Abolitionist Editor*. Urbana: University of Illinois Press, 1961.

Dorsey, Dorothy B. "Howard High School, the Outstanding Pioneer

Co-educational High School in Missouri," *Missouri Historical Review,* Vol. XXXI (April, 1937), pp. 249-266.

Finckh, Alice H. "Gottfried Duden Views Missouri," *Missouri Historical Review,* Vol. XLIII (July, 1949), pp. 334-343; Vol. XLIV (October, 1949), pp. 21-30.

Forster, Walter O. *Zion on the Mississippi.* St. Louis: Concordia Publishing House, 1953.

Gill, J. *Tide Without Turning: Elijah P. Lovejoy and Freedom of the Press.* Boston: The Beacon Press, 1958.

Graves, Mrs. W. W. "Land of the Osages—Harmony Mission," *Missouri Historical Review,* Vol. XIX (April, 1925), pp. 409-418.

Hall, Thomas B. "John Sappington," *Missouri Historical Review,* Vol. XXIV (January, 1930), pp. 177-199.

Hazlett, James A. "The Troubles of the Circuit Rider," *Missouri Historical Review,* Vol. XXXIX (July, 1945), pp. 421-437.

Hill, Leslie Gamblin. "Moral Crusade: the Influence of Protestantism on Frontier Society in Missouri," *Missouri Historical Review,* Vol. XLV (October, 1950), pp. 16-34.

Hockaday, John A. "A History of Westminster College," *Missouri Historical Review,* Vol. II (October, 1907), pp. 41-46.

Kirkpatrick, R. L. "Professional, Religious, and Social Aspects of St. Louis Life, 1804-1816," *Missouri Historical Review,* Vol. XLIV (July, 1950), pp. 373-386.

Kretzmann, P. E. "Saxon Immigration to Missouri 1838-1839," *Missouri Historical Review,* Vol. XXXIII (January, 1939), pp. 157-170.

Langehennig, Laura. "The Steamboat, Playground of St. Louis in the Fifties," *Missouri Historical Review,* Vol. XL (January, 1946), pp. 205-214.

Lanser, Roland L. "The Pioneer Physician in Missouri, 1820-1850," *Missouri Historical Review,* Vol. XLIV (October, 1949), pp. 31-47.

Loeb, H. W. "One Hundred Years of Medicine in Missouri," *Missouri Historical Review,* Vol. XIV (October, 1919), pp. 74-81.

Lynch, William O. "Influence of Population Movements on Missouri Before 1861," *Missouri Historical Review,* Vol. XVI (July, 1922), pp. 506-516.

McKee, Howard I. "The Marion College Episode in Northeast Missouri History," *Missouri Historical Review,* Vol. XXXVI (April, 1942), pp. 299-319.

McKee, Howard I. "The School Law of 1853, Its Origin and Authors," *Missouri Historical Review,* Vol. XXXV (July, 1941), pp. 539-561.

McLarty, Vivian K., ed. "A Missionary's Wife Looks at Missouri: Letters of Julia Barnard Strong 1836-1839," *Missouri Historical Review,* Vol. XLVII (July, 1953), pp. 329-343.

McMillan, Margaret and Monia Cook Morris. "Educational Opportunities in Early Missouri," *Missouri Historical Review,* Vol. XXXIII (April, July, 1939), pp. 307-325, 477-498.

McMurtrie, Douglas C. "The Early Career of Joseph Charless, the First Printer of Missouri," *Missouri Historical Review,* Vol. XXVI (July, 1932), pp. 342-353.

Mahan, George A. "David Nelson and Marion College," *Missouri Historical Review,* Vol. XXI (January, 1927), pp. 185-187.

Mangold, George B. "Social Reform in Missouri During the Last Century," *Missouri Historical Review,* Vol. XV (October, 1920), pp. 191-213.

Missouri, A Guide to the "Show Me" State. New York: Duell, Sloan and Pearce, 1941.

Mullett, Charles F. "Lowry, Doctor John J., a Frontier Physician," *Missouri Historical Review,* Vol. XXXVIII (January, 1944), pp. 127-137.

Murphy, Lawrence E. "Beginnings of Methodism in Missouri, 1798-1824," *Missouri Historical Review,* Vol. XXI (April, 1927), pp. 370-394.

Owen, Mary Alicia. "Social Customs and Usages in Missouri During the Last Century," *Missouri Historical Review,* Vol. XV (October, 1920), pp. 176-190.

Philips, John F. "The Lawyer in Missouri One Hundred Years Ago," *Missouri Historical Review,* Vol. XIII (July, 1919), pp. 377-387.

Phillips, Claude A. "A Century of Education in Missouri," *Missouri Historical Review,* Vol. XV (January, 1921), pp. 298-314.

Read, Georgia Willis. "Diseases, Drugs and Doctors on the Oregon-California Trail in the Gold Rush Years," *Missouri Historical Review,* Vol. XXXVIII (April, 1944), pp. 260-275.

Robins, Ruby Matson, ed. "The Missouri Reader: Americans in the Valley," *Missouri Historical Review,* Vol. XLV (October, 1950; January, April, July, 1951), pp. 1-15, 158-169, 275-293, 386-403; Vol. XLVI (October, 1951; January, April, July, 1952) pp. 46-63, 162-171, 262-275, 363-379; Vol. XLVII (October, 1952; January, April, July, 1953), pp. 47-61, 148-162, 251-265, 364-375; Vol. XLVIII (October, 1953; January, 1954), pp. 59-70, 166-180.

Rothensteiner, John E. "The Missouri Priest, One Hundred Years Ago," *Missouri Historical Review,* Vol. XXI (July, 1927), pp. 562-569.

Schlafly, James J. "Birth of Kansas City's Pioneer Church," *Missouri Historical Review,* Vol. XLIV (July, 1950), pp. 364-372.

Schmidt, Joseph H. "Recollections of the First Catholic Mission Work in Central Missouri," *Missouri Historical Review,* Vol. V (January, 1911), pp. 83-93.

Shoemaker, Floyd C. *Missouri and Missourians.* Vols. I and II. Chicago: The Lewis Publishing Company, 1943.

Shoemaker, Floyd C. "Missouri, Heir of Southern Tradition and Individuality," *Missouri Historical Review,* Vol. XXXVI (July, 1942), pp. 435-446.

Shoemaker, Floyd C. "Missouri's Tennessee Heritage," *Missouri Historical Review,* Vol. XLIX (January, 1955), pp. 127-142.

Shoemaker, Floyd C. "The Pioneer." *Missouri Historical Review,* Vol. XIX (January, 1925), pp. 241-255.

Simmons, Lucy. "The Rise and Growth of Protestant Bodies in the Missouri Territory," *Missouri Historical Review,* Vol. XXII (April, 1928), pp. 296-306.

Spencer, Joab. "John Clark, Pioneer Preacher and Founder of Methodism in Missouri," *Missouri Historical Review,* Vol. V (April, 1911), pp. 174-177.

Spencer, Joab. "Methodist Church Early History in Saline County," *Missouri Historical Review,* Vol. VI (October, 1911), pp. 14-33.

Spencer, Joel. "Reverend Jesse Walker, the Apostle of the Wilderness," *Missouri Historical Review,* Vol. II (July, 1908), pp. 261-278.

Spotts, Carl Brooks. "Mike Fink in Missouri," *Missouri Historical Review,* Vol. XXVIII (October, 1933), pp. 3-8.

Spotts, Carl Brooks. "The Development of Fiction on the Missouri Frontier, 1830-1860," *Missouri Historical Review,* Vol. XXVIII (April, July, 1934), pp. 195-205, 275-286; Vol. XXIX (October, 1934; January, April, July, 1935), pp. 17-26, 100-108, 186-194, 279-294.

Squires, Monas N. "Merry-Making in Missouri in the Old Days," *Missouri Historical Review,* Vol. XXVIII (January, 1934), pp. 91-102.

Switzler, William F. "Historical Sketch of Presbyterian Church in Columbia, Missouri," *Missouri Historical Review,* Vol. III (July, 1909), pp. 300-305.

Wellman, Paul I. "Missouri as the Missionary of the American Idea," *Missouri Historical Review,* Vol. XLIX (April, 1955), pp. 217-229.

Williams, Helen Davault. "Social Life in St. Louis 1840-1860," *Missouri Historical Review,* Vol. XXXI (October, 1936), pp. 10-24.

Windell, Marie George. "Reform in the Roaring Forties and Fifties," *Missouri Historical Review,* Vol. XXXIX (April, 1945), pp. 291-319.

Windell, Marie George. "The Background of Reform on the Missouri Frontier." *Missouri Historical Review,* Vol. XXXIX (January, 1945), pp. 155-183.

Windell, Marie George. "The Camp Meeting in Missouri," *Missouri Historical Review,* Vol. XXXVII (April, 1943), pp. 253-270.

Winter, Hauser. "The Division in Missouri Methodism in 1845," *Missouri Historical Review,* Vol. XXXVII (October, 1942), pp. 1-18.

Wish, Harvey. *Society and Thought in Early America.* Vol. I. New York, London: Longmans, Green and Company, 1955.

Withers, Robert S. "The Madstone," *Missouri Historical Review,* Vol. XLIX (January, 1955), pp. 123-126.

Before the days of the department store, the peddler's wagon—a veritable general store on wheels—was a welcome sight to isolated farm families.

(Harper's Weekly, June 20, 1868)

CHAPTER X

The Growing Conflict

> . . . the whole policy of my life
> . . . was to keep slavery agitation
> out of the State. . . .
> —Thomas Hart Benton's
> letter to a friend in 1857

> Struggle on, brave men! . . . until the banner of emancipation is planted upon the capitol of your state, and one of the proudest chapters of our history will read: "Missouri led the van and the nation followed!"
> —Carl Schurz' "Doom of Slavery"
> address, August 1, 1860

Both Thomas Hart Benton and Carl Schurz were wrong about Missouri. She could not be spared the strain of struggle. Nor would slavery disappear as a bad dream in the dawn of a glorious new day. Slavery was an evil habit—once adopted, it could not be easily abandoned. Missouri was addicted; she could not be spared the pains of the return to reality—in spite of Senator Benton's efforts. The drug of slavery had its compensations and delights—particularly for the slaveowner—and the Missouri slaveholders were not ready to forego those pleasures as Carl Schurz had hoped. Missouri was suffering for her folly—but not suffering enough to quit.

The Fall of Thomas Hart Benton

The decade of the 1840's and the beginning of the 1850's mark the decline and fall of Thomas Hart Benton. The great senator had served in the United States Senate for thirty years —longer than any man to that time—before he was finally defeated. Benton's personality and political acumen had great impact not only in the state of Missouri, but at the national level as well. For the purpose of organization this section will be divided into (1) a character study of Thomas Hart Benton, (2) an analysis of several of the issues facing him late in his career as senator, and (3) the political developments at the state level in Missouri from 1840 to 1852.

The personality of Thomas Hart Benton was a major factor in his success. Although he served Missouri in the United States Senate at a time when many great men frequented that chamber, his imposing appearance, his air of confidence, his dramatic and forceful manner of speech, his erect carriage, all marked him as a man to be reckoned with.

Certainly, many facets of his complex personality were responsible for his prominence. His speaking ability made him well known throughout the nation. The galleries were crowded when it was known that Thomas Hart Benton was to discuss an important issue. Known as the "Lion of the West" for his roar which filled the Senate chamber, he delighted to put on a lengthy show—including at one point a speech three days long. Unlike the many other political figures who went to Washington during this time, Benton was not only a forceful speaker, but also an excellent writer. Throughout his career he was able to manipulate public opinion through the wide circulation of his speeches and public statements. His interests were catholic, and he cultivated men in all areas of life. The inquisitiveness of his mind and his ability to assimilate great bodies of information from voracious reading contributed to the effectiveness of his speaking and writing.

Thomas Hart Benton was also an industrious, vigorous man who did not shrink from an exhaustive campaign or the preparation of a lengthy manuscript. He rose early in the morning—usually at 4 o'clock—to begin the day with an invigorating bath, followed by a rubdown with a stiff horsehair brush wielded by his slave. His careful attention to his health may have been motivated by the early deaths of his father and five of his sisters and brothers from tuberculosis. He seems to have escaped their fate, although the exertion of lengthy speeches sometimes produced symptoms of the disease.

Certainly, one of the reasons for Benton's effectiveness in the Senate was his devotion to the legislative process. Although Benton had numerous offers to accept other positions, he declined them to retain his office as senator from Missouri. President Jackson offered him the post of minister to Russia. President Polk offered to send him on a similar assignment to France. President Van Buren requested that he act as secretary of war.

Benton refused them all to remain in the work and the limelight he loved.

If Benton had his strong points, he also displayed those qualities which caused him to be hated by many and made him one of the most controversial Senate figures of the century. Benton's arrogance and feelings of superiority sometimes led him to disdain others. He expected praise. After making a speech in St. Louis on one occasion, he was introduced to a boy who had walked 200 miles to hear him. Unimpressed, the senator characteristically informed him, "You did right." Another aspect of his makeup was an inclination to turn political conflicts into personal feuds. Dogmatic in his political views, he was contemptous of anyone who dared to disagree. He was often abusive and vindictive in his political debate. In studying the list of Benton's friends during his career it is interesting to note how frequently he made enemies of men such as John Scott, David Barton, Henry Clay, and John C. Calhoun, all of whom he had once considered his good friends. In defense of Benton it should be observed that he would sometimes make friends of old enemies. His relationship with Andrew Jackson is the outstanding example.

Thomas Hart Benton was a Democrat—in fact, he was one of the founders of Jackson's Democratic coalition which was the

Thomas Hart Benton by Alonzo Chappel. The celebrated orator and statesman served Missouri in the Senate for thirty years before his opposition to the extension of slavery cost his Senate seat.
(Courtesy State Historical Society)

forerunner of our present Democratic Party. Throughout Jackson's presidency Benton's adherence to administration positions marked him as the most faithful and effective Democratic leader in the United States Senate. In 1856 when his own son-in-law ran for President of the United States as the candidate of the new Republican Party, Benton would not support him.

His party loyalty, however, was tempered with other considerations. Probably the greatest concern of his political life was the maintenance of a sound monetary system in America. He supported Jackson in the president's attack upon the B.U.S. because he believed the bank was dangerous to the country. On a later occasion, however, although Democratic Party unity demanded that he support such ventures as the annexation of Texas, he departed from the party position when he felt it would endanger the flow of silver from Mexico, thus encouraging the use of paper money in America. Benton was a loyal Democrat, but he was also an individualist with the strength of his convictions.

Benton was a persistent advocate of those policies he considered vital to the interests of Missouri. His leadership secured the passage of the Santa Fe Bill of 1825, which provided for the federal surveying of the route to the Southwest. He finally achieved a fifty per cent reduction in the import duties for salt, so important to the westerners for curing meat. He had long been an advocate of pre-emption rights for western settlers; the Whig Congress of 1841 secured the passage of a bill legalizing the "squatter's rights" which he had upheld for many years. Benton had supported a plan for the lowering of federal land prices; Congress passed an act in 1854 providing for the gradual lowering of land prices for the less desirable federal land. All of these issues, however, were secondary to the three main political conflicts of his career. They were (1) the bank conflict which finally resulted in the destruction of the Bank of the United States, (2) his crusade for the use of hard money, and (3) his attempt to halt the expansion of slavery. The bank issue was settled in the 1830's. The hard money issue became critical in the late 30's and continued to be an item of political discussion during the 40's. The issue of slavery extension led ultimately to Benton's political defeat.

Immediately preceding the election of 1844 Benton, the western expansionist, startled his constituents by voting against the annexation of Texas. He was the only member of the Missouri delegation in Washington to do so. Benton argued that the moment was not right to annex Texas, for he feared a war with Mexico would result. Ever an advocate of hard money, he disliked the thought that a conflict with Mexico might halt the American purchase of silver from that country. Furthermore, he was opposed to the expansion of slavery into the Mexican territory. Though Benton's position on these matters was unpopular, he had sufficient political stature to secure re-election by the legislature in 1845 by an eight-vote margin.

Benton's actions from 1844 to 1851 were a constant source of irritation to proslavery Missouri Democrats who considered themselves part of the South. In 1846 he declared his approval of the Wilmot Proviso which stipulated that slavery could not be extended into territory previously part of Mexico. In this he was contesting the position of John C. Calhoun, leader of the South in the Senate. Calhoun believed that "slavery follows the flag" —wherever the American flag is taken into new territories any American citizen may go with his property, slaves included. Calhoun argued that Congress could not legally prevent the expansion of slavery into a territory and, therefore, declared the Missouri Compromise Line unconstitutional. Benton dissented, affirming the right of Congress to legislate for or against slavery. He further warned that positions such as that of Calhoun would lead only to disunion.

Benton was a slaveowner throughout his life. But he recognized slavery as an evil and would not be a part of the extension of the practice. In this he was looking to the welfare of the nation as a whole. His vision was broad and foresighted, but he lost touch with the growing, adamant proslavery faction of the Democratic Party. When this faction, sympathetic to Calhoun, became dominant in Washington in the late 1840's and in Missouri at approximately the same time, Benton was in political trouble. In Missouri, the Democratic faction opposing Benton was led by Claiborne F. Jackson and included such men as Sterling Price and David Atchison.

Benton's enemies secured the passage of a document known as the Jackson Resolutions in the Missouri legislature in 1849. These resolutions restated Calhoun's arguments that the United States constitution does not authorize Congress to halt the spread of slavery; that a citizen of the United States could take his property to any American territory; and that slavery could be prohibited only by the vote of the citizens of a territory. Thus, the resolution asserted that slavery was to follow the flag into the West unless the citizens of the territories themselves chose to prohibit it through their own constitution. The resolution ended by requesting Missouri's senators and representatives to act in conformity with the resolution. This request was a challenge to Thomas Hart Benton. He might have ignored the challenge had he chosen to do so. But Benton was not that kind of man. He charged into the fray by announcing his intention to ignore the instructions of the legislature in the Jackson Resolutions. Instead, he would

> . . . appeal to the people of Missouri—the whole body of the people—and if they confirm the instructions, I shall give them an opportunity to find a Senator to carry their wishes into effect, as I cannot do anything to dissolve the Union or to array one half of it against the other.

In his vigorous campaign throughout the state in 1849 Senator Benton charged that the Jackson Resolutions were "a mere copy of the Calhoun resolutions offered to the [United States] Senate." He declared that they were a "firebrand, intended for electioneering and disunion purposes." He charged that Calhoun wished to weaken Congress, and he predicted an attempt to break up the Union if Calhoun and his friends were thwarted in their advocacy of the expansion of slavery.

As Benton stumped the state, the opposition faction of the Democratic Party referred to Old Bullion as "Traitor," "Apostate," "Scoundrel," and "Abolitionist." Benton's enemies hoped to create such a fuss in Missouri that the old senator would be defeated in his attempt to be re-elected. The election of 1850 resulted in a three-way split in the state legislature. The largest number of delegates were Whigs. The pro-Benton Democrats were the second largest group, and the anti-Benton group was third. A combination of the Whigs and anti-Benton Democrats was enough to defeat him. Twelve days and forty ballots were required, but finally, in January, 1851, Henry S. Geyer, a Whig, was chosen to replace Thomas Hart Benton. The great man had been repudiated after thirty years in the Senate.

Thomas Hart Benton had correctly diagnosed the approaching slavery crisis for the Union, but although he had felt the pulse of the nation, he had not heard the heartbeat of his Mis-

Brilliant attorney Henry Sheffie Geyer who served Missouri in the Territorial Legislature, the General Assembly, and the United States Senate, was the leading attorney for the defense in the Dred Scott case.

(Courtesy State Historical Society)

souri constituents. He no longer had a popular national leader such as Jackson with whom he could associate himself politically. The leaders of the Democratic Party were largely allied against him. A coalition of those within and without the party toppled the Colossus.

Benton was beaten, but not broken. For another five years he struggled in vain to regain his political power. In 1852 he attempted to redeem himself politically. He entered the campaign for congressman from the first Missouri district and was elected to a two-year term in the House of Representatives. In 1854, however, he was defeated in his re-election attempt. In the election of 1855 he failed to regain his Senate seat. His final defeat occurred in the 1856 race for the governorship of Missouri. Benton spent most of his last years, before his death in 1858, in Washington, completing the manuscript of his biography. Thomas Hart Benton's thirty years as a dedicated statesman won for him a distinguished place in the history of the state and of the country he loved. The memoirs of these years were so successful that the returns from their sale satisfied all his creditors, thus preserving from any tarnish the honorable name he prized.

To complete the study of the political activities of the period 1840 to 1852, let us examine briefly the main developments in the state government. The Democratic Party, even with its internal difficulties, was able to control the choice of governors during this era. Thomas Reynolds was elected governor in 1840, John C. Edwards in 1844, and Austin C. King in 1848. Both King and Edwards completed their four-year terms, but Governor

Austin Augustus King defeated James S. Rollins to become Missouri's eleventh governor in 1848. Although a slaveholder, King opposed the extension of slavery and was elected to Congress in 1862 as a Democrat.

(Strauss Portrait, Courtesy State Historical Society)

Reynolds took his own life ten months before the end of his administration. James S. Rollins of Columbia was the only Whig candidate to threaten seriously the Democratic hold on the governor's office when he ran in 1848.

The "Soft" faction in the Democratic Party was able to secure legislative approval of its policies in 1841. In that year the legislature authorized the Bank of the State of Missouri to accept paper money from banks refusing to redeem their currency in specie. This was obviously a defeat for Benton and his supporters. Another important political development of the time was the constitutional convention of 1845. Although the convention was authorized by a vote of the people, the citizens of the state refused to accept the constitution presented to them by the convention. Thus, the Constitution of 1820 continued in effect. The last major state development before 1852 was the decision to make state loans for the construction of private railroads. At the end of King's administration the Democratic Party was severely rent by the Benton battles. The Whigs momentarily gained political power, but the Democrats continued as the majority party. The amazing strength of the Democratic Party during this time is attested to by the fact that they could continue to rule the state despite such serious internal troubles.

Slavery in Missouri

There are always certain aspects of life in another century which are more difficult to understand. Those of us who live in the twentieth century have difficulty accepting or explaining certain characteristics of life in the nineteenth century. In particular, we may be shocked by the violence and brutality of that age. The bigotry and bloodletting of the Mormon era are contrary to our present code of conduct. The frequent street mobs which destroyed presses or seized unpopular individuals are not part of our daily experience. We do not today, as did Missourians a century ago, take the entire family to witness public hangings, nor do our judges sentence criminals to public floggings. Slights of honor and thoughts of revenge do not lead us to Bloody Island. The first half of the nineteenth century was a violent time, and the institution of slavery must be understood in the context of that society.

Although both the French and Spanish governments outlawed Indian slavery, there was so little direct control over the settlers that the enslavement of Indians was practiced despite official prohibition. Black slavery began in Missouri during the French period and continued past the midpoint of the nineteenth century. In 1720 the French miner, Renault, brought into the area of Missouri his first group of black slaves to carry on the difficult work of the lead mines. Black slavery was more successful from the owner's point of view than was Indian slavery. The Indian did not adjust well to the role of a servant and constantly sought opportunities to escape. An Indian brave, who usually assigned such tasks as gardening to his squaw, did not readily adapt to the routine of agricultural labor. In addition, the Indian had less immunity to the diseases of the white man than did the black. It became the policy of both the French and Spanish governments either to allow or encourage the growth of black slavery, but to discourage the enslavement of Indians.

When Missouri became American in 1804, Amos Stoddard estimated that there were approximately 1500 black slaves in Upper Louisiana. His estimate is probably accurate since the census of 1800 shows a total 1195 slaves. The influx of southern immigrants after the Louisiana Purchase brought many more slaves into the territory. The following census figures illustrate the growth of the black population in Missouri:

Year	Black Slaves
1810	3,011
1820	10,222
1830	25,091
1840	57,891
1850	87,422
1860	114,931

The number of black slaves in Missouri tripled during the decade from 1810 to 1820. In the next two decades the black population doubled each decade. Thereafter, a substantial increase continued for each ten-year period.

An examination of census statistics clearly illustrates that slaves in Missouri were concentrated in the regions along the Mississippi and Missouri rivers. During the years 1850 to 1860 there was a great growth of the slave trade in the western counties along the Missouri River and a slight decrease in the counties bordering the river at the eastern edge of the state. In 1860 nearly one-half of the 114,931 slaves in Missouri were located in twelve counties. The accompanying illustration demonstrates the distribution and concentration of slaves in the counties of Missouri. The smaller slave population in the southern region of the state may be explained in two ways. First, the Ozarks were settled later than the river lowlands by immigrants from free states who brought no slaves to their new home. Second, the Ozarks region, for the most part, did not lend itself to economic enterprises requiring large labor crews as did the plantations of Lafayette County. It was not a plantation region; there were no vast crops of cotton, hemp, or tobacco to tend or harvest. The slaves located in southern Missouri usually worked either as household servants or in industries such as the lead mines or the iron works. In northern Missouri, the rich plains were divided into small farms which did not require many laborers.

A comparison of the ratio of slaves to white residents in several counties in 1860 will illustrate the small number of slaves in the southern part of the state. Howard County in central Missouri had 5,886 slaves in 1860 and 9,986 whites, an approximate ratio of one to two. However, in Carter County, located in the southeast, there were only 20 slaves in a population of 1,200 whites, a ratio of one to sixty. In centrally-located Lafayette County there were 6,374 slaves to 13,688 whites, again a ratio of one to two. At the same time Sullivan County in northern Missouri had only 102 slaves to 9,095 whites or a ratio of one to ninety. In general,

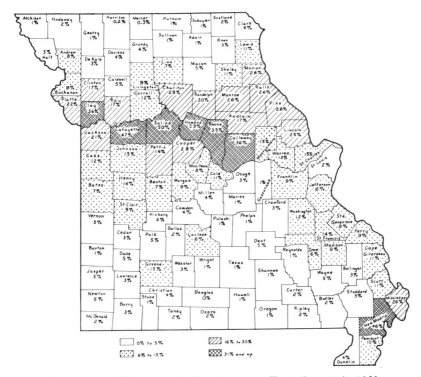

Percentage of Slaves in the Population of Each County in 1860

the slave population was concentrated between lines stretching
from Hannibal to St. Joseph on the north and from Herculaneum
to Harrisonville on the south.

It can never be doubted that slavery was an intrinsic part of
Missouri society during these important times of settlement and
economic growth. Slaves provided much of the labor to clear
the land, to grub out the stumps, to erect the homes and fences,
and to plant, hoe, and harvest the crops. Furthermore, the high
standard of living and the comforts of many early nineteenth-
century Missouri families were greatly dependent upon the labor
of black maids, cooks, nurses, handymen, and butlers. Some
slaveholders supplemented their income by hiring their slaves
out to others. The blacks contributed much, both to the original settlement and to the continually advancing standards of
living enjoyed by some slaveholding Missourians.

Some arguments have been offered to defend the institution
of slavery. Blacks who were newly-arrived from Africa needed

Slave cabin near Otterville

a period of transition during which they could be oriented to life in a new society. The time of slavery provided such an orientation period. It was also argued that the institution of slavery was actually a protection for the black. Under the system, the black was guaranteed the necessities of life without having to compete with white workers in the labor market. But such arguments cannot excuse or justify the cruelties and brutality of the system.

Under the laws of Missouri, black slaves were property, and they could be purchased and sold as such. However, the Constitution of 1820 declared that the legislature should pass laws to assure humane treatment of the slaves. But in practice a slave —who could not legally testify against a white man—had great difficulty securing the protection of the law. Certainly, a long list of offenses and cruelties can be cited. The occasional brandings and the more frequent beatings were a part of slavery. The separation of families through the sale of a parent or child brought heartache to hundreds. The misuse of slave women was a tragic consequence of the system. The slave trade, condemned even by slave-owners, caused blacks to be purchased at the auction block, crowded into jail cells, slave pens, or stockades, and often brutally marched long distances in chains. It is easier to catalogue the physical abuses than it is to describe the throttling of the genius, the frustration of the hope, and the crushing of the spirit of a whole people. Slavery was an evil institution.

The two aspects of slavery most frequently criticized—even by slaveholders—were (1) the separation of families, and (2) the slave trade. Although warm-hearted slaveholders sometimes made provisions for the families of their slaves to remain together, forced separation was an inevitable consequence of the slavery system. Many reasons such as the need to economize, business failures, the settling of estates, or the natural growth of slave families forced the owners to put their blacks on the block. Slaves were sold regularly in the area adjacent to each county courthouse. In the major slave market of St. Louis, slaves were exhibited before the critical eyes of prospective buyers at the east door of the courthouse. One contemporary described the cry of the auctioneer as, "A sound wench, sixteen years old, good to cook, iron, bake, and work." Or he might shout, "How much is offered for this woman? She is a good cook, good washer, and a good obedient servant. She has got religion." The moment of crisis came when a slave was purchased and thus separated from his family. One St. Louis professor left records of a woman who attended the slave sales in order to purchase infants whom she took from their mothers' arms and reared to be sold later for a profit. Mark Twain must have been thinking of the agony of a slave's separation from his family when he has Huckleberry Finn say, as he talks of Jim, his black friend:

> He was thinking about his wife and his children, away up yonder, and he was low and homesick; because he hadn't ever been away from home before in his life; and I do believe he cared just as much for his people as white folks do for their'n. It don't seem natural, but I reckon it's so. He was often moaning and mourning that way nights, when he judged I was asleep, and saying "Po' little 'Lizabeth! po' little Johnny! it's mighty hard; I s'pec I ain't ever gwyne to see you no mo', no mo'!"

The slave trade was the second major target of the critics of slavery. The advances of settlement into Alabama, Mississippi, Texas, and Arkansas created a new demand for slaves to be used on the huge plantations devoted primarily to the production of cotton. In 1854, advertisements in the papers of St. Louis indicated that slave traders sought to purchase gangs of 500, 1,000, and 2,500 slaves for transportation to the new cotton-growing regions. In addition to advertising, the slave traders traveled from settlement to settlement seeking to purchase any available slaves. Missouri slaveholders of the time denied a conscious attempt to produce slaves for sale in the southern market. However, they were not above selling their surplus slaves, who were carefully examined by the trader before he completed the deal.

The price of slaves was dependent upon a number of factors. Good crops and prosperity would push the market up. The number of slaves available for sale in the state also helped determine the cost, since price was directly related to supply and demand. The constant expansion of cotton plantations with the resultant demand for slaves also forced prices up throughout the slave regions of the United States. The slave dealers, having acquired a number of slaves, used all the techniques of the used car dealer a century later in preparing their slaves for resale. William Brown, a slave employed by such a dealer, described his duties as follows:

> I had to prepare the old slaves for the market. I was ordered to have the old men's whiskers shaved off, and the grey hairs plucked out where they were not too numerous, in which case he (the trader) had a preparation of blacking to cover it, and with a blacking brush we put it on. . . . These slaves were then taught how old they were. . . . After going through the blacking process they looked fifteen years younger.

Slaves so prepared for sale were then either sold individually by the trader or put up for auction.

Before 1830 slaves sold for a price of $500 or less. After 1830 there was a constant rise in slave prices so that in the 1850's field hands frequently sold for $1300 and female slaves for $1000. There are records of slaves sold for as much as $1600 during this period. The following list of prices indicates slave prices in Saline County in 1859:

Henry,	age 17,	value	$1300
Daniel,	age 36,	value	1200
George,	age 13,	value	950
Stephen,	age 8,	value	650
Addison,	age 8,	value	550
Thomas,	age 5,	value	440

The transportation of slaves to the area of their eventual sale often resulted in cruelties to the slave, but great profits for the slave trader. The horrors and hardships were so well known that owners insured obedience by threatening unruly slaves with sale to traders. A prisoner in the jail at Platte City described one of the many brutal slave dealers who made use of the facilities, and the treatment endured by the slaves in his care:

> At midnight Gen. Dorris, his son and assistants, came to the jail and ordered the slaves to get ready to leave. As it was quite cold a pair of sox were drawn over the fists and wrists of the men, in place of mittens, they were then handcuffed together in pairs and driven into the street, where they were formed into marching order behind the wagons containing the women and children—some of the former tied with ropes when considered unruly. . . .

Since slaves often tried to escape such a gang, they moved under the constant surveillance of the trader, and in mortal fear of his pistol and whip.

Most slaveholders abhorred the slave trade but salved their consciences by referring to it as a necessary evil. They perpetuated the practice they loathed by patronizing the traders and the auction block. Since no respectable member of the community would act as a slave trader, the trade was carried on by those individuals in society who were unmoved by compunction or the tragedy inherent in the operation. Some traders were not only callous, but inhumanly cruel. One escaped black slave later

"Huck Finn and Jim" by Thomas Hart Benton
(From a lithograph in the collection of the State Historical Society)

wrote of his experiences as one of a gang of Missouri slaves who marched to St. Louis under the leadership of a vicious trader named Walker. On one occasion the trader, annoyed by the wailing of one slave's baby, tore the child from the mother and, holding the infant by one leg, ran to a nearby house. There, despite the anguished pleas of the mother, he gave the child away. This same man forced a mulatto girl into concubinage and later sold her, and the four children she had borne him, into slavery.

These criticisms of the slavery system must be studied in conjunction with evidence of owners' genuine concern for their slaves. In Missouri, most slaves were closely associated with the owner's family. Although Jabez Smith of Jackson County owned 244 slaves in 1850, he is not a typical Missouri slaveholder, for most had fewer than five slaves. Under such circumstances the owner lived in close contact with his slaves. Owners with few slaves often worked side by side with their men. The children of master and slave often played and even studied together. Records of churches during the slavery period show that the slaves attended many of the churches, both Catholic and Protestant, with their masters, although they were seated separately either in a slave balcony or at the rear of the sanctuary. A few were taught to read, although this was declared illegal in 1847. Except on the hemp plantations in Platte and Lafayette counties, Missouri slaveowners did not use the harsh task system employed on the plantations farther south, where a certain amount of work was required of each slave each day. The Missouri slave was usually assigned chores in the fields, in the farmyard, or in the owner's home, but he was given Sunday as a day of rest. Frequently Saturday afternoon was a free time, too. The intimate relationship that often existed between master and slave can be observed at the burial place of Dr. William Jewell, who had his slaves buried beside him. Some masters such as Frank Blair freed their slaves. A nearly bankrupt farmer named Ulysses S. Grant quit farming in 1859 and gave his one slave freedom.

The institution of slavery was legally established both in the Louisiana Purchase Treaty and by later territorial and state enactments. In 1804 while Upper Louisiana was attached to the Indiana Territory, the territorial officials adopted a slave code similar to that used in the state of Virginia legalizing and regulating slavery. When Missouri created its new constitution in 1820, that constitution recognized the legality of slavery. The document also authorized the legislature to enact laws designed

Bill of Sale
For and in consideration of the sum of Fourteen Hundred Dollars, to me in hand paid, the receipt of which is hereby acknowledged, I have this day sold John Maclin (?) a Negro Man named Henry aged about 26 years and his wife a negro woman aged about 23 years—Both Slaves I warrant Sound in Body and mind and slaves for life—
Witness my hand and seal this Eleventh day of September eighteen hundred and fifty one
M. G. Singleton

to protect the institution; for example, statutes were suggested to exclude free blacks, from the state and to provide for the compensation of slaveholders in the event of abolition of slavery. In 1825 the state legislature adopted a slave code which provided for the details of slave treatment. Later, in 1847, a law was passed declaring that slaves could not be taught to read or write, and free blacks were excluded from the state. This act of 1847 was in direct violation of the pledge made by the Missouri legislature in 1821 that laws would not be enacted to prevent the entrance of free blacks from other states into Missouri.

The slave's actions were restricted by several laws. The black could not hold property or buy and sell without the permission of his owner. He could not legally buy or sell liquor, although historical records show that this law was not always observed. A slave could not marry in the eyes of the law. If slaves were allowed to marry legally, then division of families through the sale of some members would be more difficult to justify. A black was prohibited by law from acting as a witness in court against a white man. This restriction, too, was ignored at times, for blacks were sometimes called as witnesses. Slaves

were forbidden to hold assemblies—including church services—
without authorization and without a white person in attendance.

Although there were many prohibitions, the black, according to law, did have certain rights. The slave could not, legally,
be forced to give evidence. He could sue for his freedom if doubt
existed as to his status. He was promised an impartial jury trial
when charged with a crime. A slave found guilty of a crime was
to be punished in accordance with the degree of the crime. For
an act of rebellion, assault, or murder, he could be sentenced
either to death or to mutilation. Other crimes were usually punished by confinement in jail or by stripes. When a monetary fine
was levied against a slave, he was to pay off the fine by being
whipped, unless his owner objected. Under this system each
stripe or lash "well and truly laid on" counted for $2.

There were free blacks in Missouri as there were in all
southern states. Toward the mid-1800's an increasing number of
slaveholders, in their concern to protect loved slaves from the
evils of the system, freed their blacks. One account tells of
kindhearted—and apparently wealthy—Colonel William B. Mason who purchased a black woman and her four children, then
freed them to prevent their being sold down the river. In 1860
there were more free blacks than slaves in St. Louis, but this
heavy concentration was unusual in Missouri. Manumission of
slaves was tolerated, although not encouraged, by the state government. Permission had to be secured from the court before a
slave's freedom became legal.

Free blacks were watched constantly to prevent their inciting a slave rebellion. A freed slave lived in constant danger of
being kidnapped and returned to slavery. William Switzler, the
Columbia editor, told the story of such an abduction which had
a surprise ending for the kidnapers. In 1833 a group of Boone
County farmers abducted a free black and brought him to a
rendezvous at a landing on the Missouri River. While the party
awaited the pre-arranged arrival of a slave trader, a downpour
of meteors known as the Great Star Shower suddenly lighted up
the woods and the river. The culprits believed judgment day
had caught them in the act of enslaving and selling a free man.
Terrified and remorseful, they released their lucky captive. Free
blacks enjoyed greater independence than their enslaved brothers, but their lives were shadowed by the danger of abduction
and an uneasy awareness of constant surveillance and suspicion.

Abolitionists

Although there were people in Missouri throughout the pre-Civil War period who abhorred the institution of slavery, those who advocated its abolition were a minority. Their views were bitterly opposed and often suppressed by the irate proslavery forces. There were two kinds of abolitionists: (1) those who only advocated ending the system, and (2) those who acted illegally to spirit slaves away. The Missouri slaveholder did not discriminate between the two and considered the first as bad as the second.

Abolitionists in Missouri can be classified into three groups: (1) certain ministers and journalists of the time who used the pulpit or press to condemn slavery; (2) some politicians—particularly those from St. Louis with its large slavery-hating German population—who quietly attempted to use their political skills and influence to effect abolition; and (3) the resolute outsiders who entered the state to impress Missourians with the need to destroy the institution.

The first category of abolitionists were those associated with the churches and publications of the time. The Reverend John Clark, a Methodist minister who later embraced the Baptist Church, promoted the group known as the Friends of Humanity during Missouri's Territorial Period. The organization insisted that no one should be admitted to the Baptist Church who believed in slavery as a permanent institution. Dr. David Nelson, a Presbyterian minister, was the president of Marion College. Although he was a southerner and a former slaveholder, he was forced to leave the state in 1836 after reading a paper which suggested a system of compensated emancipation. The very next year the Reverend Elijah Lovejoy, who, like Nelson, was a Presbyterian minister, was forced to flee from St. Louis. Although Lovejoy, the editor of the St. Louis *Observer,* had criticized slavery at an earlier time, he particularly angered the St. Louisans by censuring the mob which burned to death Francis McIntosh, a black accused of stabbing a policeman. Lovejoy also called to task Judge Luke Lawless, who had publicly defended the mob's action. Although Lovejoy luckily escaped unscathed, his printing office was destroyed. A minister of the Christian Church in Chillicothe in 1855, the Reverend David White, was forced to leave his church because of pressure from people who felt he favored the abolition of slavery. The *Indus-*

Colonel George S. Park, editor of the Parkville Luminary, wealthy landowner, and patron of Park College founded in 1875. Because he published his antislavery views, Park's presses were thrown into the river.

(Courtesy State Historical Society)

trial Luminary, a Parkville newspaper, publicly deplored the institution of slavery. The editor of the paper was George S. Park, the founder of the town. Park's presses were thrown into the river by a mob in 1855. About the same time, a citizen's meeting declared a connection between the abolition movement and the Northern Methodist Church. Among the resolutions adopted at the gathering was this: "That we will suffer no person belonging to the Northern Methodist Church to preach in Platte County after date, under penalty of tar and feathers for the first offense, and hemp rope for the second."

There were also political leaders in Missouri who wanted to establish a plan of emancipation, but they wished to avoid creating havoc in the state. In the late 1820's a private meeting of political leaders was held which included both Jackson and anti-Jackson supporters. Senator Thomas Hart Benton and Senator David Barton are both reported to have attended this secret conclave. It was their intention to establish a blueprint for the emancipation of slaves in Missouri. However, the Missouri project was dropped when a racial incident in New York stirred up anti-abolitionist sentiment in the nation.

Late in his career as a senator, Thomas Hart Benton became a leader of the forces who wished to halt the spread of slavery. A group of Missouri politicians gathered about Benton in the 1850's and went farther than the senator in seeking the abolition

of slavery in this state. Among the leaders associated with this
pro-Benton faction were B. Gratz Brown, Henry Boernstein, and
Frank Blair, all three from St. Louis. Their antislavery views
were consistent with those of the large German population of the
city. Among the Germans were many who had been exiled because of their liberal political views. Having escaped from tyranny, they opposed any system which tended to exploit the individual. These politicians were not in control of government
during the 1850's, but they became government officials later
during the Civil War. It should be noted that Frank Blair did
not wish the freed blacks to remain in Missouri. As many
abolitionists, Blair favored the return of the former slaves to
Africa, or as an alternative their resettlement in Central
America.

Another group active in Missouri in the abolitionist controversy consisted of outsiders who came to the state to encourage
opposition to slavery. Theodore Weld, a professor at Oberlin College, became active in the organization known as the American
Antislavery Society and traveled about the nation speaking to
promote the aims of the society. In 1832 Professor Weld spoke
at the First Presbyterian Church in St. Louis and there met Dr.
David Nelson and Elijah Lovejoy. The American Antislavery
Society appears to have worked through these Presbyterian
leaders in the state of Missouri. However, not all in the denomi-

Francis P. (Frank) Blair, Jr., a
foe of slavery and firm unionist,
served as a general in the Union
army and later as a senator
from Missouri from 1871 to 1873.
(Courtesy State Historical Society)

nation favored their proposals, and in 1835 both Methodist and Presbyterian conferences passed resolutions opposing the Society. Another outside organization which sent literature to Missouri was the American Colonization Society which proposed that American slaves be freed and returned to Africa. The society was much disliked in Missouri, and in 1836 two teachers at Marion College were requested to leave the state for receiving literature from the American Colonization Society.

There were many other outside organizations or individuals who broadcasted their disapproval of slavery in Missouri. Their views were not met with tolerance. In 1855 an abolitionist from Leavenworth, Kansas, was seized in Weston, Missouri, and after the hair was shaved off half of his head, he was tarred, feathered, and, in frontier fashion, ridden on a rail. The episode ended in a ridiculous scene as the Weston mob held a mock auction of the abolitionist by a black auctioneer.

To this point we have discussed those groups which only advocated abolition. There were some who went further and attempted to effect abolition by freeing the slaves immediately and without compensation. There were obvious reasons why a slaveholder with thousands of dollars invested in slaves would dislike such a prospect. In the two decades before the Civil War the most damaging charge to make about a man was to call him an abolitionist. Once so classified, he was considered a slave thief. This explains the feelings that Huck Finn had while giving Jim assistance in his flight to freedom. As Huck declared, "People will call me a low down Abolitionist and despise me for keeping mum—but that don't make no difference."

The Underground Railroad was the term often employed to describe the operations of those individuals who illegally attempted to spirit slaves out of Missouri. Missouri slaveholders were vulnerable to this type of undercover activity since the state was a slave peninsula surrounded on three sides by free states (although, for a time, the status of Kansas was in question). The Underground Railroad directed slaves out of Missouri to such depots as Tabor, Grinnell, and Cincinnati in Iowa; Sparta, Godfrey, Cairo, Quincy, and Galesburg in Illinois; and Fort Scott and Ossawatomie in Kansas. In particular, the Quakers and Northern Methodists were accused of slave stealing. The Railroad operated during the 1840's but probably was more active in the 1850's. We know that Dr. David Nelson and Professor

(Courtesy State Historical Society)

Allenson Work, James E. Burr, and George Thompson, Abolitionists, in the Palmyra Jail, 1841

Moses Hunter from the Mission Institute near Quincy, Illinois, and George W. Gale and John Blanchard of Knox College at Galesburg were all active in operating the Underground Railroad.

Three episodes particularly irritated the citizens of Missouri. In 1841 two pre-ministeral students, George Thompson and James E. Burr, and a friend named Allenson Work decided to rescue Missouri blacks from slavery. They spread the word that they would give assistance to slaves at a meeting point on the Fabius River south of Taylor. The slaves informed their masters of the plot, and the three men were arrested. Slave testimony was admitted in the trial, and the young men were sentenced to from three to five years imprisonment in the state penitentiary in Jefferson City.

A more successful abolitionist plot was carried out by the celebrated John Brown in 1858. Brown was residing in Kansas at a place known as the Osage Settlement when a slave from Vernon County, Missouri, sought Brown out and implored him to rescue his family who was soon to be sold. The impetuous Brown crossed the state border the next night and freed eleven blacks.

He also seized a quantity of meat, flour, and wagons, which he declared was due the slaves for services rendered in the past, and in addition took goods which could be turned into money to provide for the slaves until they were self-supporting. One Missourian was killed in the raid. Brown led the blacks through Kansas, Iowa, Illinois, and Michigan, and finally delivered them to Canada where they were freed.

A third such episode occurred in Buchanan County in the year 1859. Dr. John Doy, captured with a group of slaves, was charged with attempting to transport them out of Missouri. He was imprisoned at St. Joseph, but a group of Kansans crossed the river, overcame the jailer, and freed Doy.

Since the activity was illegal, and those who aided escaping slaves could not safely publicize their actions, we cannot estimate with accuracy the number of slaves who were emancipated in this manner and transported to freedom in the North. The strong feeling in Missouri against slave stealers would seem to indicate that, though the number of slave thefts was probably exaggerated, they occurred frequently enough to build up widespread concern.

Missouri authorities adopted several policies to discourage such abolitionist practices. As early as 1837 the legislature had passed a law authorizing both a fine and punishment for individuals who either excited or tried to excite slaves to rebellion. In 1843 the illegal transporting of a slave from the state was declared grand larceny. Later laws were passed establishing strict regulations for the operators of ferries and steamboats to make them responsible for the transportation of any escaping slaves. The laws prohibiting blacks from attending meetings without whites in attendance were also motivated by fear of uprisings or escapes. An act of 1837 set up township patrols to travel the roads at night and to inspect slave quarters to determine if any had strayed.

In retrospect, the abolitionist movement in Missouri appears to have been a failure. The antislavery group was not able to mobilize public support for its objectives, and even those who did agree with the abolitionists were often too frightened to express themselves because of the violent reaction of the proslavery groups in control of the state. The operators of the Underground Railroad may have engaged in dangerous and exciting exploits, but they were able to free only a small number of slaves. Their activities alerted Missouri slaveholders to the dangers of the time, and encouraged increased vigilance on their part.

The Dred Scott Decision

Dred Scott was brought to St. Louis from Virginia in 1827. In time he was sold to Dr. John Emerson, an army surgeon stationed at Jefferson Barracks. When his owner was transferred to the federal arsenal at Rock Island, Illinois, Scott accompanied him. Then, when Emerson was moved again—as army personnel frequently are—Scott was transported with the doctor to Fort Snelling in the Wisconsin Territory. In 1837 Dr. Emerson returned to St. Louis where he died six years later. Dred Scott was part of the estate.

Scott attempted to purchase freedom for himself and his family, but Emerson's heirs refused. The slave decided to sue for his freedom—which was constitutionally permitted under Missouri statutes. Scott based his case upon the fact that he had lived in Illinois where slavery was forbidden by state law and in the Territory of Wisconsin where slavery was illegal according to the provisions of the Missouri Compromise line of 1820. In his first trial, held in St. Louis Circuit Court in 1846, he failed to secure his independence. In a second trial in 1850, the court ruled in his favor. The case, immediately appealed to the Missouri Supreme Court, became a political football for the next seven years.

The anti-Benton members of the Missouri Supreme Court looked upon the case as an opportunity to strike a blow against the senator and against his contention that Congress could and should halt the expansion of slavery into the territories. In 1852 the court declared that Dred Scott was not entitled to his freedom, whereupon the case was appealed to the Supreme Court of the United States. Obviously, Dred Scott did not have sufficient resources to finance such lengthy litigation. His case was considered so important that interested individuals organized to carry it through. Roswell M. Field, father of Eugene Field, and Montgomery Blair, former mayor of St. Louis, agreed to defend Scott. Senator Henry S. Geyer and former Federal Attorney General Reverdy Johnson acted as attorneys against Scott. By the time the case reached the United States Supreme Court the nation was aware of the significance of the litigation. The New

After the famous Supreme Court
decision in 1857, Dred Scott was
voluntarily freed by his master.
He died in St. Louis in September
of 1858.
(Courtesy Missouri Historical Society)

York *Tribune* was highly critical of the president and Congress
for their proslavery opinions, and the *Tribune* predicted that the
Supreme Court would hand down an opinion against the slave.

In March, 1857, Chief Justice Roger Taney and his five proslavery associates issued their opinion, denying Scott his freedom. Beyond the immediate results for Scott were the other
broad controversial aspects of the decision. The court seemed
to be following the edicts of John C. Calhoun when it declared
(1) that a black could not be considered a citizen of the United
States, and (2) that Congress does not have power to exclude
slavery from the territories.

Although there were numerous ramifications of the decision, the issue for immediate consideration was the Missouri
Compromise Line of 1820. According to the Supreme Court decision, Congress had acted illegally in attempting to halt the expansion of slavery into the greater part of the Louisiana Purchase region. Furthermore, if the decision were correct, Congress
could not in the future halt the expansion of slavery in the territories by legislative action.

Dred Scott was amazed at the publicity given his case.
When it was revealed that Mrs. Emerson, the widow of Scott's
owner, had married an abolitionist congressman from Massachusetts, the publicity caused her to arrange immediately for his
freedom. Although the well-mannered, intelligent ex-slave was
given opportunities to make a lecture tour in the North, he refused all overtures.

Meanwhile, Thomas Hart Benton was much disturbed over the court decision. He immediately prepared a denunciatory manuscript of 130 pages with 60 extra pages of appendices. Benton charged into the affray with the words, "I am one of the few —no longer in power, but still in armor when the works of our fathers are in danger." Clay and Webster were gone, but Benton recalled the circumstances and the justifications for the earlier congressional enactments. Benton declared that the "court had no authority to decide such 'political subjects'." But he was a defeated senator. The proslavery wing of the Democratic party held sway in Washington and had used a Missouri lawsuit to legalize the expansion of slavery.

Bleeding Kansas

By the 1830's most Missourians had lost their early prejudice against the prairies as areas for homesteading. The people of Missouri, particularly those residing along the western border, were aware of the fertile lands of the Indian country immediately to the west. In the 1840's Missourians began to agitate for the opening of this land to settlement. In 1847 the Missouri legislature sent a request to Congress for the extinction of Indian titles and the development of the area as a new territory. Two years later, in 1849, the Jackson Resolutions called upon Congress to

The St. Louis Court House in 1840, the site of the first scenes in the famous Dred Scott trial, in sessions held in 1847, 1850, 1852, and 1854
(From an old lithograph by Charles Overall, Courtesy State Historical Society)

use the principle of "squatter sovereignty"—letting the residents of the territory decide by their vote—whether the area would be free or slave. Under the provisions of the Missouri Compromise of 1820 all territory in the Louisiana Purchase north of 36° 30' was to be free of slavery. However, the Jackson Resolutions proposed that the line might now be discarded if the settlers so voted. Missourians reasoned that Kansas would be occupied by slave-holding settlers from Missouri who would insure the slavery status of their new home.

The South was pleased with the possibility that a new slave state might be brought into the Union. The admittance of California into the Union in 1850 as a free state had given the North a majority of two senators in the Senate. Since there was some doubt that potential states in the New Mexico region would be slave, southerners were delighted with the possibility of rescinding the line of 1820.

Senator Stephen A. Douglas of Illinois proposed a bill in 1854 for the establishment of two new territories. He suggested that the Indians be removed from the region directly west of Missouri and Iowa and that the area be divided into two new territories, Kansas and Nebraska. He further suggested that the principle of "squatter sovereignty" be employed in these new territories in determining the status of slavery. It was commonly believed that immigrants from the free state of Iowa would occupy Nebraska, which would therefore be free, while Kansas, settled by Missourians, would be slave.

Senator Stephen Douglas, of the free state of Illinois, was probably not so much interested in the slavery issue as he was in establishment of territorial government in the western regions which would facilitate the building of a transcontinental railroad from Chicago to California. By adding the "squatter sovereignty" provision, he assured himself the support of the South. His bill, known as the Kansas-Nebraska Act of 1854, passed both houses of Congress and was signed by President Pierce. Of the Missouri delegation in Washington all senators and representatives voted in favor of the bill with the exception of Thomas Hart Benton, who was then in the House of Representatives.

Except for Benton and his few close associates, Missouri Democratic leaders supported the Kansas-Nebraska Act. Even the opposition party, the Whigs, seems to have supported the Act, since 50 of the 60 Whigs serving in the state legislature met to declare their approval of the bill. Missouri in 1854 welcomed the possibility of establishing a new proslavery sister on her western border.

Many northerners, and New Englanders in particular, were disturbed at the passage of the Kansas-Nebraska Act. Some spoke of the repeal of the Missouri Compromise Line as "violation of a sacred pledge." In Massachusetts, dissatisfaction over the act was so great that the state legislature chartered a company to encourage the emigration of antislavery settlers into Kansas. Although several such companies were organized in the North at this time, the best known was the New England Emigrant Aid Society.

During 1854 great numbers of Missourians rushed into Kansas seeking the best settlement sites along streams and near woods and establishing such towns as Kickapoo, Atchison, Lecompton, and Leavenworth. The Missouri settlers who went to Kansas did so under the urging of several prominent Missouri politicians, especially Senator David R. Atchison and former Attorney General B. F. Stringfellow. These leaders and the newspapers of western Missouri declared the necessity of rescuing Kansas from the grasp of the New Englanders. Those who could not go to Kansas as settlers were urged to join one of the many new Missouri societies organized to win the victory in Kansas by whatever means necessary. The organizations took many names. One group called itself the Platte County Self-Defensive Association; others were known as the Blue Lodges, the Social Bands, the Sons of the South, and the Friends of Society. The purpose of these western organizations is clear from the following quotation taken from the Liberty *Democratic Platform* in the issue for June 27, 1854:

> Shall we allow such cutthroats and murderers as the people of Massachusetts are to settle in the territory adjoining our own State? NO! If popular opinion will not keep them back, we should see what virtue there is in favor of arms.

The first election in Kansas was held November 29, 1854. The territorial governor, Andrew H. Reeder, understood the intentions of many Missourians when he announced that only Kansas residents would be allowed to vote. In the meantime Senator Atchison traveled through western Missouri calling upon people to vote in the Kansas election in order to prevent the abolitionists from seizing the new state. He said, when speaking

David Rice Atchison, president pro tempore of the United States Senate in 1849, is considered by many to have been president for a day when the inauguration (March 4, 1849) of President Taylor was delayed until Monday, March 5.
(Courtesy State Historical Society)

to a group at Weston on November 6, "You can without any exertion, send 500 of your young men who will vote in favor of your institutions." On election day some 1700 Missourians crossed into Kansas and insisted upon the right to vote. The officials of the polls were either sympathetic to the Missourians' interests, or intimidated by their numbers, and allowed them to cast their ballots. A total of 2883 persons voted and well over half were Missourians. The proslavery candidate for Congress was elected overwhelmingly. It appears, however, that he would have won even without the illegal ballots, since the other two candidates received only a scattering of votes. Missouri had won the first round in the fight for control of Kansas.

The next election in Kansas was held on March 30, 1855, to name delegates to the territorial legislature. In the two months preceding the polling there was great activity in western Missouri in preparation for this election. Even students of the University of Missouri showed interest by sending a delegate to Kansas to cast a vote for slavery. Between 4,000 and 5,000 armed Missourians with flags and banners rode or walked across the border to call their ballots in the March election. An antislavery journalist noted that they had "guns upon their shoulders, revolvers stuffing their belts, bowie knives protruding from their boot-tops." Although there was much liquor in evidence among the group, they were reported to have been otherwise a well-behaved delegation of voters. When the polls were closed, a total of 6,307 persons had voted, a remarkable circumstance in view of the fact that there were only 2,095 eligible voters in Kansas at that time. As anticipated, the proslavery candidates were once again the overwhelming victors in the election. Senator Atchison, who had led a large group across the border, said later:

> We had at least seven thousand men in the Territory on the day of the election, and one-third of them will remain there. . . . The pro slavery ticket prevailed everywhere. . . . Now let the Southern men come on with their slaves. Ten thousand families can take possession of and hold every acre of timber in the Territory of Kansas, and this secures the prairie. . . . We are playing for a mighty stake; if we win, we carry slavery to the Pacific Ocean.

The Missourians attempted to rationalize their actions by noting that Massachusetts had sent people to Kansas in order to have them vote against slavery. Furthermore, they noted that a person was qualified to vote if he were present in the territory and *intended* to remain there. Thus, intention was important in establishing the right to vote. We can only note that the greater number of voters in the Kansas elections changed their intentions quickly after calling their vote, for most returned to Missouri.

By the fall of 1855 the tactics of the Missourians seemed to be succeeding in Kansas. The Kansas territorial delegate to Congress was proslavery. The territorial legislature established a severe slave code to protect the institution of slavery. The proslavery legislature forced the removal of Governor Reeder, who did not always agree to their actions. The Missouri newspapers gloated over the defeat of the northern abolitionist foes. The following remarks appeared in the Canton *North East Reporter* on April 5, 1855:

> The importance of this victory cannot be too highly estimated. Had the abolitionists carried Kansas, the next step would have been to undermine and destroy the institution of slavery in Missouri . . . With emissaries under the garb of religion, and coworkers with the political designation of *free-soilers*, they have been making war upon our rights heretofore; and having such secret enemies in our midst, it was thought Missouri would fall an easy

prey to their diabolical schemes, so soon as besieged
on three sides by their fanatical army.

During 1855 the antislavery forces in Kansas began to grow,
fed by a great stream of settlers from the populous North. Under
the capable leadership of Dr. Charles Robinson and Jim Lane
they refused to recognize the proslavery government that had
been established. Disregarding the laws and attempting to ignore
the legal authority of the elected legislature, the free-state forces
proceeded to hold elections of their own, in which they chose
their own delegate to Congress, elected delegates to the constitutional convention, and ratified the free-state constitution.

By December, 1855, Kansas had two governments. The proslavery government at Lecompton was the legal government
recognized by the Democratic administration in Washington. The
illegal antislavery government, which had no authorization from
Washington, had its headquarters at Topeka. The proslavery
forces felt that the constant influx of northern emigrants placed
them at a disadvantage. Such influential writers as John Greenleaf Whittier and Horace Greeley were encouraging these emigrants and were upholding the cause of abolition. Whittier described the Kansas situation in the following poem:

> We cross the prairies as of old
> The pilgrims crossed the sea,
> To make the West, as, they the East,
> The homestead of the free!
>
> *   *   *
>
> Upbearing, like the Ark of old,
> The Bible in our van,
> We go to test the truth of God
> Against the fraud of man.

Whittier was thinking about Missouri voters in the Kansas election when he wrote the last line. Many northerners responded
to such emotional appeals and came flocking to Kansas carrying
with them the new Sharp's rifle. At this point emotional debate
sparked physical violence.

When the proslavery group in Kansas sensed that the tide
was running against them, they determined upon a policy of intimidation. The antislavery groups were ready to reply in kind.
In the late fall of 1855, when the crisis came, the tall, imposing
former Senator Atchison of Missouri emerged as the natural
leader of the proslavery forces. Atchison was not afraid of vio-

lence. As early as September 24, 1854, he had written to his associate, Jefferson Davis:

> We will before six months rolls around, have the Devil to pay in Kansas and this State. We are organizing to meet their organization. We will be compelled to shoot, burn and hang, but the thing will soon be over. We intend to 'Mormonise' the Abolitionists.

The Missourians were referred to as "Border Ruffians" after one of their group knocked down with his fist the governor of the Kansas Territory. Senator Atchison and his associates gleefully adopted the name along with a plan of action. Anxious to prevent enlargement of the antislavery population of Kansas, they threatened to halt the westward movement of Kansas immigrants via the Missouri River. On one occasion, the steamer *Arabia* was stopped at Lexington, and rifles intended for antislavery emigrants in Kansas were removed. Thereafter, the antislavery forces made a policy of directing their Kansas-bound emigrants through the free state of Iowa. Another incident occurred in December, 1855, when a group from Clay County seized the United States arsenal at Liberty and removed both arms and ammunition. Army officials from Leavenworth came to Liberty immediately to demand the return of the arms. No

Kansas City in 1852
(Dana, United States Illustrated, Courtesy State Historical Society)

arrests were made when all, save approximately $400 worth of arms, were brought back to the arsenal.

The following three incidents are typical of the savage encounters which occurred in the border warfare during the years 1855 and 1856. In May, 1856, a large band of Missourians surprised the town of Lawrence, an antislavery stronghold, bringing with them five artillery pieces to intimidate the Kansans. In this attack the hotel, the printing offices of the town, and several private homes were destroyed, and several men were killed.

The fanatic abolitionist, John Brown, determined to make a retaliatory raid, attacked the proslavery settlers living at Dutch Henry's Crossing on Pottawatomie Creek. Five men were murdered. The brutality of the killings led to a great outcry in Missouri and the South. A Missouri band, the Westport Sharpshooters led by reporter H. C. Pate, vowed to capture Brown. In a short maneuver John Brown and his men surrounded and captured the Westport Sharpshooters. Pate described in his newspaper the encounter with Brown: "I went to take old Brown and old Brown took me." The Missourians, however, were to have their revenge, for in August, 1856, they marched in great numbers against John Brown's headquarters at Ossawotamie, set fire to the town, and left it a blackened ruin.

In October, 1857, a second territorial election was held in Kansas for the selection of members of the state legislature. By this time the antislavery forces had grown strong enough to win, and therefore to establish a legal government sympathetic to their views. During the three years 1857 to 1860 intermittent warfare continued. The Jayhawkers, as the Kansans were known, made numerous raids into Bates, Vernon, Barton, and Cass counties. These incursions were opportunities for horse stealing, general thievery, and sometimes murder. During John Brown's 1858 foray into Vernon County he rescued a number of slaves. Another Kansas raider who caused great concern in the border counties was James Montgomery, a hothead from Fort Scott, who attempted to crush slavery by threatening to raid and seize slave settlements. Governor Denver of Kansas, Governor Stewart of Missouri, and, at the same time, the United States army troops stationed along the Kansas-Missouri border used their influence and power to attempt to halt the raids.

Intermittently throughout the Civil War period conflict erupted between Kansas and Missouri. It was not until the end

Jefferson City in 1859 by E. Robyn

of the Civil War that a durable peace was established. In retrospect, the foregoing episodes in Bleeding Kansas were the result not only of Missouri attempts to preserve slavery, but of the growing concern throughout the nation over the expansion of slave territory. Both North and South had a stake in Kansas. Missouri was the closest neighbor. Missourians fought to make Kansas slave as they were, but the tides of emigration from the North eventually won the day.

The Election of 1860

The decade before the Civil War was a time of great change in the party structure in the United States. The Whig Party died in 1855. The Democratic Party developed a wide and bitter split. A new American Party appeared in 1856, but it lasted only a few years. Many smaller groups such as the Free Soil Party and the Constitutional Union Party sprouted during this decade. This burgeoning of parties resulted from the growing prominence of the slavery issue in national politics, the continuing influence of Thomas Hart Benton, and the growing feelings of a body of Missourians that something must be done to attempt to save the Union, which they believed to be in peril. Finally, in 1860, the Republican Party, which included fragments from each of the previously-named parties, entered the Missouri election. Let us consider chronologically, beginning in the year 1852, the politics of this time leading up to the crucial election of 1860.

In 1852 a slaveholding Democrat from Chariton County named Sterling Price ran for governor and was elected. Price was well known in Missouri for his military leadership during the Mexican War. He had resigned from the United States House of Representatives in order to lead Missouri troops to Santa Fe. During Governor Price's term two events are of greatest importance. First, the Kansas border troubles began. Governor Price made it clear that his sympathies lay with those Missourians who attempted to make Kansas a slave state. A second important development occurred in 1855 when the state legislature met to select a senator at the end of David Atchison's term. The delegates could not come to an agreement, and because of this stalemate Missouri had only one voice in the United States Senate during the years 1855 to 1857.

At the conclusion of Governor Price's term the Whig Party collapsed because of internal dissension over slavery and other issues. A new grouping called the American Party was organized to take the place of the Whigs. This party is often known in American history as the Know-Nothing Party since it was a secret organization whose members answered, when quizzed about their party, "I know nothing." The Know-Nothing Party was a bigoted organization, militantly anti-Catholic, anti-Irish, and anti-German. Fortunately, it was short-lived.

In the election of 1856 an anti-Benton Democrat from St. Louis named Trusten Polk won the governor's post by defeating Thomas Hart Benton. Polk resigned the governorship shortly after his victory when the state legislature selected him as a United States senator. He was succeeded briefly by Lieutenant-Governor Hancock Jackson of Randolph County. In 1856 a special election was held to select a new governor. Robert M. Stewart of St. Joseph was the candidate for the anti-Benton Democrats. All other political factions in Missouri, including former Whigs and Benton Democrats, united in support of the candidacy of James S. Rollins of Columbia. The campaign was bitterly fought, and the final count indicated that Stewart won by a margin of only slightly more than 300 votes.

During the Stewart administration the Governor supported the institution of slavery as being constitutional, but he also insisted on the preservation of the Union. Stewart had been an ardent promoter of the Hannibal-St. Joseph Railroad. Although, as governor, he was forced to recognize the fact that the railroads of the state were not meeting their obligations, he opposed the seizure of the roads, and the state did not foreclose during his administration. Stewart concluded his administration with the following plea to the state: "I would here, in my last public official act as Governor of Missouri, record my solemn protest against unwise and hasty action, and my unalterable devotion to the Union, so long as it can be made the protector of equal rights."

A major change in immigration into Missouri during the last years before the Civil War was an important factor in the election of 1860. The influx of great numbers of Germans and a new wave of people from the northern states created a body of voters who were hostile to slavery. In 1860 the German population in Missouri constituted about ten per cent of the total; immigrants from the North formed about fifteen per cent of the population. While these groups were not large enough to control state politics, they did elect certain leaders in the St. Louis area who upheld their ideas. They also were able to provide leadership later during the Civil War when the proslavery state government was forced out.

The election of 1860 was probably the most crucial American election in the nineteenth century. The new Republican Party, with its platform calling for an end to the expansion of slavery, nominated Abraham Lincoln of Illinois for president.

Trusten Polk, elected the twelfth governor of Missouri in 1856, resigned after one year in office to serve in the United States Senate. He and his fellow senator from Missouri Waldo P. Johnson were expelled from the Senate for secessionist activities in January, 1862, and both served as officers in the Confederate army during the Civil War.

(Strauss portrait, Courtesy State Historical Society)

Francis P. Blair, B. Gratz Brown, and other Missourians of similar abolitionist sentiments organized the party in Missouri in 1860 with the support of the large German population in St. Louis.

The Democratic National Convention in 1860 was a fiasco which led to a split in the party. The Southern Democrats supported John Breckenridge of Kentucky for president, while the Northern Democrats supported Stephen Douglas of Illinois. The split in the party resulted from differing opinions over the same well-gnawed bone of contention—the extension of slavery to the territories. The southern Democrats accepted the Calhoun view that slavery extension could not be halted. The northern Democrats declared that "squatter sovereignty" should determine the issue. In Missouri the Democrats were split along the same lines, although the issue was more confused by the fact that the Douglas Democrats in Missouri nominated a man for governor named Claiborne Jackson, who in fact, held to the Calhoun view with regard to slavery expansion. However, since Jackson was supported by the *Missouri Republican,* which in spite of its name was a Douglas Democrat paper, Jackson did not openly declare his position.

The fourth party both nationally and in Missouri was known as the Constitutional Union Party. It sought to settle the differences between North and South through compromise, and wanted above all to avoid war.

Each of these four parties entered the election campaign for governor in 1860. A plurality of Missourians cast their votes for Douglas for president and Claiborne Jackson for governor. The gubernatorial candidate of the Constitutional Union Party was runner-up; he and Jackson received over eighty-five per cent of the ballots cast in the election.

The victorious Douglas Democrats and the runner-up Constitutional Union Party supported more moderate views than the extreme antislavery stand of the Republicans, or the radical conviction that "slavery follows the flag" of the Breckenridge Democrats. The Missourians' choice of the two moderate parties demonstrates their rejection of either radical stand. If the election was a true indication of their feelings, Missourians did not want to bolt the Union.

There were those who spoke openly of secession from the Union when administrations changed in January, 1861. But re-

Robert Marcellus Stewart was elected to the state Senate in 1846 on the Democratic ticket. In his ten years as a state senator, he was instrumental in the promotion of Missouri's first major railroads. In 1857 S t e w a r t narrowly defeated Whig James S. Rollins to become governor.

(Courtesy State Historical Society)

tiring Governor Stewart expressed his opposition to this: "Missouri to surrender her prosperity in exchange for the mad chimera of secession, to be followed by revolution, battle, and blood? Never!" Newly elected Governor Claiborne Jackson, however, was not so fearful of secession. He believed that great effort should be exerted to settle differences peacefully, but he added:

> The destiny of the slaveholding States of this Union is one and the same. So long as a State continues to maintain slavery within her limits, it is impossible to separate her fate from that of her sister States who have the same social organization. . . . Missouri will not be found to shrink from the duty . . . *to stand by the South.*

BIBLIOGRAPHY

Atchison, Theodore C. "David R. Atchison," *Missouri Historical Review,* Vol. XXIV (July, 1930), pp. 502-515.

Benet, Stephen Vincent. *John Brown's Body.* New York, Toronto: Rinehart and Company, 1958.

Blanton, B. F. "True Story of the Border War," *Missouri Historical Review,* Vol. XVII (October, 1922), pp. 57-61.

Blum, Virgil C. "The Political and Military Activities of the German Element in St. Louis 1859-1861," *Missouri Historical Review,* Vol. XLII (January, 1948), pp. 103-129.

Bradford, Priscilla. "The Missouri Constitutional Controversy of 1845," *Missouri Historical Review,* Vol. XXXII (October, 1937), pp. 35-55.

Buckmaster, Henrietta. *Let My People Go: the Story of the Underground Railroad and the Growth of the Abolition Movement.* New York, London: Harper and Brothers, 1941.

Chambers, William Nisbet. *Old Bullion Benton: Senator from the New West.* Boston: Little, Brown and Company, 1956.

Fitzgerald, Fred. "Daniel Dunklin," *Missouri Historical Review,* Vol. XXI (April, 1927), pp. 395-403.

Green, James F. "James S. Green," *Missouri Historical Review,* Vol. XXI (October, 1926), pp. 41-44.

Herklotz, Hildegard R. "Jayhawkers in Missouri 1858-1863," *Missouri Historical Review,* Vol. XVII (April, July, 1923), pp. 266-284, 505-513; Vol. XVIII (October, 1923), pp. 64-101.

Kirkpatrick, Arthur R. "Missouri on the Eve of the Civil War," *Missouri Historical Review,* Vol. LV (January, 1961), pp. 99-108.

Kirschten, Ernest. *Catfish and Crystal.* Garden City, New York: Doubleday and Company, 1960.

Lewis, Lloyd. "Propaganda and the Kansas-Missouri War," *Missouri Historical Review,* Vol. XXXIV (October, 1939), pp. 3-17.

Luthin, Reinhard H. "Organizing the Republican Party in the 'Border Slave' Regions: Edward Bates' Presidential Candidacy in 1860," *Missouri Historical Review,* Vol. XXXVIII (January, 1944), pp. 138-161.

McClure, C. H. "Early Opposition to Thomas H. Benton," *Missouri Historical Review,* Vol. X (April, 1916), pp. 151-196.

Malin, James C. *John Brown and the Legend of Fifty-Six.* Philadelphia: The American Philosophical Society, 1942.

Meigs, William M. *The Life of Thomas Hart Benton.* Philadelphia and London: J. B. Lippincott Company, 1924.

Merkel, Benjamin G. "The Abolition Aspect of Missouri's Anti-Slavery Controversy 1819-1865," *Missouri Historical Review,* Vol. XLIV (April, 1950), pp. 232-253.

Merkel, Benjamin G. "The Slavery Issue and the Political Decline of Thomas Hart Benton," *Missouri Historical Review,* Vol. XXXVIII (July, 1944), pp. 388-407.

Merkel, Benjamin G. "The Underground Railroad and the Missouri Borders 1840-1860," *Missouri Historical Review,* Vol. XXXVII (April, 1944), pp. 271-285.

Morison, Samuel Eliot and Henry Steele Commager. *The Growth of the American Republic.* New York, London: Oxford University Press, 1942.

Nelson, Earl J. "Missouri Slavery 1861-1865," *Missouri Historical Review,* Vol. XXVIII (July, 1934), pp. 260-274.

Newhard, Leota. "Beginning of the Whig Party in Missouri 1824-1840," *Missouri Historical Review,* Vol. XXV (January, 1931), pp. 254-280.

Nichols, Alice. *Bleeding Kansas.* New York: Oxford University Press, 1954.

Parrish, William E. "David Rice Atchison: Faithful Champion of the South," *Missouri Historical Review,* Vol. LI (January, 1957), pp. 113-125.

Parrish, William E. "David Rice Atchison, Frontier Politician," *Missouri Historical Review,* Vol. L (July, 1956), pp. 339-354.

Parrish, William E. *David Rice Atchison of Missouri.* Columbia: University of Missouri Press, 1961.

Ray, P. O. "The Retirement of Thomas Hart Benton from the Senate and Its Significance," *Missouri Historical Review,* Vol. II (October, 1907; January, 1908), pp. 1-14, 97-111.

Rollins, C. B. "Some Impressions of Frank P. Blair," *Missouri Historical Review,* Vol. XXIV (April, 1930), pp. 352-358.

Ryle, Walter H. "Slavery and the Party Realignment in Missouri in the State Election of 1856," *Missouri Historical Review,* Vol. XXXIX (April, 1945), pp. 320-332.

Shoemaker, Floyd C. *Missouri and Missourians.* Vol. I. Chicago: The Lewis Publishing Company, 1943.

Shoemaker, Floyd C. "Missouri's Proslavery Fight for Kansas 1854-1855," *Missouri Historical Review,* Vol. XLVIII (April, July, 1954), pp. 221-236, 325-340; Vol. XLIX (October, 1954), pp. 41-54.

Smith, William E. "The Blairs and Fremont," *Missouri Historical Review,* Vol. XXIII (January, 1929), pp. 214-260.

Snyder, J. F. "Battle of Osawatomie," *Missouri Historical Review,* Vol. VI (January, 1912), pp. 82-85.

Snyder, J. F. "The Democratic State Convention of Missouri in 1860," *Missouri Historical Review,* Vol. II (January, 1908), pp. 112-130.

Stevens, Walter B. "A Day and Night with 'Old Davy'; David R. Atchison," *Missouri Historical Review,* Vol. XXXI (January, 1937), pp. 129-139.

Thomas, Raymond D. "A Study in Missouri Politics, 1840-1870," *Missouri Historical Review,* Vol. XXI (January, April, July, 1927), pp. 166-184, 438-454, 570-580.

Trexler, Harrison A. *Slavery in Missouri, 1804-1865.* Baltimore: The Johns Hopkins Press, 1914.

Trexler, Harrison A. "Slavery in Missouri Territory," *Missouri Historical Review,* Vol. III (April, 1909), pp. 179-198.

Trexler, Harrison A. "Value and Sale of the Missouri Slave," *Missouri Historical Review,* Vol. VIII (January, 1914), pp. 69-85.

Twain, Mark (Samuel L. Clemens). *The Adventures of Huckleberry Finn.* Cleveland, New York: The World Publishing Company, 1947.

Viles, Jonas, ed. "Documents Illustrating the Troubles on the Border, 1858, 1859, 1860," *Missouri Historical Review,* Vol. I (April, July, 1907), pp. 198-215, 293-306; Vol. II (October, 1907), pp. 61-77.

Violette, Eugene Morrow. *A History of Missouri.* Cape Girardeau, Missouri: Ramfre Press, 1951 ed.

CHAPTER XI

The Civil War

I will never see chains fastened upon my country! I will
ask for six and a half feet of Missouri soil in which to
repose, but [I] will not live to see my people enslaved!
—proclamation by General
Sterling Price,
November, 1861

In the agonizing moments of the Civil War crisis many
absurd things were said in Missouri—and elsewhere. It was a
time of bravery, bravado, and plain nonsense. The road to war
and the battle paths themselves were paved with falsehoods. In
New England it was commonly believed that Missourians were
all either illegal voters or border ruffians. In the South it was
commonly believed that Missouri was so dedicated to the expansion of slavery that she would undoubtedly stand with the Confederacy. The Radical Unionists of the time declared that the
Civil War was a conflict solely to crush black slavery. General
Price melodramatically announced that he was fighting to keep
white Missourians from enslavement. Not one of these views
was really correct. There were, of course, important economic,
social, and constitutional differences between North and South,
but both sides exaggerated the hostility and misread the intent of
the other. The Civil War stands as a tragic monument to the pig-
headedness of people. In the midst of all this gullibility and dis-
tortion we can see Missourians at their best and at their worst.

Choosing Sides

Abraham Lincoln of Illinois was elected President of the
United States in November, 1860. The slave states of the South,
seething with hatred for Lincoln and fearing that their property
rights and the institution of slavery were in jeopardy, began to
secede from the Union. By March, 1861, seven states of the
lower South had broken their ties with the United States of
America. Although Lincoln earnestly requested the states to

Governor Claiborne Fox Jackson is best known for his unsuccessful attempt to lead Missouri into the secessionist camp in 1861. He is also noted for the fact that he successively married three daughters of Dr. John Sappington.
(Courtesy State Historical Society)

return and promised in his inaugural address that he would not destroy the institution of slavery where it already existed, his pleas were futile.

The slave states which had not seceded were now forced to make a difficult decision. The states of the upper South—called the border states—had many ties with the North. Furthermore, they recognized that should a civil war result it would likely be fought first in the border states. Four trends of opinion were prevalent in Missouri at this time. There were those who favored secession in order to stand with the South. There were some whose devotion to the Federal Government was so great that they would prefer to relinquish the institution of slavery, if necessary, to remain in the Union. There were others who believed that slavery in Missouri was secure and that secession was unnecessary. Still other Missourians advocated immediate abandonment of slavery and a break with the traditions and alliance of the South.

Of these various groups in Missouri, the advocates of secession had the greatest need for immediate action. If a rebellion is to be successful, the rebels must act in unison. The secessionists of Missouri recognized this and sought to join their like-minded associates in the South.

The members of the Missouri General Assembly elected in November, 1860, convened on December 31, 1860, only eleven days after the secession of South Carolina. The Breckenridge

Democrats in the Missouri legislature were the largest group, but they did not have a majority, and even within their ranks there were those who had second thoughts about secession. The Douglas Democrats, Constitutional Unionists, and Republicans, of course, were not ready to secede.

Governor Claiborne Jackson, the author of the proslavery Jackson Resolutions of 1849 which had caused so much difficulty for Thomas Hart Benton, had close ties with the political leaders of the secessionist states. The governor informed the legislature that he believed Missouri should remain in the Union so long as her rights were protected by constitutional guarantees. He did request that the legislators consider and decide whether Missouri should continue her present relationship with the Federal Government in Washington. Fearful that Jackson's intention was to encourage the secessionist groups to secure the passage of legislation withdrawing Missouri from the Union, the moderates in the state legislature obtained acceptance of a bill calling upon the citizens of Missouri to elect delegates to the state convention. This convention would discuss Missouri's status in the Union and recommend possible action to be taken to formalize this status. The recommendation would then be submitted to the people for approval. The moderates designed this cumbersome and time-consuming system to avoid precipitous action by the legislature which the citizens might later regret.

On February 18, 1861, the people of Missouri elected ninety-nine delegates to the special convention called to consider the momentous question of secession. Although they lacked the power to control the government, the Democratic faction supporting secession had been the largest of four groups in the state legislature. The election results on February 18 demonstrated that Missourians had changed their minds since the preceding November when they had chosen a plurality of Beckenridge Democrats to represent them in the legislature. Of the 140,000 votes cast in the election, 110,000 votes went to candidates who supported the Union. Only 30,000 votes were received by secessionist candidates. Not a single advocate of secession was elected a member of the convention.

The state convention met originally in Jefferson City, but the moderate delegates, apprehensive that the secessionist members of the legislature would unduly influence the convention, successfully maneuvered a change of location. The convention adjourned to hold its meetings at the Mercantile Library in St. Louis, the stronghold of Union sympathy in the state.

Most of the delegates to the convention can be described as conditional Unionists. That is, they wished to remain in the Union, but they feared developments which might force the state to withdraw at a later time. White-haired former Governor Sterling Price was chosen chairman of the convention; Hamilton Gamble of St. Louis was appointed to head the main committee. Gamble's committee presented a report declaring loyalty to the Union and expressing hope that the attempts being made at that time to compromise the differences between North and South would be successful. The committee further reported that they saw no reason for Missouri to secede. The Gamble committee also went on record as opposing any federal coercion of the seceding states. This report was adopted by the convention, which adjourned to meet again at the call of the executive committee.

Certainly this state convention of 1861 was an example of master strategy on the part of the Union forces. The governor and the strong secessionist forces in the legislature had been thwarted. The citizens of Missouri appear to have been overwhelmingly opposed to secession. This does not mean, of course, that they were opposed to slavery, but they did not wish to separate themselves from the Federal Union.

On April 12, 1861, the South fired on Fort Sumter, precipitating the bloody war which was to rage for another four years. President Lincoln issued his request to the governors for 75,000 men to defend the Union against the secessionists. To Lincoln's request for four Missouri regiments, Governor Claiborne Jackson, whose sympathies were with the South, replied indignantly, "Your requisition, in my judgment, is illegal, unconstitutional, and revolutionary in its objects, inhuman and diabolical, and cannot be complied with. Not a man will the State of Missouri furnish to carry out such an unholy crusade." It is clear from Governor Jackson's answer that his southern sympathies were so strong that his leadership in the state would be likely to incline Missouri toward secession.

Jackson's refusal to send troops into federal service was followed by four significant developments. First, on April 20, 1861, a group of some 200 men quietly seized the federal arsenal at Liberty, Missouri, and proceeded to remove all the guns and ammunition stored there. This was an obvious attempt on the

part of the secessionists to prepare for the battle they anticipated. Second, the governor called a special session of the legislature to assemble at Jefferson City on May 2. Jackson addressed this Assembly, reminding them of the strong ties and
mutual interests of Missouri and the South. Apprising the legislators of Missouri's duty to prepare to defend herself and her
friends, the governor requested legislative action to provide for
the adequate arming of the militia forces of the state. Third, the
governor instructed the state guard to meet in camps throughout the state, beginning on May 3, for six days of training. Some
800 men were requested to gather at Camp Jackson in St. Louis
under the direction of General Frost. Fourth, Jackson wrote to
Jefferson Davis, president of the Confederacy, requesting the
immediate transmission of guns and ammunition to St. Louis so
that the state guard gathering there might be properly armed
and thus able to seize the well-stocked federal arsenal. We can
see in these four events the governor's determination, despite
the obviously moderate opinion of the people of Missouri, to overwhelm the federal forces in the state and mobilize both the legislature and the state guard to stand with the South.

St. Louis attorney and congressman Francis P. Blair, Jr.,
better known as Frank, was as radical as Jackson, but Blair was
a Unionist who felt that secession must be avoided at all costs.
He was the outstanding leader of the Republican Party in Missouri. During the election of 1860 he organized a group known
as the Wide Awakes to act as sergeants-at-arms at Republican
campaign meetings. The gangs of hoodlums or hotbloods of the
opposition who sometimes invaded political gatherings of the
time were discouraged by the heavy leaded sticks of Blair's
guards.

Frank Blair and the Republican Party were strongly supported by the German and Irish citizens of St. Louis. The pro-
Union, anti-secessionist views of a large segment of the German
population were expressed in the *Anzeiger des Westens,* on January 12, 1861:

> We stand by the Union no matter what may turn
> up, because only in and through the Union is St.
> Louis great, a prospering city and Missouri a state
> of growing wealth.

When Governor Jackson refused the president's request to
provide troops for federal service, Blair offered his Wide Awakes
as well as other pro-Union volunteers. A group of Blair's boys

were mustered into the federal service and armed early in 1861. These units of pro-Union volunteers were called the Home Guards.

Blair feared the seizure of the St. Louis arsenal by Jackson's forces, and determined to defeat the governor's plot. His influence in Washington helped him secure the transfer of Captain Nathaniel Lyon to St. Louis from Fort Riley, Kansas. On February 6, Lyon arrived to assume command of the arsenal located in the southern part of St. Louis. He and Blair immediately planned the strategy responsible for thwarting Governor Jackson's scheme. Blair and Lyon were handicapped by the mild attitude of General W. S. Harney, the superior army officer in the St. Louis area and personal friend of Jefferson Davis. Harney, anxious to avoid offense, acted in a conciliatory manner toward Governor Jackson and his associates. Blair, apprehensive of the effect of Harney's leadership, secured his temporary withdrawal to the national capital. In the general's absence, Captain Lyon was in charge of the military forces in St. Louis.

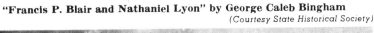

"Francis P. Blair and Nathaniel Lyon" by George Caleb Bingham
(Courtesy State Historical Society)

To insure that the valuable guns and munitions in the St. Louis arsenal remained in Union hands, Lyon armed his own forces and then transferred the surplus of armaments to Illinois via steamboat. Next, in musical comedy fashion, he donned the garb of an old lady and rode through the encampment of the state guard which the militiamen called Camp Jackson. Lyon was disturbed by the evidences of Confederate sympathy at the camp—even the streets were named for Jefferson Davis and General Beauregard—and, after consultation with Frank Blair and other members of the St. Louis Union Committee of Safety, he decided to seize Camp Jackson.

This decision has been a most controversial one in Missouri history. The munitions from the arsenal were safe from rebel hands. Lyon had a force of 10,000 regulars and volunteers in the area while the militia numbered only 800 men. Although the militiamen were obviously sympathetic with the Confederacy, an attack upon them might well anger those Missourians who gave grudging or conditional allegiance to the Federal Union. Despite these considerations, Lyon and Blair decided to attack.

On May 10, 1861, General Frost, a West Point classmate of Lyon and the commanding officer at Camp Jackson, sent a message to Captain Lyon. Frost had heard rumors of an attack, and denounced the move as unwarranted. Lyon refused to accept the message, surrounded the camp, and forced the surrender of the outnumbered Missouri state guard. The captured militiamen were lined up to be escorted by Union troops to the arsenal.

As the procession of federal troops and their prisoners made its way down Olive Street, curious citizens gathered to watch the somber parade. Insults and anti-German taunts from unfriendly spectators were followed by a pistol shot and a rain of rocks and debris. A soldier dropped. The panicky troops answered the order to fire by aiming low into the fleeing crowd. Fifteen bystanders and two soldiers were killed. Shock and then turmoil followed the episode. A wave of anti-German feeling swept the city and resulted in several street fights and more bloodshed. After a few days, the city settled down and even the many terrified southern sympathizers who had fled St. Louis in the midst of the confusion returned to their homes.

The seizure of Camp Jackson resulted in immediate countermoves by the state government. The legislature, which was then in session, acted in short order to pass a bill placing all able-bodied Missouri men in the state guard and appropriating $2,000,000 for military expenses. The state was divided into eight military districts with a brigadier-general in charge of each district. Ex-Governor Sterling Price, the much-loved old veteran of the Mexican War, agreed to serve as the commander of the militia with the rank of major general. Price had been opposed to secession, but the abrupt seizure of Camp Jackson caused him to side with the governor.

General Harney returned from his trip to Washington shortly after the Camp Jackson affair. Wishing to allay the fears of Missourians in St. Louis and elsewhere concerning his intentions, he entered into a conference with Sterling Price. These two men of good will published the Price-Harney Agreement, which stated that General Harney, to avoid exciting the fears of the citizens, would not move troops about the state. Price agreed to keep order in the state and to protect the interests of all.

Frank Blair and Captain Lyon were infuriated with what seemed to them Harney's appeasement of the southern sympathizers. Particularly galling was Harney's promise to restrict the federal troops to St. Louis. Blair, adopting the same policy used by Sam Adams before the American Revolution with the committees of correspondence, requested that Unionists throughout the state notify him of any offenses or attacks against them. When a group of such complaints were received, they were sent to Washington with the request that General Harney be removed for failure to protect the Unionists of Missouri. President Lincoln responded by sending Blair an order, to be presented at his discretion, removing Harney from his command. Frank Blair wasted no time in delivering the order. On May 30, 1861, at the removal of General Harney, Nathaniel Lyon was promoted to brigadier-general and became the commander of the federal forces in the Missouri area.

Governor Jackson and Sterling Price, perhaps because they recognized the superior training and armament of the federal troops at St. Louis, wished to avoid an immediate conflict. On June 12, Jackson and Price met Lyon and Blair at the Planter's House in St. Louis where they conferred for nearly five hours. Jackson expressed his desire to have Missouri assume a neutral position in the Civil War. The governor offered to demobilize his newly-formed militia, halt the further introduction of armaments into the state, and put down any insurrection, if Lyon

(From Dacus, and Buell, A Tour of St. Louis, 1878)

The Planters' House on Fourth Street between Chestnut and Pine, St. Louis

would promise to restrict his troops to St. Louis and would agree to demobilize the Home Guard which Blair had encouraged in several communities in the state. Lyon and Blair refused to enter into such an agreement. Finally, Lyon is reported to have made the following cold-blooded answer:

> Rather than concede to the State of Missouri the right to demand that my Government shall not enlist troops within her limits, or bring troops into the State whenever it pleases, or move its troops at its own will into, out of, or through the State; rather than concede to the State of Missouri for one single instant the right to dictate to my Government in any matter, however unimportant, I would see . . . every man, woman, and child in the State dead and buried.

Then Captain Lyon dismissed his two guests from Jefferson City by saying, "This means war. In one hour one of my officers will call for you and conduct you out of my lines." Jackson and Price did not wait the hour before leaving. Realizing that federal troops would soon follow them to Jefferson City, they rushed home, taking time only to burn the Pacific Railroad bridges behind them at the Gasconade and Osage rivers.

In fairness to Lyon it should be said that he had correctly assumed Governor Jackson's intentions to ally with the South. If, under such circumstances, federal troops were kept in St. Louis, the vital Missouri River route to California, Oregon, and the West would really be in Confederate hands. The obstinate, adamant Lyon would not allow it. He was sworn to uphold the best interest of the United States.

Upon his arrival at the capital, Governor Jackson immediately announced to the citizens of Missouri the federal government's intention to occupy the state and called upon 50,000 Missourians to enroll in his new militia force, the state guard, to resist the invasion. This was Claiborne Jackson's declaration of war against the United States. By the time Nathaniel Lyon and his 1700 men disembarked from the steamboats on which they had pursued Jackson to Jefferson City, the governor, his army, and his chief officers had fled to Boonville. Meeting no resistance, Lyon and his troops took possession of the capital on June 15, 1861.

Claiborne Jackson, Lieutenant-Governor Thomas C. Reynolds, Sterling Price, and the leaders of the state militia had resolved to fight with the Confederacy. Frank Blair and the Home Guard had chosen to side with the federal forces. It was yet to be determined how the remaining citizens of Missouri would choose.

General Lyon and the Federal troops under his command disembarked at Jefferson City, June 15, 1861.

(Courtesy State Historical Society)

In some of the southern states fear of a high Republican tariff, or of northern-elected Republican administration policies were important causes for the secession which led to war. However, the tariff issue was not a critical one in Missouri and, although the state did not vote Republican, there was no great panic on the part of Missourians over what would happen to the Union under Republican leadership.

There are three basic explanations for the development of war in Missouri. First, since the war was national in scope, all states ultimately had to take a stand. Although some states— particularly border states such as Missouri—hoped to remain neutral, neutrality was impossible. Sparked by irresponsible leadership and fed by popular hysteria, the war spread across the nation like a grass fire on a windswept prairie. Involvement was inescapable.

Second, concern over state's rights more than fear for the institution of slavery led Missouri into the conflict. Few Missouri slaveholders believed their property rights were in immediate danger. The Republican platform of 1860 and President Lincoln himself in his inaugural address declared that the institution of slavery would not be disturbed where it already existed. Attention in Missouri tended to be focused on such issues as the proper method for determining the free or slave status of a territory, and on the relative authority of Congress and the states. This fight to decide whether Congress or the inhabitants should exclude slavery in a territory—or whether it could be excluded at all—was a long struggle, and Thomas Hart Benton was one of the first casualties of the conflict. Related to the issue of state's rights was the problem of secession itself. If a state disagreed with federal policy, could she legally dissolve her ties with the Union? A German soldier in Lyon's army made a profound analysis of the causes of the war in his diary. John T. Buegel wrote on September 3, 1861, as follows:

> Slavery came into consideration only in so far as the South wanted to make territory which was still available open to the institution of slavery. The South knew well enough that this would never happen, so they believed they had the right to secede from the North. This was the main cause of the war. The main question, therefore, was whether or not one or several states had the right to separate from the Union. The South claimed this right, the North denied it. So this great question could be

decided only by force of arms. The [Black] hardly
came into consideration.

Third, the impetuous activities of such radical Missourians
as Frank Blair and Claiborne Jackson precipitated an early crisis
in the state. Their provocative actions forced others to take a
stand—others who would have much preferred to remain neutral.
Pride and prejudice led by impetuosity pushed a reluctant state
into the ring in 1861.

The Armies

Most of the highest officers of the Confederate and Union
armies were personally acquainted; several had been at West
Point together. Occasionally former friends would command opposing forces in a battle. The Union and Confederate armies had
much else in common. Both used ill-trained men and sustained
great casualties. Those soldiers who survived several engage-
ments received their best training in the field, and officers of
both sides found their armies improving as the war progressed.

Union and Confederate soldiers alike were often ill-clad and
poorly equipped. In the beginning of the war, many units organized by patriotic individuals were not even issued uniforms.
The following description of the members of the Missouri state
guard in the fall of 1861 demonstrates this point:

> In all their motley array there was hardly a uni-
> form to be seen. . . . There was nothing to distin-
> guish their officers, even a general, from the men
> in the ranks, save a bit of red flannel or a piece of

"General Sigel's Transportation in the Missouri Campaign"
(From Knox, Camp-fire and Cotton-field, 1865)

cotton cloth, fastened to the shoulder or to the arm
of the former.

Some units began the war in impressive uniforms, but the rigors
of battle and travel soon rendered even the best-tailored regiments almost indistinguishable from those who had come to the
army straight from the farm. One Union soldier from St. Louis
wrote on June 25, 1861:

> The majority of our regiment was in a deplorable
> condition. We resembled a rabble more than sol-
> diers. Each one wore whatever clothes he chose to
> wear. They had become torn on the march. Some
> had no trousers any more. In place of trousers,
> they had slipped on sacks. Others had no shoes or
> boots any more, and were walking on the uppers or
> going barefooted. Still others had no hats or caps
> and used flour sacks for head covering.

Although we usually think of the Confederates as clothed in gray
and talk of the Union men as the boys in blue, the uniform colors
were not always consistent. Colonel Sigel's company was routed
at the Battle of Wilson's Creek by a Louisiana unit he had mistaken for the gray-clad First Iowa Infantry. The colonel himself
credited his escape to the blue blanket and yellow slouch hat he
wore, which resembled the garb of the Texas Rangers. A battle
must be complicated indeed when the commanding officers are
unable to distinguish friend from foe.

The soldiers' rations depended upon the time of the year, the
successes or failures of the military unit, and the vigor or aggressiveness of the supply officers. Corn meal, beans, and coffee
were the staples for both armies. Garden vegetables, corn from
the fields, and fruit from orchards along the road of march
added some variety to their meals. The soldiers were supplied
with beef or pork when animals could be secured. George A.
McKee tells of the cow he contributed reluctantly to General
Price during the latter's withdrawal from Lexington:

> Price retreated southward. All through the evening
> and far into the night they marched past, doing us
> no damage except to eat up a cow of mine. I had
> traded a pup for a pig; the pig grew, and I traded
> it for a calf; the calf grew to be a nice cow, and
> Price's men ate her.

Civilians were paid by Union troops in vouchers which were
later redeemed by the government. Confederate forces in the

(Frank Leslie's Illustrated Newspaper, November 2, 1861)

"Cooking in Camp—The Kitchen of the Fremont Dragoons at Tipton, Missouri"

state gave "Missouri scrip," which later proved worthless, in return for supplies. But redeemable or not, pieces of paper were of little use to civilians whose families were hungry. Northern units tended to be better fed than southern units, but most field soldiers during the four years of strife became acquainted with hunger—the traveling companion of war.

Both Union and Confederate armies were enlarged by men who wished to be close to the action and who were sympathetic to the cause of the unit to which they attached themselves. Runaway slaves often stayed with the Union Army performing menial chores for their board. The camp followers moved with the army, ate army rations, and, although they were usually unarmed, they even marched to battle with the soldiers. The undisciplined, untrained, camp followers panicked easily and, at times when it was important to retreat rapidly or to conduct a fast maneuver, they were often in the way. After the Battle of Wilson's Creek some 1,000 fleeing civilians, refugees, and camp followers, on foot, on horseback, and in wagons, clogged the already filled highway to Rolla.

In those days of uncertain communications and slow transportation, both southern and northern officers sometimes found themselves dangerously short of munitions—especially ammunition. When possible, resourceful leaders improvised. There are

(Frank Leslie's Illustrated Newspaper, October 5, 1861)

Rebel prisoners in the dungeon of the state house at Jefferson City

instances of Confederates loading their cannon with nuts, bolts, harness rings, and even gravel. General Price, during a period of organizing and training his troops in extreme southwest Missouri, resorted to making his own shot with handcarved bullet molds and lead from the Granby mines.

Both sides in Missouri were troubled with unruly units which refused to follow orders and engaged in looting and arson. Jim Lane's Kansas troops pillaged and burned Osceola. Quantrill and his marauders, perhaps chafing under army discipline, left Price's troops to ravage the countryside.

At the beginning of the war it was common for men to enlist for ninety days. These short-term enlistments were a severe handicap to those generals who discovered in the midst of a major campaign that a large number of troops were due for discharge.

In the Civil War, military units as large as 2,000 men marched into battle to the drummer boy's cadence. The defensive units usually stood two deep and held their fire until the offensive group was within close range. Because the guns of the time were awkward to load and ammunition was precious, officers instructed their men to fire low to make each shot count.

The guns were equipped with bayonets, but most troops were unskilled in their use. After the first exchange of fire, battles developed into savage hand-to-hand combat. Guns were wielded as clubs, and sabers slashed and flashed through the smoke of the artillery fire.

Since so many of the men were unprepared for combat, and since the Civil War encounters were so brutal and bloody, it is understandable that many of the soldiers ran from battle and deserted the armies. Both sides reported a large number of such deserters. Price recruited many new troops after his victories at Wilson's Creek and Lexington; he moved south from the Missouri River with 22,000 men. Two-thirds of the troops were unarmed and unorganized, and reports of an approaching Union contingent scared many away. Twelve thousand men were under Price's command when he crossed the Osage River, but by the time he arrived in Springfield his forces had shrunk to 8,000 men. Before the Battle of Wilson's Creek General Lyon exhorted his men, "it's no part of a soldier's duty to get scared." One mem-

"The Fremont Body-Guard—Second Charge of the Detachment, under Major Zagonyi, on the Retreating Rebels in the Forest beyond Springfield, Missouri, October 25"

(Frank Leslie's Illustrated Newspaper, November 23, 1861)

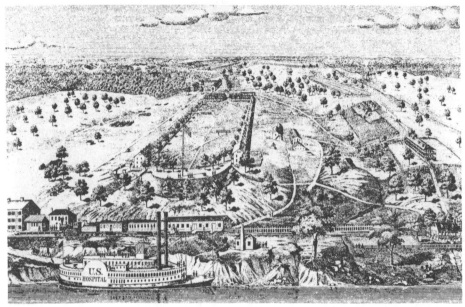

United States General Hospital, Jefferson Barracks, Missouri, 1864. Notice the hospital ship in the foreground and the wagon on the left hauling wounded up from the dock.

ber of the Iowa forces probably expressed more candidly than most soldiers his true feelings—"How is a man to help being skeered when he is skeered?"

Because field hospitals were primitive or, in some cases, non-existent, doctors and medical supplies scarce, and transportation to army medical centers slow and uncomfortable, there was an extremely high mortality rate among casualties of both sides. Our high powered rifles of today shoot bullets at such speed that heat from air friction sterilizes the surface of the projectile. Civil War balls and bullets, traveling at a slower speed and contaminated with a variety of bacteria, often introduced germs which made minor wounds mortal. Amputations and other surgery were performed with unsterilized instruments, and incisions were often dressed with lint scraped from old sheets. The resultant infections claimed thousands of lives. Diseases such as dysentery, measles, and malaria raged in the crowded army hospitals, taking an even greater toll of men than did the battle-field injuries. The combination of these hazards made the Civil War the costliest in American history.

Early Battles of the War in Missouri

Governor Jackson, accompanied by the immediate members of his staff and those other state officers who were outspoken secessionists, withdrew from Jefferson City never to return to the Missouri capital. The state guard forces were ordered to form at Boonville in an attempt to hold that important site overlooking the Missouri River. Brigadier General Lyon, leaving only 300 men to hold the capital city, followed the retreating Jackson to Boonville. At this time Sterling Price became ill and could not provide leadership for the Missouri forces at Boonville. In his place, Governor Jackson personally directed the defenses of the city.

All the state guard at Boonville were ill-trained and were clearly no match for the regular army troops under the command

"Departure of General Lyon and his command from Boonville, Missouri, for the Arkansas border"

(Courtesy State Historical Society)

General Franz Sigel, a native of Germany and adopted St. Louisan, survived many Civil War battles and became a newspaperman and civic leader after Lee's surrender.

of General Lyon. Since he felt his troops were not ready, Colonel John S. Marmaduke protested the assignment, but the governor insisted on facing Lyon. When Lyon approached Boonville, Governor Jackson and Colonel Marmaduke confronted the Union Army with a small militia force of 400 to 500 men. In the resulting skirmish six miles downriver from Boonville on June 17, 1861, Marmaduke's men were routed after a short battle with Lyon's army. In their haste to leave Boonville, the state guard left part of their supplies including 1,200 pairs of shoes, which were important booty to an army of foot soldiers.

The victory at Boonville was of great importance in Union strategy. Lyon was determined to hold the Missouri River which was the chief channel of transportation and communication between the North and such western areas as Kansas, California, and Oregon. Lyon divided the state and attempted to prevent the Confederacy from recruiting or securing supplies north of the Missouri by patrolling the river with gunboats. In addition, he ordered his forces to destroy all boats and rafts along the river to preclude surreptitious crossings by Confederate recruits, recruiters, or suppliers. He also established guards to protect and supervise all major crossing points such as ferries. Then, to complete his control of Missouri's transportation facilities, Lyon seized the railroads.

The Federal Government also began to recruit soldiers in Missouri and to establish garrisons at St. Louis, Rolla, Boonville, Hermann, Jefferson City, and at Bird's Point in the bootheel. Thus, in the summer of 1861 federal forces were well situated to control the state.

Lyon's next concern was to prevent Governor Jackson and General Price from uniting their troops with those of the Confederate General Benjamin McCulloch in Arkansas. He ordered the Union regiments, largely German troops under the direction of Colonel Franz Sigel, to move by way of the Pacific Railroad to Rolla. There they were organized to march to southwest Missouri in order to cut off the Price-Jackson forces from joining McCulloch.

Most contemporary observers noted the number of Germans, mostly from the St. Louis area, in the northern army. These German-Americans provided both excellent troops and important leaders during the Civil War. They were a source of much irritation to the Confederates who considered them foreign invaders. The Confederate soldiers—just as those of every war—wrote many songs and verses ridiculing their enemy. The following, entitled "I Fight Mit Sigel" was a favorite among the rebel troops.

> Ven first I comes from Lauterbach
> I works sometimes by bakin',
> Und next I runs my beer saloon,
> Und den I try shoe-makin',
> But now I march mit musket out
> To safe dot Yankee eagle,
> Dey dress me up in soldier clothes
> To go and fight mit Sigel.

Sigel's forces met those of the southward-moving Jackson at Carthage on July 5, 1861. Jackson's forces numbered some 4,000 armed men; Siegel had forces slightly over 1,000. At this battle Captain Joseph O. Shelby, of later fame, was in charge of the state cavalry. After a brief engagement, Sigel retreated in the face of the larger state forces. It is fortunate that Sigel withdrew as early as he did, since 6,000 reinforcements arrived later in the day to swell the pro-southern army. At the battle it is estimated that Sigel lost thirteen men killed and thirty-one wounded, while the state guard sustained thirty deaths and 125 wounded with forty-five missing. Sigel withdrew to Springfield to await reinforcements.

In the meantime General Price, having recovered from his illness, returned to Carthage from a conference in Arkansas with General Benjamin McCulloch. McCulloch hesitated before granting Price's request for assistance against Lyon, for the Confederacy had not yet officially accepted Missouri. By the time McCulloch did reluctantly send forces to Missouri, Sigel's defeat at Carthage made his immediate assistance unnecessary, and he withdrew temporarily into Arkansas.

Since Price's green troops were in need of training and his ammunition supply dangerously low, he moved the state guard to the extreme southwestern corner of the state. At Cowskin Prairie he set up camp and spent three weeks drilling his troops and replenishing his ammunition stores from the lead mines at Granby.

General Lyon had difficulty transporting his army south from Lexington to Springfield because of floods, but finally on July 13 the general arrived in Springfield, a city of 2,000 people.

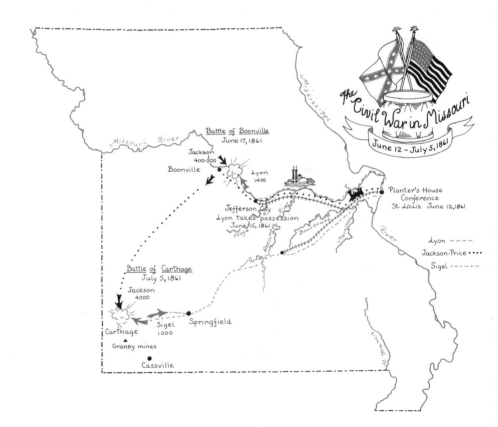

The little red-bearded general was escorted into the city by a ten-man bodyguard of German-American soldiers in ornate uniforms complete with white-plumed hats. Lyon, upon examining his intelligence reports, found himself in a precarious situation. The combination of secessionist troops in the area had his army of 4,000 men greatly outnumbered. General Fremont had not sent the reinforcements from St. Louis which he had requested. The forces opposing him, which now had gathered at Cassville, included 5,200 Missouri state guard troops together with 2,700 Confederate troops and an additional 2,200 state militiamen from Arkansas—a total force of over 10,000 men under the command of General Benjamin McCulloch. In addition, approximately 2,000 men were traveling with the Confederate Army without arms but sympathetic to southern aims and anxious to be part of the southern forces. Lyon carefully weighed his alternatives. At one point he wrote to his superior in St. Louis, "Prudence seems to indicate now the necessity of withdrawing, if possible, from the country and falling upon either St. Louis or Kansas." However, he was moved by several other considerations. He was reluctant to desert the sizable pro-Union population in Springfield, and he feared that if he withdrew to Rolla, as some of his officers suggested, the Confederate cavalry would attack and destroy the rear guard of his retreating army.

It was his decision to make a surprise attack upon the enemy. In this way he believed he would either win or so weaken the enemy forces that they would be unable to follow his retreat. Lyon organized his troops and in the late afternoon of August 9, the Union forces began to move slowly out of Springfield. The men were given special rations and told to prepare for a night of marching. As fortune had it, the rain that night caused the Confederate forces, located some twelve miles southwest of Springfield on the banks of Wilson's Creek, to withdraw their pickets. Thus, Lyon was able to move his forces to the battle scene under the double protection of night and rain. When the Confederate forces awakened at 5:30 a.m., they found their enemy upon them.

The Federal strategy called for Colonel Sigel and his men to move around the enemy and attack from the south, while Lyon came upon the forces from the north. In the bloody encounter that followed, with cavalry and infantry charge, bayonet attack, and the blast of artillery fire, there was great carnage on both sides. However, the superior numbers of the Confederates became an important factor and, as the battle neared noon, the forces of Sigel were routed. Lyon's forces attempted to overwhelm the enemy in charge after charge, but by noon the forces of the North had nearly exhausted their ammunition and General Lyon himself lay dead on the battlefield. The northern forces, now under the command of Major Sturgis, withdrew. The battle was over.

After six hours of savage fighting the total casualty list reached 2,330—twenty-five per cent of the federal forces and ten per cent of the rebel forces. From Lyon's army 233 men were killed, 721 wounded, and 291 missing. McCulloch's army suffered 265 dead, 800 wounded, and 30 missing. The battlefield was a nightmare. As one observer described it:

> All over this level spot and down over the edges of
> the hill lay the dead, their faces white against the
> gray rock and the green grass.

The total casualties for the North were 1,235 and for the South 1,095. As the Yankee camp song described:

> In a little old creek bottom
> Three hundred yards around,

Lyon's charge at the Battle of Wilson's Creek
(Courtesy Missouri Historical Society)

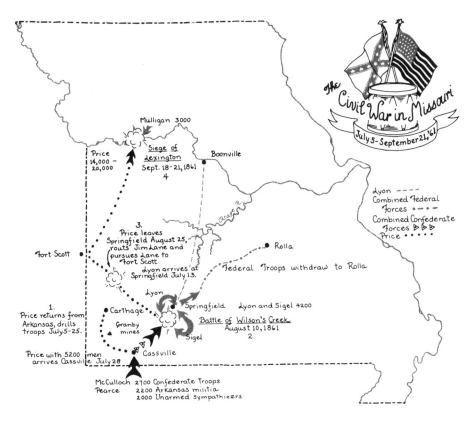

Mulligan 3000

Price
14,000 —
20,000

Siege of
Lexington
Sept. 18-21, 1861
4

Boonville

3.
Price leaves
Springfield August 25,
routs Jim Lane and
pursues Lane to
Fort Scott
Lyon arrives at
Springfield July 13.

Fort Scott

Lyon

1.
Price returns from
Arkansas, drills
troops July 5-25.

Carthage

Granby
mines

Springfield   Lyon and Sigel 4200

Battle of Wilson's Creek
August 10, 1861
2.

Sigel

Rolla

Federal Troops withdraw to Rolla

Lyon — — — —
Combined Federal
Forces • — • —
Combined Confederate
Forces ▷ ▷ ▷
Price • • • • •

Price with 5200 men
arrives Cassville July 28.

Cassville

McCulloch 2700 Confederate Troops
Pearce   2200 Arkansas militia
              2000 Unarmed sympathizers

Was thirteen hundred of the bravest men
A-laying on the ground.

    Those wounded who survived the twelve-mile trip to Spring-
field were housed in any available building in the city. A woman
who nursed the wounded at the Bailey Hotel said:

> They were unloaded, covered with blood and dust.
> . . . I had nothing to work with but a washpan and
> my handkerchief. The first thing I did when a
> wounded soldier was brought into the house was
> to wash his face. . . . As fast as the men died with-
> in the building, . . . the bodies were thrown out the
> window and hauled down on the Jordan for burial.

    The southern forces were technically victorious. But because
they had suffered horrible losses and were without ammunition,
they could not pursue the enemy limping back toward Springfield.

    The state guard's defeat at Boonville had been a great dis-

(From Frank Leslie's Illustrated Newspaper, February 1, 1862)

"The Campaign in Missouri —the Dark Side of War—Refugees from Southern Missouri, Driven from Their Homesteads by the Rebels, Encamped near Gen. Siegel's [sic] Division at Rolla"

appointment to Confederate sympathizers. Their governor had been chased from his capital and their state army had been pushed aside; not even the incident at Carthage gave the Rebels of Missouri hope. Now, however, after the Battle of Wilson's Creek, there was a renewed optimism among the secessionists, for they felt that "Old Pap" Price and his troops had displayed the great fighting ability Missourians had traditionally assigned to themselves. No doubt this tradition of military prowess stemmed from Missouri's victories in the Mexican War. However, the costly victories over the federal troops were quite different from the almost bloodless expedition of Doniphan fourteen years before.

About midnight after the Battle of Wilson's Creek a great mass of weary soldiers and frightened civilians could be seen trekking out of the little city of Springfield along the road to Rolla. Fleeing before the Confederate troops they knew would soon be upon them, they trudged or limped along on foot, or lurched along in wagons and carts to escape the southern army. It was seven days before the remnants of Lyon's army, untouched by the opposition forces, finally arrived at Rolla, there to regroup and to prepare for new action. Left behind in Springfield, some 1,600 wounded men lay in the churches, schools, homes, and the new courthouse receiving the medical attention of a federal surgeon and a southern doctor.

Meanwhile, "Old Pap" Price was determined to take the offensive. General McCulloch, who had a dim view of both the Missouri forces and the Missouri people, refused to join Price in a northern invasion. As Price marched northward, his numbers swelled by enlistments of those Missourians who now felt assured of a Confederate victory. After chasing Jim Lane and his forces back to Kansas, Price marched directly to Lexington, on the Missouri River. He intended to cut off that valuable water route to federal use, secure more recruits from north Missouri, and secure necessary supplies as well by seizing Lexington.

The federal officer in charge at Lexington was Colonel James A. Mulligan, who had joined the federal service as the leader of the Chicago Irish Brigade. Mulligan had some 3,000 men at Lexington, but he learned with consternation that General Price's army numbered at least five times as many. Mulligan immediately requested reinforcements, but General John C. Fremont again failed to send reinforcements in time.

Mulligan decided to defend the Masonic College Hall, which was located on a prominence and had been fortified with trenches. Price seized the one available steamboat, thus cutting Mulligan off both from escape and from the reinforcements which finally did arrive. Price bombarded the entrenched Irish for two days with artillery fire—including blasts from "Old Sacramento," the twelve-pound cannon he had brought back from Chihuahua during the Mexican War. In the meantime, the federal troops had been surrounded and cut off from all supplies and water. After two days of bombardment, Price adopted a new technique. Bales of hemp, soaked in water to prevent their being set afire, were rolled up the hill in front of the advancing soldiers, thus protecting them from Federal fire. Since Mulligan's forces were without water and had almost exhausted their ammunition, they had no hope of winning the battle. To avoid needless suffering, Colonel Mulligan finally surrendered on September 20. As one observer analyzed the Battle of Lexington:

> The opposing forces were so far apart, and so well protected, the one by earthworks and the other by

hempbales, that their small arms were ineffective;
and but little damage was done by the round shot
of the mounted guns on either side. Lexington was
not captured by hard fighting, but by well planned
stratagem and well-maintained seige.

The Battle of Lexington was important to the morale of the
Missouri state guard, but it was also important because of the
supplies captured there. General Price reported to Governor
Jackson that he had seized the following:

> The visible fruits of this almost bloodless victory
> are very great—about 3500 prisoners, among whom
> are Colonel Mulligan . . . and 118 other commis-
> sioned officers; five pieces of artillery and two
> mortars; over 3000 stands of infantry arms, a large
> number of sabers, about 750 horses, many sets of
> cavalry equipments, wagons, teams, and ammuni-
> tion; more than $100,000 worth of commissary
> stores, and a large amount of other property.

The greater number of those who were captured took an
oath promising never to fight against Confederate forces again;
others were merely released. As one female Secessionist observed: "In some instances, where the men captured were citizens
of the town they were laughingly handed over to their wives to
be kept out of future trouble."

John C. Fremont was named the commander of the Western
Department on July 3, 1861. Fremont was one of the most
famous men in America at that time. He had been the Republican candidate for president in 1856, and earlier he achieved popularity as "the Pathfinder" for his leadership in directing an
army unit to California at the outset of the Mexican War. Fremont was well known in Missouri for another reason. He had

Confederate soldiers using
hemp bales as breastworks
in the Siege of Lexington
(From Musick, Stories of
Missouri, 1897)

(From Frank Leslie's Illustrated Newspaper, October 12, 1861)

The Siege of Lexington, September 18-21, 1861

secretly married Jessie Benton, the seventeen-year-old daughter of the famous senator. From the very beginning, Fremont's command at St. Louis was a succession of errors. During the summer of 1861, when each day was crucial, he procrastinated for at least two weeks before taking his command at St. Louis. Once there, he failed to reinforce Lyon at Springfield with the disastrous results described above. His reinforcements for Mulligan at Lexington arrived too late.

In partial defense of Fremont, it can be said that he planned a major military move down the Mississippi River and did not wish to disperse his forces. However, his reluctance to support his officers in the field led to bitter criticism. Although he had originally been a close friend of Frank and Montgomery Blair, the Blairs soon became disillusioned and angered. Lincoln was not only perturbed by Fremont's reluctance to support his men, but he was also incensed by Fremont's order of August 30, which declared that southern sympathizers convicted of carrying arms would be shot and their slaves freed. Lincoln, recognizing his

(Frank Leslie's Illustrated Newspaper, October 14, 1861)

Camp Zagonyi, encampment of Fremont's army on the prairie near Wheatland, Missouri

need for border-state backing, did not wish to begin a wave of retaliatory shootings which would offend many people in the border states and which might cause needless concern to those slaveholders who supported the Union. Lincoln countermanded the order and removed Fremont from his command only 100 days after the general had taken control of the Western Department.

Before Fremont received notice of his removal, he had transported his "Army of the West" to Springfield, where he hoped to force a battle with Price. Price feared being cut off from the Confederacy and retreated once more to extreme southwest Missouri. Major Charles Zagonyi and a force of 150 men preceded Fremont to Springfield and forced a state guard contingent of 1,000 to retreat from the city. Before Fremont could engage Price in battle, the order removing him from command was delivered. The federal troops then made their way back up the road to Rolla while Price returned to occupy the city of Springfield during the winter months of 1861-1862.

General Price appears to have been greatly perturbed over his failure to assemble a large army of Missouri troops. In November, 1861, he issued a long and melodramatic appeal to the citizens of Missouri. The silver-maned old general demanded to know why they had failed to provide 50,000 men for his army as Governor Jackson had requested. He informed Missourians that this was the moment of crisis for the state, and that their service was needed immediately. Intimating that they would be reimbursed later from Union property in the state if their possessions were taken, he stated that those who were patriotic would answer his call despite danger to property left at home. He closed his appeal with these words:

> Are you coming! Fifty thousand men! Missouri shall move to victory with the tread of a giant! . . . Come on, my brave boys, fifty thousand heroic, gallant, unconquerable Southern men! We await your coming.

General Price called in vain. Whether deterred by federal control, or by fear of property loss, or by the long casualty lists from the first battles, Missourians failed to rally to "Old Pap" Price. He never was able to raise more than half his quota.

Brigadier General Samuel R. Curtis, a West Pointer who was

"The Fremont Body-Guard—the First Charge of a Detachment of 150 of Fremont's Body-Guard under Major Zagonyi, at Springfield, Missouri, on the Rebel Garrison 2,000 strong, October 25"
(Frank Leslie's Illustrated Newspaper, November 23, 1861)

a congressman from Iowa when war developed, was placed in charge of the Union forces gathered at Rolla. Curtis, an aggressive, intelligent commander, pressed the battle against Price. When Curtis moved his force of 10,000 men down the road to Springfield in February, 1862, Price was forced to desert the city, moving first to Cassville and later into Arkansas. General Earl Van Dorn, another West Point graduate, was in charge of the Confederate troops west of the Mississippi River. Van Dorn combined Price's army of Missouri state militia with the Confederate forces under General Benjamin McCulloch and added some 1,000 Creek, Cherokee, and Choctaw Indians from the Oklahoma Territory. Curtis' troops had increased to 10,500 men; Van Dorn's army numbered 25,000. From March 6 to 8, in a three-day battle which raged around the Elk Horn Tavern at Pea Ridge, Arkansas, the Union army finally forced the Confederates to retreat. Despite reports of General Price's reluctance to halt the battle, the southern army withdrew.

The Union had attained a great victory there at Pea Ridge; but both sides sustained heavy casualties. Although Confederate losses were not calculated, the northern forces suffered casualties of over 1,300 men, including eight Union soldiers who were scalped by the war-painted tribesmen. Forced from his state, Price now took those Missouri troops who remained faithful to join the Confederate service east of the Mississippi River. The following camp song describes the outcome of the battle and the reaction of Price to the defeat:

> An' with that dread confusion
> We was forced to leave the ground,
> The rollin' storms of iron balls
> Was cutting thousands down.
>
> To see our friends a-fallin'
> It did us so provoke,
> The sun was dim, the sky was hid
> With clouds of rollin' smoke.
>
> Old General Price rode down the line,
> His horse in swiftest pace,
> An' as he told us to retreat
> The tears rolled down his face.

The Battle of Pea Ridge was more important in the long run than the Battle of Wilson's Creek. By this victory, the Union army had excluded the state guard from Missouri. Although

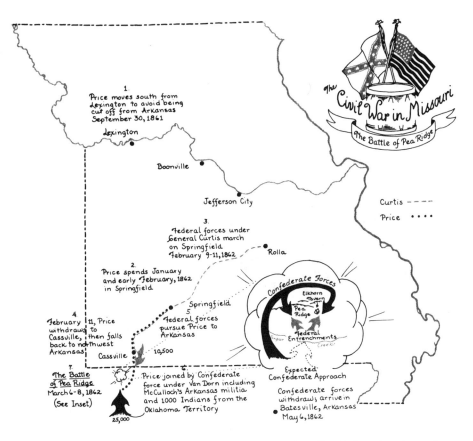

1.
Price moves south from Lexington to avoid being cut off from Arkansas September 30, 1861

Lexington

Boonville

Jefferson City

Curtis - - - -

Price • • • •

3.
Federal forces under General Curtis march on Springfield February 9-11, 1862

Rolla

2.
Price spends January and early February, 1862 in Springfield

Springfield

4.
February 11, Price withdraws to Cassville, then falls back to northwest Arkansas

5.
Federal forces pursue Price to Arkansas

Cassville

10,500

7.
The Battle of Pea Ridge March 6-8, 1862
(See Inset)

25,000

Confederate Forces

Elkhorn Tavern

Pea Ridge

Federal Entrenchments

Price joined by Confederate force under Van Dorn including McCulloch's Arkansas militia and 1000 Indians from the Oklahoma Territory

Expected Confederate Approach

Confederate forces withdraw; arrive in Batesville, Arkansas May 6, 1862

several later attempts were made by the Confederates to seize the state, federal control of Missouri was never relinquished throughout the war. Price's defeat sealed the doom of the Claiborne Jackson government. Those Missourians sympathetic to the Confederacy lived in a Union-occupied state for the duration of the war and were unable to assist effectively the cause in which they believed. Missouri was won for the Union at Pea Ridge.

Political Chaos

Both Governor Jackson and General Price were greatly encouraged by the victory at Wilson's Creek. Governor Jackson proceeded to call for a meeting of the state legislature to be held at the Masonic Hall in Neosho October 21, 1861. Only ten senators and thirty-nine representatives appeared. Despite the fact that this number was insufficient to make the assembly legally competent to transact business, the delegates, in compliance with

Although a southerner by birth, Hamilton Gamble remained loyal to the Union. He stood firm against the radical element among the Unionists and, despite ill health, gave wise and effective leadership as provisional governor from July 31, 1861 until his death in 1864.

(*Courtesy State Historical Society*)

Governor Jackson's request, adopted "an act declaring the political ties heretofore existing between the state of Missouri and the United States of America dissolved." This act was signed by the governor three days later at Cassville. Having thus seceded from the Union, the Jackson government applied for and was granted, on November 28, 1861, admission to the Confederacy. Obviously, this act of secession was illegal, both because a quorum had not existed and because the legislature had decided earlier that so momentous a decision should be voted on by the people. Since the greater part of Missouri was occupied by federal forces at the time, and since the seceding groups were never able to control the state again, the act of secession was, in fact, meaningless.

In that troubled time the need for effective state government was acute. At their meeting in St. Louis earlier in the year, the delegates to the state convention had established an executive committee with the power to recall the convention in the event that another meeting proved necessary. Convention president Sterling Price and twenty other delegates, swayed from their stand against secession by the Camp Jackson affair, had joined the state guards and were fighting the Federal troops. The remaining delegates had chosen to stand with the Union.

The executive committee called upon the state convention to meet at Jefferson City on July 22, 1861. In nine days of meetings, the delegates made several important decisions. After selecting a Robert Wilson, who had been the vice president of the convention, to succeed Sterling Price, the convention declared the chief state offices vacant and proceeded to appoint Hamilton R. Gamble as provisional governor, Willard P. Hall as provisional lieutenant-governor, and Mordecai Oliver as provisional secretary of state. Originally, it was announced that these men would serve until the next election, scheduled for November of 1861, when new officials and a new legislature would be chosen.

Obviously, this state convention had no authority to take such action, since Governor Jackson was the popularly-elected chief of state. However, in the time of war, legality is frequently supplanted by expediency, and, in so acting, these Missouri politicians established an illegal provisional government to fill the breach left by the secessionist exiles. The delegates also passed a bill to repeal Governor Jackson's earlier act which raised a militia and appropriated military funds. In retrospect, we must admit that the actions of the state convention were unprecedented, brash, and illegal. However, since federal troops in Missouri upheld the actions of the convention, no one could argue.

The southern sympathizers in Missouri, who had hoped that the state convention would support Governor Jackson and his followers, were bitterly disappointed when the delegates repudiated the secessionists. This rejection did not deter Thomas C. Reynolds, the lieutenant-governor, exiled in Arkansas, from declaring himself governor of the state at the death of Claiborne Jackson in December, 1862. Reynolds' gesture was an empty one, however, for he had no power in Union-occupied Missouri.

The state convention had picked a competent new governor in Hamilton Gamble. Gamble, a former Virginian who had settled in Howard County, was much respected in the state. He was a man of integrity and stability who gave excellent leadership during a chaotic time.

Gamble, faced with a multitude of problems, called the state convention together for their third meeting in St. Louis in October, 1861. The convention took action on five important matters. First, because of the confusion and disorder in the state, the delegates decided to postpone the elections originally set for November, 1861, until August, 1862. Second, to ease the state's financial crisis it was decided to institute a rigid new economy move abolishing many state offices and cutting by twenty per cent the salaries of all state officials. Third, the convention made arrangements for the government to sell $1,000,000 worth of bonds and to issue $1,000,000 worth of so-called "defense warrants," which would circulate as money. Fourth, provisions were made for the organization of a new state guard, to be called the Enrolled Missouri Militia, which would be armed by the federal government and would assist in maintaining order in the state. Fifth, the convention adopted an oath of loyalty to the federal constitution and to the state constitution of Missouri which all civil officials of the state were required to take within forty days on pain of removal from their offices. By these actions, the convention established a basis for a loyal group of state officials and provided the necessary finances to operate their government of questionable legality.

Governor Gamble, concerned over the approaching August election, called the state convention to Jefferson City for a fourth time in June, 1862. In deference to his wishes the convention agreed to call off the election of state executive officials and to hold an election only for the selection of members of the state legislature in November. Gamble was also troubled over voter qualification. Since many Missourians were known to be sympathetic to the South, he feared a voter revolt in the November election. The legislature, too, was apprehensive over the possibilty that a pro-secession vote might throw the state into chaos and endanger their own political plans. Therefore, the convention adopted a new series of test oaths. One oath was to be taken by all citizens before they were qualified to vote. A second oath was to be sworn by all candidates for public office. The third oath was to be taken by all attorneys, public school teachers, school trustees, clergymen, jury members, officials of corporations, and the president, professors, and curators of the University of Missouri. In each of these oaths, the individual swore his allegiance to the constitutions of the United States and of Missouri, declared that he had not taken up arms against either the United States government or the provisional government of Missouri since the date December 17, 1861, and affirmed that he did not "give aid and comfort to the enemies thereof." By using these oaths, the leaders of the state convention believed they could disenfranchise southern sympathizers and prevent the election of a secessionist legislature.

In the meantime, the question of emancipation had become

the major political issue in Missouri. General Fremont had stirred up the controversy when he issued his proclamation of August, 1861, which warned that Missouri secessionists who were found guilty of aiding the Confederacy would have their slaves taken from them and freed.

Lincoln, who was anxious to avoid offending the large body of loyal slaveholders in the border states, was infuriated by Fremont's tactless introduction of the emancipation issue, and countermanded the order. Lincoln wished to encourage compensated emancipation in the border states, and hoped that Missouri would be the first state to adopt the policy. In March, 1862, he secured Congressional approval for the plan in a resolution which passed both houses of Congress. He told Senator Henderson of Missouri:

> We can't get through this terrible war with slavery existing. You've got sense enough to know that. Why can't you make the border States members see it? Why don't you turn in and take pay for your slaves from the government? Then all your people can give their hearty support to the Union. We can go ahead with emancipation of slaves by proclamation in the other States and end the trouble.

Senator Henderson then sponsored a bill authorizing the expenditure of $20,000,000 to compensate border-state slaveholders. Under this plan, slaveowners were to receive approximately $300 per slave. The House passed a similar bill late in 1862, but stipulated that only $10,000,000 should be spent. A House-Senate conference committee adopted a compromise sum of $15,000,000. It is unfortunate that three Missouri congressmen, believing the sum of $300 per slave to be inadequate, were among those who kept the House of Representatives from passing this forward-looking legislation. Had the compromise bill been passed, it might very well have set a precedent which would have allowed for an early settlement of the war.

The Unionist Party, which developed in 1861 and controlled Missouri during the war, included the few Republicans who had organized their party in Missouri in 1860 and those Democrats, former Whigs, and Free Soilers who decided to stand with the Union.

Because of the difference of opinion between General Fremont—who was also a politician seeking support for his candidacy for the presidency in 1864—and Lincoln, there was a division of the Unionists into political factions in Missouri. The factions, which took differing views on the method or importance of emancipation, received colorful names. The Charcoals, or Radical Unionists, who were strongest in the St. Louis area, demanded immediate emancipation. The Claybanks favored emancipation, but wished to effect it in a slow and orderly manner with compensation if possible. The Chocolates opposed emancipation. The Snowflakes were not immediately concerned about emancipation, but were more interested in legislation affecting the white people of the state. In the election of 1862 the Charcoals were elected in great numbers, although the total number of votes cast was small because of the test oath. Missouri was now on its way to proclaiming emancipation, but the exact technique or method was yet to be established. The legislature which convened in December, 1862 was frustrated in its attempts to free the slaves by the provision in the Constitution of 1820 requiring that slaveowners be compensated. Because the financial resources of the state were barely adequate to meet ordinary governmental expenses, the legislature requested the federal government to provide $25,000,000 to reimburse the slaveowners. Congress failed to take such action.

Governor Gamble, concerned over the inability of the legislature to evolve a plan for emancipation, called the state convention to meet for a fifth time. This assembly in Jefferson City in June of 1863 came forth with a plan for freeing the slaves. Under the suggested system, all slaves were to be freed in Missouri on July 4, 1870. However, slaves over forty years of age were to remain with their masters as indentured servants for the rest of their lives.

The Radical Unionists of Missouri were still not satisfied. If slavery were an evil system, they reasoned, why not destroy it immediately? In September, 1863, they held a Radical Unionist state convention in Jefferson City and there determined to send a delegation to Washington, D. C., to speak to President Lincoln. A committee of seventy Radical Unionists, under the leadership of Charles Drake, traveled to the capital with great national publicity and there addressed Lincoln:

> If you, Mr. President, felt that your duty to your country demanded that you should unshackle the slaves of the rebel states in an hour, we see no

earthly reason why the people of Missouri should not, from the same sense of duty, strike down with equal suddenness the traitorous and parricidal institution in their midst.

They then demanded that the president (1) use his authority to secure the immediate abolition of slavery in Missouri, (2) remove General Schofield from command in Missouri, (3) send new federal troops to Missouri to take the place of the Enrolled Missouri Militia loyal to Governor Gamble, and (4) use his authority to deny the franchise to Confederate sympathizers in Missouri.

During the fall of 1863 Lincoln had many sharp critics in the nation. The war was not going well. Since by his Emancipation Proclamation issued in 1862 he had already declared the slaves of the seceded states to be free, Radical leaders throughout the North were clamoring for the immediate manumission of the border state slaves. Lincoln was fully aware of the complexities of the situation. After five days he replied to the Missouri delegation with the following statement:

> We are in civil war. In such case there is always a main question, but in this case that question is a perplexing compound—Union and slavery. It thus becomes a question not of two sides merely, but of at least four sides, even among those who are for the Union, saying nothing of those who are against it. Thus, those who are for the Union but not without slavery; those for it without but not with; those for it with or without but prefer it with; those for it with or without but prefer it without; among these again is a subdivision of those who are for gradual but not immediate, and those who are for immediate, but not for gradual, extinction of slavery.

The president, at the same time, refused to take action to free the slaves in Missouri or to remove the general or to send new troops to the state, although he did agree that the voting restrictions should be maintained.

The Radical Unionists in Missouri did not forget Lincoln's refusal of their demands. In 1864 when the Republican Party held its convention—for war and political reasons the party was known as the National Union Party—the delegation from Missouri was the only one to oppose the re-election of Lincoln. The

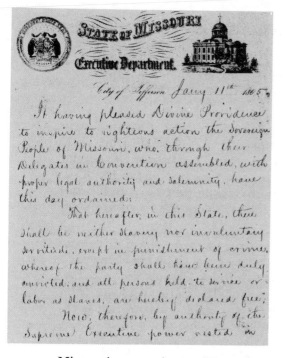

The Emancipation Proclamation of Missouri, January 11, 1865
(Courtesy State Historical Society)

Missourians nominated Ulysses S. Grant, but later changed their vote when the other convention delegates supported the president.

On January 31, 1864, Governor Gamble died. He had given strong leadership during a trying period in Missouri history. He was succeeded by Lieutenant-Governor Hall, who served until the election of the next governor. During 1864 the legislature authorized the calling of a new state constitutional convention. This convention met in St. Louis on January 6, 1865, and was overwhelmingly controlled by Radicals. Only five days after the convening of the conference, the delegates passed a resolution declaring the end of slavery in Missouri. Thus, the institution of slavery was destroyed in Missouri even before the United States adopted the Thirteenth Amendment to the federal constitution.

By the election held in November, 1864, the Radicals were so strong that they won control of the legislature and elected Thomas C. Fletcher as governor. Fletcher was the first popularly-elected governor to serve since the election of Claiborne Jackson. However, his election did not necessarily represent the will of the majority, since he was chosen under a voting system which denied the franchise to Confederate sympathizers in Missouri.

Order Number Eleven

The border warfare which followed the opening of Kansas had largely abated by 1860, but there still were those on both sides of the boundary who burned with a passion to revenge the destruction and slaughter of the unforgotten raids. With the outbreak of the Civil War it was possible for the earlier raiders to join either the northern or the southern forces and, in the guise of soldiers, to satisfy their lust for vengeance which had been frustrated by the concerted efforts of the governors of Kansas and Missouri and the intervention of federal troops.

Fiery-eyed, fanatic John Brown was dead now, hanged after his capture while leading a slave uprising in Virginia in 1859. The Brown legend lived on in the haunting popular camp song, "John Brown's Body." The song was even sung in proslavery areas of Missouri, but with altered words. The refrain ended:

Governor Gamble doesn't want to go to Heaven;
He's afraid he'll meet John Brown.

Though Brown was no longer a threat to slaveholders and Missouri, he was survived by a thieving crew of bloodthirsty leaders such as James Montgomery, Jim Lane, and Dr. Charles Jennison. In July of 1861, as an advance group for the Union army, a band under Jennison's leadership arrived in Harrisonville. Although there was not an enemy soldier within its limits, the marauders sacked the town. The citizens of western Missouri knew the terror was upon them again.

George Caleb Bingham, the artist, was the state treasurer of the provisional government in Jefferson City. When he learned that the brutal Dr. Charles Jennison was allowed to organize the Seventh Kansas Cavalry, he wrote in protest to Missouri's congressmen indicating his disbelief that such a criminal as Jennison could undergo "a complete transition from the condition of an outlaw, abhorred and avoided by honorable minds, to that of an officer in the United States Army." The governor of Kansas also was apprehensive of what would occur when Lane's forces organized. Governor Gamble of Missouri shared their concern and expressed his fear of a renewed border conflict. The forebodings of all three men were realized when, in the fall of 1861, the Seventh Kansas Cavalry invaded Jackson County and remained there in occupation, sacking, looting, and murdering suspected southern sympathizers and those who dared to disobey them.

General Halleck in St. Louis wrote to his superior officer in Washington:

> The conduct of the forces under Lane and Jennison has done more for the enemy in this State than could have been accomplished by 20,000 of his own army. I receive almost daily complaints of outrages committed by these men in the name of the United States, and the evidence is so conclusive as to leave no doubt of their correctness. It is rumored that Lane has been made a brigadier-general. I cannot conceive of a more injudicious appointment. It will take 20,000 men to counteract its effect in this State, and, moreover, is offering a premium for rascality and robbing generally.

On September 23, 1861, Lane, having been chased back to Fort Scott by General Price, recrossed the border after Price had moved the major part of his forces north to Lexington. The Kansas looters who became known as Jayhawkers, or as "Red Legs" for the red morocco leggings they wore, are reputed to have seized $1,000,000 in goods at Osceola, an important river distribution point. The complete destruction of Osceola by fire was followed by the sacking of Butler and Parkville.

William Quantrill was the man who appointed himself as the avenger of these raids. Quantrill was a slight young man in his early twenties with wavy reddish hair and heavy-lidded pale blue eyes. The son of a school master, he himself while still a teenager had taught school in Illinois and Indiana. After moving to Lawrence, Kansas, in the midst of the border troubles, he had taken part in some of the incursions into Missouri, even helping to steal slaves on one occasion. During the war he changed sides in the border struggle and became one of Missouri's most notorious bushwhackers, and a hero to slaveholders and southern sympathizers in the state. In 1862 he received a Confederate commission as a captain, and led his men in the sack of Aubrey, Kansas, in March, 1862, and in an October raid on Olathe, where they shot down settlers "like so many hogs."

General Thomas Ewing was the officer in charge of the border region and carefully discussed with his superior officer, General Schofield, the countermeasures to be taken. General Ewing was sensitive to the reasons for the outbreak of violence. He described the background of the troubles in the following portion of a letter to General Schofield:

SIR: About one half of the farmers in the border tier of counties of Missouri in my district, at different times since the war began, entered the rebel service. One-half of them are dead or still in the service; the other half, quitting from time to time the rebel armies, have returned to these counties. Unable to live at their homes if they would, they have gone to bushwacking, and have driven almost all avowed Unionists out of the country or to the military stations. And now, sometimes in squads of a dozen and sometimes in bands of several hundred, they scour the country, robbing and killing those they think unfriendly to them, and threatening the settlements of the Kansas border and the towns and stations in Missouri.

In an attempt to curtail the activities of the guerrillas, General Ewing ordered the arrest of women known to be the wives or close relatives of the Missouri Quantrill band.

These wives, mothers, and sisters of the notorious group were jailed in a decrepit brick building in Kansas City. On August 14 the three-story structure collapsed; four of the women were crushed to death and many more were severely injured. News of the tragedy enraged the members of the Quantrill gang. Determined to avenge the lives of their womenfolk, Quantrill and his followers organized a group of 450 men from Jackson County. One of the leaders of the Quantrill group was "Bloody Bill" An-

To General Thomas Ewing fell the impossible task of guarding the long boundary between Missouri and Kansas with an insufficient number of troops. His solution to the problem was made notorious by George Caleb Bingham's painting "Order Number Eleven."
(Courtesy State Historical Society)

derson, whose wife was killed in the Kansas City accident. After riding all night, the army of avengers invaded the sleepy town of Lawrence at the break of day. Following Quantrill's order to "kill every man big enough to carry a gun," the Quantrill forces went from house to house brutally murdering the men of Lawrence, often in the presence of their wives and children. After only two hours in the city, some 150 Lawrence men had been cruelly dispatched and 185 buildings destroyed by fire. While this was happening Quantrill enjoyed his breakfast in the lobby of a hotel. Quantrill was frustrated in his attempt to carry Senator Jim Lane back to Missouri to be hanged when Lane sprang from his bed and fled in his nightshirt to hide in a cornfield. When reports of approaching federal troops reached him, Quantrill and his men sped away from Lawrence leaving "eighty widows and 250 orphans" in the crushed city.

The accounts of the Lawrence massacre soon spread through Missouri, the Midwest, and the nation. Impassioned cries were made in Kansas for avenging raids into Missouri. General Thomas Ewing had the impossible task of guarding with insufficient forces the long boundary between Missouri and Kansas. Undermanned, yet anxious to fulfill his responsibility and to put a halt to the fratricidal tit-for-tat between Kansas and Missouri, General Ewing issued, at Jim Lane's blunt command, "Order Number Eleven." Under the terms of this edict, residents who lived beyond one mile of the main towns in Jackson, Cass, Bates, and parts of Vernon Counties were ordered to evacuate the area within fifteen days. Many farm families fled to Harrisonville and Pleasant Hill for sanctuary. Not only were the farm families required to leave, but they were instructed to take all grain and hay to the nearest military station, where it would be accepted for safekeeping by the commander. All other products were to be destroyed. Ewing issued the order to prevent any further raids originating in the region, for the guerrillas now would be unable to secure supplies.

Jim Lane had another motive for promoting the issuance of the despised edict. The Kansas cavalry unit under the leadership of vicious "Doc" Jennison helped enforce the order with brutality and ruthless vandalism. The hated "Jayhawkers" stole what they could and put the torch to the rest. Prairie fires completed the devastation. For a hundred miles, the smoke-stained chimneys, scorched grass, and blackened stumps were all that remained of hard-won homesteads. For years after the war, Bates and Cass counties were known as the "Burnt District."

George Caleb Bingham, who was a member of General Ewing's staff, later played an important part in publicizing the harsh enforcement of Order Number Eleven. Bingham had protested the edict and warned Ewing, "If you persist in executing that order, I will make you infamous with pen and brush as far as I am able." Bingham went on to paint his famous "Order Number Eleven," depicting the brutality with which the edict was enforced. General Schofield, Union commander of the department of Missouri, later defended General Ewing, indicating that he had earlier agreed to the order. General Halleck spoke of the edict as "within the recognized laws of war." General Ewing later said of artist Bingham that he had "so little understanding of the necessities of war that before he would commandeer a mule or load of corn from a farmer in the line of march, he would first have to consult the Constitution to see that he was within the law."

"Order Number Eleven"

George Caleb Bingham (Courtesy State Historical Society)

Clearly, the conditions along the Kansas frontier were so serious that strong action was necessary. There is no justification for the harshness with which Order Number Eleven was enforced, yet, while many people were forced from their homes and great destruction of property resulted, the evacuation did sharply curtail border troubles. The suffering of the innocent always accompanies war, but for some reason hidden in human nature, the glitter of brass buttons and the cheers of victory are often remembered longer than the instances of injustice and suffering. In the folklore of west Missouri, Quantrill, the savage killer, became a hero. He has been remembered both in legends and verses:

> They came to burn Lawrence, they came not to stay.
> They rode in one morning at breaking of day,
> With guns all a-waving and horses all foam,
> And Quantrill a-riding his famous big roan.
>
> Oh, Quantrill's a fighter, a bold-hearted boy,
> A brave man or woman he'd never annoy.
> He'd take from the wealthy and give to the poor,
> For brave men there's never a bolt to his door.

A ballad such as this makes one wonder what Robin Hood was really like.

Later Battles of the War

After Pea Ridge both the Confederate and Union governments transferred their major forces to the theater of war east of the Mississippi. Missouri was left in the hands of federal troops garrisoned in towns and forts throughout the state.

The battles in Missouri between the conflict at Pea Ridge in March, 1862, and the beginning of a short-lived invasion by General Price in September, 1864, resulted either from recruiting operations on the part of the Confederacy or the hit-and-run raids of Confederate guerrillas. The term "bushwhacking" is descriptive of the kind of war fought in Missouri during that period. Small forces, usually mounted, would sweep down on an unsuspecting settlement to punish those who disagreed with them politically, to plunder, and sometimes to kill. It was a time of intimidations of towns, of families, and of individuals. The Confederate guerrillas who carried on this war would usually disappear into the woods and then resume their normal agricultural occupations when federal forces arrived to put down the trouble.

Another activity characteristic of this kind of conflict was sabotage. Rebels discovered that cutting telegraph wires, burning railroad bridges, and shooting at passing trains was relatively simple and not very dangerous. Guerrilla warfare is difficult to crush since locating the enemy is often impossible.

Missouri had a bad reputation in the nation when war erupted in 1861. All during the Kansas troubles northern journalists had reported in profusion and with detail the illegalities and brutalities of Missouri units in Kansas. Northern officers stationed in Missouri during the Civil War, believing that the citizens of Missouri were not to be trusted, treated them harshly. It is true that a strong body of Missourians favored the Confederacy. Since it was impossible for these southern sympathizers to support the Confederacy so long as Union troops occupied strategic places in the state, most tried to follow a policy of neutrality. The suspicious northern officers, failing to appreciate this neutrality, were often hostile and sometimes cruel in their dealings with the people of the state.

Since a large part of Missouri's population came from the South originally, it was to be expected that many would sympathize with the Confederacy; yet, to General Price's chagrin, his dramatic call to arms failed to rouse near the number of Missourians he had anticipated. After the defeat of the Confederate forces at Pea Ridge, Colonel Joseph C. Porter traveled to northern Missouri to recruit men for the Confederate Army. He established a recruiting camp near Monticello in Lewis County in the spring of 1862. Although he succeeded in enlisting over 2,000 volunters, he was able to arm only a fourth of his recruits. Furthermore, he was unable to transport his men across the Missouri River, since the federal forces had destroyed all boats and were in command of all the ferries. When Porter attempted to cross the river near Fulton he was halted by Colonel Odon Guitar from Columbia and forced to retreat into the northeast corner of the state. Colonel John H. McNeil's forces finally met Porter's well-situated army at Kirksville. Although McNeil had an army of only 1,000 men, they were well armed, and in a short time the Confederate forces were routed. Casualties for the North amounted to five killed and thirty-two wounded. Although the estimates of the Confederate forces vary, it is certain that Porter lost a much larger number of his untrained soldiers. As a result of the battle, Colonel Porter was forced to curtail his activities.

Another battle associated with Confederate recruiting in

General Odon Guitar of Columbia accompanied Doniphan to Santa Fe, and later made a trip to California during the gold rush. His brilliant and lucrative career as a criminal lawyer, interrupted by the Civil War, was resumed in 1864.

(Courtesy State Historical Society)

Missouri occurred on August 11, 1862, at Independence. There Rebel Colonel Upton Hayes and a group of 150 recruits, together with a body of recruits under Colonel Hughes and the notorious Quantrill, charged a federal force under the leadership of Colonel James T. Buel. In this conflict the federal force was destroyed.

The battle at Lone Jack in Jackson County on August 16, 1862, was a third encounter occasioned by Confederate recruitment. Colonel Vard Cockrell led a Rebel force of 3,200 men; Union Major Emory S. Foster commanded fewer than 800 men. The uneven contest waged for almost five hours before the Confederates finally abandoned the position.

All facts considered, it can be said that the North was successful in discouraging the recruitment of Confederate soldiers in Missouri. There were those units, of course, who would march south from Missouri to join the Confederate Army. However, the constant surveillance by Union troops and the occasional battles kept these units to a minimum.

In guerrilla warfare with behind-the-line attacks and marauding units separated from the main armies, there are many problems of discipline and of justice. Missouri history during the Civil War presents examples of reprisal killings and pathetic executions. Both sides were guilty of this bloodletting. In September, 1862, Brigadier General Lewis Merrill held prisoner eleven men who had been captured for the third time after taking oaths that they would not oppose the Federal Government. According to federal accounts, they were apprehended in the acts of robbery and murder. Since Missouri was filled with Confederate sympathizers, the federal officers felt it necessary to deal harshly with men found guilty of violating their oath, and sentenced the eleven to death. One of the condemned wrote the following note to General Merrill, pleading for mercy in his faulty frontier English:

> general for god sake spare my life for i am a boy
> i was perswaded to do what i have done and forse i
> will go in service and figt for you and stay with
> you douring the war i wood ben figting for the
> union if it had been for others.

The general refused the plea, and on September 25, a solemn parade of men was marched to a point one half mile south of Macon, blindfolded, and executed by a firing squad. The *Missouri Republican* in its description of the execution analyzed the reason for this harshness by stating, "It is understood all bushwhackers found guilty of this offense will be similarly dealt with."

A second example of harsh military justice occurred at Palmyra in 1862. Confederate Colonel Joseph C. Porter had seized and carried away a number of northern sympathizers while raiding the city of Palmyra. All of the captives were later released with the exception of Andrew Allsman, a Union sympathizer with many enemies in the community. Union Provost Marshal Strachan published a notice giving Colonel Porter ten days to release Allsman and threatening that if, at the end of that ten days, Allsman did not appear the federal forces would execute ten prisoners who had formerly served in Porter's unit. Although evidence indicates that Allsman was released by Porter's troops, he never arrived at Palmyra. When the grace period had expired, Colonel John McNeil selected ten men from Ralls, Lewis, and Scotland counties to execute in reprisal. On the morning of October 18, the ten hostages were transported to the fairground at Palmyra seated in coffins. After the execution, the procession of coffins was slowly driven through the city of Palmyra. Obviously, Colonel McNeil was attempting to give the Confederate sympathizers of that area an object lesson to discourage any further Confederate activities.

A third example of the brutality of the Missouri war is associated with the little village of Centralia. On September 27, 1864, "Bloody Bill" Anderson with 350 Confederate guerrillas invaded the town. After robbing the people and the stores of the community, the bushwhackers remained to greet the Columbia stagecoach and to steal the property of the passengers. The outlaws in uniform then placed ties across the track of the Northern Missouri Railroad and halted the train from St. Louis, stripping all 150 passengers, including twenty-three federal soldiers, of their possessions. After plundering the train, Anderson set it afire and sent it off down the track, where two and one half miles farther it left the track and plunged into a field. Anderson's men then proceeded to shoot down in cold blood the twenty-three federal soldiers who had been on the train. That afternoon when Major A. V. E. Johnson arrived with Union forces, the guerrillas surprised the Union party in an ambush. Out of a force of approximately 150 men, 123 federal troops were killed. Only four bushwhackers were killed and three wounded. After Anderson's escape, seventy-nine of the dead were buried in a long trench near the railroad in Centralia. Anderson is notorious also for the human scalp tied to his saddle and for the many atrocities linked to his name.

The last major military episode in Missouri during the Civil War was the raid by "Old Pap" Price in the fall of 1864. Most military activities of the war occurred east of the Mississippi after Wilson's Creek. However, in 1864, General Price, aware that many Union troops had been moved to the eastern theatre, decided to make one more invasion of Missouri. In his five-week raid of the state, Price severely frightened federal officers in Missouri and aided the Confederacy by forcing the Union officers in the state to recall some 6,000 men from the Georgia campaign.

Price's Confederate force of 12,000 men entered the state in Ripley County in the southeast. The General maneuvered his troops for an intended attack upon St. Louis. A force of approximately 1,200 federal troops under General Thomas Ewing faced Price at Pilot Knob in Iron County. Before Ewing's outnumbered men were forced to retreat, they engaged the rebel forces in battle and succeeded in inflicting over 1,000 casualties.

General Price continued to march north but, made apprehensive by the toll inflicted by Ewing, he abandoned his St. Louis objective and swung west toward Jefferson City. Since Thomas

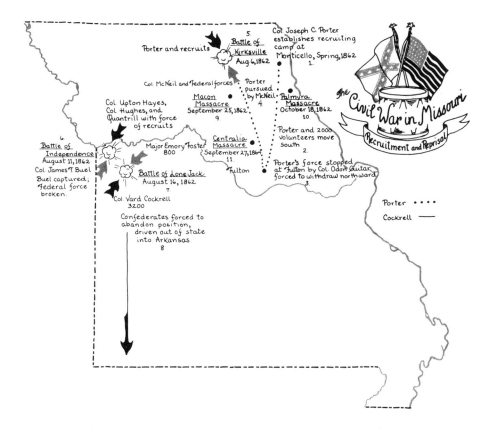

Col. Joseph C. Porter establishes recruiting camp at Monticello, Spring, 1862
1.

Porter and recruits

5.
Battle of Kirksville
Aug 6, 1862

Col. McNeil and Federal forces

Porter pursued by McNeil
4.

Palmyra Massacre
October 18, 1862
10.

Macon Massacre
September 25, 1862
9.

Col. Upton Hayes, Col. Hughes, and Quantrill with force of recruits

Centralia Massacre
September 27, 1864
11.

Porter and 2000 volunteers move South
2.

Porter's force stopped at Fulton by Col. Odon Guitar, forced to withdraw northward
3.

Fulton

6.
Battle of Independence
August 11, 1862
Col. James T. Buel Buel captured; Federal force broken.

Major Emory Foster
800

Battle of Lone Jack
August 16, 1862
7.

Col. Vard Cockrell
3200

Confederates forced to abandon position, driven out of state into Arkansas
8.

The Civil War in Missouri
Recruitment and Reprisal

Porter · · · ·

Cockrell ———

C. Reynolds, who had succeeded to the governorship of the Confederate government of Missouri at Claiborne Jackson's death, was traveling with Price's army, it was assumed that Reynolds intended to seize the state government. A large federal force gathered at Jefferson City frustrated the plan, and caused Price to bypass the capital and move on to western Missouri. During their march across the state, units of Price's army fought skirmishes at Glasgow and at Lexington. Sterling Price was forced by expediency to make use of such vicious guerrilla groups as those of Quantrill, "Bloody Bill" Anderson, and George Todd. The colorful ex-planter General Jo Shelby from Lafayette County, who had recruited and raided in Missouri intermittantly throughout the Union occupation, fought with Price in the raid of 1864. Shelby was in charge of the seizure of Glasgow, but he was forced to evacuate immediately in order to move to Independence with Price.

General Sterling Price, former
governor of Missouri (1853-
1857), was swayed from his
conditional Unionist stand by
the Camp Jackson affair to
fight for the Confederacy.
(Courtesy Missouri Historical Society)

The crucial battle of the campaign, sometimes called the "Gettysburg of the West," occurred at Westport October 21-23, 1864. At Westport, Price found his army caught between two strong federal forces. One army was led by Major General Samuel R. Curtis; the other force, which followed him from Lexington, was under the leadership of General Alfred S. Pleasonton. The battle was fiercely fought along the rocky banks of the Big Blue River. At a moment when Curtis feared he would be unable to move Shelby's troops situated at the top of a rocky hill, a "feeble old man" came along to show the general an easier way to ascend the prominence. This assistance, together with the greater numbers in the federal armies, finally led to the defeat of Price. He ordered a rapid march southward and arrived in Arkansas in November. Price's army had marched 1,434 miles in the campaign and had fought forty-three skirmishes.

The Confederate soldiers—just as those in any war—used the safety valve of humorous song to lessen the tension of daily peril. They followed "Old Pap" Price and General Jo Shelby into Missouri with high hopes of victory and contempt for the Yankee foe. The following rebel song expresses both:

> The Union folks up in the North
>   Are getting much afraid
> That something's coming from the South,
>   They think it is a raid.
> Now I will tell you what it is,
>   If you will just keep cool;

Its got long ears and a long sleek tail,
    And is called Joe Shelby's mule.

Oh! once I went to see old Abe
    And found him in a rage,
Because this mule had started north,
    And had just crossed Osage.
Indeed his anger knew no bounds,
    Said I, "Sir, pray keep cool;"
"I can't," said he, "I've lost so much
    By Shelby's long-eared mule."

Old "Rosey"* got a long dispatch,
    Which came from 'way down east,
To take some thirty thousand men
    And try to catch the beast.
To obey orders he was bound,
    But he called old Abe a fool,
For he had no halter strong enough
    To hold Joe Shelby's mule.

Some say our state did not secede,
    But let me tell you now,
That if she did or if she didn't,
    We'll have her anyhow.
Let us alone, we'll do the same,
    That is the Southern rule;
If that won't do we'll pack the state
    Down South on Shelby's mule.

*General William S. Rosecrans, Union Commander of Missouri stationed at
St. Louis during Price's raid.

**Confederate Gen. Joseph
Shelby raised and com-
manded the "Iron Brig-
ade" of Missouri cavalry
from Lafayette County,
Missouri.**
*(Courtesy State Historical
Society)*

Shelby's fabulous beast disappointed his admirers. Price and his men proved unable to seize a single major federal position. General Sterling Price's last campaign was a failure.

Missouri's Part in the Conflict

The Civil War was neither won nor lost in Missouri. Neither the Confederate nor the Union government considered the military activities west of the Mississippi of vital significance. This is not to say that Missouri's role was unimportant. Her location on the strategic Mississippi and Missouri rivers made control of the state requisite to the maintenance of communications with the West and to the use of the rivers for transportation. Militarily, however, after the Battle of Wilson's Creek the commanders of the opposing forces considered the war in Missouri a side show. The citizens of Missouri would not have agreed. For Missourians, the war did not end with Wilson's Creek or Pea Ridge. It continued in an ugly string of vicious battles provoked frequently by robber bands masquerading as soldiers and in a multitude of skirmishes between Confederate recruiters and federal forces.

The complete history of the war, of course, can never be written. Nor can we fully appreciate the anxiety, the occasional wry humor, the sorrow, the suffering, the suspense of those four years. The tales of only a few Missouri battles have been recounted here. There were over 400 others—Newtonia, Athens, Belmont, Syracuse, Marshall, Miami, Monroe City—each as important as Wilson's Creek to the men who stopped a bullet or a bayonet in the encounter.

Missouri gave more men, in proportion to her population, than any other state in the nation. One hundred nine thousand Union soldiers were Missourians; 30,000 citizens of Missouri marched with the Confederates. Together, these soldiers constituted sixty per cent of the men eligible for military service in the state. Fourteen thousand Missourians gave their lives for the Union. Figures are not available for the losses sustained by the Missourians who joined the South; however, of the 5,000 who formed the first and second Missouri brigades of the Confederate Army after the Battle of Pea Ridge, only 800 survived the war, and half of those were sick or wounded when Lee surrendered to Grant in April of 1865. Missourians fought and died on the battlefields of the South at Vicksburg, Shiloh, Corinth, and

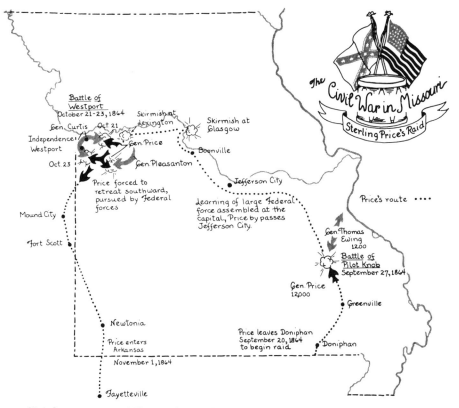

Battle of Westport
October 21-23, 1864
Gen. Curtis   Oct 21
Skirmish at Lexington
Skirmish at Glasgow
Independence
Westport
Gen. Price
Boonville
Oct 23
Gen. Pleasanton
Jefferson City
Price's route   ••••
Price forced to retreat southward, pursued by Federal forces
Learning of large Federal force assembled at the capital, Price by passes Jefferson City.
Mound City
Gen. Thomas Ewing 1200
Fort Scott
Battle of Pilot Knob September 27, 1864
Gen. Price 12,000
Greenville
Newtonia
Price leaves Doniphan September 20, 1864 to begin raid.
Price enters Arkansas
November 1, 1864
Doniphan
Fayetteville

Chickamauga. Missourians followed Sherman in his march through Georgia.

Men of Missouri not only marched in the armies of the North and South, but led them as well. General Sterling Price and General Joseph O. Shelby distinguished themselves in the service of the Confederacy. Abraham Lincoln's two most successful generals, Ulysses S. Grant and William Tecumseh Sherman, were both residents of St. Louis at the outbreak of the war. Grant and Sherman were both onlookers in the crowd during the riot following Lyon's capture of Camp Jackson.

The war brought out the best—and the worst—in Missourians. There was Colonel Richard H. Weightman, who, as he lay dying at Wilson's Creek, was less concerned with the severity of his wound than with its effect upon his men's morale. And then there were the vicious Quantrill, Anderson, and Todd who left in their wake a trail of atrocities, arson, and murder.

The battlefields, littered with the white bones of fallen horses and foul with the stench of death and decay, remained for long months as a reminder that war is more gore than glory.

BIBLIOGRAPHY

Adamson, Hans Christian. *Rebellion in Missouri: 1861. Nathaniel Lyon and His Army of the West.* Philadelphia: Chilton Company, 1961.

Anderson, Frank. "Missouri's Confederate State Capitol at Marshall, Texas," *Missouri Historical Review,* Vol. XXVII (April, 1933), pp. 240-243.

Austin, Robert A. "The Battle of Wilson's Creek," *Missouri Historical Review,* Vol. XXVII (October, 1932), pp. 46-49.

Bek, William G., ed. "The Civil War Diary of John T. Buegel," *Missouri Historical Review,* Vol. XL (April, July, 1946), pp. 307-329, 503-530.

Blum, Virgil C. "The Political and Military Activities of the German Element in St. Louis 1859-1861," *Missouri Historical Review,* Vol. XLII (January, 1948), pp. 103-129.

Borland, William P. "General Jo Q. Shelby," *Missouri Historical Review,* Vol. VII (October, 1912; January, 1913), pp. 10-19, 146-148.

Breihan, Carl W. *Quantrill and His Civil War Guerrillas.* Denver: Alan Swallow, 1959.

Brownlee, Richard S. *Grey Ghosts of the Confederacy: Guerrilla Warfare in the West, 1861-1865.* Baton Rouge: Louisiana State University Press, 1958.

Carr, Lucien. *Missouri, a Bone of Contention.* Boston, New York: Houghton, Mifflin and Company, 1888.

Castel, Albert. "The Bloodiest Man in American History," *American Heritage,* Vol. XI (October, 1960), pp. 22-25, 97-99.

Castel, Albert. *A Frontier State at War: Kansas, 1861-1865.* New York: Cornell University Press, 1958.

Cross, Jasper W. "The Mississippi Valley Sanitary Fair," *Missouri Historical Review,* Vol. XLVI (April, 1952), pp. 237-246.

Culmer, Frederic A. "Brigadier Surgeon John W. Traders' Recollections of the Civil War in Missouri," *Missouri Historical Review,* Vol. XLVI (July, 1952), pp. 323-334.

Doerschuk, Albert N. "Extracts from War-time Letters 1861-1864," *Missouri Historical Review,* Vol. XXIII (October, 1928), pp. 99-110.

Edwards, John N. "Shelby's Expedition to Mexico," *Missouri Historical Review,* Vol. XIV (October, 1919; January, April-July, 1920), pp. 111-144, 246-264, 470-493; Vol. XV (April, 1921), pp. 545-560; Vol. XVI (October, 1921; April, 1922), pp. 146-157, 428-456; Vol. XVII (October, 1922; January, April, 1923), pp. 77-95, 187-197, 348-357; Vol. XVIII (January, April, 1924), pp. 250-277, 438-453; Vol. XIX (April, 1925), pp. 438-471.

Fitzsimmons, Margaret Louise. "Missouri Railroads During the Civil War and Reconstruction," *Missouri Historical Review,* Vol. XXXV (January, 1941), pp. 188-206.

Frick, John H. "Recollections of the Civil War," *Missouri Historical Review,* Vol. XIX (July, 1925), pp. 630-654.

Gentry, North Todd. "General Odon Guitar," *Missouri Historical Review,* Vol. XXII (July, 1928), pp. 419-445.

Grover, George S. "Civil War in Missouri," *Missouri Historical Review,* Vol. VIII (October, 1913), pp. 1-28.

Grover, George S. "Major Emory S. Foster," *Missouri Historical Review,* Vol. XIV (April-July, 1920), pp. 425-432.

Grover, George S. "The Price Campaign of 1864," *Missouri Historical Review,* Vol. VI (July, 1912), pp. 167-181.

Grover, George S. "The Shelby Raid, 1863," *Missouri Historical Review,* Vol. VI (April, 1912), pp. 107-126.

Herklotz, Hildegarde R. "Jayhawkers in Missouri 1858-1863," *Missouri Historical Review,* Vol. XVII (April, July, 1923), pp. 266-284, 505-513; Vol. XVIII (October, 1923), pp. 64-101.

Hesseltine, W. B. "Military Prisons of St. Louis 1861-1865," *Missouri Historical Review,* Vol. XXIII (April, 1929), pp. 380-399.

Holcombe and Adams. *An Account of the Battle of Wilson's Creek or Oak Hills.* Springfield, Missouri: The Springfield Public Library and the Greene County Historical Society, 1961 (Centennial Edition).

Huling, Polly. "Missourians at Vicksburg," *Missouri Historical Review,* Vol. L (October, 1955), pp. 1-15.

Kirkpatrick, Arthur R. "Missouri in the Early Months of the Civil War," *Missouri Historical Review,* Vol. LV (April, 1961), pp. 235-266.

Kirkpatrick, Arthur R. "Missouri on the Eve of the Civil War," *Missouri Historical Review,* Vol. LV (January, 1961), pp. 99-108.

Kirkpatrick, Arthur R. "Missouri's Secessionist Government, 1861-1865," *Missouri Historical Review,* Vol. XLV (January, 1951), pp. 124-137.

Larkin, Lew. *Bingham: Fighting Artist.* St. Louis: State Publishing Company, 1955.

Larkin, Lew. *Vanguard of Empire: Missouri's Century of Expansion.* St. Louis: State Publishing Company, 1961.

Laughlin, Sceva Bright. "Missouri Politics During the Civil War," *Missouri Historical Review,* Vol. XXIII (April, July, 1929), pp. 400-426, 583-618; Vol. XXIV (October, 1929; January, 1930), pp. 87-113, 261-284.

Lee, Bill R. "Missouri's Fight over Emancipation in 1863," *Missouri Historical Review,* Vol. XLV (April, 1951), pp. 256-274.

Lewis, Warner. "Civil War Reminiscences," *Missouri Historical Review,* Vol. II (April, 1908), pp. 221-232.

McCausland, Susan A. Arnold. "The Battle of Lexington as Seen by a Woman," *Missouri Historical Review,* Vol. VI (April, 1912), pp. 127-135.

McDougal, H. C. "A Decade of Missouri Politics—1860 to 1870. From a Republican Viewpoint," *Missouri Historical Review,* Vol. III (January, 1909), pp. 126-153.

McLarty, Vivian Kirkpatrick, ed. "The Civil War Letters of Colonel Bazel F. Lazear," *Missouri Historical Review,* Vol. XLIV (April, July, 1950), pp. 254-273, 387-401; Vol. XLV (October, 1950), pp. 47-63.

Merkel, Benjamin G. "The Abolition Aspect of Missouri's Anti-Slavery Controversy 1819-1865," *Missouri Historical Review,* Vol. XLIV (April, 1950), pp. 232-253.

Mudd, Joseph A. "What I Saw at Wilson's Creek," *Missouri Historical Review,* Vol. VII (January, 1913), pp. 89-105.

Mudd, Joseph A. *With Porter in North Missouri.* Washington: The National Publishing Company, 1909.

Nelson, Earl J. "Missouri Slavery 1861-1865," *Missouri Historical Review,* Vol. XXVIII (July, 1934), pp. 260-274.

Parrish, William E. "General Nathaniel Lyon: a Portrait," *Missouri Historical Review,* Vol. XLIX (October, 1954), pp. 1-18.

Penn, Dorothy. "George Caleb Bingham's 'Order Number Eleven'," *Missouri Historical Review,* Vol. XL (April, 1946), pp. 349-357.

Philips, John F. "Hamilton R. Gamble and the Provisional Government of Missouri," *Missouri Historical Review,* Vol. V (October, 1910), pp. 1-14.

Potter, Marguerite. "Hamilton R. Gamble, Missouri's War Governor," *Missouri Historical Review,* Vol. XXXV (October, 1940), pp. 25-71.

Randall, J. G. and David Donald. *The Civil War and Reconstruction.* Boston: D. C. Heath and Company, 1961.

Rea, Ralph R. *Sterling Price: The Lee of the West.* Little Rock: Arkansas Book House, 1959.

Schrantz, Ward L. "The Battle of Carthage," *Missouri Historical Review,* Vol. XXXI (January, 1937), pp. 140-149.

Shoemaker, Floyd C. *Missouri and Missourians.* Vol. I. Chicago: The Lewis Publishing Company, 1943.

Shoemaker, Floyd C. "The Story of the Civil War in Northeast Missouri," *Missouri Historical Review,* Vol. VII (January, April, 1913), pp. 63-75, 113-131.

Sigel, Franz. "Military Operations in Missouri in the Summer and Autumn of 1861," *Missouri Historical Review,* Vol. XXVI (July, 1932), pp. 354-367.

Simonds, May. "Missouri History as Illustrated by George Caleb Bingham," *Missouri Historical Review,* Vol. I (April, 1907), pp. 181-190.

Smith, William E. "The Blairs and Fremont," *Missouri Historical Review,* Vol. XXIII (January, 1929), pp. 214-260.

Snyder, J. F. "The Capture of Lexington," *Missouri Historical Review,* Vol. VII (October, 1912), pp. 1-9.

Stevens, Walter B. "Homecoming of Shelby's Men," *Missouri Historical Review,* Vol. XIX (July, 1925), pp. 604-610.

Stevens, Walter B. "Lincoln and Missouri," *Missouri Historical Review,* Vol. X (January, 1916), pp. 63-119.

Stewart, Douglass. "When the Civil War Invaded Livingston County," *Missouri Historical Review,* Vol. XXI (October, 1926), pp. 50-55.

Stewart, Faye L. "The Battle of Pea Ridge," *Missouri Historical Review,* Vol. XXII (January, 1928), pp. 187-192.

Sweet, Benjamin F. "Civil War Experiences," *Missouri Historical Review,* Vol. XLIII (April, 1949), pp. 237-250.

Swindler, William F. "The Southern Press in Missouri 1861-1864," *Missouri Historical Review,* Vol. XXXV (April, 1941), pp. 394-400.

Tasher, Lucy Lucile. "The Missouri Democrat and the Civil War," *Missouri Historical Review,* Vol. XXXI (April, 1937), pp. 402-419.

Thomas, David Y. "Missouri in the Confederacy," *Missouri Historical Review,* Vol. XVIII (April, 1924), pp. 382-391.

Thomas, Raymond D. "A Study in Missouri Politics 1840-1870," *Missouri Historical Review,* Vol. XXI (January, April, July, 1927), pp. 166-184, 438-454, 570-580.

Violette, Eugene Morrow. "The Battle of Kirksville Aug. 6, 1862," *Missouri Historical Review,* Vol. V (January, 1911), pp. 94-112.

Violette, Eugene Morrow. *A History of Missouri.* Cape Girardeau, Missouri: Ramfre Press, 1951 ed.

CHAPTER XII

The Aftermath of War

Oh, yes, you are wonderfully fond of me now; but you will
soon choose a Confederate brigadier to succeed me.
—Senator Carl Schurz
circa 1870

Due to the efforts of political leaders such as Thomas Hart
Benton and Andrew Jackson, the Democratic Party became the
majority party in Missouri before the Civil War. However, since
many Missouri Democrats were pro-Confederate in sentiment,
the party split during the war. Democrats with southern sympathies were forced to keep silent under federal occupation;
Democrats loyal to the Union allied themselves with the Republicans to form the Union Party. When the necessity of alliance
passed with the war, the Republicans and Democrats parted ways
once more. The peacetime struggle for political power was
resumed.

In the turbulent days following the conflict, "waving the
bloody shirt" was a favorite political technique of some Radical
Republicans. By intimating that Democrats were responsible for
the tragic bloodletting of the war, these politicians hoped to discredit the Democratic Party. "Scratch a Democrat and you find
a rebel" was a Republican slogan in the election of 1868. The
Radicals used another technique against the Democrats—by
passing laws to disenfranchise Confederates and Confederate
sympathizers, they hoped to hold the Democratic vote in Missouri
to a minimum.

Those Republicans who advocated forgiveness, conciliation,
and fair play opposed the vindictive policies of the Radicals. Republican Senator Carl Schurz, a man of principle, led a split in
his own party in 1870 because he believed that former Confederates should be re-enfranchised. He had the courage to do what
he believed was just, despite the knowledge that a split would
weaken his own party and that the enfranchisement of rebels
would strengthen the Democratic opposition.

As Schurz predicted in the statement quoted above, the re-vitalized Democratic Party praised him and his associates at the time of their stand, but, in 1875, when the Democrats regained control, they elected Francis M. Cockrell to replace Schurz in the United States Senate. True to Schurz' prophecy, Cockrell had been a brigadier general in the Confederate Army.

The Constitution of 1865

We have observed the growing political dissension within the Union Party during the Civil War years. Governor Gamble and those associated with him became known as the Conserva-tive Unionists. They advocated compensated emancipation of slaves and some disenfranchisement of Confederate sympathiz-ers. The Radical Unionists, dissatisfied with these half measures, favored immediate manumission of the slaves and adoption of stronger measures disenfranchising friends of the South. There were, of course, many in Missouri who were still sympathetic to the Confederacy as late as 1865. The following Ozark folksong describes their feelings about the war:

> I'm glad I fit against it,
> I only wish we'd won,
> And I don't want no pardon
> For anything I done.
>
> I cain't take up my musket
> An fight 'em any more,
> But I aint a-goin' to love em,
> An' that is sartin shore.

The Radicals, after winning a sweeping victory at the state level in 1864, immediately secured the approval of the General Assembly for the election of a constitutional convention. The authorization act, passed by the legislature in November, 1864, requested that the proposed convention adopt amendments to the constitution freeing the slaves of Missouri, restricting the fran-chise "to loyal citizens," and "such other amendments as might be deemed essential to the promotion of the public good."

The constitutional convention was held in St. Louis at the Mercantile Library Hall during the last days of the Civil War from January 6, 1865, to April 10, 1865. The armistice at Appo-mattox was signed only one day before the sixty-six delegates adjourned the convention.

Charles D. Drake, a St. Louis lawyer, was the leading figure of the convention. He was an intense, intelligent, dogmatic, aggressive man who had held a variety of political views in Missouri. At various times he had defended the institution of slavery as just, tolerated slavery as necessary, and advocated gradual emancipation. By 1865 he was calling for immediate manumission, and labeling men who disagreed with him "traitors." Because Drake was so successful in dominating the convention and in injecting his will and convictions into the constitution, the document is known in Missouri history as Drake's Constitution. Punsters among historians, comparing the disenfranchisement section to a harsh legal code written by Draco and adopted in ancient Greece, have referred to the Ironclad Oath as the "Draconian Code."

Although it was fifty per cent longer than the Constitution of 1820, most provisions of the Constitution of 1865 were similar to those of the earlier charter. Two minor changes were the establishment of two-year terms for the chief state officials, and the greater emphasis placed upon education, banks, and corporations. These were minor matters, however, in the political conflict of that time.

The three major developments coming out of the constitutional convention of 1865 related to (1) emancipation, (2) removing certain state officials from their positions, and (3) limiting the franchise. The first two items were passed as ordinances; the last was made part of the new constitution.

Emancipation was the most pressing matter for the convention. The war appeared to be nearing an end. The Radicals—who became known as Radical Republicans—wished to act immediately on the matter of manumission. Five days after the beginning of their deliberations the following emancipation ordinance, which made no provision for reimbursing the slaveowners, was passed by a vote of sixty to four:

> That hereafter, in this State, there shall be neither slavery, nor involuntary servitude, except in punishment of crime, whereof the party shall have been duly convicted; and all persons held to service or labor as slaves are hereby declared free.

Through the adoption of this ordinance Missouri was the first slave state to renounce slavery officially. The delegates considered this manumission provision their major accomplishment, and at the time of signing of the ordinance held a celebration

Charles Daniel Drake, leader of the Radical Republicans from 1865 to 1871, served from 1867 to 1870 in the United States Senate where he was a vocal supporter of the radical program of reconstruction.
(Courtesy State Historical Society)

which included singing by an abolitionist group known as "The Hutchison Family," who were invited to "invoke the . . . magic of vocal music in aid of the political ardor of the great occasion."

A second major development growing out of the constitutional convention of 1865 was the passage of an "Ousting Ordinance." The delegates believed that the Missouri supreme court would declare their emancipation ordinance and other acts unconstitutional. In order to prevent this, they passed a bill which removed all state judges, circuit attorneys, sheriffs, and county recorders—a total of over 800 Missouri officeholders. Radical Republicans were then named to fill the vacant offices.

A third major accomplishment was the adoption of the so-called Ironclad Oath. Although an oath had been adopted for the qualifications of voters in Missouri as early as 1862, the Radicals felt that it did not exclude enough Confederate sympathizers. The Ironclad Oath, which was part of the new Constitution of 1865, declared that any Missourian "who had ever been in armed hostility to the United States," or "has ever given aid, comfort, countenance, or support to persons engaged in any such hostility," or "has ever disloyally held communication with such enemies" was to be denied the franchise. In all, some eighty-six acts were listed as reasons for denial of voting rights. In the Registry Acts, the constitution stipulated that Missouri was to be divided into voting districts, and only those citizens who were properly enrolled and had sworn the oath would be permitted to vote. Another restriction in the constitution specified that certain professional people in Missouri would be prohibited from practicing their professions or serving in civil or honorary positions because of their past activities. Clergymen particularly seem to have come under suspicion during the war years. Judge James Mc-Ferran of Gallatin wrote in June, 1862, when the first oath was being considered for adoption:

> The question now is, whether ministers of the Gospel and school teachers shall take this oath. I think if there is any class in the State that ought to be put under the solemnity of an oath, it is the ministers of the Gospel. Of all the men in the state who have contributed to bring about the evils now on us, I think there is no class that is so responsible as ministers of the Gospel. The minister always does his work effectually; and whenever he gets to be a politician and gets among his flock, he instills poison into their minds, and all the arguments of politicians and orators can never remove it.

Lawyers, teachers, officers of corporations, and church officers were also victims of discrimination, for the Constitution of 1865 denied them the right to act in their normal capacities if they refused to take the oath.

The Constitution of 1865 can best be explained in Charles Drake's own words. He declared:

> We intend to erect a wall and a barrier, in the shape of a constitution that would be as high as the eternal heavens, deep down as the very center of the earth, so that they [Conservatives] shall neither climb over it nor dig under it, and as thick as the whole territory of Missouri so that they shall never batter it down nor pierce through it; and never shall put upon the colored race the disqualifications which have borne them down in times past.

The severity of the constitution caused even some Radicals to vote against it. For a time Governor Fletcher, a Radical, refused to support it. The old Whigs such as William S. Switzler and James S. Rollins were outspoken critics. One interesting and illegal aspect of the ratification of the constitution was the provision that only those individuals could vote for or against ratification who could qualify to vote under the oath which was part of the constitution. In other words, citizens were prevented from voting against a document which would prevent them from voting! On the last day of the convention of 1865, Charles Drake had secured the delegates' approval of an ordinance which allowed Missouri soldiers to vote although they were stationed in army posts in other states. The votes of these soldiers secured the adoption of the constitution. In Missouri itself, despite the disenfranchisement of an estimated one-third of the population, the constitution failed to pass by 965 votes. However, when the soldiers' votes were added to the Missouri totals, the constitution was ratified on June 8, 1865, by a vote of 43,670 to 41,808, and became effective July 4, 1865. The approval of the constitution, despite strong opposition from many former Whigs, from a number of Conservative Unionists, and from the Germans of St. Louis who disapproved a restriction on alien voting, may be due in part to anger over Confederate guerrilla activities. The bushwhacking which had caused property loss and bloodshed in Missouri in 1864, continued in 1865, and may have provoked ballot box revenge.

Enforcement of some parts of the constitution was difficult. The provision for oath taking angered many professional people, some of whom either ignored or openly defied the law. Father John A. Cummings, a Catholic priest serving a church in Louisiana, Missouri, by his refusal to take the oath was upholding Father Pierre De Smet's announcement made earlier:

> The priests are generally agreed that, on principle, such an oath cannot be taken, because our authority does not emanate from the State, and we cannot, without compromising the ecclesiastical state, consent to take it. No Catholic priest in Missouri will take it.

Father Cummings was arrested, fined, and jailed when he refused to pay his fine. The case was appealed to the United States Supreme Court, which ruled in 1867 that the Missouri oath for professional activity was unconstitutional. The "Ousting Ordinance" was also difficult to enforce. Two members of the Missouri supreme court, Judges William V. N. Bay and John D. S. Dryden, refused to relinquish their positions. Governor Fletcher employed militia officers and police to force the two men from their courtrooms and to seize their records.

Drake's Constitution lasted only ten years. In its treatment of Confederate sympathizers, the constitution was a document

THE OATH OF LOYALTY
PRESCRIBED BY
THE CON2TITUTION, ADOPTED IN 1865.

"The Ironclad Oath," 1865
(Courtesy State Historical
Society)

I, Joseph W. McClurg, do solemnly swear, that I am well acquainted with the terms of the third section of the second Article of the Constitution of the State of Missouri, adopted in the year eighteen hundred and sixty five, and have carefully considered the same; that I have never, directly or indirectly, done any of the acts in said section specified; that I have always been truly and loyally on the side of the United States against all enemies thereof, foreign and domestic; that I will bear true faith and allegiance to the United States, and will support the Constitution and laws thereof, as the supreme law of the land, any law or ordinance of any State to the contrary notwithstanding; that I will, to the best of my ability, protect and defend the Union of the United States, and not allow the same to be broken up and dissolved, or the Government thereof to be destroyed or overthrown, under any circumstances, if in my power to prevent it; that I will support the Constitution of the State of Missouri; and that I make this oath without any mental reservation or evasion, and hold it to be binding on me.

J. W. McClurg

Subscribed and sworn to before me this 23rd day of August, 1866.

of revenge. Like many decrees enacted in hate and designed for revenge, it did not survive the conciliation of peacetime. In some states where a large Republican electorate lived, politicians were able to maintain their popularity by blaming the Democrats for the Civil War, but this tactic did not work well in Missouri. There were too many Confederate sympathizers and too many fair-minded Republicans who opposed unjust or unnecessarily severe legislation.

Radical Republican Rule

One of the most complex aspects of the history of Missouri is the study of the political parties which operated in the state during the years 1850 to 1870. Not only were there several parties, but there were also many factions within parties, each group contending for its own solution to the problems of slavery, slavery extension, and union or disunion. The scene is one of a great tangle, and in this maze of parties, factions, and cliques there is no easy understanding of the whole.

Contemporary sources, for example, speak of Benton Democrats, anti-Benton Democrats, Free Democrats, National Democrats, Douglas Democrats, and Breckenridge Democrats. The Republicans were at various times divided into Radical Republicans and Liberal Republicans. In addition, there were other groups known as the Whigs, the American Party, the Free Soil Party, the Union Party, the Conservative Unionists, and the Radical Unionists. In examining the biographies of certain prominent Missourians during this time, it appears that they changed their parties almost as frequently as their shirts. Charles Drake was at various times a Whig, a Know-Nothing (American Party), a Democrat, a Radical Unionist, and a Republican. Frank Blair was a Democrat, a Free Soiler, a Free Democrat, a Republican, and a Conservative Unionist. The Democratic Party does not appear to have held a grudge against him, for in 1868, shortly after he returned to the party, he was the Democratic candidate for vice president of the United States. Students of history who study both the period of the Civil War and the tumultuous years preceding and following the conflict must keep in mind that, to the statesmen of that time, the issues appeared so important and were so controversial that parties were split over differences which today we might consider minor.

Although we have just noted the great number of political parties during this time, the picture can be simplified by noting that basic political structure in effect during the war years. The Republicans entered the Missouri election of 1860, but they constituted a small group. The Democrats at the same time were split between the Breckenridge group—sympathetic to the South —and the Douglas Democrats. When the war erupted, most Breckenridge Democrats sided with the South, and with the failure of the state guard to hold Missouri, these pro-Confederate Democrats were unable to take part in political leadership in the state. Some Douglas Democrats, such as Governor Jackson himself, sided with the Confederacy; others of the party defended the Union. In 1861 the Unionist Party, embracing both Republicans and Democrats who supported the Federal Government in the conflict, was established in Missouri. Abraham Lincoln encouraged this fusion of Republicans and loyal Democrats and ran for re-election in 1864 on a Union Party ticket which included a Democrat—Andrew Johnson of Tennessee—as the candidate for vice president. The Union Party was the controlling party in Missouri during the war years.

In time, a difference of opinion developed within the Union

Party. Some politicians who favored the immediate emancipation of slaves were highly critical of both Governor Gamble and President Lincoln. These politicians, known as Radical Unionists, also demanded sterner measures to disenfranchise Confederate sympathizers. On the other hand, Unionists who opposed harsh and hastily enacted legislation and who supported Lincoln and Gamble were known as the Conservative Unionists. When the war was over, there was no longer a pressing military need for political cooperation on the part of the Unionists, so in 1866 a group of Unionists broke away to form the Democratic Party of Missouri. Those Radical Unionists who wished to disassociate themselves from the unpopular Union president, Andrew Johnson, began calling themselves Radical Republicans. By the year 1868 the Union Party was dead. Pre-war Democrats and many Conservative Unionists such as Frank Blair joined the newly reorganized Democratic Party. The Republican Party then absorbed both the Radical Unionists and some members of the Conservative Unionists. These Radicals—whether known as Radical Unionists or Radical Republicans—were in political control of Missouri from 1864 to 1870. However, the moderate elements within the Republican Party were restless and, in time, secured the overthrow of the Radical leaders in Missouri government.

We have already noted the leading part played by Charles Drake in the creation of the new Constitution of 1865. Drake tended to lose political power after the writing of the constitution, and other individuals in the party became more important. Thomas C. Fletcher, a Radical, served as governor from 1864 to 1868, during the closing months of the conflict and the difficult years of adjustment immediately following the war. During this time, which has been called the Reign of Terror, there was a continuation of the criminal activities which had been carried on by guerrilla units during the war years. Fletcher gave assistance to those communities victimized by the marauding gangs which roamed the state during 1866 and 1867, calling out the militia to halt the bandit activities in Jackson and Lafayette counties. Another major concern of the Fletcher administration was the enforcement of the constitutional provisions regarding the franchise. The Registry Acts of 1866 and 1868 set up the mechanism whereby only registered citizens who took the oath prescribed by the constitution were allowed to vote. Obviously, the Registry

Joseph Washington McClurg, with two partners, ran the "Big Store on the Osage" at Linn Creek in Camden County before joining the Union army. With his election in 1868, McClurg became the second native Missourian to serve as governor.

(Courtesy State Historical Society)

Acts were unpopular in those areas of Missouri where former rebels were numerous.

In the election of the legislature in 1866 the Conservative Union Party, led by Frank Blair, and the reorganized Democratic Party opposed the Radical Unionists. However, the Ironclad Oath and the registry procedures worked so successfully for the Radicals that they were able to overwhelm their opposition. After the election the Radicals had twice as many members in the state legislature as did all other groups combined.

In the state election of 1868 the Conservative Unionists merged with the Democratic Party. Despite the united front of their opposition, the Radicals once again won the election, but their candidate for governor, Joseph W. McClurg of Linn Creek, was the last Radical to hold the gubernatorial office. During McClurg's term the Radical governor and legislature followed a conservative financial policy, paying off state financial obligations at the same time that they made advances in the field of higher education. Under McClurg's administration the Rolla School of Mines was authorized, the Agriculture School for Missouri was attached to the University of Missouri, and teacher training institutions were established at Kirksville and Warrensburg. Despite the support of Radical leaders, a constitutional amendment to grant black suffrage failed to win approval from the voters.

At this time dissension was simmering in the Republican Party. A number of outspoken Republicans, opposed to the harsh treatment accorded the Confederate soldiers and southern sympathizers, demanded a change to a more tolerant policy, both at the state and national level. Carl Schurz, a native of Germany who had been forced to leave his homeland after the Revolution of 1848, became a leader of the dissenting Republicans. Schurz came to the United States in 1852, and immediately immersed himself in the study of American history and government. By 1857, only five years after his arrival in America, he had become so involved in politics that he was the Republican nominee for lieutenant governor in Wisconsin. In 1867 he moved to St. Louis to assume the editorship of the *Westliche Post*. Only two years later, in 1869, he was chosen United States senator from Missouri. After serving in the northern army during the war, Schurz made a study of the South and of the reconstruction policies instituted immediately following the war. He was an outspoken opponent of any policy of oppression or disenfranchisement of the Confederacy or individual Confederates. Schurz wanted the Civil War to be forgotten. He was not alone in his criticism of the Radicals and their harsh treatment of the rebels.

The great crisis for the Republican Party in Missouri came in 1870. Carl Schurz, in conjunction with B. Gratz Brown and two other St. Louis newspapermen, William Grosvenor of the *Missouri Democrat* and Joseph Pulitzer of the *Westliche Post*, organized the opposition to Drake's Radical policies. The legislature, under prodding by the moderates, produced a constitutional amendment repealing the Ironclad Oath, and authorized its submission to the people for their vote of approval or disapproval in the election scheduled for November.

Meanwhile, in August, 1870, when the Republicans held their state convention in Jefferson City, the resolutions committee of the convention was dominated by moderates who shared the views of Schurz. The committee presented a resolution to the convention putting the Republican Party on record as supporting the immediate withdrawal of test oath qualifications for voting. The Radicals and the convention refused to adopt it. At that point Carl Schurz and some 250 delegates dramatically withdrew from the state convention to establish their own Liberal Republican Party. The Radicals were appalled at this move, since a split in the party would forecast its downfall. Drake and his

German-born statesman and journalist Carl Schurz represented Missouri in the United States Senate from 1869 to 1875 and acted as secretary of the interior under President Hayes.

(Courtesy State Historical Society)

associates called the walkout of the Schurz Republicans "one of the most audacious schemes of political knavery known in the history of American politics; a flagrant act of desertion [sic] for a trivial and unjustifiable cause; a transaction of deception, misrepresentation, and fraud." The Radicals could see their castle crumbling around them.

By withdrawing from the state convention, Schurz, Brown, and their associates had forced the Republican Party to take a stand on the question of enfranchisement of former rebels. The Radical Republicans nominated Joseph W. McClurg for another term as governor of Missouri and flaccidly advocated the return of the franchise at some time in the future to those who were then disqualified. The Liberal Republicans chose B. Gratz Brown as their flag bearer and demanded the immediate abandonment of the Ironclad Oath.

As one would anticipate, the Democrats were delighted at the division in the Republican ranks. In order to encourage the split, the Democrats adopted a policy of supporting the Liberal Republican nominees for office at the state level. By helping the Liberal Republicans win the state offices, the Democrats correctly anticipated that they would greatly weaken the Republicans as a whole and make Republican reunion unlikely. This policy of refraining from the nomination of candidates for state offices has been referred to as the "Possum" policy, since the Democrats temporarily "played dead." Brown's position with

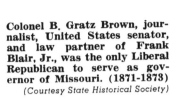

Colonel B. Gratz Brown, journalist, United States senator, and law partner of Frank Blair, Jr., was the only Liberal Republican to serve as governor of Missouri. (1871-1873)
(Courtesy State Historical Society)

regard to the enfranchisement of Confederates was the position of the Democratic Party as well. In May, 1870, Brown had declared concerning the Radical Republican administration:

> . . . you rest beneath a charter of constitutional state government that is in its text only a bundle of disfranchisements of black and white, whose discriminations are founded upon the color of skin and the oaths of the vanquished.

Brown intended to destroy such bases for discrimination.

Brown previously had been, at various times, a Whig, a Benton Democrat, a Republican, and a Radical Unionist. The *Missouri Republican* jested in its issue of July 2, 1870, that B. Gratz Brown should please most people in Missouri since he had taken so many sides on political issues. Charles Drake, probably more enraged than anyone else at the split in the party, declared in December, 1870, "He [Brown] has gone to the Democracy and may the Lord have mercy on his soul."

When the ballots were counted in 1870, Brown was the easy victor in the contest for governor. However, of his 104,000 votes, only about 45,000 to 48,000 were cast by Liberal Republicans; the other Brown votes came from Missouri Democrats. In the congressional election that year the Democrats rode the tide of victory to capture five of Missouri's ten seats in Congress. The Liberals captured two and the Radicals, three.

By the end of 1870 the three main political problems of the

prewar and postwar period were solved. Those three issues were (1) secession, (2) emancipation, and (3) suffrage for Confederates. The secession issue had been solved in 1862 at Pea Ridge. With federal forces occupying the state, talks of secession in Missouri after 1862 were purely academic. The emancipation question was answered in 1865 when the constitutional convention of that year declared the manumission of all Missouri slaves. The suffrage issue was finally resolved in 1870 with the election of a Liberal Republican state administration and with the popular endorsement of the amendment removing the Ironclad Oath from the Missouri constitution. William Switzler, the editor of the *Missouri Statesman,* declared in the November 18, 1870 issue:

> The fetters which were forged in 1865 by the Drake constitution have fallen from the wrists of 75,000 white men and the ballot is free. Infamous registry laws, odious test oaths, venal and villainous registry officers will be known to our state no more.

The Radical Republicans, failing to see that Missouri and Missourians could not be divided permanently by their respective stands in the Civil War, had by their actions so alienated not only the ex-rebels, but also fair-minded people throughout the state, that the Radicals were sure to lose power when all regained the right to vote.

The Liberal Republicans

B. Gratz Brown was the first and only candidate of the Liberal Republican Party to serve as governor of Missouri. Brown, a firm foe of slavery, had been a leader of the Benton Democrats in the state legislature from 1854 to 1859, but his strong opposition to secession led him into the Republican Party in 1861. After service as an officer in the Union army, Brown, from 1863 to 1867, represented Missouri in the United States Senate where he exerted all possible influence to effect the passage of an emancipation proclamation for border-state slaves. B. Gratz Brown was a man of strong convictions, but he, like Carl Schurz and Frank Blair, believed in conciliation. His desire for amity between the various political parties was expressed with Jeffersonian style in his inaugural address when he reminded the legislators:

> We are all Republicans—
> We are all Democrats.

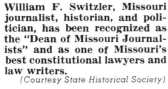

William F. Switzler, Missouri journalist, historian, and politician, has been recognized as the "Dean of Missouri Journalists" and as one of Missouri's best constitutional lawyers and law writers.
(Courtesy State Historical Society)

A development which must have been particularly troubling to a man of justice and honor occurred during Brown's administration. The Ku Klux Klan reared its sheet-draped head early in 1870. Klansmen, intending to insure white supremacy, rode the backroads of the bootheel, cloaked or masked to conceal their identity, terrorizing the blacks and some whites of the area and sometimes committing acts of violence. The Klan spread rapidly, and was soon active in such widely separated places as Boonville and Bloomfield. In Stoddard County members of the secret society moved about in groups as large as fifty. Lawless and violent members of the Klan, taking advantage of the society's disguise, used the night rides as opportunities for horse thievery, general robbery, and occasional murders. Governor Brown sent agents about the state to investigate reports of crimes committed by the mounted terrorists, and, on several occasions, called out the militia to curtail Klan activities.

During Brown's term as governor, the legislature selected his former law partner, Frank Blair—now a Democrat—as the senator from Missouri to fill the vacancy left by Charles Drake. Drake, having fallen from political power and favor, had resigned his Senate seat to accept an appointment as chief justice of the

United States court of claims. The hated registry system which
had dominated the Missouri election system since 1866 was
destroyed by laws passed under Brown's administration. Under
the handicap of a Democrat-dominated General Assembly and
the continued split in the Republican Party, B. Gratz Brown
served his state well from 1871 to 1873.

During Brown's two-year term there was great concern
within the Republican Party over the division of its membership
and several earnest attempts to unite the two groups were made.
The failure of these reunion efforts was due to Liberal dissatisfaction with the conduct of the administration in Washington
and their refusal to support President Grant.

St. Louis was the scene of one corrupt phase of Grant's
tenure. To supervise the collection of the whiskey excise tax in
the St. Louis area, President Grant appointed a Missourian
named John McDonald. The choice was a poor one. McDonald,
William McKee—part owner of the *Missouri Democrat*—and
several Republican officials formed a ring which remitted about
half the whiskey tax money to Washington and divided the remainder with the distillers. At the height of their illicit activities
the members of the ring deprived the government of approximately $500,000 a year.

Although General Babcock, President Grant's personal secretary, was involved in the scandal, Grant may not have had personal knowledge of the ring. However, during a St. Louis visit
in 1874, the president was so naive as to accept from the leaders
of the ring the gift of a buggy and a team of handsome horses
adorned with golden breast plates inscribed with his name. Na-
ivete was not one of General Babcock's qualities, for when he
discovered a flaw in a $2,400 four-carat diamond shirt stud pre-
sented to him by the grafters, he returned it to the donors to be
replaced by a finer stone. The people of St. Louis were not so
easily hoodwinked as Ulysses S. Grant seems to have been. There
were rumblings and rumors of corruption for several years before
the scandal was publicly exposed in 1874.

Although the Liberal Republicans did not have all the details
of the whiskey ring by 1872, they were aware of several other
corrupt situations in the Grant administration, including an attempt to corner the gold market and corruption in federal assistance to transcontinental railroads. Since the Liberal Republicans
of Missouri were known throughout the country as a reform

Kentucky-born Silas Woodson was admitted to the bar at the age of twenty-one years and only two years later was elected to the Kentucky Legislature. After moving to St. Joseph, Missouri, where he established a law firm, he became active in the Democratic party and won the governorship in 1872.
(Courtesy State Historical Society)

group, it was natural that Republicans of other states who objected to the extremes of reconstruction and who censured the Grant administration would seek to follow successful and inspiring reform leaders such as Brown and Schurz of Missouri.

On May 1, 1872, a national convention of Liberal Republicans was held at Cincinnati, Ohio. With Senator Carl Schurz of Missouri as the presiding officer, the convention adopted a platform critical of Grant, and nominated Horace Greeley, the editor of the New York *Tribune,* for president and B. Gratz Brown, the Missouri governor, for vice president. The national Democratic Party in 1872 watched the Liberal Republicans closely. Convinced that an enduring split in the Republican Party would materially help their chances of eventual victory, the Democrats, to encourage the establishment of the Liberal Republicans as a permanent party, agreed to support the national ticket of Greeley and Brown in 1872.

On the state level back in Missouri, the election of 1872 provided an example of continuing cooperation between the Liberal Republicans and the Democrats. The two parties held their convention together in the state capital in August, 1872. Agreeing not to compete for the same offices, the two parties divided the several positions to be filled by election. Since a Liberal Republican had been elected governor in 1870, the Democrats were

given the chance to nominate one of their own men—Silas Woodson of St. Joseph—for governor in 1872. In the election which followed, the Liberal Republicans and Democrats won another victory over the greatly-weakened Radical Republicans. During
Governor Woodson's two years as the chief executive of Missouri,
the Liberal Republican Party disintegrated. By 1874, the Democrats stood alone. Woodson's administration was noted for economy and for a lowering of state taxes from their wartime levels.
During Woodson's term of office the state normal school at Cape
Girardeau was authorized (1873).

At the national level, in the election of 1872, the defeat of
the Liberal Republican ticket of Greeley and Brown spelled the
doom of the Liberal Republican Party. The Liberal Republicans
were never as large a group in Missouri as the Democrats, and
the political developments after 1872 show that, in essence, the
Liberal Republicans had given the Democratic Party the victory
by splitting the Republican forces. When the Liberal Republican
Party disappeared between 1872 and 1874, the members of the
defunct party moved into the Republican and Democratic folds.

The Constitution of 1875

Governor Silas Woodson secured authorization from the legislature for an election in 1874 in which the citizens of Missouri
could express their desire for a new constitution. Missourians
indicated by a narrow 283 vote margin that they favored the
drafting of a new charter; no doubt, the margin would have been
much greater had not the despised Ironclad Oath been abolished
by constitutional amendment in 1870. The constitutional convention assembled in Jefferson City on May 5, 1875, with sixty
Democrats, six Republicans, and two Liberals as delegates. Since
the Democratic majority was so overwhelming, there was no significant party difference in the convention.

The sixty-eight delegates worked diligently until August 2,
1875, when the completed document was presented to the people
of Missouri. Upon investigation, the citizens of Missouri found
the very detailed charter to be twice as long as the Constitution
of 1865.

In order to explain the aims of the constitution framers, it
is necessary to note certain circumstances of the period which
influenced the delegates. First, the legislatures between 1865
and 1875 had been increasingly occupied with so-called "special

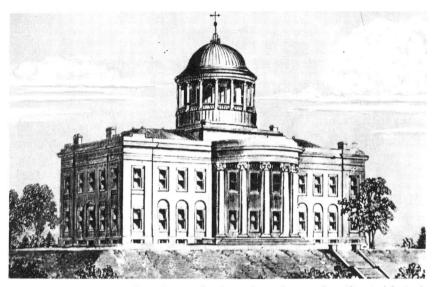

(From Stevens, The Center State; Courtesy State Historical Society)

The State Capitol, Jefferson City, 1876. This capitol building, completed in 1840, replaced the first publicly-owned capitol, which was destroyed by fire in 1837.

legislation," which referred to bills adopted for the assistance of an individual or a particular group, granting either immunity from other legislation or certain preferential treatment. During the decade 1865-1875, these special legislation bills constituted at least half of the acts passed during legislative sessions. A second concern of the legislators were the problems of regulating the corporations which were part of the newly-accelerated growth of industry. Of special interest to the constitution writers was the development and the financing of railroads. We have already noted that the state had, in effect, financed the construction of the first railroads in Missouri with large grants of money during the 1850's. In the years immediately after the Civil War many county courts, sometimes without the voters' approval, had issued bonds to finance the construction of the railroads through the territory under their jurisdiction. Often the railroads went bankrupt, and the citizens were thus defrauded. A third matter of concern to intelligent, dedicated political leaders throughout the country was the exposed corruption associated with government service. Reformers were shocked and troubled by the fact that highly influential legislators at the national and state levels had been involved in the wave of scandals during the Grant administration. The distrust of legislators which resulted from these revelations is manifested in the restrictions placed upon them in the new constitution.

Fourth, the panic of 1873, incurred by reckless speculation after the war, brought unemployment and bank and business failures to Missouri. As a consequence, there was great solicitude in the state for solvency and the avoidance of bankruptcy at the state level. Fifth, with the passing of the prejudice against free education there was a heightened interest in the establishment and financing of schools for the children of Missouri. Sixth, the rapid growth of urban centers in Missouri—particularly in St. Louis and Kansas City—made necessary new laws for the regulation and representation of the large cities.

The various changes made in Missouri's constitution were influenced largely by the six factors and historical circumstances mentioned above. Examination of the Constitution of 1875 reveals that the special legislation which allowed preferential treatment to individuals was curtailed by the careful outlining of the procedures for the passage of bills and by the outlawing of special legislation in thirty-two specified categories.

Legislative interest in the growth of industry can be seen in the twenty-seven sections dealing with corporations—thirteen of which were related to the establishment, operation, and regulation of railroads.

A study of the portion of the constitution dealing with the legislature reveals that the writers of the constitution in 1875 did not have the great confidence in legislators which the framers of the 1820 charter displayed. In the decade preceding the drafting of the new constitution, the legislature tended to meet almost annually, which resulted in excessive legislation and extra expense for the state. To discourage unnecessary legislation and to economize, the charter authorized the General Assembly to meet in regular session only once in every two years, and a strict limitation was imposed on expenditures for mileage, stationery, etc., by the legislators.

At the same time that the power of the legislature was restricted, the governor's hand was strengthened. Where earlier only a majority vote was necessary to override a governor's veto, under the Constitution of 1875 a two-thirds vote of each house of the legislature was required. The governor's term was returned to four years, but he was not allowed to succeed himself. Of great importance was the power granted to the governor allowing him to veto separate items in appropriation bills.

The fear of insolvency can be read in the new limitations placed upon the state, counties, cities, and towns, preventing them from using public credit to assist in the construction of railways and setting maximum taxation levels for their governments. Recalling the heavy debt which resulted from the earlier railroad bonds, a debt level of $250,000 was set for the state government. The government could not obligate itself beyond that level unless the citizens agreed to an increase in indebtedness by a two-thirds vote.

In the area of education the constitution established "Separate free schools . . . for the education of children of African descent," recognized the University of Missouri as a responsibility of state government, and continued the policy of reserving one-fourth of the state revenues for education.

Since the growing number of large cities in Missouri had governmental problems distinct from those of the smaller towns, the writers of the Constitution of 1875 introduced the home rule charter provision which made possible the writing of their own charters of government for cities of over 100,000 inhabitants. While the legislature was still dominated by the rural population, a new formula for the representation of cities allowed a slightly louder voice in state government for city dwellers. The constitution also provided for the establishment of the St. Louis court of appeals to handle the great burden of cases in that area, and allowed the city of St. Louis to withdraw from St. Louis County and become a county in itself.

The executive mansion where Missouri governors resided from 1834 to 1871
(Courtesy State Historical Society)

The Constitution of 1875, unanimously adopted by the delegates at the end of their convention and overwhelmingly accepted by the citizens of Missouri, became the effective charter of government in Missouri on November 30, 1875. It remained the law of the state for seventy years until a new constitution was drafted in 1945.

The Resurgence of the Democratic Party

The Democratic Party recaptured control of the state and enjoyed a period of renewed strength and success from 1874 to the end of the century. Despite instances in which the Republicans combined forces with the People's Party and the Greenback Party in an attempt to secure victory, the Republican opposition maneuvered in vain to defeat the Democrats. The political battles of the time were waged over (1) regulation of railroads, (2) rapid lowering of the state debt, (3) issuance of cheap money and the resultant inflation, and (4) lawlessness in Missouri.

In 1870 O. H. Kelley came to Missouri to organize a new group named the Patrons of Husbandry—better known as the Grange—to provide a source of educational and social experience for farmers. When farm men gathered at Grange meetings, discussion inevitably focused on the problems which weighed most heavily on their minds. In that day—as in this—the farmer's most pressing problems were financial. The farmers of the 1870's were suffering from a decline in prices for farm products. They also complained of exploitation by railroads, grain elevators, and commission companies, and protested the high prices of manufactured goods. The sharing of their common worries and the airing of their mutual protests and complaints led to a pooling of ideas and resources to effect a solution to their common problems. The Grange initiated a number of projects designed to alleviate rural economic strain: cooperative buying to secure lower prices, the founding of banks where money might be secured at low rates of interest, and the establishment of manufacturing plants where farm implements might be purchased at reasonable prices. The Grange soon developed into a booming organization and, by 1875, 2,009 Grange chapters existed in Missouri—more than in any other state in the Union at that time.

The Grange activity which most interests us here was the

organization, largely by Grange members, of a new political party known as the People's Party. In an organizational convention at Jefferson City in September, 1874, the delegates nominated Major William Gentry of Pettis County as candidate for governor, and chose a complete state ticket of candidates. The People's Party adopted a reform platform demanding that there be no increase in the state debt, that railroad corporations be carefully regulated, that free public schools be encouraged, and that taxes and tariffs be lowered. The party, obviously much concerned over the heavy state debt, particularly stressed the need for economy.

The Republicans, recognizing an opportunity in 1874 to capitalize on this new political party, adopted the old "Possum" policy which the Democratic Party had used so successfully in 1870, and declared their intention to support the state ticket of the People's Party.

Reformer Carl Schurz, the Republican senator from Missouri, indicated his approval of a coalition between the Republican Party and the People's Party. Schurz made a passionate address in St. Louis in September of 1874, in which he chided the Democratic Party, demanding to know what they had accomplished "with the power . . . derived from the unselfish and generous movement of 1870?" Of course, Schurz was referring to the fact that the resurgence of the Democratic Party in Missouri was due to Liberal Republican insistence upon re-enfranchisement of former Confederates. Referring to the gangs of outlaws which were terrorizing the state, the senator then added:

> Good government! What has become of the reputation of the state under your rule, when the newspapers of the East and West, as well as our own, are alive with accounts of highway robbery and murder in Missouri, which the government showed itself utterly impotent to repress and punish?

In a letter to James S. Rollins, Carl Schurz wrote in August of 1874, "The movement inaugurated by the farmers seems to promise well, and if the convention called on the second of September acts judiciously, the chances will be decidedly good." Senator Schurz was overly optimistic. The Democratic candidate for governor, Charles H. Hardin of Mexico, Missouri, was able to win an election victory by a sizable margin in 1874.

Hardin wrestled with serious financial problems during his administration. Civil War expenses and the costs of the earlier

During the administration of Governor Charles Henry Hardin (1875-1877) the Constitution of 1875 was drafted and adopted.

(Courtesy State Historical Society)

railroad construction had encumbered the state with a debt of $36,094,908. By cutting expenses in half, Governor Hardin was able to make decided progress in relieving Missouri's burden of indebtedness.

A second serious problem of the Hardin administration was the result of great invasions of grasshoppers or "Rocky Mountain Locusts" which swarmed into Missouri during the years 1874-1877. The locusts arrived in such numbers that they darkened the sky and filled the air for miles around with the sound of millions of munching insects. The St. Louis *Republican* described the invasion of 1874:

> A glance upward toward the sun revealed them filling the air as far as vision could extend, as thick as snowflakes in a storm, and they drifted along with the breeze, and fluttered down at your feet occasionally or lit on your nose, with as much unconcern as if they had been part of the elements.

Cornsilk, young wheat kernels, and the stems of cotton were the locusts' first target. When these were consumed they would eat almost anything—tree bark, canvas, hoe handles—even each other. One farmer with an unquenchable sense of humor remarked that the hoppers had eaten everything he had "but the mortgage." In 1875 Governor Hardin set aside the third day of June as a day "for humble and devout prayer, and to otherwise observe the day as one for fasting and prayer" to seek divine intervention in halting the plague. In short order a series of rains arrived and the harvest of 1874 was saved. Since Missouri's northern neighbor was not so fortunate, one of Hardin's critics charged that the governor had "prayed the grasshoppers clear out of Missouri and up into Iowa." The following three years the locusts returned to Missouri inflicting tremendous damage and increasing the woes of the beleaguered farmers before the plague ended in 1877.

The election of Francis M. Cockrell to replace Carl Schurz as a Missouri senator in Washington occurred in 1875, during Hardin's administration. Cockrell, like Thomas Hart Benton, served his state in Congress for thirty years.

The Greenback Party, so named because of the members' opposition to Republican withdrawal of Civil War greenbacks from circulation, appeared in Missouri in 1876. The distribution of the Civil War greenbacks had produced great inflation, with accompanying higher prices for farmers. The recalling of the greenbacks from circulation caused deflation and a drop in prices for farm commodities. The lower farm income resulting from the combination of deflation and overproduction by farmers during this period evoked great complaints from the rural areas of the West. The Greenback Party prescribed the immediate printing of more paper money as the cure for the nation's economic ills. The Greenbackers were outspoken in their hatred of gold and silver money and in their praise of paper. With fervor they sang their hymn:

> Thou, Greenback, 'tis of thee,
> Fair money of the free,
>   Of thee we sing.
> And through all coming time
> Great bards in every clime
> Will sing with joyful rhyme,
>   Gold is not king.

In 1876 there were three slates of candidates in Missouri; the Greenback Party, the Republican Party, and the Democratic Party all contended for state offices. Once more, Missourians elected a Democratic governor. John S. Phelps of Springfield, a man of intelligence and long experience, had served as a military leader in the Union army. During his four years as governor of

John Smith Phelps (left), a native of Connecticut, moved to Springfield, Missouri, after having been admitted to the bar at twenty-one years of age. He led Phelps' Regiment for the Union at Pea Ridge and served as military governor of Arkansas for a time during the Civil War. In 1865, Phelps won the acquittal of "Wild Bill" Hickok who had shot a professional gambler on the Springfield square. Attorney Phelps acted as governor from 1877 to 1881.
(Courtesy State Historical Society)

Johnson-countian Francis M. Cockrell (right) formed a law partnership with Thomas T. Crittenden after his release from a Union prisoner of war camp in April, 1865. In 1874 he succeeded Carl Schurz in the United States Senate, where he served for thirty years.
(Courtesy State Historical Society)

Attorney Thomas Theodore Crittenden (left) fought with the Union army as a lieutenant colonel during the Civil War, but he chose former confederate Brigadier General Francis Cockrell as his law partner in Warrensburg when peace was declared. Crittenden served as governor from 1881 to 1885 and as consul general in Mexico from 1893 to 1897.
(Courtesy State Historical Society)

Missouri he was able to continue the reduction of the state debt and to secure greater appropriations for education.

In 1880 the Democratic Party in Missouri chalked up another victory when Thomas T. Crittenden of Warrensburg was chosen governor. During Crittenden's term as chief executive he achieved national fame by his campaign to rid Missouri of outlaws. While he is best known for his defeat of the James brothers, also brought to justice during his administration were the Meyers gang in New Madrid County, the Mason gang in Adair County, and the Lewis gang in Jasper County.

Some of the desperate marauders who made Missouri notorious for sixteen years following the Civil War had ridden with the wild guerrillas during wartime and had been untamed by peace. Fourteen spectacular bank robberies, a daring holdup at the Kansas City fair, and a series of train robberies terrorized Missourians and frustrated law officers. The cold-blooded murder of the conductor and an escaping passenger during a train ambush near Winston in 1881 was the final outrage which led to the end of the criminal careers of the James boys. Governor Crittenden, after securing promises of up to $50,000 from several railroads to be used as reward money, published, in July, 1881, a proclamation offering $5,000 as a reward for the arrest and conviction of those outlaws who had been responsible for the train robberies and, in particular:

> for the arrest and delivery of said Frank James and Jesse W. James and each or either of them, to the sheriff of said Daviess County, I hereby offer a reward of Five Thousand Dollars ($5,000.00), and for the conviction of either of the parties last aforesaid of participation in either of the murders or robberies above mentioned, I hereby offer a further reward of Five Thousand Dollars. . . .

In 1882 the bait of the reward money drew Charles and Robert Ford, members of the James gang, into negotiations with Clay County officials to arrange the capture of Jesse James. Robert Ford, during a call on Jesse James, who was living in St. Joseph under the assumed name of Thomas Howard, shot his former comrade in the back. This bit of treachery inspired the well-known lines:

> Jesse James was a lad that killed many a man,
> He robbed the Danville train,
> But the dirty little coward that killed Mr. Howard,
> Has laid poor Jesse in his grave.

The Ford brothers, who surrendered to law enforcement officers, were convicted of first degree murder, but were immediately pardoned by the governor. Although Governor Crittenden's strategy was indisputably successful in ending the reign of terror, he was criticized both in the state and the nation for his obvious collusion with criminals. After Frank James, accompanied by Major J. N. Edwards, dramatically walked into Governor Crittenden's office to surrender himself on October 5, 1882, the governor withdrew the reward offer. The total cost of apprehending the outlaw bands was approximately $20,000, but since the governor never revealed the recipients of the rewards, the full story of the negotiations leading to the destruction of the James gang is not known.

Governor Crittenden was unsuccessful in securing authorization for the construction of a branch prison to relieve the overcrowded conditions at the Jefferson City penitentiary, but the governor was successful, as his predecessor had been, in further reducing the Missouri state debt during his term of office.

In the election of 1884 the Republicans and Greenbacks in Missouri cooperated in the creation of the Fusion ticket by which they agreed to support each other's candidates. In view of the fact that the national Republican Party was inclined toward monetary policies in direct conflict with Greenback desires, this fusion is most remarkable. However, even so remarkable a merger failed to conquer the Democratic Party. St. Louis Democrat John S. Marmaduke, son of M. M. Marmaduke who served as governor of Missouri in 1844, was elected the chief executive of the state. Since John S. Marmaduke was a veteran of Confederate service, his election to the governor's post led to some grumbling within the Democratic Party. From the Civil War until 1884 there appears to have been an unwritten agreement among Missouri Democrats that major positions should be divided between both Union and Confederate veterans. Although with the election of Marmaduke some Democrats felt that the pro-Union faction was being slighted, the difficulty within the party was not sufficiently severe to cause serious trouble.

Governor Marmaduke repeated his predecessor's plea for a branch prison, but the request for enlarged penal facilities was refused once more. However, the legislature increased state support of education, so that one-third of state revenue was appropriated for public schools. During this period there was con-

John S. Marmaduke (right), son of former Governor M. M. Marmaduke, a general in Sterling Price's Confederate army, became active in politics after the close of the war. He was elected governor in 1884 and died in office in 1887.

(Courtesy State Historical Society)

David Rowland Francis distinguished career as mayor of St. Louis won for him the governorship of Missouri in 1889. In 1916 President Wilson appointed Francis the ambassador to Russia, in which capacity he served during the turbulent years of World War I and the Russian revolution. On one occasion he held off a bolshevik mob at gunpoint on the steps of the American embassy.

(Courtesy State Historical Society)

Meredith Miles Marmaduke (right) was governor of Missouri for nine months after Thomas Reynold's death in February of 1844. His brief term proved him to be a wise and efficient administrator. At the time of the Civil War Marmaduke remained loyal to the Union although two of his sons served in the Confederate Army.

(Strauss portrait, Courtesy State Historical Society)

siderable interest in prohibition, and the temperance movement was gaining strength. In 1887, the legislature passed a local option law which authorized any county or city of over 2,500 population to call an election to determine whether intoxicating beverages could be sold within their boundaries. Following the passage of this local option law in 1887 there were many county elections throughout the state, and by 1889 fifty of Missouri's counties were dry.

After Governor Marmaduke died in office in 1887, the term was completed by Lieutenant-Governor Albert P. Morehouse of Maryville.

In 1888 four parties campaigned for state offices—the Democratic Party, the Republican Party, the Prohibition Party, and a new organization of farmers and union members called the Union Labor Party. David R. Francis, who had come to the attention of Missouri voters for his work as mayor of St. Louis, was the capable, effective man nominated by the Democratic Party and elected by the people. Governor Francis, a loyal friend of the University of Missouri, successfully exerted a great effort to provide funds for university endowment. After the old major academic building on the campus was destroyed by fire in 1892, the Governor immediately proceeded to Columbia to arrange for temporary housing and the continuance of classes. When a special session of the legislature was called in 1892 to provide money for the rebuilding of the university, the legislators considered relocating the school. Attractive offers were received from several cities. There was considerable sentiment in the legislature for moving the university to Sedalia, but ultimately Columbia was selected after the people of Boone County offered $50,000 to assist in the rebuilding of the main structure.

The many changes in textbooks from year to year in the public schools of Missouri had evoked much criticism. Therefore, in 1891 a state commission was established to select texts and to negotiate the price of the books. Governor Francis proudly noted that the commission had saved the citizens of Missouri approximately sixty-one per cent of the former costs of textbooks.

Another innovation favored by the governor was the adoption of the Australian, or secret, ballot. Prior to this time, because voting had been conducted openly, a voter could not maintain secrecy. During his term as mayor of St. Louis, Francis had been able to save money for the city, at the same time that he extended city services. As governor, Francis upheld his enviable record as a financial manager when, despite a lowering of state taxes during his administration, the state debt was reduced to $6,680,000 by the end of his term.

In summary, for Missouri Confederate soldiers and their sympathizers the years immediately following the Civil War were difficult ones. Most Confederates returned home and attempted to resume life where they had left it before the great conflict. Rebels often found the Unionist citizens of their home communities cool, and sometimes hostile, toward them. They had forfeited their right to vote by fighting for the South. A few, like Sterling Price, Jo Shelby, and John N. Edwards, gallantly galloped off to Mexico to offer their services to troubled Maximilian. Jo Shelby became a freighter of supplies in Mexico, Sterling Price acquired a plantation near Vera Cruz, and newspaperman John Edwards started a paper called the *Mexico Times*. But Mexico wasn't Missouri, Maximilian was overthrown, and all three were home by 1867.

During the five years immediately following Appomattox, when Confederates and their cohorts could not legally vote, the Republicans held sway in Missouri. Although the Unionist and Republican administrations in Missouri were in most respects honest, efficient, and forward looking, they were responsible for harsh treatment of Confederates and Confederate sympathizers and engendered much ill will and criticism among former Confederates and fair-minded citizens of Unionist sympathies as well. The removal of voting restrictions in 1870 was secured with the help of Liberal Republicans. The rebels, who were largely Democrats, came "crawling out of the brush" in the elections of the 1870's and Missouri became Democratic again. Times changed. In 1893 Jo Shelby was a federal marshal for the western district of Missouri—upholding the Constitution of the United States. Once in control, the Democratic majority continued to dominate Missouri politics until the end of the century.

BIBLIOGRAPHY

Barclay, Thomas S. "Test Oath for the Clergy in Missouri," *Missouri Historical Review*, Vol. XVIII (April, 1924), pp. 345-381.

Barclay, Thomas S. "The Liberal Republican Movement in Missouri," *Missouri Historical Review*, Vol. XXI (October, 1926), pp. 59-108.

Botsford, J. S. "Administration of Missouri Governors: Governor Joseph W. McClurg," *Missouri Historical Review*, Vol. VI (July, 1912), pp. 182-191.

Grissom, Daniel M. "Personal Recollections of Distinguished Missourians—B. Gratz Brown," *Missouri Historical Review,* Vol. XIX (April, 1925), pp. 423-426.

Guese, Lucius E. "St. Louis and the Great Whisky Ring," *Missouri Historical Review,* Vol. XXXVI (April, 1942), pp. 160-183.

Kirschten, Ernest. *Catfish and Crystal.* Garden City, New York: Doubleday and Company, Inc., 1960.

Loeb, Isidor. "Constitutions and Constitutional Conventions in Missouri," *Missouri Historical Review,* Vol. XVI (January, 1922), pp. 189-246.

McDougal, H. C. "A Decade of Missouri Politics 1860-1870—from a Republican Viewpoint," *Missouri Historical Review,* Vol. III (January, 1909), pp. 126-153.

Magnuson, Warren G. "Pharaoh Had It Easy," *American Heritage,* Vol. XI (October, 1960), pp. 39-41, 79-81.

March, David D. "Charles D. Drake and the Constitutional Convention of 1865," *Missouri Historical Review,* Vol. XLVII (January, 1953), pp. 110-123.

March, David D. "The Campaign for the Ratification of the Constitution of 1865," *Missouri Historical Review,* Vol. XLVII (April, 1953), pp. 223-232.

Peterson, Norma L. "The Political Fluctuations of B. Gratz Brown: Politics in a Border State," *Missouri Historical Review,* Vol. LI (October, 1956), pp. 22-30.

Randall, J. G. and David Donald. *The Civil War and Reconstruction.* Boston: D. C. Heath and Company, 1961.

"Selections from the Autobiography of Governor T. T. Crittenden," *Missouri Historical Review,* Vol. XXVI (October, 1931; January, April, 1932), pp. 3-11, 142-152, 241-255.

Shoemaker, Floyd C. *Missouri and Missourians.* Vols. I and II. Chicago: The Lewis Publishing Company, 1943.

Shoemaker, Floyd C. "Some Colorful Lawyers in the History of Missouri 1804-1904," *Missouri Historical Review,* Vol. LIII (April, 1959), pp. 227-237.

Stevens, Walter B. "The Political Turmoil of 1874 in Missouri," *Missouri Historical Review,* Vol. XXXI (October, 1936), pp. 3-9.

Switzler, William F. "Constitutional Conventions of Missouri 1865-1875," *Missouri Historical Review,* Vol. I (January, 1907), pp. 109-120.

Thomas, Raymond D. "A Study in Missouri Politics 1840-1870," *Missouri Historical Review,* Vol. XXI (January, April, July, 1927), pp. 166-184, 438-454, 570-580.

Thompson, Cyrus. "Reminiscences of Official Life in Jefferson City 1865-1875," *Missouri Historical Review,* Vol. XXIII (July, 1929), pp. 550-567.

Violette, Eugene Morrow. *A History of Missouri.* Cape Girardeau, Missouri: Ramfre Press, 1951 ed.

Zornow, William. "Missouri Radicals and the Election of 1864," *Missouri Historical Review,* Vol. XLV (July, 1951), pp. 354-370.

CHAPTER XIII

Economic Growth, 1860-1910

I shot a deer—put a bullet thro' his brain—
And gutted him and et him where now it's Sixth and Main . . .
—"Recollections of Kansas City"
by C. L. Edson

Some cities such as Joplin and Kansas City went through a dramatic growth in the late nineteenth century. Joplin did not exist at the end of the Civil War; by 1900 it was the fourth largest city in Missouri with a population of over 26,000. The boom at Kansas City was even more remarkable. In 1860 only 4,418 Missourians inhabited the little river town; by 1910 Kansas City was second only to St. Louis with a population of 248,381 citizens. Latter-day poet, C. L. Edson, has captured in his verse the speed of transition at Kansas City as the people exchanged riverboats for railroads, pack trains for packing houses, and fur traders for flour millers. There were only a few years, relatively speaking, between the blood lust of Quantrill and the luxury of Quality Hill. The first train arrived in Kansas City in 1865. In 1900 the eyes of the nation were focused upon this Missouri river city as William Jennings Bryan was renominated for president at the Democratic National Convention there. Kansas City never. had an adolescence—it sprang almost directly from infancy to adulthood. Although Kansas City is not typical of the development in all parts of the state, it does demonstrate the amazing economic growth of the times.

Population and Industry

After the war, the return of those who had fled the troubled state during the conflict and a new influx of northerners and foreign immigrants stimulated the economy and boosted population statistics. In 1860 Missouri ranked eighth in the Union in

(Dacus and Buell, A Tour of St. Louis. . . . 1878)

Newly-arrived emigrants (shown here at Union Depot, St. Louis) were sometimes exploited by salesmen or tricksters.

population; by 1870 it had climbed to fifth place. Although her sister states were experiencing a similar growth, Missouri held her place as the fifth most populous state until 1910 when she dropped to seventh.

Year	Total Population	Pct. Increase Over Previous Census
1860	1,182,012	73.3
1870	1,721,295	45.6
1880	2,168,380	26.0
1890	2,679,185	23.6
1900	3,106,665	16.0
1910	3,293,335	6.0

During this time of expansion, the black population was increasing only slightly. Since the number of white citizens was growing much more rapidly, there was a decrease of the percentage of blacks in the population of the state. In 1860 ten per cent of Missouri's population was black; in 1910 that percentage had dropped to 4.8. It should be noted that the population of the Ozark area, which had attracted few settlers before the Civil War, also increased rapidly during the postwar period. The most sparsely populated region of the state until the end of the century was the southeast section.

Despite the spurt of population growth in Missouri at the end of the Civil War, the increase in number of inhabitants never again equaled the prewar boom. The population grew steadily in the last half of the nineteenth century, but at a constantly diminishing speed.

With the development of railroads and the expansion of the West, it was to be expected that some Missourians would leave the state to settle elsewhere. We have noted earlier the large numbers of Missourians who were among the first settlers in such territories as Texas, Oregon, and California. The migration of Missourians continued. Despite this exodus, up to the year 1900 Missouri gained more settlers each year than she lost. To illustrate the mobility of her native-born, in 1860 only one out of six persons born in Missouri lived outside the state; in 1910 one of three native Missourians had left their home state. Migrant Missourians were known for their loyalty to their native state. Like many Texan emigrants in our own time who praise the Lone Star State but choose to live elsewhere, Missourians were a source of comment in the West for their devotion to Missouri. From California comes the following nostalgic verse sung in the nineteenth century by homesick Missouri emigrants:

> Pike, O! Pike, it is my name,
> Missourer is my nation,
> Pike County is my dwelling-place,
> And Pike is my salvation!

As the following statistics indicate, the cities of Missouri also experienced a rapid expansion in population immediately following the Civil War:

	1860	*1870*
St. Louis	160,773	310,864
Kansas City	4,418	32,260
St. Joseph	8,932	19,565

St. Louis almost doubled in population during the decade; Kansas City experienced a dramatic population increase of over

(Photo (1940) by Pohl, Missouri State Highway Department)

Watkin's Woolen Mill, erected by Waltus L. Watkins in northeast Clay County in 1861, remained in operation until the 1880s.

sevenfold. The number of the inhabitants of St. Joseph more than doubled from 1860 to 1870.

The period from 1860 to 1910 brought a constant flow of foreign immigrants into the state. Although in actual numbers there was an increase of European immigrants in this period, because that increase was not nearly so large as the general expansion in population the foreign-born constituted a smaller percentage of the population at the end of the period than at the beginning. The European-born in Missouri constituted fourteen per cent of the population in 1860; by the year 1910 they comprised only seven per cent.

Immigrants from Germany still composed the largest group of foreign-born at the end of the period. New citizens from Ireland and Great Britain formed a sizable segment of the immigrant population, which was further swelled after the turn of the century by Russian and Italian arrivals.

St. Louis remained the chief industrial and commercial center of the state. In addition to the industries established earlier, such as those concerned with the manufacturing of lead, iron, and leather products, and the brewing of beer, the city surged ahead in several new areas. For example, it became an important center for the manufacture of chemicals, medicines, and even streetcars. By the year 1890, the latter industry alone employed 3,000 workers. Another new postwar industry was created with the establishment of the first shoe plant in 1872. Twenty-five years later St. Louis had twenty-six shoe factories providing jobs for 5,500 workers. Paving bricks, sewer pipe, and white lead were also important products of St. Louis plants in this period. Missouri was the chief manufacturer of tobacco products in the Union in 1890, and most of the tobacco processing plants were located in St. Louis. In those years before the cigarette was popular, many Americans chewed tobacco. In the manufacturing plant, tobacco was mixed with honey or licorice, and sugar, spices, and rum. The St. Louis manufacturers produced products of such appealing trade names as Sweet Buy and Buy, My Wife's Hat, Revenge, and Wiggletail Twist.

Kansas City's population decreased during the Civil War, but a great influx of new citizens in the first five years after the conflict raised her to the rank of second city in the state. Her location near the confluence of the Kansas and Missouri rivers made Kansas City a natural supply depot for the West. Even before the war, the wagonmakers, saddlers, and blacksmiths of the city had been kept busy by the demand for their products from westbound immigrants. However, the industry which did more than any other to stimulate the growth of Kansas City was meat packing. Kansas City was well situated to serve as a slaughtering point for animals brought from Texas or from the ranches of the Great Plains region. In 1866 a bridge had been constructed across the Kansas River and three years later a railroad bridge was built across the Missouri providing the city with direct rail connections to Chicago and the western United States. By 1877 seven railroads operated through Kansas City.

The high meat prices of the late 1860's provided a strong incentive for enterprising Texans to round up the longhorn cattle available in west Texas and drive them north to a railhead for shipment to packing houses. In 1868 the Texas cattle were driven via the Chisholm Trail to Abilene, Kansas, from where they were shipped to Kansas City by railroad. In the year 1867 only slightly over 4,000 cattle were slaughtered; in 1870, one year before the building of the first stockyards, the Kansas City packers processed 21,000 cattle and 36,000 hogs. The Texas

(From Joseph G. McCoy, Historic Sketches of the Cattle Trade, 1874)

"Dressing Beeves—Plankinton and Armour, Kansas City, Missouri"

longhorn was an animal which originally had been raised for cowhide rather than table beef. The animal was lank and stringy on the plains of west Texas, and after it had been driven all the way to Kansas its meat certainly could not be considered prime. Although packers recognized that longhorn beef was not satisfactory fresh, they soon learned that it was excellent for canning. As late as 1879 Plankinton and Armour, the leading meat packer of the city, was still processing Texas longhorns. In 1880 the introduction of refrigerator cars greatly stimulated the development of the packing industry. New slaughterhouses were built by such companies as Morris and Butt (later Wilson and Company), Kingan and Company (Cudahy), and Swift. In the year 1900 the packers of Kansas City processed 4,555,950 head of livestock.

Flour milling developed in Kansas City in the 1870's. The first elevator was built in 1871, and mills were constructed shortly thereafter. Since the plains of Kansas were ideal for the production of wheat, Kansas City was well located for processing the wheat and for shipping the flour. The wheat industry was much improved when in 1874 the Mennonite immigrants into Kansas brought from Russia a hardy, hard winter wheat. Although the development of milling techniques to accommodate this new, harder wheat required several years, the time was well spent, for flour from the Russian wheat was soon preferred over that from the conventional grain.

Poet C. L. Edson graphically describes the economic background of Kansas City:

> Ships made Carthage, gold made Nome,
> Grain made Babylon, the wars built Rome,
> Hogs made Chicago with their dying squeal,
> Up popped Pittsburgh at the birth of steel;
> Come, Kansas City, make your story brief:
> "Here stands a city built o' bread and beef."

St. Joseph went through a period of expansion similar to that experienced by Kansas City at the end of the Civil War. Like Kansas City, St. Joseph was an outfitting center for western travelers; it too became the site of packing houses. In 1866 when drovers from Texas attempted to drive some 260,000 longhorn cattle through southwest Missouri to the railhead at Sedalia, they were deterred by irate farmers, and redirected north through Kansas to the railroad center of St. Joseph A bridge was constructed across the Missouri River at St. Joseph in 1873.

"View of West Kansas City, Looking from the Upper Town. . . ." Compare this view of Kansas City in 1881 with the 1852 scene pictured on page 339.
(From Frank Leslie's Illustrated Newspaper, June 4, 1881)

Stockyards were built in 1887, but were not a financial success until 1895 when Gustavus Swift purchased the yards and established a major packing house there. An indication of the growth of the stockyards can be seen in the following statistics. In 1896, 36,893 livestock were slaughtered in St. Joseph; in 1898 the total reached 225,984. By 1900, 397,967 animals were butchered at the St. Joseph stockyards. Both Kansas City and St. Joseph served as important slaughtering centers for the entire nation during the late nineteenth century.

The smaller cities of Missouri also grew during the period, and frequently established industries similar to those in the larger metropolitan areas. For example, most cities in Missouri had mills for the production of flour, and many had slaughterhouses of their own. Hannibal on the Mississippi was noteworthy for the manufacture of boats and of tobacco products. The economy of Springfield was stimulated by the arrival of the Atlantic and Pacific Railroad in 1870. In addition to supplying the usual frontier-town services, Springfield produced cotton and woolen goods and manufactured wagons and carriages for the population of southwest Missouri during the last half of the century.

Washington, Missouri, was the site of two of Missouri's most distinctive industries. Franz Schwartzer of Austria established

Stafford and Pringle Carriage and Wagon Manufacturers established in 1869 on the corner of Clay and Washington in Chillicothe, Missouri

(Courtesy State Historical Society)

A skilled craftsman making
zither at Washington, Missouri The manufacture of
zithers at Washington was
discontinued in the 1950's.
(Courtesy State Historical Society)

a zither factory in 1866. Six years later Henry Tibbe began to
produce and market the corn cob pipes—still manufactured in
Washington today—which have been dubbed picturesquely "Missouri meerschaums."

Mining towns of the West were famous throughout the
nation for their phenomenal growth and their sensational rowdi-
ness. Sam Clemens of Hannibal need not have traveled to Virginia
City to view this bit of Americana firsthand, for in the 1870's he
might have "roughed it" with the lead miners of Missouri in the
southwest corner of the state. In August of 1870, E. R. Moffett
and J. B. Sergeant discovered a rich vein of lead while prospect-
ing near Joplin Creek. News of the discovery drew scores of
prospectors eager to stake claims and exploit the ore in the
area. Some were successful and gave their mines such colorful
names as "Once More," "Bonehead," "Blue Goose," "Navy Bean,"
"Never Sweat," and "Quick Seven."

The settlement established at Joplin, which served as a supply center for the miners, was incorporated as a city of 4,000
people by the year 1873. The following year, the miners were
excavating approximately 200 tons of lead each week and the
proprietors of the American House Hotel proudly exhibited a
4,000 pound chunk of pure galena. It is remarkable with what
speed the new community was able to establish itself. By late
1875 Joplin had constructed educational facilities to meet the

(From Nathan H. Parker, Missouri As It Is in 1867)

"Interior View of Blow and Kennett's Lead Furnace, Granby, Missouri"

needs of her 1,620 school children. Within two years of incorporation, Joplin had twelve dry goods and clothing stores, twelve blacksmith shops, five hotels, sixteen physicians, sixteen lawyers, two banks, and seventy-five saloons. Later dubbed the Klondike of Missouri, Joplin was a rip-roaring mining town. In 1876 the proprietor of Blackwell's Bar arranged to provide for his patrons outdoor entertainment in keeping with the character of the community. In the apparent absence of a humane society, Blackwell brought a cinnamon bear from Arkansas to pit against six blooded bulldogs. In a scene reminiscent of the Roman arena 1200 settlers and miners gathered to witness the mortal contest, which was won by the bear. Television westerns probably would have seemed tame to the citizens of nineteenth-century Joplin.

In this period when a steel web of railroads was being woven across the face of the nation, there was a great demand for railroad ties. Missouri oak, sassafras, sycamore, and hickory trees were chopped into ties at camps along the Niangua and Osage rivers. The tie industry provided work for hundreds of Missourians; each camp employed from 300 to 500 men. The ties were floated down the Niangua and the Osage to Bagnell where they were loaded onto railroad cars. Each tie "hacker" was reported to have cut forty to fifty ties per day; companies sometimes floated as many as 4,500 ties downriver in one great solid stream of timber.

Although there is evidence that blacksmiths in the St. Louis region were using coal as early as 1809, commercial exploitation of Missouri's coal deposits did not begin until 1840 when 10,000 tons were mined. By 1850 the annual yield of mines had increased tenfold. In the second half of the century, the yearly production of coal averaged 1,000,000 tons, and until 1874 Missouri was the first coal producer west of the Mississippi. Soon after the turn of the century, the annual Missouri output exceeded 3,500,000 tons. Expansion of coal mining was, no doubt, influenced by the growth of steamboat lines and railroads, both of which converted from wood to coal in the late 1850's and 1860's. General Jo Shelby operated a coal mine near Clarksburg in the 1870's, but abandoned the enterprise when the price per ton dropped to an unprofitable level.

Although bricks had been manufactured and used in Missouri since the building of the John Price residence in Ste. Genevieve shortly after 1800, the structural brick industry did not reach its peak until the last decade of the nineteenth century. Seventy-six metropolitan brick yards produced bricks worth $683,775 in 1860. In 1890, the peak year, almost $3,000,000 in bricks were being manufactured in 277 establishments. By 1900,

A Tie Raft below the Mill Dam, Camden County, circa 1906. Ties were lashed together to form a raft, then floated downstream to a shipping point.
(Courtesy State Historical Society)

(Courtesy State Historical Society)

Using horsepower in mining coal from a pit near the Gravois road in 1856

the number of brickyards had decreased to 256, and the output had shrunk to a little over $1,600,000. The bricks were made by the "soft-mud" process using hand molding until molding machines were introduced in the 1880's, at which time the large yards converted to machines.

Commercial quarrying of building stone began at Carthage in 1880 and contributed to the growth of the city. The abundant uniformly gray, coarsely crystalline limestone is easily quarried and has been used to construct many impressive buildings across the country, including the state capitol building at Jefferson City. Carthage stone, which is used as marble when it is highly polished, is said to be the only true gray "marble" available in the United States.

The iron industry continued to have a strong effect upon the Missouri economy until 1900. James B. Eads of St. Louis used Missouri iron in the armored gunboats which he built for the Union during the Civil War. The Ashebrans furnace near Ironton and the Maramec Iron Works, which had expanded operations between 1857 and 1875, were important iron manufacturing centers, although the latter was forced to close later due to financial difficulties. By the end of a half century of iron production, for miles around the iron works thousands of acres of Missouri forests had been cut twice over and burned for charcoal to fire the furnaces. When the shortage of readily accessible charcoal became acute, many furnaces were dismantled and moved closer to St. Louis where coal and coke could be obtained as a substitute. Because the firing of furnaces with coal and coke introduced impurities, the move was not a successful one, and iron production declined in Missouri at the end of the century.

The expanding industries of the state, which required an increased labor supply, were served by the rapidly growing population of the cities. In the late nineteenth century a growing number of these industrial workers organized themselves into unions to help secure their goals of higher wages, shorter hours, and better working conditions.

The Palmyra *Spectator* of February 27, 1890 reported the following instance of labor difficulties:

> Seventy-five girls employed in the overall factory of Tootle, Hosea and Co., at St. Joseph, recently struck for higher wages. They were receiving 55 cents and 80 cents per dozen for two grades of over-alls and demanded 65 and 90 cents. After a two hour consultation their demand was complied with and they resumed work.

Not all labor problems in Missouri were so easily resolved. The history of organized labor and its attempts to secure its aims is a long tale of struggle and violence.

In the year 1866 there were at least five labor unions in the St. Louis area. The painters, molders, the ship carpenters and caulkers were organized, and a General Workers Union was also in existence. Eight years later there are records of organizations of bricklayers, masons, plasterers, mechanics, and blacksmiths. During the 1880's some 5,000 laboring men in the St. Louis area were members of the Knights of Labor. The American Federation of Labor granted a charter to the St. Louis Central Trades and Labor Union in 1887, and four years later the Missouri State Federation of Labor was organized at a Kansas City meeting.

The major show of strength by organized labor during this period occurred in the year 1877. Railroad workers in the East had gone on strike after a wage reduction. The walkout quickly spread to all parts of the country, and a Working Men's Party was organized in St. Louis to give sympathy and support to those railroad employees in the area who desired to strike. In a mass meeting the workers adopted a resolution which declared: "we will stand by them in their most righteous struggle against robbery and oppression." Encouraged by this support, the railroad workers in St. Louis and East St. Louis halted the movement of freight into St. Louis. The unions were well led during the strike of 1877. The labor leaders insisted that there be no destruction of property, and they arranged the patrolling of saloons by workers to prevent trouble from inebriated strikers.

When, in a show of strength, delegations of workers marched through the city requesting other laboring men to cease their toil, a large number of the working people of St. Louis responded. Both Mayor Overstolz and Governor Phelps were disturbed at the effectiveness of the strike and fearful that the mass assemblies of laboring men might result in property destruction or physical violence. In an attempt to crush the strike, the mayor raided union headquarters and jailed the union leaders. Although the walkout finally ended after a week of demonstrations with little gain for the workers, organized labor had demonstrated its strength to the people of Missouri.

The St. Louis streetcar workers' strike of 1900 was a tragic episode in the annals of management-labor relations. Mayor Ziegenhein failed to offer any leadership in the mediation of the difficulty. Strikebreakers were recruited and armed by the company, and in the ensuing battles between strikers and company thugs, fifteen men were killed.

During the administration of Governor Francis, the Missouri Labor Commissioner informed the legislature that mining companies in the state were paying their employees with pasteboard checks which could not be cashed for five to ten years, but could be redeemed in merchandise from the store owned by the companies. Under this system, the employees were forced to purchase the necessities of life from the company store, which often exploited the situation by charging exorbitant prices. The state legislature in 1891 corrected this injustice by passing a law making this exploitation illegal and requiring companies to pay their men in checks which were immediately redeemable in cash.

After the establishment of the Missouri Bureau of Labor Statistics in 1879, the state legislature gradually began to pass more laws protecting the working man. In particular, in the 1890-1910 period, laws were passed to regulate child labor, to protect a worker's right to join a union, and to set an eight-hour day for men in mining, smelting, and public works.

In retrospect, industry grew rapidly and became strong in

"Back Home, April 1865," a mural by Tom Lea in the Pleasant Hill Post Office

the late nineteenth century; organized labor was not so successful. The railroad walkout of 1877 gained little for the strikers; the bloody St. Louis streetcar strike of 1900 was lost by the union. Even public opinion was often anti-union. Cases of injustice and exploitation, however, were being brought to the attention of the lawmakers of the state, and legislation beneficial to labor was passed in the decades preceding and following the turn of the century.

Agriculture

The Civil War had a devastating effect on Missouri agriculture—particularly in the southern half of the state where fighting was more frequent and in the western tier of counties south of Jackson County which had been put to the torch after the issuance of Order Number Eleven. The marauding of armies, the plundering and arson of bushwhackers, and the desertion of homesteads by civilian refugees or army-bound farmers all hampered Missouri agriculture. Farm buildings, machinery, crops, orchards, and livestock were stolen or destroyed. On many of the farms which were spared destruction, neglect and rampant weeds cancelled out years of hard labor. However, once the war was over, with new determination and enthusiasm Missourians dedicated themselves to the rebuilding of a flourishing agriculture. There were some changes. Hemp and tobacco, both of which had been dependent upon slave labor, were no longer important crops. However, the increased use of machines made hand labor less important for the production of crops such as corn, wheat, and oats.

During the nineteenth century the rural population of Missouri continued its steady climb until it reached its peak in 1900, when approximately 2,000,000 people were considered rural by the United States Census Bureau. At the same time, since the farm population was not growing so rapidly as the urban population, the per cent of the total population engaging in agriculture decreased regularly. In 1880, 74.8 per cent of Missouri's population was rural according to Census Bureau statistics; and in 1910 the percentage of rural population had dropped to 57.5. As one would anticipate, with a growing farm population more and more of Missouri's land was placed in cultivation during the latter half of the century. In 1860, 45.4 per cent of Missouri's total land was in use, and thirty years later 70 per cent was under cultivation. This increasing utilization of Missouri's land resources can be seen also in the statistics of the number of individual farms. During 1860 there were 92,792 farms in Missouri; by 1890 the Census Bureau reported 238,043 individual farms in the state.

The postwar Missouri farmers, struggling to regain wartime losses and to re-establish their farms, were in no mood to endure harassment from Texas cattlemen. The high cattle prices after the Civil War had motivated many Texas cowboys to round up the unclaimed herds of longhorns roaming west Texas and drive them to shipping points for sale in the East. In 1866 an attempt was made to move great herds numbering about 260,000 from Texas to the nearest railhead, which happened to be at Sedalia, Missouri.

The farmers of southwest Missouri opposed the drovers, not only because they wished to preserve the grass for their own livestock, but also because they feared a recurrence among their cattle of Texas fever which had followed an earlier drive in the 1850's. The introduction of a disease-carrying tick into Missouri had resulted in 1858 in a loss of $100,000 worth of stock in Vernon County alone. Thus, when the new Texas herds appeared, the farmers took the law into their own hands, stampeding, stealing, or shooting the longhorns. After capturing the drovers, the irate farmers either forced them into Indian territory or, in several instances, lynched them. This reception deterred the cattle drivers, who sought new routes—such as the Chisholm

(Joseph G. McCoy, Historic Sketches of the Cattle Trade, 1874)
"Armed Mobs Beat Texas Drovers"

Trail—to new railheads or slaughtering points. The publicity concerning these acts of violence did nothing to enhance the already questionable reputation Missourians had gained nationally during the border warfare with Kansas and the guerrilla activities of the Civil War.

The most striking development in agriculture after the Civil War was the increased use of new machinery. Although improved plows, disk harrows, reapers, and straddle-row cultivators were available before the war, the many new machines—new sulky plows with wheels and a seat for the driver, corn planters, end gate seeders, spring tooth rakes, binders, threshing machines, hay balers, hoisting forks, and corn shellers—made farming much more productive. In the period before the Civil War some Missouri farmers had transformed their agricultural operation from one of self-sufficiency to one of producing for the market. After the Civil War, the increased yields resulting from the use of machines and improved techniques, the rapidly developing systems of transportation, and the resultant breakdown of isolation all encouraged production for the market.

When, however, the farmer produced for market and departed from the old, more diversified type of agriculture, he was more susceptible to harm from a low market price. The several depressions during the first half of the century affected the Mis-

The Maple Grove Poultry Yards at Fayette, circa 1902

Steam Plow in Chariton County, circa 1902

Loading Hay, circa 1903

Stacking Hay with a horse-powered pulley, circa 1903

Horse-drawn McCormick Reaper, circa 1904
(Courtesy State Historical Society)

Strawberry Picking in Missouri, circa 1904
(Courtesy State Historical Society)

souri farmers much less seriously than did the later panics, since
the prewar farmers, who produced almost all of their food and
much of their clothing and home furnishings, did not purchase
many consumer goods. After the Civil War, however, when the
farmer needed the products of industry, he was much more vulnerable to the price cycle. Thus, during this time the farmers
formed various new organizations to attempt to solve their financial problems.

Corn continued as the chief crop in Missouri throughout the
period. In the post-Civil War years there was a greatly enlarged
production of corn in the western counties beginning with Bates
and extending to the north border of the state. At the same time
that this crop was more frequently planted in the western area
of the state, the production of wheat and oats was increased in
the eastern part of north Missouri. Before the war, cotton was
produced mainly to provide housewives with fiber for home-
woven textiles. After the Civil War, commercial production of
cotton was stimulated by the reclamation of the bootheel area
after the turn of the century. In 1880 Missouri produced approximately 20,000 bales of cotton. By 1910 this production
reached nearly 60,000 bales.

A dramatic development occurred in southeast Missouri
early in the twentieth century. In 1905 an ingenious lumber company representative named Otto Kochtitzky suggested that an
attempt be made to drain the marshy regions of southeast Missouri. The area was low and had been heavily overgrown by
forests. Much of the land was owned by lumber companies who,
after cutting the trees, found themselves left with uninhabitable
swampland. Since the companies were anxious to utilize the
area, Kochtitzky was able to secure backing for his plan. In 1905
the legislature authorized the establishment of an organization
under the engineering leadership of Kochtitzky to survey and
plan the drainage of the region.

Out of this authorization the Little River Drainage District
was founded to build ditches and levees in the region. In order
to secure proper drainage it was necessary to excavate a canal
to divert the Little River into the Mississippi. At the same time,
levees were created to retain the flood waters of the Mississippi
and St. Francis rivers. Next, ditches were dug at mile intervals
through the low areas, and drainage barriers were constructed
to hold the runoff. The $13,000,000 cost was met by collecting an

Otto Kochtitzky
(From Otto Kochtitzky, The Story of a Busy Life; Courtesy Mary Kochtitzky)

acreage assessment of from four to forty dollars. The original area of 550,000 acres was so successful agriculturally that the plan was adopted in other sections of the bootheel region. The new, highly fertile agricultural area which was reclaimed by these drainage programs and made available to southeast Missouri farmers has contributed greatly to the wealth of the state.

The United States Congress in 1862 passed the Morrill Act

Digging Drainage Ditch Number One, Little River District, Southeast Missouri. Notice the workman standing atop the ninety foot boom (arrow).
(From Otto Kochtitzky, The Story of a Busy Life; Courtesy Mary Kochtitzky)

which granted certain federal lands to the states to finance the development of agricultural and mechanical education. Because of the turmoil of the Civil War, Missouri did not respond immediately to the offer; however, in 1867 Missouri finally selected some 244,000 acres of land in southern Missouri for this purpose. Under the terms of the grant the land could not be sold for less than $1.25 an acre. Since other blocks of land were available at lower prices, it was difficult to dispose of the federal acreage. For example, the Springfield *Express* for June 3, 1881, advertised 25,000 acres of land in Oregon County for only fifty cents per acre.

Undaunted by the difficulties encountered in the sale of the federal grant, the state legislature in 1870 established the College of Agriculture at Columbia. Despite grand plans and legislative enthusiasm, the agriculture department was slow to develop; as late as 1888 there were only seven students in agriculture. Criticism of the ineffectiveness of the program at the University of Missouri led to a reorganization of the department. The introduction of new leadership and the opening of the first agricultural experiment station in 1888 was a great stimulus to scientific farming in the state. By the year 1908 the enrollment in the agriculture department at Columbia had climbed to 446 students.

Scientific farming methods were encouraged by other or-

Drainage canals near Kennett, Missouri
(Courtesy Massie-Missouri Commerce)

(Courtesy State Historical Society)

John Husmann's vineyard at Hermann, circa 1900 Notice the heavily-laden vines in the foreground.

ganizations such as the Grange, the Agricultural Wheel, and the Farmers' Alliance, which disseminated information concerning new agricultural techniques. In addition, the fairs of the state encouraged the improvement of agriculture and animal husbandry by offering prizes for the best crops and animals. As early as 1853 a fair was held at Boonville which drew agricultural entries from many central Missouri counties. The State Agricultural Society sponsored fairs in Boonville in 1854 and 1855, and St. Louis held annual agricultural fairs from 1866 to 1904. The present state fair at Sedalia was not initiated until the year 1901.

In addition to an increase in the production of the leading crops in Missouri—corn, wheat, and oats—there was new interest after the Civil War in dairying, poultry production, and fruit growing. The Ozark Highlands were not properly suited to the intensive production of corn and wheat, but they were excellent for grazing and for the culture of certain fruits, particularly apples and grapes. Swiss immigrant Hermann Jaeger settled in Newton County where in 1867 he produced a new hardy grape by crossing Virginia grapes with the wild Ozark variety. Jaeger developed a large vineyard near Neosho with his hybrid, which proved very successful. Some years later, when Jaeger learned that a grape louse was inflicting great damage in the vineyards of France, he suggested the adoption of cuttings from the wild Ozark grapes to give more resistance to the French vines. When his suggestion was favorably received, Jaeger sent seventeen carloads of grape cuttings to France. Jaeger's plan, which was a great success, won for the Missouri grape grower the cross of the French Legion of Honor for his service to French agriculture.

Livestock breeding in Missouri also expanded rapidly during the late nineteenth century. The number of cattle in the state tripled between 1860 and 1890, while the swine and mule population doubled. Throughout this time Missouri was famous both in America and in Europe as a source of mules. Missouri was also a well-known producer of saddle horses in the nineteenth century. During the late 1800's the area around Mexico, Missouri, was known as one of the saddle horse centers of the world. Missourian Tom Bass, who was born as a slave in 1859, became world-famous as a horse trainer and was recognized for his unusual training abilities at the World's Fair in Chicago in 1893.

Missouri mules at the 1903 fair

(Courtesy State Historical Society)

(Photo by George Ford Morris, Courtesy State Historical Society)

Tom Bass up on Belle Beach

The Bass stable, which attracted to Mexico a host of dignitaries including three presidents, turned out many prize-winning horses. But the one Tom Bass loved best was Belle Beach, acclaimed in her day as the world's champion saddle mare. Probably the best known horse in Missouri history was named Rex McDonald. The handsome ebony stallion, who sold for $6,000 when he was eight years old, "defeated every horse ever shown against him," and at the St. Louis Fair in 1903 was given the title of the champion saddle horse of America.

Several individuals should be recognized for their contribution to the development of Missouri agriculture. From 1865 to 1911 Norman J. Colman, editor of *Colman's Rural World* and later first United States secretary of agriculture, promoted adoption of crop rotation and other scientific agricultural techniques through the distribution of his journal. Colman is reputed to have written the Hatch Act of 1887, which was introduced into Congress by William Henry Hatch of Hannibal and authorized the establishment of agricultural experiment stations in each state.

The introduction of agriculture as an elementary and secondary school subject in Missouri around 1900 also had a great impact in circulating the latest agricultural methods. Two other services to farmers were initiated toward the end of the century. Weekly crop bulletins were issued beginning in 1889. Free delivery of rural mail, first attempted in Randolph County in 1896, soon spread to the other parts of the state.

In spite of experiment stations, innovations in technique and machinery, better seed, and greater accessibility to markets, farming still was a difficult and often unrewarding occupation. The droughts and the depressions of the last half of the nineteenth century produced great trials for farmers. During the mid-1890's, corn sold for as little as twenty cents a bushel, wheat forty-three cents a bushel, and oats eighteen cents a bushel. Many farmers who held mortgages signed when wheat brought $1.50 a bushel lost their land during the 1870's and the 1890's.

The farmer of the late nineteenth century often felt victimized by the railroads upon which he depended for the transportation of his goods. The rail lines charged special low rates to long-distance, large-volume shippers, and sometimes offered rebates to customers who transported a specified tonnage within a certain length of time. The individual farmer, who shipped relatively small volumes of freight comparatively short distances, did not share in these favorable terms. In some instances the railroads refused to print their rates, which were subject to change without notice, and charged some farmers more than others. Often the commission houses, which sold the farmer's grain or livestock for a percentage of the selling price, charged exorbitant rates. Thus, the farmer felt that he was at the mercy of either the commercial carrier or the middleman, and he sought redress of his grievances through legislation. The farmers of this period were continually sponsoring laws to supervise railroads and other monopolies.

A new woe for the farmers came in the 1870's in the form of invasions of Rocky Mountain locusts, or grasshoppers, which descended on the state in frightful numbers. After the wells had been covered to keep the water from contamination, little else could be done to preserve possessions and crops from the plague. The burning of damp haystacks to deter the insects by smoke

Norman J. Colman, Publisher of Colman's Rural World.
(Courtesy State Historical Society)

proved futile. An assortment of ingenious locust-exterminating machines failed to decrease substantially the insect hordes. In their despair, Missouri farmers even considered squashing the grasshoppers to produce grasshopper oil, or possibly preparing them for human consumption. Luckily, the locust invasions stopped after 1877, sparing the Missouri farmers the addition of grasshoppers to their diet. The locusts were followed in the western counties of Missouri—particularly Jackson—by an invasion of rats which destroyed much of the crops.

Despite the depredation of war, despite plagues of low prices, locusts, rats, and Texas trespassers, and despite exploitation by some commercial carriers and middlemen, the Missouri farmer still utilized the resources of the state to build a flourishing agriculture. But he did this with the aid of new techniques and machines, new experimental and educational facilities, and interested journalists and legislators.

Bland and Money Reform

Farmers are often stereotyped as tradition-bound conservatives, slower than their city cousins to adopt innovations or suggest changes. Actually, the most radical political and economic proposals in the last half of the nineteenth century were made by farm organizations or parties. Farmer-dominated groups advocated government ownership of the railroads, and the telegraph and telephone systems. They also supported the graduated income tax and adoption of the secret ballot. The most persistent radical demand of the farmers of this period was for the creation of inflation through manipulation of the money system.

Both gold and silver coins had been minted before the Civil War. According to an economic theory known as Gresham's law, when two mediums of exchange are in circulation, the more valuable medium will be hoarded while the less valuable medium will be used in commercial transactions. Due to a fluctuation in the price of metals in the 1850's, silver dollars contained more than one hundred cents' worth of silver, so people saved the silver dollars or melted them and sold the metal. When they wished to buy something, they used gold coins. This hoarding took most silver coin out of circulation.

Inflation is caused by a sudden increase of money in circulation or a great expansion of credit. In 1862 the Federal Government, in order to finance the Civil War, issued $450,000,000 in paper money. These "greenbacks", as the currency was called, were not redeemable in gold or silver and were based solely upon the credit of the United States Government. The introduction of this large sum of money combined with wartime economic expansion produced inflation.

Prices generally are influenced by two factors, the amount of money in circulation and the total goods and services available. During the war, the large number of greenbacks in circulation combined with a wartime shortage of goods and services pushed prices up. During periods of inflation farmers usually prosper and debtors are able more easily to repay debts incurred in normal times or periods of deflation.

After the war, the Federal Government decided to withdraw the greenbacks from circulation gradually. This constriction of the money supply combined with a postwar boost in production forced prices down sharply. Both farmers and debtors suffered from this deflation and many were unable to meet their obligations.

Those who were hurt by deflation strongly opposed the withdrawal of greenbacks and advocated the issuance of additional paper money. The members of the Greenback Party of the 1870's, who favored inflation and were greatly concerned over the gradual withdrawal of paper money, made this the most important

William Henry Hatch, during his seven terms as a congress-man from Missouri, sponsored over 50 acts beneficial to American agricultural interests.
(Courtesy State Historical Society)

issue in their attempts to secure political power in the 1870's. In 1878, although Congress did authorize a halt in the withdrawal of greenbacks from circulation, the government refused to resume the printing of additional greenbacks.

Since their plan for the wide distribution of greenbacks was thwarted, the advocates of inflation turned next to the "free silver" scheme. Gold had been used for many years at an approximate equivalence with silver of 1 to 15 or 1 to 16. This means that fifteen or sixteen times as much silver by weight was required to equal a given value of gold. When the commercial value of gold fell just before the Civil War, silver dollars had passed out of circulation because they were more valuable than gold dollars. In the last half of the century, the discovery of new silver mines in the West forced the price of silver down rapidly. Because of this fluctuation in the value of precious metals and the subsequent hoarding of the more valuable coins, many government leaders in Europe and America believed that a single standard of money was preferable; that is, only one metal should be used in a monetary system. In 1873, silver was dropped by the United States as a monetary standard.

The silver miners, incensed by the removal of silver as a standard and distressed by the lowering of the price of the metal, were able to convince certain political leaders from the Midwest that the "free and unlimited coinage of silver at the ratio of 16 to 1" would provide both inflation and higher prices. Thus, the miners would receive more money for their silver and the farmers would command higher prices for their crops. Among those who came to advocate the free coinage of silver was a congressman from Lebanon, Missouri, named Richard P. Bland.

Congressman Bland was elected to Congress for his first of twelve terms in 1872. Bland, who had worked in Nevada during the 1850's before returning to Missouri after the Civil War, was well acquainted with silver mining. His outspoken leadership of the free silver movement earned for him the nickname "Silver Dick." In 1877 he proposed an act authorizing the free and unlimited coinage of silver at 16 to 1. The act, finally known as the Bland-Allison Act of 1878, was passed over President Hayes' veto; but since it was amended before passage to authorize the secretary of the treasury to purchase only $2,000,000 to $4,000,-000 worth of silver each month, Bland did not secure the "unlimited coinage of silver" he wished.

The free silver issue was popular among Missourians. All Missouri's representatives in Congress voted for the passage of the Bland-Allison Act, and even Missouri's four Republican congressmen voted to override the veto of Republican President Hayes. However, in spite of the expectation of Bland and others that the passage of the law would give assistance to Missouri debtors, it did not in fact do so. Since the secretary of the treasury declared that the Federal Government would redeem silver dollars in gold, the silver dollars traveled at the same value as the gold dollars, and there was, in effect, one standard. The amendment limiting the amount of silver to be purchased each month prevented inflation, and the Republican administration was able to continue its sound money policies in spite of the intentions of Congress.

Congressman Bland of Lebanon continued for nearly a quarter of a century as a leading spokesman for the free silver movement. When the depression of the 1890's developed, Bland and his money ideas became more popular. In fact, he was considered one of the leading candidates for the Democratic nomination for the presidency in 1896, and on the first three ballots he received more votes than any other candidate. Eloquent William Jennings Bryan, however, was able to stampede the convention with his famed "'Cross of Gold" speech, and Bland withdrew on the fifth ballot. Free silver ceased to be a national issue after 1900.

A nineteenth-century campaign ribbon worn by a supporter of Richard P. Bland and free silver
(Courtesy State Historical Society)

Transportation

By the turn of the century, the steamboat had relinquished her throne as the queen of transportation in Missouri. Regal steamers still glided up and down the Mississippi and Missouri rivers, but the locomotive wore the crown as king of transport. Railroads could operate through the winter when the steamboats were imprisoned by river ice. Trains could travel faster and were easier to keep on schedule than the temperamental river queens, and they did not so frequently threaten passengers with the danger of fiery disaster. Locomotives did not require highly paid pilots to guide them—it was far easier to run a train down two iron rails than to navigate the unpredictable Missouri.

As the railroads stretched back and forth across the state binding it together with cords of commerce, those river towns which were not served by railroads went into a decline; once-flourishing river ports such as LaGrange, Glasgow, and Lexington no longer were thriving centers of commerce. Since they had become railroad terminals, St. Louis and Kansas City continued their steady growth. New towns, such as Moberly and Sedalia, sprouted along the right of way, encouraged by the opportunities for commerce afforded by the railroads. Because of construction difficulties encountered in hill country, there were fewer railroads serving the Ozark Highlands.

(From the Collection of the Boatmen's National Bank of St. Louis)

Although the steamboat lost first place as transporter of Missouri's goods, the levees of the rivertowns continued to be busy late into the century. The Jennie Howell is pictured above loaded with 2456 bales of cotton in January, 1873.

In his poem "Where the West Begins," Kansas City poet C. L. Edson has captured this transportation transition:

> Little Kansas City, when its bones were green as
>   gristle,
> Swapped its catfish seaport for a locomotive
>   whistle. . . .
> The River was the sponsor for those towns upon
>   the shore,
> The River was their wet nurse but it suckles them
>   no more;
> Their landings all have languished where the weeds
>   and willows wave,
> Their dream of catfish commerce is a legend in the
>   grave,
> And the river towns are dust upon the Kansas City
>   pave.
> The Iron Mare is mother of the epoch here begun—
> And the city, Kansas City, is the railroad's son.

Railroad mileage in Missouri more than doubled during the 60's and 70's and increased by fifty per cent in the 1880's. The rate of railroad expansion in Missouri can be seen in the following chart listing the miles of railroad track in Missouri in the designated years.

Year	Miles
1852	5
1860	817
1870	2000
1880	4007
1890	6126
1900	6887
1910	9019

The depression-plagued 1890's brought a temporary lull in building; however, after 1900 another spurt of railroad construction added over 2100 miles of track.

In a time when the railroads promised to provide those channels of communication so important to the development of each section of the state, it was natural for citizens to desire rail connections for their communities. Because railroad construction was expensive, railroad promoters went to the counties, cities, and townships in an attempt to secure financial support. The units of local government, eager for connections, were often led to promise large sums of money in order to secure railroad services. Since so large a sum of state money had been lost in the building of the first railroads, the Constitution of 1865 forbade the state government to provide public funds for railroad expansion. The county, city, and township governments, which were not restricted by this law, gave $17,000,000 to railroad

"The St. Louis Levee in 1870's" by O. E. Berninghaus
(Courtesy August A. Busch, Jr.)

FIRST TRAIN ARRIVING AT TIPTON 1858

This mural by W. Herbert Duncan in the state capitol depicts the arrival of the first Missouri Pacific train at Tipton in 1858.

companies during the years 1866 to 1873. In some instances, county courts provided large sums of money for these projects without securing public approval by election.

Such illegal debts caused community troubles when the railroads failed to construct lines as they had promised or when depressions occurred—such as that beginning in 1873—so that the local governments could not meet their bond obligations. The courts of Missouri, during the last quarter of the nineteenth century and the first third of the twentieth century, heard many cases involving claims against railroads and cities for breach of contract or nonpayment of obligations.

One example of this was the attempt to build the Missouri and Mississippi Railway from Glasgow on the Missouri River in Howard County through Chariton, Macon, Knox, and Clark counties to the northeastern corner of the state. The four latter counties and Chariton township in Howard County issued bonds to a total of $934,600, which were then given to the railroad company. The road was begun in 1869, but work was at a standstill in 1873. Although the railroad was never completed, the citizens of the counties went on paying taxes for decades in order to redeem the bonds which had been issued. In a similar railroad case, the residents of St. Clair County, which issued bonds during this period, were obliged to continue payments until 1938.

One of the most unfortunate episodes in the history of these locally-sponsored railroads occurred in Cass County in 1872. After several railroad companies had secured large grants of money from the county governments, the citizens discovered that the bonds were being handled suspiciously. Three county officials—a judge, a circuit attorney, and a Harrisonville councilman—were indicted for the misuse of large sums of public funds. To escape the fury of the citizenry, the officials boarded a train for Kansas City. A mob of forty to fifty irate citizens halted the train at Gunn City, dragged the fleeing men from the cars, and lynched them. Later attempts to indict the mob leaders failed, and no one was ever convicted of the crime.

One can never doubt that the railroads were economically valuable to the growing state. Railroads increased the price of land wherever they were built. By offering cheaper, faster transportation of goods and passengers, they encouraged the development of industries and the growth of cities. Unfortunately the railroads, misusing their power and importance, were sometimes guilty of discrimination and exploitation. While few people have denied the importance of railroads in the late nineteenth century,

A nineteenth-century Hannibal and St. Joseph train in the Grand River Valley

(Courtesy State Historical Society)

many have condemned the railroads for their tactics and their policies.

The most frequent complaints against the railroads stemmed from activities such as discriminating between customers in fixing rates, bribing of public officials, price cutting to secure a monopoly and then profiteering once the monopoly was effective, and violating promises made to towns and communities. The plea for government regulation of the railroads was the chief cry of the Grange during the 1870's; farm groups and others dependent upon railroads continued to demand legislative action throughout the rest of the century.

Although the constitution which Missouri adopted in 1875 provided for the passage of regulatory legislation dealing with railroads, Governor Crittenden believed that the railroads had been unjustly abused and should not be subject to any new restrictive legislation. However, Governor John Marmaduke, who disagreed with his predecessor, prodded the legislature into adopting a new set of railroad regulations in 1887. These laws made illegal disproportionate rates for short and long hauls, outlawed rate discrimination, and set up certain regulations for the connecting of railroad lines.

Dramatic developments in the field of communications occurred in Missouri during the latter half of the nineteenth century. William A. Davis, assistant postmaster at St. Joseph, designed the first railway postal car in the world. His plan and design were approved by postal authorities, and the separation, distribution, and bagging of overland mail was initiated on cars of the Hannibal and St. Joseph Railroad in 1862. The system spread over the country and has had an important effect in speeding postal service in the nation.

The telephone appeared in Missouri in the late 1870's to supplement the communications revolution introduced by the telegraph three decades earlier. The Hannibal telephone exchange, which was set up in 1878, has been given the distinction of being the first in Missouri and the second in the world. Later in the same year, a telephone system was installed in St. Louis, and in 1879 an exchange was established in Kansas City. The first trans-Missouri call was made by Kansas City Mayor Jimmie Jones from St. Louis to the office of the Pacific Mutual Telegraph Company in Kansas City on October 12, 1885.

The rivers of Missouri, so instrumental in attracting her

The switchboard of the Columbia Telephone Exchange in March, 1898. The service had about 85 subscribers. Toll connections were available only to Centralia.
(Courtesy State Historical Society)

settlers and later in serving as highways for the transport of their goods, became, with the advent of the railroad, an obstacle in the path of the iron horse. Missouri-born poet T. S. Eliot describes this transition in the role of the river in "The Dry Salvages":

I think that the river
Is a strong brown god . . . sullen, untamed, and intractable.
Patient to some degree, at first recognized as a frontier;
Useful, untrustworthy, as a conveyor of commerce;
Then only a problem confronting the builder of bridges.

In the period before the Civil War, many wooden bridges had been constructed over the smaller rivers of the state, both for railroad trestles and for wagon crossings, but none had straddled the Mississippi or the Missouri rivers. Immediately after the war there was a new interest in bridge building in Missouri. The first bridge to span the Mississippi to Missouri was built at Quincy, Illinois, and was first crossed by trains in 1868. Three years later a railroad bridge was built at Hannibal, and in 1874 the masterpiece of James B. Eads formed a highway across the Mississippi from St. Louis to Illinois. Bridges spanning the Missouri River were built at Kansas City in 1869, at St. Charles in 1871, at Leavenworth in 1872, and at Glasgow in 1879.

(Harper's Weekly, October 7, 1869)

The first bridge across the Missouri River at Kansas City, 1869

The noblest bridge of all is the product of a St. Louis genius, James Buchanan Eads. With no formal training, Eads became one of America's most famous and successful construction engineers of the nineteenth century. At the age of twenty-two he designed a double-hulled boat outfitted with derricks and diving equipment and became a partner in a salvage company. For years Eads himself explored the bed of the Mississippi, Missouri, Ohio, Tennesseee, and Cumberland rivers raising the cargoes and fittings of submerged wrecks.

Prior to the Civil War, Eads joined the group of St. Louis liberals who opposed secession—Blair, Bates, Franz Sigel, and Eads' cousin, B. Gratz Brown. Anxious to serve the Union and convinced of the importance of the rivers in the conduct of the war, Eads signed a contract to construct seven ironclad river gunboats for the federal forces. Employing 4,000 men in shifts around the clock seven days a week, he was able to launch the first armored boat sixty-five days after the signing of the contract. Despite obstacles woven of red tape, interservice rivalry, and governmental inefficiency, the entire fleet was ready for action in a little over three months and served the Union well at

Fort Henry, Fort Donelson, Island No. 10, Vicksburg, and Mobile Bay.

Before the Civil War, the Mississippi had been Eads' livelihood; after the war, the river became a challenge. Eads realized that the continued growth of St. Louis was dependent upon communication and rail connections with the East. The Mississippi, which had been the city's helpmate in the steamboat age, became a threat to her future with the ascendance of the railroads.

The communications problem had been solved with the laying of a telegraph cable across the bed of the river. Eads proposed to solve the transportation problem by building a magnificent bridge across the Mississippi to carry the railroads of the East to his city. The can't-be-doners greeted Eads' proposal with derision. Building a bridge above the confluence of the Mississippi and Missouri was one thing, but spanning the one-third-mile-wide river at St. Louis? Impossible! Fortunately, Governor Hall and the legislature had more imagination and faith than did Eads' critics, and the state government approved his proposal in 1864.

Had he needed only to vault the obstacle of the river, Eads' job would not have been half so difficult. But he was forced first to surmount the opposition of Chicago interests, of northern railroads, of rival river cities, and of steamboat companies. Then the shakedown methods of greedy suppliers added cost and delayed construction. But Eads had a plan and project and all the combined forces of vested interests could not stop him.

The two-level bridge was designed with a lower deck for the flow of railroad cars and an upper level highway for other traffic. Eads planned to construct his bridge of three basic arches, the central arch, a 520 foot span, to be flanked on either side with a 502 foot arch. In order to support the immense structure, it was necessary to build great piers in the river. The largest pier was built of 45,000 tons of granite on bedrock ninety feet below the bed of the river.

To construct these supports, Eads adopted the pneumatic caisson process whereby men worked under pressure far below the surface of the river. Diving was not the advanced science that it is today and caisson disease or "the bends," caused by too rapid a decrease in air pressure on surfacing, resulted in fourteen fatalities and two cases of permanent paralysis. To

James B. Eads

(Engraving by A. H. Ritchie, (Courtesy State Historical Society)

lessen this hazard, Eads reduced the work day to two shifts of forty-five minutes each.

As the bridge neared completion, the Mississippi steamboat interests suddenly became concerned that clearance was only fifty-five feet above water level when the river was high. The smokestacks of some Mississippi steamboats towered as high as 105 feet. The protests of the steamboat interests were heard in meetings held in Washington, D. C., and for a time it appeared that the bridge company would be forced to build, circumventing the main bridge, a canal with its own drawbridge to allow the ships with high funnels to pass. Fortunately, this proposal was allowed to die in a confusion of hearings.

Finally, after seven years of work and an expenditure of $10,000,000, Eads' blueprint was reality. At the opening ceremonies on July 4, 1874, a one-hundred gun salute and a fifteen mile parade added to the festivities which were climaxed by General Sherman's driving the last spike in the presence of President Grant, six governors, and a huge crowd of St. Louis citizens and tourists.

The cheers had barely faded before Eads' fertile mind had fashioned a new project. Steamboats were having difficulty using the mouth of the Mississippi below New Orleans because of the build-up of sandbars on the bed of the river. Undaunted by the scoffing of trained engineers, Eads designed jetties which forced the current to scour the bed, thus deepening and widening the channel.

New York University has honored James B. Eads by including him in the Hall of Fame of great Americans. His most appropriate monument, however, is the beautiful bridge still spanning the Mississippi at St. Louis.

In their enthusiasm for the development of railroads, Missourians did little in the last half of the nineteenth century to improve their roads. Although stumps had been removed, bridges built, and some roads had been graveled during the post-Civil War years, as late as the year 1910 ninety-five per cent of Missouri's highways were still dirt. The state-authorized toll roads, improved and maintained by individuals who would then collect a fee from those who traveled the road, were still in use as late as 1925.

Missourians were not motivated to develop their roads until the advent of the automobile. The first car in Missouri created a sensation in 1891. By 1903 a state registration system had been set up and a nine mile an hour speed limit had been established. In 1904 many handsome "horseless carriages" were on display at the World's Fair in St. Louis. It is difficult to state accurately

The Eads Bridge as it appears in Frank Nuderscher's mural in the state capitol

(Massie-Missouri Commerce)

the number of cars in use in Missouri during the early years of the century, but by 1911 the state registration of automobiles totaled 16,387. The number of car owners multiplied amazingly in the next few years, and the automobile users were the loudest advocates of good roads.

During the last half of the century a new frontier was opened when men of imagination and daring began to take to the skies. A number of these pioneers were Missourians. We have already mentioned the remarkable balloon flight of Pike County scientist John Wise from St. Louis to New York state in 1859. Wise, "America's leading mid-Victorian aeronaut," after thirty years of planning, proposed a transatlantic balloon flight for 1873. The vehicle for this fantastic trip was a huge whaleboat attached to a balloon of 400,000 cubic foot capacity. Just before the ascent, Wise, because of a disagreement with his backers, was replaced by another pilot. The "transatlantic flight" ended in Connecticut, forty-one miles from New York. Captain Wise was drowned six years later when his balloon fell into Lake Michigan.

Major Albert Bond Lambert, a balloonist and enthusiastic supporter of air flight, helped found the St. Louis Aero Club which did much to interest Missouri in the new frontier of the skies. In 1907 the first "Great American Air Meet" was held in St. Louis under the sponsorship of the Club. Dirigibles were first raced in America at the Aero Club Meet in St. Louis in 1908. In 1910, the first international aviation meet was held at Kinloch Park between Ferguson and Florissant. Ex-President Theodore Roosevelt took his first plane ride at this meet, and a French pilot named Le Blanc set a new record by flying his machine at the incredible speed of sixty miles an hour.

In the period from 1860 to 1910, Missouri's population continued its steady climb upward, but at a speed much reduced from the precipitous ascent prior to the war. Although the population of Missouri's rural areas was growing it increased at a slower rate than that of her booming cities. Her agriculture, maturing from slave labor to a mechanized industry and from self-sufficiency to market production, was utilizing more of her land resources. The clang, clatter, chug, and boom of the machine age could be heard in her rapidly expanding cities laced together by silver ribbons of railroad track.

(Courtesy State Historical Society)

Few Missourians owned "horseless carriages" before 1910. A two horse-power fringe-topped surrey suited these young Cass Countians in 1903.

Missouri's children had ridden and bridged her rivers. Drawn by smoking iron horses, they had raced across her plains. Then at the dawn of a new century, an awed and proud Missouri saw her more daring sons explore the possibility of a highway in the sky.

BIBLIOGRAPHY

Beebe, Lucius and Charles Clegg. *Hear the Train Blow.* New York: Grosset and Dunlap, 1952.

Billington, Ray Allen. *Westward Expansion: a History of the American Frontier.* New York: The Macmillan Company, 1949.

Bratton, Sam T. "Coal in Missouri," *Missouri Historical Review,* Vol. XXII (January, 1928), pp. 150-156.

Clevenger, Homer. "Railroads in Missouri Politics 1875-1887," *Missouri Historical Review,* Vol. XLIII (April, 1949), pp. 220-236.

Clevenger, Homer. "The Farmers' Alliance in Missouri," *Missouri Historical Review,* Vol. XXXIX (October, 1944), pp. 24-44.

Cole, Lela. "Early Tie Industry Along the Niangua River," *Missouri Historical Review,* Vol. XLVIII (April, 1954), pp. 264-272.

Cozzens, Arthur B. "The Iron Industry in Missouri," *Missouri Historical Review,* Vol. XXXV (July, 1940), pp. 509-538; Vol. XXXVI (October, 1941), pp. 48-60.

An early twentieth-century telephone
(Courtesy Southwestern Bell Telephone Company)

Donnelly, Phil M. "Rural Free Delivery Service in Missouri," *Missouri Historical Review,* Vol. XXXV (October, 1940), pp. 72-80.

Dorsey, Florence. *Road to the Sea: the Story of James B. Eads and the Mississippi River.* New York: Rinehart and Company, 1947.

Drury, John. *Midwest Heritage.* New York: A. A. Wyn, Inc., 1948.

Ellis, Roy. *A Civic History of Kansas City, Missouri.* Springfield, Missouri: By author, 1930.

Fitzsimmons, Margaret Louise. "Missouri Railroads During the Civil War and Reconstruction," *Missouri Historical Review,* Vol. XXXV (January, 1941), pp. 188-206.

Gates, Paul W. "Railroads of Missouri 1850-1870," *Missouri Historical Review,* Vol. XXVI (January, 1932), pp. 126-141.

Gibson, A. M. "Lead Mining in Southwest Missouri After 1865," *Missouri Historical Review,* Vol. LIII (July, 1959), pp. 315-328.

Hutcheson, Virginia Sue. "Cattle Drives in Missouri," *Missouri Historical Review,* Vol. XXXVII (April, 1942), pp. 286-296.

Jones, John J. "The Morrill Lands of the University of Missouri," *Missouri Historical Review,* Vol. LI (January, 1957), pp. 126-138.

Jordan, Samuel M. "Farming as It Used To Be and as It Is in Missouri," *Missouri Historical Review,* Vol. XXII (October, 1927), pp. 13-29.

Kirschten, Ernest. *Catfish and Crystal.* Garden City, New York: Doubleday and Company, 1960.

Lanterman, Alice. "The Development of Kansas City as a Grain and Milling Center," *Missouri Historical Review,* Vol. XLII (October, 1947), pp. 20-23.

Leach, J. A. "Public Opinion and the Inflation Movement in Missouri 1875-1879," *Missouri Historical Review,* Vol. XXIV (April, July, 1930), pp. 379-413; 568-585; Vol. XXV (October, 1930), pp. 116-146.

Meriwether, Lee. "Labor and Industry in Missouri During the Last Century," *Missouri Historical Review,* Vol. XV (October, 1920), pp. 163-175.

Missouri, a Guide to the "Show Me" State. New York: Duell, Sloan and Pearce, 1941.

Mumford, F. B. "William H. Hatch," *Missouri Historical Review,* Vol. XVIII (July, 1924), pp. 503-506.

Popplewell, Frank S. "St. Joseph, Missouri, as a Center of the Cattle Trade," *Missouri Historical Review,* Vol. XXXII (July, 1938), pp. 443-457.

Renner, G. K. "The Kansas City Meat Packing Industry Before 1900," *Missouri Historical Review,* Vol. LV (October, 1960), pp. 18-29.

Riegel, R. E. "The Missouri Pacific," *Missouri Historical Review,* Vol. XVIII (October, 1923; January, 1924), pp. 3-26, 173-196.

Roberts, Clarence N. "History of the Structural Brick Industry in Missouri," *Missouri Historical Review,* Vol. XLVII (July, 1953), pp. 318-328.

Shoemaker, Floyd C. *Missouri and Missourians.* Vols. I and II. Chicago: The Lewis Publishing Company, 1943.

Violette, Eugene Morrow. *A History of Missouri.* Cape Girardeau, Missouri: Ramfre Press, 1951 ed.

Violette, Eugene Morrow. "The Missouri and Mississippi Railroad Debt," *Missouri Historical Review,* Vol. XV (April, 1921), pp. 487-518; Vol. XVI (October, 1921), pp. 90-118.

White, Edward J. "A Century of Transportation in Missouri," *Missouri Historical Review,* Vol. XV (October, 1920), pp. 126-162.

White, L. M. "Heart of the Saddle Horse Story of Missouri," *Missouri Historical Review,* Vol. L (January, 1956), pp. 121-131.

Fifty years ago, these telephone linemen drove to work in a mule-drawn service wagon.   *(Courtesy Southwestern Bell Telephone Company)*

CHAPTER XIV

Social Development, 1860-1910

> The arc lights were turned on for the first time Tuesday night, and although they are not yet in good running order, they give a splendid light. . . . Palmyra is surely getting there, and not very slowly either.
>
> —Palmyra *Spectator,*
> December 4, 1890

Once, Missouri had been the isolated Wild West. By 1875 Missouri was a state of growing metropolitan areas and progressive towns and villages, closely tied to the other states of the Union through improved channels of transportation and communication. As the far West developed and proud cities began to line the Pacific shore, Missouri's central location became important. By 1882, Missourians could travel by rail to either coast. Missouri merchandise could serve all parts of the nation, and the citizens and goods of the East could meet those of the West in Missouri. Five national political conventions were held in the state from 1888 to 1904. Although Missourians had played big league baseball as early as 1876, by 1902 St. Louis had one team each in the American and National leagues. In 1904 St. Louis dazzled the world with the Louisiana Purchase Exposition. Missourians, sharing the pride of the citizens of Palmyra, felt that they were moving into the spotlight. Missouri, no longer isolated and provincial, was becoming intimately associated with the main political, economic, and cultural activities of the nation.

Religion

The years of the Civil War were bleak ones for the churches of Missouri. The slavery issue had rent the Baptist, Methodist, and Presbyterian denominations before the outbreak of hostilities. During the years of conflict, many church buildings were

Interior View of the Abbey Church of the Immaculate Conception, Conception, Missouri, circa 1900
(Courtesy State Historical Society)

destroyed, either in military battles or by the vandalism of bush-whackers. Members of the Freedom Association of Baptists in southwest Missouri owned approximately thirty churches in 1860. In 1866 only seventeen of these church buildings remained. At the same time that the war crumbled physical walls, it built up invisible barriers of enmity between former church associates of differing political sympathies. The brutality and chaos of the wartime—so religious leaders of the day testified—contributed to a general lowering of morals. The horror, hate, and violence of warfare not only destroyed much of that which had been accomplished by the churches in a half century of work, but also prevented five years of progress the religious organizations might otherwise have realized.

At the end of the Civil War the constitutional provision that clergymen must take an oath of loyalty caused great concern to men of the cloth. A writer of the time estimated that only fifty of the 450 Baptist ministers in Missouri could take the oath in 1865. At a conference of Southern Methodist clergy in St. Louis in 1865 twenty ministers revealed their intention to take the oath, but fifteen adamantly declared that they would preach without it. Archbishop Kenrick, who firmly opposed the oath, led the Catholic priests of the state in a refusal to conform to the constitutional enactment. At Rolla, Father Gallagher was imprisoned and later released. When Father Cummings of Louisiana also was arrested for refusing to take the oath, Archbishop Kenrick provided $10,000 to appeal his case to the United States Supreme Court, which finally declared the Missouri enactment illegal.

The most striking characteristic of Missouri churches after peace had been established was their steady growth. There was a constant, and in some cases, remarkable enlargement in membership lists and in church facilities in the last quarter of the century. The census bureau has provided a valuable statistical picture of Missouri's denominations in its reports for the years 1890 and 1906. By studying these reports we can learn the relative size and rate of growth of the main church bodies in Missouri.

	1890		1906	
		Per cent of		Per cent of
	Number of	Total Church	Number of	Total Church
	Members	Members in Mo.	Members	Members in Mo.
Baptist	159,371	21.7%	218,353	18.2%
Congregationalist	7,617	1.0%	11,046	.9%
Disciples of Christ	97,773	13.3%	166,137	13.9%
German Evangelical Synod	25,676	3.5%	32,715	2.7%
Lutheran	27,099	3.7%	46,868	3.9%
Methodist	162,514	22.1%	214,004	17.8%
Presbyterian	53,510	7.3%	71,599	6.0%
Protestant Episcopal	8,828	1.2%	13,328	1.1%
Reformed	586	.1%	1,284	.1%
United Brethren	4,361	.6%	3,616	.3%
Other Protestant	16,960	2.3%	23,166	1.9%
Roman Catholic	162,864	22.1%	382,642	31.9%
Latter Day Saints	3,189	.4%	8,042	.7%
All Other Bodies, Including Jewish	5,491	.7%	6,439	.5%

Although the Roman Catholic Church was the largest individual church in the state during the indicated period, the combined Protestant denominations (the first eleven groups in the table) constituted a 76.7 per cent majority in 1890. This majority shrank to 66.9 per cent in the next sixteen years, during which the Roman Catholic Church experienced a dramatic growth. Several factors contributed to this development. The work of the Catholic Church was most effective in the large city, and Missouri was slowly becoming more urban. In addition, the membership of this church was much increased when a large influx of immigrants from the Catholic areas of Europe poured into the state. The Baptists and Disciples of Christ enjoyed the largest increases in membership among the Protestant churches of Missouri from 1890 to 1906.

The Jewish population of Missouri was still relatively small. In 1869 the new Reformed group, *Shaare Emeth,* was organized in St. Louis by some members of the *Emanu-El* and *B'nai B'rith* congregations. The new fellowship established their synagogue at Seventeenth and Pine. By 1890, the 3,018 Jews of Missouri were organized into nine congregations maintaining six houses of worship.

The following statistics show the percentage of total church membership constituted by each of the seven largest churches in the three most populous cities of Missouri in 1906.

	Kansas City	*St. Joseph*	*St. Louis*
Baptist	1.4%	9.8%	3.6%
Disciples of Christ	12.1%	8.4%	1.6%
Lutheran	2.5%	2.5%	5.5%
Methodist	16.2%	16.2%	6.3%
Presbyterian	7.9%	8.0%	3.3%
Protestant Episcopal	3.6%	3.0%	1.8%
Roman Catholic	31.0%	39.5%	69.0%

According to the census from which these statistics were taken, there were twice as many protestants (66.2 per cent) as Catholics (31 per cent) in Kansas City in 1906. Of the church membership of St. Joseph, 56.4 per cent were Protestant and 39.5 per cent Catholic. St. Louis had been a Catholic stronghold from the beginning, and with the entrance of many new immigrants the Catholic membership climbed to 69 per cent of the church-affiliated citizens of St. Louis. Protestants constituted 29.5 per cent of the total St. Louis church membership.

Another aspect of the growth of churches during the late nineteenth and early twentieth centuries in Missouri is the organization by blacks of many new churches—largely Baptist or Methodist.

Since the construction of houses of worship usually did not match the speed with which churches were organized, new congregations often worshipped in homes, in school buildings, or in courthouses for many years before a denominational place of worship was built.

In the years after the Civil War the Sunday school movement gained many supporters in America. This increased popu-

Jewish Synogogue, Kansas City, circa 1900
(Courtesy State Historical Society)

larity may be explained by noting a new approach to Christian conversion and growth. After the war there was less emphasis on the emotional outdoor camp meeting, although these continued until the end of the century and are sometimes held even today. More frequently, protracted meetings were held in a school or church building with less emphasis on extreme emotionalism. When the church could nurture the faith of the next generation through Sunday school work and Bible studies, the sensational and sometimes uncontrollable camp meeting was not so necessary. Sunday schools flourished, and an adult interest in Bible studies is indicated by the fact that in the year 1902 in eleven counties of Missouri there were more students enrolled in the Sabbath schools than there were school-age children in those counties.

A continuing interest of the churches was the establishment of academic schools and colleges. Since the fast-growing public school system provided for the secular elementary education of their children, protestants placed particular emphasis upon the development of colleges. Missouri Catholics were interested not only in church-sponsored institutions of higher education, but also in Catholic schools for younger children.

The February 1, 1851, issue of the diocesan paper *Shepherd of the Valley* expressed the fear that the public school would endanger the faith of its pupils. Thus, the Catholic Church centered its concern and its finances in developing a Catholic school system which would educate and, at the same time, protect the faith of their children.

Evidence of increasing cooperation between the various denominations may be seen in this period. "Union" churches were built to serve several denominations in a number of Missouri towns. In Bates County, Southern Methodists, Missionary Baptists, Cumberland Presbyterians, and Christians constructed a common house of worship in 1866. "The Union Evangelical Church" of Springfield had a membership from several denominations. In 1899, for a union service at the Christian church at Versailles, Episcopal Bishop E. R. Atwill organized a choir from every denomination in the city. From a merger in 1870 of the Old School and the New School Presbyterians came the Missouri Synod with 175 united congregations. Methodists, Baptists, and Presbyterians cooperated in sponsoring special services. Ministerial alliances began to be formed toward the end of the century; the Springfield Ministerial Alliance was founded in 1885 for all pastors of the city without distinction of race or color.

There was controversy as well as cooperation among the churches of Missouri during the postwar years. Debates between speakers of different denominations were popular in many communities. Eldorado Springs was the site of a ten-day debate in 1895 between a Mormon and a minister of the Church of Christ. The enthusiasm with which such debates were attended is intimated in the following notice from a Baptist publication, the *Word and Way,* for October 10, 1908:

> Mr. Roberts is a weak man in debate but fairly represents the hardshell faction of the Campbellite church, and if any of the brethren want to witness a regular Campbellite Waterloo, then come over to Dadeville and see a man with a cold water hope catch it good and plenty.

As has been true of churches through the ages, the religious organizations of Missouri were concerned about the conduct of people during the period. In 1895 a Methodist committee declared: "We have reason to believe that some of our people indulge in practices and amusements . . . positively against the rules of the church." In particular, this Methodist committee in southwest Missouri was disturbed over the frequency with which Methodists engaged in dancing, drinking, swearing, and playing cards. In some churches the guilty ones were removed from the church rolls for failure to abide by established rules of conduct. The *Christian Evangelist* for February 22, 1883, tells of one church where "four brethren and sisters came forward and confessed their sins, promised a better life and were restored to fellowship." An emphasis upon temperance was another characteristic of the Protestant churches in the latter half of the century. Although promotion of temperance was usually spearheaded by Baptist and Methodist leaders, Bishop Hawks of the Protestant Episcopal Church was also influential in the work in Missouri.

The demand that Christians observe certain rules of conduct was not new; however, an interest in world missions was a new concern of Missouri churches in the late nineteenth century. In 1876 two Methodist leaders of Missouri—Eugene Russell Hendrix and Bishop Enoch Mather Marvin—toured China, Japan, India, and Turkey to examine the mission activities and opportunities in the Far East. Contributions were made by major denominations for the establishment and support of Asian missions and for continued work among the American Indians.

The churches also found opportunities for service closer to home. Orphanages were established in St. Louis by the Missouri Baptists in 1882 and by the Disciples of Christ in 1889. A Lutheran hospital was built in St. Louis in 1867. Springfield became a center for church-sponsored hospitals. St. John's hospital was established by the Sisters of Mercy in 1891, Springfield hospital opened in 1905 and was later controlled by the Baptists, and Burge Deaconess Hospital was incorporated in 1906 under the direction of the Women's Home Missionary Society of the Methodist Church.

Toward the end of the century, a new sympathy for the working man and interest in the labor union movement could be seen in certain church publications of the state. An Ozark region journal, the *Western Methodist*, declared in 1907:

> We believe in the principles of trade unions. So far as we can see there was no other way, in our modern industrial organization, for labor to protect itself against the deepest oppression on the part of capital.

The Catholic publications of the day were particularly vocal in support of the establishment of organizations to protect the interests of the working man.

Since congregations were often small and there was a scarcity of clergymen, all churches adopted a policy whereby one clergyman might serve several congregations. Until about 1870 the majority of pastors were serving more than one church. It is also true that among the Baptists and some of the Methodists, ministers often held other jobs during the week. In 1874, of the twenty-five ministers in the Shoal Creek Baptist Association, only one did not have another job besides his church work. In the latter quarter of the century, particularly as the century neared its end, the denominations—including Baptist and Methodist—began to place greater emphasis upon specialized training for their ministers.

The clergy, respected and prominent people in all communities, were invited into parishioners' homes where they were entertained with the best available to the householder. It was considered a privilege to accompany the clergyman for a part of the way to his next place of ministry. In the rural areas and in the small churches sermons were simple but sincere, and the fast-growing congregations around the state witnessed to the effectiveness of the preaching described in the old hymn:

> On listening to his words apart,
> They noted not his homely coat,
> But his appeals from burning heart,
> And not from manuscript or note.

Despite their growth and influence, the churches of Missouri were not without opposition. When Robert G. Ingersoll, America's leading agnostic in the late nineteenth century, toured the country delivering spellbinding lectures on topics such as "Some Mistakes of Moses," he attracted a disciple from Lamar, Missouri, a lawyer named G. H. Walser. In 1881, after he had been criticized in Lamar for his unorthodox beliefs, Walser established the town of Liberal in Barton County as a refuge for freethinkers. Walser advertised his settlement as follows:

> We have neither priest, preacher, justice of the
> peace, or other peace officer, no church, saloon,
> prison, drunkard, loafer, beggar, or person in want,
> nor have we a disreputable character. This cannot
> be truly said of any Christian town on earth.

The Christians of southwest Missouri, scandalized by what they called a "Godless town of Infidelity" in their midst, immedi-

The First Methodist Church of Sikeston, Scott County, Missouri, circa 1900
(Courtesy State Historical Society)

ately sent missionaries to Liberal. These Christians settled next to Liberal and so irritated Walser and his associates that they built a barbed wire fence to keep out the missionaries. The freethinkers invited people from around the world to attend their Liberal Normal School and Business Institute located in a $6,000 structure known as the Universal Mental Liberty Hall and Opera House. Few responded, however, and the school soon failed financially.

Within a decade of the founding of Liberal, the leaders of the town turned to spiritualism, and Walser himself married a medium. However, spiritualism was discredited when a fire developed in a house occupied by a charlatan who regularly held seances. The citizens who rushed into the house to quench the fire found various devices used to deceive patrons by simulating spirits. Both freethinking and spiritualism lost their appeal, and these unorthodox groups gave way to the Protestant churches which moved into the town. Universal Liberty Hall itself was sold to the Methodists for a Sunday school. Neither Civil War nor agnosticism was able to impede the progress of Missouri churches for long.

Education

During the Civil War there was an almost complete disruption of the educational system in Missouri. Only in St. Louis and a few other population centers were school activities continued. Armies found that school buildings were ideal for use as barracks and as hospitals; used in this way, the buildings often deteriorated and were frequently destroyed. The state government, pressed for funds, was forced to discontinue financial support of the schools. Local school taxes were collected by only a few communities during the hostilities. Many teachers left their pupils to enter military service, and the conflict of political sympathies within communities made school operations all the more difficult. Even after the cessation of hostilities, it was not easy to re-establish an educational system. In those communities of strong Confederate sympathies, the antagonism of the residents toward the Radical government often resulted in hostility toward the public school system. Another obstacle in the path to reconstruction of the educational system was the loyalty oath which was required of all teachers and which prohibited persons of Confederate sympathies from teaching school in the state.

Once the first difficult postwar years had passed, the last decades of the nineteenth century brought increasing growth and strength to the public school system of Missouri. In the early days of statehood, political leaders gave enthusiastic verbal support to the concept of universal education, but those same politicians were usually reluctant to authorize increased taxes to finance a public school system. The state officially recognized its responsibility for educating the children of Missouri in 1820, but did not provide tax money until 1853, when one-fourth of the revenue of the state was reserved for public education. In 1887 appropriations for schools were increased to one-third of all general revenue funds.

With such financial encouragement, new school districts and new schools developed rapidly. During the late 1870's an average of 250 school districts were organized each year in Missouri. In the 1880's and 1890's the trend continued at a lower rate with the formation of thirty-five new school districts on an average every year.

The effect of financial support and the establishment of new school districts can be seen in the statistics indicating the percentage of the school-age population in Missouri public schools. In 1860, forty-four per cent of the eligible students in Missouri were pupils in the public schools. This percentage increased to forty-six per cent in 1870, to sixty-five per cent in 1880, and to seventy-six per cent in 1900.

With the renewed interest in schools came a recognition of the need to educate the black children of the state, who were now no longer slaves. In 1866 the state government authorized the establishment of separate schools for blacks in districts where twenty or more school-age black children resided. This segregated school system was to persist in Missouri for nearly a century.

The establishment of high schools was another important development during this period of educational growth. We have mentioned earlier the construction of the first public high school in St. Louis in 1853. In 1864 St. Joseph reopened its high school which had been established earlier, but had been discontinued for a time during the war. The first high school in Kansas City was founded in 1867. Thus these three largest cities of the period were, appropriately, the leaders in the establishment of public high schools. By the year 1890, four-year high schools were operating in thirty towns in Missouri, and more than 100 towns had two-year or three-year high schools. The greatest encouragement of high schools came after the turn of the century when the state legislature authorized the development of consolidated school districts in 1901. By the year 1910 it is estimated that there were approximately 400 schools in Missouri which offered study beyond the elementary level.

The University of Missouri assumed leadership in examining the qualifications of Missouri high schools, and announced in 1890 that twenty-three high schools in the state were accredited. By 1899 there were twenty-seven first class high schools, twenty-eight second class high schools, and sixty-five third class high schools on the approved list. The University continued to act in this capacity until the responsibility for accreditation was passed on to the Department of Education in the year 1903.

Although there were improvements in education during the late nineteenth century, most elementary schools, especially in rural areas and small towns, changed little from the postwar days. The dirt floors were covered with wood and the school

Central High School in Chillicothe, as it appeared in 1883, is typical of city school architecture in the period. The building was razed in 1923.

(Courtesy State Historical Society)

furniture was somewhat improved over that in the schools of the first half of the century. The old benches, which were little more than planks on legs, were replaced with desks and benches with backs. The open fireplaces of the earlier schools were being supplanted by coal or wood-burning iron stoves, but drinking water was still carried into the schoolroom in a bucket and was drunk from a common dipper.

Learning was largely by rote, for few pupils had paper or pencils in the 1860's and 1870's. However, those children with sufficient resources owned slates for use at their desks. Toward the end of the century, small blackboards were hung in each classroom and textbooks were made available to the pupils. Great emphasis was placed upon training in spelling, reading, and ciphering. Spelling matches were not only held in the schools, but were community social events as well. The Louisiana *Journal* on April 23, 1875, reported, "Warrensburg promises a grand spelling match for Johnson County to come off on the 20th of May. The best speller is to get forty acres of land for a prize."

In the years immediately following the Civil War, one could find students of all ages from five to twenty and over in the classrooms. Although twenty years was the maximum age for free attendance of the public schools, veterans past twenty were allowed to return to the schools and attend without tuition a period of time equal to the length of their service in the Union Army.

(Courtesy State Historical Society)

"The Badly Arranged School Room," an illustration from the 47th Report of Public Schools of the State of Missouri, 1897.

Often the strict discipline of the schools was maintained by whipping or knocking heads together. An old Ozark folksong reminisces:

> Still sits the schoolhouse by the road
> Close by the old oak tree,
> Where many a boy has took a dose
> Of grim old hickory tea.

Other teachers used more ingenious punishments to preserve discipline or to encourage mastery of lessons. One teacher in Lawrence County cut letters from newspapers and forced students with spelling difficulties to eat them. Unruly boys were sometimes compelled to don bonnets and sit with the girls.

While the decades after the Civil War were a time of rapid expansion of the public school system, they were also a period of increased concern with standards in education. The Missouri State Teachers Association, which had been organized in 1856, acted as a leader in calling for the raising of educational standards. In 1873 the MSTA requested the legislature to authorize the lengthening of school terms. In 1877 state law was changed to provide that public schools in Missouri must meet for at least five months each year; in 1889 the school year was lengthened to seven months, and in 1909 to eight months. The MSTA was also interested in professional training for teachers. It requested the establishment of normal schools for those desiring to enter the profession, and teachers' institutes for the training of those who were already engaged in teaching. William Lucky of Fayette, the first president of MSTA, and Joseph Baldwin of Kirksville were outspoken educational leaders who called for state support of normal schools.

Baldwin in the year 1867 established North Missouri Normal School at Kirksville as a private teacher-training institution. That same year, 1867, the legislature earmarked money for a department of education at the University of Missouri in Columbia. In 1870 the state legislature acquired Joseph Baldwin's normal school for a state-supported teacher-training institution to serve

A star pupil recites as a fellow classmate weeps on the "dunce box" in this scene from a nineteenth-century classroom. Notice the rough furniture and the bare feet of the pupils.

(*Harper's Weekly, September 12, 1874*)

(Courtesy State Historical Society)

This log school house in Barry County was built ten miles southeast of Cassville in 1894. The teacher and her pupils posed for this photograph in 1914.

north Missouri, and appointed the founder the first president. A normal school for south Missouri was finally located at Warrensburg in 1871, although Sedalia was given careful consideration as a location. In 1873 the state established a third teacher training school at Cape Girardeau to serve the southeast section of the state. After the turn of the century two other state teachers colleges were established—one at Springfield and the other at Maryville, both of which first opened their doors to students in the year 1906. During the latter half of the century, St. Louis continued to operate its own teacher-training school which later became known as Harris Teachers College.

Since most teachers in the field had not yet received specialized training, the state passed a law in 1891 requiring every teacher to attend an institute taught by the county superintendent and consisting of at least two weeks of training in pedagogy. Since many county superintendents of the time were not themselves well qualified, there were many complaints about the ineffectiveness of these county institutes. In 1903 the legislature changed the law to require a three-day conference of teachers before the beginning of each school year.

The last half of the nineteenth century was also a time of growth for the University of Missouri. Before 1867, the University depended upon tuition fees and income from an endowment fund to meet operating expenses. In 1867 the legislature appropriated $10,000 for the president's home and allotted one and three-fourths per cent of the state revenue remaining after the twenty-five per cent grant to the public schools had been deducted. Since Columbia was located in an area where many Confederate sympathizers lived, pro-Union individuals in the legislature were sometimes suspicious of the University during the reconstruction years. This distrust can be read in the loyalty oaths required of the University president, professors, and members of the board of curators by the radical postwar government.

In 1870 the state legislature instituted the College of Agriculture at Columbia and established the School of Mines and Metallurgy at Rolla as a branch of the University. These facili-

A Model Rural School on the campus of the State Normal School, Kirksville, Missouri, 1909

(Courtesy State Historical Society)

Walter Williams was a newspaper editor in Boonville, Columbia, and Jefferson City
before he became Dean of the
Missouri University School of
Journalism in 1908 and President of the University in 1931.
(Courtesy State Historical Society)

ties were to be financed in part by the land grant made to the
states in 1862 under the Morrill Act. When a fire at Columbia
destroyed the main building on the campus in 1892, consideration
was given to moving the school from Columbia; but the decision
was made to rebuild the University on the original site, where it
stands today. The outstanding president of the University of
Missouri during this time was Richard Henry Jesse, who served
from 1891 to 1908. The enrollment increased substantially during
President Jesse's tenure, and greater emphasis was placed upon
the development of teacher training. Walter Williams, editor of
the Columbia *Herald,* was chosen as the first dean of the School
of Journalism when it was founded in 1908.

The establishment of Lincoln University at Jefferson City
is an interesting episode in the history of education in Missouri.
The Sixty-second and the Sixty-fifth regiments of the United
States Colored Infantry, which were stationed in Texas at the
end of the Civil War, were concerned about the need for educational institutions for former slaves. Under the leadership of
Lieutenant R. B. Foster, a white officer, and J. Milton Turner, a
Missouri black of great leadership and speaking abilities, a fund
of $6,000 was collected from the soldiers' discharge pay to estab-
lish a school for blacks. With Lieutenant Foster as the first

president and teacher of the newly organized Lincoln Institute, classes began in the fall of 1866 in Jefferson City. Since the Institute trained black teachers for the public schools of Missouri, the state of Missouri agreed in 1870 to make annual contributions to the school. Finally, in 1879 the Missouri General Assembly assumed control and financial support of the college.

There was a continued growth in the number of private colleges in the state in the last half of the nineteenth century. Drury College was established as a Congregational-related institution in Springfield in 1873. Park College at Parkville was organized in 1875 by a Presbyterian minister and educator, John Armstrong McAfee, with the financial help of George S. Park of the Parkville *Industrial Luminary*. The school was designed to enable needy students to acquire a college education by performing the tasks necessary for the operation of the college. The United Presbyterian Church assumed financial responsibility for Tarkio College in Atchison County in 1885. Three years later Missouri Valley College was founded at Marshall by the Cumberland Pres-

Thomas Hart Benton's mural painted for Lincoln University in Jefferson City
(Courtesy Lincoln University)

byterian Church. Just as in the first half of the nineteenth century, after the war many small colleges were organized, lived for a few years, and then became defunct. These failures of privately sponsored colleges were due to inadequate financial resources and the depression periods in the last half of the century.

The state of Missouri recognized its responsibility for providing help for its citizens afflicted with special problems. We have noted the establishment of the Missouri School for the Deaf and State Hospital Number One for the mentally ill at Fulton prior to the war. The state also acknowledged the importance of the work being done at the privately sponsored Missouri Institute for the Education of the Blind at St. Louis, and granted state funds for the support of the school in 1855. In the last decades of the century the legislature, aware of overcrowded facilities at the state hospital in Fulton, established three more havens for the mentally ill: State Hospital Number Two at St. Joseph opened in 1874, State Hospital Number Three at Nevada in 1885, and cottage-plan Hospital Number Four at Farmington in 1903. A state school for retarded children and for youngsters afflicted with epilepsy began operations at Marshall in 1901. Four years later the Missouri State Sanatorium was opened at Mt. Vernon to provide facilities for victims of pulmonary tuberculosis. For boys and girls who had experienced difficulties in adjusting to society, the state established in 1889 a state training school for boys from ten to sixteen years of age at Boonville and an industrial home for girls from seven to twenty years of age at Chillicothe.

It is obvious from the multitude of educational activities after the war that the citizens of Missouri were now dedicating a greater portion of their resources to education than ever before. This popular support of an institution is always, at least partially, due to the leadership of certain devoted individuals. Dr. William Torrey Harris, superintendent of schools in St. Louis from 1868 to 1880 and later the United States commissioner of education, was nationally known for his important role in the progress of public education. Under his leadership the St. Louis schools adopted the study of natural science as a part of the curriculum, taught a phonetic system of reading, and introduced the kindergarten to Missouri. In this latter development Miss Susan Blow, who offered her services free to the city, should be recognized for

Susan Elizabeth Blow went to Germany to study the teaching methods of Froebel before she established a school in St. Louis to train kindergarten teachers. This portrait of Miss Blow is from a mural by Gari Melchers in the governor's reception room in the state capitol.
(*Courtesy Massie-Missouri Commerce*)

establishing the public school kindergartens in St. Louis. Later her methods and accomplishments in Missouri were studied and imitated in other parts of the United States. James M. Greenwood, superintendent of schools in Kansas City from 1874 to 1914, should also be noted as an outstanding educational leader and an important organizer in the MSTA and in the National Education Association.

The Louisiana Purchase Exposition

Despite the steady growth of her population and the development of a flourishing economy, St. Louis suffered from an inferiority complex at the turn of the century. In 1870 St. Louis was the fourth city in the nation and one rung ahead of Chicago, but in 1880 the announcement that her fast-growing sister city on Lake Michigan had passed her brought great gloom to St. Louis. When plans were started to hold a Columbian Exposition in 1892 to celebrate the 400th anniversary of Christopher's great discovery, St. Louis applied for permission to host the exposition; however, to the dismay of all public-spirited St. Louisans, the fair was assigned to Chicago.

(Courtesy State Historical Society)

One of the many elaborate palaces at the Louisiana Purchase Exposition in 1904

Not to be outdone, St. Louis citizens took the first steps, in 1898, to organize an exposition to commemorate the Louisiana Purchase. The original backers suggested that such an exhibition would stimulate the economic development of the city, as well as provide certain buildings which might later be used by St. Louis institutions. Pierre Chouteau, a direct descendant of Marie Therese Chouteau, the "Mother of St. Louis," was named chairman of the committee of 200 to plan the exposition, and former Governor David R. Francis accepted the position as head of the executive committee. Grand plans were instituted.

The committee determined to make the exposition larger and more elegant than Chicago's earlier production. Twelve hundred and forty acres of Forest Park—an area twice the size of the Chicago fairgrounds—were chosen for the site. The municipal government of St. Louis and the Federal Government each matched the $5,000,000 provided by private citizens of the city to finance the fair; and the states, territories, and possessions of the United States, and the nations of the world were invited to sponsor buildings or exhibits. A favorable response from all of the states except Delaware, and from sixty-two foreign countries gave the exposition a universal flavor, with living specimens of the world's peoples from Pygmies to Patagonians.

The original plans called for a 1903 opening, but construction difficulties forced postponement until 1904. This revised date was quite appropriate since Upper Louisiana—of which St. Louis had been the capital—was not officially transferred to the United States until 1804, the same year in which Lewis and Clark began their expedition. The great fair was officially opened when President Theodore Roosevelt pressed a button in Washington, D. C., on April 3, 1904.

The fairgrounds were adorned with a six-acre rose garden and over 1,200 pieces of statuary. All types of architecture were represented from the skin tent of a Patagonian to a reproduction of the French Trianon at Versailles. Visitors could stroll through the home of a Chinese mandarin, walk the streets of a German village of the Tyrolean Alps, or skim over the fairground lagoons

Fair visitors could stroll through an alpine village in Forest Park at the fabulous fair of 1904.   *(Courtesy State Historical Society)*

in Venetian gondolas. By night, the major buildings were outlined with thousands of electric light bulbs whose reflections joined those of the stars twinkling in the dark waters of the lagoons.

Almost 20,000,000 tourists—country folk and city dwellers alike—an average of 100,000 per day, jammed the streets of the fair, marveling at such wonders as Palaces of Electricity, Education, Transportation, Agriculture, Mines, Machinery, and Manufacturers, a full scale Philippine village, an exotic Japanese garden, priceless art collections, and a colossal floral clock. The curious could gaze at totem poles and the latest railroad locomotives, or hear such speakers as Woodrow Wilson, then the President of Princeton University. Fair visitors were impressed by the wonders of the inventive genius of man. Included in the hundreds of industrial exhibits were such advanced developments as a machine for the home which kept food cold on the hottest days, a stove which cooked with electricity, a gleaming model bathroom complete with oriental rug, and a Swift Rambler automobile of sixteen horsepower selling for $1,350. The latest im-

The miracle of electricity outlined the fair buildings with magic by night.
(Courtesy State Historical Society)

provements in the Victor Talking Machine were lauded by one reporter for having removed "the tinny, mechanical sound noticeable in the earlier and in inferior talking machines." "High fidelity" and "stereophonic sound" were not found in the phonographs or the vocabulary of Missouri in 1904. A guidebook to the exposition prophesied, "It may well turn out that the new age of Electricity—as in a sense superseding steam—will date from this Fair."

To lure people to the exposition, fair officials proclaimed such days as Emancipation Day, Stenographers' Day, Rural Letter Carriers' Day, and one enigmatically called the House of Hoo-Hoo Day. According to tradition, the fairgoers also were the first Americans to enjoy ice cream cones, which are said to have been invented by a St. Louis waffle vender at the exposition. The popularity and excitement of the fair inspired a tune that was sung, hummed, and whistled from Seattle to Sarasota in 1904 and has become a favorite bit of musical Americana:

> When Louie came home to his flat
> He hung up his coat and his hat,
> He gazed all around but no wifey he found,
> So he said where can Flossie be at?
>
> A note on the table he spied,
> He read it just once then he cried.
> It ran Louie dear, its too slow for me here,
> So I think I will go for a ride.
>
> Meet me in St. Louie, Louie,
> Meet me at the Fair,
> Don't tell me the lights are shining
> Any place but there.
>
> We'll dance the hootchie-kootchie,
> I'll be your tootsie-wootsie,
> If you'll meet me in St. Louie, Louie,
> Meet me at the Fair.

The fair closed after 184 days, an unqualified success. A total expenditure of nearly $50,000,000 had been made, but the exposition had remarkably stimulated the economy of the city. The original backers of the movement—the businessmen of the city—made money, the city secured a better water system and an art museum, Washington University became the recipient of three new buildings, and St. Louisans were satisfied that they had outshown Chicago as fair-givers and hosts to the world.

Lawlessness

The years following the Civil War were vividly described as the Reign of Terror. Many of the men who had ridden with marauding guerrilla bands during the war learned, with the advent of peace, that thievery was easier than labor. Defying justice, they brazenly snatched their livelihood from law-abiding, hard-working fellow citizens. The outlaws of Missouri not only preyed upon the people of their own state, but they carried out acts of violence and robbery in other states as far removed as Minnesota and Kentucky. Perhaps one of the circumstances which encouraged such lawlessness was the uneasy transfer of authority from military to civilian officials. As the military withdrew, the civil officials who remained were often weak. Especially in counties where a major part of the population had been Confederate sympathizers and were discontented with the postwar Radical government, county officials refused to cooperate with the state government and were lax in the administration of their posts. This attitude was an invitation to outlaws to take the offensive.

Missouri's first train robbery was at Gad's Hill in Wayne County in 1874.
(Triplett, Life and Times of Jesse James)

The most common crime was horse theft, which was committed with about the frequency with which automobiles are stolen in our own day. Good horses, always in demand since they provided the chief method of transportation, could be easily sold. Presenting no ignition key problem, they could be easily seized. The bandits soon discovered that daylight bank robbery was also a lucrative activity and that train hijacking was frequently even more profitable. In 1866 the robbery of a savings bank in Liberty began a string of bank holdups in other towns such as Gallatin, Lexington, and Kansas City. The first railroad robbery, which occurred at Gad's Hill in Wayne County in 1874, proved so lucrative that a series of train hijackings followed over the next seven years. In the famous robbery at Winston in 1881, four men took control of the train, seized the valuables of the passengers and crew, and shot the conductor and a passenger who did not cooperate.

The Ku Klux Klan was organized in the state as early as 1868. The society became particularly active in southeast Missouri in the 1870's; in October, 1871, Governor Brown was forced to call out the militia in an attempt to put down the organization in Dunklin and Stoddard counties. Contemporary accounts describe the Klansmen, who were known as Dead Men, as wearing long black gowns with white stripes. One investigating officer reported that criminals from neighboring states had crossed into the bootheel region and adopted the Klan garb and techniques. In this way, outlaws could carry on marauding activities under the protection of disguise. After the militia restored order in Dunklin and Stoddard counties in 1871, the Klan appears to have moved west to Butler and Ripley counties. Since the Klan was a secret organization, it is difficult to secure records which give us much information about its activities. but contemporary accounts affirm that men in Klan garb were guilty of violence and murder.

The honest citizens of the community, who were always disturbed at such outbreaks of lawlessness, were of course stirred far more by the taking of a life than by material loss. When the appointed officials failed to bring men to justice or to provide the necessary protection, it was inevitable that citizens would organize themselves in order to protect their property or their lives. Many groups of vigilantes such as the Honest Men's League

The symbol for the Anti-Horse Thief Association became a warning to the lawless.
(Courtesy State Historical Association)

of Marshall, the Regulators of southeast Missouri, or the Anti-Horse Thief Association were active in Missouri in the late nineteenth century. The last named group, which first appeared in northeast Missouri before the Civil War, was the most successful, and continued as an important association into the twentieth century. Known as the A.H.T.A., it was established "To protect the Innocent and bring the Guilty to Justice." Members were expected to search diligently for two days after an act of thievery to find clues or evidence which might lead to the apprehension of the criminals. Most vigilance committees, such as the Independence vigilantes of 1866 and the Warrensburg vigilantes of 1867, acted only for a short period of time and then disbanded.

There is an example in Missouri history of a vigilance group which became an outlaw band. The Ozarks—particularly Christian and Taney counties—continued to be plagued with terrorism for two decades after the Civil War. These threats to law and order came from organized bands who flaunted their contempt for justice and were seldom convicted. Nat Kinney, a 6-foot 7-inch former Union officer, moved to Taney County after the war. Kinney—a former Springfield saloon operator who established the first Sunday school in Taney County—called a meeting of the leading citizens of the area to organize a vigilance group to enforce the law. Since the organizational meeting occurred at a timberless hilltop, or knob, called a bald, the group became known as the Bald Knobbers. Members of the organization were sworn to keep the secrets of the society and to do all possible to bring criminals to justice. As the new members of the organization were sworn in, they were solemnly reminded, "Should you willfully and knowingly violate this oath in any way, you subject yourself to the jurisdiction of twelve members of this order, even if their decision should be to hang you by the neck until you are dead, dead, dead."

The Bald Knobbers began as a self-appointed law-enforcement agency. On one occasion they took two men from the county jail at Forsyth and hanged them. Soon the organization degenerated into a pack of bandits when thrill- and plunder-seeking men of the community joined the group and when some of the original members—including Nat Kinney—turned outlaw. Whipping, stealing, and threatening, the Bald Knobbers began to terrorize the community. This intimidation forced some residents to leave the area. One exile wrote:

> Adieu to old Kirbyville, I can no longer stay.
> Hard times and Bald Knobbers has driven me away.

After several citizens had been murdered, a group known as the anti-Bald Knobbers organized and requested help from Governor Marmaduke. Adjutant General J. C. Jamison was sent to Forsyth in April, 1886, and was successful in forcing the organization to disband. Jamison's victory did not spell the end of the Bald Knobbers, however, for new groups had sprung up in Christian County. When several Bald Knobbers murdered two men in 1887, county officials were so infuriated that they called a grand jury and indicted eighty people. During August of 1887 newspapermen and curious spectators crowded the little town of Ozark to observe and report the trials of the Bald Knobbers. Most of the defendants were fined and released, but three were hanged in May of 1889 after Governor Francis refused clemency.

The **Anti-Horse Thief Association** pursued thieves great distances over rough country.

(Triplett, Life and Times of Jesse James)

The citizens of Missouri often called upon their governors for help in their fight against the mounting menace. Governor Fletcher called out the militia in Jackson and Lafayette counties in 1866; Governor McClurg authorized the militia to assist the sheriff at Gallatin in 1870; Governor Woodson in 1873 offered $2,000 reward for the arrest of Frank and Jesse James. Despite these efforts, lawlessness continued, and charges became more and more frequent that the Democratic administration was not seriously attempting to maintain law and order. Actually, there were former Confederates, even in the state legislature, who sympathized with the James brothers. Finally, however, in 1881, Governor T. T. Crittenden took action. His offer of $5,000 reward for the arrest and $5,000 reward for the conviction of Frank and Jesse James or their associates led to suspicion and treachery within the outlaw ranks, and within a year all major members of the gang either had been seized or were dead. Jesse himself was shot by one of his own men while standing on a chair dusting a picture in his St. Joseph hideout. Frank James surrendered to the governor. Frank was acquitted in the dramatic murder trial that followed at Gallatin, Missouri.

After "Cole" Younger — another alumnus of Quantrill's raiders—was released from a Minnesota prison, he and Frank James successfully capitalized on their notoriety by appearing in a Wild West show. For many years James, whom Republicans referred to as "the Democratic Pet," was a source of political controversy. Even as late as 1912, when the Republican Party was split by Theodore Roosevelt, the Republican faction in Missouri, hoping to discredit Roosevelt, declared that Frank James was supporting him. Although James' previous life of crime was a well-known fact, he lived his later years quietly in western Missouri where he died in 1915 at the age of seventy-two years.

Society

For a time after the Civil War, some Missourians were unable to forget the bitterness of that conflict. The Confederate flag waved above the Clay County courthouse until 1870. Most Missourians, however, were too much concerned with the problems of living to nurture unpleasant memories of the past. The rapidly changing industrial technology of the day opened vistas unknown a few years earlier. Although telegraph lines stretched across Missouri before the Civil War, the postwar period brought other important innovations. The gas lights which had been installed in Kansas City in 1867 were replaced by electric arc lights in 1881. St. Louis had a telephone exchange in operation in 1878. Subscribers were solicited for Kansas City's telephone system in 1879. After the turn of the century, such vehicles as the Success Auto-Buggy began to revolutionize many aspects of life from church-going to courting.

Literature

The newspapers of Missouri were instrumental, not only in the dissemination of news, but also in the introduction of ideas and in the influence of popular opinion in the state. Missouri was blessed with a number of outstanding journalists during the late nineteenth century period. Joseph R. McCullagh, editor of the St. Louis *Globe-Democrat,* was recognized throughout the United States for his accurate, though frequently sarcastic, journalism. Eugene Field, a fledgling reporter, wrote this of McCullagh:

> This talk about the journalists that run the East is bosh.
> We've got a Western editor, that's little, but, O gosh!
> He lives here in Miszoora, where the people are so set
> In ante-bellum notions that they vote for Jackson yet;
> But the paper he is running makes the rusty fossils swear,—
> The smartest, likeliest paper that is printed anywhere!
> And best of all, the paragraphs are pointed as a tack.
> And that's because they emanate
> From Little Mack.

Joseph B. (Little Mack) Mc-Cullagh edited the St. Louis Globe-Democrat from 1871 to 1896. This Irish-born newspaperman was known throughout the nation as one of the founders of the "new journalism" which furnished the readers with fair and accurate reports of the news.
(Courtesy State Historical Society)

McCullagh did not have the field to himself in St. Louis. Joseph Pulitzer, a Hungarian-born reporter who first worked in St. Louis on the *Westliche Post,* established the *Post-Dispatch* in 1878. Pulitzer later moved to New York to enlarge his newspaper holdings with the New York *World* and *Evening World,* but he retained ownership of the *Post-Dispatch,* which the Pulitzer family continues to operate today. The coveted Pulitzer prize was established and endowed by Joseph Pulitzer in his will. Both McCullagh and Pulitzer exposed many examples of municipal graft in the city they served, and became commentators on national issues as well. At the other side of the state William Rockhill Nelson built a great newspaper empire around the Kansas City *Star.* He was a constant agitator for the improvement of the city, and many advances in such areas as streets, parks, architecture, and museums were directly related to the efforts of this tireless journalist.

Missouri produced several great writers in the last half of the nineteenth century. Foremost, of course, was Samuel L. Clemens of Hannibal, better known as Mark Twain. When he was forced to leave school at the age of twelve because of the death of his father, Clemens became a printer and writer on his brother's paper until 1853. After more than a decade of traveling about the country supporting himself as a journeyman

Through his conservative Kansas City Star, which he edited from 1880 to 1915, William Rockhill Nelson campaigned for civic improvements and clean city government.

(Courtesy State Historical Society)

Joseph Pulitzer, who used his St. Louis Post-Dispatch and his New York World to fight for civil service reform and clean city government, was elected to the Missouri House of Representatives in 1870, although he was under the legal age and a Republican from a Democratic district.

(From Seitz, Joseph Pulitzer, His Life and Letters, Copyright Simon and Schuster, Inc. Used by permission.)

printer and writer, he first gained acclaim for his story, "The Celebrated Jumping Frog of Calaveras County," which he wrote in 1865 during a period of residence in California. *Roughing It* retells his experiences in the Old West. Clemens' boyhood in Hannibal, Missouri, embellished by a vivid imagination and irrepressible sense of humor, is presented in his most popular works, *Tom Sawyer* and *Huckleberry Finn.* His apprenticeship and career as a river pilot furnished his pseudonym, Mark Twain (an expression meaning two fathoms deep) and the background for *Life on the Mississippi.*

Novelist Winston Churchill spent his pre-college days in St. Louis where he was born in 1871. Author of at least eleven novels, including the best-selling *The Crisis,* Churchill first met success in 1899 with *Richard Carvel.*

Prolific author Rupert Hughes, a native of Lancaster, Missouri, produced a wide variety of literary works—novels, plays, short stories, biographies—as well as musical compositions. His 1904 novel, *The Whirlwind,* has a Missouri setting.

Another writer of note was the above-mentioned Eugene Field, who began his work as a reporter on the St. Louis *Journal,* but served several other papers in Missouri before finally moving to Chicago in 1883. Field is probably best known for his two children's poems, "Little Boy Blue" and "Wynken, Blynken, and Nod."

Journalist Eugene Field, affectionately known as "the children's poet," is best known for his With Trumpet and Drum and Poems of Childhood. This portrait is from a mural in the governor's reception room of the state capitol.
(Courtesy Walker-Missouri Commerce)

In the first decade of the twentieth century, Harold Bell Wright used the Ozark hill country as the scene of his two best sellers, *Shepherd of the Hills* (1907), and *The Calling of Dan Matthews* (1909). The picturesque red frame Bennett's Mill near Bennett Spring is the site where Wright wrote much of *The Calling of Dan Matthews* and is the prototype of Gordon's Mill in the novel. In the "Shepherd of the Hills country" near Branson, Wright fans may see Uncle Matt's cabin, Uncle Ike's Post Office, Mutton Hollow, Sammy's Lookout, and statues of several of the leading characters of Wright's book.

A literary magazine of wide influence and popularity was a product of St. Louis-born editor William Marion Reedy. After periods of service on the staffs of several St. Louis papers, Reedy acquired in 1896 the ownership of *The Mirror*, which he had edited for three years. *Reedy's Mirror* gained international fame for its proprietor, who is recognized today as one of the leading figures in American literature in the period from 1895 to 1920. Through his *Mirror* Reedy introduced or encouraged such Missouri authors as playwright Zoe Akins, novelist Fanny Hurst, and poet Sara Teasdale.

Missouri's outstanding playwright of the period was Augustus Thomas of St. Louis, whose most successful play was entitled *In Mizzoura*. Thomas, who worked in New York at the height of his popularity, is credited with helping free the American stage from European domination.

Another important source of literature in Missouri was the group of men who organized the St. Louis Philosophical Society and produced the *Journal of Speculative Philosophy*. This journal, under the editorship of St. Louis Superintendent of Schools William Torrey Harris, became the forum for the presentation of philosophical treatises by America's leading thinkers in the late nineteenth century.

Art

Missouri claims two famous artists of the nineteenth century. George Caleb Bingham, considered the most important painter of the American scene in the mid-nineteenth century, was active professionally from about 1840 until his death in 1879. Bingham was for a brief time professor of art at the state university in Columbia. He had long been closely associated with James Rollins, the "Father of the University of Missouri," who helped finance the young artist's early training. Bingham is best known for his genre painting—scenes from everyday life in Missouri—and his sensitive portraits. Bingham lived his later years in Kansas City, where he died in 1879.

Samuel Langhorne Clemens (Mark Twain) journeyman-printer, river pilot, writer, lecturer, and humorist is pictured in this mural from the governor's reception room in the state capitol.

(Courtesy Massie-Missouri Commerce)

Carl Ferdinand Wimar, after moving to St. Louis from Germany in 1843, became an apprentice in a sign shop where he began to develop his latent artistic talent. An inheritance later enabled him to study painting in Dusseldorf, Germany. He later returned to America and traveled among the Indians photographing and studying many phases of Indian life. This study tour enabled Wimar to paint the acclaimed Indian portraits and scenes for which he is best known. His last works were four historic scenes from Missouri history, and portraits of George and Martha Washington, Edward Bates, and Thomas Hart Benton in the dome of the St. Louis courthouse. Wimar died shortly after completing these paintings in 1862.

Sports

As in most of the United States, baseball was the popular sport in Missouri after the Civil War. In 1876 the St. Louis Browns joined the National League. The next year, however, when some of the St. Louis players were charged with throwing games, the team dropped its National affiliation. In 1899 the St. Louis Cardinals were organized in the National League, and three years later the St. Louis Browns became affiliated with the American League. Baseball games were enthusiastically attended throughout the state, and many minor leagues were started. Either through amazing batting power or appalling defensive playing, the scores were often unusually high; a typical score resulted in 1873 when Carthage defeated Joplin by a score of 67 to 17.

Despite some objection from church leaders who felt that it was a brutal and immoral sport, football gained many fans during the late nineteenth century. The University of Missouri organized its first football team in 1890 and first played the perennial rival, the University of Kansas, the next year. When the Missouri team traveled south to play the University of Texas in 1896, the squad took the opportunity to make an unauthorized tour of Mexico. As early as 1897 Warrensburg played the University of Missouri; and two years later Kirksville formed her first football team. The Missouri Intercollegiate Athletic Association, including such schools as St. Louis University, Warrensburg, and Kirksville, was established in 1900. In 1907 the Missouri Valley Conference was organized with Washington University and the University of Missouri as member schools. Basketball, which developed late in the nineteenth century, was

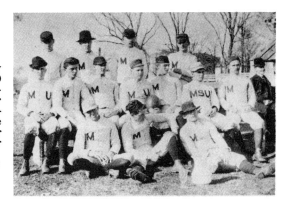

The Missouri University Football Team of 1890 went on the field unprotected by helmets or padding, but their waterboy provided an ironware pitcher and goblet for their b e t w e e n-quarter drinks.
(Courtesy State Historical Society)

The natty St. Louis Browns of 1884 were the first team ever managed by Comiskey.
(Courtesy State Historical Society)

The basketball team at Springfield Normal in 1908 wore knickers.
(Courtesy Don Payton, Southwest Missouri State College)

adopted by the colleges later than football. Missouri University played its first intercollegiate basketball in 1907, defeating Central College.

Prize-fighting, another popular spectator sport in the late nineteenth century, retained the flavor of the earlier period of Missouri's history. Until the 1890's, most of the contests were fought with bare knuckles, and for many rounds which were much longer than those today. A fight in St. Joseph is reputed to have gone 110 rounds; it was not unusual for two men to fight for four to five hours. A brutal fight on Chouteau's Island at St. Louis in 1873 led to severe criticism of prize-fighting in the state, and in the year 1874 the Missouri state legislature enacted a law prohibiting prize-fighting, boxing, or sparring exhibitions. After the passage of this law, however, fights were still held by those who were willing to defy the law by using a ruse which allowed "private" clubs to sponsor their own matches. St. Louis was one of the chief prize-fighting centers in America during the last half of the nineteenth century.

Bicycling became so popular in the 1890's that some livery stables complained that "young men who used to take their girl friends driving every pleasant Sunday afternoon take them bicycling instead, at a much smaller expense." Growth of Y.M.C.A.'s and various athletic clubs evidenced the growing interest in sports, and roller skating and bowling gained fans in the 1880's and 1890's.

Entertainment and Recreation

Those of us who live in an age of television should be impressed by the number and variety of entertainers who came to Missouri during the pre-movie days. Opera houses were built in all county seats and many other of the smaller communities. While its name might suggest magnificent architecture and luxurious appointments, in truth the small town "opera house" was usually little more than a barn-like structure with a stage. In the metropolitan centers, however, the palatial opera houses were worthy of their name. In Kansas City, Coates Opera House, built in 1871 at a cost of $105,000, was known for its elegance until it was eclipsed by the opening a few years later of the Tootle Grand Theater in St. Joseph. The Grand Opera House, built in 1885, was only one of many well-appointed theaters in St. Louis; the Louisiana Purchase exhibition added another ele-

The California, Missouri, Opera House in 1903

gant theater—the Garrick—in 1904. Although admission to the opera house was usually listed in terms of cash, the Joplin miners could pay for tickets with wheelbarrows of lead ore.

The post-Civil War period has been called the golden age of the professional stage in the state. To the delight of Missouri audiences, Sarah Bernhardt, Edwin Booth, and even John L. Sullivan—after he left the prize-fighting ring—performed in local theaters. Oscar Wilde lectured before Missouri audiences, and Walter Damrosch presented Wagnerian opera. Music lovers had an opportunity to hear many of the world's greatest voices, including Caruso, Adelina Patti, and Madame Schumann-Heink. St. Louisans were introduced to Gilbert and Sullivan's operettas in an open air theater—a foretaste of the Municipal Opera so popular today. Thespian societies composed of stage-struck local residents were organized as early as the 1830's and 1840's in towns such as Jefferson City, Palmyra, and Boonville, and many of these amateur groups continued into the twentieth century.

Traveling groups of actors, musicians, and entertainers of all kinds toured the hamlets. One agency which brought a wide variety of singers, lecturers, actors, and musicians to the towns and cities of the Midwest was the Chautauqua. The citizenry of

Missouri communities flocked to the huge tent of the Chautauqua for entertainment and information. Missourians were still enthusiastic patrons of the numerous circuses which toured the state. County fairs were also growing in popularity; by 1891 there were thirty being held annually in the state. Kansas City began holding its livestock show, the forerunner of the American Royal, in 1872.

Because of their size, Kansas City and St. Louis had recreation and cultural facilities which were not available in most communities. About 1860 Henry Shaw of St. Louis opened his lovely gardens to the citizens of the city. Under the terms of Shaw's will his estate became, in 1889, the privately endowed Missouri Botanical Garden, famous for its varied, massive, and exotic flower displays. Forest Park in St. Louis, the second largest park in the country, was dedicated in 1876. Two years later, the Veiled Prophet parade and festivities were begun in St. Louis. Kansas City's Swope Park, a gift to the city from devoted citizen Thomas Hunton Swope, was dedicated in 1896.

For the many Missourians who delighted in dancing, the country dance in hall, barn, or home was still popular. To the tune of the fiddle, Missourians still danced or skipped to such old favorites as "Buffalo Gals," "Old Dan Tucker," "Turkey in the Straw," and "Pop Goes the Weasel." The minuet was rarely danced after the Civil War, but the waltz, schottische, and polka were popular, as well as the two-step and the cakewalk, which were added in the 1890's.

In the years just before and after the turn of the century, the pathos, the haunting beauty, and the intricate rhythms of black work songs, spirituals, and blues melodies began to evolve into jazz, which many musicologists consider the only truly American contribution to music. The talented black composers of a long list of jazz classics lived in St. Louis at the turn of the century: Scott Joplin, originally of Sedalia, wrote the "Maple Leaf Rag"; Tom Turpin published a series of intricate compositions for the piano including the "Harlem Rag" and the "St. Louis Rag." W. C. Handy, "the dean of American jazz composers," compiled a collection of blues songs that had as their nuclei the melodies Handy had heard on the wharves and in the cotton fields, during his wanderings. Handy's most famous composition is the mournful and perennially popular "St. Louis Blues."

Although many would object if we described the political conventions of the late nineteenth century as entertainment, the frequent conventions with their impassioned oratory did provide a source of money and of some diversion for Missourians. In 1876 the Democratic convention met in St. Louis, and Samuel Tilden of New York was nominated for president. Joseph Mc-Cullagh, Eugene Field's "Little Mack," called Tilden "Slippery Sam." In 1888 Grover Cleveland was tapped as the Democratic standard-bearer at the party's national convention in St. Louis. In 1896 two conventions were held in St. Louis—McKinley was chosen candidate for president on the Republican ticket, and the People's Party nominated William Jennings Bryan (already the Democratic nominee). In 1900 it appeared that the Democratic Party convention scheduled for Kansas City would have to be relocated when Convention Hall there burned only months before the date of the meeting, but the vigorous leaders of the city pooled their efforts and constructed in three months a new convention hall, which became known as the "ninety-day wonder." In 1904 the Democratic Convention revisited St. Louis.

The churches of Missouri recouped their Civil War losses and moved ahead in the establishment of congregations and the construction of church buildings in the postwar period. The spirit of cooperation which could be seen among several denominations did not preclude a fondness among some groups for theological debate. The larger denominations evidenced a growing awareness of the opportunities for service, both in the support

The Chautauqua tent sheltered a variety of cultural offerings
(Courtesy State Historical Society)

of foreign missions across the world and in the founding of hospitals and orphanages in their home communities. Church interest in education continued. The Protestant emphasis centered on higher education; the Roman Catholics of Missouri established a comprehensive educational system for all their children. A concern for public morals was manifested among all the church groups, with some denominations and church leaders placing particular stress on the value of temperance in regard to intoxicating beverages. An interest in the plight of the working man and a resultant support for the trade union movement was manifested among several denominations late in the century.

In the first half of the nineteenth century the settlers were involved in the physical trials of clearing land, building homes, making roads, and developing an economy; therefore, education was not part of the experience of most young citizens of frontier Missouri. By the last half of the century, however, the growing economy, the resources of government, and the interest of the people encouraged the development of a comprehensive public education system. Most of the private academies disappeared. Some of the churches continued to establish their own elementary and high schools, but the major growth in education during this half century was in the field of public education. Additional financial support from the state, the establishment of teacher training institutions, and an intensified interest in standards all contributed to the growth and improvement of Missouri's educational system.

Improved communications and the greater circulation of newspapers not only brought national and world news to Missourians, but also introduced them to the trends of thought and conduct that were prevalent across the country. Missourians enjoyed the sports, saw the shows, and sang the songs which were entertaining their fellow Americans from East to West. Missouri was losing its distinctive frontier flavor in the growing urban standardization of the late nineteenth century. The St. Louis exposition acquainted both rural and urban Missourians with foreign lands and the wonders of the machine age. The fair also inspired a new pride in being, not only Missourians, but Americans.

(Courtesy State Historical Society)

Banker R. B. Price of Columbia and his family of tennis players, circa 1900

BIBLIOGRAPHY

Barclay, Thomas S. "Test Oath for the Clergy in Missouri," *Missouri Historical Review,* Vol. XVIII (April, 1924), pp. 345-381.

Brashear, Minnie M. "The Anti-Horse Thief Association of Northeast Missouri," *Missouri Historical Review,* Vol. XLV (July, 1951), pp. 341-348.

Burke, Harry R. "Eugene Field's Newspaper Days in St. Louis," *Missouri Historical Review,* Vol. XLI (January, 1947), pp. 137-146.

Byars, W. V. "A Century of Journalism in Missouri," *Missouri Historical Review,* Vol. XV, (October, 1920), pp. 53-73.

Caldwell, Dorothy J. "A Look at the Missouri State Teachers Association 1856-1956," *Missouri Historical Review,* Vol. LI (October, 1956), pp. 31-41.

De Menil, Alexander Nicolas. "A Century of Missouri Literature," *Missouri Historical Review,* Vol. XV (October, 1920), pp. 74-125.

Field, Roswell. "Eugene Field, a Memory," *Missouri Historical Review,* Vol XLIV (January, 1950), pp. 147-167.

Forbes, Cleon. "The St. Louis School of Thought," *Missouri Historical Review,* Vol. XXV (October, 1930; January, April, July, 1931), pp. 83-101, 289-305, 461-473, 609-622; Vol. XXVI (October, 1931), pp. 68-77.

Haswell, A. M. "The Story of the Bald Knobbers," *Missouri Historical Review,* Vol. XVIII (October, 1923), pp. 27-35.

Hubach, Robert T. "St. Louis, Host of Celebrated Nineteenth Century British and American Authors," *Missouri Historical Review,* Vol. XXXVIII (July, 1944), pp. 375-387.

Hulburt, Ray G. "A. T. Still, Founder of Osteopathy," *Missouri Historical Review,* Vol. XIX (October, 1924), pp. 25-35.

Johns, George S. "Pulitzer, Joseph," *Missouri Historical Review,* Vol. XXV (January, April, July, 1931), pp. 201-218, 404-420, 563-575; Vol. XXVI (October, 1931; January, April, 1932), pp. 54-67, 163-178, 267-280.

Jones, John J. "The Morrill Lands of the University of Missouri," *Missouri Historical Review,* Vol. LI (January, 1957), pp. 126-138.

Kirschten, Ernest. *Catfish and Crystal.* Garden City, New York: Doubleday and Company, 1960.

Krohn, Ernst C. "A Century of Missouri Music," *Missouri Historical Review,* Vol. XVII (January, April, July, 1923), pp. 130-158, 285-320, 440-463.

Lyon, Peter. "The Wild, Wild West," *American Heritage,* Vol. XI (August, 1960), pp. 32-48.

McCarty, Mary L. "Recollections of Kansas City 1866-1916," *Missouri Historical Review,* Vol. XLV (October, 1950), pp. 35-46.

Mangold, George B. "Social Reform in Missouri During the Last Century," *Missouri Historical Review,* Vol. XV (October, 1920), pp. 191-213.

Missouri, a Guide to the "Show Me" State. New York: Duell, Sloan and Pearce, 1941.

Morris, Lucile. *The Bald Knobbers.* Caldwell, Idaho: The Caxton Printers, Ltd., 1939.

Morris, Monia Cook. "Teacher Training in Missouri Before 1871," *Missouri Historical Review,* Vol. XLIII (October, 1948) pp. 18-37.

Sechler, Earl T. *Our Religious Heritage: Church History of the Ozarks 1806-1906.* Springfield, Missouri: Westport Press, 1961.

Settle, William A., Jr. "The James Boys and Missouri Politics," *Missouri Historical Review,* Vol. XXXVI (July, 1942), pp. 412-429.

Seymour, Harold. "St. Louis and the Union Baseball War," *Missouri Historical Review,* Vol. LI (April, 1957), pp. 257-269.

Shoemaker, Floyd C. "Mark Twain: America's Most Widely Read Author," *Missouri Historical Review,* Vol. XXIX (April, 1935), pp. 165-168.

Shoemaker, Floyd C. *Missouri and Missourians.* Vols. I and II. Chicago: The Lewis Publishing Company, 1943.

Simmons, Lucy and P. O. Selby. "Northeast Missouri State Teachers College and Its Founder, Joseph Baldwin," *Missouri Historical Review,* Vol. XXII (January, 1928), pp. 157-170.

Spilman, John F. "History of Sylvan School, Lawrence County," *Missouri Historical Review,* Vol. L (October, 1955), pp. 30-43.

Stevens, Walter B. *Centennial History of Missouri 1820-1921.* Vol. I. St. Louis, Chicago: The S. J. Clarke Publishing Company, 1921.

Stevens, Walter B. "McCullagh, Joseph B.," *Missouri Historical Review,* Vol. XXV (October, 1930; January, April, July, 1931), pp. 3-9, 245-253, 425-431, 576-584; Vol. XXVI (October, 1931; January, April, July, 1932), pp. 40-53, 153-162, 256-266, 374-386; Vol. XXVII (October 1932; January, April,

July, 1933), pp. 50-62, 151-156, 257-261, 337-343; Vol. XXVIII (October, 1933; January, April, 1934), pp. 38-42, 125-129, 206-210.

Stevens, Walter B. "The New Journalism in Missouri," *Missouri Historical Review*, Vol. XVII (April, July, 1923), pp. 321-330, 470-478; Vol. XVIII (October, 1923; January, April, July, 1924), pp. 55-63, 197-211, 404-414; Vol. XIX (October, 1924; January, April, July, 1925), pp. 105-113, 325-337, 427-437, 675-688.

"The World's Fair at St. Louis." *The World's Work*, Vol. VIII (August, 1904).

White, John Turner. "The Bald Knobbers," *Missouri Historical Review*, Vol. XXXV (July, 1941), pp. 570-573.

Windell, Marie George. "The Camp Meeting in Missouri," *Missouri Historical Review*, Vol. XXXVII (April, 1943), pp. 253-270.

CHAPTER XV

Progressive Missouri

Men gave bribes and thought nothing of it; . . . legislative halls were made dens of thieves, while the conscience of the people was asleep. Then came the revelations, and the people awoke. . . .

—Joseph Folk's speech
"Era of Conscience," 1909

At the turn of the century the verb "boodle" became part of the vocabulary of most Missourians. The term meant to secure money by corrupt means—particularly the selling of votes and influence by legislative officials.

Joseph W. Folk, circuit attorney in St. Louis in 1900, startled the people of his city and of the state with his revelation of boodling in the St. Louis government. The corrupt Democratic Party of St. Louis under the control of Colonel Ed Butler, the millionaire blacksmith, lived to regret the choice of Folk as a candidate for office. The sensational revelations by Folk and his parade of witnesses made the St. Louis attorney the popular hero of Missouri. Folk, in time, was able to win the governorship of the state and to challenge the Democratic Party leaders, who used such names as "Fungus Folk," "The Missouri Messiah," or "St. Joe" to ridicule Folk for his reforming zeal.

Joe Folk was not the only reformer in America at the turn of the century. Similar reformers appeared in every state. These Progressives, as they were known, who were to be found in both major political parties, ushered in a new era of governmental concern for the citizen, consumer, and little man.

The Populist Movement

Throughout the late 1880's and the first half of the 1890's the legislative halls in America rang with the voices of unhappy farmers protesting their lot. There was much to complain of— low prices for their hard-won products of the soil, high and discriminatory freight rates, oppressive mortgages, high interest rates, and finally the drought which robbed them of their crops. Throughout the South and the Midwest, anxious farmers gathered in new organizations to consider what should be done, to frame documents of protest, and ultimately to enter the political contests of the time in an effort to secure redress of their grievances. Although some farmers attempted to improve their situation through the establishment of cooperatives for buying and selling, most farmers seemed to place their confidence in legislation as a source of their salvation. Missouri's farmers took their part in the protest of this period; their complaints were a major current in the political maelstrom during the late 1880's and early 1890's.

There had been a succession of farmers' protest parties in Missouri: first, the People's Party, created by Grangers for the election of 1874; second, the Greenback Party of 1876-1878; third, the Greenback Labor Party in the elections of 1880, 1882, 1884; and fourth, the Union Labor Party in the elections of 1888 and 1890. None of these parties was ever sufficiently powerful to control Missouri's government. However, they were strong enough to focus the attention of the major parties on their demands, and sometimes they were able to encourage a policy change in the larger groups.

During the late 1880's two new farmers' organizations were active in the state: The Agricultural Wheel, established in late 1886 in Mississippi County; and the Farmers' Alliance, founded in 1887. The state was ripe for these groups, and in 1888 the Alliance claimed 13,000 Missouri members. The two organizations, so similar in program, merged in the year 1889, taking the name Farmers' and Laborers' Union of Missouri. The Union was split over the question of whether the group should attempt to become a political party in Missouri or whether it should try to influence the parties already in existence. In the election of 1888 ten members of the Alliance were elected to the legislature. Under the liberal leadership of Governor Francis, laws were passed outlawing railroad pools, trusts, and combinations. One of the more interesting laws which had the support of the farmers' organizations was a statute stipulating that a producer of watermelons could ride free on a train transporting his melons and could sell them to people en route without extra charge by the railroad.

After Missouri's first publicly-owned capitol burned in 1837, this building, completed in 1840 (see the illustration on page 423), was built to house the state government. Shown here after extensive remodeling and enlargement in 1888, it was destroyed by fire in 1911.

For the election of 1890 the Farmers' and Laborers' Union of Missouri adopted an interesting technique at a meeting in Sedalia. Rather than establish a separate political party, the Union adopted a platform which it asked all Missouri political candidates to sign. Some of the more important planks in this platform were resolutions calling for the lowering of interest rates—some members were paying from 10.8 to 14.4 per cent interest—the lowering of salaries for state officials, and the extension of the Australian ballot to all communities of the state. The farmers themselves passed a resolution declaring that they would not support any candidate who refused to uphold the principles enunciated in their platform. This technique at first glance appeared to be highly effective, since of the successful candidates, 105 of the 141 members of the state House of Representatives, twenty-four of the thirty-four members of the state Senate, and all fourteen Missouri congressmen had agreed to support the Sedalia platform.

But the farmers were not satisfied with the legislative results of their political activities. American legislative processes are slow. The farm crisis continued, and farm leaders still sought a political panacea. Beginning in 1891 a series of meetings were held to consider the establishment of a political party which would combine the votes of the unhappy farmers with those of the dissatisfied workers of the city. The People's Party, often called the Populist Party, which was the result of these meetings, adopted a platform at the gathering in St. Louis in 1892. This platform was considered radical in its demands for: (1) the creation of inflation either by the printing of paper money or by the free and unlimited coinage of silver in the definite ratio of 16 to 1; (2) government ownership and operation of the railroads; (3) a graduated income tax; (4) shorter hours for labor; and (5) the direct election of United States senators by the vote of the people. The preamble to the Populist Party platform clearly illustrated the point of view of its members:

> . . . we meet in the midst of a nation brought to the verge of moral, political, and material ruin. Corruption dominates the ballotbox, the Legislature, the Congress, and touches even the ermine of the bench. . . . The newspapers are largely subsidized or muzzled, public opinion silenced, business prostrated, homes covered with mortgages, labor impoverished, and the land concentrating in the hands of the capitalists. . . . The fruits of the toil of millions are boldly stolen to build up colossal fortunes for a few. . . .

These Populists—as the members of the People's Party were called—were determined to organize a third party in all the states and to enter the national election.

In Missouri the People's Party was organized on the state level at a meeting in Sedalia in June, 1892. Leverett Leonard, who was serving as the president of the Farmers' and Laborers' Union of Missouri, was chosen as the People's Party candidate for governor. At the state level the party called for a number of important reforms: an eight-hour working day; liability laws to make employers responsible for injuries to workers; the outlawing of child labor; the halting of the system whereby Missouri convicts were leased as industrial workers; the reduction of salaries for state officials; the abolition of the State Railroad Commission, which they felt to be ineffective; and the granting of the franchise to women.

The Farmers' and Laborers' Union of Missouri did not officially endorse the People's Party, although it was obvious that they favored the party. In the campaign of 1896, when the Democrats advocated the free coinage of silver, the Populists lost one of their chief issues. Although many farmers and workers were sympathetic to Populist aims, the party was not large enough to secure victory, and not a single Populist candidate for office was elected in 1892.

In 1894, the Populists' second attempt in Missouri politics was only slightly more successful. Two members of the party were able to capture seats in the Missouri House of Representatives, and some ten others were elected to county offices in the state. However, by taking votes from the Democratic Party in this election, the Populists may have played an important role in helping Republicans secure control of the legislature.

The climax of the long attempt of the farmers to secure redress of their complaints through political action occurred in 1896. On that occasion the Populist views on free silver were heartily embraced by the Democratic Party, which adopted a free silver platform and nominated the capable William Jennings Bryan as their candidate. When this occurred, the Populists were in a dilemma. Since the Democrats now upheld their chief position, the Populists had to decide whether they should endorse the Democratic candidate or name their own nominee. After duly considering the matter at their national convention in St. Louis, the party determined to support Bryan. The Populists did choose their own candidate for vice president. Although Bryan was defeated, the Populists could take some comfort from the fact that they had succeeded in forcing one of the national parties to adopt their money proposals.

A few Populists secured seats in the state legislature in 1898, but thereafter the party slowly sickened and died. In 1892 many farmers had delighted in singing the following song as they left their former political affiliations to join the new Populist Party:

> I was raised up in the kind of school,
>   Good-bye, my party, good-bye.
> That taught to bow to money rule,
>   Good-bye, my party, good-bye.

In the years after the election of 1896 those same farmers were forced to bid farewell to the languishing People's Party and rejoin the parties they had earlier deserted.

(Courtesy State Historical Society)

The Hall of Representatives of the Old Capitol

The Spanish-American War

Cuba was still a Spanish colony in 1890. Spain had lost most of her American empire by that time, but she had been able to retain control of the island despite regular revolutionary uprisings by the Cuban people. During the 1890's the American press reported in vivid detail the rebellions, concentration camps, starvation, and brutalities in Cuba. Many newspapers of the time dramatized these situations and encouraged American intervention in behalf of the islanders. In all honesty, we should admit that some Americans were anxious for an opportunity to make Cuba an American colony. Others, more mindful of economic interests than of the liberation of the oppressed, wished to secure better access to Cuban sugar. In any event, America was certain to be watchful of any developments on an island only ninety miles off the Florida coast.

Tales of Spanish tyranny awoke among many Missourians a keen sympathetic interest in Cuba. Beginning in 1895, meetings were held in such cities as Kirksville, Sedalia, Columbia, and Kansas City to discuss the Cuban situation and to explore the possibilities of American recognition of the rebels and assistance to their cause. In the same year a secret organization with close ties to the Cuban junta, or revolutionary government, was established in St. Louis for the purpose of encouraging Missourians to enlist in the Cuban army and of coordinating the activities of those citizens of the state who wished to aid the Cuban rebels. The thirty to fifty Missouri volunteers recruited each week from the St. Louis region were supplied food, clothing, and arms—but no money—and were sent to Cuba.

By March, 1896, a total of 150 recruits had sailed from Missouri. One of these volunteers was Captain T. Rosser Roemer, who, as a colonel, served for a year in the rebel army until he was assigned the task of delivering messages from the Cuban rebel commander to the junta in New York. Alone, Roemer set off from Cuba in an open sixteen-foot sailboat to the Bahamas, from where he continued to New York. When his mission had been accomplished, Roemer was granted leave to return to St. Louis, where friends and Cuban sympathizers hailed him as a hero and feted him with a banquet and parade.

In 1897, St. Louis physician Foster S. Winn, moved by reports of their need for medical help, volunteered his services to the rebels and sailed for Cuba at his own expense. Perhaps moved as much by the spirit of adventure as by compassion, twenty students of the Missouri Medical College in St. Louis also set off for the troubled island.

Cuban sympathizers who stayed home promoted the rebel cause by sending to Congress petitions advocating recognition of Cuban independence or by gathering money and supplies to be used for Cuban relief.

All of these activities demonstrating Missouri interest in the Cuban revolution occurred before the United States had declared war on Spain. There are several reasons which might explain Missouri's intense concern with Cuban affairs. First, a thriving commerce had developed between Missouri and Cuba. Cuba purchased large quantities of grain and flour from Kansas City millers and grain dealers; and, in addition, St. Louis merchants purchased great quantities of Cuban products such as tobacco, coffee, and sugar for distribution to much of the West. Second, aside from their economic ties with Cuba, Missourians, appalled at the tales of atrocities coming from the little island, were motivated, like many of their fellow-Americans, by humanitarian sentiments. Furthermore, the concept of "Manifest Des-

(St. Louis Daily Globe-Democrat, May 5, 1898)

The First Regiment under Colonel Edwin Batdorf was recruited in St. Louis. Here the men of the First are shown marching to Jefferson Barracks.

tiny" had been widely accepted in Missouri as early as the War of 1812. In 1898 Missouri Congressman James Beauchamp Clark —better known as Champ Clark—expressed this concept of "Manifest Destiny" when he said, "we intend, at all hazards and at whatever cost, to thoroughly dominate the western world." Missouri had mixed motives—economic interests, compassion, and national pride—for promoting the Spanish-American War.

In Washington, Missouri's congressmen reflected by their actions the feelings of many of their constituents. Both Senator Cockrell and Senator Vest urged the immediate recognition of the rebel government in Cuba, and joined their Democratic associates in castigating Republican President McKinley, whom they felt to be acting too slowly to assist the rebels. Representative Charles Cochran of St. Joseph melodramatically charged in January, 1898, "The administration is practically joining hands with Spain to crush the Cubans."

The sinking of the American battleship, the *Maine,* on February 15, 1898, which resulted in a loss of 260 American lives, was blamed upon Spain and added impetus to the growing sentiment for war. As war fever rose, groups of men throughout the state began to organize volunteer military units to be prepared to go to Cuba, or Puerto Rico, or perhaps even the distant Spanish-held Philippine Islands. It is reported that these volunteer units were assembled in many towns of the state and were known by such titles as "The Sons of Veterans," "The Naval Reserves," and "The Busch First Regiment of St. Louis." The enthusiastic units immediately offered their services to the state. But when Adjutant General Bell announced that only the State National Guard would be organized and sent into federal service, some groups disbanded; many of the volunteers enlisted in the government forces; others, hoping to be taken as a unit into a state regiment, continued to drill.

Governor Stephens, who had been vacationing in California, rushed home to Missouri to direct the preparations for the war that now seemed inevitable. Unfortunately, since the legislature had provided only $10,000 a year for the support of the troops, the state militia was in poor condition. These appropriations had been so inadequate that units had been forced to request supplemental funds from cities and individuals in order to meet their expenses. The governor had instructed Adjutant General Bell to do whatever was necessary—and permitted by peacetime law— to prepare the guard for mobilization. Bell then ordered the reconditioning of guard munitions and the filling of the ranks of the various regiments.

On April 25, 1898, despite the reluctance of President McKinley, and with the affirmative vote of every Missouri congressman present, war was declared. Back home in Missouri, the few who had feared war were now outshouted as the state greeted the declaration with a joyous outburst. The news was celebrated in St. Louis, Kansas City, Joplin, Sedalia, Lamar, Jefferson City, Hillsboro, and many other Missouri towns with the ringing of bells, the shooting of guns, and scenes of frenzied rejoicing.

The men of the state militia expected to be called into action immediately, but Governor Stephens informed the impatient troops that they would be sent to federal duty as soon as President McKinley's request was received. The governor pointed out that there was little money available to finance the mobilization, but he assured the citizens that the credit of the state would be used and that "the movement of the men will not be delayed."

On April 29, 1898, Missouri was requested to provide five regiments of infantry and one battery of light artillery. Frugal Governor Stephens, although greatly hampered by the lack of ready funds, hesitated to incur the expense of a special legislative session to obtain appropriations. Instead, he hoped to secure an offer from the Federal Government to transport the men to a

(Courtesy State Historical Society)

The boys of Company "L" of the 2nd Regiment pose for their picture before leaving for Jefferson Barracks. The 2nd Regiment was brought to full strength by companies from such widely separated cities as Joplin and Jefferson City.

federal camp, feed, clothe, and equip them. When the United States Government, although agreeing to pay for the transportation of the units to a federal point, refused to finance the subsistence of the men for more than six days prior to their mustering into federal service, Governor Stephens decided to spare the state the expense of financing a camp by allowing the units to remain in their home towns until the call to muster to a federal camp arrived.

Meanwhile, state militia colonels organized Battery A of light artillery at St. Louis, the First Regiment at St. Louis, the Second Regiment at Joplin, the Third Regiment at Kansas City, the Fourth Regiment at St. Joseph, and the Fifth Regiment also at Kansas City. At first there was great enthusiasm in the state, but as time went on, the recruiters began to have difficulty in securing full units. The Jefferson City *Daily Tribune* remarked in print that young Missourians seemed to be more willing to volunteer to play in a band or to command companies than to carry on other military duties in the infantry or cavalry. The paper declared, "One county has organized three brass bands. The Dons [Spaniards] could hardly stand an attack of American country bands massed in a hollow square all playing a 'Hot Time in the Old Town Tonight'."

Finally, anticipating an immediate muster call from Washington, Governor Stephens ordered Battery A and the First Regiment to move their men to Jefferson Barracks in St. Louis. The other regiments were to follow within the next two weeks. When the first units arrived at the camp they soon became aware of the results of Governor Stephens' money-saving policies. No preparations had been made for the comfort of the soldiers, who were finally situated in leaky tents with insufficient bedding-straw and blankets, and fed scanty, poorly prepared food. In their discomfort and disgust, the soldiers decided to call their place of assembly "Camp Stephens," in honor of their parsimonious governor. The Kansas City *Times* reported that Sunday, May 9, was observed in Camp Stephens as a day of fasting and prayer —"Fasting because there was nothing to eat—prayer for the eatables to come."

Governor Stephens, obviously proud of his ability to save money during this time of war preparations, announced that the mobilization of the Missouri militia had cost only $3,050. Whether the soldiers and citizens of the state appreciated his economy is questionable. The governor not only was anxious to avoid waste of money in Missouri, but he created a stir by insisting that the Federal Government pay an unreasonable price for the uniforms which the Missouri troops took with them into federal service.

The Missouri units were sent to Chickamauga Park, Georgia; Camp Alger, Virginia; or Jacksonville, Florida, after they were mustered into federal service. The men found camp conditions remarkably bad. At Chickamauga, typhoid fever resulted from contamination of the water supply by the camp waste. Spoiled, tough beef, rotten potatoes, and maggot-infested bacon brought many complaints. The circumstances for the troops were all the more complicated by the clothing situation. Before the state militia had left Missouri, the state government had issued old, nearly worn-out uniforms. Governor Stephens demanded that the Federal Government pay Missouri full price for the uniforms. When the Federal Government refused to pay the price demanded by Governor Stephens, Adjutant General Bell ordered the Missouri men to retire to their tents and disrobe. Some of the soldiers wrapped themselves in blankets until the squabble was settled and uniforms were supplied. The Fourth Missouri Regiment under the direction of Colonel H. H. Corby adopted an interesting — and successful — technique for securing their uniforms. When President McKinley visited Camp Alger on May 28, Corby assembled his men and paraded them dressed in "ragged civilian clothes" before the chief executive. This ingenious performance stimulated the military officials to action, and three days later the Fourth Regiment received complete uniforms.

The Spanish-American War was a short one. Of the Missouri units in federal service, only Battery A of the light infantry from St. Louis was placed on the front lines. The unit was ordered to embark from Newport News, Virginia, on July 28, on an old freighter. The United States, expecting the Spanish to surrender before Americans had secured control of Puerto Rico, was rushing troops to the island. The circumstances for transportation of the men were most uncomfortable. As Captain Rumbold described it, "There are 780 men in the steerage, eighteen inches to a man. You can imagine how it smells. There are 700 head of horses and mules, and these are on either side of the officers' quarters." No sooner had the unit disembarked in Puerto Rico and placed its guns in firing position than the armistice was announced. Thus, none of the Missouri units actually took part in the fighting during the three and one-half months' war.

Of course, individual Missourians in the regular United States Army and Navy were involved in battle. Missourians

Camp Stephens (Jefferson Barracks) named for the conservative Governor Lon V. Stephens whose failure to provide adequate housing, bedding, and food provoked bitter complaints from the volunteers

(Courtesy State Historical Society)

proved to be effective flag raisers. St. Louisan Frank Fulton of the Sixteenth Infantry was slightly injured when he planted the first flag on San Juan Hill. Edward P. Stanton, another citizen of St. Louis, distinguished himself by being the first to raise Old Glory over Manila Bay. An ensign from Kirksville won the New York *Herald's* $100 prize for being the first to plant an American flag on Cuban soil when he raised the Stars and Stripes at Diana City. Among the Missourians to be distinguished in this war was a young lieutenant, John J. Pershing, whose bravery on the field at El Caney brought him the attention of General Leonard Wood and a recommendation for a promotion. Pershing was later to be honored with great commands.

The role that some Missouri women played in the Spanish-American War has often been neglected. The offers of many Missouri women to volunteer for service as army nurses was at first politely refused; but by mid-summer of 1898, with malaria and typhoid fever raging in the army camps, the government reversed its policy and not only accepted with gratitude earlier offers, but made an appeal for additional nurses. The Daughters of the American Revolution responded to this appeal by paying the full expenses for sending thirty nurses to camps at Chicka-mauga, Tampa, and Santiago. One of these volunteers, Dr. Toland, died of typhoid fever in Cuba. Thirty-six young women of St. Louis, thirteen of whom were students at the St. Louis Training School for Nurses, also volunteered their services. The sacrifice of these Missouri girls and women who endured the privation of primitive camps and the hazards of dread fevers in the service of their country and humanity has too often gone unnoticed.

During the war, 8,083 Missouri militiamen served in the United States forces. Of this number, 107 died of disease, eight died in accidents, and 135 deserted. When the number who were serving in the regular federal forces is added to this figure, Missouri contributed 11,600 soldiers and sailors. Only four states in the Union contributed a greater number of fighters. The interest of young Missourians in this war can be seen in the fact that one-sixth of the students at the state university volunteered for service.

The war had important economic and political results for Missourians. Economically, the war produced higher prices and helped the farmers, who had been suffering from depressed prices for nearly a decade. In addition, the absence of so large a number of men from the state created a demand for labor and this cut down unemployment. Government purchasing, encouraged by the establishment of a quartermaster's department in St. Louis, increased state income substantially. Contracts for food brought $100,000 weekly into the state. The army bought thousands of dollars worth of shoes, drugs, and hay from Missouri merchants and manufacturers. Packing houses in St. Louis and Kansas City alone supplied 3,750,000 pounds of meat, and the National Biscuit Company furnished 610,000 pounds of hardtack. A Neosho timber contractor filled an order for 50,000 black walnut gun stocks.

Kansas City and St. Louis mule dealers, realizing that the army would require great numbers of mules and horses for the war, attempted to form a combine to force up the price of the animals. The army became aware of this profiteering and threatened to stop buying in Missouri. As a result, the combine dissolved, and the army resumed its purchasing on the open market. It is estimated that the army purchased over $500,000 worth of mules and horses in the state during 1898. This government business hastened the return of prosperity which had fled during the depression days of the nineties.

Lon V. Stephens of Boonville was a banker and editor before his election as governor in 1896.
(Strauss portrait, Courtesy State Historical Society)

Politically, the plight of the soldiers during the Spanish-American War provided an issue for both parties. Governor Stephens was blamed for the inadequate preparations and for the insufficient provisions for the militia and was attacked for his policies of attempting to name his friends as officers in the military units. The Republican state platform of 1898 declared:

> We call attention to the fact that the parsimonious treatment of the National Guard of this state by the Democratic Legislature has brought shame upon the State of Missouri, leaving our brave volunteer soldiers without supplies and dependent on charity to keep them from starving before being mustered into United States service.

On the other hand, Governor Stephens referred to the deplorable conditions in federal camps for which he blamed the Republican administration in Washington when he greeted the returning militiamen: "We know of the silent but fierce battle in which you have been engaged with neglect, filth, incompetency, corruption, and disease." Some Democrats even charged that the Republican administration had kept Missouri troops out of battle because they did not wish the Democratic state of Missouri to receive military glory. The war intensified the political conflict in the state, and public dissatisfaction with the conduct of the Democratic administration during the mobilization period probably strengthened the Republican cause in the election of 1900 and the years which followed. This awakened public interest also resulted in better support of the National Guard in Missouri.

The "splendid little war," as Ambassador to England, John Hay, described the Spanish-American conflict, had one salubrious effect on the state of Missouri and the nation as a whole. As the sons of Union and Confederate veterans fought side by side under the American flag, the old Civil War wound began to heal. The St. Louis *Republic* for May 15, 1898, proclaimed: "This war has wiped out sectionalism. Sectionalism is dead forever. The Mason and Dixon line has been removed."

Corruption

At the turn of the century St. Louis, the fourth largest city in the United States, was plagued with the cancer of corruption in its municipal government. Many of the largest metropolitan centers in the nation were similarly afflicted during this period. Two men diagnosed the malady; one published the diagnosis, the other attempted to effect a cure. The former was Lincoln Steffens, a writer for *McClure's Magazine;* the latter was Joseph W. Folk, a lawyer of St. Louis.

During the 1890's the standards of conduct in St. Louis government were lowered as first one and then another illegal and immoral practice was allowed. The government of St. Louis was vested in the two houses of the municipal assembly—the council and the house of delegates. Certain unscrupulous members of the assembly organized what became known as the Combine, an organization of lawmakers who agreed to work together in securing the passage or defeat of certain legislation in return for adequate bribes. The Combine, in its systematic businesslike way, set up prices to standardize bribery in the city. Thus, a company which wished permission to relocate a railroad switch or which wanted to purchase a state railroad franchise could determine the cost of securing the necessary legislative approval by consulting any leader of the Combine. For a greasing of their palms the Combine would agree to pass or to defeat bills according to the desires of the briber. When income from their legislative thievery dwindled, the Combine would introduce a bill designed to threaten a St. Louis industry, and then agree to kill the bill for a proper reward.

Members of the Combine later, in testimony before a grand jury, admitted receiving incomes of $25,000 a year from their iniquitous enterprise. One councilman confessed to accepting $50,000 for a single vote. This system of bribery in the city legislature led to other corrupt practices—blackmail, payroll padding, profiteering on public improvements, and profiteering on city contracts.

Although the existence of such an illegal organization was well known among the business people of St. Louis, and although the newspapers attempted to alert the citizens, the practice continued for nearly a decade. Since prominent and powerful men of the city were indulging in the bribery, public indignation was not sufficiently strong to halt the practice.

The political boss in St. Louis was Colonel Edward Butler, a blacksmith who had risen to the position of a millionaire politician through his crafty manipulations. Butler had organized the two houses of the municipal assembly so that he had control of a two-thirds majority in each house, which was sufficient to override any mayor's veto. Butler, the boss of the Democratic

Party in St. Louis, had organized groups of subordinate politicians who used "repeaters" to control the outcome of elections.
By hauling vans of repeaters from one polling place to another,
the Democrats were able to secure the election of handpicked
candidates in St. Louis, which was normally a Republican city.
Butler, who had some power over the Republican Party, too, in
some instances connived with Republicans. In the long run, he
was more interested in boodle than he was in party.

As the election of 1900 drew near, Boss Butler and his Democratic associates, deciding that they would appear in the election
as reformers, adopted the slogan, "No more Ziegenheinism." Republican Mayor Ziegenhein, who had been a most incompetent
mayor, became famous for his response to a group of citizens
who approached him complaining that their street lights were
not working. "You have the moon yet, ain't it?" was the mayor's
reply. In attempting to don a mask of reform, the Democrats
asked a young Tennessee-born St. Louis lawyer named Joseph W.
Folk to be their candidate for circuit attorney. Folk had enjoyed
much good publicity in St. Louis in his arbitration of the railroad
strike of 1898. After repeated requests that he run for office,
Folk finally accepted, but he added, "If elected I will do my duty."
The Democratic committeemen, having heard such platitudes
before, were unimpressed. Folk was nominated and elected circuit attorney for the Eighth Missouri District in 1900.

It was not long before Folk had alienated Butler and his
followers. Folk refused to appoint associates suggested by Colonel Butler, and when a group of Republicans and Democrats were
charged with illegal registration at the prior election, Folk insisted upon prosecution. However, it was not until the year 1902
that Folk became aware of the extent of the operations of the
Combine. Through a brief news story, he learned that the members of the municipal assembly had been promised large sums of
money in return for their votes on a railroad franchise action.
In a search for evidence, Folk quickly subpoenaed one hundred
persons to testify before a grand jury. As he had hoped, two of
those requested to testify decided to admit their part in the conspiracy. By the time Folk discovered the bribery money hidden
in safety deposit boxes in the city, the Combine was in serious
trouble and several leading members were on their way to Old
Mexico to escape justice.

Although Attorney Folk knew that Ed Butler was head of

the corrupt political Combine, he had difficulty in securing an indictment. Finally, the attorney received information that Butler had offered two members of the board of health $2,500 for their granting a garbage contract to a company in which he owned a large share of stock. Although Boss Butler was convicted of bribery, he escaped the penitentiary when the decision was reversed by the Missouri supreme court because of a technicality.

The scandal continued to grow and to engulf more and more people. During Folk's investigation of one boodle-tainted deal, he uncovered the facts in another scandal—the Central Traction Dealings—which had occurred four years earlier in 1898. A Kansas City promoter named R. M. Snyder had come to St. Louis, and by spending a total of $300,000 in bribing, wining, and dining members of the municipal assembly, had managed to secure an exclusive permit to operate a streetcar line in St. Louis. The existing streetcar lines were, therefore, at the mercy of Snyder. They could either sell out to him on his terms, or purchase his permit at whatever price he would set. One week later Snyder sold his exclusive franchise for $1,250,000. Without laying one inch of track, the briber had realized a profit of nearly $1,000,-000.

New York reporter Lincoln Steffens came to Folk's city in

In 1904 Missouri went Republican, but Democrat Joseph W. Folk was elected governor when his reputation as a reformer won for him many Republican votes.

(Courtesy State Historical Society)

1902 and wrote a revelation of the prevalent corruption under the title "Tweed Days in St. Louis." When Steffens' story focused the attention of America on the actions of the courageous young attorney, Folk became a national personality. At the turn of the century a journalist named Finley Peter Dunne was the writer of a column in which he commented on the happenings of the day in the words of a perceptive and loquacious Irishman, Martin Dooley. This is what Mr. Dooley had to say about Joseph Folk in 1903:

> . . . Folk is th' noblest chaser iv thim all. Set him on a boodler's trail an' he's a whole pack iv trained bloodhounds. With tireless energy an' exalted enthusiasm he chases a boodler up hill an' down dale, into th' woods, across th' pasture, around th' barn, back iv th' pig pen an' into th' hin house, where he pins him to th' wall with a pitchforruk. 'Villain,' says Folk to th' boodler, 'villain, confess now an' I'll be lenient with ye. Confess to all yer infamies an' all yer thousand-dollar bills an' all yer associates in fraud and corruption, an', so help me, I will ask the coort to give ye not more than 40 or 50 years,' says Folk, as he deftly wiggles th' pitchforruk in th' boodler's vitals. 'I do confess,' says th' boodler. . . . And now that I have confessed will ye have th' kindness to pull th' harpoon out iv me vitals an' let me take me chances with the Missouri Supreme Court.' Thus th' Missouri boodlers confess to Mr. Folk, Hinnissy. He's th' man that ought to be probing th' postoffice department at Washington. He's the champion prober iv Missouri boodlers.

Folk earned Mr. Dooley's praise by obtaining thirty-nine indictments during his period as circuit attorney, but securing convictions was another matter. Many of the cases brought to trial by Folk were later thrown out by the Missouri supreme court, and only nine of the boodlers from St. Louis were ever sentenced to the penitentiary. As Lincoln Steffens wryly remarked, "The whole machinery of justice broke down under the strain of boodle pull."

Joseph Folk performed a valuable service for the citizens of St. Louis. He proved that their municipal assembly was controlled by nine men in the council and nineteen in the house, all of whom worked together under the leadership of Colonel Edward Butler. Attorney Folk was even able to publicize the so-called "Thieves' Oath," to which the members of the Combine swore:

> I do solemnly swear before Almighty God that in associating myself and in becoming a member of this Combine, I will vote and act with the Combine whenever and wherever I may be so ordered to do so. And I further solemnly swear that I will not at any place or at any time reveal the fact that there is a Combine, and that I will not communicate to any person or persons anything that may take place at any meeting of the Combine.
>
> And I do solemnly agree that, in case I should reveal the fact that any person in this Combine has received money, I hereby permit and authorize other members of this Combine to take the forfeit of my life in such manner as they may deem proper, and that my throat may be cut, my tongue torn out, and my body thrown into the Mississippi River.
>
> And all this I do solemnly swear, so help me God.

Folk also dared to reveal that many of the leading professional and businessmen of the city and members of the wealthiest segment of the population were involved in schemes to defraud the city. To Joe Folk the statement "I will do my duty" was no platitude. To Lincoln Steffens' chagrin and contempt, the people of St. Louis did not immediately destroy the Butler political machine. Boss Butler, still an important power in the politics of St. Louis, continued to be consulted by both Republican and Democratic leaders. However, the publicity which Joseph Folk received for his campaign to cleanse the municipal government of St. Louis made him a well-known figure in Missouri and led to his election as governor of the state in 1904.

The Progressive Movement and Missouri Government

Periodically in American history, the demand of the people for reform legislation swells with a flood of corruption and grievances, crests in the passage of reform measures, and then ebbs in apathy. In the years after the Civil War there were examples of moral decay in national government, in state government, in business, and in many social areas of life. In the last decade of the nineteenth century and the early years of the twentieth century a new wave of reform legislation crested in America. The reform movement was known by various names; the most popular one at the turn of the century was Progressivism.

(Courtesy State Historical Society)

The stately Jasper County Courthouse, constructed of Carthage stone in a style characteristic of government buildings in the nineties, was completed in 1895 during Governor Stone's term.

Politics and Progressivism

The Progressive movement grew from several roots. First, although the Populist movement of the 1890's soon withered and died, the need for reform from which the Populists sprang still existed. Second, organized labor, which was becoming stronger in the late years of the nineteenth century, fed the Progressive movement with frequent calls for a reform of existing government or business practices. A third group which contributed to the Progressive movement were the journalists known as "Muckrakers," who nurtured Progressivism with startling revelations of the scandals in American life. Joseph Folk's eulogist, Lincoln Steffens, was the uncrowned King of the Muckrakers. Steffens, who shocked the American people with his descriptions of municipal corruption in his book, *The Shame of the Cities,* singled out St. Louis as one of the most corrupt city governments in

America. Another basis for the development of the Progressive movement was the increasing social consciousness of the churches of America who came to see the importance of applying their Gospel in the concrete, everyday situations of life. Out of these several separate movements of Populism, organized labor, sensational journalism, and church concern, came a new demand for reform in America.

It must be made clear that Missouri was not unique in the new interest in reform. The Progressive movement was a national development, and young political leaders who advocated programs of progressive reforms appeared from coast to coast. In New York, Charles Evans Hughes led the Progressive crusade; Wisconsin's leader was Robert LaFollette; Hiram Johnson provided reform leadership in California. By adopting Progressive measures, Missourians were in step with American reformers across the nation.

The Progressive movement cannot be assigned to any one party or to any small number of men. Both Democrats and Republicans had their Progressives; Woodrow Wilson and Theodore Roosevelt, although members of different parties, can both be considered Progressives. Not only did Progressives subscribe to varying party loyalties, but they also held a variety of views concerning the necessary reforms and the methods of securing them.

Despite differences of opinion, most Progressives tended to favor most of the following reforms. Loathing the old system of open, oral voting, they demanded both the Australian ballot, and the direct primary to give all citizens a voice in the selection of nominees. The reformers also called for constitutional provisions to allow for the initiative and the referendum, so that the citizens might themselves initiate needed legislation and pass it by referendum if the legislature failed to respond to popular demand. Progressives were also outspoken in their criticism of the manner in which United States senators were chosen. The critics, declaring that the state legislatures all too frequently appointed wealthy men, intimated that the United States Senate was a "millionaires' club" because people with great wealth could purchase their election to the Senate. To remedy this situation, the reformers advocated the direct popular nomination and election of senators. Also attacked was the sale of intoxicants. Many churches and organizations of the time, noting evil consequences of the widespread sale of liquor and its relationship to crime, insanity, and other social problems, advocated prohibition as a technique for improving society. Still other Progressive demands called for woman suffrage, the graduated income tax, stricter labor laws to protect the interests and health of the workman, increased aid to public education, the improvement of eleemosynary institutions, the discouragement and control of monopolies, and the cleansing of governmental operations at all levels. Missouri had many reformers who demanded such changes in the state and who supported these general aims of the Progressive movement.

We will not here follow in detail the elections of the period 1892 to 1916, but it should be stressed that a pattern can be seen in the election results of this time. From 1892 until 1904 the Democratic Party gradually lost its dominance in Missouri politics. There are probably several reasons for its slowly decreasing strength. The normal amount of dissatisfaction and friction within the party alienated a few. The reports of corruption in St. Louis and in the state legislature were certain to hurt the Democratic cause. In addition, there were Democrats during the 1890's and in 1900 who disagreed with the party platform on such issues as the free coinage of silver and the condemnation of imperialism at the end of the Spanish-American War. At the

Champ Clark from Louisiana, Missouri, took his seat in the United States House of Representatives in 1893. Accompanying him up the steps of the national capitol was his son, Bennett, who later served as senator from Missouri. This pioneer news photograph was taken by Walter B. Stevens.
(Courtesy State Historical Society)

With only a two-year interval, Champ Clark served in Congress from 1893 to 1921, and as speaker of the House from 1911 to 1919. In 1912 he was a leading candidate for the Democratic presidential nomination.

(Portrait by Edmonston, Courtesy State Historical Society)

time when these differences were weakening the Democratic Party, the Republicans seem to have gained nationally because of the easy victory over Spain during a Republican administration. Furthermore, "Teddy" Roosevelt, a popular Republican president at the beginning of the twentieth century, no doubt made the Republican cause more attractive to Missourians.

The rejuvenated Republican forces in the state were able to secure a Missouri victory for their presidential candidate in 1904 when Roosevelt carried the state. That same year, Democratic reformer Joseph W. Folk of St. Louis was chosen governor. However, since all other state offices and a majority of the legislative seats were won by the Republicans, Folk's election in 1904 cannot be considered a Democratic victory. It was a personal triumph. From 1904-1920 the two major parties in the state were almost evenly matched, and two of the governors—Hadley, a Republican, and Gardner, a Democrat—were forced to work with legislative houses controlled by the opposition party.

During the period of our consideration in this chapter (1892-1920), more of Missouri's senators and representatives were Democrats than Republicans. Missouri did send two Republicans to the United States Senate—the first since Reconstruction days —William Warner of Kansas City (1905-1911) and Selden Spencer of St. Louis (1910-1925). The Democratic senators of the time were probably more controversial individuals. Senator Vest

Governor William Joel Stone
of Nevada began his political
career as prosecuting attorney of Vernon County in 1872
and ended it as United States
senator in 1918.

*(Strauss Portrait, Courtesy State
Historical Society)*

(1879-1903) was particularly noted for his fight to maintain the
Yellowstone region as a national park. Although Senator Cockrell (1875-1905) was a Democrat, he was particularly outspoken
in his criticism of Democratic President Cleveland and Cleveland's money policies, just as Senators William Stone (1903-
1918) and James A. Reed (1911-1928) were outspoken in their
opposition to the foreign policies of Woodrow Wilson. Champ
Clark from Pike County was the first and only Missourian to
serve as speaker of the United States House of Representatives.
He served with distinction from 1911 to 1919, and he contended
with Woodrow Wilson for the Democratic nomination for president in 1912.

The Stone Administration

William J. Stone, a lawyer and one time prosecuting attorney
from Nevada, was chosen as the Democratic governor of Missouri
in 1892. He had served in the United States Senate in the trying
days leading to American entrance into World War I, and is one
of the most unusual and outstanding Missouri political leaders.
A man of independence, courage, and resourcefulness, Stone was
one of twelve senators who refused to grant President Wilson the
authority to arm American merchant ships, although his stand
made him one of the most hated members of the Senate. In the

hysteria of the time Stone insisted that war with all its horrors must be avoided if at all possible.

During Stone's administration as governor of Missouri, he was able to secure larger appropriations for the educational and eleemosynary institutions of the state. New buildings were authorized at Missouri University, the Rolla School of Mines and Metallurgy, Lincoln Institute, and Warrensburg Normal, as well as for several of the other state institutions. Because of the bankruptcy of several building and loan associations, the state legislature established procedures for the examination of the books of such organizations and of banks. The legislature also passed new laws to regulate the operation of mines for the greater protection of the workers, and to insure for Missouri laborers the right to join a union. Because of the well-publicized election frauds in St. Louis and Kansas City, the legislature, in a special session called by the governor, enacted new, detailed laws to prevent voting frauds.

After Andrew Taylor Still, the founder of osteopathy, had established the American School of Osteopathy in Kirksville in 1892, an increasing number of Missourians had become osteopaths. During Governor Stone's administration the legislature

Free delivery of rural mail was first attempted in Randolph County in 1896.
(Courtesy State Historical Society)

passed a bill to approve and license the practice of osteopathy in the state. Governor Stone vetoed this measure, but it was finally passed in 1897 during the administration of Governor Stephens, who had been treated by Dr. Still.

In the election of 1896, the voters were requested to indicate on their ballots whether they favored moving the state capital to Sedalia where land and money were available for the construction of a new capitol building. The proposal was defeated by a two to one vote, and the City of Jefferson remained the seat of the government of Missouri.

The Stephens Administration

In 1896 the successful contender for the governorship was Democrat Lon V. Stephens of Boonville, a former lawyer, editor, and banker who was known as an expert in financial affairs. Stephens was sympathetic with the view expressed at that time by many, particularly farmers, that greater economy should be exercised in state government. During his term as governor, Stephens took pride in his economy measures which resulted in reducing the state debt to below the two million dollar mark.

Certain of the laws passed during the Stephens administration show the impact of Populist ideology upon government. In 1897 the General Assembly passed a law subsequently approved by the governor, making railroads liable for injuries to a worker although the accident was caused by the negligence of another employee. The legislature established employment offices to assist those who sought work, and passed legislation to curtail child labor. Bakery and confectionary firms were forbidden by law to require more than a six-day work week, and a bill was enacted which established an eight-hour work day for miners. To control the loan sharks in the state the legislature passed an act prohibiting the charging of an interest rate higher than two per cent per month. Additional laws were enacted to regulate the operation of trusts or monopolies in the state.

In 1897, in answer to many complaints of ill treatment and inadequate facilities in penal, mental, and other institutions of the state, a board was created to visit all such public institutions and to make recommendations for future policy. These reports subsequently led to a number of improvements in Missouri's institutions in the next administrations.

During Stephens' term several new Missouri organizations were established. The General Assembly authorized appropriations for a state fair at Sedalia, which was first held in 1901. In the same year, the legislature assumed support of The State Historical Society of Missouri by appropriating $4500 for its work.

We have already noted that Governor Stephens was severely criticized for his policies during the Spanish-American War. These policies invoked so great and bitter an outflow of journalistic venom that one member of the General Assembly proposed the outlawing of criticism of the governor in the legislature. This proposal was not adopted, but it is an indication of the heated political conflict of the time.

The Dockery Administration

In the election of 1900 the Democratic candidate, Alexander M. Dockery, of Gallatin, was chosen governor. Dockery had practiced medicine in Chillicothe as a young man and then moved to Gallatin where he became a banker. Active in Democratic politics, he was chosen congressman in 1882 and served for sixteen years in Washington, where he was elevated to the post of speaker pro tempore of the House. Dockery served his term in Jefferson City during an exciting period in Missouri history—when the Louisiana Purchase Exposition was being held in St. Louis and Joseph Folk was revealing the degradation of St. Louis politics. It was also a time of scandal in the state legislature. In 1891 a bill had been introduced to repeal an earlier act prohibiting the sale of baking powder which contained alum. The earlier law had excluded all but one company from the sale of baking powder in Missouri. When the repealing act came to a vote in 1901 it failed to pass, and the speaker of the House publicly declared that lobby interests had killed the bill. A grand jury investigation in Cole County was begun. Since this investigation occurred while Attorney Folk was attempting to halt the boodling activities in St. Louis, Folk gave assistance to the state prosecution in ferreting out bribe takers. It soon was learned that Lieutenant-Governor John A. Lee had received $8,500 in a meeting at the Laclede Hotel in St. Louis in 1901 in return for a promise to kill the repeal action. Lee had kept $1,500 for himself and distributed $1,000 to each of seven state senators. When the facts in the case were publicized, Lieutenant-Governor Lee resigned and agreed to testify in court. No one was convicted in the incident, although the details were publicized throughout the state and the affair led to public suspicion of the state administration.

Physician Alexander M o n r o e Dockery of Gallatin served in the United States House of Representatives from 1883 to 1901 and as governor from 1901 to 1905.

(Courtesy State Historical Society)

When, during Dockery's term as governor, the state was able to pay off all outstanding bonds in 1903, a great gathering of state officials met to celebrate the day with speeches, band music, and a forty-four gun salute. Certainly the procession of governors from the Civil War to 1903 should be given credit for their financial wisdom and restraint in having successfully paid off forty-four million dollars of debts. Governor Dockery was able to announce at the end of his term that the Missouri tax rate was then the lowest in the Union.

The Dockery administration brought forth certain needed reforms of the day, including the founding of juvenile courts, the creation of a board of arbitration and mediation to help settle labor disputes, and a staff of factory inspectors to examine the manufacturing establishments of the state to observe the circumstances of labor and report infractions of the law.

The Folk Administration

The election of 1904 was a time of great conflict within the Democratic Party. Joseph W. Folk, the reforming attorney from St. Louis, was disliked by many leaders of the Democratic Party who felt that he had hurt the party by his revelations of corruption. The brewery and railroad interests of the state also opposed him. When Folk announced his candidacy in 1904 he immediately received the support of many rank-and-file Democrats across the state, but he found few party leaders willing to back his candidacy. The revelations of scandal in the legislature during the Dockery administration, which evidenced a need for house cleaning at the state level, made Folk all the more appealing to the voters. Despite all the best efforts of the Democratic Party leaders from Kansas City and St. Louis, Folk was nominated on the first ballot of the Democratic convention in 1904. He then secured the adoption of a platform built around the "Missouri Idea," which meant that the party was dedicated to the abolition of bribery in government.

The Democratic candidate for president in 1904 was Alton B. Parker, a colorless judge who opposed Bryan's money policies. The Republican candidate was the colorful, effervescent, dynamic Teddy Roosevelt. Faced with this choice, great numbers of Democrats stayed at home. When the results were tallied, Missouri had for the first time since Reconstruction voted for a Republican candidate for president. Joseph W. Folk, however, who received many Republican as well as Democratic votes, was elected governor. All other state offices and a majority of the seats in the legislature were filled with Republicans. John McCutcheon, the cartoonist for the *Chicago Tribune*, drew a well-known cartoon entitled "The Mysterious Stranger" to portray Missouri's unusual election results in 1904.

"The Mysterious Stranger," a famous cartoon by John McCutcheon appeared in the November 10, 1904, issue of the Chicago Tribune the day after the Republican victory in Missouri.

Folk considered himself a Progressive, and his first message to the General Assembly listed the many reforms he felt necessary for Missouri. Although Folk had a Republican legislature during his first two years in office, he was able to secure the passage of a large body of reform legislation during his whole term as governor. The Alum Law of 1899 was repealed. The legislature also passed a law forcing lobbyists to register and thus to operate in the open. The statute of limitation was extended from three to five years on bribery cases, making easier the conviction of legislators who had accepted boodle. A new railroad law was passed to establish freight rates, thereby reducing some rates in Missouri from fifteen to forty per cent. Folk secured the passage of a compulsory school law which applied to all children between the ages of eight and fourteen. The legislature also established two new teachers' colleges—one at Maryville and the other at Springfield. A new primary election system was established which gave Missouri's voters the power to determine nominees. Governor Folk secured in the second half of his administration the passage of a bill to provide for the initiative and the referendum, making possible the proposal and adoption of laws directly by the people of Missouri. This is only a partial list of the legislature's reform acts.

Probably the most controversial aspect of Governor Folk's administration was his attempt to enforce the Sunday closing laws. Although he was not an advocate of prohibition himself, he insisted that the laws must be obeyed and ordered state agents to raid the popular beer gardens of St. Louis to halt the Sunday sale of intoxicants.

Herbert S. Hadley was the attorney general for the state during Folk's administration. Only two months after taking office, Hadley brought suit against the Standard Oil Company of New Jersey charging that Missouri had been divided into two halves with Standard Oil of Indiana in control of the sale of oil north of the Missouri River and Waters-Pierce Oil Company controlling the oil trade south of the river. The only alternative company available was the Republic Oil Company, which, like Standard of Indiana and Waters-Pierce, was a subsidiary of Standard of New Jersey. Hadley, after revealing that ninety-five per cent of Missouri's oil business was controlled by one trust, brought suit in 1905. The testimony in the case continued for more than two years, and it was reported that John D. Rockefeller was so anxious to avoid testifying at the Missouri trial he disguised himself in a wig and departed the country. In March, 1906, Standard Oil admitted that a trust had been established. Finally, in December of 1908, the three companies were fined $50,000 each. Standard Oil was denied the right to do business in Missouri, and Waters-Pierce was ordered to sever its ties with Standard Oil. As a consequence of this case, Missouri petroleum prices, long inflated by the monopoly, dropped, resulting in an estimated savings to Missourians of approximately $600,000 a year. Attorney General Hadley received much publicity and praise for his handling of the case.

Governor Folk was an excellent speaker and a fine administrator, but he was not a good politician. He lacked the warm personality which attracts votes, and he refused that close association with party leadership which insures party support. The party leaders were happy to be rid of him at the end of his term in 1908. Although he ran for other offices later, he was never again chosen to an elective position by the people of Missouri.

The Hadley Administration

In 1908 Herbert S. Hadley became the first Republican governor since B. Gratz Brown in 1870. Hadley was a handsome, capable man with an enviable prosecuting attorney record (Jackson County) of 122 convictions to only six acquittals. In the remarkable Republican state victory in 1904 he had been chosen attorney general, in which office he secured fame throughout the United States for his victory in the Standard Oil case discussed above, as well as other successful antitrust suits against International Harvester and certain lumber companies. He added further luster to his record by securing an out-of-court agreement for the lowering of insurance rates in Missouri and for successfully prosecuting eighteen railroad companies for infractions of Missouri laws.

As governor of Missouri he had a Republican legislature during his first two years, but a Democratic legislature during the last two. Hadley was able to secure the levying of a new oil tax to help meet the need for increased revenue, but the legislature refused to authorize other new taxes he requested. To insure honest elections in Kansas City and St. Louis, the governor established bipartisan election boards. The bureau of vital statistics for the recording of births and deaths, and a state food and drug commission were also established during Hadley's administra-

In 1911 Governor Herbert S.
Hadley led a twenty-six automobile caravan of state officials across the state to pick a
route for an all-weather cross-
state highway from Kansas
City to St. Louis.
(Courtesy State Historical Society)

tion. In addition, new laws were passed regulating working hours
and conditions for women. During Hadley's administration the
Sixteenth Amendment to the Federal Constitution was ratified,
providing for a graduated federal income tax. Hadley was disappointed in being unable to secure legislative approval of his
plan to create a state public service commission for the regulation of utilities, or to effect passage of workman's compensation
to insure payment to the worker for injury suffered on the job.

In 1911 a lightning-sparked blaze destroyed the capitol building in Jefferson City. During the remainder of his term, Hadley
directed the first steps in preparing for the erection of a new
capitol. The people of Missouri agreed to finance a new capitol
in an election in August, 1911. Ground was broken in 1913; and
the building, constructed of Carthage and Phoenix stone from
southwest Missouri, was completed and dedicated in 1924.

The Major Administration

In the election of 1912 Elliott Woolfolk Major was the successful Democratic candidate for the governor's office. Major,
who had been the Missouri attorney general during the Hadley
administration, had continued the antitrust suits which had been
pressed by Hadley during his own term as attorney general.

Major was so successful in his antitrust crusade that he secured $500,000 in fines for the Missouri State Treasury. Like Folk and Hadley, Elliott Major was an outspoken Progressive who sought to utilize the forces of state government to protect citizens and consumers from those who would exploit them.

The accomplishments of the Major administration indicated his ties with Progressivism. Probably his most important achievement was the establishment of a state public service commission to regulate the public utilities operating in Missouri. The five-member commission was specifically assigned to examine critically the utilities of the state in order to protect the consumer from exorbitant rates and at the same time to see that the companies were permitted to receive a fair profit for their invesment. Since the inspection of railroads was assigned to the new commission, the previous office of railroad and warehouse commissioner was abolished.

During Major's term of office the state passed new education acts which provided larger sums of money for the schools of Missouri, particularly in the rural areas and in the smaller communities of the state. Major, who was also interested in road improvement, secured the establishment of a state highway department in Missouri and instituted a novel "Good Road Days" scheme. Under this program, during two days in August, 1913

A graphic picture of Missouri's capitol building, completed in 1840 and remodeled in 1888, as it burned from a lightning-set blaze on February 5, 1911. A temporary capitol built at a cost of $51,000 housed the state government until completion of the present structure.

(Courtesy State Historical Society)

Governor Elliott Woolfolk Major
focused attention on the need for
road improvements by asking citizens to work on the roads during
Good Road Days.
(Courtesy State Historical Society)

and 1914, 250,000 men of Missouri gave their time to improve
Missouri roads. Although these two days obviously were not the
complete answer to Missouri's road problem, they did focus the
attention of the citizens of Missouri on the need for better roads.

In 1916, the legislature finally abolished the contract labor
system used in Missouri's prisons. Before this time the state had
sold contracts to certain Missouri companies giving those companies the privilege of using prisoners for labor in return for the
maintenance of the convicts. Under the system there was great
exploitation of the prisoners, who often were neither adequately
clothed nor fed. The state then established a system of prison
industries which provided work for the inmates, furniture and
supplies for other state institutions, and some financial support
for the prisons.

During Major's administration, the present state flag, designed by Mrs. R. B. Oliver of Cape Girardeau, was adopted as
Missouri's official banner.

The Gardner Administration

In the election of 1916, Democrat Frederick D. Gardner,
president of the St. Louis Coffin Company, was chosen governor
of the state. Gardner served during a difficult period with all
the problems of World War I and an increasing state debt. The
Progressive governors of the state, in their desire to protect the
citizens and consumers, established many new boards and agencies to carry on this work. Such agencies, of course, were expensive, and the governors had been unable to secure the passage

of new legislation to pay for the added expense. As a result, the debt mounted steadily until it reached two million dollars in 1916. The Republicans, who attempted to make the deficit an issue in the election of 1916, probably would have had greater success had not Democratic candidate Gardner himself been an outspoken critic of deficit financing. Governor Gardner promised that, if elected, he would institute new measures to force the legislature to live within its means.

As soon as he took office, Gardner demanded that the legislature pass new taxes. Among the taxes levied was one on corporations, another on inheritance, and still another on income. These taxes, together with certain minor levies, brought in sufficient revenue to pay off Missouri's indebtedness during Gardner's term.

The governor was so intent upon sound financing that he dared to veto a law providing pensions for needy blind people when the legislature refused to pass a tax law to finance the large expenditure the pensions would require.

Mrs. Marie Elizabeth Watkins Oliver, ninety years young, with the original state flag.
(Courtesy State Historical Society)

Several important advances were made during his term. The state park system and a single board to direct the prisons were established. A state tax commission was instituted to adjust and equalize property values throughout the state, as well as to carry on certain assessment duties.

National Reforms

The reform movement can be seen at the national level in the amendments to the Federal Constitution which were adopted during the second decade of the twentieth century. In 1913, federal income taxes were made legal and the election of United States senators was shifted from the state legislatures to the people. In 1919 the states adopted another amendment which outlawed the manufacture and sale of beverage alcohol. This Prohibition Amendment and the subsequent difficulties of enforcement will be discussed in the next chapter. In 1920 still another reform amendment which granted women the right to vote was added to the United States Constitution.

The movement toward woman suffrage was active in Missouri fifty-three years before the adoption of the federal amendment. In 1867 the legislature was petitioned to grant the women of Missouri the franchise; two years later, a national convention of advocates of woman suffrage was held in St. Louis. At various times in the century Missouri organizations proclaimed the wisdom of allowing women to vote—the Populists, the Farmers' Alliance, the Missouri State Teachers Association, the Prohibitionists, and other organizations openly espoused woman suffrage. However, when the proposal to give women the right to vote in Missouri was submitted to the eligible male voters in 1914, the proposition failed.

Two years later, women gathering in St. Louis made a dramatic attempt to impress the virtue of woman suffrage upon the Democratic National Convention meeting in the city. Over seven thousand women dressed in white with yellow parasols, streamers, and sashes formed a double line for ten blocks along Locust Street. The male delegates to the convention were forced to walk between these silent witnesses to the need for widening the franchise. One observer called this display the Golden Lane and wrote the following descriptive poem:

A Suffragette Parade in 1907
(Courtesy State Historical Society)

Silence! My but it did talk
Marching down the Golden Lane.
Fast the delegates did walk,
Marching down the Golden Lane!
But they couldn't get away
From the "Women's Votes" display.
They'll all recall for many a day
Marching down the Golden Lane.

The would-be voters' demonstration won for them only vague reference to the need for woman suffrage in the Democratic platform.

The next year, 1917, Mrs. William C. Fordyce addressed the state legislature on behalf of the women of Missouri. By her presence she demonstrated the persistence of the weaker sex in demanding the franchise. She challenged the legislators:

Gentlemen, fifty years ago my grandmother came before the Missouri Legislature and asked for the enfranchisement of women; twenty-five years ago my mother came to make the same request; tonight I am asking for the ballot for women. Are you going to make it necessary for my daughter to appear in her turn?

Finally, in 1919, an amendment to the United States Constitution authorizing women to vote was distributed to the states. Governor Gardner called a special session of the legislature, and by action of this body Missouri became the eleventh state to ratify the amendment. It became part of the United States Constitution in August, 1920.

The decade before and the two decades after 1900 were an important era in Missouri history. By the late nineteenth century Missouri had huge urban areas with the industrial productivity and cultural developments which are the by-products of urbanization. Missouri also suffered the metropolitan maladies of urban political machines, election thievery, and legislative bribery. The years from 1890 to 1920 were a fight arena with billings of combines versus conscience, corruption versus courage, and rascals versus reformers. In this struggle, both political parties were split, for Progressive measures usually threatened the well-entrenched in both parties. Slowly the voters began their demand for government regulation of those aspects of society in need of reform. Missouri began to regulate its utilities, to establish working hours and conditions for many of the laborers, to inspect factories and mines, to provide greater sums of money for schools and institutions, and to reform those political practices which made corruption possible. The forces of corruption and of tradition were not easily destroyed. For the spectator the struggle was an engrossing one.

BIBLIOGRAPHY

Clevenger, Homer. "The Farmers' Alliance in Missouri," *Missouri Historical Review,* Vol. XXXIX (October, 1944), pp. 24-44.

Geiger, Louis G. *Joseph W. Folk.* Columbia: The Curators of the University of Missouri, 1953.

Hicks, John D. *The Populist Revolt.* Minneapolis: The University of Minnesota Press, 1931.

Houghton, N. D. "Initiative and Referendum in Missouri," *Missouri Historical Review,* Vol. XIX (January, 1925), pp. 268-299.

Kirschten, Ernest. *Catfish and Crystal.* Garden City, New York: Doubleday and Company, Inc., 1960.

Long, Hazel Tutt. "Attorney General Herbert S. Hadley *versus* the Standard Oil Trust," *Missouri Historical Review,* Vol. XXXV (January, 1941), pp. 171-187.

Miller, William T. "The Progressive Movement in Missouri," *Missouri Historical Review,* Vol. XXII (July, 1928), pp. 456-501.

Missouri, a Guide to the "Show Me" State. New York: Duell, Sloan and Pearce, 1941.

Morris, Monia Cook. "The History of Woman Suffrage in Missouri 1867-1901," *Missouri Historical Review,* Vol. XXV (October, 1930), pp. 67-82.

Neilson, James Warren. "Congressional Opinion in Missouri Concerning the Spanish-American War," *Missouri Historical Review,* Vol. LI (April, 1957), pp. 245-256.

(Courtesy State Historical Society)

Although the Woman Suffrage Association of Missouri was formed in 1867, its members did not achieve their goal until 1919 when Governor Gardner signed the Woman Suffrage Act into law.

Oliver, R. B. "History of the State Flag of Missouri," *Missouri Historical Review,* Vol. XIII (April, 1919), pp. 226-231.

Reddig, William M. *Tom's Town.* Philadelphia and New York: J. B. Lippincott Company, 1947.

Scott, Mary Semple, ed. "History of Woman Suffrage in Missouri," *Missouri Historical Review,* Vol. XIV (April-July, 1920), pp. 281-384.

Shoemaker, Floyd C. *Missouri and Missourians.* Vol. I. Chicago: The Lewis Publishing Company, 1943.

Steffens, Lincoln. *The Shame of the Cities.* New York: Sagamore Press, Inc., 1957.

Violette, Eugene Morrow. *A History of Missouri.* Cape Girardeau, Missouri: Ramfre Press, 1951 ed.

Waldeck, Ruby Weedell. "Missouri in the Spanish-American War," *Missouri Historical Review,* Vol. XXX (July, 1936), pp. 365-400; Vol. XXXI (October, 1936), pp. 25-56.

CHAPTER XVI

War and Prosperity

> . . . Eddie Jacobson and I made plans to open a men's
> furnishing goods store in Kansas City. . . . During the first
> year of operation we sold over seventy thousand dollars'
> worth of merchandise and had a good return on our invest-
> ment.
>
> —Harry S Truman's
> *Memoirs*

On May 6, 1919, like thousands of other Missourians who had
fought in World War I, a field artillery captain from the 35th
Division returned to his home town as a civilian. Harry Truman
was ready to begin life anew. Eight weeks after his discharge
he married Bess Wallace, his blue-eyed childhood sweetheart
from Independence. Deciding that a change of vocation was in
order, he sold the farm machinery and the livestock on his 600
acre farm at Grandview for over $15,000. With this capital,
Harry Truman opened a haberdashery on Twelfth Street in Kansas City near the Muehlebach Hotel, in partnership with his wartime buddy, Eddie Jacobson.

Wheat was selling for $2.09 a bushel, and corn for $1.38 in
Missouri of 1919. With high prices such as these, there were
many who could afford the sixteen dollar silk shirts available at
the Truman-Jacobson haberdashery on Twelfth Street. Two
years later, however, when the price of wheat dropped to $.90
and corn to $.40 a bushel, buyers for high-priced haberdashery
became scarce. When the farmers of an agricultural state are
squeezed by low prices, the small businessmen are sure to feel
the pinch. In 1921 Harry Truman's business venture failed.

Many Missourians had experiences similar to those of army
veteran Truman. Farmers who had purchased expensive land,
machinery, and livestock during and immediately after World
War I had great difficulty making payments on their obligations
during the twenties when farm prices skidded. For many city

dwellers, however, the 1920's brought improvement in wages and easy credit. Eager-to-lend banks and loan companies found plenty of customers. Money—earned or borrowed— in the hands of the wage earner created a demand for consumer goods and housing. Industry hummed with activity and building and related trades prospered. Even Harry Truman, after his bitter experience with business failure, was able to realize a good income from the sale of memberships in the Kansas City Automobile Club, and as the general manager of the Community Savings and Loan Association of Independence. But the palace of prosperity, built on the sands of credit and speculation, housed only the city dwellers; the farmers stood outside in the cold rain of hard times. By the end of the decade, the financial storm worsened, sweeping away the foundations of prosperity and bringing the castle tumbling down on the heads of those who had reveled in its comforts.

Missouri's Part in World War I

World War I started in Europe in 1914 when two great alliances of proud and imperialistic nations—England, France, and Russia versus Germany and Austria-Hungary—were thrown into battle by the assassination of an Austrian prince and the exchange of international threats which followed the incident.

The United States was not part of the alliance scheme, and President Woodrow Wilson immediately declared America's intention to remain neutral. Because the United States was the world's leading industrial power, both sides sought her war goods and other exports, and as a result of America's trade with the combatants she became involved in the war despite her declaration of neutrality. Since under international law neutral nations could sell goods to belligerents, for a time the United States shipped supplies to both sides. Soon, however, both Britain and Germany began to violate America's rights by intercepting her ships. Each combatant declared the waters surrounding her enemy to be a battle zone, which meant that any ship entering the area would be in danger of attack. Since England's large navy controlled the Atlantic, and thereby was successful in prohibiting shipments to Germany, the Germans and Austrians were unable to buy many war supplies in America. As a result, the United States was trading almost exclusively with one side. The largest number of foreign-born in America—and in Missouri— were of German descent. As might be expected, some German-

Americans favored Germany in the European struggle, and protested our trade with Germany's enemies, declaring that the provision of assistance to only one side was a violation of our neutrality.

The character, as well as the size, of Britain's navy gave her another advantage over Germany. Because the British navy was composed primarily of surface craft, she was better able to follow the rules of international law requiring warships to evacuate the passengers and crews of merchant vessels before sinking them. On the other hand, submarines were predominant in the German navy. Because they might be destroyed while surfacing to give warning, the submarines sank British and French ships on sight without allowing evacuation of the people aboard. Germany tried to avoid trouble with America by placing notices in New York papers warning Americans of the dangers involved in traveling on ships of belligerent nations. When some Americans ignored this caution and President Wilson refused to issue official prohibition of such travel, American lives were lost. These American casualties of German U-boat attacks, of course, aroused indignation and inspired anti-German feeling across the nation.

In May of 1915 the deaths of 124 American citizens in the sinking of the British ship *Lusitania,* and other ship sinkings in 1916, evoked so intense a response from the American people and drew so strong a protest from President Wilson that the Germans, anxious to avoid American entrance in the war, stopped using submarines for a time. However, in January of 1917 the German high command, deciding to starve out the British as part of a final assault against Germany's enemies, announced that they were resuming submarine warfare and would destroy any ships carrying cargo to England. Although England had similarly violated our rights of neutrality, President Wilson by 1917 had become sympathetic to the cause of England and France. Wilson seems to have believed that German victory in the European war would have been contrary to America's best interests. When the Germans renewed their sub warfare in 1917, President Wilson called upon the Senate for permission to arm American merchant ships.

William J. Stone, former governor of Missouri, was representing the state in the United States Senate in 1917. When the president requested permission to arm American merchant ships,

Senator Stone, who was chairman of the foreign relations committee, was one of the Senate leaders in opposition to Wilson's plan. Stone and eleven other senators engaged in a filibuster to block passage of Wilson's bill. President Wilson, outraged at the actions of what he described as a "little group of willful men," tongue-lashed the senators for their stand.

Senator Stone was a man with the strength of his convictions. Although he recognized the fact that his part in the filibuster might ruin him politically in Missouri, he deplored war and cried out:

> I cannot vote to send our boys into this conflict, to involve our country in this struggle, the end of which we cannot see, and the results of which to our country and our civilization we cannot prophesy. I cannot so vote until further efforts have been made to avert the fearful sacrifices.

Senator Stone's position was not a popular one. The sentiment of the American people echoed President Wilson's growing sympathy for Britain and France. The anti-German feeling in-

The steam frigate U.S.S. Missouri burned at Gibraltar in 1843. The U.S.S. Missouri pictured below was active from 1901 to 1922 and served during World War I.

(Courtesy Mariner's Museum, Newport News, Virginia)

spired by the loss of American life in U-boat attacks was intensified by a barrage of British-planted stories of German atrocities.
Since Britain had cut the American cable from Germany early
in the war, this propaganda battle was decidedly one-sided and
very effective. German sabotage of war goods being manufactured in America and German use of poison gas on the battle-
field added more fuel to the fires of hatred.

Stone's voice was lost in the clamor of the crowds who
sought war in 1917. Although he was condemned in Missouri and
the nation for his stand, Stone acted in what he considered to be
the best interests of America and his state. Stone in 1917 stood
in much the same position as Thomas Hart Benton at the outset
of the Mexican War. Both men could see a bloody conflict approaching; both did their best to avert it. Both men were assailed for their actions and came to know the anguish of standing
firm in an unpopular position. Both, when the will of the majority was victorious and war was declared, did their best to bring
the conflict to a rapid and successful conclusion.

On April 2, 1917, after three American merchant ships had
been sent to cold Atlantic graves by German subs, President
Wilson asked Congress for a declaration of war to make the
world "safe for democracy." Actually, since Britain and France
were allied with totalitarian Czarist Russia, the preservation of
democracy could not logically have been a major issue. President
Wilson, however, who knew that he needed strong ideological
appeals to unite the American people, gave Americans a cause
and a crusade when he challenged them to champion democracy
and to win "the war to end all wars."

Missouri was a half step ahead of Congress in answering
the president's appeal. On April 5, 1917, 10,000 Missourians
gathered at the St. Louis Coliseum for an American loyalty rally.
A series of resolutions which had been composed by prominent
citizens of St. Louis were presented to Governor Frederick D.
Gardner, who read them to the assemblage. The resolutions
ended:

> We stand for the honor of our flag, for the rights
> of Americans on sea and on land, and in full pro-
> tection of everyone [sic] of those rights, and to
> that end are in favor of immediate and compulsory
> universal military service and adequate means to
> secure, when the war shall end, lasting world peace.

Then the governor vehemently declared:

> The resolutions are adopted. *This is no time for*
> *slackers, copperheads or soft pedalists. If there are*
> *any such among us, it is our duty to drive them out*
> *and brand them as traitors.*

Hours later, on April 6, 1917, word arrived that Congress had formally declared war on the Central Powers—Germany and Austria-Hungary.

Missourians responded to the call of their country with dedicated enthusiasm. During the war years, four Liberty Bond drives were held to help finance the tremendous cost of the war. Each state was given a quota of bonds her citizens would be asked to buy. Missourians oversubscribed all four drives; in the third drive they purchased 152 per cent of their quota. Missourians also contributed generously to such organizations as the Red Cross, Y.M.C.A., Young Men's Hebrew Association, the Salvation Army, and the Knights of Columbus, all of which provided services for American soldiers.

Since it was necessary for the United States to send great quantities of food to its allies in addition to feeding its own fighting men and civilians, food was a critical item during World War I. Governor Gardner, recognizing that the "burden of war will be placed on the shoulders of the farmer," immediately organized the Missouri Council of Defense under the leadership of Dean F. B. Mumford of the College of Agriculture at the University of Missouri. With Dean Mumford's coordination and $100,-000 supplied by the state government, a broad program was established to encourage Missourians to produce more food and to waste less. The 12,000 members of the Council reached every village in the state, and the effects of their efforts are evidenced by the rise in Missouri's rank from fourteenth state in value of crops produced in 1916 to fifth rank in 1917. Abolition of waste was another aim of Dr. Mumford's organization. With the encouragement of the Council, one million Missourians signed the Hoover pledge to conserve food. Wartime inspired many slogans, including one calling for "the patriotism of the clean garbage can." The success of this slogan can be seen in the fact that from April, 1917, to May, 1918, the garbage in St. Louis was reduced by over 12,000,000 pounds! Under Dr. Mumford's outstanding leadership, Missouri's Council of Defense was one of nine in the country given an "A" rating. Not one of the other eight councils

A "pep-talk" poster from World War I
(Courtesy State Historical Society)

had an appropriation of under $1,000,000. The Missouri Council spent only $76,986.47 for all its activities.

Missouri's first family set an example of patriotism for the citizens of the state. Mrs. Gardner, heeding the advice of the Defense Council, planted the backyard of the executive mansion with a "thrift garden" to supply her household with vegetables. The Gardners' son, William, cut short his college career and went to France with an ambulance unit from the University of Missouri.

The members of the medical profession in Missouri answered the appeal for professional help in army and Red Cross hospitals at home and abroad. Almost 1,500 Missouri doctors—one-third of them from St. Louis—closed lucrative practices to offer their services to the nation. Kansas City supplied more doctors and nurses than any other city of its size in the country. Twenty-five per cent of the volunteer physicians were sent overseas, where five were killed and two were taken prisoners of war.

The women of Missouri demonstrated their patriotism in numerous ways—knitting, sewing hospital garments, and making surgical dressings for the Red Cross; planting and cultivating "thrift gardens"; selling Liberty Bonds; preparing appetizing meals with substitutes and with restraint; and last—but not least in expenditure of energy—seeing to it that their families cleaned their plates. As *Life Magazine* of February 21, 1918, pointed out in a whimsical plea to conserve apples, "Nowadays even children must be taught to be patriotic to the core."

Several Missouri inventors were able to aid their country by the products of their genius. The Lexington *News* lauded A. A. Kellogg of Clinton, Missouri, who:

> invented an instantaneous detonator for shells, which is creating havoc with German wire defenses, trenches and emplacements. Heretofore the fuses on shells made contact explosions impossible, but this Missourian's invention is doing the work quickly and all Henry County is proud of its inventor.

A native St. Louisan and graduate of St. Louis University and Washington University Medical School discovered a successful treatment for those exposed to poison gas. Julien A. Gehrung's discovery, adopted by the French army, saved the lives of thousands of gas victims and restored sight and hearing to many more.

Another citizen of St. Louis is credited with making possible the crossing of the Meuse River in the critical Argonne-Meuse drive. Captain S. S. M. Smith adapted the invention of his commanding officer, Colonel L. J. Lambert of St. Louis, to form a footbridge of canvas floats stretched over folding frames. Once this footbridge was secured, a heavier-duty pontoon bridge was easily constructed.

Even some Missouri animals captured the attention of the press by their contributions to the war effort. The Missouri mule was hailed as an indispensable help in winning the war and was paid this tribute by a Minnesota reporter:

> He kept the heavy artillery right up to the front with the attacking infantry. He went without his oats and waded through mud and over filled-in shell holes. . . . The Missouri mule took his share of the gas and shell shock. He slept out o' nights in the rain and cold. He kept his "hee haw" muffled at critical moments. He pulled and pulled—my, how he pulled when put to it.

A little dog named "Wrinkles" provided some welcome chuckles for the men at the front and, through the newspapers, for the

Missourian George Creel
served as chairman of the
Committee on Public In-
formation during World
War I.
*(Courtesy State Historical
Society)*

folks at home, when he was decorated for valor by France and
Italy. Wrinkles was the faithful pet of Sergeant Archie Boyd of
Grant City, who, serving as a sniper, was sent far ahead of the
lines. Although wounded three times by shrapnel, Wrinkles
never hesitated to perform his duty of delivering messages between Sergeant Boyd and his commanding officer.

Much of the enthusiasm and patriotism demonstrated not
only by Missourians but also by Americans across the country
was stimulated through the distribution of inflammatory literature by a national committee whose head, George Creel, was a
native of Missouri and former Kansas City editor. Creel, as
chairman of the Committee on Public Information, was assigned
the task of stirring up the war fever in America, which he accomplished through atrocity-laden pamphlets, newspaper reports,
posters, and even movies. His best-known war propaganda movie
was entitled "The Kaiser, the Beast of Berlin." George Creel
later admitted that many of the revelations thus distributed
were manufactured and had no basis in fact. Creel also organized
groups of "Four-Minute Men," who were prepared to present to
any organization a four-minute speech on the war effort. Some
4,000 Missourians acted in this capacity, and the programs of
many groups in the state included such patriotic oratory.

Occasionally, Missourians were carried away in a passion of patriotism and were guilty of violating the rights and disturbing the peace of those whose loyalty they suspected. Some of the older German-born residents who still preferred to speak and read their native language were most frequently the targets of these misguided zealots. Fortunately, except for the destruction of the presses of a German newspaper in Cape Girardeau, these isolated incidents of injustice were minor, but the fact that they occurred at all is regrettable.

The Missourians who most convincingly proved their loyalty were, of course, those men who braved artillery fire, bombs, grenades, and poison gas to fight for the ideals to which they were dedicated. Historians who have computed the total number of Missourians in the war indicate that 156,232 men from Missouri acted either as officers or enlisted men in the military service. Approximately half of these served overseas. Missouri casualties numbered 11,172, and approximately three per cent of all Americans killed in battle were from Missouri.

Many of the National Guard troops from Missouri had served under General John J. Pershing in Mexico during 1916 in the futile attempt to capture the outlaw revolutionary, Pancho Villa. The next year after returning to Missouri, the entire Guard of 14,756 officers and men was called up for duty, mobilized at the rifle range near Nevada, and placed in federal service in August, 1917. A number of the Missouri troops were made part of the 35th Division, which included both Kansas and Missouri Guard units. Other of the Guard members were attached to the 42nd (Rainbow) Division. Missourian Brigadier General Harvey C. Clark cited the record of the "Brave 35th" in these words:

> [The division was] moved to the Argonne and for six days participated in the fiercest fighting of this, the greatest and decisive battle of the war. The 35th Division was the razor edge of the advancing American wedge; it bore the brunt, and four picked divisions of the Prussian Guards . . . were thrown in its way only to be routed.

In the thick of this fight was the spectacled young captain from Independence, Missouri, Harry Truman, who reported years later in his memoirs that his men fired 3,000 rounds of seventy-five millimeter ammunition from four a.m. to eight a.m. on September 26, 1918. The division was able to push the Germans back

"The Glory of Missouri in War," a painting by the French artist Charles Hoffbauer, decorates the east wall of the House of Representatives in the Missouri State Capitol.

seven miles, but the cost of victory was high. Of the 8,000 casualties of the division, 4,561 of the wounded and 675 of the fatalities were Missourians. The Rainbow Division was also active in France, and among the Missourians of the 42nd, forty-two were wounded and seventeen were killed.

Of course, many men who were not members of the National Guard joined the army, navy, or marine corps during World War I. In May of 1917 the selective service system began drafting eligible and physically fit men between the age limits of 21 and 31. By the end of the war, the selective service system had called 92,843 Missouri men into service. These drafted Missourians, especially those in the 89th Division, the 210th Engineers, the 232nd Field Signal Battalion, and the black units known as the 805th, 806th, and 817th Pioneers, distinguished themselves on the front lines in France. The "Fighting 89th" Division has been called "one of the most successful divisions in the American army in France." Of the seven Congressional Medals of Honor won by members of the unit, three were awarded to Missourians. A total of 387 men of Missouri were cited for unusual service and awarded honors by America, Great Britain, France, Italy, Belgium, Japan, Russia, Roumania, and Montenegro.

After the National Guard was called to federal service, there was need for military groups to be organized to deal with any

General John J. Pershing, a native of Linn County, Missouri, was commander-in-chief of the American Expeditionary Force during World War I and played a significant role in the defeat of the Germans.
(Courtesy State Historical Society)

emergencies arising within the state. At the governor's call, a Home Guard was organized of some 6,000 men, who served until the end of the conflict.

Missouri produced not only fighting men, but also some of the leading wartime officers and civilian officials. General John J. Pershing was chosen by President Wilson as the commander of the American Expeditionary Force. Pershing, born at Laclede in Linn County, was a graduate of West Point with valuable experience in Cuba and the Philippines during and after the Spanish American War. The unified Allied Command under Marshall Foch by which all the armies were directed from a central agency was insisted upon by General Pershing. The American general's insistence upon the Allies' assuming the offensive contributed to the successful assault upon the German lines in 1918. Pershing returned to America a hero.

In 1911 Enoch H. Crowder of Edinburg, Missouri, attained the highest position in the United States army's legal department, in which capacity he made significant changes in the administration of military justice. He also wrote the selective service bill which established the military draft in the United States shortly after the declaration of war against Germany in 1917.
(Courtesy State Historical Society)

Among the other Missourians who served with distinction in places of great importance was Major General Enoch Crowder, who was born in Grundy County in the town of Edinburg. Crowder, who had received both a military education at West Point and a legal education at the University of Missouri, wrote the selective service bill which established the military draft in the United States. And as Provost Marshal General during the war, Crowder administered the selective service system. One of the chief officers in the United States Navy during World War I was Commander Joseph K. Taussig of St. Louis. Commander Taussig was in charge of the first flotilla of American destroyers to serve in European waters. We should also note that former Governor David R. Francis was Ambassador to Russia during World War I and during the troubled years of the Russian revolution. Assistant Secretary of War Edward R. Stettinius and Secretary of Agriculture David E. Houston, both of St. Louis, were also among a long list of Missourians who served in governmental positions of high responsibility during this critical time.

On November 11, 1918, an armistice was signed near Compiegne, France, quieting the guns along the front and cheering both the men in the trenches and their loved ones anxiously awaiting their return. When peace was a reality the commander of the 35th Division, Major General Peter E. Traub, exhorted the people of Missouri:

> Now let me preach a little sermon. When the boys come back remember that brass bands and ice cream aren't the only things to a real welcome. Get busy and do something worthy—provide each returning soldier with a job. . . .

General Traub's exhortation was heeded. When the men of Missouri came marching home, they were greeted not only with cheers and confetti, but with special homecoming editions of the newspapers full of such ads as:

> *Your job awaits you*
>
> Rice-Stix Dry Goods Company

> *Everyone of you who left this*
> *store to take up arms . . .*
> *will find a hearty welcome—*
> *and your job—awaiting you.*
>
> Famous-Barr Company

A Missouri Welcome Home Committee, World War I

*For all employees who left this
company to enter the service . . .
a BETTER position than the one
they left awaits them.*
        Acme Cement Plaster Company

Buddy come back to your good old job. . . .
        Statler Hotel

To those of her boys who could never return, Missouri could offer neither reward nor adequate monument—only her undying gratitude.

Prohibition

In their zeal to improve society, the reformers of the nineteenth century called upon the American people to institute many reforms such as the abolition of slavery, the establishment of hospitals for the mentally ill, the granting of woman suffrage, the improvement of prisons, and the outlawing of child labor. Toward the end of the century, the temperance movement became one of the most widely-supported of the reform activities. Two particular organizations spearheaded the attack upon the liquor industry—the Women's Christian Temperance Union (better known as the W.C.T.U.) and the Anti-Saloon League. These two national organizations were joined by many Missouri churches in the fight to bring "prohibition" to the state.

Two Missouri women were especially active in the W.C.T.U. at the turn of the century. Mrs. Clara Cleghorn Hoffman, who was elected the first president of the Missouri W.C.T.U. in the 1880's, remained active in the organization for twenty-five years. Mrs. Hoffman was a delegate to the world's temperance conference in London in 1895 and served as a lecturer for the W.C.T.U. in Europe and in many states of the Union. Mrs. Carry Nation, who lived at various times in the Missouri towns of Holden and Belton, achieved national fame for her unorthodox and violent attacks upon the liquor industry. Mrs. Nation's first marriage, to an alcoholic physician, had been a nightmare. As a result of this experience, Carry Nation dedicated herself to the destruction of the intoxicant trade. In lecture tours and stage appearances she proclaimed the evils of drink and castigated those in society who profited from the sale of liquor. Her rapier tongue was not her only weapon in the assault. Mrs. Nation's zealously-swung hatchet wrecked numerous saloons and incurred many fines, which she was able to pay with the income from her lecture tours.

The Anti-Saloon League, founded in 1893, was the most effective organization in the prohibition movement. The League, which clearly indicated that it was an organization to influence legislation, supported politicians who would further the prohibition cause. With the support of many Protestant churches in America, the organization had an abundance of dynamic leaders and sufficient finances to carry on a nationwide publicity campaign. The following statement, printed in 1912, is typical of the approach used by the Anti-Saloon League:

> The American People have been hysterically trying to mop up the deluge of paupers, blind, . . . criminals, etc., . . . which have flowed from the faucet of the liquor business, the saloon. Better to stop the faucet.

The League commissioned and distributed many posters, and placed numerous newspaper ads in communities across the nation. The following ad, designed to show the saloons' corrupting influence on youth, was circulated by the League in 1908:

WANTED—BOYS FOR CUSTOMERS

Most of our old customers are rapidly dropping out.
Ten committed suicide last week.
Twenty are in jail—eight in the chain gang.
Fifteen were sent to the poorhouse. One was
    hanged.
Three were sent to the insane asylum.
Most of the rest are not worth fooling with;
    they have no money.
WE NEED FRESH YOUNG BLOOD

The League also quoted a Missouri lawyer in 1908: "I have defended forty-one men and women for murder, and nineteen out of twenty of the crimes were caused by whiskey."

These materials were widely read in Missouri and were ultimately to have an impact upon the thinking of the citizens of the state.

Missourians had been aware of the liquor problem before the organization of the Anti-Saloon League. In 1887 the state legislature had passed an act establishing local option in Missouri. Under the local option plan, the citizens of any county or city of 2,500 or more population could vote to halt the sale of liquor within their jurisdiction. Elections in counties and cities within them sometimes had opposite results, thereby creating "wet" cities in "dry" counties and vice versa. In effect, this made the act meaningless. In the year 1917, ninety-six of Mis-

A Local Option Election at Independence in 1888
(Frank Leslie's Illustrated Newspaper)

souri's counties were dry, and the remaining nineteen wet. With only two exceptions the wet counties were located along the Mississippi and Missouri rivers. It is interesting to observe, however, that sixteen wet towns were situated in dry counties; for example, Kansas City and Springfield allowed liquor sales although they were located in counties where intoxicants were outlawed. On the other hand, some cities such as Kirkwood and Webster Groves were dry, although St. Louis County was wet.

The local option arrangement continued in Missouri until the adoption of nationwide prohibition with the passage of the Eighteenth Amendment to the federal constitution in 1920. The prohibition movement, which was already strong in Missouri in the late nineteenth century, constantly gained momentum in the first two decades of the twentieth century. In 1910 the citizens of Missouri turned down by a margin of 218,000 votes a proposal to make the entire state dry. Six years later, when Missourians voted again on total prohibition for the state, the measure failed by only 122,000 votes. By 1918 opposition to the same proposal had a margin of only 73,000 votes.

During the years of political conflict over prohibition, many churches and Sunday schools exhorted their members to abstain from liquor and to support prohibition. The following Ozark folk song indicated that some church people failed to heed the exhortation of their religious leaders:

> The cunnin' old brewer was cheerful and meller,
> Says he, I admire this Sunday School feller,
> He's true to his church, to his party he's truer,
> He talks for the Lord, but he votes for the brewer!

The Anti-Saloon League exerted constant pressure upon Congress to authorize national prohibition. Missouri's two senators split on the issue. The fiery James A. Reed of Kansas City became one of the leading enemies of the League, but William Joel Stone supported prohibition because of the pressure of letters and telegrams from his Missouri constituents. Congressman Richard Bartholdt from the brewery center of St. Louis was a leading enemy of prohibition in the House of Representatives. When Congress approved proposal of the Eighteenth Amendment to the United States Constitution in 1917, twelve of Missouri's Democratic congressmen in the House of Representatives voted in favor, while one Democrat and two Republicans opposed. When the amendment was subsequently

James A. Reed followed a brilliant two year career (1898-1900) as prosecuting attorney of Jackson County with two terms as a reform mayor of Kansas City. He later represented Missouri in the United States Senate from 1911 to 1929.

(Courtesy State Historical Society)

submitted to the several states, the Missouri General Assembly on January 16, 1919 ratified it by an overwhelming majority—22 votes to 10 in the Senate and 104 votes to 36 in the House. Prohibition was to continue in effect for another fourteen years.

There were many in Missouri and in every state who opposed the amendment. In particular, the German-American Missourians, whose beer gardens had been a tradition imported from the old country, were unhappy with prohibition. The many German brewers were doubly distressed by the outlawing of their product. In order to counteract the effective promotional literature of the Anti-Saloon League, the brewers and distillers organized the German-American Alliance. In Missouri the brewers, stressing their conviction that prohibition was an infringement upon personal liberty, formed the Association Against the Prohibition Amendment and published a paper known as the *Minute Man*. The Association even commissioned a play entitled "The Passing of Hans Dippel," the tearjerking story of a good, warm-hearted German saloon keeper whose business was ruined by the drys.

The Anti-Saloon League remained active in Missouri even after the Eighteenth Amendment had been adopted. In 1922, the Reverend W. C. Schupp, who was superintendent of the League in Missouri, pledged, "Our organization will [continue to] fight Senator James A. Reed and other candidates who have furnished wet leadership . . ."

The Anti-Saloon League in Missouri emphasized two arguments during and before the 1920's. First, the League attempted to prove that Missouri was poorer because of the liquor traffic within the state. As early as 1912, the League contrasted dry Kansas with wet Missouri, noting that Kansas wages were higher, Kansas appropriated more money for education, more Kansans owned automobiles, and Kansans enjoyed greater per capita wealth. The second argument, which was used with telling effectiveness at the time of the anti-German feeling during and immediately after World War I, was that the breweries in America were largely controlled by Germans. In 1917 the League declared, "German brewers in this country have rendered thousands of men inefficient and are thus crippling the republic in its war on Prussian militarism . . . The brewers are helping the enemy."

Whatever gain the League realized from these arguments quickly melted in the heat of scandal. It was suddenly revealed that the Reverend W. C. Schupp, who was superintendent of the League, had used his great influence to secure alcohol permits for his son's firm, the Druggists Cooperative Company, which was accused of breaking the prohibition laws by improper sale of alcohol. Even more shocking to his dedicated followers was the charge that Superintendent Schupp had been accepting protection payment from bootleggers and arranging for raids on competitors of his bootlegger clients. Schupp, who reported that he was stepping down because of "broken health," resigned his position in 1923 after the state attorney general investigated the situation.

Another development which worked against the interests of the prohibitionists was the increase of crime during the 1920's. With many citizens seeking forbidden liquor, there was a ready market for those bootleggers, rum-runners, and "alky-cookers" who were willing to break the law. Of course, since bootlegging and the operation of saloons called "speakeasies" or "blind pigs" was an illegal business activity, those who engaged in these practices could not ask protection from law enforcement officials. This situation was ideal to encourage gangsters to move into the state either to take part in the production and sale of liquor or to threaten others who did so. Although they tended to congregate in Kansas City and St. Louis, these gangsters and gangs became a menace to the entire state.

For over two decades the crayon of cartoonist Daniel Fitzpatrick decorated the editorial pages of the St. Louis Post-Dispatch with graphic comments on the political scene. Many originals of Fitzpatrick's cartoons are now in the collections of the State Historical Society of Missouri in Columbia.

St. Louis Post-Dispatch, Nov. 15, 1926 (Courtesy State Historical Society)

THE SOURCE.

Such underworld characters as gambler Solly Weissmann and John Lazia in Kansas City and gunman Blackie Armes in St. Louis were much feared. Gangs of outlaws in the St. Louis area were known by such names as the Cuckoos, the Bergers, the Sheltons and Egan's Rats. When bootlegging or gambling activities failed to provide enough excitement or profit, the gangsters turned to kidnapping wealthy Missourians. In 1931 Dr. Isaac D. Kelley, a wealthy St. Louis physician, was kidnapped and terrorized for eight days before he was released. A year earlier a more profitable kidnapping was perpetrated at Kansas City when Mike Katz of the drugstore chain was snatched from his sports roadster on Ward Parkway. Ike Katz was forced to deliver $100,000 to the criminals for the safe release of his brother. The harsh justice and quick tempers of the underworld triggered bloody gang wars and brazen assassinations in both of Missouri's largest cities.

This proliferation of crime in Missouri strengthened the arguments of the brewers and distillers against prohibition. August A. Busch argued that prohibition was hurting the law-abiding brewers, while it allowed the underworld and law-breakers to flourish. Shortly after the election of Franklin Delano Roosevelt, a constitutional amendment repealing prohibition was proposed. In an election in August of 1933 to select delegates to the state constitutional convention required for action on the proposed amendment, Missourians voted 503,642 to 156,961 in favor of repeal. The temperance workers had been defeated. Missouri and the rest of the states decided to abandon what Herbert Hoover had called the "Noble Experiment." The prohibition movement is instructive in that it shows the strength of reform in America in the early years of the century. However, the citizens of Missouri—and the nation—appear to have deserted the reformers. Each advocate of prohibition for the improvement of society might have adopted Carry Nation's epitaph:

She hath done what she could.

The Republican Twenties

Missouri throughout its history has been primarily a Democratic state. However, opposition parties—particularly the Republican Party—have always been present to challenge Democratic rule. In 1920 the citizens of Missouri were unhappy with the Democratic Party for several reasons.

First, President Woodrow Wilson, with thrilling words of idealism, had led America into World War I to preserve democracy and to end all future international conflicts. The war had put such a financial and emotional strain upon the American people and had taken so bloody a toll of Americans that by 1920 Wilsonian idealism was no longer so popular. A second reason for the Republican resurgence was the difference of opinion within the Democratic Party concerning American entrance into the League of Nations. President Wilson, the great political scientist, fervently supported the newly created League of Nations, which had been designed to settle international difficulties once the war was over. Opposition Republicans and isolationist Democrats in Washington opposed American membership in the League. Democratic Senator James A. Reed of Missouri, who disagreed with President Wilson over the advisability of joining the League, led an internal fight within the state Democratic Party. Such a family argument never helps a party on election day. Third, many minor items irritated and agitated the citizens of Missouri in 1920. While consumer prices were high, farm prices had dropped to a low point during the summer of 1920, and the farmer was feeling the pinch of this unfavorable market situation. The party in power—guilty or not—usually is blamed for a recession or depression. Finally, to the dissatisfaction of most Missourians, state taxes had been raised to a new high during the administration of Governor Gardner.

All these factors contributed to the sweeping Republican victory in the Missouri election of 1920.

"The Housing Situation at Jefferson City," Fitzpatrick, St. Louis Post-Dispatch, January 7, 1921
(Courtesy State Historical Society)

The Hyde Administration

Arthur M. Hyde was the first of the three Republican governors elected in Missouri during the 1920's. Hyde, like earlier Republican Governor Herbert S. Hadley, was a Progressive in sentiment. An ardent follower of Theodore Roosevelt, Hyde had bolted the Republican Party in 1912 when Roosevelt attempted to secure election with his Progressive Party. Governor Hyde, who had practiced law and operated an automobile agency in Trenton, Missouri, had also gained administrative experience as mayor of Princeton in Mercer County.

Republican candidates were successful in securing election to all the state offices open in 1920. Both houses of the legislature in Jefferson City had a Republican majority, and fourteen of Missouri's sixteen congressional seats were won by the G. O. P.; even popular James Beauchamp "Champ" Clark was defeated in this election.

Governor Hyde had drawn up many proposals to improve the organization of government in Missouri. Although his plans for simplifying and streamlining the structure of the state govern-

Arthur Hyde, who had operated an automobile business
in Trenton, Missouri before
his election as governor of
the state in 1920, was aware
of the growing importance
of the automobile and the
need for improved roads in
Missouri.

(Courtesy State Historical
Society)

ment were acceptable to the legislature, most of the reorganization proposals were rejected by the voters in referendums. Despite this setback, the Hyde administration effected some important changes in the state.

With the automobile becoming more important to the
citizens of Missouri, there was a growing awareness in the state
of a need for good, all-weather roads. Under Governor Gardner
the state had taken two important steps to improve the roads.
With the Hawes Act of 1917, Missouri accepted federal aid to
build Missouri roads, agreeing to provide matching funds. Three
years later, after much planning and publicity, the voters of the
state authorized a bond issue of $60,000,000 for the grading and
surfacing of roads. Governor Hyde continued the program of
road improvement begun by his predecessor. The Centennial
Road Law of 1921 established procedures for developing a state
highway system and provided for a state highway commission
to supervise the construction and maintenance of these highways. The act outlined a total road system of 7,640 miles of
which 1,500 miles were to be hard-surfaced. The Centennial Act
was known as the act which "lifted Missouri out of the mud."
Hyde secured more money for roads in 1924 with the levying
of a tax on gasoline of two cents per gallon and a fifty per cent
increase in motor registration fees.

As a true Progressive governor, Hyde was particularly concerned with education and with eleemosynary institutions. Under
his leadership, a State Children's Home was established at

Carrollton, and a single board was organized to direct all the state hospitals. The legislature passed a new pension system for Missouri's blind which provided $300 per year for sightless citizens who had an annual income of less than $600. In addition, the state increased its support of public education. In the fiscal year 1921-22 over $14,000,000 of state money was appropriated to finance educational facilities at all levels. During this period the college for blacks at Jefferson City became known officially as Lincoln University. During Governor Hyde's administration a state law was enacted requiring each county of more than 100,000 population to construct a high school for blacks.

The financial condition of Missouri was excellent when Governor Hyde took office. Since the high taxes which Governor Gardner had been forced to levy had proved more than adequate for state needs, Hyde had the happy opportunity to recommend tax reductions. The property tax was reduced from fifteen cents to seven cents per $100 valuation; the income tax was reduced by a third; and the corporation franchise tax was cut in half.

During Hyde's administration the Missouri veterans of World War I—as did the veterans in all states—sought a bonus.

The late pioneer Lamar Ford dealer Ed Stephens and his fellow travelers experience the joys of motoring in early twentieth-century Missouri.
(Courtesy The Lamar Democrat)

Because of the voting power of the large number of veterans and because of public sympathy for the proposal, it was difficult for the legislature to refuse the request. A bonus was granted allotting each veteran $10 for each month of service up to a maximum of $250. Under this schedule, nearly $15,000,000 was distributed to veterans in eighteen months.

Since the Constitution of 1875 was in need of many changes, Governor Hyde called a constitutional convention in 1922-23 to recommend modifications in the basic law. Although many changes were proposed by the convention, the recommendations were largely ignored by the citizens, who approved only six of the proposals.

In the election of 1922 the voters of Missouri restored Democratic control of both houses of the state legislature and elected Senator James A. Reed to another term. Democrat Reed of Kansas City had been Missouri's representative in the United States Senate since 1911. Known as the Stormy Petrel, he had made his reputation in Missouri as a colorful and vigorous trial lawyer. Reed, like many other Americans of the day, ridiculed what he considered to be the fantastic reforms of the time; he hated prohibition as much as he despised the League of Nations. In 1920 Wilson's control over the Democratic Party in Missouri had been so strong that Senator Reed was refused a seat as a delegate to the national Democratic convention in San Francisco. Two years later, when Reed ran for re-election in Missouri, former President Wilson said, "I hope and confidently expect to see him repudiated by the Democrats in the primaries." Despite Wilson's opposition and the "Rid Us of Reed" Clubs organized by Wilson supporters in Missouri, Reed was able to secure re-election. Three important factors favored him. The Kansas City *Star,* which opposed the League of Nations, gave him assistance. The strong city machines in Kansas City and St. Louis supported him, and Republicans across the state— particularly the beer-drinking German Republicans of St. Louis —voted for the renegade Democrat who had courage enough to assail the "Democratic messiah," Wilson. Reed's 50,000 vote majority demonstrated that many Missourians, suspicious of any foreign entanglements after the horror of the war, approved his opposition to American membership in the League of Nations.

This same election of 1922 marked the beginning of the long and fruitful career of Representative Clarence Cannon, who was

Representative Clarence Cannon of Elsberry, who was first elected to Congress in 1922, became a national authority on parliamentary procedure. He had long service as the chairman of the House Appropriations Committee. *(Courtesy State Historical Society)*

to become one of the nation's experts in the fields of parliamentary procedure and public finance.

The Baker Administration

Because the Democrats were still divided nationally in 1924, and the superficial prosperity of the 1920's had increased the popularity of the incumbent Republican Party, Republican Calvin Coolidge was easily elected president. Missouri followed the nation once more and elected as governor former State Superintendent of Schools Sam A. Baker. A graduate of the State Normal College at Cape Girardeau and Wesleyan College, Baker had served as public school principal at Jefferson City and Joplin, superintendent of schools at Piedmont, Richmond, and Jefferson City, president of the Missouri State Teachers Association, and vice president of the National Education Association. All other state officials were Republicans after this election, although the Democrats were able to control the Senate of the Missouri legislature.

In the American political structure a president or governor can be frustrated in his leadership if an opposition party controls one or both houses of the legislature. During Governor Baker's administration a clique of lawyers in the Democratic Senate steadfastly refused to adopt many needed reforms. Thus, a new banking code, new criminal law, and proposals for the establishment of a state police system, were all defeated by this Senate group. Baker was successful, however, in securing the passage of two important proposals. In 1926 a program of workingmen's compensation was finally adopted after a fifteen-year struggle. Although the law was not all that the unions had hoped for, it was a major step toward greater protection of the

Like his predecessor Governor Baker, Republican Governor Caulfield held office during a period when the Senate was controlled by the Democratic Party and he, too, experienced difficulty in securing support for his proposals.

(Courtesy State Historical Society)

workers. A commission was established to administer the law and to make rulings on the many requests for compensation. Under the original law the company was liable for a sum up to $250 for the first sixty days of incapacitation resulting from work injuries. Those who were incapacitated for a longer period of time could appeal to the commission for further assistance. Baker's second victory was the passage of a law which authorized the raising of $75,000,000 for road construction. This second major bond issue adopted by Missourians for road improvements during the 1920's illustrates the interest of the citizens of Missouri in the development of a state highway system. Missouri's excellent highway system developed out of the willingness of Missourians in the 1920's to provide large sums of money for construction.

Governor Baker, because of his former profession, was especially interested in education; but he was defeated by the legislature in his efforts to establish a permanent school fund for more satisfactory financing of Missouri's schools. The governor was able, however, to secure passage of an act which required the teaching of both the United States and the Missouri constitutions in the public schools of the state.

Governor Baker not only had difficulty with the Democratic Senate, but he also met opposition from members of his own party who were dissatisfied with many of his appointments. Despite his differences with Republican leaders in the state, at the time of the national Republican convention in 1928 Baker was considered as a candidate for the vice presidency. He tasted defeat once more when frustrated in his attempts to secure this nomination.

The Caulfield Administration

In 1928 Herbert Hoover was elected president in a great landslide over the colorful Democratic candidate, wisecracking Al Smith of New York. The Republican presidential candidate's overwhelming victory helped the candidacy of Republican Henry S. Caulfield, who was elected to the governorship of Missouri the same year. Caulfield was a St. Louis lawyer who had previously served one term in Congress. The Democrats were able to retain their control of the Senate during Caulfield's administration, and after the election of 1930 they were able to regain control of the Missouri House of Representatives as well. Under these circumstances, Governor Caulfield had difficulty, just as did his predecessor, in securing support for his proposals.

The governor, who saw a need for reorganizing Missouri's government, hoped to encourage this reorganization through the establishment of a state survey commission, which was appointed in 1929. This commission, after studying all the activities of state government, recommended a bold, new plan of improvement. The commission deplored the conditions in the penitentiaries and hospitals of the state, and severely criticized the educational standards in Missouri. It recommended the spending of $192,000,000 in a ten-year period for reorganization and im-

Former State Superintendent of Schools Sam A. Baker was especially interested in education during his administration as governor and was responsible for securing the passage of an act requiring the teaching of the United States and the Missouri Constitutions in the Missouri public schools.

(Courtesy State Historical Society)

provement of conditions. Unfortunately, the plan was offered just as depression settled over America, and the financial crisis prevented immediate action on the proposals.

Although handicapped by an opposition legislature and by financial difficulties, Governor Caulfield was able to introduce several innovations and improvements during his administration. The state highway patrol, with only six captains and forty-nine patrolmen for the entire state, was established in 1931. The agency was much needed, as the roads of the state, which were becoming more heavily traveled yearly, required supervision. Highway construction was a major activity during Governor Caulfield's term of office. In a single year the state had been able to place a hard surface on 1,200 miles of roads. This road building gave work to many unemployed Missourians during the early years of the depression. The governor informed the legislature that 10,000 Missourians had been employed in road construction during a single biennium.

The conditions in Missouri's schools prodded the legislature into passing a new school law in 1931, which authorized equalization funds, making possible the financing of at least a minimum program for every school district in the state. Under this plan, educational funds from the state treasury were granted to those districts financially unable to provide for the necessary expenses of an adequate school program. This system has been a major factor in improving the level of education in some of the more isolated rural parts of the state. Because of this and other new expenses, the state adopted a graduated income tax in 1931 on all incomes over $1,000 a year after authorized deductions. The income tax ranged from a low of one per cent on $1,000 taxable income to four per cent on incomes above $9,000 after deductions.

The depression which came to Missouri during Governor Caulfield's term prevented the enactment of the many reforms he had planned for the state and forced him to reduce the salaries of state employees and to veto those appropriation measures which would have authorized overspending. During Governor Caulfield's administration, Missouri began a program of direct relief for her needy citizens. In addition to some funds provided by the Federal Government, $250,000 of state funds were distributed to needy Missouri farmers, primarily for the purchase of seeds and feed.

A census is taken each ten years in Missouri. The results of the census of 1930 showed that Missouri was not growing as rapidly as the other states in the Union. As a consequence, Missouri lost three of her sixteen seats in Congress, and the state was forced to redraw its congressional districts. The Democratic legislature during the second half of Caulfield's administration passed a measure establishing the congressional districts in such a manner that eight of the thirteen districts were Democratic in orientation. Republican Governor Caulfield, of course, objected to this redistricting and vetoed it. As a result of this veto, Missouri was unable to hold district elections in 1932, and all Missouri congressmen were elected at large. The vigorous campaign of Franklin D. Roosevelt culminated in a resounding victory for the Democratic Party at the national level. A similar Democratic sweep of the state during this election resulted in a solid Democratic delegation from Missouri in the United States House of Representatives.

In summary, Missouri had Republican governors during the 1920's and in 1928 even elected Republican Roscoe C. Patterson of Springfield to the United States Senate. Missouri appears to have turned to the Republicans primarily because of national, rather than state issues. The Republican governors of the 1920's were progressive, forward-looking men who attempted as best they could to continue the process of reform and reorganization of government. Despite Republican victories, Missouri's Democratic Party retained much of its strength. With the exception of the period 1920-22, the Democratic Party controlled the state Senate all during the 1920's, and constituted a majority in both houses of the legislature in the years 1922 to 1924 and 1930 to 1932. Examination of the platforms of the two parties during the twenties reveals that both were anxious to build roads, to pass workmen's compensation, and to streamline government, although party politics sometimes prevented the passage of reform legislation, since each party wanted to receive credit for the reforms. Both parties condemned the Ku Klux Klan, which was resurrected in the twenties as a nationalistic, reactionary group of sheet-draped bigots who intimidated blacks, Jews, Catholics, pacifists, evolutionists, and anyone else who disagreed with their concept of patriotism. It appears that the political leaders of the 1920's were more interested in reform than were the people themselves, who rejected reform opportunities in several referendums during the decade.

The Boom

Population and Industrial Growth

Historians have dubbed the decade following World War I the "Roaring Twenties." The name is a descriptive one, for the years resounded with the raucous symphony of lathe and press, automobile horn and airplane engine, hammer and riveter, jazz-band and gangster's gun. In general, it was a time of urban growth and of superficial industrial and business prosperity built upon credit, extravagant speculation, and reckless install-ment buying. In these years the radio first brought the jazz of the speakeasy and the voice of the president into American homes. It was also the decade when the automobile replaced the horse and buggy for most Missourians, and thousands of miles of all-weather roads were laid across the state. The social habits of the decade were those of a people in reaction against the earlier idealism of the Progressives which had not brought Utopia, and against Woodrow Wilson's war crusade which had not ended international squabbling. The prosperity of the twenties was confined to the metropolitan areas of the state—there was no boom time for the farmer.

Census figures in 1920 and 1930 clearly indicate that Mis-souri was not growing as rapidly as other states in the Union. Missouri had dropped from fifth most populous state in 1900 to ninth rank in 1920, with a population of 3,404,055 in the latter year. This was an increase of only 3.4 per cent over the popu-lation of 1910. This population increase was the smallest in any decade since Missouri had become a state. In 1930 Missouri had a population of 3,629,367 and ranked tenth among the states. The rate of growth in Missouri during the 1920's increased slightly to a rate of 6.6 per cent.

Although Missouri's population was edging up slightly, the number of people on the farms of the state was continuing to decrease. Between 1910 and 1920, 77,366 Missourians left the farms and rural villages of the state. In 1920 the census bureau calculated that the urban population accounted for 46.6 per cent of the state's total population, while rural population ac-counted for 53.4 per cent. Since the twenties were a time of trouble for Missouri farmers it is understandable that the migration from rural to metropolitan areas continued. By 1930, 51.2 per cent of Missouri's population was urban. For the first time in Missouri's history over half of her inhabitants were residents of cities of 2,500 or more.

Some cities such as Springfield and Kansas City manifested great growth. For example, Springfield grew 45.2 per cent between 1920 and 1930, and the population of Kansas City increased 23.2 per cent during the decade. The growth of St. Joseph, however, had virtually halted. The development of suburban communities near St. Louis indicates the movement of people into that metropolitan area. For example, University City experienced a population growth of 280 per cent between 1920 and 1930. The population of the suburban municipality reached 25,809 in 1930.

There was a constant industrial growth in Missouri during the 1920's. With an output of $1,594,208,338 worth of goods in 1919, Missouri ranked tenth in the nation in the total value of products manufactured. Ten years later the value of Missouri

This print entitled "Missouri Sawmill" was made by Fred Geary of Carrollton, Missouri, whose original woodcuts and tools are now housed in the collections of the State Historical Society. *(Courtesy State Historical Society)*

products rose to $1,917,115,275, but because of bigger increases in other states Missouri dropped to eleventh rank in the nation. During this same decade, 1919 to 1929, there was an increase in wages, particularly to employees of manufacturing industry. In 1919 wages amounted to $196,515,353; by 1929 they had risen to $240,368,692.

There was an increasing trend in Missouri for industry to congregate in the largest metropolitan centers. For example, in 1919, 57.76 per cent of the manufacturing establishments in the state were located in the twelve largest cities; by 1929, the percentage of industries in the first twelve urban areas had climbed to 71.73 per cent. While it is true that greater industry was concentrated in urban centers such as St. Louis and Kansas City, there was at the same time a tendency for shoe and clothing manufacturers to move their plants to the smaller towns where production costs were lower and wages cheaper.

Part of the diversification of industry during the 1920's resulted from the Eighteenth Amendment to the United States Constitution. Some brewers, prohibited by law from continuing their former production, turned to the manufacture of such diverse items as refrigerator cabinets, truck bodies, baker's yeast, and soft drinks.

The Plight of the Farmer

The farmer was caught in a trap between diminishing farm income and increasing costs of consumer goods and taxes. For example, in 1919 corn had sold for $1.38 and wheat for $2.09 a bushel. Encouraged by these high prices and by the ease of obtaining bank loans, many men who owned their farms mortgaged them to buy additional acreage. Unfortunately, the high prices for farm commodities did not last. Between 1920 and 1931 the price of corn averaged $0.68 and wheat $1.11 a bushel. By the end of 1931 corn and wheat prices had dropped still further to $0.33 and $0.45, respectively. Other farm commodities were similarly affected.

At the same time that the farmer was receiving less for his crops, his taxes continued to climb. In 1913 taxes for state, county, and local purposes averaged $0.14 per acre. By 1928-29 they averaged $0.47 per acre. The farmer also discovered that the industrial boom in the country kept the prices of his consumer goods high. It is little wonder then that those Missouri

"A Sign of the Times"
October 24, 1926
Fitzpatrick, St. Louis Post-
Dispatch, (Courtesy State
Historical Society)

farmers who had purchased farms at high prices found it difficult to meet their mortgage payments.

There were a number of farm organizations, such as the
Grange, the Farm Bureau, and the Farmers Union, which were
active in Missouri during this period. The Farm Bureau played
an important role in Missouri agriculture by sponsoring county
agents who in turn introduced the newest farming techniques in
each county. The Farm Bureau was the leading spokesman for
farmers in Washington, D. C., during the 1920's and 1930's; it
still plays a major role in shaping national agricultural policies.

An organization which displayed dramatic new power was
the Missouri Farmers Association, commonly known as the
M.F.A. William Hirth is probably more responsible than anyone
else for the establishment of the M.F.A. Hirth edited a publication known as the *Missouri Farmer and Breeder* which advocated the establishment of farm cooperatives to improve the
bargaining power of the farmers. In 1914 a group of seven
farmers met near Brunswick in Chariton County to establish a
farm club with the intent of putting Hirth's plan into action.
By pooling their binder twine order, they purchased 1,150 pounds
of twine at a great saving. Encouraged by this success, they investigated the purchase of other commodities at wholesale prices.
The idea soon spread and other farm clubs were organized, until

by 1916 there were approximately 500 similar clubs in the state. The next year, these clubs held a state convention at which they established the Missouri Farmers Association and adopted the following resolution:

> We direct the attention of the Farm Clubs of the state to the building of farmer's cooperative elevators and also to the forming of livestock shipping associations.

From this beginning, the M.F.A. developed into one of the major economic groups in the state.

It is interesting to note that William Hirth, who had been a member of the Farmers' Alliance during the 1880's and who had supported the candidacy of William Jennings Bryan for president in 1896, had long traveled within the main stream of the farmers' protest movement. His publication, renamed *The Missouri Farmer,* became the chief organ of the M.F.A.

During the 1920's, the M.F.A. established many exchanges where farmers might buy necessary farm goods and sell produce, and in addition, branched out into such enterprises as livestock shipping associations, grain elevators, and creameries. In 1930 Missouri farm clubs numbered 2,500. By 1930, the M.F.A. was operating 375 exchanges, 300 shipping associations, two milk plants, one mill, and one oil company with twenty-four bulk stations. Through these cooperative efforts, the farmers of Missouri attempted to work their way out of the economic trap of the 1920's.

Banks

During this period of agricultural depression and industrial growth there was a growing uneasiness among Missourians concerning the stability of the banks of the state. Most of us today whose savings are insured by the Federal Government fail to appreciate the great concern bank patrons once felt for the safety of their deposits. In the 1920's the banks were reckless in lending money for the purchase of expensive land or to finance industrial or residential growth. When a bank invests large sums in enterprises which later fail, the bank itself may be forced into bankruptcy. Depositors in the 1930's had no guarantee that they would be able to secure their money from their bank. When bank patrons live in fear of such developments, a rumor may stampede the depositors into a run on the bank as the frightened people attempt to withdraw their funds before the bank closes its doors.

The stock market in 1929 caused many people—Missourians included—to lose their faith in money institutions, and resulted in a sharp increase in the number of bank failures in the state. In 1923 only one Missouri bank failed, in 1926 there was a slight increase—seven banks closed their doors. From 1929 through 1932 — the years immediately following the crash — over 300 Missouri banks and trust companies failed. The despair of depositors whose life savings were wiped out, the bitterness of retired Missourians whose income from bank dividends was gone, the suspicion in which bank officials were held by the victims of failures, and the suspense of those whose savings accounts were as yet intact—all this was part of the Missouri banking picture at the beginning of the great depression.

Roads

Missouri devoted great energy and expenditures to the construction of roads during the 1920's. As we have noted, the road improvement projects were late to develop because the earlier settlers used means of transportation which did not require an elaborate road system. Before the Civil War, the rivers were the most convenient avenues of commerce; after the Civil War and through World War I the railroads provided the necessary transportation for goods and people.

Several factors near the turn of the century encouraged the improvement of roads. The decision of the United States postal department to operate a system of rural free delivery made necessary the development of roads which were passable in all seasons. The introduction of the automobile with the meteoric rise in automobile ownership created an interest in, and demand for, improved roads. In 1911 there were 16,387 automobile vehicles registered in Missouri; by 1920 the number had grown to 297,008, and by 1930 to 763,375. Offers of federal assistance provided a further encouragement to highway development in Missouri. Beginning in 1916, and with supplemental appropriations in 1921, 1922, and 1928, federal money was granted to Missouri for the construction of rural post roads, a national road for interstate use, and for the restoration of roads and bridges damaged by the destructive floods of 1927.

With the passage of the $60,000,000 bond issue for construction of roads in 1920 and the Centennial Road Law of 1921, the roadbuilding program for the state took a sudden spurt

Chillicothe Square, 1910

forward. Until this time the construction and maintenance of roads in Missouri had been the responsibility of the counties. A second bond issue for $75,000,000 authorized in 1928 was supplementetd by gasoline taxes and automobile license fees. These same sources of income continued during the 1930's. By 1940 Missouri was fifth in the nation in miles of improved highways. At the same time, Missouri's two-cent gas tax was the lowest in the country.

Entertainment

In 1921 WEW, the first radio station in Missouri, began operation under the auspices of St. Louis University. The next year a station was established at Jefferson City. When its listeners were requested to inform the station by mail if they had received the broadcast, Missourians as far away as Poplar Bluff, Gallatin, St. Louis, and Kansas City responded. Since radios were expensive—from $150 to $250—the listening audience was not large at first. Other pioneer radio stations in Missouri were KSD and KMOX in St. Louis and WDAF in Kansas City. The early programs were confined largely to the playing of music and the reading of market reports. In 1923 a speech delivered in St. Louis by President Warren G. Harding was broadcast to the lucky few who clustered around their crystal sets and heard through their earphones the voice of the president for the first time.

The vaudeville programs and touring plays of the golden age of the theatre were largely replaced by the moving picture during the second decade of the century. During the early twenties, since motion pictures were silent, Mary Pickford, Gloria Swanson, Rudolph Valentino, Charlie Chaplin, and Clara Bow, the "It" girl, flickered across the screen to the accompaniment of organ or piano music played in the theatres. In 1928 the presentation of "Lilac Time" starring Colleen Moore introduced motion pictures with sound to Missouri.

Beginning in 1919, operetta fans among St. Louis residents and visitors might view productions held under summer skies at the nation's first outdoor theatre—the Municipal Opera Theatre in Forest Park. The St. Louis symphony orchestra—second oldest in the nation—presented public concerts during the 1920's. A Kansas City orchestra also performed during the period, although the Kansas City Philharmonic was not organized until the 1930's. Some touring companies presented such vaudeville performers as comedians Jack Benny, Eddie Cantor,

Chillicothe Square, 1923.

The contrast between these two views of downtown Chillicothe shows dramatically the rapid growth of automobile ownership in Missouri during the second decade of the century.

(Courtesy State Historical Society)

Circus Scene by Fred Geary.
Twentieth-century Missourians continued to enjoy circuses as their ancestors had since the early days of statehood.

and George E. Jessel, cowboy star Tom Mix, and dancer Bill Robinson to entertain Missouri audiences.

In 1927 the state legislature repealed the earlier law which prohibited commercial boxing in Missouri. Interest in the sport increased, and Jack Dempsey is reported to have held an exhibition fight at Excelsior Springs. The big sports thrill for Missourians in the twenties came in 1926 when the St. Louis Cardinals defeated the New York Yankees in the World Series. Grover Cleveland Alexander pitched on two consecutive days to win the series for the Cardinals. Two other players were special heroes of Missouri ball fans during the period. Roger Hornsby of the St. Louis Cardinals was the leading hitter in the National League from 1920 to 1925, and George Sisler of the St. Louis Browns was the leading batter and named the "most valuable player" in the American League in 1922. The Cardinals succeeded in capturing the National League pennant again in 1928, but were defeated in the World Series when the Yankees were victorious in four straight games. In collegiate athletics Missouri University withdrew from the Missouri Valley Conference in 1927 to join the Big Six made up of Kansas University, Iowa State College, Kansas State College, Nebraska University, and Oklahoma University.

Missourians still enjoyed dancing, although the older, more sedate dances were giving way to the Charleston, Fox Trot, Black Bottom, and Shimmy, especially in the large cities and college towns. Player pianos tinkled "Dardanella," "Rhapsody in Blue," "Valencia," and "Yes, Sir, That's My Baby." Such melodies as "When Day Is Done," "Ol' Man River," "Tea for Two," and "Who" were introduced by musicals and movies and became favorites of Missourians down to the present day.

The State Park System

During the 1920's the state of Missouri began to purchase and improve attractive and unusual areas of the state to be transformed into parks for the pleasure of Missourians and tourists. In the year 1924, during the administration of Governor Hyde, Missouri established seven parks. The first parks were Bennett Spring in Laclede and Dallas counties, Round Spring in Shannon County, Big Spring in Carter County, Alley Spring in Shannon County, Deer Run in Reynolds County, Indian Trail in Dent County, and Mark Twain in Monroe County. In 1926 Meramec State Park in Franklin County was added to the system. That same year the Old Tavern at Arrow Rock in Saline County was purchased, and the Daughters of the American Revolution, with the assistance of the state, remodeled the building for use as a restaurant, hotel, and museum. Three other properties were added to the state list in 1926: the Chesapeake Fish Hatchery in Lawrence County, the Sam A. Baker State Park in Wayne County, and the Montauk State Park in Dent County. The last park acquired during the twenties was Roaring River State Park near Cassville, which was the gift to the people of the state from a St. Louis resident.

The little village of Bagnell on the twisting Osage River was transformed into a center of furious activity when the engineers and construction workers began the building of a dam there in August, 1929. The Union Electric Light and Power Company of St. Louis, requiring additional facilities for the generation of power, secured permission to dam the Osage River at Bagnell. The massive dam, 2,543 feet long and extending 148 feet

Work on Bagnell Dam, which houses Missouri's largest hydroelectric plant, was begun in August, 1929. In July, 1930 the river was closed off and preparations were made for the construction of the power house.

above the bedrock of the Osage River, created the 129-mile-long Lake of the Ozarks. The lake's 1,300 miles of wooded shoreline extend through Camden, Morgan, Miller, Benton, Henry, and St. Clair counties. Bagnell Dam and other dams, such as that built in 1912 at Forsyth which created lovely Lake Taneycomo, were important to Missouri not only for the generation of electric power, but also for promotion of Missouri as a vacation center. The resort industry of Missouri has developed at a steady rate, and today constitutes one of the important money-making activities in the state.

Lindbergh and the "Spirit of St. Louis"

War often awakens interest in and speeds development of a recent invention. The war in Europe had this effect on the airplane. Improvements in flying machines and new uses for aircraft were devised during the war and in the years following the armistice. When regular air mail was instituted in the 1920's, among the first companies to provide this service was the Robertson Aircraft Corporation of St. Louis, which secured the franchise to carry mail between St. Louis and Chicago in 1925. One of the pilots whom they hired was a tall, youthful-looking Minnesotan named Charles A. Lindbergh, a first lieutenant in the 110th Observation Squadron of the Missouri National Guard. Lindbergh divided his time between making the mail runs to Chicago, giving lessons in flying, and participating in the activities of the National Guard unit. In this time before elaborate navigational instruments were available and before the airplane itself had been perfected, navigation problems and mechanical difficulties were not unusual. Lindbergh was forced to make two emergency jumps from his plane during his brief career as a mail pilot.

In 1926 a French aviation enthusiast named Chevalier Raymond Orteig offered a $25,000 prize for the first pilot to cross the Atlantic non-stop from New York to Paris. Lieutenant Lindbergh accepted the challenge and carefully outlined a plan for the flight, but this required money. Summoning his best sales technique, Lindbergh approached leading St. Louis businessmen. He promised to refund their money if the flight were successful; and pointed out that such a feat would bring fame to St. Louis and establish the already air-minded city as an aviation center. Although Lindbergh discovered some St. Louis businessmen reluctant to risk their money or his life, he found his first backer in Major Albert B. Lambert—a civic leader and air travel enthusiast who had maintained an airport at St. Louis at his

Bagnell Dam in 1931

(Courtesy State Historical Society)

own expense since 1920. After Lambert's first pledge of $1,000, Lindbergh was able to secure the necessary funds from other citizens of St. Louis including Earl Thompson, J. D. Wooster Lambert, Bill and Frank Robertson, Harry H. Knight, Harry F. Knight, Harold M. Bixby (who was president of the St. Louis Chamber of Commerce), and E. Lansing Ray (editor of the St. Louis *Globe-Democrat*). With the contributions of these St. Louisans and $2,000 from his own pocket, Lindbergh had the $15,000 necessary to carry out his plans.

There was no time to lose, since other flyers were reported to be making preparations to attempt the non-stop flight. Lindbergh traveled to San Diego, California, where he purchased and tested a Wright Whirlwind. This he flew across the continent with only one stop at St. Louis before touching down in New York.

On May 20, 1927, at 7:52 in the morning, Lindbergh took off in his *Spirit of St. Louis,* which was heavily loaded with 300 gallons of gasoline. The plane cleared the rain-softened field with considerable difficulty and slowly climbed into the mist of a damp gray morning. He guided the plane northeast over Long Island, then to Nova Scotia, and finally joined the clouds over the unbroken expanse of the north Atlantic.

Will Rogers, the beloved humorist, wrote a witty newspaper column in the twenties, but the morning of May 20, 1927, was no time for humor. He wrote, "No attempt at jokes today . . . a slim, tall, bashful, smiling American boy is somewhere over the middle of the Atlantic ocean, where no human being has ever ventured before . . ." The famous insurance company, Lloyd's of London, had indicated when Lindbergh took off from New York that the chances were ten to three that he would never be seen again.

Undaunted by such odds, Lindbergh flew eastward through fog and moonless night, over icebergs, black ocean, and island mirages. After the sun had risen and the fog cleared, his task was eased considerably. By flying low over the surface of the water, Lindbergh could determine wind direction and velocity by watching the path of the foam blown from the crest of the ocean whitecaps. Finally, he sighted the coast of Ireland, flew over south England, and at last brought the *Spirit of St. Louis* down in Paris on May 21, 1927. He had crossed 3,600 miles of Atlantic Ocean in only 33 hours and 30 minutes. Sustained by five sand-

(Courtesy Massie-Missouri Commerce)

In 1927 Charles Lindbergh became a national hero and brought fame to St. Louis for his non-stop flight across the Atlantic from New York to Paris in his plane called "The Spirit of St. Louis."

wiches, two canteens of water, and an indomitable will, Lindbergh had conquered the Atlantic skies.

Charles Lindbergh was not the first to cross the Atlantic on a non-stop flight. Two British pilots—Captain John Alcock and Lieutenant Arthur Whitten Brown—had first accomplished the feat eight years before in June of 1919. But no pilot had ever been the object of the adulation which the modest young American received. Perhaps it was because he braved the Atlantic skies alone; perhaps it was because the world, weary of corruption and disillusioned by a costly war which had not brought peace, was ready for a clean-cut hero with a schoolboy grin. Whatever the reason, Charles Lindbergh became the world's hero. He was wildly cheered and nearly mobbed in Paris, Brussels, and London. The United States Government assigned the *U.S.S. Memphis* to return the flyer and his ship to America, where he was awarded the Distinguished Flying Cross in Washington, D. C., and rode down New York's Broadway in a snowstorm of confetti and good wishes. The St. Louis *Post-Dispatch* sold 40,000 extra copies of the paper announcing Lindbergh's success, and on Friday, June 17, when he flew the *Spirit of St. Louis* home to Lambert Field, the city's champion emerged from the cockpit to the deafening huzzas of thousands of eager St. Louisans. A huge welcoming parade, followed by a luncheon and banquet, made the homecoming complete. On Sunday he thanked St. Louis with an exhibition flight over Forest Park.

Lindbergh's victory yielded two rewards for St. Louis; it increased the interest of her citizens in air travel and it furthered the establishment of the city as one of the leading air centers in the nation. The very next year St. Louis adopted a $2,000,000 bond issue to buy and maintain the St. Louis-Lambert Municipal Airport.

As a memorial of Lindbergh's epic flight and the part that St. Louis played in the realization of his triumph, Lindbergh's trophies remain on exhibit today in the Jefferson Memorial collection in Forest Park.

In summary, Missourians accepted with enthusiasm President Wilson's challenge to "make the world safe for democracy." The eligible men sailed for the mud and peril of the front lines in France. The Missourians at home did their bit by cultivating "thrift gardens," conserving coal, cleaning their plates, contributing time and money to agencies serving the soldiers, buying far more than their allotted share of Liberty Bonds, and, in some cases, assuming positions of high responsibility in government service.

In a wave of idealism and reform the prohibition of the sale of intoxicating beverages was made a part of the American Constitution with the ratification of the Eighteenth Amendment in 1919. The "Noble Experiment" proved difficult to enforce and to the dismay of its supporters eventuated in the nurture of crime and criminals. A second, more successful, reform was the granting of woman suffrage with the adoption of the Nineteenth Amendment in 1920.

A split in the Democratic Party over the advisability of American participation in the League of Nations, and the false prosperity of the twenties under national Republican administrations, weakened Democratic control in the state and resulted in a series of progressive Republican governors in the twenties. Despite hindrance from party politics, advances were made on the state level during the decade: a dramatic improvement of roads, the establishment of a state highway patrol, increased interest and financial aid to schools, improvement in the administration and the services of the eleemosynary institutions, the acquisition of land for many state parks, legal protection for the injured worker, and at the end of the era, state aid to the hard-pressed farmers and the unemployed.

Missouri's population and industrial growth moved steadily upward during the decade, but at a slower rate than that of her sister states. Urban expansion continued until, by 1930, for the first time Missouri's urban population exceeded that of her rural areas.

The postwar prosperity of the city dweller was not shared by the farmer, who once more turned to cooperative ventures to lessen his distress.

The radio and moving picture revolutionized entertainment in Missouri, and the development of parks and artificial lakes provided not only recreation and electric power for Missourians, but a new resort industry for the state as well.

By the end of the decade, the banks of Missouri were beginning to feel the effects of that financial storm which broke on Wall Street in New York and, blown by the winds of panic, thundered across the nation raining despair on city and farm alike. Dark days were upon Missouri—and the nation.

BIBLIOGRAPHY

Daniels, Jonathan. *The Man of Independence.* Philadelphia, New York: J. B. Lippincott Company, 1950.

Davis, Kenneth S. *The Hero: Charles A. Lindbergh and the American Dream.* Golden City, New York: Doubleday and Company, 1959.

Derr, Ray. *Missouri Farmers in Action.* Columbia: Missouri Farmer Press, 1953.

Epperson, Ivan H. "Missourians Abroad—George Creel," *Missouri Historical Review,* Vol. XII (January, 1918), pp. 100-110.

Epperson, Ivan H. "Missourians Abroad: Major John J. Pershing," *Missouri Historical Review,* Vol. XI (April-July, 1917), pp. 313-323.

Kirschten, Ernest. *Catfish and Crystal.* Golden City, New York: Doubleday and Company, 1960.

Lindbergh, Charles A. *We.* New York, London: G. P. Putnam's Sons, 1927.

McCain, William D. "Papers of the Food Administration for Missouri 1917-1919 in the National Archives," *Missouri Historical Review,* Vol. XXXII (October, 1937), pp. 56-61.

Mahan, George A. "Missourians Abroad—Rear Admiral Robert E. Coontz," *Missouri Historical Review,* Vol. XIII (July, 1919), pp. 372-376.

Missouri, a Guide to the "Show Me" State. New York: Duell, Sloan and Pearce, 1941.

Odegard, Peter. *Pressure Politics: The Story of the Anti-Saloon League.* New York: Columbia University Press, 1928.

Reddig, William M. *Tom's Town: Kansas City and the Pendergast Legend.* Philadelphia, New York: J. B. Lippincott Company, 1947.

Ridings, J. Willard. "Missourians Abroad—Edward R. Stettinius," *Missouri Historical Review,* Vol. XIII (October, 1918), pp. 36-43.

Shoemaker, Floyd C. *Missouri and Missourians.* Vol. II. Chicago: The Lewis Publishing Company, 1943.

Shoemaker, Floyd C. "Missouri and the War," *Missouri Historical Review,* Vol. XII (October, 1917; January, April, July 1918), pp. 22-31, 90-110, 180-194, 240-257; Vol. XIII (October, 1918; July, 1919), pp. 1-35, 319-360.

Stevens, Walter B. "Missourians Abroad—David R. Francis," *Missouri Historical Review,* Vol. XIII (April, 1919), pp 195-225.

Sullivan, Mark. *Our Times: The United States 1900-1925.* Vol. V and VI. New York: Charles Scribner's Sons, 1937.

Truman, Harry S. *Memoirs.* Vol. I. Garden City, New York: Doubleday and Company, 1955.

Violette, Eugene Morrow. "Missourians Abroad—Major General E. H. Crowder," *Missouri Historical Review,* Vol. XII (July, 1918), pp. 224-239.

CHAPTER XVII

Missouri in the Great Depression

A sinister and ominous shadow is raising its ugly head in
an attempt to destroy the sanctity of our highest court.
—Governor Lloyd Stark, 1938

If we are going to starve, let's starve out where people can
see us.
—The Rev. M. Owen H. Whitfield, 1938

Twin ghosts plagued the people of Missouri during the
1930's. The political specter of corrupt machine rule took up
residence in Kansas City, but the economic specter of depression roamed the state bringing misery to thousands. These
apparitions were not new to Missourians, but they had grown
more powerful and terrifying since their previous visits to the
state. It took the combined powers of Jefferson City and Washington to exorcise the evil spirit of political corruption, but even
the cooperative efforts of the state and federal governments
failed to banish completely the specter of financial distress. It
was not until the advent of terrible Mars, in the guise of World
War II, that the ghost of depression fled.

The Pendergast Machine

In 1889 a citizen of Kansas City coined the slogan, "Make
Kansas City a Good Place to Live in." This catch phrase, dan-
gling preposition notwithstanding, became the goal of William
Rockhill "Baron" Nelson and his Kansas City *Star*. While Nelson
was working to beautify and civilize the packing house city, he
made millions with his two-cent papers, which could be purchased
at a discount for ten cents a week. Eugene Field, acting as an
editor of the competing Kansas City *Times,* bantered the *Star*:

Twinkle, twinkle, little *Star*.
Bright and gossipy you are;
We can daily hear you speak
For a paltry dime a week.

While Baron Nelson was creating a newspaper empire in Kansas City, an Irish family from St. Joseph founded a political dynasty which was an important force in the metropolis for a half century. The Pendergast family came to Missouri in 1857 when Michael Pendergast, his wife, and first-born son James, settled in St. Joseph. In 1876 Jim Pendergast, grown to manhood, moved to larger, more rapidly developing Kansas City, where he entered the saloon business at St. Louis Avenue and Mulberry Street. It was here that the friendly, open-handed Irishman became known as a man of his word, an excellent organizer, and a political leader. By 1892 Pendergast, whose statue stands today in Mulkey Square, was a power in Democratic politics, who could deliver the votes in the First Ward. At the death of James Pendergast in 1911, the machine he founded was a major force in Kansas City government.

The development of a political machine in Kansas City is not an isolated case in American history; similar political organizations appeared in most of the new urban centers. Lincoln Steffens, whom we met earlier in our discussion of St. Louis politics, has left descriptions of corrupt machines in Minneapolis, Chicago, Pittsburgh, Philadelphia, and New York. The political bosses of the time, although they sometimes used fraudulent tactics to win elections and to exploit government, often performed valuable services in the growing cities. The political boss became the protector and spokesman for the new immigrants who crowded into the growing slums of the metropolis. The political boss often carried on a relief agency of his own long before the Federal Government began to provide funds for unfortunates. Despite a few such saving aspects of machine politics, however, it must be admitted that the tactics of the machine were often intended to destroy the principles of democracy, and that machine politics contributed to corruption in city life.

Jim Pendergast's brother, Tom, followed him to Kansas City in 1890. Short, muscular, black-mustachioed Tom had a sharp mind which proved useful when he assumed the dual role of bookkeeper in the Pendergast saloon and political understudy of his older brother. Tom began his career as a public employee in 1896 when he was named deputy marshal for Jackson County. He later served as superintendent of streets in Kansas City, and held office as a city councilman from 1911 to 1916. When Jim died in 1911, Thomas J. Pendergast became head of the faction known as the Jackson Democratic Club. He soon proved his political sagacity in creating a larger and a stronger organization than that which his brother had controlled.

Another Irishman of great political ability was Joseph B. Shannon, who came to Kansas City with his mother and seven brothers and sisters in 1879. The studious Shannon was noted for his scholarly interests and particularly for his amazing breadth of knowledge concerning our third president, Thomas Jefferson. Democrat Joe Shannon, a dedicated student of political tactics, became Tom Pendergast's chief intra-party rival.

There are several versions describing the origins of the names adopted by the two rival Democratic factions in Kansas City. The authenticity of these several versions is in doubt, but it is only necessary for us to know that for whatever reason, Pendergast's political group was called the Goats, and Shannon's faction the Rabbits. Shannon and Pendergast became known for their violent primary election campaigns, in which mobs of each faction threatened the other and where deceit and trickery were employed to cast and count votes. In spite of the brawls which preceded primary elections, the two political leaders would usually form an alliance after the contest and divide the patronage until the next bloody encounter at primary time.

Neither city skyscraper nor city political machine is constructed overnight. Thomas J. Pendergast, called Tom, "T. J." or "Boss," devoted many years of loving attention to the creation of his political faction. He made friends, gave jobs to them or their relatives, and carefully cultivated the new rising political personalities of his district. As the years went by, Tom, with his brother Mike and other members of the family, slowly enlarged their control over the city. By 1924 Tom Pendergast was the chief figure in the Democratic Party in Kansas City.

In many ways the Pendergast operation was routine and unpretentious. Boss Pendergast had his headquarters at 1908 Main Street in a dingy second-floor office, where he sat at a great roll-top desk and conferred day after day with those who sought financial help or political positions. Tom Pendergast's job may not seem to have been attractive. But he loved politics, and he became wealthy in his position of authority. Pendergast had several very profitable legal businesses. His pre-mix concrete company sold millions of dollars worth of quality concrete for building city projects. His corporations sold wholesale liquor,

**Pendergast Headquarters,
1908 Main Street,
Kansas City, Missouri**
*(© St. Louis Post-Dispatch,
used by permission)*

asphalt, and concrete pipe. His garbage trucks were granted the garbage collection contracts for the city at a handsome fee. His brother Mike operated an oil company which was "fortunate enough" to receive much of the city oil trade.

With control of the city government, Pendergast could, by one system or another, influence the letting of lucrative city contracts and could convince contractors in the city to use Pendergast concrete. In 1928 Mayor Beach of Kansas City, who was carrying on a feud with city manager McElroy, referred to a builder who was compelled to tear out the concrete footings for a new structure because the city inspector declared that they had been damaged by frost. Actually, the mayor stated, the concrete was defective only because it had not come from T. J. Pendergast.

Through business devices of this kind a boss could reap great fortunes. A 1928 robbery of Pendergast's Kansas City mansion revealed how profitable such business enterprises can be. Included in the loot were jewels valued at $150,000 and 480 pairs of silk hose from the trousseau of Pendergast's daughter, Marceline. The Pendergasts' lavish tours of the United States and their expensive European vacations were also indicative of the financial rewards of political power.

Tom Pendergast made no secret of his political success. Said he, as quoted by Federal District Attorney Maurice Milligan:

> I'm not braggin' when I say I run the show in Kansas City. I am Boss. If I was a Republican they would call me leader.

During the 1920's Tom Pendergast had such control over Kansas City politics that he could defy the reform elements in the city. In 1925 civic-minded citizens proposed a new charter for the city which would establish the most modern type of city government, the city manager system. The reformers reasoned that a new streamlined nine-man council would be more difficult for a boss to control, and they believed that a competent city manager would operate the city for efficiency, rather than for patronage. To their amazement, the new-charter advocates learned that Tom Pendergast favored their proposal. When the charter came to a vote in 1925, Pendergast's followers marked their ballots for the reform plan, which was overwhelmingly adopted.

Immediately after the election, the reformers learned the truth. Pendergast's power was so great that he not only controlled the council, but he also handpicked for city manager a mild-looking, successful Kansas City bakery owner named Henry F. McElroy. The new city manager was able to use his position and his ties with Pendergast to dominate the city administration.

The impressive Pendergast Mansion, at 5650 Ward Parkway, Kansas City, Missouri, contrasts strikingly with the dingy, second-floor office where Boss Pendergast conducted his daily affairs.

(© *St. Louis Post-Dispatch, used by permission*)

As a consequence, the city manager system had the opposite effect from that desired by its original supporters; and the hold of the Pendergast machine on Kansas City affairs was strengthened by the new charter of 1925. Another political development increased Boss Pendergast's authority in the state of Missouri. When the census of 1930 revealed that Missouri was not growing so rapidly as the other states in the Union, she lost two of her seats in Congress. Republican Governor Caulfield rejected by veto the congressional districts drawn by the Democratic legislature. Consequently, in the election of 1932 all candidates for Congress ran "at large" in the state and, therefore, required support in all sections of the state. Democratic office holders swarmed to Kansas City to secure the blessing of Boss Pendergast, thus increasing his influence at the state level.

When the Democratic candidate for governor in 1932, Francis M. Wilson of Platte City, died less than a month before the election, the Democratic Party was immediately forced to select a new candidate. The Democratic State Committee under the influence of Tom Pendergast selected Circuit Judge Guy B. Park, from Platte City, as the new Democratic candidate. Park proved his reputation as a strict party man who could be relied upon to follow the leaders. During his four years in Jefferson City the state capitol building became known as "Uncle Tom's Cabin."

As the strongest single political voice in Kansas City, Jackson County, and Missouri, Pendergast had numerous chances to exploit Kansas Citians, and equally abundant opportunities to benefit the residents of his city. With his direction and that of his underling, city manager H. F. McElroy, Kansas City adopted a new Ten Year Plan under which fine new roads, city buildings, and a new municipal airport were built, and even little Brush Creek was widened and paved in its path through the residential district of Kansas City. School bond issues passed. Under McElroy's management, deficits disappeared. The city gave many appearances of progress and efficient leadership.

In the midst of this construction a few people observed that the concrete company owned by Mr. Pendergast seemed to have most of the concrete business, but who could complain when the construction activity clearly demonstrated that Kansas City was making progress during a time when much of America seemed to be suffering a decline? Many people in America, critical of the inefficiency of democracy during the crisis of the depression, spoke words of praise for the machine-run city. Even the Kansas City *Star* for a time lauded city manager McElroy for his enlightened administration. In 1938 Benito Mussolini granted Boss Pendergast the Order of the Crown of Italy for his service to the Italians of Kansas City.

The recognition of two facts may dim somewhat the accomplishments of the machine and its financial wizard, Mr. McElroy. First, this was the depression era, and federal funds were generously allotted to the states and cities for improvement projects to provide work for the unemployed. The state director of the Public Works Administration, Matthew Murray, was a Pendergast man who channeled funds into Kansas City. Second, city manager McElroy's acumen was more easily understood when it was revealed that he sometimes made deficits disappear by shifting funds from department to department.

At its best, the Pendergast machine was a servant to many Kansas Citians. The precinct worker greeted the newcomer to

In 1938 an ambassador of Benito Mussolini presented Tom Pendergast with the Order of the Crown of Italy for his service to the Italians of Kansas City.

(© St. Louis Post-Dispatch, used by permission)

his district, made arrangements to have the gas, water, and electricity turned on, and assisted the new resident in registering to vote. If a member of the precinct had difficulty with the police, the precinct worker provided bail, or often tried to secure a lighter punishment. Those who were in need of coal, food, or clothing recognized the precinct worker as one who would often provide assistance. In a big impersonal city where individual citizens felt a need to be part of a group and where immigrants and others battled for status, it was comforting for many people to be associated with an organization which seemed interested in them and offered them protection. The importance of this factor is seen in the continuing strength of the Pendergast machine after its leader was imprisoned and election fraud was revealed. It was natural—and calculated, of course—that the recipients of machine kindnesses would feel an obligation to the organization on election day. The strength of the machine was based upon its large body of adherents in the community.

There was another side to Goat activities. Machine workers who were dedicated to the cause sometimes became overzealous in the rough and tumble of Kansas City politics. The year 1934 was a crucial one for Pendergast, since a reform movement in Kansas City known as the National Youth Movement organized both reform Democrats and Republicans in an attempt to topple the machine. On election day, cars of hoodlums roamed the streets to intimidate the reform-minded citizens of the city and to defeat the N.Y.M. *Star* reporters, and N.Y.M. officials and workers were shot or beaten. When the day was over four people had been killed and eleven injured. Politics in Kansas City was an activity of deadly seriousness. Pendergast's candidate for mayor won the election by a margin of 59,000 votes.

A show of force was not necessary two years later when the machine won another overwhelming victory. The Kansas City *Star* said hopelessly in November, 1936, "An honest election here Tuesday is absolutely impossible." Looking back on the election, *Star* writer William M. Reddig wrote in his book *Tom's Town,* "There were between fifty and sixty thousand illegal votes from Kansas City in the election of November, 1936." The election tactics employed by the machine were revealed in the election fraud trials of 1937. For example, the names of deceased persons were not deleted from the voting rolls, and these "cemetery commuters" continued to vote for decades. Loyal machine

"Dead Men and Vacant Lots"
Fitzpatrick, St. Louis Post-
Dispatch, September 22, 1934
(Courtesy State Historical Society)

DEAD MEN AND VACANT LOTS.

members listed fictitious names as residents of their homes and business establishments, and even vacant lots were recorded as the domiciles of non-existent voters. The machine then sent flocks of men from polling place to polling place on election day to cast votes for these "registered voters." In 1936 the Pendergast machine was able to secure 41,805 votes in two Kansas City wards, the total population of which, including little children, was only 38,401.

Another unfortunate aspect of Kansas City politics was the development of ties between the machine and Johnny Lazia, Big Charley Carollo, and his associates. Ex-convict Johnny Lazia was the leader of the North Side Democratic Club. Lazia had previously been sentenced to twelve years in the Missouri state penitentiary for armed robbery. After serving only eight months and seven days, he returned to his north side area of Kansas City where he acted as the political chief. Maurice Milligan told how Pendergast wrote to Democratic political leader James A. Farley on May 12, 1933, in an attempt to halt the successful prosecution of Lazia for income tax evasion: "Now, Jim, Lazia is one of my chief lieutenants and I am more sincerely interested in his welfare than anything you might be able to do for me now or in the future." Lazia and city manager McElroy worked out a system whereby Lazia was to attempt to control the criminal element in the city and to prevent major crimes. In return Lazia was granted a voice in police policy. Milligan declared in his book:

> . . . more than sixty ex-convicts had been placed on the police payroll at the request of Johnny Lazia. In 1934 one-tenth of the entire police force in Kansas City had criminal records.

Milligan later linked Lazia to the underworld by his charges at the trial of Lazia's bodyguard, Big Charley Carollo, in 1939. Milligan declared that Carollo

> . . . took over the authority exercised by Lazia in his lifetime, relative to gambling and rackets carried on in Kansas City . . . the defendant became the collector of the lug [payment] that was imposed on the gambling rackets of Kansas City who paid large sums of money monthly for the privilege of carrying on gambling games unmolested by the police officers of the city.

Nattily-dressed Johnny Lazia, regal in his spats, gloves, and cane, became rich. But he was not successful in controlling crime in the city. Lazia himself was machine gunned to death in gangland fashion in 1934.

CRIME AND POLITICS

Fitzpatrick, December 9, 1934, the St. Louis Post-Dispatch
(Courtesy State Historical Society)

THE PLIGHT OF KANSAS CITY

In Kansas City all of the city groups—voters, underworld, and even businessmen—were asked to cooperate. The businessmen of Kansas City discovered that it was prudent to keep in step with the machine. Those who attempted to fight the machine might find their property taxes suddenly raised, their buildings condemned by city inspectors as unfit for use, or their requests for building permits denied. In Kansas City, a lethargy developed among some citizens who felt that nothing could be done to halt the abuses or to protect themselves and their rights.

However, many Kansas Citians who did not object to gambling pointed to the many fine new buildings and other projects, the increased importance of their city in state affairs, and the orderliness of machine rule. They continued as friends of the organization even through the troubled times at the end of the decade.

Tom Pendergast, shrewd politician and astute businessman, seemed for many years to be invincible. He had a weakness, however — an uncontrollable passion for gambling — particularly horse racing—which he later admitted had been part of his life since he left St. Joseph. Pendergast was not satisfied to place small bets, and, particularly during the thirties, he began to wager incredible sums of money. Like all gamblers, he frequently lost. In 1935 alone his losses exceeded $600,000. As a result, his need for money grew. As was admitted in federal court, these losses led him to seek new sources of money and to conceal the true income of his many corporations to avoid paying taxes.

Pendergast's power at the city, county, and state level was at its height during the 1930's. But when the agents of the Federal Government began to close in on him, he was in trouble. Neither his gun-toting supporters, nor the grateful recipients of his patronage, nor the Democratic hopefuls he had supported, nor the fortune he had gleaned from his many enterprises could save him from the Bureau of Internal Revenue. In May, 1939, Tom Pendergast was sentenced to fifteen months in the federal penitentiary for income tax evasion.

The New Deal in Missouri

Missourians had seen hard times before. The panics of 1837, 1873, and 1893 had brought low farm prices, unemployment, bankruptcies, and bank failures. But the Great Depression of the 1930's made the earlier financial crises seem mild by comparison. In the nineteenth century most Missourians had lived on farms or in small towns with garden plots, a few chickens, and a fruit tree or two. During periods of depression, clothes might have to be darned, purchases curtailed, and luxuries foregone— but few went hungry. By 1930, however, 51.2 per cent of Missouri's population were city dwellers, dependent upon wages to purchase the barest necessities. The stock market crash had resulted in business and bank failures in every state. Millions were thrown out of work across the nation. While Missouri did not suffer to the degree that the more highly industrial states did, Missourians did not escape the drastic effects of the depression. The easy credit of the twenties had tempted many to buy on the installment plan the things they desired. Homes, cars, and furniture were repossessed when jobless workers were unable to meet payments. Many city dwellers' savings which were not lost in bank failures were eaten up buying food for hungry families and paying rent during prolonged periods of unemployment.

Still the cities continued to grow. By 1940 the percentage of urban population had risen to 51.8. The census returns of 1940 show that greater numbers left the counties north of the Missouri River to move to the cities than did the inhabitants of the Ozarks area. There was also a movement of people from the Old Plains section south of Kansas City to the urban areas. The Ozarks and the river counties tended to hold their own population and, in some cases, to gain residents.

When the depression struck, President Hoover, who feared that federal doles would degrade the recipients and lead to reckless "pork barrel" spending, recommended that the local government and community charities feed and provide relief for their own needy. One estimate indicates that in 1932 St. Louis was feeding one out of every ten families. The percentage of families on relief was only slightly lower in Kansas City. The hard-pressed cities soon found that they could not finance such operations. Unemployed men and boys joined the "Starvation Army," riding the rails from town to town in search of work. One author reports small groups of desperate men, women, and children searching the St. Louis dumps for food scraps. Bitter, wretched men slept in parks or doorways and wrapped themselves in newspapers, which they called "Hoover blankets" for the man on whom they blamed their distress.

President Hoover took several steps to alleviate the financial crisis. The Reconstruction Finance Corporation was established

"One Person Out of Every Ten" Fitzpatrick, St. Louis Post-Dispatch, January 16, 1938
(Courtesy State Historical Society)

to aid banks and businesses in trouble, with the intent of safeguarding savings and securing workers' jobs. Hoover instituted new public works projects for the improvement of rivers and harbors and to channel two and a quarter billion dollars into the economy. Several of Republican President Hoover's proposals were defeated by the Democratic Congress, and those which were passed proved inadequate to resolve so severe a financial crisis.

The unemployed, frightened and miserable, were in no mood for half measures. Just as the Populists, Muckrakers, and Progressives at the turn of the century had called for government action to solve the problems of the day, the reformers of the 1930's decided that government intervention was the answer. When dynamic, sympathetic Franklin Delano Roosevelt promised in his campaign that, if elected, he would "try something," unhappy Missourians decided to give him an opportunity to do so. In the presidential election of 1932 the citizens of Missouri gave Mr. Roosevelt the largest popular plurality—460,000 votes—ever polled by a presidential candidate in the state.

Immediately upon taking office after his landslide victory, President Roosevelt introduced his "New Deal" and began the process of experimentation to attempt to improve conditions in the nation. Hundreds of new policies were designed to pump money into the sagging economy and bring relief to those who were in difficult financial straits. This direct assistance to the citizens increased the importance of the Federal Government and decreased the prestige of the state government in the eyes of the recipient. In spite of this, however, the Federal Government did carry on many projects in conjunction with state officials, using the principle of matching state with federal funds for special projects. Thus, while the authority of the Federal Government grew more than that of the state government during the thirties, the national authority either forced or lured the states into accepting new financial responsibilities. The long-term result of the New Deal—still evident decades later—was to involve government much more directly in the economy. Having intervened once, the government could never again seem indifferent or disinterested when a segment of the nation was in economic distress.

Not all agreed that the New Deal experiments were desirable. Over 500,000 Missourians cast their ballots for Hoover in 1932. The Republican opposition of course could be expected to condemn some of Roosevelt's proposals. However, in Missouri, Roosevelt policies were criticized also by leading Democrats. Senator Bennett Champ Clark disliked the NRA (which the United States Supreme Court later declared unconstitutional) and the AAA—Roosevelt's major programs for business and agriculture. Former Democratic Senator James A. Reed, who despised the growing power of the Federal Government, actively opposed the re-election of Roosevelt in 1936. The New Deal seems to have pleased a majority of Missourians, however, for Franklin D. Roosevelt was able to win decisive victories in Missouri each of the four times he sought the presidency.

Roosevelt declared that the New Deal was designed to bring the three R's—relief, recovery, and reform. Admitting that mistakes might be made in the adoption of new policies, he called for bold experiments. These experiments resulted in the expenditure of great sums of money; for example, during the years 1933 to 1937 the Federal Government made non-repayable grants to Missouri totaling $862,880,012. By pouring such great sums of money into each of the states, President Roosevelt, if he could not end the depression, at least made it endurable, and in the process he set the precedent for federal intervention into more and more aspects of American life.

The Workers of Missouri in the Thirties

The most pressing problem President Roosevelt faced on taking office was the feeding of twelve to fifteen million hungry, unemployed Americans. Since the resources of local agencies were running low, in some cases almost exhausted, the Federal Emergency Relief Administration (FERA) was set up to provide for the immediate material needs of the jobless.

To preserve the skills and self respect of the unemployed, a program of work-relief was soon instituted under the supervision of the Civil Works Administration (CWA). The agency was established to furnish immediate employment for those on relief. Within one month 89,500 men and 6,000 women were at work on jobs furnished by the CWA program in Missouri. This emergency agency, designed to provide temporary work primarily on local projects, passed out of existence in March of 1934.

Under the Public Works Administration, instituted in 1933, the Federal Government in cooperation with local organizations or units of government provided work on hundreds of federal and non-federal major projects. Although the workers were not required to be hired from the relief rolls, PWA projects indirectly relieved unemployment by stimulating business. A total of 361 federal projects such as dams, canals, streets and highways, and post offices or federal buildings in Bowling Green, Cameron, Hannibal, Independence, Joplin, Neosho, and Perryville were completed in Missouri. Of 560 non-federal projects in the state 510 buildings were erected, including a thirty-one-story city hall and nine schools in Kansas City. With the help of the PWA, St. Louis built two elementary schools, a high school, eighteen hospital projects, and added a municipal auditorium and a civil courts building to her skyline. The state constructed new buildings and repaired existing structures at her penal and eleemosynary institutions at a cost of over five million dollars. Other state and local projects included streets and highways, sewer systems, water systems, railroad construction, and recreation projects.

In 1935 the Works Progress Administration, later the Work Projects Administration and better known as the WPA, was set up to furnish jobs for those on the relief rolls. Local supervision and cooperation with the Federal Government in financing was encouraged whenever possible. Highways, roads, and streets; buildings such as schools, gymnasiums, hospitals, and court-

CIVIL
WORKS
PROGRAM

"Regenerating the Amer-
ican Workingman" Fitz-
patrick, St. Louis Post-
Dispatch, December 13,
1933

*(Courtesy State Historical
Society)*

houses; recreational facilities such as parks, tennis courts, golf courses, and swimming pools; sewage disposal plants; water supply systems; airport projects; sewing, weaving, gardening, and canning projects; library programs, and the production of books for the blind in Braille are among the accomplishments of the WPA in Missouri.

The National Youth Administration (NYA), first established as a branch of the WPA in 1935, became an independent agency in 1939. The NYA provided financial assistance through work on useful projects for unemployed young people who desired to continue their education, and furnished vocational guidance and placement for Missouri youths leaving school. For those interested in further education, the colleges, universities, and high schools of Missouri cooperated with the agency in a program of student aid. For out-of-school youths, a placement service was operated in cooperation with the state employment offices, and jobs in construction work, clerical services, or home economics were offered.

In April of 1933 the Civilian Conservation Corps was instituted to help young unemployed and untrained men not provided for by other agencies. Men between the ages of eighteen and twenty-three years, who were not on probation or parole, and who came from needy families, were eligible for jobs performing construction tasks or conservation work in national and state forests and parks. The young men lived in CCC camps and received a minimum of $30 a month in salary, $22 of which they were required to send to their dependents. The development of Mark Twain State Park at Florida and extensive construction at Big Spring, Roaring River, Bennett Spring, and Washington state parks, Dr. Edmund A. Babler Memorial Park, Henry Shaw Gardenway, and in the Cuivre River recreation area were accomplished by the men of the CCC. Camps of the CCC were also located in state forests at Sullivan, Ellington, and Salem, and in national forests and parks in Missouri where reforestation, wildlife conservation, and soil erosion projects were carried out. CCC projects were continued in Missouri until 1941.

Another New Deal program designed to help the workingman was social security. Under this system, a tax levied on wages was set aside to be used later for compensation during periods of unemployment or for old age assistance after retirement. As a part of the bill, the state government was invited to share in the expenditures necessary to provide old age pensions, aid to dependent children, and other forms of assistance and re-

Although Fitzpatrick usually praised New Deal relief measures, he was sometimes critical of the loafing involved in federal projects. St. Louis Post-Dispatch, February 26, 1936

(Courtesy State Historical Society)

lief. State cooperation in the social security program is discussed later in this chapter.

During the early 1930's, fear of bank failure was one of the chief concerns for most Missourians. A rumor or a bit of gossip led to runs on banks when depositors lined up to demand the return of their money. Since banks normally have a large part of their deposits out on loan, the bank runs frequently led to bank failures. In 1931 and 1932, 182 Missouri banks and trust companies went bankrupt. As soon as President Roosevelt assumed office he closed the banks of the nation to prevent their being forced into bankruptcy by panicky depositors. Those which were in sound condition were allowed to reopen. The enactment of legislation to establish the Federal Deposit Insurance Corporation was a big step toward restoring confidence in the banking structure of the state. Under the FDIC, bank deposits were insured to a sum of $5,000. As a result, many Missourians heeded President Roosevelt's advice to take their savings from under their mattresses to a bank, where they could at last be sure their deposits would be safe.

In the 1930's legislation was enacted under the National Industrial Recovery Act (NIRA) and the Wagner Labor Act to protect the right of workers to organize and to bargain collectively. During the depression many attempts were made to organize unions in Missouri. At the same time, many companies, operating under financial strain, either cut wages or refused to grant increases. The workers, on the other hand, with their newly-formed unions wished to demonstrate their strength to force the companies to grant higher wages and better working conditions. Many strikes occurred, particularly in the years 1935 to 1939. For example, in the year 1935 alone there were forty-five strikes in Missouri involving 16,438 workers.

The tiff miners of Washington County called a strike in 1935. Tiff, or more technically, barite ore, is dug in Crawford, Franklin, Jefferson, St. Francois, and Washington counties, the last named producing approximately three-fourths of the state's output. The mineral, used in paints, enamels, textiles, chemicals, glass, linoleum, and rubber products, had been dug for decades with the crudest of tools and techniques. After locating a deposit, whole families would proceed to dig up the ore with pick and shovel from pits usually five feet wide and several feet deep. Occasionally, deposit depths would reach thirty to forty

(Photo by Townsend Godsey, Courtesy State Historical Society)

The W.P.A. encompassed a wide variety of projects. These women, working on a flag from the Mexican War, were two of twenty who restored the battle flags in the state museum in Jefferson City.

feet, and in this case a crude windlass would be used to haul the ore to the surface in buckets. When machinery was introduced, greatly increasing the supply of tiff and, therefore, decreasing its price to $3.50 a ton, the miners, demanding an increase to $5.50 a ton, refused to dig. After several weeks the company agreed to come to terms and increased the price to $5 a ton. Despite this settlement, the living conditions of the tiff miners were not much improved and three years later were shockingly described by Jane Whitbread in the article "Missouri Misery," appearing in the *Nation* for October 1, 1938. The poorest housing, almost non-existent medical care, a high rate of illiteracy, and starvation wages were reported. Pinkeye, goiter, tuberculosis, diabetes, and a case of severe burns went untended. Parents and children were digging side by side for an average of $5 a week to support families of ten to twelve. Even as late as 1941 the average wage of a tiff miner's family was reported to be less than $20 a week and free rent.

In 1937 the new and vigorous union known as the CIO called a strike in the Ford plant at Kansas City. Prolonged struggle between labor and Ford caused new economic dislocation in the Kansas City community. Finally, Pendergast's shrewd city manager, Henry F. McElroy, went to Detroit to confer with Henry Ford. When McElroy returned, he happily announced:

> Everything's lovely, and the goose hangs high,
> Soon you will see the Fords rolling by.

McElroy was wrong, just as many other economists and politicians were mistaken in believing that the economic crises of the thirties would pass easily. In Kansas City the strike continued into 1938 with picket line struggles, shootings, and stonings.

Another long and bloody strike occurred in southwest Missouri in 1935 when the International Union of Mine, Mill, and Smelter Workers called a strike in the Joplin area. The company refused to come to terms with the union and hired other workers. The case was appealed to the National Labor Relations Board, which finally handed down a decision in 1939 declaring that the workers had a right to organize, and forced the company to rehire the strikers.

Rural Missouri in the Thirties

In 1932 the total income for rural America had dropped so that farmers had only one-half the purchasing power they had enjoyed a decade earlier. In 1932 the farmers received only fifty-six per cent of the prices paid for farm commodities immediately before World War I. While farm income was down, the cost of manufactured goods had spiraled to approximately 107 per cent of the prices charged in 1914. In 1932 cash income for many Missouri farmers had fallen below the sum needed to pay their property taxes. The farms of many such Missourians were sold for taxes, and the former owner sometimes remained as a tenant on land that had been in his family for generations. Farmers who had purchased land at high prices during World War I and immediately thereafter were hard pressed to repay the loans in the twenties and thirties. The farmer's crisis can be seen in other figures. A forced transfer of 2,700,000 acres resulted when approximately 18,000 farms were seized by foreclosure action in Missouri during the years 1930 to 1934.

At the same time that commodity prices were low, agricul-

Missouri Farm Scene in the Thirties by Fred Geary

ture was becoming more mechanized. The tractor became a necessary implement in the 1930's. Thus, the farmer required new
sums of money to mechanize at the same time that he was unable
to secure reasonable prices for his products. Severe drought
further complicated the farm situation during the thirties. In
1930, 1934, and 1936 drought withered the crops, dried up ponds,
creeks, and wells, and crazed the parched land like an old plate
left too long in an oven. Unusually intense heat increased the
misery of man and beast. In 1934 the residents of Columbia, Missouri, sweltered twenty-six days in temperatures over 100° and
thirteen days in heat over 105°. Two years later another heat
wave scorched Columbia with thirty-nine days over 100° and
thirteen days over 105°. The summer of 1936 was made even
more unpleasant by great swarms of grasshoppers which invaded
the state. When the county agents of Missouri distributed a
poison bran mash to curtail the grasshopper damage, those farmers who used the bait were able to save some of their crop. It
was estimated that the grasshoppers that summer stripped the
crops on approximately 1,000,000 acres of Missouri farm land.

President Roosevelt authorized his secretary of agriculture,
Henry A. Wallace, to bring forth an immediate program designed
to improve the farmers' plight. In 1933, shortly after the begin-

ning of Roosevelt's administration, Congress passed the Agricultural Adjustment Act, which was intended to boost farm prices. Under this act, farmers were paid to curtail their acreage of the basic crops. By decreasing the supply, the government intended to force prices upward. The AAA plan of 1933 was the basic law for farmers until 1936, when it was declared unconstitutional by the United States Supreme Court. Congress then passed the Soil Conservation Act, under which farmers were to be compensated for planting crops which were soil conserving (such as clover, alfalfa, or lespedeza) instead of crops which were soil depleting (such as corn, wheat, cotton, or tobacco). This law would have an effect similar to that of the AAA, since the acreage of market crops would be decreased. This program, with modifications after 1936, became the basic continuing federal agricultural program.

Neither the AAA nor the soil conservation program was successful in drastically reducing production, because the development of mechanized farming and the use of fertilizer made possible increased production on decreased acreage. However, the government did establish a system of purchasing the surplus, thus forcing prices up to certain so-called parity levels. In effect, the Department of Agriculture was trying to raise prices to such a level that the farmers would have as much purchasing power as they had in the prosperous years from 1910 to 1914. The intervention of the government into the agricultural economy did effect a rise in prices so that farm income improved during the thirties. It was estimated that by 1937 farm prices had increased sixty-seven per cent over the prices paid in 1932. However, farm income did not surge upward dramatically until the beginning of World War II.

Many Americans have been critical of the agriculture program introduced during the thirties. It was frequently charged that the program tended to favor the large landowner more than the small landowner. The program did cost the farmer some of his independence by making him more and more dependent upon federal governmental decisions. It is also charged, as noted above, that the program failed to control production effectively. Despite these criticisms, the farm community in Missouri and elsewhere has been unwilling to relinquish the basic features of the program.

The severity of the economic crisis for farmers drove them

to mob action on several occasions during the early thirties. In August and September of 1935 crowds of defiant and desperate farmers gathered in Daviess, DeKalb, Clinton, and Nodaway counties to halt or obstruct the foreclosure and sale of mortgaged farms. Through the Farm Credit Administration, the Federal Government did provide money during the 1930's to help farmers refinance their mortgages at low interest rates and thus prevent foreclosures. These policies apparently were successful in encouraging farm ownership, for statistics show that farm tenancy declined during the late thirties.

As they were first introduced, the agricultural plans of the AAA and the Soil Conservation Act worked to the advantage of the owner of the land, but the system failed to ease the plight of the tenant farmer or sharecropper. In the southeast section of the state—particularly the bootheel—the land was farmed largely by sharecroppers and tenants who lived in great poverty. The fertile flat fields of the bootheel were really part of the South. Like much of the South after the Civil War, the land had been divided into plots which were tilled by sharecroppers—about ninety per cent of whom were blacks—who lived from year to year without making economic progress. Under the sharecrop system the tenant was given a shack, a team, seed, and the necessary tools and implements to produce cotton. During the year the sharecropper could secure the food, supplies, and clothing he needed on credit from his landowner. After the cotton was picked and brought to the gin, the profits were to be equally divided by the landowner and the sharecropper. However, after the tenant paid his bill for the previous year, there was little money left.

The sharecroppers were restless in the 1930's. Drought and low cotton prices had made their meager lives even more miserable. The increased use of power machinery made it possible for landowners with sufficient capital for mechanization to farm great areas without tenant help. Federal agricultural policies required the landowner to share with his tenants the government bounty for reducing the amount of land under cultivation. Therefore, more and more landowners, realizing that the sharecrop system was decreasing their potential income, informed the tenants that they were no longer wanted as sharecroppers. Many were invited to remain as day laborers for seventy-five cents to a dollar a day when they were needed.

Labor organizers who had been active in the South moved

Fitzpatrick's Sympathetic Sketch of "Missouri's Refugees" appeared in the St. Louis Post-Dispatch on January 15, 1939.
(Courtesy State Historical Society)

into the bootheel region and began to organize the unhappy sharecroppers for action against the landowners. As soon as this was known, some of the landowners ordered the tenants to leave the land by the first day of 1939. The Reverend Mr. M. Owen H. Whitfield, who was associated with the Southern Tenant Farmer's Union, suggested that the evicted tenants camp on the state property along the highways to focus attention on their plight. For five days the motorists driving along U. S. Highway 61 in January, 1939, were shocked to discover over a thousand ragged men, women, and children, shivering in the rain and snow and icy blasts of winter, huddled around fires and lining the highway for about eighty miles from a point near Sikeston almost to the Arkansas line.

The dramatic protest of the strikers was partially successful. Governor Stark intervened with the owners to reach a settlement. Approximately half of the strikers returned to their former houses at the invitation of the landowners. The remainder, however, were forced by state and county officials into a new camp site, which the tenants called Homeless Junction, near Sikeston.

Some of these sharecroppers were aided by the Resettlement

Administration, which engaged in several activities such as the relocation of farmers whose land was not productive; the issuing of temporary loans for feed and seed and five-year loans for equipment, feed, and livestock; and the adjustment of farm debts to prevent foreclosures. Resettlement projects in Dent, Lincoln, Miller, Pettis, New Madrid, Camden, and Butler counties, land conservation projects in the Lake of the Ozarks, Cuivre River, and Montserrat recreation areas, the Missouri game and arboretum project in Boone County, and rehabilitation demonstration farms in twenty-five counties were among the accomplishments of the agency.

One of the most publicized projects of the Resettlement Administration was La Forge Farms established in New Madrid County in 1937. The Federal Government purchased the land, constructed the buildings, and loaned money for the purchase of feed and livestock and for the establishment of a cooperative association for the settlement of 100 families. Each family was provided a five-room house, a barn, a food cellar, a deep well,

In this bootheel scene in the thirties a sharecropper gazes at his new home under construction.

(Courtesy State Historical Society)

and sanitary facilities. After two years, the farmers were repaying their loans from the sale of crops and livestock, and were canning and storing food for winter. The average property wealth of the La Forge project residents rose from $28 to $1,473.71. By December, 1940, ninety-seven families of the original 100 remained in the settlement, and the Federal Government had realized an eighteen per cent return on its investment.

After the sharecroppers' dramatic demonstration in 1939, a program was designed by state, federal, and local officials to construct 500 homes for former tenants. Each family received a house, built and furnished for $800, a three-fourths-acre garden plot, and a common pasture which was shared with the other families.

The Farm Security Administration (FSA) was also set up to assist low income farm families with loans, technical assistance, and encouragement. The Resettlement Administration and the FSA were instrumental in alleviating the distress of almost 113,000 Missouri farm families between 1935 and 1939.

The Rural Electrification Administration (REA) was another agency which served the interests of Missouri farmers. Created as an emergency agency in May of 1935, the REA was given permanent status by the Rural Electrification Law of 1936 and became a division of the federal Department of Agriculture in 1939. The REA administers long-term loans to farmer's cooperatives, public power districts, and public utilities for the construction of high line electric service facilities. That the agency contributed significantly to the electrification of Missouri's farms can be seen in the fact that it served over 33,000 Missouri farms in 1939.

Democratic Control

The great depression which passed over the United States in the 1930's like an evil shadow soon darkened the economic outlook in all parts of the country. In Missouri—and all her sister states—the financial crises could be seen in bank failures, in unemployment, in mortgage foreclosures, and in the poverty of great multitudes. Normally, a depression works to the advantage of the party which is out of power at the national level and to the disadvantage of the party controlling the White House at the time of its occurrence. Herbert Hoover, a Republican, was the occupant of the White House at the time of the stock market crash and the onset of the subsequent depression. Although Hoover, in his concern for the unfortunate, attempted to alleviate the suffering of the people, he was anxious to avoid action which might permanently damage the economy. His well-meaning actions were far from adequate to halt the spreading economic plague, and by 1932 the American people were anxious for a change—which meant a Democratic administration.

Senator James Reed of Kansas City had dreams of capturing the presidency, and the dominant Pendergast faction in the state supported his aspirations in 1932. Reed's views, however, were not popular at the time. Instead of calling for more government intervention to ease the effects of the depression, Reed wanted less. He declared, "What we need is to recognize the government cannot take care of the people, that the people must take care of government." The Democratic convention turned its back on the fiery senator from Missouri and jubilantly nominated Governor Franklin Delano Roosevelt of New York, who asserted that government should act with dispatch to assist needy citizens.

In 1932 Roosevelt won a crushing victory over Hoover, who carried only six states of the Union. In Missouri, Roosevelt won nearly a half million vote lead over his Republican opponent— the largest plurality of any presidential candidate in Missouri history. The Democrats were not only successful in supporting their presidential candidate in Missouri, but made a clean sweep of the state offices as well. Only seventeen lonely Republicans —seven of them holdovers in the Senate—were to be found in the entire Missouri General Assembly in January, 1933.

The Democratic nominee for governor in 1932 was Francis M. Wilson of Platte City. A little less than one month before the November election, Wilson died. The State Democratic Committee, which was dominated by the Pendergast forces at the time, met and selected as their candidate Guy B. Park of Platte City, a party regular and a close associate of Francis Wilson. The strength of the Democratic political drive in 1932 can be seen in Park's victory, for although he was virtually unknown in the state a month before the election, when the ballots were counted in November, 1932, Park was elected with a larger plurality than any previous candidate for governor.

It should be noted that Bennett "Champ" Clark was elected to the United States Senate in 1932. Clark, the son of the former speaker of the House of Representatives and, like his father, a

Swept into office on the coat-tail of the Roosevelt victory, Governor Guy B. Park stressed economy in state expenditures and cooperation with New Deal policies.

(Courtesy State Historical Society)

polished politician, was one of the founders of the American Legion and derived much of his support from the veterans of the state. As was noted earlier, Missouri's delegation to the House of Representatives was cut to thirteen in 1932. Since the legislature had failed to divide the state into districts, all the congressmen were elected at large, and in the Roosevelt landslide thirteen Democrats were chosen. From 1904 to 1930 the Republican Party had been a strong competitor for the formerly dominant Democratic Party. With the sweeping victory of Roosevelt in 1932, Missouri's Republican Party received a serious setback; and, although it subsequently defeated the Democratic Party in a few instances since 1932, for the most part, Missouri continued to lean Democratic.

Governor Park served as chief executive of the state during four trying years. The economic distress of many citizens led to demands for relief and financial assistance. The depressed economic conditions forced the state to seek new sources of revenue. The circumstances surrounding Park's choice by the State Democratic Committee led to many charges that he was controlled by the Kansas City boss. Each of these situations made his administration more difficult.

As governor of the state, however, he soon discovered that the Roosevelt administration in Washington, by adopting dramatic new policies to rejuvenate the American economy, would provide large sums of money to be spent in Missouri. As we have seen, the enactments of the Federal Government gave great and welcome assistance to the struggling states, and Missouri was given large sums of money for the many projects described in the previous section.

A number of changes were made during Park's administration. School appropriations were exempted from the governor's right to veto items in appropriation bills. The department of the budget was established at the state level to consolidate budgeting procedure and to supervise state expenditures. A state system of centralized purchasing was adopted, which allowed the state to purchase in quantity at lower prices.

Probably the most controversial act of Park's administration was the passage of a general sales tax in 1934. This one half of one percent tax was much criticized, since it hit both rich and poor. However, since the property owners of the state were burdened by a great tax drain at the same time that property was less productive of income, no other tax seemed feasible. Although it was intended to be levied for only two years, the tax was extended and increased in subsequent years.

In 1935 the Missouri General Assembly passed a law to provide old age pensions for those Missourians who were over seventy years old and were unable to earn a living. As originally enacted, the law provided for a monthly payment of $30 to each pensioner and a total of $45 to married pensioners. Later the Federal Government provided additional support for the state

Bennett Champ Clark, one of the founders of the American Legion, was strongly supported by the veterans of Missouri in his election to the United States Senate in 1932.

(Courtesy State Historical Society)

pension program, and during Governor Stark's administration the federal and state systems were merged under the state social security commission.

The growing power of the Pendergast machine was clearly manifest at the state level in the 1930's. Harry Truman secured, with the support of the Kansas City faction, his election as United States senator in 1934 when he defeated the Republican incumbent, Roscoe Patterson of Springfield. Another example of the power of the Pendergast faction was the appointment of R. Emmett O'Malley as state superintendent of insurance under Governor Park. O'Malley subsequently became involved in an insurance scandal which rocked Jefferson City.

A leading candidate in the election of 1936 was Lloyd C. Stark of the town of Louisiana in Pike County. Stark had been an officer in World War I and a successful businessman, with a nursery of nationwide fame. In the 1932 election, Pendergast had refused Stark's request for support. Finally, in 1936, the Kansas City political leader granted his approval of Stark's candidacy. Another Democratic primary candidate for governor in 1936 was William Hirth, the well-known leader of the Missouri Farmers Association. During the campaign, Hirth denounced State Superintendent of Insurance O'Malley for certain agreements made with fire insurance companies, and implied that O'Malley was guilty of bribery. Lloyd Stark defeated Hirth and won both the Democratic nomination in August and the final election in November.

When Roosevelt ran for his second term in 1936, Missouri was once more in the Democratic column. As might be expected, all state officials were Democratic, and the legislature was dominated by the Democratic Party.

During Governor Stark's term, a number of significant state developments occurred. A retirement system was adopted for the public school teachers of the state, and the state conservation commission was established to centralize the state offices concerned with the conservation of Missouri's wildlife.

In 1937 the state began a project to construct a new, much-needed office building in Jefferson City with an appropriation of $850,000. In 1937, the one per cent sales tax was boosted to two per cent to help pay for the continued increase in state expenses during the depression years. The state used the additional revenue for direct relief to the people, for old age assistance, and for the maintenance of the many state institutions. The monies expended for public education were also greatly increased after the institution of the sales tax. In 1933, before the sales tax, Missouri appropriated only $3,500,000 for her schools. In 1935, when the tax was first levied, Missouri school appropriations totaled slightly under $7,400,000. In 1937 the school funds amounted to over $12,500,000; and by 1939, state appropriations to education had been increased to over $13,400,000.

One of the most important reforms instituted by Franklin D. Roosevelt was the establishment of the Social Security Administration in 1935. As adopted by Congress, the social security system placed a tax upon wages, and the proceeds were then used to give the worker insurance protection for periods of unemployment and for retirement. It originally stipulated that workers retiring at the age of sixty-five would receive a monthly payment depending, in size, upon the past contributions of the

State Auditor Forrest Smith (left) gives the first old age assistance check to Jesse B. Farmer of Callaway County in 1935. Smith became popular in the state for his letters beginning "Dear Pensioner."
(Photo by Townsend Godsey, Courtesy State Historical Society)

recipient. As part of the complex social security plan, the Federal Government gave grants to the states which they were to administer to help care for dependent children, blind and crippled citizens, and state old age pensioners. During Governor Stark's term, Missouri established a social security commission to administer relief in the state. Never before in American history had government assumed such great responsibility for the immediate welfare of citizens. This increased governmental concern for those in want not only assisted the afflicted directly, but also pumped badly needed money into the depressed economy.

State cooperation with federal assistance agencies, which was discussed earlier, continued during Governor Stark's administration.

The Rise of Harry S Truman

On May 8, 1884, in the west Missouri town of Lamar, Harry Truman was born, the descendant of typical Missouri settlers who had made their way west from Virginia and Kentucky. The proud father, John Truman, planted a pine tree to commemorate the happy event of his first son's birth. Sixty-one years later that pine towered skyward when Harry Truman was inaugurated as president of the United States. The John Truman family moved about several times during the early years of their marriage, residing at Belton, then at Grandview, and finally at Independence where Harry Truman was educated in the public schools and where his real estate salesman father became known as a strong Democrat.

Because of his poor eyesight and his fear of damaging his glasses, young Harry was unable to join in the rough and tumble play of the neighborhood boys. In his *Memoirs,* the former president relates the information that because he was unable to see well enough to bat, he acted as umpire in the neighborhood baseball games. Despite his minor handicap and a bout with diphtheria which left him paralyzed for several months, the future president had a happy small town boyhood with a host of playmates, a closely-knit affectionate family, and the pets, chores, and adventures of every lucky, late-nineteenth century Missouri boy.

The Missouri lad became an avid reader. By the time he reached his middle teens, he had read every book in the Independence Public Library and the family Bible three times over.

Harry Truman found history particularly engrossing, and he credits his early interest in the principles of leadership and government to his study of the lives of great men and nations. Through the years of his political career he had many opportunities to test his theory that current events have their counterparts in the past and that the problems of today may be solved by applying the successful solutions—or avoiding the mistakes —one may learn from history.

Although not valedictorian of his class, seventeen-year-old Harry Truman was a good student who wished to continue his education after his graduation from high school in 1901. Since his father had suffered financial reverses and could not afford to send his son to college, the young graduate hoped for an appointment to West Point or Annapolis. Unfortunately, his poor eyesight disqualified him, and he was forced to take a job.

Harry Truman saw a cross section of American society and economy during his first years out of high school. In an assortment of jobs such as railroad construction timekeeper, mail room worker for the Kansas City *Star,* and bank employee he met all kinds of Missourians from hobos to bank presidents, and he learned what it was like to work for a living. He became painfully aware of many of the economic and social problems of people aspiring to rise in America. For several years the boy from Independence lived the typical life of a young man starting out in the big city. He worked as a bank clerk at the National Bank of Commerce and later at the Union National Bank in Kansas City. A sedate boarding house was "home." Most weekends were spent in Clinton where the elder Trumans were living at the time, but Sunday mornings in the city were spent at the Benton Boulevard Baptist Church. The tedium of routine was relieved by evenings viewing vaudeville shows at the Grand Theatre or the Orpheum.

In 1905 the young bank clerk joined Battery B of the National Guard of Kansas City. This association in the National Guard later became a matter of great importance to him. His many friends in the Guard were an important help in his political career, and Guard activities provided an opportunity to demonstrate his leadership abilities when war came a decade later.

In 1906 Harry Truman left the bank to operate his Grandmother Young's large farm at Grandview. After the deaths of his grandmother in 1909 and his father in 1914, Harry continued to manage the family farm, and during the prosperous pre-World War I days he appears to have been quite successful. One evidence of his prosperity was his purchase of a $600 second-hand, dark, four-door, four-cylinder Stafford touring car. The handsome automobile was noted for the fact that it could run as fast as sixty miles per hour, although few roads in Missouri were built for such reckless speeds!

Harry Truman was a busy young farmer during the years when World War I began. In addition to directing the operation of a 600-acre farm, he was active in the Farm Bureau and the Masonic Lodge in Belton, and he continued to make a trip every week to Kansas City to drill with his National Guard unit. Harry Truman was a conscientious, well-informed farmer who used a crop rotation system to attempt to increase his production of corn, wheat, and oats. He raised Angus cattle and Hampshire hogs.

As often as his busy schedule permitted he drove his Stafford to Independence to visit his childhood friend, Bess Wallace. In 1916 Harry Truman was thirty-two years old, living with his mother and sister as a successful farmer on his mother's fertile Missouri farm. Perhaps his strong sense of responsibility to the family kept him a bachelor so long. Perhaps her numerous beaux discouraged the suitor of blue-eyed, blonde Bess Wallace. Whatever the reason, the courtship was a long one.

In 1916 Harry Truman displayed some of his father's inclination to speculate when he invested money in both oil drilling and zinc mining in Oklahoma. The zinc mining venture resulted in a $7,000 loss, but the oil drilling was interrupted by the outbreak of World War I. Later, the companies which bought Harry Truman's interests struck one of the largest oil pools ever opened in Kansas.

When Governor Gardner called up the Missouri National Guard in 1917, Truman was elected first lieutenant by the men from Battery F—a unit made up of Kansas City boys, many of whom were Irish. When the unit was sent to Fort Sill, Oklahoma, the troops were in need of a canteen at which the men might purchase personal items. Lieutenant Truman and Kansas City comrade Eddie Jacobson assessed each man in the regiment two dollars to purchase merchandise for the canteen, which under the Truman-Jacobson management was so profitable that

(Courtesy State Historical Society)

Farm Home Near Independence Where President Harry S Truman Formerly Lived

in six months each man was refunded his initial investment plus his share of $15,000 profits.

Lieutenant Truman's battery, part of the soon-to-be-famous 35th Division, was shipped to France on March 30, 1918. In May, Harry Truman was promoted to captain, and in August the 35th Division was assigned to the front in the province of Alsace, where they took part in the battles of St. Mihiel and in the Meuse-Argonne drive. Under fire in France, Captain Truman won the respect and admiration of his men.

The thirty-five year old officer was returned to the United States with the unit early in 1919. After six weeks of civilian life—and twenty-seven years from the date of their first meeting—Harry Truman and Miss Bess Wallace were married in the Trinity Episcopal Church of Independence.

Immediately following his return from France, Truman decided to leave farming to enter business. His experience in operating the army canteen gave him confidence that he could successfully operate a store in Kansas City. In partnership with his wartime friend, Eddie Jacobson, Truman opened a haberdashery near the corner of Twelfth and Baltimore in Kansas City. The store, open from eight in the morning till nine at night, catered to the many people who populated that busy section of the city, including a number of Truman's wartime buddies.

For various reasons, however, the store failed. Because of his many debts, Harry Truman could have claimed bankruptcy, but instead he and his family remained in debt for another two decades until their last obligation was repaid.

In 1927 the Pendergast faction in Kansas City sought a candidate for judge of the Jackson county court—the administrative board which directs the business of the county. Tom Pendergast, whose nephew James had been a fellow officer with Truman during World War I, recognized Truman as a likely candidate. He had many friends in Kansas City, Independence, and Grandview and as a veteran with a good record and as a Protestant Mason, he was immune to the anti-Catholic prejudice stirred up by the Ku Klux Klan. Thus, while it cannot be doubted that Pendergast's approval was invaluable in securing election, Truman had certain qualities which made him a valuable ally for the Boss. He was elected to the court in 1922 along with another Goat candidate, Henry F. McElroy. Although Truman was defeated in the election of 1924, he was elected to the office of presiding judge of the Jackson county court in 1926, and continued in that position until 1934.

During his eight years as the political leader in the Jackson County courthouse, Truman was noted for his effective building program. It appears that while Boss Pendergast insisted upon controlling county patronage, he did not always meddle in county affairs. Judge Truman secured the bond issues and authorization to build $20,000,000 worth of badly needed highways and public buildings in Jackson County. The total expenditure during his period as county judge has been estimated at over $60,000,000. The plans and progress of the road program were supervised by bipartisan engineers, who found no scandal associated with this remarkable building project.

In 1934 Missourians had an opportunity to choose a new United States senator or to re-elect the Republican incumbent Roscoe C. Patterson of Springfield. Tom Pendergast hoped to elect his own man to the post; however, Senator Bennett Champ

Harry S Truman of Independence was elected to the United States Senate in 1934 after serving eight years as presiding judge of the Jackson County Court. *(Courtesy State Historical Society)*

Clark, also attempting to influence the election, backed the nomination of Jacob L. Milligan of Richmond. When the first two potential candidates approached by Tom Pendergast refused the honor, he turned to Harry Truman as his man.

The Democratic primary in 1934 was a wild and noisy affair. Boss Tom had not been a strong supporter of President Franklin Delano Roosevelt at the time of his election. By 1934 Pendergast realized that he could not successfully oppose F. D. R.'s policies. With the great distribution of federal funds for relief, there were obvious advantages in maintaining good relations with Washington. As Pendergast realistically observed, "You can't beat five billion dollars." Harry Truman, who from the beginning had been enthusiastic about Roosevelt's reform measures, carried on a strong campaign in favor of the New Deal in 1934. In this election Jacob L. "Tuck" Milligan and John J. Cochran of St. Louis were Truman's chief opposition. As might have been anticipated, the opponents charged that Truman was a tool of the Pendergast machine. Said Tuck Milligan, "Why, if Harry ever goes to the Senate, he will grow callouses on his ears listening on the long-distance telephone to the orders of his boss." In 1934 the Pendergast machine was at its height and could deliver great majorities, although their methods of delivery were subject to suspicion. At the same time, one must take into account Truman's many friends and the vigorous campaign he undertook, making six to sixteen speeches daily in support of President Roosevelt's New Deal.

The hotly-contested primary election was won by Truman with a margin of 40,000 votes over Cochran, who ran second. Truman had been the recipient of some 137,000 votes in Jackson County. The other candidates for the same office combined had fewer than 11,000 votes in that county. In the November election, Truman won a seat in the United States Senate, defeating the incumbent Republican Senator Patterson by a majority of over 250,000 votes.

Characteristically, Truman read the biographies of every senator available and studied all the information he could find on the Senate before leaving for Washington. Like most new senators, Harry Truman was in the news only infrequently during his first term; however, he did receive some publicity for hearings conducted to study the railroads, in which he became known as the defender of the railroad unions. Senator Truman's earnestness and dedication to his job won him the respect and friendship of many of his associates. His second term in Washington, which proved to be quite eventful, will be discussed in a following chapter.

In retrospect, Harry Truman should be remembered as an effective and skillful politician whose administration of affairs in Jackson County contributed remarkably to the growth, development, and financial solvency of the county. While these accomplishments were realized without scandal, we must assume that Truman, an alert, intelligent politician, knew of the suspicious activities associated with the machine. Presumably, he believed that accepting the help of the organization was necessary to his success as an office-seeker. As a result, when Tom Pendergast was sent to prison and the inside story of his machine was broadcast to the world, Truman found himself a victim of guilt by association.

The Pendergast Machine and Governor Stark

During the election campaign of 1936 many charges were made of corruption in Jefferson City. William Hirth, the Democratic aspirant for governor, was outspoken in his demand for

(© *St. Louis Post-Dispatch, used by permission*)
Lloyd C. Stark (right) requested and received Tom Pendergast's (left) support when he was candidate for governor in 1936.

an investigation of the state government. Hirth's bid for the Democratic nomination was unsuccessful; but the victorious candidate, Lloyd C. Stark, pledged "absolute honesty" during his administration and took up the fight against corrupt government. Stark, who had been elected with Pendergast's help, and Maurice M. Milligan, the federal district attorney for the Western District of Missouri, were the two leaders who ultimately exposed and secured the conviction of Pendergast. The three issues which led to the downfall of the Kansas City boss were fraudulent voting activities in Kansas City, an insurance scandal in Jefferson City, and Pendergast's failure to pay his federal income tax.

Of the November election of 1936 the Kansas City *Star* stated, in "numerous precincts and probably one entire ward, ghosts outnumber the legitimate voters." District Attorney

Milligan determined to take action against the machine. At the time of his appointment, federal officials had been careful to search for ties between Milligan and the political organization in Kansas City. There were none. One month after the election, Milligan began to present his evidence of election illegalities before Judge Albert L. Reeves and Judge Merrill E. Otis of the federal courts in Kansas City. To avoid machine pressure on the federal grand jury, Milligan insisted that the jurymen be non-residents of Kansas City. The district attorney, who had seized many of the ballot boxes from the precincts in question, presented the ballots, books, and records before the grand jury. In the very first ballot box which Milligan opened in court, ninety-five ballots originally marked as straight Republican had been changed to straight Democratic ballots. This was just the beginning. In ballot box after ballot box, similar cases were revealed. Milligan also reported the election farce which had occurred in one Kansas City precinct where, "Instead of counting the ballots, that precinct captain read from a memorandum which he held in his hand the number of votes arbitrarily allotted to the Democratic candidates and the number conceded to their Republican opponents."

This evidence of electoral fraud resulted in 278 indictments for illegal election activities. The financial resources of the Pendergast machine were strained in providing bail and lawyers to defend their workers. However, the federal courts in Kansas City continued to dispense justice; ultimately 259 of the 278 defendants were found guilty.

While these trials were going on, District Attorney Milligan's name was submitted to the United States Senate for re-appointment. Senator Harry Truman of Missouri, in damning words, opposed Milligan's re-appointment. Said Senator Truman:

> I say, Mr. President, that a Jackson County, Missouri Democrat has as much chance of a fair trial in the Federal District Court of Western Missouri as a Jew would have in a Hitler Court or a Trotzky follower before Stalin.

By opposing Milligan, Truman opened himself to attack as a defender of Pendergast corruption. The two federal justices, Judge Reeves and Judge Otis—both Republicans—obviously objected to the insinuation that their decisions were motivated by political malice. Reeves answered Truman by declaring that the

Senator's denunciation of the court "was a speech of a man nominated by ghost votes, elected with ghost votes, and whose speeches probably are written by ghost writers." In the midst of these verbal clashes, Milligan was reappointed.

District Attorney Milligan gave Governor Stark credit for playing an important role in exposing and convicting the law-breakers in the Kansas City organization. In 1937 the governor finally secured a new law from the legislature which provided for state appointment of a new election board. As a result of this change, there was a purging of the election registration books in the city. In 1936 nearly 270,000 names were recorded; after all the ghosts had been exorcised in 1937, only 216,000 names remained. Two years after the state officials had acted to purge the Kansas City voting rolls, the governor further weakened the machine by securing the passage of a new bill providing for state control of the Kansas City Police Board.

Another scandal which had occurred during Governor Park's administration, and was exposed under Governor Stark, contributed to the decline of the Pendergast faction. R. Emmett O'Malley, a close associate of Boss Pendergast, had been appointed state superintendent of insurance by Governor Park in 1933. At that time, a sum of over $9,000,000 was controlled by the courts in a rate dispute between fire insurance companies and the state of Missouri. Until a decision could be made, the courts declared that the money should be impounded. The insurance companies, of course, wanted the money. Through intermediaries Charles R. Street and A. L. McCormack of St. Louis, O'Malley and Pendergast made an agreement with agents of the seventeen insurance companies involved in the case. In secret negotiations carried on in Chicago, Boss Pendergast agreed to secure release of the $9,000,000—of which the insurance companies were to receive eighty per cent—in return for a bribe first set at $500,000, but later raised to $750,000. In a series of dramatic episodes, the intermediaries delivered black bags of currency to the boss in Kansas City, who usually dealt in cash to avoid income tax problems. On one occasion Pendergast, who received $330,000, generously kept only $250,000 for himself and divided the other $80,000 between McCormack, his courier, and O'Malley. The Federal Government became aware of the scheme through certain discrepancies in the books of the Chicago insurance executives and traced the money to Pendergast. The

(© St. Louis Post-Dispatch, used by permission)

A Post-Dispatch photographer captured Tom Pendergast's reaction just as he was told Governor Stark had described him as "a sinister and ominous shadow." Pendergast and Stark exchanged barbs in 1938 when they supported rival candidates for the Missouri Supreme Court. Stark's man won.

above-mentioned details were revealed when A. L. McCormack confessed to federal officials in Kansas City.

In 1937 Governor Stark, suspecting irregularities in the office of the state superintendent of insurance, fired O'Malley and secured the help of leading federal officials—including Attorney General Frank Murphy and J. Edgar Hoover—in an investigation of O'Malley's affairs. In the ensuing trial O'Malley was found guilty of bribery and was sentenced to a year and a day in prison and a $5,000 fine. When the trial concerning the insurance bribes led to his indictment on Good Friday, 1939, on a charge of income tax evasion, the evidence was so overwhelming that Pendergast entered a plea of guilty. The former political power was fined $10,000 and was sentenced to fifteen months in the federal penitentiary at Leavenworth and five years of probation. One by one, the leading Goats were penned. Police

Chief Otis P. Higgins in Kansas City, also found guilty of evading his income taxes, was sentenced to two years in the federal penitentiary. Big Charley Carollo, who had become head of the Kansas City crime syndicate after the 1934 machine-gun assassination of Johnny Lazia, was sent to prison for a total of eight years for income tax evasion and perjury. City Manager H. F. McElroy died before charges were brought against him. As a result of these developments, Tom Pendergast was forced to end his political career, for even after he emerged from prison he was forbidden to take part in political activities. The leadership of the Jackson Democratic Club then passed to Tom's nephew, James M. Pendergast.

Encouraged by the spectacular publicity which accompanied their defeat of the Pendergast machine, both Milligan and Stark attempted to secure the Democratic nomination to the United States Senate in 1940, when they opposed Harry S Truman in his bid for a second term.

Depression Society

Entertainment

We have noted earlier that the development of new and more rapid methods of transportation and communication contributed to a certain standardization in the society of the individual states. During the thirties, this trend continued as millions of Americans listened to the same radio programs, attended the same movies, played the same records or piano rolls, and read the same magazines and newspapers. In 1939 the 849,300 radios in the state brought the news, ideas, humor, and music from cities across America into the homes of Missourians. Even in a time of depression, thousands of Missourians were able to spare the modest price of admission to the movies; most small cities in Missouri boasted at least one motion picture theatre. "Talkies" were improving during the thirties, and toward the end of the decade the marvel of technicolor was introduced to movie patrons. Especially popular among Missouri moviegoers were the men and women from the home state who reaped fame and fortune in the golden fields of Hollywood. Jean Harlow, Ginger Rogers, Joan Crawford, Betty Grable, Ellen Drew, Wallace and Noah Beery, Jack Oakie, and William Powell were all former Missourians on filmland's roster.

During several years' residence on a farm near Marceline,

Missouri, a young native of Chicago became interested in sketching barnyard animals. After several years of high school and art training in Chicago and a stint of ambulance driving in France, he returned to Missouri and a job as a commercial artist in Kansas City where he had, for a time, attended Benton Grammar School. Experiments in animation, which began in Kansas City, led Walt Disney to Hollywood and, eventually, to fame. During the decade of the thirties, Artist Disney won his second Academy Award for his full-color animated cartoon *The Three Little Pigs*. The hit song from the show, "Who's Afraid of the Big Bad Wolf," became a sort of battle song in the campaign of the people against depression. The victorious struggle of the story's heroes against the wolf at their door seemed to symbolize for many the plight of the American people and their eventual triumph over economic disaster. The comical antics of the porcine stars added a welcome ray of humor in the dark days of the depression.

The venerable St. Louis Symphony Orchestra continued during the thirties and was joined by sister organizations in the state. In 1932 the Co-operative Orchestra—later the Kansas City Philharmonic—began its history under the direction of Karl Krueger. Little symphonies were organized in Fulton, Jefferson City, and other cities during the thirties. The Sedalia Little Symphony, established in 1935, gained a reputation for excellence under the leadership of Abe Rosenthal. In 1939, the St. Louis Grand Opera was instituted to present opera on a non-

Disney movies—animated and live —have taken rapt audiences to exotic lands, into scenes of yesterday, and through the pages of literary classics. A sensitive portrayal of the wonders and beauties of the world around us has won for the Disney nature series the gratitude of viewers and the praise of critics. By entertaining and informing millions in the past three decades, Missouri-reared Walt Disney and his co-workers have had a profound influence on American culture.

(© *Walt Disney Productions*)

profit basis. Three Missourians whose careers bloomed during the decade thrilled opera and concert audiences with their beautiful voices. Nevada was the birthplace of Marion Talley; Gladys Swarthout came from Deepwater in Henry County; and Helen Traubel was a daughter of St. Louis.

Art

The opening of the William Rockhill Nelson Art Gallery in Kansas City in 1933 was one of the most important cultural advances during the thirties. Editor Nelson's valuable art collection, housed in a beautiful new structure, was made available to the multitude of Missouri art lovers.

Missouri's best-known contemporary painter is Thomas Hart Benton, grandnephew of the famous senator of the same name. Born in Neosho in 1889, Benton attended military school and drew cartoons for the Joplin *American* before studying painting at the Art Institute of Chicago and the Academie Julien in Paris. He first attracted national attention in 1931 by his mural of contemporary America in the New School for Social Research in New York City. In 1935, Mr. Benton executed his controversial murals in the Missouri State Capitol Building. His realistic portrayals of noted and notorious characters in Missouri history evoked both praise and protest. The initial furor has subsided, but each Missourian visiting his State Capitol judges for him-

(Photo by Townsend Godsey, Courtesy State Historical Society)

The photographer caught Thomas Hart Benton at work in July, 1936, painting the mural in the House Lounge of the State Capitol.

self the merits of the dramatic representations of Frankie and Johnny, the James Boys, and Huck Finn and his friend Jim.

Thomas Hart Benton served as director of the department of painting in the Kansas City Art Institute from 1935 to 1941. In 1937 he wrote, and illustrated with his own paintings, his autobiography, *An Artist in America.*

Murals and other works of art commissioned by the WPA did much to encourage young artists during the period of economic difficulty.

Sports.

Baseball continued as the most popular athletic event, with teams in all communities. During the 1930's the St. Louis Cardinals won the National League pennant in 1930, 1931, and 1934. In the latter two years, they won the World Series as well. Frankie Frisch and Ducky Medwick of the Cardinals were judged the most valuable players in the National League in 1931 and

1937 respectively. Pepper Martin and the two Dean brothers, "Dizzy" and "Daffy," were the idols of the sports lovers. Paul "Daffy" Dean succeeded in pitching a no-hit game in the year 1934. While the Cardinals in the National League were wonderfully successful, the St. Louis Browns in the American League were noted for their inability to win games, which inspired the catchy St. Louis slogan, "First in shoes, first in booze, and last in the American League."

During the thirties the installation of lights on many high school athletic fields in Missouri attracted large crowds for evening football games. High school baseball also became popular, and the tournaments were enthusiastically attended. During the decade, several Missourians were honored for athletic achievements. Henry Armstrong, a black St. Louis fighter, became the welterweight and lightweight champion of the world in 1938. Helen Stephens from Fulton, Missouri, ran in the 1936 Olympics in Berlin to set a new Olympic record in the one hundred meter run. In the same year, Paul Christman of the University of Missouri's champion football team was recognized as M.U.'s first All-American player.

Religion

As the total population of Missouri continued to grow in the twentieth century, the membership of the churches in the state also increased. The census returns for 1936 show the growth of each of the religious groups. The Roman Catholic Church continued as the largest single church and maintained the same percentage of the total church membership in Missouri. The next two largest groups were the Baptists and Methodists, both of which increased in total number of members although their total percentage of all Missouri church members decreased.

It is interesting to note the appearance of several churches which were not listed in the religious census of 1906. The Assemblies of God established their national headquarters in Springfield, Missouri, and had organized many new congregations in the state by 1936. Another group of approximately the same size which has flourished in twentieth-century Missouri is that group identified as the Church of Christ. These two, as well as the smaller Church of the Nazarene and other pentecostal groups, place greater emphasis upon the second coming of Christ and the workings of the Holy Spirit. In a time when the older Protestant churches became more dignified and formal, the new churches emphasized informal, direct, emotional experience. The Reorganized Church of Jesus Christ of Latter Day Saints, with its national headquarters at Independence, has established new congregations in various parts of the state during the century.

(Courtesy Massie-Missouri Commerce)

A view at Unity Farms in South Kansas City

It is significant that the number of members in the Jewish congregations of Missouri had greatly increased by 1936. In the religious census of 1906 the total membership of the Jewish synagogues was not large enough to be listed individually, but by 1936 there were 83,358 Jewish members of synagogues, constituting almost six per cent of the membership of religious groups in the state. A much smaller religious body is that organization known as the Unity School of Christianity which maintains its impressive, spacious headquarters on a large acreage in south Kansas City.

	Number of Members in 1936	Per Cent of Total Church Members in Mo.
Assemblies of God	10,613	.8%
Baptist Bodies	225,542	16.2%
Churches of Christ	10,078	.7%
Congregational and Christian Churches	10,323	.7%
Disciples of Christ	108,374	7.8%
Evangelical and Reformed Church	39,231	2.8%
Jewish Congregations	83,358	6.0%
Latter Day Saints, Reorganized Church	15,011	1.1%
Lutheran Synod	83,674	6.0%
Methodist Bodies	186,125	13.4%
Presbyterian Bodies	62,477	4.5%
Protestant Episcopal Church	20,559	1.5%
Roman Catholic Church	432,344	31.0%
All Other Bodies	105,151	7.5%
Total	1,392,860	100.0%

During the 1930's there were several religious developments at the national level which had an impact upon Missouri churches. In 1931 the Congregational churches and the Christian churches reached an agreement to merge their two organizations. Three years later the Evangelical churches and the Reformed churches united. At the end of the decade, in 1939, the Methodist churches in America merged to form one great denomination and thus to heal the split which had been created within the denomination by the Civil War.

One of the most prominent religious figures of the 1930's was Reinhold Niebuhr, who was born in Wright City, Missouri, on June 21, 1892. After attending Eden Theological Seminary in St. Louis and receiving from Yale University a bachelor of divinity degree in 1914 and a master of arts degree in 1915, the young theologian was ordained to the ministry of the Evangelical Synod of North America. As a pastor among the factory workers of Detroit, he became a champion of the working man. Niebuhr joined the faculty of Union Theological Seminary in New York in 1928, where he taught philosophy of religion and applied Christianity until 1960. In 1939 Professor Niebuhr became the fifth American to deliver the Gifford lectures at Edinburgh University. Reinhold Niebuhr, the author

Sara Teasdale, who was born and reared in St. Louis, won acclaim for her lyric poetry.
(Courtesy State Historical Society)

of a long list of perceptive and provocative books of philosophy and ethics, has also edited several religious and political periodicals. Upon his retirement, Professor Emeritus Niebuhr accepted the position of research associate in the Institute for War and Peace Studies at Columbia University.

The remarkable Niebuhr family also includes Richard Niebuhr, who has had an eminent career as a professor of theology and Christian ethics at Yale Divinity School, and Ursula M. Niebuhr who has been the head of the Department of Religion at Barnard College, Columbia University, since 1946.

Literature, 1910-1940

Reedy's Mirror, published in St. Louis, served as a showcase for a long list of twentieth century authors during the first two

Author Homer Croy skillfully pictured the rural scenes familiar to him through his boyhood experiences on a farm near Maryville, Missouri.
(Courtesy State Historical Society)

Author Vance Randolph's under-
standing of the Ozark hill people
enabled him to prepare the val-
uable multi-volume collection of
Ozark Folksongs published by the
State Historical Society.
*(Portrait by Rose O'Neill, Courtesy
State Historical Society)*

decades of the century. Three of the best known of these authors
Missourians by birth or residence, were Sara Teasdale, Fannie
Hurst, and Homer Croy. Miss Teasdale, a poet as fragile and
lovely as her poems, spent her first thirty years in St. Louis.
After her marriage in 1914, she moved to New York, where most
of her poetry was written. Her best known works are *Helen
of Troy and Other Poems* (1911), *Rivers to the Sea* (1915),
Love Songs (1917), *Flame and Shadow* (1920), *Dark of the
Moon* (1926), and the posthumously published *Strange Victory*
(1933).

Homer Croy drew from his boyhood on a farm near Maryville, Missouri, for his stories of rural life in *Boone Stop* (1918),
Turkey Bowman (1920), *West of the Water Tower* (1923), and
R.F.D. No. 3 (1924). Other novels of the period by Homer Croy
include *They Had to See Paris* (1926), *Fancy Lady* (1927),
Caught (1928), *Coney Island* (1929), *Headed for Hollywood*
(1932), and *Sixteen Hands* (1938).

Fannie Hurst was reared in St. Louis, where she graduated
from Washington University. Like her fellow-Missourian Homer
Croy, her short stories and novels have been widely read. Among
her best known works are *Humoresque* (1918), *Lummox* (1923),
Back Street (1931), and *Imitation of Life* (1933).

Poet, dramatist, and critic Thomas Stearns Eliot, grandson
of the founder of Washington University, William Greenleaf
Eliot, received his elementary and high school education in his

In addition to her charming sketches for children, Rose O'Neill produced several well-received serious works in which her sensitive drawings are comparable to those of Edwin Abbey, the noted English artist.
(Courtesy State Historical Society)

native St. Louis. A graduate of Harvard, Eliot also studied at the Sorbonne in Paris and at Oxford University. He became a British citizen in 1927. *The Lovesong of J. Alfred Prufrock* (1917), *The Waste Land* (1922), *Ash Wednesday* (1930), *Murder in the Cathedral* (1935), *Four Quartets* (1940-43), and *The Cocktail Party* (1950) are among his best-known poems and verse-dramas. T. S. Eliot, who edited and published *The Criterion* in London, is acknowledged to have had a greater influence on English poetry than any other writer in the first half of the twentieth century.

Life in the small towns and in the hills of Missouri inspired a long list of books during the 1930's. Vance Randolph resided in Pineville in McDonald County for ten years while he studied the folkways of the Ozarks. The result of this study was a series of works on the hill people and their home: *The Ozarks* (1931), *Ozark Mountain Folk* (1932), *From an Ozark Holler* (1933), and *Camp on Wildcat Creek* (1934).

Rose Wilder Lane, living at her home in Mansfield since 1920, used the Ozark small town as the setting for her collection of short stories, *Old Home Town* (1935). The Ozarks were the locale of her novels *He was a Man* (1925), *Hill Billy* (1926), and *Cindy* (1928).

Missouri fox hunting provided the background for *the Voice of Bugle Ann* (1935), a novel by MacKinlay Kantor. Elizabeth Siefert (Mrs. John Gasparotti) of Moberly began her popular series of novels with *Young Doctor Galahad* (1938), which won a $10,000 prize from Dodd, Mead, and Company. Best-seller *Kings Row* (1940), written by Henry Bellamann of Fulton, Missouri, provided the plot for a successful movie in 1942. Mary Margaret McBride, renowned radio personality, wrote of the scenes of her Paris, Missouri, childhood in *How Dear to My Heart* (1940).

Missouri proudly claimed two Pulitzer Prize winners in 1935. The award for drama was won by Zoe Akins, a native of Humansville, for her adaptation of Edith Wharton's *The Old Maid.* The Pulitzer Prize novel for the year was *Now in November,* the first published work of twenty-four-year-old Josephine Winslow Johnson of Webster Groves.

The rugged pioneer life of her childhood served as the source for Laura Ingalls Wilder's series of eight books which may be considered classics in children's literature: *Little House in the Big Woods* (1932), *Farmer Boy* (1933), *Little House on the Prairie* (1935), *On the Banks of Plum Creek* (1937), *By the Shores of Silver Lake* (1939), *The Long Winter* (1940), *Little Town on the Prairie* (1949), and *These Happy Golden Years*

Rose O'Neill's popularity was enhanced by the appeal of her "Kewpie Dolls."
(© Permission through the courtesy of Joseph L. Kallus, Brooklyn, New York)

(1943). In 1894 Mrs. Wilder moved to the Mansfield area of her beloved Ozarks, where she made her home until her death at the age of ninety in 1957.

Also remembered chiefly for her children's work is Rose O'Neill, the creator of the "Kewpie," which for almost a quarter century was an important part of American childhood and American art. Her home at Bonniebrook Farm forty miles south of Springfield is said to have been the birthplace of the Kewpies and the scene of many of their adventures. A Rose O'Neill collection is exhibited in the museum at the School of the Ozarks.

Langston Hughes, the black poet and novelist, was born in Joplin in 1902. His early works included a novel, *Not Without Laughter* (1930), and books of poetry entitled *The Weary Blues* (1926), *Fine Clothes to the Jew* (1927), *The Dream Keeper* (1932), *Shakespeare in Harlem* (1942), and *Freedom's Plow* (1943). He has written mainly about black life. In 1960 he was awarded the Spingarn medal for his contribution in literature. This is an award made annually by the National Association for the Advancement of Colored People to a person who has reached the highest achievement in his field of activity.

Lecturer Dale Carnegie, a native of Nodaway County, is best known for his book-long formula for success, *How to Win Friends and Influence People* (1936).

The WPA Writer's Program sponsored the production of the excellent and valuable *Missouri: a Guide to the "Show Me" State,* which was first published in 1941. This volume contains within its covers a vast collection of Missouriana.

The 1930's witnessed the rise in Kansas City of a shrewd and successful political boss, Tom J. Pendergast. By favors and fraud T. J. extended his power and influence until it pervaded the state capitol itself. At the close of the decade, reform-minded Governor Lloyd Stark and courageous District Attorney Maurice M. Milligan joined forces to end the rule of Boss Tom.

Suffering from the pangs of depression and dissatisfied with the measures the incumbent Republican administration had taken to relieve their distress, Missourians returned to the Democratic fold in the thirties. Among the successful Democratic candidates in the state was the man destined to be the first president from Missouri. Harry S Truman arrived in Washington in 1934 to begin a notable career in the nation's capitol.

The New Deal of the 1930's as described by its author, Franklin D. Roosevelt, had a three-fold goal—relief, recovery, and reform. The alphabet agencies of the Roosevelt administration did bring about reform in some areas of Missouri life and were successful in relieving, to an extent, the distressing symtoms of depression. However, recovery from the economic plague of depression was not realized in eight years of New Deal vitamins and soothing syrup. It was not until the bitter medicine of world war was forced upon America that she experienced a more lasting cure for her economic illness.

Governor and Mrs. Lloyd C. Stark and Daughters Mary and Katherine Celebrate a Birthday in the Executive Mansion.

(Courtesy State Historical Society)

BIBLIOGRAPHY

Bailey, Eutopia O. "Small Town in Missouri Twentieth Century Fiction," *Missouri Historical Review,* Vol. XLIX (April, July, 1955), pp. 230-248, 328-341.

Brashear, Minnie M. "Missouri Literature Since the First World War," *Missouri Historical Review,* Vol. XL (October, 1945; April, 1946) pp. 1-20, 330-348; Vol. XLI (January, 1947), pp. 241-249.

Coghlan, Ralph. "Missouri—a Threat and a Promise," *The Nation,* Vol. CXXXV (November 2, 1932), pp. 422-424.

Daniels, Jonathan. *The Man of Independence.* Philadelphia and New York: J. B. Lippincott Company, 1950.

Milligan, Maurice M. *The Missouri Waltz: the Inside Story of the Pendergast Machine by the Man Who Smashed It.* New York: Charles Scribner's Sons, 1948.

Missouri: a Guide to the "Show Me" State. New York: Duell, Sloan and Pearce, 1941.

"Missouri Mills," *Time,* Vol. XXVI (September 9, 1935), p. 17.

Reddig, William M. *Tom's Town: Kansas City and the Pendergast Legend.* Philadelphia and New York: J. B. Lippincott Company, 1947.

Ridpath, Ben Morris. "The Case of the Missouri Sharecropper," *The Christian Century,* Vol. LVI (February 1, 1939), pp. 146-148.

Shoemaker, Floyd C. *Missouri and Missourians.* Vol. II. Chicago: The Lewis Publishing Company, 1943.

Simmons, Mrs. George B. "How the New Deal Affects a Missouri Farmer," *The Saturday Evening Post,* Vol. CCVII (August 25, 1934), pp. 23, 78, 80-81.

Truman, Harry S. *Memoirs.* Vol. I. Garden City, New York: Doubleday and Company, Inc., 1955.

Violette, E. M. and F. E. Wolverton. *A History of Missouri.* St. Louis: State Publishing Company, 1955.

CHAPTER XVIII

Missouri in the Forties

I just had to learn to double clutch the big truck and now
there's nothing to it.
                          —Mrs. Ralph Lewis,
                          Kansas City truck driver, 1944

When Missouri and the nation were plunged into a great
global conflict in the 1940's, the war effort soon became the pre-
occupying concern of all. Young men, and some not-so-young
men, either enlisted or were drafted into military service and
were transported to all parts of the globe where they tangled
with the armies of Japan, Germany, and Italy. For those who
remained at home there were many adjustments, too. Mrs.
Lewis became a night-time truck driver at the medical depot in
Kansas City, where she learned the system of depressing the
clutch twice in shifting truck gears. Many other Missourians
had to learn unfamiliar techniques such as "double clutching"
to adapt themselves to the new demands of the time.

In the midst of this struggle, political life continued. The
Republican Party which had gone into eclipse during the 1930's,
appeared with new strength in Missouri. During the turmoil of
supporting and supplying their men in war, Missourians voted
to write a new constitution, which was adopted as the governing
document for the state. One of Missouri's sons was placed in
the White House by the death of the aging veteran leader, Franklin D. Roosevelt. Missouri's president was to lead not only the
United States, but much of the world in the very troubled postwar years when the Soviet Union attempted to exploit the period
of postwar difficulty to its own advantage.

Donnell and Donnelly

During the 1940's Missouri had two governors with similar
names, who, interestingly enough, found themselves in similar
situations. The first was Forrest C. Donnell, a Republican, who

found himself facing a Democratic General Assembly during the first half of his term. The second was Phil M. Donnelly, a Democrat, who during his four years as governor had a Republican General Assembly. Both were capable leaders during the hectic wartime and postwar years.

The election of 1940 is significant in several respects. In Kansas City a non-partisan group, under the dynamic leadership of former Senator James A. Reed and his wife, finally defeated the Pendergast machine. In addition, the election was precedent-setting at the national level, for in 1940 Franklin D. Roosevelt was the first American president to be elected to a third term. In choosing a candidate for United States senator from Missouri, the Democratic voters had to choose between three leading primary candidates—incumbent Harry S Truman, former Governor Lloyd C. Stark, and Federal District Attorney Maurice M. Milligan—all well-known, controversial figures in Missouri. Senator Truman's two main competitors were leaders in the exposure of the Pendergast machine. Although both Stark and Milligan made capital of their role in bringing Pendergast to justice and were outspoken in opposition to the machine-sponsored candidates, they never accused Senator Truman of illegal conduct. Milligan was careful to declare, "At no time did the finger of suspicion ever point in the direction of Senator Truman." In spite of such statements, Senator Truman's name was linked with Pendergast. Speaking of the campaign of 1940 in his memoirs, Harry Truman stated:

> I realized that attempts would be made to link my name with the misdeeds and misfortunes of Pendergast and to make it appear that I was the product of a corrupt political machine.

In answer to such charges Senator Truman declared, "Tom Pendergast never asked me to do a dishonest deed. He knew I wouldn't do it if he asked it." Still, the image of Harry Truman as a tool of the Pendergast machine persisted. Pendergast himself, who had on occasion referred to Senator Truman as his "office boy," apparently shared this view. Truman's unshakable loyalty to his one-time supporter did nothing to correct the distorted image. After Pendergast's conviction, the senator had declared, "Pendergast has been my friend when I needed it. I am not one to desert a ship when it starts to go down."

His association with Pendergast was not the only obstacle

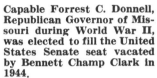

Capable Forrest C. Donnell,
Republican Governor of Missouri during World War II,
was elected to fill the United
States Senate seat vacated
by Bennett Champ Clark in
1944.
(Courtesy State Historical Society)

in Harry Truman's path to the nomination. The large city newspapers of the state—with the exception of the Kansas City
Journal—were opposed to his candidacy. He had no established
organization and no personal funds to finance an expensive campaign. With the help of a staff of volunteers, the contributions
of individuals across the state, and his characteristic energy
and determination, Harry Truman took his campaign to the
people. Stressing his solid support of the New Deal and his
close friendship with organized labor, he toured the cities and
villages of seventy-five counties. His strenuous campaign proved
effective. Senator Truman was renominated by a margin of
8,000 votes, and in the November, 1940, election regained his
Senate seat.

In the same election two St. Louis men were competitors in
the race for governor of the state. Democrat Lawrence Mc-
Daniel, a candidate with the strong support of Mayor Dick-
mann of St. Louis, was opposed by Republican Forrest C. Donnell, a capable, intelligent St. Louis lawyer. Donnell, a Phi Beta
Kappa scholar, had graduated at the head of his college and law
school classes at the University of Missouri. When the ballots
were counted in 1940, Donnell had 3,613 more votes than Mc-
Daniel. There were immediate charges by the State Democratic
Committee of "glaring and widespread irregularities, actual

buying and trading of votes, open and brazen frauds perpetrated at the very ballot box." Several leaders of the Democratic Party, particularly C. M. Hulen who was chairman of the Democratic state committee, decided upon a strategy calculated to wrest the governor's post from Donnell. According to the Missouri constitution, the speaker of the House of Representatives was assigned the duty of examining the election returns and publicly announcing the names of the duly elected individuals. The Democratic leaders decided that Speaker Morris Osburn of Shelby County should refuse to announce the name of Donnell as having won the election until the legislature could establish a committee to look into voting irregularities. The Democratic legislature, when it convened in January, 1941, authorized the naming of a committee of six Democrats and four Republicans to investigate the election charges. In the meantime, Donnell was not authorized to take office. Some Democrats, including Governor Lloyd Stark, who vetoed the bill establishing the committee, and state Senator Allen McReynolds of Carthage, opposed the Democratic strategy. The attorney general then declared that the governor could not prevent the legislature from establishing the committee, but he could deny them funds to carry on their investigation.

The major newspapers of the state—particularly the St. Louis *Post-Dispatch*—were outspoken in their denunciation of the Democratic maneuver. Finally, Donnell filed a mandamus suit before the state supreme court to force Osburn to announce him as the winner of the election. The seven Democratic judges of the supreme court voted unanimously to order Osburn to announce Donnell the winner, and after forty-four days of delay, Forrest Donnell was finally sworn in as governor on February 26, 1941. The committee investigation of election fraud continued for about two months after the inauguration; however, when the recount showed that Donnell had received an even larger vote than the previously recorded one, the inquiry was dropped. Governor Donnell did not hold a grudge. His efforts to get along with the Democratic legislature were remarkably successful, considering the bizarre manner in which his administration began.

During Donnell's four years as governor, the United States was involved in the greatest war in the history of the world. Because of war production and the resultant prosperity, state reve-

"By Hook or Crook" is the title of Fitzpatrick's cartoon showing the delayed attempt of the Democrats to pull their dead mule and candidate McDaniel to a victory in the race for governor. St. Louis Post Dispatch January 3, 1941.
(Courtesy State Historical Society)

nues increased. Thus, although Donnell became governor of a state nearly four million dollars in debt, at the end of his term the state treasury contained a surplus. One important reform adopted during Donnell's administration was a measure to insure secrecy in balloting. Since Missouri ballots were numbered, it was possible for election officials to compare the ballot number with the voting rolls and thus to determine how each individual had voted. In 1941 the legislature authorized a new procedure in voting. A two-inch black patch, which can only be removed by direction of the court, is placed on the ballot over the number. When a voter's privacy is thus assured, he is immune to pressure from those who would influence his vote. Two laws passed during this time were related to marriage. The first law passed in 1941 required applicants for marriage licenses to have a blood test for the detection of syphilis. The second law was enacted to discourage the so-called "marriage mills" along the Missouri border where non-residents could be married without the waiting period required by other states. The new law passed in 1942 established a three-day waiting period between the acquisition of a license and the marriage ceremony. Another development during Governor Donnell's administration was the establishment of a council of national defense to direct the citizens of the state in the war effort. In 1942 Missourians voted to authorize a constitutional convention. In 1943 and 1944 constitutional convention delegates met in Jefferson City and drafted a new fundamental law which was ratified by the people in 1945.

On the national level in 1944, Democrat Franklin D. Roosevelt, who had already served an unprecedented three terms, was re-elected with former Senator Harry S Truman as his vice-president. In Missouri, retiring Governor Forrest Donnell captured the Senate seat vacated by Bennett Champ Clark. Donnell was the first Missouri Republican to serve in the United States Senate since the defeat of Senator Patterson of Springfield in 1934. In the race for governor, Phil M. Donnelly of Lebanon was the Democratic candidate. It is interesting to note that attorney Jean Paul Bradshaw, the Republican candidate for governor in 1944, was also from the city of Lebanon. In their mutual home town each of the two candidates received exactly 1,731 votes, but in the state at large Mr. Donnelly was victorious. Donnelly's pleasant personality and ability to work with the opposition party were most important, since his legislature was Republican dominated.

Governor Donnelly was the first chief executive to act under the new constitution adopted in 1945. As governor he was able to secure passage of a number of acts important to the welfare of the state. In 1946 a merit system was established in several departments of state government. Under this system, advancement was to be governed by merit, rather than by political influence. In 1947 the King-Thompson Utility Anti-Strike Law was passed which outlawed strikes resulting in the halting of utility company operations. The law proved very unpopular with unions. Another act of great importance was the Hawkins School Reorganization Law of 1948. Leading educators of Missouri, as well as the legislature recognized that the level of education in the state would be improved by the reorganization and enlargement of school districts. The Hawkins Law was designed to encourage such reorganization plans. These plans occasionally caused difficulty in communities which would have preferred to retain their small schools, but the process of reorganizing was accelerated by the law.

When Harry Truman left his Senate seat to become vice president in 1945, Governor Donnelly appointed Frank P. Briggs of Macon as his successor. In the senatorial race the following

One week before Hitler's invasion of Poland this cartoon appeared in the St. Louis Post-Dispatch. Fitzpatrick, St. Louis Post-Dispatch, August 25, 1939.
(Courtesy State Historical Society)

NEXT!

year, Republican James P. Kem of Kansas City defeated Briggs in his bid to retain the Senate seat. In the late 1940's, as a result, for the first time since David F. Jewett and Carl Schurz represented her in Washington in the early 1870's, Missouri had two Republicans in the United States Senate.

Missouri and World War II

On September 1, 1939, German Fuehrer Adolph Hitler and his highly-trained, well-equipped army followed a series of aggressive acts by an invasion of helpless Poland. After this outrage, the British and French finally abandoned their attempts to pacify the Nazi leader and declared war on Germany. Since the United States was not part of the European alliance system when war erupted in Europe, President Roosevelt, in a scene reminiscent of 1914, declared our neutrality. However, the vicious, indefensible acts of Hitler against the Jewish people and his ruthless conquest of Austria, Czechoslovakia, and Poland provoked a strong anti-German sentiment in America. Since the Axis powers—Germany, Italy and Japan—had formed an alliance in 1939, the Japanese attack upon Pearl Harbor on December 7, 1941, threw this country into a war not only against

Japan, but also against her allies Germany and Italy. World War II therefore was fought on widely scattered fronts from the islands off the coast of Alaska to the swamps of New Guinea, and from the sands of North Africa to the rolling woodlands of North Europe.

Twentieth-century warfare, fought on a global scale with modern weapons and advanced technology, requires of the combatants an intense concentration of effort and an efficient utilization of all resources. Those Missourians who remained at home during the war became well aware of the need to produce and to conserve for the war effort. Donald M. Nelson, originally from Hannibal, was put in charge of the Washington, D.C. office of the War Production Board, in which post he was given the responsibilty for increasing American productivity necessary to the war effort.

St. Louis was the hub of the most populous of the thirteen ordnance districts established in the nation. Ninety-five per cent of the military ammunition and explosives used by American forces around the world were manufactured in the St. Louis district, which extended from the Mississippi to the Rockies and from the northern border of Missouri to the Gulf of Mexico. Sixty-five per cent of all ordnance produced in this district was manufactured within a hundred-mile radius of St. Louis.

In St. Louis proper all varieties of ammunition were produced, from rifle bullets to blockbuster bombs. St. Louis firms also manufactured pre-fabricated railway bridges, blasting machines, portable machine repair shops, airplanes, gliders, and hundreds of less spectacular but necessary items of supply.

The chemical companies of St. Louis, one of the world's leading chemical centers, played an important role in the war effort. Lambert Pharmaceuticals supplied the armed forces with a lotion called M-5 which was used as a protection against blister gas. Monsanto produced classified chemicals for the services, and as early as 1943 was manufacturing experimental rocket motors for testing purposes, and producing launching propellant chemicals.

In Kansas City, the American Royal arena was converted into an assembly line for the manufacture of gliders. The workers of the North American Aviation plant in Kansas City built two of every three Mitchell bombers flown by American pilots. Twenty-five per cent of the walnut gunstocks used to manufac-

The finances of Kansas City were in chaos in 1940 when L. P. Cookingham was named city manager by a nonpartisan reform group. Such great financial improvement was made in three years that Kansas City received an achievement award from the Municipal Finance Officers Association in 1943. City Manager Cookingham served Kansas City from 1940 to 1959.

ture rifles for American soldiers were purchased in Kansas City. The stockyards supplied tons of Kansas City's famous beef for service menus. Gasoline trains, trucks, and semi-trailers were other products of 394 Kansas City plants which supported the war effort.

Missouri factories outfitted servicemen from head to toe. The Schueter Manufacturing Company of St. Louis supplied the steel helmets worn by American fighting men of all ranks. The International Shoe Company was kept humming producing service combat boots. Kansas City clothing factories such as those of the H. D. Lee and Nelly Don companies furnished items of apparel from undershorts to flying suits for the men in uniform.

Operations outside the two great metropolitan areas of the state also contributed to the war effort. To provide raw materials for the multitude of war industries, the lead and zinc mines of southwest and southeast Missouri were operated at full capacity.

Several new military installations were constructed in Missouri and those already in existence were improved and enlarged. The largest new army installation was begun in Pulaski County near Waynesville in 1940. With the selection of this site for a new army installation, the village of Waynesville, population

648, was suddenly transformed into a beehive of activity. After 304 farm families had been relocated, the construction companies moved in bringing thousands of workmen. One resident of Waynesville described his house during the construction period: "I had twelve double beds in three rooms. There was hardly enough space between beds for walking." At a nearby hotel the workers occupied beds in eight-hour shifts around the clock. Those who were unable to secure shelter in hotels or homes occupied garages and even hen houses. Only five months after the army announced the beginning of the construction, the weekly payroll at Fort Leonard Wood totaled $1,380,000. This influx of workers and paychecks, and the need of new farms for those whose property had been purchased for the army post boosted farm land values in the area from fifteen to forty per cent and encouraged the establishment of many new businesses in the general area of the fort.

Another camp established in Missouri was Camp Crowder, construction of which was begun near Neosho in August of 1941. Four months later, 21,000 people employed at the post were dividing a weekly payroll of $650,000.

In addition to the new installations, the existing army post —Jefferson Barracks at St. Louis—was renovated and enlarged for use during the war. The colleges and universities of the state also made their facilities available for specialized training of men in the various branches of the services, and, as a result, there were uniforms on almost all campuses during the war.

The Ordnance Works located at Weldon Springs, another large war construction project, was an important supplier of TNT for American forces. One year from its beginning in October of 1940 the plant was employing over 8,000 workers.

The Missouri farmer rallied to the support of his nation in 1941 as he had a quarter century earlier. The farmer was hampered somewhat by a shortage of farm labor. Many men had left the farm to enter military service. Others—men and women alike —had left the rural areas for the higher income opportunities of the metropolitan war plants. All but three rural counties in the state lost from 3.6 to 32 per cent of their population during the war years. The population of Phelps and Pulaski counties increased 20.5 and 15.5 per cent, respectively, because of the economic opportunities offered by Fort Leonard Wood. Mississippi County gained 0.7 per cent, continuing a twenty-year trend of

Fort Leonard Wood, located southwest of Rolla, Missouri, was the training center for the Seventh Corps. Pictured above is a small section of the Sixth Division area at the Fort.

population growth influenced by expanding cotton production.

To compensate for these losses of trained rural manpower, the farmer drew on new sources of labor. Family cooperation in field work increased, with mothers and children taking the place of hired hands. Grandmothers and nine-year-olds were reported driving tractors. Urban youths were recruited during school vacations. City boys were trained to assist with chores and field work; girls helped busy farm mothers with their household duties. Farmers aided each other by pooling their efforts and swapping work. Even the business and professional men of the small towns closed shop to help in the fields during rush seasons.

Despite the handicaps of labor and machinery shortages and gas and tire rationing, Missouri farmers succeeded in greatly increasing production to meet the tremendous needs of a nation at war. These increased yields were largely the result of the wider adoption of improved farm practices such as application of limestone and commercial fertilizers, terracing, contouring, construction of deep ponds, proper crop rotation, the establishment of grass waterways, and the use of hybrid seed. The following figures show the increase in the production of the listed commodities from 1939 to 1943.

Cattle	48%	Soybeans	651%
Hogs	55%	Milk cows	20%
Corn	11%	Chickens	29%
Oats	22%		

To fill the ranks left vacant by enlisted men and draftees, women took on work which had previously been considered strictly masculine. In addition to performing all manner of jobs in war plants, Missouri women operated street cars, drove trucks and tractors, rode dairy routes, and even acted as "section Jennies," maintaining rail beds for the vital railroad transportation system.

Missouri citizens, urban and rural alike, further cooperated in the war effort by joining the Civilian Defense Corps and the Red Cross, by contributing to a long list of private service organizations, by collecting scrap, by cultivating victory gardens, and by canning foods to stretch ration stamps. Missourians also responded to a series of patriotic appeals for funds and purchased a total of $3,114,591,770 worth of war bonds in eight statewide drives.

The Civilian Defense Corps of World War I had stressed the building of civilian morale. In World War II the Civilian Defense Corps emphasized civilian protection, for air raids and even invasion were considered a possibility. By July, 1942, a total of 400,000 Missourians had volunteered for civilian defense work. In addition to supervising several statewide blackouts and training leaders in safety techniques and emergency procedures, the Corps promoted the salvage of vital materials in a series of drives. School children collected waste paper, scrap metal, and old rubber. Housewives washed and flattened tin cans to be converted into war materials, and saved kitchen grease to be used in the production of explosive nitroglycerin.

The "thrift gardens" of World War I reappeared in Missouri vacant lots and backyards as "victory gardens" during World War II. Neighborhood families in Kansas City tended victory gardens on the site of the beautiful flower garden William Rockhill Nelson once planted for his daughter Laura. In order to preserve needed commodities, the government established a rationing system. Automobile tires, cars, shoes, farm machines, gaso-

(Courtesy State Historical Society)

**"The Sowers" from Thomas Hart Benton's war series "Year of Peril,"
now in the collections of the State Historical Society.**

line, sugar, meat, and many other commodities were rationed. The ingenuity of family cooks was tested when only fifty "points" of canned goods per month per person was allowed— and a can of tomatoes cost twenty points! In place of scarce and point-consuming steaks and chops, St. Louis butchers offered unrationed shark's meat at $.45 a pound.

On the highways, a thirty-five-mile-an-hour speed limit was established to conserve gas and tires. When a patriotic motorist noted someone exceeding the limit, it was appropriate to remind the transgressor with the victory honk—three short blasts followed by a long one—Morse code for V. Salesmen during this time often had to pool cars in order to make their rounds. During the war a crash in Camden put the only taxicab and, therefore, the town's entire taxi service, out of operation for the duration.

Greatly increased interest in the Red Cross was evident in Missouri, particularly in the early years of the war. Adult membership multiplied almost five times and enrollment in the Junior Red Cross increased more than threefold. Members rolled band-

Following his successful leadership during World War II, the highly-respected Omar N. Bradley became the chairman of the Joint Chiefs of Staff.

(Courtesy State Historical Society)

ages, knitted sweaters, made up soldiers' kits, worked at blood collection centers, and took courses in first aid and home nursing.

The enlistment of many fathers in military service and the employment of mothers, and even grandmothers, in war plants deprived thousands of young Missourians of a normal family-centered childhood. The disruption of home life had an impact on the young people of Missouri. Particularly in the metropolitan areas sharp increases in vandalism and other forms of juvenile delinquency were viewed with alarm. School and law enforcement agencies also expressed concern over the decrease in school attendance. Curfews and the establishment of chaperoned "Teen Towns" were employed in an attempt to modify the effect of loosened family supervision.

A total of approximately 450,000 Missouri men and women served in the armed forces between the declaration of war on December 8, 1941, and the Japanese surrender on September 2, 1945. Included in this number were eighty-nine generals and admirals.

Among those Missourians who distinguished themselves for their leadership in the war was General Omar N. Bradley who grew up in Clark and Moberly, Missouri. General Bradley successfully led troops in Tunisia, Sicily, and France and was made commander of the million-man Twelfth Army in Germany. Bradley was a calm, sensitive, humble man, who was loved by the soldiers in the ranks. A conservative, astute leader, he can be given a great part of the credit for the success of the American invasion of France and Germany in 1944 and 1945. After the cessation of hostilities General Bradley became the chairman of the joint chiefs of staff in Washington. General Maxwell D. Taylor of Kansas City gained fame for a fearless trip to Rome to confer with Italian officials hours before the invasion of Salerno. General Taylor, decorated for personal bravery at the front in Normandy, later was given high commands during the Korean Conflict in the 1950's.

Lamar, Missouri, a town of 3,000 in the 1940's, boasted a president, three rear admirals and the commander of the coast guard women's reserve among her sons and daughters. During the last year of the war Harry S Truman, a native of Lamar, occupied the White House. Rear Admiral Charles A. Lockwood, Jr. of Lamar was the commander of the United States submarine fleet in the Pacific, while his friend Rear Admiral Freeland A. Daubin commanded the Atlantic submarine fleet. Rear Admiral Thomas Selby Combs was the third member of the "Lamar triumvirate" of admirals, and Lieutenant Commander Dorothy C. Stratton of Lamar served as director of the SPARS.

On September 2, 1945, after three years and nine months of sacrifice and struggle, Americans listened to a description of the surrender ceremonies broadcast from Tokyo Bay. Douglas

"The U.S.S. Missouri in Tokyo Bay" from the mural by William Knox in the state capitol.

(Courtesy Massie-Missouri Commerce)

MacArthur and American and Japanese officials signed the formal surrender aboard the U.S.S. *Missouri,* and then the nation heard Missouri's first president say:

> ... From this day we move forward ... toward a
> new era of security at home. With the other United
> Nations we move toward a new and better world of
> peace and international good will and coopera-
> tion. ...

The Constitution of 1945

During the 1930's and the early 1940's there was a growing feeling in the state that the Constitution of 1875 should be abandoned and a new constitution written. The Constitution of 1875, which had been amended sixty-one times, was difficult to use. The constitutional convention of 1922-1923 had recommended the adoption of some twenty-one amendments. Only six of the suggested amendments won the approval of the voters. Before the election of 1942, farm organizations, labor unions, educational and other professional groups, and civic organizations united behind the attempt to authorize a constitutional convention. The calling of a convention was approved by a margin of over 100,000 votes in 1942.

The eighty-three delegates to the convention were selected in two groups. The first group of district delegates was made up of one Democrat and one Republican from each of the thirty-four senatorial districts in the state. A second group of fifteen delegates-at-large was elected on a slate which had been agreed upon by the leaders of the two major parties. The delegates-at-large included seven Republicans, seven Democrats, and one anti-New Deal Democrat. Politically, the convention was almost evenly balanced between the two parties. The delegates worked as individuals more than as representatives of political or economic groups. The convention, conservative in its approach to government, wished to retain the main elements of the old constitution. Interestingly, the older delegates tended to be more willing to modify the set patterns and procedures of government than the younger men who had had less political experience.

The meetings of the convention were open to the public, and unlimited debate was allowed. This is in striking contrast to the secrecy of the Founding Fathers who wrote the American Constitution in 1787. Although the constitution framers in Missouri in 1943-44 opened their doors to any new suggestions and,

An Aerial View of the State Government Buildings in Jefferson City

in fact, solicited proposals from the citizenry, they were able to carry on the important work of the convention without a filibuster and without undue political maneuvering. The convention began its sessions on September 21, 1943, and completed the work on September 29, 1944. The document was then submitted to the citizenry on February 27, 1945, at which time sixty per cent of the voters indicated their approval of the new constitution. It accordingly became effective in 1945.

As we have noted earlier in discussing the constitutions of 1820, 1865, and 1875, the basic structure of government has remained constant. Missouri continues with a government divided into three branches—legislative, executive, and judicial. The legislative power is vested in a General Assembly, which includes a Senate and a House of Representatives. The executive power is exercised by the governor and his administrative associates. The judicial responsibility is centered in the court system of the state. Thus, the major divisions of Missouri government have not changed since the first state constitution was written in 1820.

The Constitution of 1945 is longer than the unamended version of the Constitution of 1875. One would expect this since the responsibilities of the state had grown and the complexity of city government, education, and welfare activities required many new regulations. There are several major differences between the Constitution of 1945 and its predecessor.

First, the basis for representation was modified. Although Missouri was becoming increasingly urban, the rural areas had always dominated the legislature. Under the Constitution of 1945 the new basis for representation in the Senate gives the cities slightly more voice in Jefferson City. However, the rural citizens of the state still have a larger representation in the House.

Second, a somewhat unusual aspect of the Constitution of 1945 was a "nonpartisan plan" for the election of judges, first adopted by amendment in 1940. Under this plan the supreme court judges, the judges of the courts of appeals, and the judges in the circuit and probate courts of St. Louis City and Jackson County, as well as the judges of the St. Louis court of criminal correction, all are originally appointed by the governor from a list of three names submitted by a nonpartisan judicial commission. At the next regular general election after he has served for a year the judge must stand for election or be replaced. If he files for the office, no other name is placed on the ballot. Voters can vote either for or against retention of the judge. If a judge is defeated in an election, the governor and the nonpartisan commission begin the process over again.

Third, under the new constitution the justice of the peace courts which had frequently been presided over by untrained men were replaced by magistrate courts which were to be staffed by licensed lawyers. Fourth, the state superintendent of schools was no longer to be elected. Under the Constitution of 1945 the bipartisan eight-member state board of education was given the power to select the head of Missouri's public school system—now known as the commissioner of education.

The Legislature

The legislative branch of government in Missouri, as in all other states but Nebraska, consists of a bicameral General Assembly. The Senate is the smaller body with only thirty-four members—one from each of thirty-four senatorial districts. These districts are established primarily on the basis of population. Although there is some attempt to draw the districts so

The present Missouri Executive Mansion, the residence of the governor and his family, was constructed in the years following the Civil War and completed in 1871. It was first occupied by Governor and Mrs. B. Gratz Brown. The structure is considered to be the finest example of French-Italian architecture still standing in America. *(Courtesy Walker-Missouri Tourism)*

that the number of residents within them is approximately equal, some gerrymandering is practiced. In order to reduce districting for party advantage, a variation of twenty-five per cent above or below one-thirty-fourth of the population of the state has been set as a maximum. Despite this maximum variant, there are inequalities of representation. For example, the residents of the predominantly rural twenty-ninth senatorial district, which is experiencing a growth in population, is probably "under-represented;" while the senatorial districts of the City of St. Louis, which are undergoing a population loss, may be "over-represented." Senators are chosen for a four-year term. One-half of the membership of the body is elected every two years. The odd-numbered senatorial districts elect their senators in leap years. The even-numbered senatorial districts select their senators at the intervening biennial elections. A senator is required to be at least thirty years old, a voter of the state for three years, and a resident of the district from which he is elected for at least one year. The lieutenant-governor acts as the president of the Senate. However, the president pro tempore of the Senate, who is selected from the senators by the members of the majority party, exercises great political power, since it is his responsibility to assign the senators to committees. Most of the work of the Senate is handled by some two dozen Senate committees which review proposed legislation and recommend certain measures for passage.

Representation in the House of Representatives is more closely associated with geographic or political divisions of the state. For example, each county is assured of at least one member in the House, whereas in the Senate many senators represent a number of counties. A rather complex formula has been established to determine representation in the House. After each census, the population figure for Missouri is divided by 200 and this number then is considered the state ratio of representation. The number of delegates to the House from each county is determined by establishing how many times the ratio can be divided into the population of the county. If there are less than two and one-half ratios in the county, then that county receives one representative. A county with two and one-half ratios is allotted two representatives. Three representatives are assigned that county which has four ratios. A county with six ratios will send four representatives to Jefferson City. An additional representative is allowed for each two and one-half ratios beyond six. This system works to the advantage of the sparsely populated rural counties which have the same representation as those counties in which the number of residents is many times greater, but still under the two and one-half ratios required for two representatives.

Members of the House of Representatives are chosen every two years at the regular biennial elections. They must be at least twenty-four years old, have been eligible to vote in the state for at least two years, and have resided in the district for one year before the election. Although the Constitution of 1945 set legislative salaries at $125 per month, an amendment in 1960 permitted them to be raised by the General Assembly. Today, both senators and representatives receive an annual salary of $8,400 plus expenses of $10 per day during session as well as a mileage allotment for travel between Jefferson City and the residence of the legislator, twice a month. The leading official of the House of Representatives is known as the speaker of the House. He is originally chosen at a caucus of the majority party and then officially elected by the House. The speaker is responsible for the appointment of members to all committees (about four dozen in number), and the naming of committee chairmen. Beginning in 1963, as a result of the 1960 census, the size of the Missouri House of Representatives was increased to 163. As in many other states, the legislature in Missouri is so constructed that rural citizens have greater representation than do city residents. The House of Representatives is highly rural in its outlook.

As in the other states, legislative acts must be submitted to the governor for his approval or veto. The same is true in Missouri. However, the Missouri governor has a power known as the item veto which allows him to delete items from any appropriation bill except those for the support of the public schools. Theoretically, the legislature can override a veto by the governor; however, in practice it happens only rarely.

A major problem in Missouri is the length of sessions of the

The Senate in Action

(Courtesy Massie-Missouri Commerce)

Governor Phil M. Donnelly was one of only four Missouri Chief Executives to be elected for two full terms, 1945-1949 and 1953-1957. The other three two-term governors were John Miller, 1825-33; Warren E. Hearnes, 1965-73; and Christopher S. Bond, 1973-77 and 1981-
(Courtesy State Historical Society)

General Assembly. In this century the legislatures have been faced with the need to conduct an increasing amount of business. Under the Constitution of 1945 the legislators gather on the first Wednesday after the first day of January following a general election. In 1952 a constitutional amendment set the date of May 31 as the last possible day of a session. Eight years later, in 1960, the legislative sessions were extended to July 15. However, even with this new extension of time, the legislators still find they are unable to complete much of their work within the regular session. As a result, governors are frequently forced to call the legislature back into special sessions. To allow additional time to consider the many pieces of legislation submitted, the legislature now holds annual sessions beginning each January.

The Executive

The executive branch of the state government is not so highly centralized in one person as is the executive branch of the Federal Government. Still, the governor of the state is a powerful official with great appointive power, control of the state militia, authorization to enforce the laws of the state, the responsibility of maintaining peace and order, the right to call special sessions of the legislature, the obligation to recommend needed legislation to the General Assembly, and the right to veto legislation and items of appropriation. The governor is elected for a four-year term directly by the people in the general election held at the same time the presidential elections occur. The candidate for governor must be thirty years of age, a citizen of the United States for at least fifteen years, and a resident of Missouri for at least ten years. Until revised in 1965 the Missouri Constitution provided that the governor could not serve two consecutive terms. The governor, who receives a salary of $55,000 per year, is also provided the use of the executive mansion, and chauffeur and maid service. In the event of death or resignation, the governor is succeeded by the lieutenant-governor, who serves at a salary of $30,000 per year.

The governor as an executive has less authority over the government than does the president of the United States, since many of the chief officials of the executive branch of the state government are elected, not appointed by him. The state treasurer, the attorney general, the secretary of state, and the state auditor all are chosen by the people to serve for four-year terms. All of these officials are elected at the same time as the governor except the state auditor, who is chosen at the off-year election—between presidential elections. Since these officials are selected by the people, not by the governor, they do not necessarily feel an obligation to support or cooperate with the governor. In spite of this theoretical opportunity for conflict within the state government, the several state officials usually work together efficiently to carry out the obligations of their offices.

The governor, with the consent of the Senate, appoints the officials of a number of departments which serve under his direction: revenue, state highway, agriculture, public health and welfare, conservation, education, business and administration, corrections, and labor and industrial relations. The first six departments named are established as authorized in the constitution; the last three have been created by statute. The state highway commission, the conservation commission, the board of education, and the labor and industrial relations commission are agencies directed by bipartisan boards.

In addition to the departments just listed, the governor has other state agencies which are directly subject to his control. He is in charge of the state highway patrol, the state military department, the liquor control department, the division of civil defense, and several boards of election commissioners and police commissioners for the more densely populated areas of the state.

In general, it can be said the Missouri government has op-erated with little scandal and apparently with reasonable efficiency through the years—the O'Malley insurance scandal during the Park administration being a notable exception to the rule. In an organization the size of state government one can anticipate some evidence of either illegal or unethical conduct at times. The character of Missouri state government has been excellent, in an over-all view.

The Judiciary

The Missouri court system is similar to those in many American states. At the top of the judicial structure is the su-preme court, a body of seven judges who sit in Jefferson City. Not only is the supreme court the highest tribunal in the state and the place of appeal for the state, but the body also has general control over the lower courts of Missouri, establishing rules and procedures for all. The judges of the supreme court receive a salary of $50,000 per year and serve for terms of twelve years. Below the supreme court are three courts of appeals—one in Kansas City, one in St. Louis and another in Springfield. The three judges who sit in each court of appeals receive salaries of $47,500 per year. Below the courts of appeals are located the forty-two circuit courts of the state. These judicial circuits vary in size from one to a maximum of five counties. The circuit court judge, who moves from county courthouse to county court-house in his district, receives a salary of $45,000 per year. In addition to the circuit courts, Missouri has two courts of common pleas—one located at Cape Girardeau and the other at Hannibal. In most situations these courts act in the same manner as circuit courts. Below the circuit courts are the magistrate courts, one of which is located in each county. These courts are the lowest courts of the state, similar to the justice of peace courts in other states. In those counties where the court activity requires them, several judges preside at the different divisions of the magistrate courts. There is also in each county a probate court which is given the responsibility of carrying out the intent of wills and

The Missouri State Capitol, Jefferson City.
(Walker - Missouri Tourism)

settling the estates of deceased citizens. In addition, the City of St. Louis has a special court of criminal correction, which handles the many cases in that metropolitan center that involve violations of state law. Judges of the appeals and supreme courts serve for twelve-year terms. Circuit court judges serve for six years, and all other judges have four-year terms.

As noted earlier, the unusual characteristic of Missouri's judicial system is the method used in selecting judges. The complicated procedure is obviously intended to remove politics from the selection of judges. Although political factors are less important under this system, the political affiliation of a judge still is, at times, a factor in his selection. For example, from 1940 to 1950 the governors always selected judges of their own political party. Since 1950, however, the governors have sometimes selected judges from the opposition party.

Like most other constitutions, that of Missouri has a bill of rights which guarantees certain basic rights to the citizens. Among those prerogatives protected are religious freedom, freedom of speech, freedom of press, freedom of assembly, and the right to keep and bear arms. In addition, the citizens of Missouri are guaranteed an open trial with the right to defend themselves and to secure justice. Missouri citizens are also assured of the initiative and the referendum through which they may initiate and pass legislation. Furthermore, the state legislature may refer matters to the citizens for their approval or rejection.

Although the structure of government in Missouri may seem complex and cumbersome at first glance, the intricate mechanism has operated in a remarkably efficient manner through the years and continues to serve Missourians well. Despite this efficiency, some changes in the governmental system of Missouri will prove to be judicious. As the legislative load increased, an annual session of the General Assembly was found to be imperative. The equalization of representation within the state would also seem to be in order. The conscientious citizen of Missouri must remain alert to the need for change in the interest both of efficiency and justice.

A Missouri President

Men of Missouri such as Thomas Hart Benton, Edward Bates, B. Gratz Brown, Richard Bland, Champ Clark, and Stuart Symington have been prominent candidates for the presidency, but only one Missourian has occupied that high position of trust and leadership. It is appropriate that we discuss in some detail the administration of this one Missouri president.

During his second term in the United States Senate, Harry S Truman achieved national fame as chairman of a committee to investigate the conduct of the national defense program. It has been estimated that the recommendations of the committee and its revelations of waste, inefficiency, and fraud saved the American taxpayers approximately $15,000,000,000.

In 1944 a haggard and weary Franklin D. Roosevelt became a candidate for the presidency a fourth time. Because many delegates to the Democratic convention of that year opposed the renomination of Vice-President Henry A. Wallace, great pressure was exerted upon the president to name a new vice-presidential candidate. In the considerations of this choice the senator from Missouri was prominently mentioned, and Harry Truman was ultimately chosen by the Democratic convention with the blessing of F. D. R.

PROGRESS CHART OF A BILL
THROUGH THE MISSOURI LEGISLATURE*

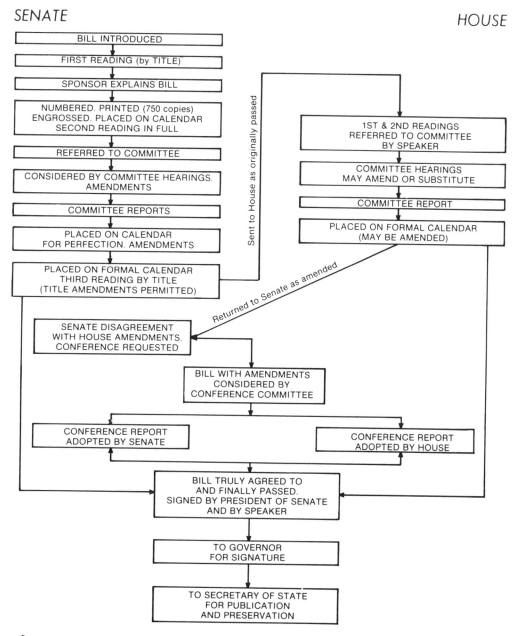

SENATE

HOUSE

BILL INTRODUCED

FIRST READING (by TITLE)

SPONSOR EXPLAINS BILL

NUMBERED. PRINTED (750 copies)
ENGROSSED. PLACED ON CALENDAR
SECOND READING IN FULL

REFERRED TO COMMITTEE

CONSIDERED BY COMMITTEE HEARINGS.
AMENDMENTS

COMMITTEE REPORTS

PLACED ON CALENDAR
FOR PERFECTION. AMENDMENTS

PLACED ON FORMAL CALENDAR
THIRD READING BY TITLE
(TITLE AMENDMENTS PERMITTED)

Sent to House as originally passed

1ST & 2ND READINGS
REFERRED TO COMMITTEE
BY SPEAKER

COMMITTEE HEARINGS
MAY AMEND OR SUBSTITUTE

COMMITTEE REPORT

PLACED ON FORMAL CALENDAR
(MAY BE AMENDED)

Returned to Senate as amended

SENATE DISAGREEMENT
WITH HOUSE AMENDMENTS.
CONFERENCE REQUESTED

BILL WITH AMENDMENTS
CONSIDERED BY
CONFERENCE COMMITTEE

CONFERENCE REPORT
ADOPTED BY SENATE

CONFERENCE REPORT
ADOPTED BY HOUSE

BILL TRULY AGREED TO
AND FINALLY PASSED.
SIGNED BY PRESIDENT OF SENATE
AND BY SPEAKER

TO GOVERNOR
FOR SIGNATURE

TO SECRETARY OF STATE
FOR PUBLICATION
AND PRESERVATION

* The chart shows the bill as being introduced in the Senate. Should the bill be introduced in the House, practically the same procedure is followed in reverse order.

Although the tremendous strain of the war years could be seen on the face and figure of the president, the American people in 1944 were unwilling to change their leadership in the midst of the global conflict. When Roosevelt was re-elected, his running mate Harry S Truman of Missouri became the vice-president. Only a little more than three months after the inauguration, Americans across the nation were startled by the solemn newsflash: "The President of the United States is dead." Several hours later, a grave-faced Missourian took the oath of office in the White House and became the thirty-third president of the United States. The next day Harry Truman, visiting with his senatorial friends, expressed his reaction to this turn of events:

> I don't know if any of you fellows ever had a load
> of hay or a bull fall on [you] . . . last night the
> whole weight of the moon and stars fell on me. I
> feel a tremendous responsibility.

The people of America knew very little about their new president. Some recalled that he had been associated with a discredited political machine in Missouri. Others linked his name with the Senate investigating committee and remembered him as a man who demanded honesty in the fulfillment of war contracts. After thirteen years of strong, dynamic direction from Roosevelt there was a feeling of concern lest the new man prove to be inadequate for the demands of the hour. America waited fearfully to discover the quality of leadership possessed by their new president.

In his years in the White House the Truman image emerged. The president was a man of determination who would fight long and hard for the legislation he favored. As an ardent reader of history, he wished to avoid the mistakes of the tragic post-World War I period. Truman revealed himself as a thoroughgoing disciple of Roosevelt who intended to continue and expand the reform legislation begun under the New Deal. Truman also cast an image as a man who enjoyed politics and engaged in political activity with all his strength. Late in his administration he also displayed a characteristic dogged loyalty when he faithfully stood by the associates and cronies who brought dishonor to his name by their own misdeeds. Finally, President Truman appeared as a happily married man with simple American tastes, an abiding love for and loyalty to his wife and daughter, and a volatile temper when his loved ones were criticized. His early mornirg walks, his piano playing, and his delight in vigorous campaigning became symbols of the presidency during his nearly eight years in the White House.

President Truman brought a number of Missourians to Washington after he assumed his high office: banker John W. Snyder, Democratic political leader Robert Hannegan, his press secretary Charles G. Ross, his naval aide Commodore J. K. Vardaman, his military aide Major General Harry H. Vaughan, and Stuart Symington. At a meeting of the Alfalfa Club in the nation's capital in September, 1945, the following song describing the Missouri invasion of Washington was sung to the tune of "Meet me in St. Louie, Louie":

> Bob Hannegan, Snyder and Ross
> Reported at once to the Boss—
> Three men from St. Louie
> No friends of Tom Dewey
> Just helping put Harry across.
> Missouri has now come of age,
> Her sons hitting every front page.
> Jake Vardaman too,
> Arrived from St. Loo,
> Then Symington stepped on the stage.
>
> Don't meet them in St. Louie, Louie,
> Meet them here not there,
> When the dear old White House called them
> They dug up their fare.
> They boarded Greyhound busses—
> Weren't they the lucky cusses?
> You can't meet them in St. Louie, Louie,
> They're all here, not there.

It is doubtful that any president in American history excepting Lincoln assumed the mantle of leadership under as difficult circumstances. When Harry Truman became president the war in Europe was reaching its final stages, but victory in the Pacific conflict seemed far from won. The president was immediately faced with two tremendous tasks—the complex diplomatic negotiations with Russia and Britain associated with the ending of the European War, and the leadership of the allies to a final victory over Japan. After the war was over there were the thorny problems of peace treaties and the establishment of an effective international organization to prevent future wars. At home he was faced with the demands for an immediate disbanding of the army, since the veterans were anxious to return to

Missouri's Only Native-Born Son to Reach the White House—Harry S Truman

(Portrait by Leo Stern, courtesy State Historical Society)

their homes and families. Yet President Truman knew that too sudden a withdrawal and demobilization might well defeat us in the securing of peace terms. At the same time, the nation was struggling with such ugly problems as soaring prices, strikes in major industries, a great shortage of housing facilities, and racial conflict. It was a time that called for firm and wise leadership.

When President Truman had served in the Senate during the thirties, the Democratic Party had overwhelming majorities in both houses. In the crisis of the great depression, congressmen were so anxious for solutions to national problems that they gave willing assent to many daring new reforms. As a result, Franklin Roosevelt was able to secure almost any legislation he requested during the decade of New Deal experimentation. President Truman wished to continue the liberal reforms of the thirties. During the forties, however, the economic distress of the nation was no longer acute. Furthermore, the Democratic majority in Congress was not so overwhelming, and during part of Truman's administration the Republicans controlled both houses of Congress. Thus, when President Truman presented his program, which he dubbed the Fair Deal, it was not so readily welcomed as the New Deal had been a decade earlier.

As part of his program, the president sought to remove the Taft-Hartley Act, which had been passed by the Republican Congress over his veto in 1947. He wished to establish a Fair Employment Practices Commission, which would work to end discrimination in hiring on the basis of race, creed, or national origins. He hoped to build TVA-type projects on rivers in several parts of the United States. He advocated a new farm plan which would allow for greater flexibility in market prices, while retaining government subsidies to maintain agricultural income. President Truman also formulated plans for health insurance, universal military training, and federal aid to the public schools. Had these programs been adopted, the Fair Deal would have made a major impact upon American history, as Roosevelt's New Deal had earlier. However, Congress was more conservative during the forties. Although Truman blasted the Republican Eightieth Congress as a "do nothing", uncooperative body, he found that the Democratic Congresses which followed the Eightieth were also unwilling to accept the proposals listed above.

Although he was disappointed by the rejection of the major points of his program, President Truman did realize success in several aspects of domestic affairs. He secured the settlement of several major strikes by intervening in the conflicts, and, in one case, by threatening to draft railroad workers. On the whole, however, it should be noted that Mr. Truman was sympathetic to the demands of labor. The president led the opposition against the Taft-Hartley Act, which labor leaders called a "slave labor law." Actually, the law was not the threat that labor leaders believed it to be; and, although it was a sharp party issue at the time of its adoption, the act became less and less an object of controversy as the years passed. President Truman was successful in securing an extension of social security benefits, an increase in the minimum wage level, and federal funds for slum clearance projects. The president also was able to maintain a sizable army in order to defend our commitments abroad despite great pressure from servicemen who wished to return to civilian life.

President Truman may not be remembered for his domestic policies, but he will certainly have an important niche in American history for the monumental foreign policy of his administration. In general, it can be said that foreign policy overshadowed domestic policy in the first decade and a half after World War

II. Americans were aware that in an era of atomic weapons and intercontinental bombers wrong decisions in foreign policy could lead to national disaster. Some of the strong isolationist sentiment which had been prevalent in America before World War II remained after the global conflict. President Truman disagreed with this isolationism and firmly believed that America could no longer remain aloof from the troubles and alliances of the world. It was, therefore, the task of the president so to guide the nation that she could take her place in the councils of the world powers, rather than crawl back into her shell as she had after the First World War. Cognizant of the failures of Wilson and the Republican presidents of the twenties, President Truman attempted to lead the nation into a position of international responsibility. In doing so, he was careful to work with the Republican leaders of the Senate to secure their support.

When the United Nations was organized in San Francisco in April, 1945, prominent Republicans and Democrats alike supported American participation. When President Truman left the White House in January, 1953, the nation, firmly committed to international cooperation, was part of an alliance of free nations pledged to resist attack from the Communist foe facing them. President Truman had finally won the victory over the proponents of isolationism. The significance of this accomplishment cannot be overestimated.

In July, 1945, President Truman traveled to Potsdam in Germany to meet with Stalin and the new British prime minister Clement Attlee. At this meeting the president requested the Soviet Union to enter the war against Japan. From our present vantage point, this request may seem to have been a mistake. However, at that time, American military leaders predicted that an invasion of Japan would cost millions of American casualties. The president, wishing to have as much help as possible in bringing the Japanese war to an end, promised Russia certain territorial advantages in Asia in return for Soviet intervention. We actually did not need Soviet help to defeat Japan, but the president discovered this only after concessions to Stalin had been made. Six weeks later, the explosion of the most powerful weapon the world had ever known brought the Pacific theatre of war to an unexpectedly abrupt halt.

Although the fighting was formally ended on September 2, 1945, when General McArthur and representatives of the defeated

(Official U. S. Navy Photograph—Courtesy State Historical Society)

On September 2, 1945, General MacArthur and Japanese officials signed the formal surrender ending World War II aboard the U.S.S. Missouri.

Japanese government signed the surrender aboard the U.S.S. *Missouri,* the years following were a time of great diplomatic conflict. The United States found living with a victorious Soviet Union increasingly difficult. Under Stalin's control, the Russian communist state proceeded to establish communist puppet regimes in eastern Europe, to organize communist subversion in western Europe, to attempt to push its way through Greece and Turkey to gain a foothold on the Mediterranean, and to establish Red regimes in such Asian areas as Korea, China, and the rich regions of southeast Asia. The United States tried to conciliate and maintain friendly relations with Russia; but less than two years after the fighting ended in Europe, the Truman administration felt obliged to take a strong stand against the Soviets. Some have referred to this stiffening of resistance as Truman's "get tough" policy. In 1947 Congress supported the Truman Doctrine, under which the United States provided military and economic assistance to Greece and Turkey to help them withstand Soviet pressure. As a result, both nations were saved from Red domination. In 1948, when the Communist Party threatened to overthrow the governments of western Europe, the president secured adoption of the Marshall Plan, which funneled money into Europe to rejuvenate their economies, thereby reducing the threat of communism.

In 1948, when the Russians attempted to cut off the American, British, and French sectors of West Berlin from needed Western supplies, President Truman authorized the Berlin Airlift, which dramatically demonstrated to the world our intention to hold our position in Berlin. For ten months the city was supplied by air, and then the Russians abandoned their attempt to starve out the allied forces. In 1949 President Truman led the United States into the North Atlantic Treaty Organization (NATO), an alliance of the major Western powers pledged to fight together in the event of Soviet aggression. American entrance into this alliance was a most unusual development; from the time of President Washington's administration until President Truman's term, the United States had never taken part in a European alliance during peacetime. The nation was ignoring Washington's advice that we avoid all such European alliances. But circumstances had greatly changed since the eighteenth century. In an age of A-bombs and rockets, it was no longer possible for America to remain aloof. The North Atlantic Treaty Organization became a major force in containing the Soviets during the postwar years.

President Truman's very effective basic European policy was followed by both of his successors, President Dwight D. Eisenhower and President John F. Kennedy. President Truman's Asian policy, however, was not so successful. The United States did not have such loyal and strong allies in Asia as she did in Europe. The communists of Asia were highly organized, and frequently exploited the corruption, inequalities, and obvious weaknesses of the existing governments. As a result, there was a dramatic enlargement of communist control in Asia during President Truman's administration. In China the communist forces of Mao Tse-Tung swept across that populous nation, pushing aside the Nationalist Chinese armies. Although some in America spoke of these Chinese Reds as "agrarian reformers," they soon revealed themselves as ruthless Marxists by their bloody and brutal policies of crushing the upper and middle classes. In the loss of China to the Reds, one-fourth of the world's population was suddenly placed under communist control. While it is unfair to blame the Truman administration for this loss—obviously, the Chinese themselves had something to say about the matter—still it is true that the weak American policy was unable to prevent the catastrophe.

Another great shock in Asia came a year later when Red North Korean armies invaded South Korea. It appears that the Reds believed America would not defend Korea. At this moment President Truman made one of his most difficult decisions. Remembering the earlier invasion of Manchuria in 1931, which ultimately led to other acts of aggression, President Truman ordered American troops into Korea to push back the aggressors. The war in Korea was a long, frustrating, victory-less war in which we did not use all of our military weapons and could not attack enemy bases in China whose "volunteers" had joined the North Korean aggressors. Although the president was highly criticized for his unwillingness to order an all-out war and for his recall of General Douglas MacArthur, who advocated full-scale combat with all weapons available, the Truman deci-

The University of Missouri tower was dedicated in 1926 as a memorial to students of the university who gave their lives in World War I. In 1952 the student union wing was opened in honor of Missouri students who fell in World War II.

(Courtesy Massie-Missouri Commerce)

sions, in retrospect, seem correct. America was not ready for a war with China. As another Missourian, General Omar Bradley, expressed it, a war with China would have been "the wrong war, at the wrong place, at the wrong time, with the wrong enemy."

Many Americans will remember our Missouri president best for one of two aspects of his administration. It was Truman who was forced to make the decision in 1945 to drop the first atomic bombs on Japan. He made the decision in the belief that a show of strength, while it would kill thousands of Japanese, might lead Tokyo to make peace immediately, thus sparing millions of American and Japanese lives which might have been lost in a bloody invasion of Japan. The president's decision to drop the bomb led to world-shaking explosions at Hiroshima and Nagasaki and to the signing of a surrender treaty less than a month thereafter.

Americans will also remember Harry Truman for his amazing campaign for re-election in 1948 at a time when many members of his own Democratic Party opposed him. A left-wing

At the dedication of his birthplace at Lamar, Harry Thuman displayed his old campaign ability to please the crowd.

(Courtesy Hadley K. Irwin—Missouri State Park Board)

(Courtesy State Historical Society)

Harry, Bess, and Margaret Truman—First Family from Missouri—as Painted by Greta Kempton

group in the Democratic Party formed the Progressive Party and nominated their own candidate, Henry A. Wallace, for president. Southern Democrats who disliked Truman's civil rights ideas seceded from the party to form the so-called "Dixiecrats" and chose Governor Strom Thurmond of South Carolina as their standard bearer. With the Democrats split three ways and the nation unhappy with high prices, the Republican candidate, Thomas E. Dewey, appeared to be the sure winner. Undaunted by his poor prospects and the lack of enthusiasm for his campaign within his own party, Harry Truman proceeded to tour the country by train. Speaking in his own direct and sometimes earthy manner, he lashed relentlessly at the Republican Congress in cities across the nation and then went home to Independence to await the results. Although all the polls and political pundits predicted a Dewey victory, when the ballots were counted, Harry S Truman had been narrowly re-elected on the basis of his own vigorous campaign. This victory, which some historians have called the Miracle of 1948, can be explained only by the energetic campaign and astute political maneuvering by Missouri's president.

At the close of his second term in the White House, President Truman decided to retire to his white frame home in Independence. As Missouri's leading political figure, he continued to take an active part in political affairs, and his passion for election conflict led him to intervene in conventions and campaigns intermittently throughout his retirement. Harry Truman will be remembered both as an irrepressible politician and as a dedicated statesman whose wise leadership in the field of foreign policy set new and noble precedents in American history. He died December 26, 1972.

The 1940's brought into the light of public favor the Republican Party of Missouri, which had been eclipsed by the Democrats throughout the decade of the New Deal. Missouri voters elected a Republican governor in 1940, and chose a majority of Republican legislators for the General Assembly in 1942, 1944, and 1946. For the first time since the 1870's, Missourians were represented by two Republican senators in Washington from 1947 to 1951.

The hoary old Constitution of 1875, encumbered with sixty-one amendments, was retired by the voters of Missouri. A streamlined charter composed of eighty-three delegates elected from across the state was adopted in 1945.

When their nation was faced with world war for the second time in less than twenty-five years, 450,000 men and women of Missouri donned uniforms to fight for freedom. Missourians such as General Omar Bradley and Donald R. Nelson provided leadership for the armed forces and their civilian suppliers. Missourians at home—in factory and on farm—produced the tremendous volume of materiel necessary to wage global war. And, in the final months of conflict, a Missourian in the White House made the decision to employ a fantastic new weapon which both ended the war and ushered in the atomic age.

BIBLIOGRAPHY

Bradley, Omar N. *A Soldier's Story.* New York: Henry Holt and Company, 1951.

Daniels, Jonathan. *The Man of Independence.* Philadelphia and New York: J. B. Lippincott Company, 1950.

Dysart, Marjorie. "Missouri's Namesakes of the Navy," *Missouri Historical Review,* Vol. L (April, 1956), pp. 225-234.

Gist, Noel P., et al., eds. *Missouri: Its Resources, People and Institutions.* Columbia: The Curators of the University of Missouri, 1950.

Gruber, Bertha, Beatrice Thrapp, Juliet M. Gross, Dorothy Dysart Flynn, and Gerard Schultz. "Missouri and the War," *Missouri Historical Review,* Vol. XXXVII (October, 1942; January, April, July, 1943), pp. 40-56, 169-183, 297-314, 416-429; Vol. XXXVIII (October, 1943; January, April, July, 1944), pp. 44-62, 170-191, 305-324, 430-451; Vol. XXXIX (October, 1944; January, April, July, 1945), pp. 53-74, 200-223, 333-353, 479-504; Vol. XL (October, 1945; January, April, July, 1946), pp. 61-89, 215-244, 358-406, 531-545; Vol. XLI (October, 1946; January, 1947), pp. 56-76, 184-191.

Karsch, Robert F. *The Government of Missouri.* Columbia: Lucas Brothers Publishers, 1961.

Kirschten, Ernest. *Catfish and Crystal.* Garden City, New York: Doubleday and Company, Inc., 1960.

McCandless, Carl C. *Government, Politics, and Administration of the State of Missouri.* St. Louis: Educational Publishers, Inc., 1949.

Milligan, Maurice M., *The Missouri Waltz: the Inside Story of the Pendergast Machine by the Man Who Smashed It.* New York: Charles Scribner's Sons, 1948.

Peltason, Jack Walter. *The Missouri Plan for the Selection of Judges.* Columbia: University of Missouri, 1945.

Reddig, William M. *Tom's Town: Kansas City and the Pendergast Legend.* Philadelphia and New York: J. B. Lippincott Company, 1947.

Schultz, Gerard. *Some Effects of the War on Rural Life in Missouri 1939-1945.* University of Missouri College of Agriculture Bulletin, No. 401 (April, 1946).

Truman, Harry S. *Memoirs.* Vols. I and II. Garden City, New York: Doubleday and Company, Inc., 1955.

Violette, E. M. and F. E. Wolverton. *A History of Missouri.* St. Louis: State Publishing Company, 1955.

Windell, Marie George. "As Benton Sees the War," *Missouri Historical Review,* Vol. XXXIX (July, 1945), pp. 460-467.

CHAPTER XIX

Space-Age Missouri

For the first time in history Americans were able to watch
a French television program as it was being broadcast.
—Springfield *Leader and Press,*
July 12, 1962

The transmission of a program from France directly to
America, where it was carried by Missouri's eighteen television
stations, was a technological first symbolic of the amazing scientific advances of the post-World War II years. This development
was made possible by the July, 1962, orbiting of Telstar—a
three-foot-diameter satellite which picked up television signals
on straight-traveling microwaves and relayed them over the
curve of the earth to receiving stations a hemisphere away.

Once Missourians lived in semi-isolation which encouraged
regional idiosyncrasies. The twentieth-century scientist ended
that isolation. The automobile, radio, airplane, and television
have so stimulated travel and so improved communications that
Missourians learn of world events almost as they happen, and
find their culture losing its distinctiveness as a consequence of
the free flow of information and influence from around the world.

The rise of television made a major impact on many aspects
of society from politics to slang. The movies suffered immediately from the competition. The building which was once a motion
picture theatre in the heart of Camdenton became a grocery
store; other small theatres across the state were converted to
churches or warehouses. Appliance dealers thrived on the market
which developed after Missouri's first station—KSD-TV in St.
Louis—began operations in 1947. Capable of feeding the American people any kind of cultural fare, TV has sometimes gorged
the public with get-rich-quick quizzes, Wild West melodramas,
and gangster gunplay. On the other hand, television has made it

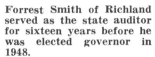

Forrest Smith of Richland served as the state auditor for sixteen years before he was elected governor in 1948.

(Courtesy State Historical Society)

possible for Americans to watch presidential candidates debate, the Metropolitan Opera perform, astronauts blast into space, and Stan Musial hit homeruns. Missourians had always lived on the main street of the Middle West; now they live on the main street of the world.

State Politics

The Republican Party slowly gained strength in Missouri after World War II. In presidential elections Missouri voters gave majority support to Democrats Harry Truman in 1948, John F. Kennedy in 1960, Lyndon Johnson in 1964, and Jimmy Carter in 1976. In contrast to those four Democratic victories, the Republicans won five presidential contests in Missouri—Dwight Eisenhower in 1952 and 1956, Richard Nixon in 1968 and 1972, and Ronald Reagan in 1980. Both houses in the General Assembly were controlled by the Democrats after World War II. Although only one Republican, Christopher S. Bond, served as governor during the period, an increasing number of Republicans—John Danforth, John Ashcroft, William Phelps, and Jim Antonio—were elected to statewide office.

The Smith Administration

In 1948 Forrest Smith was the Democratic candidate for governor of Missouri. In his earlier office as state auditor it had been his happy duty to send out the monthly checks to pensioners of the state. During the campaign in 1948 Smith had the support of organized labor and of several city political bosses. Sheriff Thomas Callanan of St. Louis and Mr. Charles Binaggio of Kansas City were notable leaders in the Smith camp. Binaggio, a former Pendergast associate, had been attempting for several years to win the Democratic leadership of Kansas City from James Pendergast. In 1946, during this struggle for power, an echo of the machine tactics of the 1930's was heard in Kansas City. A *Star* reporter, suspecting voting irregularities, made a private investigation of the balloting. After reviewing his findings, a grand jury indicted several Binaggio associates for vote-fraud conspiracy. Federal prosecution was thwarted in the case when the fraudulent ballots disappeared from the county courthouse where they were being held as evidence.

Newspapers and newsmagazines of the time linked Binaggio's name with the Capone crime syndicate in Chicago and the gambling interests of Missouri. It was reported that Binaggio secured between $100,000 and $200,000 from these groups to help finance Smith's campaign. Politician Binaggio allegedly promised the contributors that Governor Smith would, in return for their financial support, release the stiff state controls over the Kansas City and St. Louis police forces and thus give the gamblers greater freedom. Apparently Binaggio overestimated his influence on the gubernatorial candidate. Forrest Smith was elected governor, but the tight controls that prohibited gambling remained. Binaggio and an associate were found murdered in the headquarters of the First District Democratic Club in Kansas City in April, 1950. Whether his failure to open Kansas City and St. Louis to the underworld or some other gangland grievance cost Mr. Binaggio his life will probably never be known. The murders are still unsolved. The unsavory aspects of the whole situation cast an unfortunate shadow upon Governor Smith, whose term in office was marked with honesty and efficiency.

During Governor Smith's administration several enactments contributed to the development of the Missouri Highway System. In 1951 the gasoline tax was raised from 2¢ to 3¢ per gallon, and larger fees were demanded for the registration of buses and trucks. The next year, the state launched a ten-year building program the goal of which was to make available a state-maintained highway within two miles of ninety-five per cent of the citizens. This ambitious and much-needed plan

greatly enlarged the responsibilities of the State Highway Commission.

Another important development during the Smith administration was the extension of social security benefits to all state
employees.

The census of 1950 revealed that Missouri was growing
less rapidly than certain other states in the Union. As a result,
Missouri lost two more seats in the United States Congress, and
it was necessary to establish new congressional districts in 1951.
In 1950 Forrest C. Donnell's term in the United States Senate
expired. Democratic leaders were unsuccessful in their attempts
to persuade former Governor Phil M. Donnelly to oppose Donnell.
Thomas C. Hennings, Jr. of St. Louis became the Democratic
candidate who defeated Republican Donnell in his 1950 bid to
retain the Senate seat.

The Donnelly Administration

In 1952, at the close of President Harry Truman's term,
the American people were restless. The Korean War, the high
cost of living, the revelations of corruption in certain Federal
Government agencies, all worked to the advantage of the Republican Party. Another advantage the Republicans enjoyed
was the popularity of their nominee Dwight D. Eisenhower,

who had gained the gratitude of his countrymen for his part in bringing the European war to a successful conclusion. In the election of 1952, presidential candidate Eisenhower received the votes of the people of Missouri, but the major state offices were won by Democrats.

Phil M. Donnelly of Lebanon ran for a second term as governor in 1952. During the campaign, organized labor was angry with the Democratic Party because Donnelly, during his first term as governor, had supported the King-Thompson Utilities Anti-Strike Law. In fact, when the proposal was considered during his first administration, Donnelly had spoken to the legislature demanding that penalty provisions be placed in the law to punish strikers who defied it. Although Donnelly did not receive labor's support, he was sufficiently popular in the state to win without their assistance.

The race for United States senator from Missouri was most interesting in 1952. Incumbent Senator James P. Kem of Kansas City was a conservative man with isolationist leanings. The two contenders for the Democratic nomination were Missouri Attorney General J. E. Taylor and Stuart Symington. President Truman, during his first term, had appointed Symington to various government positions: surplus property administrator, assistant secretary of war, secretary of the air force, and director of the National Securities Resources Board and the Reconstruction Finance Corporation. After the beginning of the Korean War, however, there was some difference of opinion between Symington and President Truman regarding the speed with which the United States should mobilize its war production. By 1952, when he announced his candidacy for the Senate, Symington's popularity with the president had waned. His opponent, Attorney General Taylor, had the support of Kansas City Democratic leaders and the blessings of President Truman as well. Stuart Symington's whirlwind campaign tour reached all areas of the state and won for him a two to one margin over Taylor. In the November election, Symington defeated Republican Kem, this time with the support of President Truman.

Governor Donnelly served his second term from 1953 to 1957. Donnelly had already demonstrated his independence and his willingness to take a stand on issues even when his position was unpopular with a major segment of the population. During his first administration, Donnelly offended organized labor. Dur-

Since he had served in the executive branch under President Truman from 1945 to 1952, Stuart Symington was no stranger to the Washington, D. C., scene when he was elected to represent Missouri in the United States Senate in 1952.

(Courtesy State Historical Society)

ing his second administration, he alienated the school teachers of Missouri. In 1953 he vetoed a state law allocating $9,000,000 to the public schools of the state, because he declared the act was illegal. The Missouri State Teachers Association and several school districts challenged Donnelly's veto of the school appropriations as unconstitutional. Their efforts were defeated when the supreme court refused to hear the appeal.

There were several significant acts passed during the second Donnelly administration. The state reorganization commission was appointed to examine and to recommend changes in the state government. This committee, known as the "Little Hoover Commission," operated under the leadership of former Governor Lloyd C. Stark. The state park board was created during the term, and the state of Missouri began to receive new grants of federal money for the construction of state highways. The two most significant developments were, first of all, the establishment of the school foundation program which was adopted by the citizenry in a referendum in 1955. A 2¢ per pack increase in the state cigarette tax was earmarked for education. This was a major step forward in securing more money for the public schools. A second major advance under Governor Donnelly occurred in 1956 when the citizens of Missouri voted $75,000,000

James T. Blair, Jr., the son of a Missouri Supreme Court justice, served as governor from 1957 to 1961.
(Courtesy State Historical Society)

in bonds to be used to construct new buildings at the state universities, colleges, and penal and eleemosynary institutions.

Perhaps it should be noted here that "The Missouri Waltz" became the official song of the state in 1949 during the Smith administration, and the flowering dogwood was adopted as the official tree of the state in 1955.

The Blair Administration

In 1956 the Democratic nominee for governor was James T. Blair, Jr., of Jefferson City. Blair, the son of a supreme court judge, had acted as city attorney and as mayor of Jefferson City, and had served two terms as the lieutenant-governor of the state. During World War II, Air Force Lieutenant Colonel Blair was decorated several times for meritorious service. After his election, the governor surprised the people of the state by refusing to move into the executive mansion, which was badly in need of remodeling. Blair's successful insistence on the improvement of the mansion led to the following poem set to a tune which was popular at the time:

> This old house is full of spiders,
> This old house is full of rats,
> This old house ain't fit for entertaining
> Good old Democrats.

This old mansion is in tatters,
This old place needs lots of work,
If I'd have known it last November
I'd have run for county clerk.

The administration of Governor Blair was a time of some reorganization in Jefferson City. Governor Blair was highly critical of the procedures employed to create a budget, and he felt that he could not, on the basis of the information available to him, request a budget for the biennium. Therefore, he asked the legislature to appropriate money for one year of state expenses. In the meantime, he secured permission to establish a budget office under the direct supervision of the governor. When the legislature met in 1959, Blair presented a more detailed budget which he felt correctly interpreted the needs of the state.

During Blair's administration, record budgets were approved by the General Assembly. In 1959, the legislature levied a new two per cent use tax on items purchased outside Missouri, but the state lost this source of revenue when the tax was ruled unconstitutional the following year. Governor Blair, who was very much interested in the state mental health program, was able to secure money for improvements in that department. In 1960, the citizens of Missouri adopted an amendment to the constitution giving the legislators the right to set their own salaries. This act made possible the raising of the scandalously low salaries of the legislators. In 1960 Senator Thomas C. Hennings, Jr. died in office, and Governor Blair named Lieutenant-Governor Edward V. Long to complete the term. Two years later, on July 12, 1962, the people of Missouri were shocked by the news that retired Governor and Mrs. Blair had been the victims of lethal carbon monoxide fumes accidentally blown into their Jefferson City home from the exhaust of a car in the attached garage.

The Dalton Administration

In 1952 and 1956 Missourians had supported Eisenhower, but Democrat John F. Kennedy carried the state by 10,000 votes in 1960. In the same race, Edward Long was elected for a full term in the Senate and John M. Dalton was selected as governor. The only important Democratic loss in the election was one congressional seat in southwest Missouri.

Governor John M. Dalton was born in Vernon County in western Missouri, was educated in Boone County, and practiced law in Dunklin County after graduation from the University of Missouri. He was chosen as the attorney general of Missouri in 1952, re-elected in 1956, and advanced to the governor's chair in 1960.

Governor Dalton came to the chief post of responsibility in Missouri at a time when the state needed new sources of revenue. His administration was in much the same circumstances as that of Governor Gardner in 1916. Gardner's predecessors had established many fine new programs, but had failed to provide sufficient funds to finance these innovations. Like Governor Gardner, Governor Dalton was forced to go to the legislature to request new tax monies to maintain necessary state service.

The Missouri General Assembly appears to have been impressed with the efficiency, honesty, and equity of the new budget division as reorganized under Governor Blair. The subsequent budgets were only moderately trimmed by the legislature, despite the fact that both Governor Blair and Governor Dalton presented record high budgets. The General Assembly approved Governor Dalton's budget of $1,267,359,623 presented in 1961. To provide such funds, the legislature had to pass new taxes. The two per cent use tax was re-authorized, with a few changes to insure its constitutionality. Liquor taxes were raised fifty per cent. Cigarette taxes were raised from 2¢ to 4¢ per pack. Gasoline taxes were elevated from 3¢ to 5¢ per gallon with 1¢ of the increase allocated for state highway development and the other cent allotted to the cities and counties. The governor secured the passage of another controversial measure which established the withholding system for the collection of income taxes. The schools of the state benefited from a generous increase in aid, which was boosted from $185 to $321 per pupil per year.

A point system for automobile drivers' licenses was established to encourage responsible driving and to reduce the toll of traffic accidents. The legislature also passed a new fair employment practices act which set up a commission to hear grievances in cases involving discrimination in hiring. The fair employment practices commission was given authority to go to the courts to force companies hiring fifty or more people to end discriminatory practices. Another important enactment of

John M. Dalton of Dunklin County served two terms as Missouri's attorney general before he was elected governor in 1960.
(Courtesy State Historical Society)

the General Assembly occurred when the salaries of legislators were boosted from $1500 to $4800 per year. Although there were cries in the state that the legislators were engaging in a salary grab, this increase in salary may well encourage and enable a larger number of qualified Missourians to run for the legislature, thereby improving the quality of government over the years. Finally, the state's congressional districts were revamped, since Missouri's lagging population increase, as revealed in the census of 1960, had the effect of reducing her congressional delegation from eleven to ten.

The Hearnes Administration

After a bitter battle within the party for the gubernatorial nomination, the Democrats won an easy victory in Missouri in the 1964 general election. In the primary, Lieutenant Governor Hilary A. Bush was supported for the governorship by Governor John Dalton and the political leaders who had helped elect Dalton. Secretary of State Warren E. Hearnes was the gubernatorial choice of the St. Louis party heads. Dubbing the traditional leaders of the party as the Establishment, Hearnes carried on a vigorous campaign and finally secured the Democratic nomination. In November, Hearnes easily defeated Republican Ethan

Warren E. Hearnes was elected governor in 1964 after having previously served as the Secretary of State.

Shepley, former chancellor of Washington University, for the governorship.

In other races in 1964 Democratic candidates were elected to all the major state offices. Senator Stuart Symington, the incumbent, defeated Jean Paul Bradshaw, the Republican challenger. Both houses of the legislature again received heavy democratic majorities. In Missouri, President Lyndon Johnson crushed Republican presidential candidate Barry Goldwater by a vote of 1,164,344 to 653,535.

When Warren E. Hearnes, a forty-one-year-old native of Charleston, took the oath of office on January 11, 1965, he was the youngest governor in fifty-six years. Because of the split within his party Hearnes faced a difficult situation. In spite of the wounds remaining from the 1964 primary, the Democratically controlled legislature cooperated with the governor on most matters. The 73rd General Assembly passed (1) a public accommodations bill outlawing racial discrimination in resorts, hotels, restaurants, and public places; (2) an authorization for the establishment of nine new centers for the training and treatment of the mentally retarded; (3) a measure providing for the establishment of state-supported four-year colleges at Joplin and St. Joseph to be known as Missouri Southern College and Missouri Western College; (4) an authorization for a mandatory chemical test for drivers suspected of intoxication; and (5) a constitutional amendment permitting a governor to succeed himself—this constitutional change subsequently was ratified by the voters.

In the election of 1966 the Democrats easily retained control of state government. However, the election of 1968 produced several Republican surprises. Richard M. Nixon, the Republican candidate for president, carried the state by 20,000 votes. Another Republican, John P. Danforth, won the Attorney General's office. In the 1968 race of the U. S. Senate, Thomas F. Eagleton defeated two other Democrats, Edward V. Long (incumbent) and True Davis. Warren E. Hearnes was the first governor to be elected to a second consecutive four-year term since John Miller was re-elected in 1828.

During his second term Governor Hearnes found it more difficult to secure the legislation which he requested. He did receive permission from the General Assembly to build toll roads, but the project was dropped because of constitutional problems. Other enactments were the passage of bills increasing welfare payments, the providing of medical insurance for older citizens, the establishment of new congressional districts, the requiring of a safety inspection for all motor vehicles, and the authorization of increased funds for the public schools and for public higher education. Governor Hearnes' administration greatly increased spending for welfare, for protecting the environment, and for education, although it was a time when state funds were scarce.

The beginning of a Republican resurgence in Missouri occurred in 1970. In the election that year, John P. Danforth, the Republican Attorney General, nearly captured the Missouri seat in the U. S. Senate. The incumbent, Senator Stuart Symington, retained his post by only a 37,000 vote margin. Another example of Republican popularity was the victory of Christopher S. "Kit" Bond, one of Danforth's close associates, over Haskell Holman in the State Auditor's race.

The First Bond Administration

In 1972, Republican State Auditor Christopher S. Bond became the youngest governor in the history of the state upon his election to that post at the age of 33. In the preliminaries to that same election, Missouri Senator Thomas F. Eagleton was selected

Christopher S. "Kit" Bond of Mexico was elected governor twice, in 1972 and 1980. Only thirty-three years old when he first became governor, he holds the record as the youngest chief executive in the history of the state.

as the Democratic candidate for vice president of the United States on the recommendation of the presidential candidate, George McGovern. Public pressure for his withdrawal developed after it was revealed that on three occasions he had received psychiatric treatment for exhaustion and depression, and Senator Eagleton resigned from the ticket only nineteen days after his selection.

The reorganization of the executive branch of the government, authorized by a statewide vote in 1972, was accomplished during the Bond administration. Under the new plan, 45,000 state employees are responsible to seven directors or seven commissions, who in turn report to the governor. It was the first comprehensive executive department reorganization in the history of the state.

Legislation enacted during the first Bond administration abolished the personal property tax on household goods, raised installment rates to ten percent, and established a mandatory three year term for persons convicted of a felony carried out with a gun. There were annual unsuccessful attempts to pass the Equal Rights Amendment, which was supported by Governor Bond. Proponents of the amendment were unable to generate sufficient support in the Senate to secure passage. Another area of impasse was the failure of the executive and legislative branches to agree on the location of a medium security prison. Democratic majorities controlled both House and Senate throughout Governor Bond's first term.

The state purchased the Wainwright Building in St. Louis in 1973. The historically important eighty-two-year-old structure was designed by noted American architect Louis Sullivan and was considered to be the first American skyscraper. The building was remodeled to serve as a state office building. After the death of artist Thomas Hart Benton in 1975, the state purchased his home and studio in Kansas City and has since maintained it as a state historical site.

The construction industry was active in the two largest urban centers of the state; the Convention Center in St. Louis and the H. Roe Bartle Exposition Center, Hallmark's Crown Center and the Truman Sports Complex in Kansas City were among the largest projects built during this period.

In August, 1976, for the first time in forty-eight years, the Republican Party held its national party convention in Kansas City, bringing national publicity and $8,000,000 in gross revenues to the city.

In 1975-76 the people of Missouri, in a campaign personally encouraged and supported by Governor Bond, contributed $1,800,000 in private gifts to purchase 112 George Caleb Bingham

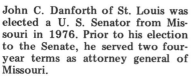

John C. Danforth of St. Louis was elected a U. S. Senator from Missouri in 1976. Prior to his election to the Senate, he served two four-year terms as attorney general of Missouri.

Joseph P. Teasdale of Kansas City was the prosecuting attorney for Jackson County before he began campaigning for the governor's post. He was elected governor in November, 1976.
(Jim Salyer, Southwest Missouri State University)

sketches. The collection of drawings by Missouri's famous nineteenth-century artist was being sold by the St. Louis Mercantile Library, and the purchase was made to keep them in the state.

The Teasdale Administration

Joseph P. Teasdale of Kansas City defeated incumbent Governor Christopher S. Bond in the November, 1976, election. Teasdale, who had earned the title "Walking Joe" by hiking across the state in an earlier unsuccessful effort to earn the Democratic nomination, carried on a vigorous campaign. Interestingly, the Republican lieutenant governor, William C. Phelps, was reelected. The competitive and distrustful relationship that developed between the governor and the lieutenant governor made Governor Teasdale reluctant to leave the state, and he did so seldom during his four year term.

Major legislative items enacted during Governor Teasdale's administration were the general revision of the state criminal code in 1977 and the streamlining of the probate code in 1980. Other significant pieces of legislation included the new death penalty law in 1977, the campaign contributions disclosure law in 1978, the repeal of the sales tax on prescribed drugs in 1978, the law regulating the generation and storage of hazardous chemicals in 1980, and the elimination of the state inheritance tax in 1980.

An accomplishment of the executive branch of the state government was the location of a new medium security prison. After years of controversy over the choice of a site, Eureka, near St. Louis, was chosen as the location of the new facility.

A major issue in Governor Teasdale's gubernatorial campaign was the operation of the Missouri Public Service Commission. Throughout his term he unsuccessfully called on the legislature to pass laws further restricting the PSC. By 1979, the governor had named all of the members of the PSC, including the controversial chairman Alberta Slavins. The most criticized decision of the PSC occurred in 1980 when it held that the Kansas City Power and Light Company could not add $164,000,000 to its rate base in order to pay for the new Iatan power plant.

The Equal Rights Amendment was considered and voted down at each meeting of the General Assembly during the Teasdale term. The legislature also refused the governor's annual request to increase taxes on corporations.

An attempt to secure approval of a state right-to-work law led to a referendum in 1978. Unions mounted a successful drive to defeat the law.

Open forum meetings initiated by Governor Teasdale were held in many communities across the state. The "Meet the

Thomas F. Eagleton, who was first elected to the U. S. Senate in 1968, previously had served terms as the attorney general and the lieutenant governor of Missouri.

Governor" sessions, as they were known, provided an opportunity for dialogue between citizens and state officials and were well received by the participants.

Two events during the Teasdale years marked a departure from earlier federal planning. In 1977 the federal government announced abandonment of plans to construct a new airport for the St. Louis area on the Illinois side of the river. This meant that Lambert Field was destined to continue as the main airport for the area. The other development was the abandonment of federal plans in 1977 to dam the Meramec River. The project had long been a center of controversy in the state.

Two trials were of particular interest in Missouri during the Teasdale years. In 1977 former Speaker of the House Richard J. Rabbitt was convicted of mail fraud and extortion and given a sentence of seven years in prison. The eleven month trial of five officials of the Progressive Farmers Association ended in 1980 with the conviction of the men for fraud and other illegal acts. It was estimated that 7000 investors had been defrauded of nearly $13,000,000.

In 1977 federal authorities announced that 3700 military and civilian personnel would be moved from Richards-Gebaur Air Force Base near Kansas City to Scott Air Base near Belleville, Illinois. The move was a blow to the economy of the area. But the decision of General Motors in 1980 to renovate their plant in the Kansas City area was a significant economic boon. This was particularly true because certain older plants in the country were being abandoned at that time. General Motors that same year announced that their St. Louis plant would be phased out and replaced by a new facility to be constructed near St. Louis.

Two tragedies of unusual proportion occurred during this period. In September, 1977, in Kansas City, twenty-four people drowned in flooding which resulted when twelve inches of rain fell in twenty-four hours. And twenty-five aged and mentally handicapped residents of Farmington's Wayside Inn lost their lives in an April 2, 1979, fire. The sudden collapse of the roof of the Kemper Arena during a storm in 1979 could have been a human disaster of immense proportion had a crowd been in the structure. Fortunately, the building was unoccupied and no injuries occurred.

The Second Bond Administration

The election of 1980 was a disappointing one for many in-

The Wainwright Building, designed in the 1890's by the great architectural pioneer, Louis Henry Sullivan (1856-1924), has been cited as the first American skyscraper. It was purchased by the state in 1973 to serve as an office building. *(Nick Decker-Missouri Department of Natural Resources)*

cumbents. Governor Teasdale lost to a hard-campaigning Christopher Bond who was determined to regain his post. Missouri followed the nation and chose Ronald Reagan over incumbent Jimmy Carter for the presidency. Senator Tom Eagleton was reelected, but Lieutenant Governor William Phelps lost his post to former Democratic Speaker of the House Kenneth Rothman. Once again, the governor and lieutenant governor were of different parties. The national trend toward the Republicans could be seen in the results of the Congressional elections, in which Republicans won four of the ten seats. Also reflecting the conservative trend, Missouri voters approved a state spending limitation proposal which was promoted by Mel Hancock of Springfield and his Taxpayers Survival Association.

Christopher S. Bond began his second term as Governor of the State of Missouri in January, 1981. He announced to the legislature and to the citizens of the state that Missouri was desperately near depletion of its financial resources. The new governor called for immediate spending cutbacks on the part of almost all state departments and agencies, and announced to the General Assembly that he could only recommend "standstill" budgets for state programs for the coming 1981-82 fiscal year.

Although both houses of the 81st General Assembly were controlled by Democratic majorities, the legislature gave strong support to the Republican governor as he attempted to steer the state through a difficult financial situation. When the General Assembly session ended in June, the House and Senate had agreed to appropriations which were very close to the recommendation made originally by the governor in January. There was a remarkable spirit of cooperation between the Republican governor and the Democratic legislature during the session.

The legislative accomplishments of the regular session of the General Assembly in 1981 include many important bills. Medicaid provisions were revised to reduce state expenditures for medical care for the poor. A Missouri Higher Education Loan Authority was established to issue tax exempt revenue bonds for student loans. The state professional licensing board regulations were completely revised. A bill passed providing compensation up to $10,000 to crime victims. All of these measures had been recommended by Governor Bond. The legislature also adopted a bill to implement the legalization of bingo for charitable purposes and one to extend the maximum weights and lengths of trucks on Missouri highways.

The regular session of the legislature was unable to come to an agreement on three major matters. First, they were unable to agree on the composition of the nine congressional districts necessitated by the population decline revealed in the 1980 census. Second, the legislature failed to provide additional tax support for education in the state. Third, the General Assembly did not pass a bill to provide additional funds to support the ailing highway system.

Agriculture

In the twentieth century there has been a growing concern over the depletion of Missouri soil resources, and increasing attempts to conserve or restore the fertility of the land. In the 1920's the University of Missouri Extension Service promoted "Clover and Prosperity". Since that time, the Extension Service has instructed farmers in crop rotation, legume planting, terracing and contour farming, use of improved seeds and plant varieties, farm pond and irrigation system construction, insecticide and herbicide application, the use of commercial fertilizers, and the "no-till" farming system for row crops.

The basic agricultural problem of contemporary Missouri and America has been the same for the past half-century. The small farmer has been caught between increasing living and production costs and a stable or sometimes decreasing income from the sale of commodities. Through greater mechanization, the large operator has been able to reduce the cost of production per agricultural unit. Thus, he has survived and often prospered, while the small farmer, with neither the large land resources nor the money to mechanize, has found himself in difficulty. As a result, many farmers have either deserted their homesteads for city life, or have continued to live on the farm while taking jobs in nearby towns and cities.

Census returns document the continuing decline of population in the most productive row crop farming areas of the state—the Bootheel and the farm counties north of the Missouri River. At the same time, farms in these areas have decreased in number and increased in size. In 1950 there were 258,000 farms in Missouri; by 1974, the number had shrunk to 116,000. On the other hand, the average size of a Missouri farm increased from 119 acres in 1900 to 169 acres in 1955 and 258 acres in 1974.

It should be noted that the type of agriculture practiced in the Ozarks often varies from that in the rest of the state. Where the growing of row crops is the most common activity in other areas, in the Ozarks, beef cattle, feeder pig, and poultry production, dairying, and fruit raising are most frequently emphasized. The development and planting of fescue grass in the Ozarks in the past half-century has particularly aided dairy and beef farmers.

One of the characteristics of Missouri agriculture has been the prominence of farmer cooperatives. The Missouri Farmers Association, which is usually known by its acronym MFA, has operated marketing programs, grain storage facilities, grocery stores, feed mills, gas and oil distribution programs, and many other services through the cooperative exchanges situated in all parts of the state. Another cooperative with strong national ties— the Farm Bureau—has provided similar services for farmers. In the November, 1980, election, the Farm Bureau played a major role in supporting the proposed amendment to the Missouri Constitution limiting state spending, which was approved by the voters of the state.

One aspect of agriculture which changed drastically in the post-World War II years was the value of land. For the decade from 1970 to 1980, it is estimated that farmland values in Missouri rose 264 percent. This average annual increase of 26.4 percent compares to a national average of 13 percent. Probably Missouri prices have increased more than the national average because the prices were so low compared to those in other states in 1970.

In summary, the expense of mechanization and the need for large volume production in an age of inflation will probably force additional tenant farmers and small farmers to leave their rural homes. The movement of the surplus rural population to urban and suburban areas need not be an unfortunate development, however, if sufficient jobs and housing are available for the new urbanites.

Population

The 1980 census returns for Missouri showed a head count of 4,917,444, a 5.1 percent increase over the 1970 total. This increase was less than half the 11.4 percent population growth of the nation during the same decade. Missouri continued to gain population in the twentieth century, but not as rapidly as other states. In 1900 Missouri ranked fifth in population in the nation; in 1960 it was thirteenth. The 1980 census showed a drop to fifteenth place as Georgia and Virginia overtook Missouri. The growth or decline of population in cities of 20,000 or more during the last decade is shown below.

Cities of 20,000 or More	Population 1980	Increase/Decrease over Preceding Census
Blue Springs	25,927	+ 282.5
Cape Girardeau	34,361	+ 9.8
Columbia	62,061	+ 5.5
Ferguson	24,740	- 14.0
Florissant	55,372	- 16.0
Gladstone	24,990	+ 6.7
Grandview	24,502	+ 40.4
Independence	111,806	+ 0.2
Jefferson City	33,619	+ 3.7
Joplin	38,893	- 0.9
Kansas City	448,159	- 11.7
Lee's Summit	28,741	+ 77.1
Raytown	31,759	- 4.6
St. Charles	37,379	+ 17.4
St. Joseph	76,691	+ 5.4
St. Louis	453,085	- 27.2
Sedalia	20,927	- 8.4
Springfield	133,116	+ 10.8
University City	42,738	- 10.1
Webster Groves	23,097	- 15.9

Population of Missouri by Counties in 1980

The upper figure represents 1980 population; the lower figure indicates percentage of gain or loss since the 1970 census. Shaded areas denote counties which declined in population between 1970 and 1980.

Notice that the two major urban centers, St. Louis and Kansas City, experienced significant population declines of 27.2 and 11.7 percent respectively. The farm counties in northwest Missouri and the Bootheel counties along the Mississippi River continued to lose residents. The dip in population in Pulaski County was a result of a decline in military personnel at Fort Leonard Wood. St. Louis residents seemed to be moving to suburban locations in St. Charles County, Franklin County, Warren County, and Jefferson County. In the Kansas City area, such neighboring cities as Blue Springs, Grandview and Lee's Summit had vigorous growth in the seventies. The general area of the Ozarks experienced an increase in population. This was particularly true near the lakes in the central and southwest part of the state. Such cities as Springfield, Columbia, Jefferson City and Cape Girardeau also registered strong growth.

The failure of the Missouri population to grow as rapidly as many of the other states has led to a decrease of representation in the United States House of Representatives. In 1950 Missouri dropped from twelve to eleven congressional districts. In 1960 the state was cut to ten representatives. In 1980 the census returns reduced the state to only nine congressional districts.

The population of the state was becoming older. When federal government officials studied age distribution in 1971 and 1979, they discovered a 13.9 percent decrease during the period in Missouri citizens age five to seventeen years. On the other hand, their study revealed that the age group sixty-five years and over had increased in numbers 10.5 percent in the same time span. Another population statistic regarding St. Louis shows a dramatic change in the years since World War II. The black population of St. Louis climbed from 13.4 percent in 1940 to 45.5 percent in 1980. In the same four decades the percent of black citizens in Kansas City increased from 10.4 percent to 27.4 percent.

Commerce and Industry

In 1979 the Missouri Division of Commerce and Industrial Development announced that during the calendar year 1978 seventy-one new industrial plants were constructed in the state and seventy-eight companies expanded their manufacturing facilities. These facilities provided 12,049 additional jobs for Missourians. This industrial growth in 1978 was typical of the industrial expansion of the post-World War II years. The trend was toward

A view of one of the first—and richest—deep shafts sunk in the Bonne Terre district
(St. Joseph Lead Company, Bonne Terre, Missour)

suburban plant locations where workers could live away from big city problems if they so desired. The larger new companies, however, requiring a larger work force, usually preferred a location in or near one of the four major industrial areas of the state—the city or environs of St. Louis, Kansas City, Springfield or St. Joseph. Smaller companies were more likely to establish themselves in out-state cities.

State officials along with local chamber of commerce staff members labored diligently to attract new industries and investment money to the state. In 1977 the state of Missouri even opened an office in Duesseldorf, West Germany, to seek foreign investments in Missouri, as well as to promote Missouri tourism and the export of Missouri products.

Since the earliest French settlers came to the area, Missouri has been important as a mining center. Ste. Genevieve, the first settlement, was established in ⅃735 because of its close proximity to the lead mines, and the so-⸱alled Lead Belt area has been mined ever since. Missouri's largest lᵣad mining concern is the St. Joseph Lead Company, which has operated continuously since 1864. Two of the company's newer mines are the Indian Creek Mine eleven miles north of Potosi and the one at Viburnum in northwest Iron County. Missouri has been first in America in the production of lead since 1906.

Mining of various minerals constitutes a major economic activity in many communities in the state. Seventeen counties

The Pony Express Stables in St. Joseph was the eastern base for the Pony Express, which in 1860 carried mail on horseback to California 1982 miles away.
(Walker-Missouri Tourism)

produce bituminous coal—ninety-six percent of which is removed by strip mining and the remainder by tunneling. Zinc production has declined sharply, but the metal is still mined in the southwestern region. Missouri is an important producer of Portland cement, with a heavy concentration of plants near Kansas City and St. Louis. Such other natural deposits as lime, silica sand, building stone, and fire clay continue to provide materials for processing and sale by Missouri companies.

A new interest in mining developed in the early 1960's with the opening of the huge iron mine at Pea Ridge near Sullivan. The Meramec Mining Company, owned jointly by the St. Joseph Lead Company and the Bethlehem Steel Company, is in charge of extracting the high-grade magnetic iron ore. The deposit is sufficiently extensive to support mining operations twenty-five years or longer.

Other less tangible resources have provided the basis for a flourishing tourism, the third-largest industry in the state. The lush beauty of her forested hills, bluff-cradled clear streams, blue lakes, churning springs, and crystal-decked caves draw floaters, boaters, fishermen, and nature-lovers. Historic sites, such as those at Hannibal, Arrow Rock, Fort Osage, Ste. Genevieve, and, of course, Kansas City and St. Louis, attract crowds of tourists yearly. Commercial enterprises such as Silver Dollar City near Branson, Six Flags over Mid-America near St. Louis, and Worlds of Fun at Kansas City, capitalizing on the throngs of vacationers, serve hundreds of thousands of fun seekers each year.

Arrow Rock Tavern, an important hotel and meeting place in the first half of the nineteenth century, was made a part of the state park system in 1926. Arrow Rock was the location of a ferry which crossed the Missouri River in mid-state.
(Walker-Missouri Tourism)

The state has also become known for the production of such items as automobiles—Missouri is second only to Michigan in auto production—soap, chemicals, electronic equipment, lawn mowers, and thousands of other items. In addition to these new products, Missouri plants continue to export and process many of the products associated with the state in the last century. Shoes, beer, drugs, electrical equipment, and chemicals are still important products of St. Louis industry. St. Joseph still exports meat and acts as the wholesale distributor for northwest Missouri and areas of the surrounding states. Kansas City remains the wheat market, milling, and packing center for much of the Great Plains. Kansas Citians are also employed in petroleum refineries, greeting card printing companies, car and truck assembly plants, clothing factories, and a wide variety of other industrial enterprises. Springfield, which is located in the chief dairy area of the state, has its huge milk and cheese-processing plants, as well as newer flourishing industries producing television sets, paper cups, and rubber belts.

Missouri and Missourians played an important part in the early development of balloons, aircraft, and spacecraft. Shortly after the turn of the century, in 1907 and 1909, the St. Louis Aero Club held meets to encourage interest in aircraft and to give aircraft enthusiasts an opportunity to race their frail vehicles and to do a little "ground flying", as early airmen referred to the swapping of flight experiences. The success of Charles Lindbergh's trans-Atlantic flight in 1927 greatly stimulated interest in aviation in

Missouri, and many airports were constructed during the 1930's. Another development during the thirties was the establishment of air service between the chief cities of the state. The airlines were stimulated by the war effort in the 1940's and achieved new popularity after the war had ended.

In contrast to lead mining, one of the state's earliest industries, is the manufacture of airplanes and spacecraft, one of the latest industrial developments in Missouri. During the last half of the 1950's, the cold war with Russia resulted in a technological competition which extended to outer space. The great emphasis which the Russians placed on the development of space science led the United States to adopt a similar crash program. In the production of vehicles for space travel, two Missouri plants made outstanding contributions—Rocketdyne (a division of North American Aviation, Inc.) in Neosho and the McDonnell Aircraft Corporation of St. Louis.

The McDonnell Aircraft Corporation experienced phenomenal growth. Organized in 1939 by J. S. McDonnell with only two employees, the corporation grew until in 1962 it was the largest private employer in Missouri. Among the better known McDonnell aircraft are the Phantom, the Banshee, the Demon, the Voodoo, and the F15 and F16. The F4H-1, known as the Phantom II, won the Bendix trophy in 1961 for a 170-minute coast-to-coast flight. This set the world's absolute speed record, up to that time, of 1,606.3 miles per hour.

In January, 1959, McDonnell was selected to build twelve spacecraft for the National Aeronautics and Space Agency. Later, eight additional spacecraft were ordered. Thirty-seven months after

A Marine helicopter fishes a Mercury capsule from the ocean. In a similar capsule—named Friendship 7—Colonel John Glenn orbited the earth three times on February 20, 1962. Designed and produced by McDonnell Aircraft Corporation of St. Louis, the Mercury capsule is one of Missouri's spaceage developments.
(Courtesy McDonnell Aircraft Corporation)

The liquid propellant engines built by Rocketdyne at Neosho provided the power for many of America's early space ventures.
(Courtesy Rocketdyne-a Division of North American Aviation, Inc.)

the St. Louis company had received the project, America's first manned and orbital flight occurred in a Mercury spacecraft designed and manufactured by McDonnell. Colonel John Glenn was the first American astronaut to be placed in orbit around the earth, although Commander Alan B. Shepard and Captain Virgil I. Grissom had earlier been carried on sub-orbital flights in the McDonnell capsule. On November 7, 1961, the government began negotiations with McDonnell for a spacecraft known as Project Gemini, designed to allow two men to orbit the earth for a week or more. Ultimately, McDonnell built all of the Gemini space capsules.

In 1967 McDonnell merged with Douglas, another airplane manufacturer, to form McDonnell Douglas Aircraft Corporation. Headquarters were maintained in St. Louis. The newly-formed corporation continued to play an important role in the space program and contributed to the Apollo team effort that placed the first man on the moon. McDonnell Douglas is also deeply involved in two of the most important new space exploration programs: America's Space Shuttle and Europe's Spacelab. In addition to space-related products, the corporation develops and manufactures a wide variety of equipment from military and commercial aircraft to a ten-megawatt solar power tower and computerized health care services.

Just as Missouri was a base for such explorers as Lewis and Clark or Zebulon Pike, the state has had a new opportunity to assist in a different kind of exploration. A little over a century ago, Missouri built wagons for the migrants who opened the West; today she is producing vehicles for pioneers in the frontier of space.

Inflation menaced all segments of the economy in the 1970's. The shrinking dollar evoked new wage demands which, coupled with rising production costs, led to strained labor-management relationships. Major strikes by such unions as the construction workers, teachers, and firefighters occurred in the Kansas City area in 1970, 1972, 1974, 1978, and 1980. A 1970 strike of the St. Louis area teamsters hurt the economy of that region. In 1978 business leaders in the state asked citizens to vote on a "right-to-work" proposal, which would have had the effect of discouraging union membership. The citizens of Missouri decisively defeated that proposal.

The growth of commerce and industry in Missouri was a great boon to the state in the years following World War II; but it also created problems. In 1980, the deadly chemical dioxin, the by-product of an industrial process, was discovered in a waste site on a farm in Lawrence County. This discovery and other similar concerns led Governor Teasdale to call a special session of the legislature that year to pass legislation regulating the disposal of hazardous industrial wastes and radioactive materials.

Education

Elementary and Secondary Education

In 1940 Missouri had 3,784,664 residents. The census taken in 1980 showed that the population had grown to 4,917,444. Since this population growth was primarily the result of the high birth rate after World War II, many new schools were necessary during the first two decades of the period. For example, Springfield was a rapidly growing community which had a 43.7 percent surge in population in the 1950's. The Springfield School System built nine new elementary schools, one junior high school, and three senior high schools in the nine years from 1953 to 1962. The obvious need for more school facilities led most Missouri communities to vote large bond issues to finance the projects during the 1950's and 1960's. But the growth rate of the school age population was not constant throughout the forty-year period, and the need for schools varied widely. In the 1970's the drop in elementary age students led school districts in the St. Louis area to sell some of their school buildings.

During the post-World War II years there was an increase in the consolidation of school districts in the rural areas. This formation of larger districts eliminated duplication of effort and expense

The new Lake Area Vocational-Technical School at Camdenton, constructed and equipped at a cost of $2.5 million, was opened March 29, 1981.
(Courtesy Dr. John Bearden-Camdenton R-III Schools)

and allowed better facilities and more specialized training than could be afforded by small rural schools. The one-room schoolhouse where ten children in eight grades were taught by one teacher largely disappeared. Critics of Missouri education charged that reorganization had not been effected rapidly enough; nevertheless, Missouri's school districts steadily became fewer and larger. While the number of school districts decreased, the number of elementary and secondary students in the public schools grew from 772,000 in 1958 to 845,000 in 1961, to 945,000 in 1980.

The schools constructed in post-World War II Missouri were vastly different from those in which young people studied fifty years earlier. Modern architecture of simple lines and easily-maintained materials were most often chosen by school planners. Aside from being better suited to the communities of contemporary homes in which they were built, schools of this modern design were more rapidly and economically constructed than the more elaborate traditional types.

The equipment provided in these schools is vastly superior to that available a half-century ago. Non-glare black or green writing boards; large well-placed lighting fixtures; desks, tables, and chairs scientifically designed and scaled to accommodate comfortably children of various age groups; all reduce fatigue and strain. Visual aids such as slide and movie projectors and classroom television sets provide opportunities to see history in the making, to learn from master teachers, and to enjoy the most honored artists. Attractive and interesting textbooks and workbooks have replaced the drabber materials of yesteryear; and pocket calculators have led to many changes in the teaching of mathematics, accounting, and the sciences.

Most Missouri schools were segregated until the 1950's. In fact, the Constitution of 1945 declared, "Separate schools shall be provided for white and colored children. . ." In 1952, before the Supreme Court handed down its historic decision, Archbishop Ritter of St. Louis desegregated the Catholic schools. In 1954 the United States Supreme Court decreed that the maintenance of separate schools for blacks and whites was contrary to the provisions of the federal constitution. As a result, the school districts of the state were under the threat of legal action unless they desegregated. St. Louis established a plan under which complete integration was to result in two years. The high schools were integrated in 1954, and the elementary and junior high schools the following year. The Bootheel, however, lagged for several years in desegregation of its schools.

Most Missouri schools were integrated with relative speed and little difficulty. But residential segregation in both Kansas City and St. Louis worked contrary to efforts for school integration. As suits were filed, federal officials called for busing to achieve better racial distribution, the construction of "magnet" schools which would attract students of both races with similar academic interests and/or abilities, and pupil exchange policies with white suburban school districts. In 1975 federal officials required the black Kinloch School District to be merged and integrated with the Ferguson-Florissant District. Then in May of 1980 Judge James H. Meredith rendered a decision with great implications, not only for black residents of St. Louis, but for all the citizens of the city and the entire state as well. Judge Meredith said that the State of Missouri was in part responsible for the racial isolation of St. Louis students. He called on state officials to submit proposals for "voluntary cooperative" integration of St. Louis City and St. Louis County schools. Further, the State of Missouri was required to pay half of the cost of the school desegregation plans. It was estimated that

the cost to the State of Missouri the first year would be
$11,000,000. It was also stipulated that the State of Missouri
would continue to be required to bear half the cost in the future.
Desegregation plans were submitted by the St. Louis School System, the U.S. Department of Justice, the Missouri State Board of
Education, and by several private organizations. Numerous legal
issues remain to be solved. Judge William Hungate assumed responsibility of the case from Judge Meredith. Judge Hungate, in the
spring of 1981, affirmed his intention to carry out the Meredith
decision.

Another education-related issue which was debated during the
1970's was student achievement and mastery of the basic skills. In
1979 a group of 3000 Missouri citizens and educators were asked
to express themselves on this issue. Asked if there were a need for
"major improvements" in "assuming mastery of basic skills by all
students" it was recorded that eighty-seven percent of the respon-
dents answered positively. The State Board of Education under
the leadership of Commissioner Arthur Mallory prepared a Basic
Essentials Skills Test (BEST) which was first used in 1978. The
test was designed to cover (1) reading/language arts, (2) mathematics, and (3) government/economics. The BEST program is now
being used throughout the state.

Another problem beset education in Missouri during this
period. Teachers' salaries were so low that many professional educators left the public schools every year for better-paying jobs in
industry or business. Commissioner Mallory wrote in 1980 that
the average salary of classroom teachers in 1967 was $6137 and in
1979 was $12,881. The commissioner pointed out that, despite
the increase, the effect of inflation had so reduced the purchasing
power of the dollar that the teacher with the 1967 salary had a
higher standard of living.

Although the public schools accommodate by far the largest
share of Missouri's students, the Catholic and Lutheran citizens
of the state have for many years operated their own parochial
school systems in many communities. The Catholic system is
much the larger of the two. As part of a national trend in the
decade from 1970 to 1980, a number of conservative religious
groups in Missouri, disturbed by what they considered the worldli-
ness of public education, organized church-related schools. Although education and construction costs have been mounting,
church-sponsored schools have continued to grow. This growth,

Dr. James Frank, President of Lincoln University 1973-1982, was elected President of the National Collegiate Athletic Association (NCAA) in 1980. Dr. Frank previously had spearheaded the successful movement to integrate collegiate athletic programs for women into the NCAA.

which represents considerable financial sacrifice, witnesses to the dedication of these church members to their belief in religion-oriented education.

Public education in America has many critics. In part this is because citizens expect so much from the system. The post-World War II years were a time of growth in numbers of students, in buildings and budgets, in teacher qualifications, and in curriculum offerings. Certainly William T. Lucky, William Torrey Harris, Susan Elizabeth Blow, and other nineteeth-century Missouri educators would be delighted with the progress of education in the state during the past one hundred years.

Higher Education

There has been an impressive growth in the number of students in higher education during the twentieth century. On a national basis, approximately four percent of college age young people (eighteen to twenty-four years old) were college students in the year 1900. The percentage had increased to twelve percent by 1930 and to thirty percent by 1950. During the 1950's the number of Missourians in this age group did not grow rapidly. In fact, the college age population actually declined during the early fifties and then climbed slowly late in the decade. Despite this decline, there was a steady one percent increase each year through the 1950's and

Dr. Barbara S. Uehling was named the Chancellor of the University of Missouri, Columbia, in 1978. Dr. Uehling, a psychologist who came to UMC from the position of Vice Chancellor of Oklahoma University is the first woman to serve as the chief administrator of a public four-year college or university in Missouri.

1960's in the proportion of college age students enrolled in institutions of higher education in Missouri.

Cognizant of this continually growing interest in higher education among the eighteen to twenty-four age group, university and college administrators braced themselves and planned for the mid-sixties, when the bumper crop of postwar babies reached college age. As the time approached, the campuses of all the state schools and many of the private institutions were the scene of construction and remodeling of dormitories, classroom buildings, libraries, student centers, and other facilities.

Missouri has a system of higher education which includes twenty-four public and thirty private colleges and universities. The two private universities in St. Louis serve a national clientele. St. Louis University, the oldest institution of higher education in the state, is particularly noteworthy for its professional schools and for the extensive microfilm collection of Vatican Library manuscripts in its Pius XII Memorial Library. Washington University has a distinguished graduate and undergraduate offering as well as professional schools for the preparation of architects, physicians and lawyers. The private colleges of Missouri not only serve an important educational function, but they also are centers of cultural activities for the Missourians living near them. In 1952 the private colleges and universities had 19,423 full-time students, while only

16,539 were enrolled in the public institutions. But the public colleges and universities experienced much greater growth than the private institutions after 1952. In 1952 the public colleges and universities enrolled only forty-six percent of the students in Missouri higher education. By 1979 they served seventy-five percent of the students.

The composition of the student body, once predominately fulltime, upper-middle-class, college-age males, began changing in the 1970's. The advent of increased female and minority enrollment, two-year college students, part-time non-residents, and adult learners—including many middle-aged women returning to complete degrees and senior citizens pursuing new interests after retirement—has altered the campus scene. Enrollment patterns were changing, but predictions were for fairly stable numbers in institutions of higher education throughout the 1980's.

In the 1960's the junior college movement was particularly strong in Missouri. Two-year colleges were to be found in Kansas City and St. Louis, Jefferson County, Neosho, Joplin, St. Joseph, Potosi, Moberly, Trenton, Union, Sedalia, and Poplar Bluff. In the 1970's those schools became known as community colleges. These new institutions were open access schools that took education to the people.

The legislature in 1963 passed legislation establishing a four-campus University of Missouri System. Added to the original programs in Columbia and Rolla were campuses in Kansas City and St. Louis. The University of Missouri-Kansas City (UMKC) was created when the state took over the privately-supported University of Kansas City. The fourth campus was the University of Missouri-St. Louis (UMSL), which was established as a new school. The decision to make state university education available in the two largest urban centers was prudent. Missouri needed the additional higher education opportunities to meet the rapidly growing demand in the 1960's and 1970's.

There were other important changes in higher education during the period. The junior colleges in Joplin and St. Joseph were given permission in 1965 to become four-year institutions—Missouri Southern State College in Joplin and Missouri Western State College in St. Joseph. With their expanding enrollments and graduate programs, the five regional state colleges—Central at Warrensburg, Northeast at Kirksville, Northwest at Maryville, Southeast at Cape Girardeau, and Southwest at Springfield—were given state per-

mission to be known as state universities. These regional universities grew rapidly in the 1960's and 1970's. It should be noted
that Harris-Stowe State College, previously supported by the St.
Louis School System, was approved for full state funding in 1979.
The remaining state-supported university—Lincoln University in
Jefferson City—established as an institution for black students,
was recognized in 1980 by the federal civil rights agency for having
enrolled an approximately equal number of black and white students.

The $7 million University Library of Southwest Missouri State University was
opened in 1980. Hammons Fountains, in the foreground, were a gift of a
former student, John Q. Hammons.
(Jim Salyer, Southwest Missouri State University)

Today it is possible for most students with ambition and ability,
but with limited means, to secure financial assistance which will
enable them to attend college. Almost all colleges, private and
public, offer scholarships to those who graduate at the upper levels
of their high school classes. In addition, the federal government
has provided money to worthy students through loans and grants.

The campuses of Missouri did not escape the wave of protest
and unrest that swept the nation in the wake of the Vietnam War.
Although the upheaval was not as extreme in Missouri as in some

of her sister states, sit-ins and other demonstrations related primarily to the war and racial issues, including some isolated cases of violence and vandalism, did occur. The belligerent idealism of the 1960's was replaced by a practical realism in the 1970's and 1980's. The war was over, the draft abolished, and civil rights legislation widely implemented. The new student generation came to campus to acquire marketable skills and to secure their future. Social critics lamented the decline of community spirit and the rise of an almost narcistic "meism." But other students of social history interpreted the change as a classic case of pendulum swing, likely to moderate with the passing of time.

Several historic events in Missouri's past of which Missourians are most proud are related to education. In 1839 the General Assembly chartered the first state university west of the Mississippi River. Eighteen years later, St. Louis Normal School (reborn in 1904 as William Torrey Harris Teacher's College) was the first teacher-training institution to be established in the trans-Mississippi West. In 1873 Susan Elizabeth Blow opened the first public kindergarten in the United States in St. Louis; and only seven years later, in the same city, Calvin Milton Woodward founded the first manual training school in the country under the sponsorship of Washington

In 1979 Dr. Henry Givens, Jr. was named the President of Harris-Stowe State College in St. Louis. That same year Harris-Stowe, previously funded and supervised by the St. Louis Public School System, received full funding as a state college.

Graceful lines suggesting a dove soaring heavenward contribute to the worshipful atmosphere of this modern Missouri church interior. Contemporary stained glass windows depicting scenes of revelation light the side aisles. *(Westminster Presbyterian Church, Springfield, Paul F. Rich, Architect)*

University. The first school of journalism in America was organized as a division of the state university at Columbia under the direction of Walter Williams in 1908. Although there are always challenges and opportunities for improvement, Missourians have reason to be proud of the development of both their public school system and higher education system in the twentieth century.

Society

Mobility is a key word in describing the development of post-World War II Missouri society. The state has excellent new roads, but these are becoming increasingly crowded. During the period 1950 to 1980, Americans became enamored of small cars and those of foreign manufacture. This demand for the small car was prompted partly by fad, but was also related to the increasing cost of gas and to the need many families felt for a second automobile. Another characteristic of highway travel was the appearance of many camping trailers, motor homes, and vehicles transporting boats to Missouri's lakes and rivers.

Television has had one of the most telling influences on postwar society. The proud owners of early sets were often disturbed

The Truman Sports Complex at Kansas City provides facilities for both professional baseball and football. Royals Stadium in the foreground is the home diamond for the Kansas City baseball team. Arrowhead Stadium in the background is the home field of the Kansas City Chief's football team.
(*Walker-Missouri Tourism*)

by "snow" on the screen and by distorted pictures of their favorite programs, but "TV" offered unparalleled opportunities for Missourians to learn of the world about them. In the early years of the new medium, it became the habit of many families to begin the day with Captain Kangaroo or Dave Garroway and to retire at night after an hour with Jack Paar. Television has proved particularly important in bringing current history into the living room. Now Missourians, from cabins in the deepest hollows of the Ozarks' hills to skyscrapers in the largest cities, can be present at the inauguration of a new president, at United Nations debates, and on the newsfronts of the world. This common ground of experience has significant implications for influencing public opinion. There is little doubt that viewing scenes of Vietnam battlegrounds from the family room couch affected American response to that

tragic conflict. The development of Telstar and other such communication satellites made possible the instantaneous reception
of accounts and pictures of events occurring anywhere in the
world and greatly enlarged the scope of our experience. It is
likely that the microwaves of television will destroy the last bul-
wark of isolationism, at home and abroad.

As one drives through the rural areas of the state the growing
number of abandoned farm homes gives evidence of the steady
migration to the urban centers. On the edges of the cities, neat
rows of houses in suburban developments witness to the growth of
the metropolitan areas. For their growing number of citizens, the
urban centers of Missouri have provided parks with swimming
pools, tennis courts, outdoor-cooking facilities, playgrounds, and
ball diamonds. The minor leagues of yesteryear are gone, but the
Little Leaguers and local softball teams entertain loyal followings
of parents and hometown fans in neighborhood parks.

Kansas Citians and St. Louisans enjoy a wide range of cultural
advantages, including fine orchestras and museums of art, history,
and science. Nor have the arts been neglected in Missouri's smaller
cities. Missourians may attend classes and view exhibits in such
cultural centers as the St. Joseph or Springfield art museums or
the Spiva Art Center in Joplin. Civic music associations in cities
across the state sponsor appearances by leading concert artists, and
symphony orchestras staffed by local musicians perform in such
cities as Joplin, Sedalia, St. Joseph, and Springfield. Little Theater
groups and collegiate drama departments present highly-polished
performances of plays and musicals by amateur casts. Professional
productions by touring companies are sponsored by civic theatre
leagues; and thousands of residents and tourists alike enjoy the
musicals produced on Missouri's two most famous stages—the
Kansas City Starlight Theater in beautiful Swope Park, established
in 1951, and the venerable St. Louis Municipal Opera in lovely
Forest Park. Encouragement of creative endeavors has been provided by the Missouri Council on the Arts, which has given both
counsel and financial assistance to art-related activities and organizations in the state.

For Missouri booklovers, the state and many cities, counties,
and educational institutions maintain excellent library facilities.
Libraries on wheels called "bookmobiles" visit many suburban
and rural communities which are not served by a permanent library.

(Courtesy Massie-Missouri Commerce)
In the striking steel and glass Jewel Box in Forest Park, the St. Louis Park Department displays selections from the almost half million plants and flowers grown in eighty acres of gardens and greenhouses.

Night classes offered by Missouri's public and private colleges and universities allow those who must work during the day to study subjects which are of interest to them or which would apply toward a college degree. For most residents of Missouri's metropolitan areas facilities are available for a full, rich life.

In this growing urban environment there are, of course, continuing problems. The crowded slum areas in the older sections of the cities have bred crime, disease, and despair. In an attempt to rejuvenate the inner city and to provide pleasant, clean housing, the cities—particularly St. Louis and Kansas City—undertook large urban renewal projects. With the aid of federal funds, blighted areas were purchased, undesirable structures demolished, and new apartments, parks, business districts, and other facilities constructed. By the end of the year 1957, St. Louis had instituted a plan for redeveloping eighty-five blocks of slums. Urban renewal has been extended to other Missouri cities—large and small—where action is needed to improve substandard facilities. A second problem during the postwar era stemmed from the difficulty encountered by cities in securing sufficient revenue to carry out their obligations to their citizens. In 1948 St. Louis secured the permission of the legislature to assess an earnings tax in the city. Through this tax, those people who earn their livelihood in the city, but choose to live in the suburbs, were forced to assist the city in paying for necessary services. The problem for St. Louis is more acute than for most cities, since she is ringed with independent incorporated communities which do not contribute to the St. Louis city budget. Springfield, Missouri's third largest city, did not have such severe financial difficulties because she was able to annex the residential zones bordering the city. As city expenses rise, other metropolitan areas may be compelled to resort to earnings taxes to relieve their financial strain.

Musicals produced on the stage of Kansas City's Starlight Theatre have entertained Missourians and their guests since 1951.

(Courtesy Massie-Missouri Commerce)

The 1954 Supreme Court decision outlawing segregation in the public schools of the nation led citizens of the state to question the propriety of excluding any American from other public and private facilities on the basis of race. Requests, and sometimes picketing, by church groups and organizations such as the National Association for the Advancement of Colored People (NAACP) encouraged some theaters, dining facilities, and hotels to lower their racial bars. The establishment of a Human Rights Commission in 1957, the passage of the Fair Employment Practices Act in 1961 to bar racial or religious discrimination in companies with fifty or more employees, the Public Accommodations Act of 1965, and the Fair Housing Law of 1972 were important steps taken to provide just treatment for black Missourians. While much remained to be done before all Missouri's citizens were treated with dignity, significant steps toward equality of opportunity had been taken.

One indication of progress in race relations is the fact that Missouri in 1969 ranked second in the nation in the number of blacks serving in state and national legislative bodies. The list of black Missourians who have played a role in state government is long. In 1980 there were four black members of the state House of Representatives from Kansas City and nine from St. Louis. The first black state senator in Missouri was Theodore D. McNeal of St. Louis, who was elected in 1960. A greatly respected man, he was later appointed to the University of Missouri Board of Curators by Governor Hearnes and to the position of president of the St. Louis Board of Police Commissioners. Those black Missourians who have served in the state senate in addition to McNeal are Franklin Payne, Raymond Howard, Lee Vertis Swinton, Gwen Giles, and J. B. "Jet" Banks. At the federal level, William Clay of St. Louis has been elected to congress six times from the First District. He is one of the organizers of the Congressional Black Caucus. Any listing of black leaders from Missouri in the post-World War II era must include the name of Margaret Bush Wilson of St. Louis, who served as the national chairman of the NAACP during the 1970's. Mrs. Wilson, an attorney, provided effective leadership for the NAACP during a time of continuing racial change in the nation.

There are other encouraging signs of black progress in Missouri society. Black men and women now hold responsible positions in businesses and financial institutions that once refused to hire per-

Gwen B. Giles of St. Louis was elected in 1977 to fill an unexpired term in the Missouri Senate. She was reelected to a full term in 1978. Senator Giles is the first black woman to serve in the Missouri Senate.

Lee Vertis Swinton of Kansas City was elected to the Missouri Senate in 1980 from the Ninth Senatorial District in Jackson County. He is the first black senator to represent the Kansas City area.

J. B. "Jet" Banks is a veteran member of the Missouri General Assembly. Elected to the House of Representatives in 1968, he served a total of eight years there. He was elected to the Missouri Senate in 1976, and again in 1980. Senator Banks is a graduate of Lincoln University.

Margaret Bush Wilson, St. Louis attorney, served as the national Chairman of the Board of the National Association for the Advancement of Colored People (NAACP) in the late 1970's and early 1980's.
(Courtesy-National Association for the Advancement of Colored People)

sons of their race. A growing number of black youth are entering college and professional schools to prepare for careers. A strong black middle class, with an increasing number of professionals, has developed. In 1980, fifty-five blacks held key positions in thirty-two state agencies. Four venerable black newspapers: the *Argus*, the *American*, and the *Sentinel* in St. Louis and the *Call* in Kansas City continue to inform and speak for black Missourians. Popular black television personalities report the news and entertain their fellow Missourians. The percentage of black Missourians who live in the central cities of St. Louis and Kansas City has decreased from seventy-six percent in 1970 to sixty-four percent in 1980, indicating that a greater number of black citizens are finding more desirable housing outside the inner city area. Many black individuals in the professions and in the fields of athletics and entertainment have distinguished themselves and brought honor to their state.

Though gains have been made, problems remain. Black unemployment is still far greater than the jobless rate for whites. The average income for black families is still significantly below that of white familes. The dropout rate among black teen-agers remains high. Many black Missourians, ill-housed and ill-nourished, are trapped in a cycle of poverty and despair. Missourians, black and white alike, cannot retire from the struggle for equality and justice so long as these conditions remain.

Elected in 1960, Theodore McNeal was the first black member of the Missouri Senate. Senator McNeal later served as a member of the University of Missouri Board of Curators and as a member of the St. Louis Board of Police Commissioners.

William Clay of St. Louis was elected to the U. S. House of Representatives from the First District in 1968. He was re-elected in the six following congressional contests. Congressman Clay was one of the organizers of the Congressional Black Caucus.

(Courtesy Massie-Missouri Commerce)
The Lake of the Ozarks "dragon" can be seen in this infra-red photograph taken from an altitude of 10,000 feet.

Missouri's population includes more citizens over sixty-five years of age than the national average. This number can be explained in part by the fact that Missouri—with its generally pleasant climate, great scenic beauty, ample recreational facilities, excellent medical centers, and low taxes—has gained a reputation as a retirement haven. Senior citizens' clubs have been organized in most cities, and some—as in Neosho—have their own buildings and recreational facilities. Condominium developments, especially in the lake areas, have attracted retirees from within and without the state. Nursing homes for those who require special care have been established by state and county governments, churches, service organizations, and private individuals. In 1957 a tragic nursing home fire at Warrenton which claimed the lives of seventy-two patients and staff members motivated the General Assembly to tighten state regulations and inspections for these facilities.

The increased leisure time enjoyed by many Missouri citizens, and the growing number of retired people in the state, have stimulated an interest in recreational centers. Missouri has developed an elaborate system of more than thirty state parks, plus historic shrines and memorials, for the use and enjoyment of residents and visitors. Swimming, boating, camping, fishing, hiking, and horseback riding in some of the loveliest settings America has to offer may be enjoyed by vacationers in Missouri. The installation of showers, restrooms, and automatic laundry equipment in many of the parks makes camping a pleasure—even for mothers.

Missouri's Conservation Commission has earned the gratitude of the hunting enthusiasts of the state. By restocking, closed seasons, and careful management, the Commission brought the whitetailed deer from near extinction in the early 1930's to a herd of hundreds of thousands. About 50,000 deer are taken annually in a nine-day open gun season, in addition to those brought down during the two-month bow-and-arrow season. With such "harvesting" the Commission considers the deer population to be in

Table Rock Dam on the White River has provided 857 miles of shoreline playground for residents and tourist guests of Missouri. After industrial manufacturing and agriculture, tourism is the third largest industry in the state.
(Walker-Missouri Tourism)

The broad tree-lined Memorial Drive in Kansas City leads to the Liberty Memorial Tower. In the background, the skyscrapers of the city rise majestically along the horizon.
(Walker-Missouri Tourism)

good balance. The Commission also undertook a restocking program of the native wild turkey. Stocking of the fishing lakes and streams, preservation of Missouri's woodlands, and protection of her wildlife are also the responsibility of the Conservation Commission. The activities of this bipartisan commission are financed through the sale of hunting and fishing permits, which are among the lowest priced in the nation, and by a one-eighth cent sales tax.

The completion of Table Rock Dam on the White River provided a huge new lake with 857 miles of shoreline, second in size only to the Lake of the Ozarks. The Truman Library, with its Benton murals and the Truman papers, is an attraction to both tourists and scholars. The development of theatrical entertainment such as that offered at the Arrow Rock Lyceum and Branson's Shepherd of the Hills Summer Theater serves well the drama fans among the areas' tourists. The developing Jefferson National Expansion Memorial located on eighty-three acres of riverfront on the original settlement site of St. Louis draws many enthusiastic visitors each year. A dramatic 630-foot-high stainless steel arch was designed for the memorial by the late great Finnish architect Eero Saarinen. Towering higher than the skyscrapers of St. Louis, the majestic arch symbolizes the "Gateway to the West."

Mechanization and urbanization are two words descriptive of the development of contemporary Missouri. For all Missourians—in city or on farm—it is a time of technological revolution. Mechanical servants perform duties and work miracles undreamed of by our Missouri ancestors. These new machines have so changed transportation, communication, agriculture, industry, and even housework that production has been increased with less direct human labor; and comforts, services, and more leisure hours have been made available to growing numbers of people. As a result, Missourians have greater educational, cultural, and recreational opportunities open to them than ever before.

Urbanization has been in part a result of the application of new machines and progressive farming techniques to Missouri agriculture. Increased production has tended to depress the market, and the small farmer with limited production facilities has been forced off the land. More and more, Missouri is becoming an urban society of modern factories and sprawling residential areas. Under these circumstances, it is desirable that the process of urbanization be carried on intelligently and systematically. The rural development program can help fit new industries to the

The gleaming Gateway Arch, tallest of America's monuments, symbolizes the role of St. Louis in the development of the West. Framed by the Arch are the Old Courthouse and the Old Cathedral.
(Walker-Missouri Tourism)

needs and resources of a community. Zoning can aid those who would develop new housing, industrial, or business facilities. The cities themselves must provide and expand the parks, libraries, schools, cultural opportunities, and social services so necessary in any urban area. If these things can be done, then the process of urbanization will be less painful, and the future can be pleasant for more Missourians.

Today, two of Missouri's daughters—Texas and California— have surpassed her in population. At times the slower pace of accomplishments might indicate that the "Mother of the West" is feeling her age. However, the slower economic growth should not be mistaken for decay. Missouri is a state with a diversified economy which can better withstand a crisis. She still has resources—such as iron ore and coal—which have hardly been tapped. Missouri is old, but not decrepit. She is a woman of experience, restraint, and cautious plans for the future, growing more sophisticated yearly, and adventurous enough to have a role in the opening of the new frontier in space.

Bibliography

Amonker, Ravindra G. and Allan D. Stone. *Missouri: Demographic-Economic Analysis.* Prepared for the Division of Budget and Planning, Office of Administration, State of Missouri. Springfield: Departments of Sociology and Economics, Southwest Missouri State University, 1980.

Amonker, Ravindra G. and Allan D. Stone. *Missouri: Demographic-Economic Profiles of Growth Regions.* Prepared for the Division of Budget and Planning, Office of Administration, State of Missouri. Springfield: Departments of Sociology and Economics, Southwest Missouri State University, 1980.

Amonker, Ravindra G. and Allan D. Stone. *Missouri: Social and Economic Indicators.* Prepared for the Division of Budget and Planning, Office of Administration, State of Missouri. Springfield: Departments of Sociology and Economics, Southwest Missouri State University, 1980.

Collier, James E. *Agricultural Atlas of Missouri.* University of Missouri College of Agriculture Bulletin, No. 645 (February, 1955).

Franklin, Inks. "Teacher Salary Increases Parallel Successful MSTA Financial Efforts," *School and Community,* Vol. XLIII (December, 1956), pp. 16-18, 20.

Gist, Noel P., et al., eds. *Missouri: Its Resources, People and Institutions.* Columbia: The Curators of the University of Missouri, 1950.

Greene, Lorenzo J., Gary R. Kremer, and Anthony F. Holland. *Missouri's Black Heritage.* St. Louis: Forum Press, 1980.

Highway Facts in Missouri: Roads, Streets, Highways. Jefferson City: The State Highway Commission, 1960.

Kirschten, Ernest. *Catfish and Crystal.* Garden City, New York: Doubleday and Company, Inc., 1960.

Massie, Gerald R., ed. *Memorable Missouri.* Jefferson City: Resources and Development Commission.

Nance, Gordon B. *Trends in Contributions to Missouri and U. S. Cash Farm Income 1924-1957.* University of Missouri College of Agriculture Bulletin, No. 708 (August, 1959).

1979-80 Report of the Public Schools: For the School Year Ending June 30, 1980. Jefferson City: Missouri State Board of Education, 1981.

1980 Census of Population and Housing, Advance Reports, Missouri. Washington, D.C.: Bureau of the Census, U.S. Department of Commerce, March, 1981.

Official Manual: State of Missouri, 1979-1980. Jefferson City: The Secretary of State, 1980.

Parrish, William E., Charles T. Jones, Jr., Lawrence C. Christensen. *Missouri: The Heart of the Nation.* St. Louis: Forum Press, 1980.

Peterson, Warren A. *Future Enrollment in Missouri Colleges and Universities:* 1965, 1970, 1975. Kansas City: Community Studies, Inc., 1960.

Rafferty, Milton D., William H. Cheek, David A. Castillon. *Economic and Social Atlas of Missouri.* Springfield: Geography and Geology Department, Southwest Missouri State University, 1975.

Rafferty, Milton D., Russel L. Gerlach, Dennis J. Hrebec. *Atlas of Missouri.* Springfield: Aux-Arc Research Associates, 1970.

The Growth of the Economy of Missouri, 1929-1960. Jefferson City: Missouri Resources and Development Commission, 1961.

Tunley, Roul. "Missouri: Four States in One," *The Saturday Evening Post,* Vol. CCXXXIII (September 3, 1960), pp. 11-13, 71, 73.

Yearbook (Issued Annually). New York: Macmillan Educational Corporation and P. F. Collier, Inc.

Lou Brock broke into the major leagues in 1962 with the Chicago Cubs, was traded to the St. Louis Cardinals in 1964, and was a Redbird star through 1979. He sparked the Cardinals to three pennants and was a World Series standout in 1964, 1967, and 1968 with his hitting and base stealing. He broke the single season major league record for stolen bases with 118 in 1974, at the same time setting another record by stealing 50 or more bases for 10 consecutive seasons. He retired as the leading all-time base stealer with 938 and as one of only 14 men in major league history to get 3000 hits in a career. *(Courtest Mark Stillwell-Southwest Missouri State University)*

Neosho-born artist Thomas Hart Benton, a grandnephew of the illustrious senator, is best known for his graphic portrayals of American life. In addition to his famed paintings in the state capitol, Benton is represented in Missouri by murals at Lincoln University and in the Truman Memorial Library at Independence.

(Courtesy State Historical Society)

St. Louisan Thomas A. Dooley turned his back on a potentially lucrative medical practice to help found MEDICO and to establish hospitals and clinics among the disease- and war-plagued people of southeast Asia and Africa. Until days before his death from cancer at the age of thirty-four, he spent his waking hours in selfless concern for others.

(Courtesy MEDICO, a Service of CARE)

George Washington Carver was born about 1864 of slave parents near Diamond Grove, Missouri. After working his way through school in Kansas and Iowa, Dr. Carver devoted almost fifty years to the betterment of southern agriculture and to the development of new uses for the products of southern farms at the Tuskegee Institute in Alabama.

(Courtesy George Washington Carver Museum, Tuskegee Institute, Tuskegee, Alabama).

Let the welfare of the people be the supreme law.

CHAPTER XX

The Legacy of a State

. . . yea, I have a
goodly heritage.
—Psalms 16:6

In mid-nineteenth century Missouri, in the days before motion pictures and television, certain enterprising artists covered long strips of canvas with paintings of daring exploits or scenic wonders. The finished canvas, wound on poles attached to either end, would be unrolled to illustrate running commentaries of adventure or travel. Viewing these panoramas, as the canvases were called, was a favorite diversion for nineteenth-century Missourians. The legacy Missouri gives to all her children—native-born and adopted—might be thought of as such a panorama depicting the material and esthetic wealth of her natural resources and the record of her past generations. The history of Missouri and Missourians unrolls from the centuries of the atlatl to the era of the space shuttle Columbia and beyond. On the long and colorful scroll are scenes and portraits which may entertain, may instruct, or may inspire Missouri's heirs.

In reviewing the long and colorful history of the state, one may make several observations which help to explain present-day Missouri. First, her location in mid-continent at the confluence of the Missouri, Mississippi, and Ohio rivers has been and continues to be a major factor in the development of the state. Until the building of the railroads, the rivers were Missouri's chief channels which conveyed settlers to her bottomland and prairies, brought merchandise to her towns, and carried the produce of her farmers to market. In the 1840's and 1850's, when her river highways funneled westbound travelers through Missouri, she became the "Mother of the West," supplying the migrant trains with wagons, harness, provisions, and some of her own sons and daughters. With the advent of the railroad the Mississippi, which had once nurtured the state, became a barrier to her progress by cutting her off from the eastern railways. Aggressive Chicago interests backed the construction of western railroads through Iowa to the far West, and the Windy City, because of her earlier rail links with the West, soon surpassed St. Louis in size. In 1874, however, with the opening of the Eads Bridge, St. Louis had finally secured an East-West link, and the goods of both were channeled through Missouri. In the twentieth century, Missouri's location continues to contribute to her economic health. Barges still haul Missouri goods on the Mississippi, and industries seeking to serve markets on both coasts find Missouri's rail and air connections and central location advantageous.

In its infancy, air travel captured the imagination of daring Missourians. One of the first airfields and several of the earliest air meets were located at St. Louis. Only thirteen years after Kitty Hawk hatched the airplane in 1903, the first United States Army aeronautical corps was established at St. Louis, which also became the base for the first regular air mail service. As Missouri's location and physical attributes once encouraged her early settlement, so in the twentieth century her central location and her freedom from mountain hazards and dangerous air currents have been influential in the encouragement of air travel within the state, and in the establishment of Kansas City and St. Louis as busy centers for continental air traffic.

A second observation which might be made is that the variety of Missouri's social and commercial ties has prevented her from casting a clear sectional image. Although Missouri originally had a strong French orientation, and later was closely tied to the South by an influx of southern immigrants, both of these cultural accents were tempered by a growing tide of settlers from the northern states and by large numbers of German and Irish immigrants who came to the state in the mid-1800's. Her supplying of goods and settlers to the new frontier areas of the West further diversified her associations. By the time of the Civil War, although sections of the state were strongly southern in sympathy, Missouri's citizens of northern and European origin had sufficient influence to prevent secession. After the Civil War, the direction of railroad extension multiplied trade and social contacts with the East and West. Thus, Missouri lost more and more of her southern orientation. Missourians today have come from so many states and have such varied economic, cultural, racial and sectional ties that the state no longer fits into any bloc.

Third, although it may pain those of us who live in the northern and southern extremes of the state to admit it, the history of the state revolves about an axis formed by the Missouri River region in mid-state with the two major urban settlements —Kansas City and St. Louis—at each extreme. The major concentrations of population, economic wealth, and governmental institutions are here. This region has been the stage on which most of the major scenes of Missouri history have been played. In this zone are located the state capital and many state eleemosynary and penal institutions. Numerous private colleges as well as seven university campuses—Washington University, University of Missouri at St. Louis, St. Louis University, University of Missouri at Columbia, Lincoln University, Central Missouri State University, and the University of Missouri at Kansas City—are all in this area. Since the central Missouri River region was originally settled by southern emigrants who brought with them elements of southern culture, much of the mid-state area is known even today as Little Dixie. The other regions of the state—the Ozarks, the bootheel, and the plains—are, of course, valuable and have contributed significantly to Missouri's development; but the region along the Missouri River has been the chief zone of historical activity.

Fourth, Missouri is conservative. She has not been a state to follow unusual new plans nor one to squander money. The state may have been influenced—along with Senator Thomas Hart Benton—by the bank failures of the territorial period. During the early years of Missouri statehood, many of her sister states incurred huge debts to build roads, canals, banks, and other projects. Missouri did not. The Bank of the State of Missouri which was established in the 1830's was a sound, conservative institution. The only occasion on which the state departed from this conservatism occurred in the 1850's when she issued nearly $25,000,000 to build railroads. Since the loans were not repaid and the state lost heavily, it was a lesson not soon forgotten by Missourians. The state government debts of the Civil War period were finally paid in 1903. Since that time, the citizens have occasionally authorized major sales of bonds for road building or improvements of state institutions, but the legislature has been reluctant to push taxes up rapidly. The state spending limitation which Missouri voters added to the state constitution in 1980 is quite consistent with the main thrust of Missouri history. As a result of such conservatism, Missouri has had delightfully low taxes in comparison to most of her sister states. But she has lacked the aggressive drive and rapid development of other states which have levied higher taxes and plowed more money into roads, schools, airports, and the encouragement of economic development.

Fifth, Missouri has had both a commercial and an agricultural economy from the first. Unlike some other agricultural states of the Middle West, even in the early days when she was primarily a rural state, Missouri had well-located major cities to carry on trade and manufacturing activities. Since the rural and urban groups have served each other, the diversified combination of agriculture and commerce has given greater stability to the state. The federal policy of granting 160 acres of land for a minimum fee (or free after 1862) gave Missouri an independent, hard-working, land-owning farm class to feed the cities and to provide raw materials and customers for her industries. Government assistance helped the farmers survive periods of agricultural depression, and today farm tenancy is declining as farms are becoming larger, more mechanized, and more productive. Many farmer tenants and small farmowners, leaving farming to the large scale operators, have moved to the metropolitan areas to fill jobs in the growing industries. Thus, although the urban population continues to gain in percentage over rural population, the state retains its dual agricultural and industrial economy.

Sixth, a review of the history of Missouri shows that while she is strongly inclined toward the Democratic Party, Missouri is not a one-party state. In Missouri, while the Democratic Party usually controls the state elections, the Republican contenders are able to defeat Democratic candidates when the current of national public opinion runs against the majority party as happened in the 1920s, the 1940s, and at the outset of the 1980s. Through the years the Democratic Party of Missouri has contributed such illustrious leaders as Senator Thomas Hart Benton, Senator Frank P. Blair, Representative Richard P. Bland, Speaker Champ Clark, and President Harry S Truman. The opposition Whigs and Republicans, who have had fewer opportunities to provide national leaders, proudly claim Edward Bates and Carl Schurz, who served with distinction during difficult years clouded by Civil War and its aftermath. In general, the dominant Democratic Party in Missouri has fulfilled its obligations in a responsible and effective manner.

As a Missourian surveys his heritage, two characteristics of the state and her history are most impressive—variety and contrast. The low, level sweep of rich bottomland forming her great river valleys, the rounded heights of the oak-mantled Ozarks, the golden carpet of her autumn prairies, the deliberate flow of her great rivers, the boiling foam-specked cauldron of her springs, all form a composite picture of Missouri's varied topography.

Her culture is equally diverse. A lifelong resident of the South would feel at home in the bootheel or in mid-state Little Dixie. Bustling Kansas City or St. Louis would suit the most confirmed city dweller from the East. A midwestern farmer would find the fields and small towns of Missouri's plains "just like home." Hill folk from the Smokies would have much—including their Anglo-Saxon origin—in common with the inhabitants of the Ozarks.

Some of the contrast evident in Missouri society is due to the happy persistence of old ways in modern days. Nimble-tongued auctioneers still perform at country sales while big city Missouri industrialists conduct business via ticker tape, cable, telephone and satellite. White frame country churches ringed with ancient trees bear quiet witness to the countryside while handsome cathedrals offer sanctuary from crowded city streets. The rhythmic shuffle and swirling color of square dancers as well as the glitter and pomp of the Governor's Inaugural Ball are part of the Missouri scene. While physics students investigate the principles of the cyclotron at Rolla, a sunbrowned, whitehaired farmer refuses to plant his potatoes until the dark of the moon.

Some of Missouri's contrasts, however, are unfortunate ones. Verdant plains and valleys yield surplus crops while eroded slopes and acres of thin, wornout soil—which should be planted with forests and grasses—provide a meager living for thousands of Missourians. Some poorly-equipped rural and inner-city schools remain to provide a sorry contrast to the handsome new schools of consolidated districts and of prosperous urban and suburban communities. The substandard housing which shelters far too many Missourians compares pathetically with the neatly clipped lawns and gleaming houses of Missouri suburbia. Challenges remain for Missouri and Missourians.

The stories of the men and women who had a role in her history are a major part of the legacy one inherits from his home state. Some Missourians originally came from other states to make their contributions. James Eads, George Caleb Bingham, or William Rockhill Nelson, for example, were among Missouri's adopted sons. Other native-born Missourians such as Samuel Clemens and George Washington Carver left the state to make their mark. Not all of Missouri's family have been heroes. The vicious mobs during the Mormon persecution, the slave traders who were ostracized even by those who patronized them, Quantrill and his blood-thirsty comrades, the hypocritical, lawless Bald Knobbers, and the bigoted members of the Ku Klux Klan played a part in the drama of Missouri's past. But the shadow of their misdeeds is banished by the light of Father De Smet's and Timothy Flint's resolute faith, Jedediah Smith's courage, Stephen Austin's vision, Mother Duchesne's and Elijah Lovejoy's dedicated concern, and Thomas Dooley's sacrificial compassion. The ignoble serves to caution and instruct; the noble serves to inspire.

Wealth and beauty, challenge and inspiration—of such is the heritage of Missouri.

Pictured are two interesting buildings from Missouri's past. The Louis Bolduc house in Ste. Genevieve was constructed after the flood of 1785. The broad porch and vertically placed logs forming the walls are characteristic of French settlers' homes of that period. In 1676, the English architectural genius Sir Christopher Wren completed the lovely church shown below, which was moved from England to the campus of Westminster College in Fulton during the years 1966-69. Known as the Winston Churchill Memorial, the building commemorates that great statesman and the historic "Iron Curtain" speech he delivered at the college on March 5, 1946. *(Walker-Missouri Tourism)*

James Stark of Kentucky moved his wife and family to Missouri in 1816 and settled in Pike County—near Louisiana—where he built the cabin shown above. Stark, skilled in the propagation of fruit trees, developed orchards and nurseries near Louisiana. Contrasting with the rustic simplicity of the Stark cabin, the Graff House in Hermann is a handsome example of the frame residences constructed by German immigrants who settled along the Missouri River in the nineteenth century. *(Walker-Missouri Tourism)*

A MISSOURI CHRONOLOGY

by
Edward Pierce

French control of Missouri, 1673-1770

1673	Marquette-Joliet expedition arrived
1682	La Salle took possession of territory for France (April 9)
1699	Settlement established at Cahokia
1700	Settlement established at Kaskaskia
1712	De Bourgmond came to Missouri
1720	Philippe Renault brought slaves to Missouri
1724	De Bourgmond built Fort Orleans
1735	Ste. Genevieve, first permanent settlement in Missouri founded
1762	Louisiana territory given to Spain by France (November 13)
1764	St. Louis founded by Laclede and Chouteau (February 15)
1767	Carondelet settled
1769	St. Charles established by Blanchette
1770	Don Pedro Piernas named Lieutenant-Governor of Louisiana territory

Spanish control of Missouri, 1770-1804

1770	Spanish government assumed control of Louisiana territory (May 20)
1770	First Catholic Church in St. Louis dedicated (June 24)
1773	Mine a Breton (later Potosi) founded
1775	Piernas succeeded as Lieutenant-Governor by Francisco Cruzat (May 20)
1778	Fernando De Leyba arrived at St. Louis as Lieutenant-Governor (June 10)
1779	Portage des Sioux established
1780	British and Indians attacked St. Louis (May 26)
1780	Cruzat replaced Leyba as Lieutenant-Governor (July 25)
1787	Florissant founded
1787	Lieutenant-Governor Cruzat succeeded by Manuel Perez (November 27)
1789	Colonel George Morgan led group to New Madrid (February 14)

	Events of Interest
1792	Zenon Trudeau appointed Lieutenant-Governor (July 21)
1793	Spanish Missouri Company founded
1793	Cape Girardeau settled by Lorimer
1793	New Bourbon founded
1797	La Charette established
1797	Moses Austin moved to Missouri
1797	Captain James S. Piggott established ferry at St. Louis (August 15)
1798	Daniel Boone moved to Missouri
1799	Lieutenant-Governor Trudeau succeeded by Carlos Dehault DeLassus (August 29)
1800	Treaty of San Ildefonso (returning Louisiana territory to France) signed (October 1)
1803	Louisiana Purchase agreement made (April 30)

		Events of Interest
U. S. Territorial Governor		
Amos Stoddard 1804	1804	United States took formal possession of Louisiana (March 10)
	1804	Louisiana divided into two parts: Territory of Orleans and Territory of Louisiana (March 26)
	1804	Lewis and Clark started expedition up the Missouri River (May 14)
James Wilkinson 1805-1806	1805	Territory of Louisiana established, seat of government at St. Louis (March 3)
	1806	Bethel Baptist Church established near Jackson
	1806	Fort Bellefontaine established
	1806	Lewis and Clark Expedition returned (September 23)
	1806	First Methodist Church in Missouri organized near Jackson
Meriwether Lewis 1807-1809	1807	First Masonic Lodge in Missouri chartered at Ste. Genevieve (July 17)
	1808	Ste. Genevieve Academy incorporated, first legally organized school in the territory
	1808	The Missouri Gazette, first newspaper in Missouri, established by Joseph Charless

U. S. Territorial Governor		Events of Interest
	1808	Osage treaty signed (November 10)
	1808	Fort Osage established (November 13)
	1809	Missouri Fur Company organized
	1809	Herculaneum laid out by Moses Austin
Benjamin Howard 1810-1812	1811	New Madrid earthquake (December 16)
	1812	Territory of Louisiana changed to Territory of Missouri (June 4)
	1812	War of 1812 (June 18, 1812-December 24, 1814)
	1812	First General Assembly of the Territory of Missouri met (October 1)
	1812	Cape Girardeau, New Madrid, St. Charles, St. Louis, and Ste. Genevieve counties organized (October 1)
William Clark 1813-1820	1813	Washington County organized
	1816	First Presbyterian Church organized in Missouri near Potosi (August 12)
	1816	Bank of St. Louis opened (December 13)
	1816	Howard County organized
	1817	Bank of Missouri incorporated (January 31)
	1817	Zebulon M. Pike, first steamboat to land at St. Louis (August 2)
	1817	First petition for statehood circulated
	1817	First Christian Church in Missouri organized in Howard County (November 22)
	1818	Cooper, Franklin, Jefferson, Lincoln, Madison, Montgomery, Pike, and Wayne counties organized
	1819	Missouri Intelligencer and Boon's Lick Advertiser established
	1819	First steamboat at Franklin, the Independence (May 28)
	1820	Missouri Enabling Act passed and approved by President Monroe (March 6)
	1820	Constitutional Convention (June 12-July 19)
	1820	Boone, Callaway, Chariton, Cole, Gasconade, Lillard (now Lafayette), Perry, Ralls, Ray, and Saline counties organized

Governor		Events of Interest	U. S. Senator	U. S. Senator
	1820	John Scott elected as Representative (September 28)	David Barton (ND) 1820-1830	Thomas Hart Benton (D) 1820-1851
	1820	Stagecoach line established between St. Louis and Old Franklin		
	1821	Masonic Grand Lodge of Missouri established (February 23)		
	1821	President Monroe proclaimed Missouri statehood (August 10)		
	1821	Trading post established at mouth of Kaw, or Kansas, River by Francois Chouteau		
Alexander McNair (D) 1820-1825	1821	Captain William Becknell started on first successful trip to Santa Fe (September 1)		
	1821	State Capitol site located at present site of Jefferson City (December 31)		
	1821	Harmony Mission established in Bates County		
	1821	St. Francois and Scott Counties organized		
	1822	The "emblems and devices" of Great Seal of the State of Missouri established		
	1822	Clay County organized		
	1823	Fayette laid out		

Governor		Events of Interest	U. S. Senator	U. S. Senator
Frederick Bates (D) 1825	1825	Lafayette visited St. Louis (April 29)	(Barton)	(Benton)
	1825	Great and Little Osage and Kansas Indians ceded all lands lying within Missouri (June 2)		
	1825	Commissioners appointed by U. S. Government to lay out Santa Fe Trail, left Fort Osage (July 17)		
	1825	Governor Bates died (August 4)		
Abraham J. Williams (D) 1825	1825	Shawnees given land outside Missouri in exchange for Missouri lands (November 7)		
John Miller (D) 1825-1833	1826	Jefferson Barracks established (July 4)		
	1826	Permanent seat of government established at Jefferson City (October 1)		
	1826	Jackson and Marion counties organized		
	1827	Lindenwood College founded, 1827		
	1829	Delaware Indians ceded all claims in Missouri (September 24)		
	1829	Branch of United States Bank established in St. Louis		
	1829	Crawford and Randolph counties organized	Alexander Buckner (D) 1830-1834	
	1831	Mormons settled in Jackson County		

Governor		Events of Interest	U.S. Senator	U.S. Senator
(Miller)			(Buckner)	(Benton)
Daniel Dunklin (D) 1833-1837	1831	Monroe County organized		
	1832	St. Louis University chartered (December 28)		
	1833	Mormons driven from Jackson County		
	1833	Carroll, Clinton, Greene, Lewis, Morgan, Pettis, Pulaski, Ripley, and Warren counties organized	Lewis F. Linn (D) 1834-1843	
	1834	Henry and Johnson counties organized		
	1835	Anzeiger des Westens, first German newspaper in Missouri, established (October 31)		
	1835	Barry, Benton, Cass, Polk, Shelby, and Stoddard counties organized		
	1836	First Jewish congregation met in St. Louis (January 1)		
	1836	State Penitentiary at Jefferson City established		
	1836	Audrain, Caldwell, Daviess, and Clark counties organized		
Lilburn W. Boggs (D) 1837-1841	1837	Platte Purchase		
	1837	Legislature incorporated 18 railroad companies; no roads built by these companies		
	1837	Missouri troops take part in Seminole War in Florida		

Governor	Year	Events of Interest	U.S. Senator	U.S. Senator
(Boggs)	1837	State Capitol burned (November 17)	(Linn)	(Benton)
	1837	United States Arsenal established at Liberty		
	1837	Bank of State of Missouri established (February 2)		
	1837	Linn, Livingston, Macon, Miller, and Taney counties organized		
	1838	Buchanan, Newton, and Platte counties organized		
	1838	Militia called out to suppress Mormons		
	1839	Iowa-Missouri boundary dispute		
	1839	Geyer Act passed (February 9)		
Thomas Reynolds (D) 1841-1844	1841	Missouri University opened (April 14)		
	1841	Adair, Andrew, Bates, Camden, Dade, Gentry, Grundy, Holt, Jasper, Osage, Ozark, St. Clair, Scotland, Shannon, Wright counties organized		
	1843	St. Joseph laid out (July 26)	David R. Atchison (D) 1843-1855	
	1844	Governor Reynolds died (February 9)		
M. M. Marmaduke (D) 1844	1844	Howard High School opened at Fayette (October 28)		
	1844	Dallas County organized		

Governor	Events of Interest	U. S. Senator	U. S. Senator
		(Atchison)	(Benton)
John C. Edwards (D) 1845-1849	1845 German Communistic Colony founded at Bethel		
	1845 Atchison, Cedar, DeKalb, Dunklin, Harrison, Hickory, Knox, Lawrence, Mercer, Mississippi, Moniteau, Nodaway, Oregon, Putnam, Reynolds, Schuyler, Sullivan, and Texas counties organized		
	1846 Mexican War (May 2, 1846-February 2, 1848)		
	1846 Regiments raised for Mexican War		
	1847 Lutheran Synod of Missouri organized		
	1847 Hannibal and St. Joseph Railroad chartered (February 16)		
	1847 State Hospital No. 1 established at Fulton (February 16)		
	1847 St. Louis first illuminated by gas (November 3)		
	1847 St. Louis connected to East by telegraph (December 20)		
	1848 Large German immigration into state begun		
Austin A. King (D) 1849-1853	1849 Jackson Resolutions introduced in State Assembly (January 1)		
	1849 Missouri Pacific Railroad chartered (March 12)		

Governor	Events of Interest	U. S. Senator	U. S. Senator
(King)	1849 William Jewell College organized	(Atchison)	(Benton)
	1849 Cholera epidemic in St. Louis with over 4,000 deaths		
	1849 Fire in St. Louis, loss of over $3,000,000 (May 17)		
	1849 David R. Atchison, president for a day (March 4)		
	1849 Butler, Laclede, and McDonald counties organized		
	1850 "Town of Kansas" (Kansas City) incorporated (February 4)		
	1850 State Medical Association organized (November 4)		
	1850 First telegraph lines in Missouri		
	1851 Christian College incorporated at Columbia (January 18)		Henry S. Geyer (W) 1851-1857
	1851 Construction of first Missouri Railroad, the Pacific, began (July 4)		
	1851 Bollinger, Dent, Pemiscot, Stone, and Vernon counties organized		
	1852 First Congregational Church in Missouri organized in St. Louis (March 18)		
	1852 Explosion of the steamboat Saluda at Lexington (April 9)		
	1852 First passenger train in Missouri operated (Pacific Railroad) (December 9)		

Governor	Events of Interest	U. S. Senator	U. S. Senator
			(Geyer)
Sterling Price (D) 1853-1857	1853 Christian University at Canton (now Culver-Stockton College) chartered (January 28)	(Atchison)	
	1853 First public high school in state opened in St. Louis (February 7)		
	1853 Eliot Seminary (now Washington University) chartered (February 22)		
	1853 Westminster College chartered (February 23)		
	1853 Reorganization of school system, state money granted for support (February 24)		
	1855 Legislature failed to elect U. S. Senator to replace Atchison	Only one U. S. Senator 1855-1857	
	1855 Central College at Fayette incorporated (March 1)		
	1855 Gasconade railroad bridge disaster (34 killed, about 100 injured) (November 1)		
	1855 Barton, Maries, and Webster counties organized		
	1856 State Teachers Association organized (May 21)		
Trusten Polk (D) 1857	1857 Polk resigned Governorship to become United States Senator	James S. Green (D) 1857-1861	Trusten Polk (D) 1857-1862

Governor		Events of Interest	U. S. Senator	U. S. Senator
Hancock Jackson (D) 1857	1857	Stephens C o l l e g e incorporated (January 17)	(Greene)	(Polk)
	1857	Dred Scott decision (March 6)		
	1857	Douglas, Howell, Iron, and Phelps counties organized		
Robert M. Stewart (D) 1857-1861	1857	St. Louis Normal School opened (October 28)		
	1858	Serious Kansas-Missouri b o r d e r trouble		
	1859	First railroad completed across state—Hannibal and St. Joseph (February 13)		
	1859	Carter County organized		
	1860	Pony Express started from St. Joseph (April 3)		
	1860	Southwest Branch of the Pacific Railroad reached Rolla (December 22)		
	1860	Christian County organized		
Claiborne F. Jackson (D) 1861	1861	Civil War (April 12, 1861-April 9, 1865)	Waldo P. Johnson (D) 1861-1862	
	1861	Worth, last and smallest of Missouri counties, organized		
	1861	Meeting of State Convention (February and March)		
	1861	Governor called special session of legislature to arm state (April 22)		

Governor	Events of Interest	U. S. Senator	U. S. Senator
(Jackson)	1861 Camp Jackson captured (May 10)	(Johnson)	(Polk)
	1861 Harney-Price agreement (May 21)		
	1861 Planters' House Conference (June 11)		
	1861 Lyon took Jefferson City (June 15)		
	1861 Battles at Boonville (June 17), Cole Camp (June 18), and Carthage (July 5)		
	1861 Hamilton Gamble appointed to succeed Governor Jackson (July 22)		
Hamilton R. Gamble (U) 1861-1864	1861 Battles at Athens (August 5), Wilson's Creek (August 10), Lexington (September 12), Springfield (September 25), Belmont (November 7), Salem (December 3), and Shawnee Mound (December 8)	Robert Wilson (U) 1862-1863	John B. Henderson (R) 1862-1869
	1861 Jackson called session of Legislature at Neosho, secession order passed (October 21)		
	1862 Battles at Pea Ridge (March 7-8), Kirksville (August 6), and Lonejack (August 16)		
	1862 Macon (September 25) and Palmyra (October 18) massacres		
	1863 Quantrill's raid on Lawrence, Kansas (August 21)		

Governor		Events of Interest	U. S. Senator	U. S. Senator	U. S. Senator
(Gamble)	1863	Order Number Eleven issued (August 25)	B. Gratz Brown (R) 1863-1867		(Henderson)
	1863	Battle of Springfield (January 8)			
	1864	Governor Gamble died (January 31)			
Willard P. Hall (U) 1864	1864	Price's raid through Missouri, Battles of Pilot Knob (September 27), Westport (October 20-23)			
	1864	Centralia massacre (September 27)			
	1865	Slavery abolished in Missouri (January 11)			
	1865	New Constitution adopted (April 10)			
Thomas G. Fletcher (RR) 1865-1869	1865	First passenger train from Kansas City to St. Louis (September 20)			
	1866	Missouri Historical Society organized			
	1866	Lincoln Institute established			
	1866	Missouri Dental College founded (branch of Washington University in 1892)			
	1867	North Missouri Normal (a private school) established at Kirksville		Charles D. Drake (R) 1867-1870	
	1867	First State appropriation for support of Missouri University made (March 11)			
	1867	Missouri Woman's Suffrage Club organized (May 8)			

Governor		Events of Interest	U. S. Senator	U. S. Senator	U. S. Senator
(Fletcher)	1867	Missouri Press Association organized (May 17)	(Drake)		(Henderson)
	1867	First Kansas City high school established			
	1868	St. Louis Insane Asylum erected			
	1869	Kansas City Board of Trade organized (February 6)			Carl Schurz (R) 1869-1875
Joseph W. McClurg (RR) 1869-1871	1869	Burlington bridge at Kansas City completed (July 3)			
	1870	State Agricultural College and Rolla School of Mines created as departments of University of Missouri (February 24)	David F. Jewett (R) 1870-1871		
	1870	Test Oath abolished			
	1870	State Normal Schools at Kirksville and Warrensburg provided for by Assembly (March 9)			
	1872	Democrats and Liberals jointly nominated state ticket	Francis P. Blair (D) 1871-1873		
B. Gratz Brown (LR) 1871-1873	1872	Law School of University of Missouri opened			
	1872	Act passed for establishment of State Hospital Number 2 at St. Joseph (March 28)			
	1872	Women admitted to all branches of the University of Missouri			

Governor	Events of Interest	U. S. Senator	U. S. Senator
Silas Woodson (D) 1873-1875	1873 State Normal School at Cape Girardeau authorized (March 22) 1873 Springfield College, now Drury, opened (September 25) 1873 School of Medicine of University of Missouri opened 1874 Eads bridge opened (July 4) 1874 Invasion of grasshoppers	Lewis W. Bogy (D) 1873-1877	(Schurz)
Charles H. Hardin (D) 1875-1877	1875 New Constitution adopted (October 30) 1875 Park College founded 1875 Creation of St. Louis Court of Appeals 1876 Public Library started in Kansas City		Francis M. Cockrell (D) 1875-1905
John S. Phelps (D) 1877-1881	1877 School of Engineering of the University of Missouri established 1877 First long-distance telephone service (Jackson to Cape Girardeau) (December 18) 1878 St. Louis City separated from St. Louis County (July 18) 1878 First American Royal Livestock Show 1878 First Veiled Prophet Celebration in St. Louis (October 8)	David H. Armstrong (D) 1877-1879 James Shields (D) 1879	

Governor		Events of Interest	U. S. Senator	U. S. Senator
(Phelps)	1880	Kansas City Star established (September 18)	George G. Vest (D) 1879-1903	(Cockrell)
	1880	Missouri Bar Association formed (December 29)		
	1880	Southwest Baptist College at Bolivar founded		
Thomas T. Crittenden (D) 1881-1885	1882	Organization of the Agricultural Wheel in Missouri		
	1882	Jesse James killed (April 3)		
	1883	Tarkio College chartered (May 19)		
	1884	Cottey College organized in Nevada		
	1884	Creation of Kansas City Court of Appeals		
John S. Marmaduke (D) 1885-1887	1885	State Hospital Number 3 at Nevada established (March 19)		
	1887	Missouri Agricultural Experiment Station established		
	1887	Local option law on liquor passed		
	1887	Governor Marmaduke died (December 28)		
Albert P. Morehouse (D) 1888	1888	Capitol remodeled at cost of $220,000		
	1888	Bald Knobbers suppressed with Kinney's death (August 20)		
	1888	Missouri Valley College founded at Marshall (June 13)		

Governor	Events of Interest		U. S. Senator	U. S. Senator
			(Vest)	(Cockrell)
David R. Francis (D) 1889-1893	1889	Missouri Military Academy founded at Mexico		
	1889	Australian ballot law made to apply to towns over 5,000		
	1889	Reform School for Boys at Boonville opened (January 15)		
	1890	William Woods College opened (September 18)		
	1891	Missouri Daughters of the Confederacy organized (January 27)		
	1891	Australian ballot extended to areas under 5,000 population		
	1892	Academic Hall, University of Missouri, burned (January 9)		
	1892	Missouri Bankers Association formed		
	1892	Kirksville College of Osteopathy and Surgery chartered (May 10)		
William J. Stone (D) 1893-1897	1894	First Missouri chapter of D.A.R. formed in Kansas City		
	1896	State School Board Association organized		
	1896	St. Louis Tornado, $10,000,000 property damage, 118 dead (May 27)		
	1896	First Missouri rural mail routes established from Cairo (October 15)		
	1896	Organization of Missouri Library Association		

Governor		Events of Interest	U. S. Senator	U. S. Senator
			(Vest)	(Cockrell)
Lon Vest Stephens (D) 1897-1901	1897	State Association of Prosecuting Attorneys formed		
	1897	Federal Soldiers Home at St. James made state institution (March 1)		
	1897	Confederate Soldiers Home at Higginsville made state institution (March 1)		
	1898	Spanish-American War (April 25, 1898-December 10, 1898)		
	1898	Missouri militia mobilized for Spanish-American War		
	1898	State Historical Society of Missouri organized		
	1899	State Hospital Number 4 at Farmington authorized by Legislature (April 4)		
	1899	Fruit Experiment Station established at Mountain Grove		
	1899	Kemper Military School officially recognized by state		
Alexander M. Dockery (D) 1901-1905	1902	Colonel Ed Butler indicted by Joseph W. Folk	William J. Stone (D) 1903-1918	
	1904	Louisiana Purchase Exposition in St. Louis opened (April 30)		
	1905	Herbert S. Hadley prosecuted Standard Oil Company		

Governor		Events of Interest	U. S. Senator	U. S. Senator
Joseph W. Folk (D) 1905-1909	1905	Acts passed establishing Normal Schools at Springfield (March 17) and Maryville (March 25)	(Stone)	William Warner (R) 1905-1911
	1905	Missouri State Sanitorium at Mount Vernon authorized (April 15)		
	1906	Missouri Historical Review established		
	1907	Missouri adopted primary election law		
	1908	Journalism School established at University of Missouri		
	1909	Springfield Court of Appeals established		
	1909	State Industrial Home for Negro Girls authorized at Tipton (June 14)		
	1911	State Capitol burned (February 5)		James A. Reed (D) 1911-1928
Herbert S. Hadley (R) 1909-1913	1911	Bonds voted for new Capitol (August 11)		
	1911	Champ Clark elected Speaker of U. S. House of Representatives		
	1911	State Poultry Experiment Station established at Mountain Grove		
	1912	First Missouri Farm Bureau organized and first county agent appointed; stationed at Cape Girardeau (August 1)		
	1912	Lake Taneycomo completed		

Governor		Events of Interest	U. S. Senator	U. S. Senator
			(Stone)	(Reed)
Elliot W. Major (D) 1913-1917	1913	Board of Pardons and Paroles created		
	1913	State Flag adopted (March 17)		
	1913	Public Service Commission provided for by Legislature (April 15)		
	1913	State Highway Department created		
	1913	Direct election of Senators authorized		
	1914	Agriculture Extension Service established		
	1915	Cornerstone of new Capitol laid (June 24)		
	1916	Missouri troops sent into Mexico after Villa, under command of John J. Pershing		
Frederick D. Gardner (D) 1917-1921	1917	World War I (April 6, 1917-November 11, 1918)		
	1917	Home Guards organized (July 17)		
	1917	Missouri National Guard called into Federal service (August 5)		
	1917	Missouri and Kansas National Guards consolidated to form 35th Division (September 28)		
	1917	Missouri Farmers' Association organized		
	1917	Missouri Council of Defense named (April 24)		

Governor		Events of Interest	U. S. Senator	U. S. Senator
(Gardner)	1919	Prohibition amendment ratified (January 16)	Xenophon P. Wilfley (D) 1918	(Reed)
	1919	St. Louis Municipal Opera made permanent	Selden P. Spencer (R) 1918-1925	
	1919	League of Women Voters organized in St. Louis		
	1919	35th Division returned to the United States		
	1919	National Woman Suffrage amendment ratified		
	1920	$60,000,000 "good roads" amendment passed (November 2)		
Arthur M. Hyde (R) 1921-1925	1921	Missouri Centennial Celebration at State Fair at Sedalia (August 8-20)		
	1921	WEW, Missouri's first radio station, started broadcasting from St. Louis		
	1921	Special session of General Assembly for passage of road legislation (begun June 14)		
	1921	Soldiers and Sailors bonus bill signed for $15,000,000 (November 11)		
	1923	Missouri State Flower—the Hawthorn—named (March 16)		
	1924	Two cent per gallon gasoline tax voted		

Governor	Events of Interest		U. S. Senator	U. S. Senator	U. S. Senator
Sam A. Baker (R) 1925-1929	1926	Workmen's Compensation Act passed	George H. Williams (R) 1925-1927	(Reed)	
	1927	Intermediate reformatory established at Algoa			
	1927	Native bluebird made official state bird	Harry B. Hawes (D) 1927-1933		
	1927	Charles A. Lindbergh crossed Atlantic in Spirit of St. Louis (May 20)			
	1928	Additional $75,000,000 authorized for roads			
Henry S. Caulfield (R) 1929-1933	1929	University of Kansas City incorporated (June 10)		Roscoe C. Patterson (R) 1929-1935	
	1930	Missouri lost three representatives by census			
	1931	Graduated income tax levied			
	1931	Bagnell Dam completed (October 19)			
	1931	State Highway Patrol created			
Guy B. Park (D) 1933-1937	1933	State convention ratified repeal of national prohibition amendment	Bennett Champ Clark (D) 1933-1945		
	1933	William Rockhill Nelson Gallery of Art opened			
	1934	Constitutional amendment passed authorizing $10,000,000 for rehabilitation program for state institutions			

Governor		Events of Interest	U. S. Senator	U. S. Senator
(Park)			(Clark)	(Patterson)
	1934	Sales tax law enacted		Harry S Truman (D) 1935-1945
	1935	Old age assistance law became effective		
	1935	Sales tax rate raised to one per cent		
	1935	"Bottle cap" mill tokens issued		
	1936	Severe drought over state		
	1937	Social Security Commission created to administer relief agencies (June 23)		
Lloyd C. Stark (D) 1937-1941	1937	Missouri Conservation Commission created (July 1)		
	1937	Death penalty changed from hanging to gas chamber		
	1937	Sales tax rate raised to 2 per cent		
	1938	Cornerstone laid for State Cancer Hospital at Columbia (December 9)		
	1939	"Sharecroppers" demonstrated in Southeast Missouri (January)		
	1939	Pendergast convicted of income tax evasion (May 22)		
	1939	Trachoma Hospital at Rolla completed (July 1)		
	1939	U. S. Government acquires site in St. Louis for Jefferson Expansion Memorial		

Governor	Events of Interest		U.S. Senator	U.S. Senator
(Stark)	1940	Amendment passed to set up non-partisan court plan	(Clark)	(Truman)
	1940	Ground broken for Fort Leonard Wood (December 3)		
Forrest C. Donnell (R) 1941-1945	1941	Assembly attempted to prevent Donnell's inauguration (January and February)		
	1941	Ground broken for Camp Crowder (August 30)		
	1941	"Balanced Farming" started in Missouri		
	1941	Lake Wappapello completed		
	1941	World War II (December 7, 1941-September 2, 1945)		
	1943	Constitutional convention met (September 21, 1943-September 29, 1944)		
	1944	Harry S Truman elected Vice President (November 7)		
	1944	General Omar Bradley of Moberly commanded troops in Europe		
	1944	Battleship Missouri christened		
	1944	Lake Norfork completed		
Phil M. Donnelly (D) 1945-1949	1945	Harry S Truman became President at Roosevelt's death (April 12)	Forrest C. Donnell (R) 1945-1951	Frank P. Briggs (D) 1945-1947
	1945	New State Constitution adopted		

Governor		Events of Interest	U. S. Senator	U. S. Senator
(Donnelly)	1945	Formal signing of Japanese surrender on deck of the battleship **Missouri** (September 2)	(Donnell)	(Briggs)
	1946	Merit system for state employees established		James P. Kem (R) 1947-1953
	1947	King-Thompson Utility Anti-Strike laws passed		
	1948	Hawkins Law for school reorganization passed		
	1948	St. Louis payroll e a r n i n g s tax levied		
	1948	Clearwater Lake completed		
	1948	Harry S Truman elected President (November 2)		
Forrest Smith (D) 1949-1953	1949	"Missouri Waltz" became official state song	Thomas C. Hennings, Jr. (D) 1951-1960	
	1950	Korean War (June 25, 1950-July 27, 1953)		
	1950	Binaggio murdered in Kansas City (April 10)		
	1950	Missouri lost two U. S. Representatives from census		
	1951	Gasoline tax increased to 3 cents		
	1952	Bull Shoals Lake completed		
	1952	Ten-year state development highway plan started		
	1952	State Division of Civil Defense created		

Governor		Events of Interest	U. S. Senator	U. S. Senator
Phil M. Donnelly (D) 1953-1957	1953	State aid for county roads increased	(Hennings)	Stuart Symington (D) 1953-1977
	1953	"Little Hoover" commission set up to study state government organization		
	1953	State Park Board created		
	1955	The flowering dogwood became official state tree		
	1955	School Foundation program passed by referendum (October 4)		
	1955	Two cent tax on cigarettes voted (October 4)		
	1956	$75,000,000 bond issue for buildings at state institutions passed		
James T. Blair (D) 1957-1961	1957	Site chosen near Moberly for medium security prison	Edward V. Long (D) 1960-1968	
	1959	Table Rock Lake completed		
	1959	Use tax on items purchased out of state passed		
	1960	Use tax ruled unconstitutional		
	1960	Missouri lost one Congressional seat by census		
John M. Dalton (D) 1961-1965	1961	New use tax passed by Assembly		
	1961	Legislators' salaries increased		
	1961	Fair employment practices act adopted		
	1961	Missouri started withholding state income tax		

Governor	Events of Interest		U. S. Senator	U. S. Senator
	1961	Cigarette and liquor taxes increased	(Long)	(Symington)
	1961	Division of Commerce and Industrial Development replaced Division of Resources and Development		
	1961	Water Resources Board established		
	1962	Gas tax increase approved by voters		
Warren E. Hearnes (D) 1965-1973	1965	Public Accommodations law		
	1965	Nine mental retardation centers authorized		
	1965	Missouri Southern College and Missouri Western College authorized		
	1965	Keystone placed in Gateway Arch		
	1966	Reapportionment of legislature		
	1966	Constitution amended to permit governor to succeed himself		
	1967	St. Louis Cardinals win World Series		
	1967	St. Louis—St. Louis County Junior College 47 million dollar bond issue authorized		
	1968	Kansas City race riots	Thomas F. Eagleton (D) 1968-	

(D)   Democrat
(LR) Liberal Republican
(ND) National Democrat
(R)   Republican
(RR) Radical Republican
(U)   Unionist
(W)   Whig

Governor		Events of Interest	U. S. Senator	U. S. Senator
Christopher S. Bond (R) 1973-1977	1973	Reorganization of Missouri executive branch	(Eagleton)	(Symington)
	1973	State buys Wainwright Building		
	1976	State buys Thomas Hart Benton home		
	1976	Republican National Convention in Kansas City		
	1976	State purchases Bingham sketches		
Joseph P. Teasdale (D) 1977-1981	1977	New state criminal code		John Danforth (R) 1977-
	1977	Kansas City flood kills 24		
	1977	New death penalty law		
	1978	Failure of right-to-work referendum		
	1980	State spending limitation passes		
	1980	Hazardous waste regulations adopted		
	1980	Meredith decrees state partly responsible for integration costs		
Christopher S. Bond (R) 1981-	1981	Higher Education Loan Authority established		
	1981	Professional licensing board regulations revised		
	1981	Crime victim compensation authorized		
	1981	Increased truck size permitted on state highways		
	1981	Missouri cut to nine congressional districts		
	1981	111 killed and 188 injured in collapse of Hyatt Regency skywalks in Kansas City (July 17).		
	1983	Funds appropriated for purchase of dioxin-contaminated Times Beach		

(D) Democrat
(LR) Liberal Rep.
(ND) National Dem.
(R) Republican
(RR) Radical Rep.
(U) Unionist
(W) Whig

618, 711, 717, 730; failure to form, 640, 726

Conservative Unionists, 406-14 **passim**

Consolidation, of schools, 492, 674, 736

Constitution, U.S., Amendments to, 386, 582, 585-86; law for teaching passed, 592

Constitutional Convention, first, 146, 150, 155, 773; delegates to, 157-58, 160; of 1845, 314; of 1865, 386, 406-8, 418; of 1922-23, 590, 684; of 1943-44, 674, 794

Constitutional Union Party, 341, 344, 350

Constitution of 1820, preparation of, 146, 150; authorized, 154; terms of, 155, 173, 178, 287, 318, 322-23, 384; discussed, 157-64; mentioned, 288, 407, 424

Constitution of 1865 (Drake's Constitution), 406-11, 413, 422, 469, 783

Constitution of 1875, discussed, 422-26; need to change recognized, 590, 684; mentioned, 428, 472, 785

Constitution of 1945, discussed, 684-86; amendment to, 690; legislative branch, 686-90; executive branch, 690-92, 797; judiciary, 692-94; school provisions, 794, 738; mentioned, 426, 669, 674

Convention Center, St. Louis, 721

Cook, John, 158

Cookingham, L. P., portrait, 677

Cooper, Benjamin, 134-35, 136, 207

Cooper County, development of, 136; school in, 138; library in, 300; organized, 773; mentioned, 173

Cooperatives, farm, 527, 599, 727

Corby, Col. H. H., 537

Cordelling, 79, 81, 191

Corn, where grown, 3, 456, 726; grown by Indians, 15, 18; by French, 90; by settlers, 239, 240, 298-99; cob pipes, 240, 445; machinery used for, 451-52; price of, 462, 598; mentioned, 2, 104, 459

Cornwell, Dean, painting by, 115

Corruption, in 1870's, 420-21, 423; in city government, 540-45, 556, 614-23 **passim**

Cortambert, Louis Richard, 272

Cote sans Dessein, 48, 132, 133

Cotton, produced, 94, 240, 456, 635; slaves for, 319; processed, 444;

mentioned, 220, 316

Cottey College, 786

Coulter, Jim, 232

Council of National Defense, 673

Counterfeiters (Bank of Niangua), 263

"Country produce," 148

County agents (Agricultural Extension Agents), 599, 633, 726

Coureurs de bois, 29, 62, 97, 99, 114, 188

Court of Appeals, in St. Louis, 425, 692, 775; in Springfield, 692; in Kansas City, 692

Court of Criminal Correction, 693

Courts, 692-93, 794

Cows, 236. **See also** cattle

Cowskin Prairie, 368

Crawford County, 243, 630, 775

Crawford, Joan, 655

Creek Indians, 378

Creel, George, 574

Creole, defined, 92; dress of, 94-6; holidays of, 98; education of, 98-101; signatures of, 100; habits of, 104-6; not revolutionaries, 108; numbers of, 138; promise to, 147; mentioned, 78, 107, 118, 119, 141, 144, 169, 193, 275

Creve Coeur, 48

Crime, before 1860, 296-98; Reign of Terror, 413, 432; Ku Klux Klan, 419, 507, 595; James brothers, 431-32; Gunn City lynching, 471; during prohibition, 584-85; mentioned, 548. **See also** Punishment, Lawlessness

Crime victim compensation, 726, 798

Criminal code, 722, 798

Crittenden, Thomas T., portrait of, 430; as governor, 431-32, 786; attitude toward railroads, 472; ends lawlessness, 510

Crowder, Enoch H., 577, 578

Crown Center, 721

Croy, Homer, 662-63

Cruzat, Don Francisco, 46, 771

Cudahy (Kingan and Company), 442

Cuivre River, 637

Culbertson Family, 121

Culver-Stockton College, 290, 780

Cumberland Presbyterian Church, 284

Cummings, Father John A., 410, 484

Currency, 258-65, 314, 463-66. **See also,** Money, Banking

Current River, 125, 238

Curtis, Samuel R., 377-78, 398

Cyclotron, at Rolla, 767

sas City, 437, 439, 597, 728, 730; of Joplin, 437, 728; of Ozarks, 439; rural, 452, 478; school age, 492; urban, 596-97, 624; chart of, 728; map of, 729; mentioned, 36, 216, 270
Populists, 526-30, 546, 522. **See also** Peoples' Party
Portage des Sioux, 48, 132, 135, 771
Portelle, Thomas, 100
Porter, Joseph C., 393, 395
"Possum" policy, 416, 427
Post, The Rev. T. M., 279
Potawatomie Indians, 126, 131
Potosi, established, 75; school in, 140; church near, 142; pictured, 147; Austin at, 221; mentioned, 177, 178, 731, 742, 771. **See also** Mine a Breton
Pottawatomie Creek, 340
Pottery, prehistoric, 15, 17, 19, 21
Powell, William, 655
Powers Phase, 20-21
Powers Fort, 21
Prairie du Chien, 134, 180
Prairie du Rocher, 33
"Prairie Park," 295
Prairie schooners, 208
Pratte, Bernard, 169, 193, 198
Preachers, 277, 281. **See also** Clergymen, Ministers, Pastors, Missionaries
Pre-emption, 310. **See also** Squatters' right
Prehistoric man, 7-25 **passim**
Presbyterian Church, first in Missouri, 142-44, 276, 279, 773; sent missionaries, 215, 279; established schools, 279; dissension in, 283-84; numbers of, 284; abolitionists in, 325, 327-28; 1860-1940, 482-90 **passim;** membership in, 484, 485, 661; mentioned, 270, 499
Presbyterian Church (Cumberland), 499
Price, John, 447
Price, R. B., 523
Price, Sterling, in Mexican War, 226-27, 342; opposed Benton, 311; elected governor, 341-42, 780; quoted, 348, 374, 377; chaired convention, 351; with Confederacy, 355-401 **passim;** agreement by, 355; at Planters' House, 355-56; in battle, 367-379 **passim;** requested troops, 376-77, 393; 1864 raid, 396-400; after Civil War, 435; portrait of, 398;

mentioned, 360, 362, 363, 379, 380, 381, 392, 401, 433, 782, 783
Price-Harney Agreement, 355
Priests, scarcity of, 87-88; Irish, 88; education by, 99, 291; pay of, 141; constitutional provision for, 161; to Indians, 216, 276; refused oath, 410; mentioned, 108. **See also** Clergymen, Missionaries
Princeton, Missouri, 587
Printing presses, by counterfeiters, 263; destroyed, 270, 315, 325, 326, 575; pictured, 271
Prisons, 560, 562, 579, 720
Pritchard, J. A., 230, 290
Probate Court, 692-93, 722
Professional Licensing Board, 798
Progressive Farmers Association (PFA), 724
Progressive Movement, 545-64, 556, 559, 587, 705
Prohibition (The Noble Experiment), interest in, 432-34; supported, 548; Amendment, 562, 582, 583, 781; discussed, 579-86; Reed's opposition to, 590; mentioned, 556, 791, 792
Prohibition Party, 434, 562
Projectile points, prehistoric, 11, 13, 13a, 13b, 15, 17, 19, 21, 23
Protestant Episcopal Church, first in Missouri, 142-43; membership in, 484, 485, 661; mentioned, 488
Protestants, in Colonial Missouri, 84-90 **passim,** 104-5; exclusion of, 101-6 **passim;** in territorial period, 142-44; missionaries, 274, 276-84 **passim;** membership in churches of, 484, 485; in prohibition, 580; mentioned, 138, 322, 490
Protohistoric Period, 20-23
Provisional government, 381-82
Public Accommodations Act of 1965, 750, 797
Public Lands, sale of, 163
Public Schools, provision for establishment of, 163; establishment of, 177; laws, 179; first public high school, 286; first in St. Louis, 289; encouragement for, 427; effect of Civil War on, 491; development of, 736-740. **See also** Education, Schools
Public Service Commission, 790
Public works, 450
Public Works Administration (PWA), 619, 627